Sex Research: Bibliographies from the Institute for Sex Research

Sex Research: Bibliographies from the Institute for Sex Research

Compiled by
Joan Scherer Brewer
and Rod W. Wright

 ORYX PRESS
In association with
Neal-Schuman Publishers, Inc.

Operation Oryx, started more than 15 years ago at the Phoenix Zoo to save the rare white antelope—believed to have inspired the unicorn of mythology—has apparently succeeded. The operation was launched in 1962 when it became evident that the animals were facing extinction in their native habitat of the Arabian peninsula.

An original herd of nine, put together through *Operation Oryx* by five world organizations now number 47 in Phoenix with another 38 at the San Diego Wild Game Farm, and four others which have recently been sent to live in their natural habitat in Jordan.

Also, in what has come to be known as "The Second Law of Return," rare biblical animals are being collected from many countries to roam freely at the Hai Bar Biblical Wildlife Nature Reserve in the Negev, in Israel, the most recent addition being a breeding herd of eight Arabian Oryx. With the addition of these Oryx, their collection of rare biblical animals is complete.

Copyright © 1979 The Institute for Sex Research
Published by The Oryx Press
3930 E. Camelback Road
Phoenix, AZ 85018

In association with Neal-Schuman Publishers, Inc.

Published simultaneously in Canada

Printed and Bound in the United States of America

Distributed outside North America by
Mansell Publishing
3 Bloomsbury Place
London WC1A 2QA, England
ISBN 0-7201-0833-0

Library of Congress Cataloging in Publication Data

Institute for Sex Research.
    Sex research.

    Includes indexes.
    1. Sex research—Bibliography. 2. Sex—Bibliography.
3. Sex customs—Bibliography. I. Brewer, Joan Scherer, 1930-
II. Wright, Rod W., 1944-   III. Title.
Z7164.S42I57 1979 (HQ60) 016.30141'07'2 78-31942
ISBN 0-912700-48-3

Contents

Poem   vi
Preface   vii
Acknowledgements   viii
Introduction   ix

I. **Sources of Sex Research Information in the United States** 1

II. **Bibliographies from the Institute for Sex Research** 9

Sex Behavior   11
  General   11
  Sex Behavior (Child)   13
  Sex Attitudes and Behavior Research (Adolescent)   15
  Sex Behavior Research (College Student)   20
  Sex Behavior (Aged)   25
  Drugs and Sex Behavior   29
  Special Groups   34

Sex Variations   43
  Bisexuality   43
  Homosexuality   45
  Sadomasochism   49
  Transvestism   53

Sexual Response Physiology   57
  Coitus and Orgasm   57

Sex Counseling   61
  Sex Counseling   61
  Sex Therapy   67
  Therapist-Client Relationships   74

Sex and Gender   77
  Gender Role Identification   77

  Hormones and Sex Behavior   84
  Transexualism   89

Marriage   93
  Marital Sex Behavior Research   93
  Trial Marriage   96
  Extramarital Sex Behavior   98

Sex Education   102
  Sex Education   102
  Sex Education Research   106

Sex and Society   113
  Anthropological Perspectives on Human Sexuality   113
  Sex Attitudes Research   118
  Sex Ethics   123
  Changing Roles of Men and Women   126

Legal Aspects of Sex Behavior   132
  Child Victims   132
  Incest   134
  Pedophilia   138
  Prostitution   141
  Rape   150
  Sex Offenses   156

Erotica   162
  Erotica   162
  Sex in the Arts   168

Research   173
  Sex Research Methodology   173
  Ethical Issues in Sex Research   177

III. **Indexes** 179
  Author Index   181
  Subject Index   200

On Quoting Authorities

Unless you've read it with your eyes
Set nothing down, nor ought surmise.
Imagination leads to lies
In Bibliography. The wise
Know well this golden rule to prize.
But if a beaten path you tread,
(You surely must if much you've read)
And needs must say what has been said,
Give your Authority—be terse—
Quote Author, Title, Chapter, Verse,
That each one to the fountain head
At once and surely may be led,
And read himself what you have read.

HENRY SPENCER ASHBEE
(Terence Deakin. *Catalogi Libroium Eroticorum.* London: Cecil & Amelia Woolf, 1964.)

Preface

Professor Alfred C. Kinsey began his research into human sexual behavior in the late 1930s while a professor of biology at Indiana University. In spite of opposition from conservative groups, he expanded his work beyond the campus and gathered a small staff to assist in conducting interviews and analyzing data. In 1947, a year before publication of the first "Kinsey Report" (actually entitled *Sexual Behavior in the Human Male*), he established the Institute for Sex Research as an Indiana nonprofit corporation in order to protect the interview records and the growing library and archives holdings as a private collection. On October 31, 1957, in a decision that is regarded as a landmark in the history of the relationship between science and law, the Southern District Court of New York supported the right of the Institute to import from abroad and to receive through the mails erotic materials for research purposes.[1] These developments permitted the Institute to realize Kinsey's plans to develop a resource collection of erotic literature and art, photographs, films, ephemeral and archival materials, and scientific literature devoted to sex research. This unique collection forms the base from which the bibliographies that follow have been compiled.

The National Institute of Mental Health, which had provided the major financial support for the Institute's research activities since 1957, recognized the importance of the collection, and in 1970 provided grant support to organize the social and behavioral sciences section and to establish an Information Service so that the research needs of scientists and scholars throughout the country could be served.[2] A second grant to provide funding to maintain the Information Service for an additional two years was awarded in 1975.[3]

During these grant years, several publications were produced in order to make the Institute's collections as widely available as possible, to encourage the development of a uniform vocabulary applicable to sex research, and to facilitate such research by aiding in the development of a communication network among scholars in diverse disciplines but with a mutual interest in sex research:

Institute for Sex Research. *Catalog of the Social and Behavioral Sciences Monograph Section of the Library of the Institute for Sex Research.* 4 v. Boston: G.K. Hall, 1975.

Institute for Sex Research. *Catalog of Periodical Literature in the Social and Behavioral Sciences Section, Library of the Institute for Sex Research, Including Supplement to Monographs, 1973–1975.* 4 v. Boston: G.K. Hall, 1976.

Brooks, JoAnn and Helen C. Hofer, comps. *Sexual Nomenclature: A Thesaurus.* Boston: G.K. Hall, 1976.

Beasley, Ruth A., comp. *International Directory of Sex Research and Related Fields.* 2 v. Boston: G.K. Hall, 1976.

The success of these publications in stimulating the already growing interest in sex research among scholars at all levels as well as among clinical workers, health delivery personnel, sex educators, and the general public led to an increase in requests to the Information Service for referrals and bibliographies. As the number of bibliographies prepared to meet the demand grew, and as the end of the financial support provided by the National Institute of Mental Health grants neared, we were challenged to take an additional step.

The present collection of most frequently requested bibliographies represents a further contribution to the Institute for Sex Research's continuing efforts to encourage basic research and to facilitate the availability to the public of accurate and current data related to human sex behavior and attitudes.

Joan Scherer Brewer

Bloomington, Indiana
October 1978

References:

1. Kenneth F. Stevens. "United States v. 31 photographs: Dr. Alfred C. Kinsey and obscenity law." *Indiana Magazine of History* 71(4):299–318, Dec. 1975.
2. Grant No. MH19348, awarded by National Institute of Mental Health, DHEW.
3. Grant No. MH19348-06, awarded by National Institute of Mental Health, DHEW.

Acknowledgements

We thank the many persons whose energy and scholarship contributed to this publication. Rebecca Dixon and Ruth A. Beasley together developed the master plan for the Institute for Sex Research Library collections and services, providing the foundation for our work. The idea to publish this volume originated with JoAnn Brooks who, along with Helen C. Hofer, developed the thesaurus used for the index. Above all, we acknowledge those authors whose cited works constitute the real worth of these bibliographies.

Extraordinary courtesies were extended by Professor Paul H. Gebhard, director of the Institute, and by Jo Huntington, assistant to the director, who made available both financial and moral support. Susan Matusak, head librarian, understood and encouraged our efforts.

Special gratitude is due Doris Weeks. Her organizational, typing, and proofreading skills kept the work going; her energy and optimism guaranteed its completion.

Finally, we are indebted to the many clerical and student workers whose labors produced the catalog cards on which these citations are based.

Introduction

SCOPE

We have attempted to provide each interested scholar with access to the subject matter at his or her level of interest. The undergraduate writing a term paper, the graduate student working on a dissertation, the author launching into the preparation of a text, senior researchers preparing a sophisticated investigation, and the teacher preparing a course curriculum should all be able to find sufficient material here for the initial if not the complete literature search necessary.

No attempt has been made to cite everything written on subject topics. These are not comprehensive bibliographies, but represent basic works, other bibliographies, and literature reviews where available, as well as contributions to the literature that might be too recent to have been cited by others or that exist only as conference papers. The lists are selective, with emphasis in most cases on current rather than historical works. Biography, fiction, and articles from the popular press have been, for the most part, excluded.

Some subject areas, such as transexualism and homosexuality, are represented here by lists that seem short in comparison with the amount that has been written on the topics because the books and articles cited contain references sufficient to lead the interested researcher more deeply into the relevant literature. Other subjects less well represented by the existence of a body of basic works have longer bibliographies in an attempt to bring the available references together for the first time.

Still another class of topics, such as "Ethical Issues," receives what might appear as short shrift because there is still so little available. We hope these lacunae will attract the attention of competent scholars interested in filling a need.

Materials range from journal articles, books and book chapters, and conference papers, to nonprint materials such as cassette tapes and films. An effort has been made to include only those works that would be available to the interested scholar. Some foreign language materials have been included, however, both for the worth of the information they present, and to remind the researcher that important work is also being done outside of this country.

Copies of inaccessible references such as articles in Slavic journals or unpublished papers are available through application to the Information Service of the Institute for Sex Research. Referrals to additional or specialized sources of information have been provided where possible.

ARRANGEMENT AND ECCENTRICITIES

The overall arrangement is by broad categories, as listed in the Table of Contents. Aspects of those broad categories are represented by individual bibliographies. Entries within each bibliography are arranged in alphabetical order by primary author.

Subject access is provided in two equally important ways: (1) directly through subject headings on individual bibliographies and (2) indirectly through the subject index. For example, the researcher interested in "Sex Ethics" should not rely solely on the citations in that individual bibliography, but must also consult the index for references to applicable citations in other portions of the collection.

Editions cited are based on those in our library, and often represent a first or foreign edition. Researchers are encouraged to determine for themselves whether more recent or translated editions are available.

Some apparent eccentricities can be traced to the still evolving state of the art of sex research. In addition to variations in spelling (e.g., "transexual" or "transsexual"), some concepts and terms have yet to be strictly defined. Terms such as "gender role," "sexual orientation," and "sexual preference" mean different things to different authors. Many of the references to studies of "transvestites" actually deal with a population that more closely resembles transexuals. We have respected the individual author's judgment about his or her own work in classifying their articles, but urge the researcher to be aware of these still to be defined boundaries.

The emphasis throughout has been to assist the researcher by making citations as helpful as possible rather than to demonstrate the scholarship of the compilers. The publication date for dissertations and theses is the date the manuscript was submitted to the author's doctoral or master's committee, and not the date it was published by University Microfilms. While this is irregular from a strict bibliographic point of view, we feel that it gives a more accurate idea of the historical context of the study. The University Microfilm order number for a dissertation, when available, is noted following the citation. Where the dissertation is cited as "unpublished," the researcher should search *Dissertation Abstracts* for an order number as the work may have been published subsequent to its acquisition by the Institute.

PURPOSE

The primary purposes of this collection are to facilitate research and to disseminate current objective knowledge about human sexuality, not to recommend self-help materials or to present any viewpoint other than that of objective scholarship.

Sex Research: Bibliographies from the Institute for Sex Research

I. SOURCES OF SEX RESEARCH INFORMATION IN THE UNITED STATES

Sources of Sex Research Information

The literature of sex research is made up of the works of anthropologists, sociologists, psychologists, psychiatrists, biologists, medical researchers, social workers, and educators. It encompasses both basic research and clinical applications. Jurists, historians, philosophers, artists, creative writers, and their critics have also produced an important segment of material. The major problem in gaining access to this literature arises from its multi-disciplinary character, because each scholar tends to write for and publish in the journals specific to his or her own discipline. Although several publications devoted specifically to sex research, therapy, and education have appeared in recent years, the amount of important material to be found outside these few specialized journals has not diminished. The conscientious researcher is well advised to understand the scope of this still emergent discipline before beginning a literature search on a particular topic within it.

Paul H. Gebhard, director of the Institute for Sex Research since 1956, has described the characteristics of sex research[1] and provided an overview of the field.[2] Documentation of the early years of sex research in the United States can be found in the history of the Committee for Research in Problems of Sex of the National Research Council, written by Sophie D. Aberle and George W. Corner,[3] and in John Money's description of the founding of the Society for the Scientific Study of Sex.[4] Kinsey, Pomeroy, and Martin review 19 major American studies conducted prior to the first "Kinsey Report" in *Sexual Behavior in the Human Male.*[5]

Edward Brecher has attempted to survey the field and to summarize the viewpoints and findings of major researchers in this country and abroad, from Havelock Ellis and others at the turn of the century to the first two studies of William H. Masters and Virginia E. Johnson in 1966 and 1970.[6]

A sociological perspective is provided by John G. Gagnon in a discussion of the interactions between significant researchers and their contemporary society,[7] and Paul Robinson brings the critical perspective of a literary historian to the writings of Ellis, Kinsey, and Masters and Johnson in *The Modernization of Sex.*[8]

Additional historical material can be found in older reference books such as the *Encyclopaedia*

Sexualis[9] and *Sex and Sex Education: A Bibliography.*[10] It is likely, however, that a complete history has not yet been written, for there are tantalizing references to early studies that were locked away in university or government files and personal archives before any findings could be disseminated.[11]

The history of the Institute for Sex Research has been recounted in books[12,13] and in doctoral dissertations.[14,15] Martin S. Weinberg, senior research sociologist of the Institute, summarized the various research projects and provided excerpts from published studies in his *Sex Research: Studies from the Kinsey Institute.*[16]

Ruth A. Beasley, coordinator of the annual Summer Training Seminar conducted by the Institute for Sex Research, has described the status of sex research throughout the world and noted some of the difficulties faced by researchers in countries where such studies run counter to the prevailing mores.[17] Gebhard outlined the criteria for a comprehensive sex research center and listed some of the individuals and groups conducting sex research in the United States, Europe, and Asia at the conference on "Sex Research: Future Directions" held at the State University of New York at Stony Brook in June 1974.[18]

ACCESS TO CURRENT RESEARCH

Current research is accessible through the various indexes and abstracts of the social, behavioral, and medical sciences, and the humanities. The Institute for Sex Research library staff keeps its collection current by searching *Biological Abstracts, Psychological Abstracts, Sociological Abstracts,* the *Social Sciences Index, Humanities Index, Abstracts of Popular Culture, Index Medicus, Dissertation Abstracts, Index to Legal Periodicals, Index to Periodical Articles Related to Law,* as well as various standard and nonstandard review sources for monographic and unpublished materials. This huge range of material is then coordinated into an integrated sex research collection by indexing the items in accordance with the terms listed in *Sexual Nomenclature: A Thesaurus.*[19] Theoretically an individual researcher could retrieve the same materials; however, experience has shown that because of the interdisciplinary nature of sex research and its specialized vocabulary, few searches produce a significant amount of on-target material. Therefore, the best present access to current research is through the Library of the Institute for Sex Research. Access to material published up to November 1975 has been facilitated by the publication of two catalogs covering the social and behavioral sciences holdings of the Library[20,21] and by the publication of this collection of bibliographies, current through 1977 and with many 1978 references.

Other bibliographic sources helpful in locating sex-related materials are available through organizations serving related fields such as family planning and marriage and family counseling. For example, bibliographies on topics within the fields of population, family planning, and related demographic aspects can be obtained from the Technical Information Service of the Carolina Population Center.[22] Directories listing other population information centers and libraries throughout the world are available from the Carolina Center and from the Public Affairs Clearinghouse.[23]

Marriage and family related topics are covered by the Inventory of Marriage and Family Literature Project, a joint venture of the Social Science Department of the University of Minnesota, the Minnesota Family Study Center, and the National Council on Family Relations.[24,25,26,27]

Data on evaluation and methods research, statistics on births, deaths, marriages, divorces, and living arrangements are available from the Scientific and Technical Information Branch of the National Center for Health Statistics.[28] Literature searches and referrals are available to agencies, research scientists, clinicians, and other professionals from the National Clearinghouse for Mental Health Information.[29]

Literature reviews and bibliographies on a number of sex-related research topics are available through the Journal Supplement Abstract Service of the American Psychological Association.[30] Bibliographies of current articles related to homosexuality, transexualism, and transvestism are published in each issue of the *Journal of Homosexuality.* Most of the articles listed there are available for a fee from the Original Article Tearsheet Service (OATS).[31] Selective bibliographies of material related to sex education and counseling are published in the *SIECUS Report.*

Other sources of information on specific topics are listed in the relevant bibliographies in this collection.

PERIODICALS

An indication of the growing importance of and interest in sex research is the rapidly increasing number of periodicals devoted to reporting on current research projects and their clinical applications. Some of the titles on the following list are also cited on the bibliographies in the body of this collection as being particularly useful in specific subject areas; others cover so broad a scope that they appear only here.

NEWSLETTERS

Sex News (m.)
("A monthly digest of news, views, events, publications and resources")
7140 Oak, Kansas City, MO 64114

Sexuality Today (w.)
("The professionals' newsletter")
2315 Broadway, New York, NY 10024

SHAR (m. except July & Aug.)
("Sexual Health and Relationships")
Box 627, Northampton, MA 01060

SIECUS Report (bi-m.)
(Sex Information and Education Council of the U.S.)
Human Sciences Press
72 Fifth Ave., New York, NY10011

Sexual Law Reporter (bi-m.)
1800 N. Highland Ave., 106, Los Angeles, CA 90028

Sex Problems Court Digest (m.)
1860 Broadway, Suite 1110, New York, NY 10023

Getting It Together
("A publication of the Youth and Student Affairs Program")
Planned Parenthood Federation of America
810 Seventh Ave., New York, NY 10019

Family Planning/Population Reporter (bi-m.)
("A review of state laws and policies")
The Alan Guttmacher Institute
515 Madison Ave., New York, NY 10022

JOURNALS

Alternatives: Marriage, Family and Changing Life Styles (q.)
Sage Publications
275 South Beverly Dr., Beverly Hills, CA 90212

Archives of Sexual Behavior (bi-m.)
("An interdisciplinary research journal")

Plenum Publishing Corporation
227 West 17th St., New York, NY 10011

Human Sexuality Update (bi-m.)
(". . . current abstracts of journal articles . . . subject index")
Haworth Press
149 Fifth Ave., New York, NY 10010

Journal of Homosexuality (q.)
(". . . devoted to empirical research, and its clinical applications")
Haworth Press
149 Fifth Ave., New York, NY 10010

Journal of Marriage and the Family (q.)
("Formerly *Marriage and Family Living*")
National Council on Family Relations
1219 University Ave. SE, Minneapolis, MN 55414

Journal of Sex and Marital Therapy (q.)
(". . . new therapeutic techniques, research on outcome . . .")
Human Sciences Press
72 Fifth Ave., New York, NY 10011

Journal of Sex Education and Therapy (semi-a.)
American Association of Sex Educators, Counselors and Therapists
5010 Wisconsin Ave., NW, Suite 304, Washington, DC 20016

Journal of Sex Research (q.)
("The publication of the Society for the Scientific Study of Sex")
208 Daffodil Rd., Glen Burnie, MD 21061

Medical Aspects of Human Sexuality (m.)
(". . . physical, psychological, and cultural components . . .")
Hospital Publications
609 Fifth Ave., New York, NY 10017

Sexual Medicine Today
(". . . published monthly by International Medical News Service, Inc.")
600 New Hampshire Ave., NW, Washington, DC 20037

Sexuality and Disability (q.)
(". . . the study of sex in physical and mental illness")
Human Sciences Press
72 Fifth Ave., New York, NY 10011

POPULAR

Forum (m.)
("The international journal of human relations")
909 Third Ave., New York, NY 10022

Sexology (m.)
("For 44 years . . . frank and authoritative sex guidance")
200 Park Ave. So., New York, NY 10003

ORGANIZATIONS

Through the years, some family planning and marriage and family counseling organizations have supported sex-related research within their scope of interest. They are still important sources of information. However, individuals with common interests specifically in sex research have begun to reach out across disciplines and organize in order to exchange information, encourage research, and develop standards specific to the subject.

American Association of Sex Educators, Counselors and Therapists
Exec. Dir.: Patricia A. Schiller
5010 Wisconsin Ave., NW, Suite 304
Washington, DC 20016

An interdisciplinary membership organization founded in 1967 for the purpose of training, education, and research in the interest of developing competency and standards for sex educators and sex counselors. Sponsors training programs; publishes a newsletter and the *Journal of Sex Education and Therapy.*

Sex Information and Education Council of the United States (SEICUS)
Pres.: Mary S. Calderone; Exec. Dir.: Ruth A. Beasley
84 Fifth Ave., Suite 407, New York, NY 10011

Founded in 1964 to develop individual and community values and attitudes basic to responsible sexuality through public and professional education, disseminate research information, and prepare educational materials. Publishes *SIECUS Report.* Catalogs describing educators' packets, books, etc., are available from Human Sciences Press, 72 Fifth Ave., New York, NY 10011.

Society for the Scientific Study of Sex (SSSS)
Exec. Sec.: Mrs. Mary Westervelt
208 Daffodil Rd., Glen Burnie, MD 21061

Founded in 1957 to foster interdisciplinary exchange in the field of sexual knowledge. Brings together individuals working in the biological, medical, anthropological, psychological, sociological, and allied fields who are conducting sexual research, whose professions involve problems relating to sex, or who are vitally concerned with sexual science. Publishes an occasional newsletter and the *Journal of Sex Research.*

The Eastern Association for Sex Therapy (EAST)
Chrmn. of Admissions: Oliver J.W. Bjorksten, M.D.
Medical University of South Carolina
80 Barre St., Charleston, SC 29401

Founded in 1974 to promote communication among professionals involved in the treatment of patients with sexual dysfunctions; to encourage collaboration in research; to define a set of standards stating the criteria of knowledge, experience, and ethics for members; and to provide a means of disseminating information related to the work of its members.

International Academy of Sex Research
Sec./Treas.: Anke Ehrhardt
Psychiatric Institute, Columbia University
722 W. 168th St., New York, NY 10032

Established in 1974 for the purpose of promoting high standards of research and scholarship in the field of sexual behavior.

National Council on Family Relations
1219 University Ave. SE, Minneapolis, MN 55414

Organized in 1938 to bring together leaders in research, teaching, and professional service in the field of marriage and the family. Sponsors conferences and publishes the *Journal of Marriage and the Family, The Family Coordinator,* and a newsletter.

Planned Parenthood-World Population
810 Seventh Ave., New York, NY 10019

National headquarters of the Planned Parenthood Federation of America, established in 1921. Affiliated local organizations are located throughout the country. Develops and maintains training programs to promote voluntary fertility control; prepares and distributes a number of publications through various divisions and committees, including: *Getting it Together, Planned Parenthood Report, Family Planning Perspectives, Family Planning/Population Reporter, International Family Planning Digest.*

References:

1. Paul H. Gebhard. "Human sex behavior research." In: *Perspectives in Reproduction and Sexual Behavior,* ed. by Milton Diamond, pp. 391–410. Bloomington: Indiana University Press, 1968.
2. Paul H. Gebhard. "Sexual behaviour, Human." In: *Encyclopaedia Britannica. Macropaedia* 16:593–601, 1974.
3. Sophie D. Aberle and George W. Corner. *Twenty-Five Years of Sex Research; History of the National Research Council Committee for Research in Problems of Sex, 1922–1947.* Philadelphia: W.B. Saunders, 1953.
4. John Money. "The development of sexology as a discipline." *Journal of Sex Research* 12(2):83–87, May 1976.
5. Alfred C. Kinsey et al. *Sexual Behavior in the Human Male,* pp. 21–34. Philadelphia: W.B. Saunders, 1948.
6. Edward M. Brecher. *The Sex Researchers.* Boston: Little, Brown & Co., 1969.
7. John H. Gagnon. "Sex research and social change." *Archives of Sexual Behavior* 4(20):111–141, Mar. 1975.
8. Paul Robinson. *The Modernization of Sex: Havelock Ellis, Alfred Kinsey, William Masters and Virginia Johnson.* New York: Harper & Row, 1976.
9. Victor Robinson, ed. *Encyclopaedia Sexualis; A Comprehensive Encyclopaedia-Dictionary of the Sexual Sciences.* New York: Dingwall-Rock, 1936.
10. Flora C. Seruya, Susan Losher and Albert Ellis. *Sex and Sex Education: A Bibliography.* New York: Bowker, 1972.
11. Karl M. Bowman et al. "Psychiatric implications of surveys on sexual behavior." *Psychoanalytic Review* 43(4):471–500, Oct. 1956.
12. Cornelia V. Christenson. *Kinsey: A Biography.* Bloomington: Indiana University Press, 1971.
13. Wardell B. Pomeroy. *Dr. Kinsey and the Institute for Sex Research.* New York: Harper & Row, 1972.
14. Paul Delbert Brinkman. "Dr. Alfred C. Kinsey and the press: historical cast study of the relationship of the mass media and a pioneering behavior scientist." Unpub. doctoral dissertation, Indiana University, 1971.
15. James Howard Jones. "The origins of the Institute for Sex Research: a history." Unpub. doctoral dissertation, Indiana University, 1972.
16. Martin S. Weinberg, ed. *Sex Research: Studies from the Kinsey Institute.* New York: Oxford University Press, 1976.
17. Ruth A. Beasley. "Current status of sex research." *Journal of Sex Research* 11(4):335–347, Nov. 1975.
18. Paul H. Gebhard. "Comprehensive sex research centers: design and operation for effective functioning." *Archives of Sexual Behavior* 4(4):447–457, July, 1975.
19. JoAnn Brooks and Helen C. Hofer, comps. *Sexual Nomenclature: A Thesaurus.* Boston: G.K. Hall, 1976.
20. Institute for Sex Research. *Catalog of the Social and Behavioral Sciences Monograph Section of the Library of the Institute for Sex Research.* Boston: G.K. Hall, 1975.
21. Institute for Sex Research. *Catalog of Periodical Literature in the Social and Behavioral Sciences Section, Library of the Institute for Sex Research, Including Supplement to Mongraphs, 1973–1975.* Boston: G.K. Hall, 1976.
22. Technical Information Service, Carolina Population Center, University Square, Chapel Hill, NC 27514.
23. Public Affairs Clearinghouse, Box 30, Claremont, CA 91711.
24. Joan Aldous and Reuben Hill. *International Bibliography of Research in Marriage and the Family, 1900–1964.* Minneapolis: University of Minnesota Press, 1967.
25. Joan Aldous and Nancy S. Dahl. *International Bibliography of Research in Marriage and the Family, Volume II,*

1965-1972. Minneapolis: University of Minnesota Press, 1974.

26. D.H. Olson and Nancy S. Dahl. *Inventory of Marriage and Family Literature: Volume III, 1973-1974.* St. Paul, MN: Family Social Science, University of Minnesota, 1975.

27. D.H. Olson and Nancy S. Dahl. *Inventory of Marriage and Family Literature: Volume IV, 1975-1976.* St. Paul, MN: Family Social Science, University of Minnesota, 1977.

28. Scientific and Technical Information Branch, National Center for Health Statistics, Health Resources Administration, 5600 Fishers Lane, Rockville, MD 20852.

29. National Clearinghouse for Mental Health Information, 5600 Fishers Lane, Rockville, MD 20852.

30. Journal Supplement Abstract Service, American Psychological Association, 1200 17th St. NW, Washington, DC 20036.

31. OATS, Institute for Scientific Information, 325 Chestnut St., Philadelphia, PA 19106.

II. BIBLIOGRAPHIES FROM THE INSTITUTE FOR SEX RESEARCH

Sex Behavior

General

CATALOGS

1 Institute for Sex Research. *Catalog of Periodical Literature in the Social and Behavioral Sciences Section, Library of the Institute for Sex Research, Including Supplement to Monographs, 1973-1975.* Boston: G.K. Hall, 1976.

2 _____. *Catalog of the Social and Behavioral Sciences Monograph Section of the Library of the Institute for Sex Research.* Boston: G.K. Hall, 1975.

DIRECTORIES

3 *(AASECT) National Register of Certified Sex Educators: Certified Sex Therapists.* Washington, DC: American Association of Sex Educators, Counselors and Therapists, 1976.

4 Beasley, Ruth, comp. *International Directory of Sex Research and Related Fields.* Boston: G.K. Hall, 1976.

ENCYCLOPEDIAS

5 Ellis, Albert and Albert Abarbanel, eds. *Encyclopedia of Sexual Behavior.* 2nd ed. New York: Hawthorn Books, 1967.

6 Lief, Harold I., comp. *Medical Aspects of Human Sexuality: 750 Questions Answered by 500 Authorities.* Baltimore: Williams & Wilkins, 1975.

7 Money, John and Herman Musaph, eds. *Handbook of Sexology.* Amsterdam: Excerpta Medica, 1977.

MONOGRAPHS

8 Barnett, Walter. *Sexual Freedom and the Constitution.* Albuquerque: University of New Mexico Press, 1973.

9 Bell, Robert R. *Premarital Sex in a Changing Society.* Englewood Cliffs, NJ: Prentice-Hall, 1966.

10 Bullough, Vern L. *Sexual Variance in Society and History.* New York: Wiley, 1976.

11 Cuber, John F. and Peggy B. Harroff. *The Significant Americans: A Study of Sexual Behavior Among the Affluent.* New York: Appleton-Century,

1965. (Paperback ed.: *Sex and the Significant Americans: A Study of Sexual Behavior Among the Affluent.* Penguin, 1966.)

12 Dickinson, Robert Latou. *Atlas of Human Sex Anatomy.* Huntington, NY: Robert E. Krieger Pub. Co., 1970. (Reprint of *Human Sex Anatomy: A Topographical Hand Atlas.* 2nd ed. Baltimore: Williams & Wilkins, 1949.)

13 Eysenck, H.J. *Sex and Personality.* Austin: University of Texas, 1976.

14 Gadpaille, Warren J. *The Cycles of Sex.* Ed. by Lucy Freeman. New York: Scribner, 1975.

15 Gagnon, John H. and William Simon. *Sexual Conduct: The Social Sources of Human Sexuality.* Chicago: Aldine Publishing Co., 1973.

16 Gebhard, P.H. et al. *Pregnancy, Birth and Abortion.* New York: Harper-Hoeber, 1958. (Paperback ed.: New York: Wiley, 1966.)

17 Gorer, Geoffrey. *Sex and Marriage in England Today: A Study of the Views and Experiences of the Under-45's.* London: Thomas Nelson, 1971.

18 Hart, Gavin. *Sexual Maladjustment and Disease: An Introduction to Modern Venereology.* Chicago: Nelson-Hall, 1977.

19 Hite, Shere. *The Hite Report: A Nationwide Study on Female Sexuality.* New York: Macmillan, 1976.

20 Hunt, Morton. *Sexual Behavior in the 1970's.* Chicago: Playboy Press, 1974.

21 Kinsey, Alfred C. et al. *Sexual Behavior in the Human Female.* Philadelphia: W.B. Saunders, 1953.

22 _____. *Sexual Behavior in the Human Male.* Philadelphia: W.B. Saunders, 1948.

23 McCary, James Leslie. *Sexual Myths and Fallacies.* New York: Van Nostrand Reinhold, 1971.

24 Masters, William H. and Virginia E. Johnson. *Human Sexual Response.* Boston: Little, Brown, 1966.

25 Oliven, John F. *Clinical Sexuality.* 3rd ed. Philadelphia: J.B. Lippincott, 1974.

26 Packard, Vance. *The Sexual Wilderness.* New York: David McKay, 1968.

27   Reiss, Ira L. *Premarital Sexual Standards in America; A Sociological Investigation of the Relative Social and Cultural Integration of American Sexual Standards.* Glencoe, IL: Free Press, 1960.

28   Robinson, Paul. *The Modernization of Sex: Havelock Ellis, Alfred Kinsey, William Masters and Virginia Johnson.* New York: Harper & Row, 1976.

29   Ruitenbeek, Hendrik M. *The New Sexuality.* New York: New Viewpoints, 1974.

30   Schmidt, Gunter and Volkmar Sigusch. *Arbeiter-Sexualität: eine empirische Untersuchung an jungen Industriearbeitern.* Neuwied und Berlin: Hermann Luchterhand Verlag, 1971.

31   Sears, Hal D. *The Sex Radicals: Free Love in High Victorian America.* Lawrence: Regents Press of Kansas, 1977.

32   Simon, Pierre. *Rapport Simon Sur le Comportement Sexuel des Français.* Paris: Pierre Charron/René Julliard, 1972.

33   Slovenko, Ralph, ed. *Sexual Behavior and the Law.* Springfield, IL: Charles C. Thomas, 1965.

34   Zetterberg, Hans L. *Om Sexuallivet i Sverige: Värderingar, Normer, Beteenden i Sociologisk Tolkning.* Statens Offentliga Utredningar, 1969:2. Stockholm: U.S.S.U., 1969.

COLLECTIONS

35   Beach, Frank A., ed. *Human Sexuality in Four Perspectives.* Baltimore: Johns Hopkins University Press, 1977.

36   Bell, Robert R. and Michael Gordon, eds. *The Social Dimension of Human Sexuality.* Boston: Little, Brown, 1972.

37   Braun, Saul, ed. *Catalog of Sexual Consciousness.* New York: Grove Press, 1975.

38   Calderone, Mary S., ed. *Sexuality and Human Values.* (SEICUS Conference on Religion and Sexuality, St. Louis, 1971.) New York: Association Press, 1974.

39   Carter, Carol Sue, ed. *Hormones and Sexual Behavior.* Stroudsburg, PA: Dowden, Hutchinson & Ross, 1974.

40   Diamond, Milton, ed. *Perspectives in Reproduction and Sexual Behavior.* Bloomington: Indiana University Press, 1968.

41   Edwards, John N., ed. *Sex and Society.* Chicago: Markham Publishing Co., 1972.

42   Gagnon, John and William Simon, eds. *The Sexual Scene.* Chicago: Aldine Publishing Co., 1970.

43   Gebhard, Paul H., Jan Raboch and Hans Giese. *The Sexuality of Women.* Library of Sexual Behavior, v. 1. New York: Stein & Day, 1970.

44   Gochros, Harvey L. and LeRoy G. Schultz, eds. *Human Sexuality and Social Work.* New York: Association Press, 1972.

45   Gordon, Sol and Roger W. Libby, eds. *Sexuality Today and Tomorrow; Contemporary Issues in Human Sexuality.* North Scituate, MA: Duxbury Press, 1976.

46   Gross, Leonard, ed. *Sexual Behavior—Current Issues: An Interdisciplinary Perspective.* Flushing, NY: Spectrum Publications, 1974.

47   Henslin, James M., ed. *Studies in the Sociology of Sex.* New York: Appleton-Century-Crofts, 1971.

48   Hurwood, Bernhardt J., ed. *The Whole Sex Catalog.* New York: Pinnacle Books, 1975.

49   Kirkendall, Lester A. and Robert N. Whitehurst, eds. *The New Sexual Revolution.* New York: Scribner, 1971.

50   Libby, Roger W. and Robert N. Whitehurst, eds. *Marriage and Alternatives: Exploring Intimate Relationships.* Glenview, IL: Scott, Foresman, 1977.

51   Lieberman, Bernhardt, ed. *Human Sexual Behavior: A Book of Readings.* New York: Wiley, 1971.

52   McCary, James Leslie and Donna R. Copeland, eds. *Modern Views of Human Sexual Behavior.* Chicago: Science Research Associates, 1976.

53   Malfetti, James L. and Elizabeth M. Eidletz, eds. *Perspectives on Sexuality.* New York: Holt, Rinehart & Winston, 1972.

54   Marshall, Donald S. and Robert Suggs, eds. *Human Sexual Behavior: Variations in the Ethnographic Spectrum.* New York: Basic Books, 1971.

55   Money, John, ed. *Sex Research: New Developments.* New York: Holt, Rinehart & Winston, 1965.

56   Morrison, Eleanor S. and Vera Borosage, eds. *Human Sexuality: Contemporary Perspectives.* Palo Alto, CA: National Press Books, 1973.

57   Oaks, Wilbur W., Gerald A. Melchiode and Ilda Ficher, eds. *Sex and the Life Cycle.* (The

Thirty-fifth Hahnemann Symposium.) New York: Grune & Stratton, 1976.

58   Otto, Herbert A., ed. *The New Sexuality.* Palo Alto, CA: Science and Behavior Books, 1971.

59   Resnick, H.L.P. and Marvin E. Wolfgang, eds. *Sexual Behaviors: Social, Clinical and Legal Aspects.* Boston: Little, Brown, 1972.

60   Rubinstein, Eli A., Richard Green and Edward Brecher, eds. *Sex Research: Future Directions.* Proceedings of the Conference, State University of New York at Stony Brook, June 5-9, 1974. *Archives of Sexual Behavior* 4(4): whole issue, July 1975. (Also published as *New Directions in Sex Research.* Perspectives in Sexuality Series. New York: Plenum, 1976.)

61   Sadock, Benjamin J., Harold I. Kaplan and Alfred M. Freedman, eds. *The Sexual Experience.* Baltimore: Williams & Wilkins, 1976.

62   Sagarin, Edward and Donal E.J. MacNamara, eds. *Problems of Sex Behavior.* New York: Crowell, 1971.

63   Shiloh, Ailon, ed. *Studies in Human Sexual Behavior: The American Scene.* Springfield, IL: Charles C. Thomas, 1970.

64   Taylor, Donald Lavor, ed. *Human Sexual Development: Perspectives in Sex Education.* Philadelphia: F.A. Davis Co., 1970.

65   Wagner, Nathaniel N., ed. *Perspectives on Human Sexuality: Psychological, Social and Cultural Research Findings.* New York: Behavioral Publications, 1974.

66   Weinberg, Martin S., ed. *Sex Research: Studies from the Kinsey Institute.* New York: Oxford University Press, 1976.

67   Winokur, George, ed. *Determinants of Human Sexual Behavior.* Springfield, IL: Charles C. Thomas, 1963.

68   Wiseman, Jacqueline P., ed. *The Social Psychology of Sex.* New York: Harper & Row, 1976.

69   Zubin, Joseph and John Money, eds. *Contemporary Sexual Behavior: Critical Issues in the 1970's.* Baltimore: Johns Hopkins University Press, 1973.

Sex Behavior (Child)

70   Bakwin, Harry. "Erotic feelings in children." *Indian Journal of Pediatrics* 38: 135-137, Mar. 1971.

71   Broderick, Carlfred B. "Preadolescent sexual behavior." *Medical Aspects of Human Sexuality* 2(1):20-29, Jan. 1968.

72   Capes, Mary. "Sexual development in childhood and its problems." *British Medical Journal* 5831:38-39, Oct. 1972.

73   Finch, Stuart M. "Sex play among boys and girls." *Medical Aspects of Human Sexuality* 3(9):58-66, Sept. 1969.

74   _____. "Sexual activity of children with other children and adults." *Clinical Pediatrics* 6(1):1-2, Jan. 1967.

75   Ford, Clellan S. and Frank A. Beach. *Patterns of Sexual Behavior.* New York: Harper & Row, 1951.

76   Gadpaille, Warren J. "Brief guide to office counseling: masturbation in preadolescent girls." *Medical Aspects of Human Sexuality* 8(9): 179-180, Sept. 1974.

77   _____. *The Cycles of Sex.* Ed. by Lucy Freeman. New York: Scribner, 1975.

78   Grimm, H. "Sexuologie des kinder- und jugendalters in vergleichend-ethnobiologischer betrachtung." *Arztliche Jugendkunde* 64(4):295-312, 1973.

79   Halverson, H.M. "Genital and sphincter behavior of the male infant." *Journal of Genetic Psychology* 56:95-136, 1940.

80   Johnson, Warren R. "Awakening sexuality of girls." *Sexual Behavior* 3(3):3-6, Mar. 1973.

81   Ribal, Joseph E. *Learning Sex Roles: American and Scandinavian Contrasts.* San Francisco: Canfield Press, 1973.

82   Sigusch, Volkmar and Thea Schönfelder. "La masturbazione nell' età infantile." *Sessuologia* 15(2):50-53, Apr./June 1974.

83   Spitz, Rene A. and Katherine M. Wolf. "Autoeroticism: some empirical findings and hypotheses on three of its manifestations in the first year of life." *Psychoanalytic Study of the Child* 3/4:85-120, 1949.

SEX BEHAVIOR RESEARCH

84   Elias, James E. and Paul H. Gebhard. "Sexuality and sexual learning in childhood." *Phi Delta Kappan* 50(7):401-405, Mar. 1969.

85   Green, Richard. "Sexual problems of children." In: *Sex and the Life Cycle,* ed. by Wilbur W.

Oaks, Gerald A. Melchiode and Ilda Ficher, pp. 19–27. New York: Grune & Stratton, 1976.

86 Kinsey, Alfred C. et al. *Sexual Behavior in the Human Female.* Philadelphia: W.B. Saunders, 1953.

87 _____. *Sexual Behavior in the Human Male.* Philadelphia: W.B. Saunders, 1948.

88 Martinson, Floyd M. *Infant and Child Sexuality: A Sociological Perspective.* St. Peter, MN: The Book Mark, 1973. (Privately published. Avail. from The Book Mark, Gustavus Adolphus College, St. Peter, MN 56082)

89 Reevy, William R. "Child sexuality." In: *Encyclopedia of Sexual Behavior,* ed. by Albert Ellis and Albert Abarbanel, pp. 258–267. New York: Hawthorn Books, 1961.

PSYCHOSEXUAL DEVELOPMENT

90 Adams, Paul L., Nancy P. McDonald and William P. Huey. "School phobia and bisexual conflict: a report of 21 cases." *American Journal of Psychiatry* 123(5):541–547, Nov. 1966.

91 Angrilli, Albert F. "The psychosexual identification of preschool boys." *Journal of Genetic Psychology* 97:329–340, 1960.

92 Arkin, E.A. "The sexual problems in early childhood (Part I)." *Journal of Sex Education* 3(4):168–172, Mar. 1951.

93 _____. "The sexual problems in early childhood (Part II)." *Journal of Sex Education* 3(5):208–217, May 1951.

94 Breiner, S.J. "Psychological principles of a sex education program for grades K through 12." *Journal of School Health* 42(4):227–232, Apr. 1972.

95 Broderick, Carlfred B. "Social heterosexual development among urban negroes and whites." *Journal of Marriage and the Family* 27(2):200–203, May 1965.

96 Broderick, Carlfred B. and George P. Rowe. "A scale of preadolescent heterosexual development." *Journal of Marriage and the Family* 30(1):97-101, Feb. 1968.

97 Capes, Mary. "Sexual development in childhood and its problems." *British Medical Journal* 5831:38–39, Oct. 1972

98 Conn, Jacob H. "Children's awareness of sex differences II. Play attitudes game preferences." *Journal of Child Psychiatry* 2(1):82–99, 1951.

99 _____. "Children's awareness of the origins of babies." *Journal of Child Psychiatry* 1(2):140–176, 1948.

100 _____. "Children's reactions to the discovery of genital differences." *American Journal of Orthopsychiatry* 10:747–754, 1940.

101 _____. "Factors influencing development of sexual attitudes and sexual awareness in children." *American Journal of Diseases of Children* 58:738–745, Oct. 1939.

102 _____. "Sex attitudes and sex awareness in young children." *Child Study* 16:86–87 passim, Jan. 1939.

103 _____. "Sexual curiosity of children." *American Journal of Diseases of Children* 60:1110–1119, 1940.

104 Conn, Jacob H. and Leo Kanner. "Children's awareness of sex differences." *Journal of Child Psychiatry* 1:3–57, 1947.

105 Eckstein, Rudolf. "Dialogue on sex: distance versus intimacy." *The Reiss-Davis Clinic Bulletin:* 38–48, Spring 1970.

106 Edwards, J.B. "Some studies of the moral development of children." *Educational Research* 7(3):200–211, 1965.

107 Fry, William F., Jr. "Psychodynamics of sexual humor: sexual views of children." *Medical Aspects of Human Sexuality* 8(9):77–80, Sept. 1974.

108 Gagnon, John H. "Sexuality and sexual learning in the child." *Psychiatry* 28(3):212–228, Aug. 1965.

109 Gardner, Richard A. "Sexual fantasies in childhood." *Medical Aspects of Human Sexuality* 3(10):121–134, Oct. 1969.

110 Heagarty, Margaret, Geraldine Glass and Helen King. "Sex and the preschool child." *American Journal of Nursing* 74(8):1479–1482, Aug. 1974.

111 Hoch, Paul H. and Joseph Zubin, eds. *Psychosexual Development in Health and Disease.* New York: Grune & Stratton, 1949.

112 Kerscher, Karl-Heinz Ignatz. *Sexualität & Erziehung: zu den Grundlagen einer emanzipatorischen Sexualpädagogik.* Giessen, GFR: Andreas Achenbach, 1974.

113 Korner, Anneliese F. "Neonatal startles, smiles, erections and reflex sucks as related to state, sex, and individuality." *Child Development* 40(4):1039–1053, 1969.

114   Kreitler, Hans and Shulamith Kreitler. "Children's concepts of sexuality and birth." *Child Development* 37(2):363–378, 1966.

115   Lando, Pier Luigi. "Sulla natura delle inibizioni e difficoltà del rapporto etero-sessuale." *Sessuologia* 15(2):12–26, Apr.-June 1974.

116   Landreth, Catherine. "Four-year-olds' notions about sex appropriateness of parental care and companionship activities." *Merrill-Palmer Quarterly* 9(3):175–182, July 1963.

117   Levin, Saul M., James Balistrieri and Mark Schukit. "The development of sexual discrimination in children." *Journal of Child Psychology and Psychiatry* 13:47–53, 1972.

118   Lewis, Melvin. "Psychosexual development and sexual behavior in children." *Connecticut Medicine* 32(6):437–443, June 1968.

119   Martinson, Floyd M. "Eroticism in infancy and childhood." *Journal of Sex Research* 12(4):251–262, Nov. 1976.

120   Montagu, M.F. Ashley. "The acquisition of sexual knowledge in children." *American Journal of Orthopsychiatry* 15(2):290–300, Apr. 1945.

121   Myers, Wayne A. "The primal scene: exposure to parental intercourse." *Medical Aspects of Human Sexuality* 8(9):156–165, Sept. 1974.

122   "Niveles de sexualidad; sexualidad infantil." *Sexualmedica* (7):69–72, May-June 1974.

123   Offer, Daniel and William Simon. "Stages of sexual development." In: *The Sexual Experience,* ed. by B.J. Sadock, H.I. Kaplan and A.M. Freedman, pp. 128–141. Baltimore: Williams & Wilkins, 1976.

124   Pietrofesa, John J. and Howard Splete. "Consultation: an effective dimension of childhood sexual development." *The School Counselor* 20(3):186–192, Jan. 1973.

125   Pomeroy, Wardell B. "An analysis of questions on sex." *The Psychological Record* 10(3):191–201, July 1960.

126   Ramsey, Glenn V. "The sex information of younger boys." *American Journal of Orthopsychiatry* 13(2):347–352, Apr. 1943.

127   _____. "The sexual development of boys." *American Journal of Psychology* 56(2):217–234, Apr. 1943.

128   Reevy, W.R. "Child sexuality." In: *The Encyclopedia of Sexual Behavior,* ed. by Albert Ellis and Albert Abarbanel, pp. 258–267. New York: Hawthorn Books, 1961.

129   Renshaw, Domeena C. "Sexuality and depression in infancy, childhood, and adolescence." *Medical Aspects of Human Sexuality* 9(6):24–45, June 1975.

130   _____. "Sexuality in children." *Medical Aspects of Human Sexuality* 5(10):63–74, Oct. 1971.

131   Rutter, Michael. "Normal psychosexual development." *Journal of Child Psychology and Psychiatry* 11:259–283, 1971.

132   Signori, Livio. "Cinema—erotismo—infanzia." *Sessuologia* 15(2):54–56, Apr./June 1974.

133   Toussieng, Povl W. "Psychosexual development in childhood and adolescence." *Journal of School Health* 35:158–165, Apr. 1965.

134   "Viewpoints: what do you advise parents on such problems as nudity before children, allowing children to visit briefly in the parents' bed, and bathroom invasion by children?" *Medical Aspects of Human Sexuality* 2(1):12–19, Jan. 1968.

Sex Attitudes and Behavior Research (Adolescent)

BIBLIOGRAPHIES

135   Baizerman, Michael et al. *Pregnant Adolescents; A Review of Literature with Abstracts 1960-1970.* University of Pittsburgh, Graduate School of Public Health, Maternal and Child Health Section; Dec. 31, 1971. (*Sharing* Supplement.) (Distributed by Consortium on Early Childbearing and Childrearing, Research Utilization and Information Sharing Project, Suite 709, 1145 19th St. NW, Washington, DC 20036.)

136   Perkins, Barbara B. *Adolescent Birth Planning and Sexuality; Abstracts of the Literature.* Consortium on Early Childbearing and Childrearing, Child Welfare League of America, 1145 19th St. NW, Suite 618, Washington, DC, 1974.

137   Stewart, Karen Robb, comp. and ed. *Adolescent Sexuality and Teenage Pregnancy: A Selected, Annotated Bibliography with Summary Forewords.* Chapel Hill, NC: Carolina Population Center, 1976.

LITERATURE SURVEYS

138   Morgenthau, Joan E. and Natalie J. Sokoloff.

"The sexual revolution: myth or fact?" *Pediatric Clinics of North America* 19(3):779–789, Aug. 1972.

139   Osofsky, Howard J. "Adolescent sexual behavior: current status and anticipated trends for the future." *Clinical Obstetrics and Gynecology* 14:393–408, June 1971.

SEX ATTITUDES RESEARCH (ADOLESCENT)

140   Bene, Eva. "Suppression of hetero-sexual interest and of aggression by middle class and working class grammar school boys." *British Journal of Educational Psychology* 28(3):226–231, Nov. 1958.

141   Brunswick, Ann F. "Adolescent health, sex, and fertility." *American Journal of Public Health* 61(4):711–729, Apr. 1971.

142   Calderwood, Deryck David. *Adolescent appraisals and opinions concerning their sex education in selected institutions.* (Thesis—Oregon State University.) Ann Arbor, MI: University Microfilms, 1970. (Order #71-2465)

143   Cristante, Francesca and Albina Luccu. "A study of adolescents' attitudes toward heterosexual affective relationships." *Archivio de Psicologia, Neurologia e Psichiatria* 33(2–3):237–260, Mar. 1972.

144   Gilligan, Carol. "Sexual dilemmas at the high-school level." In: *Sexuality and Human Values,* ed. by Mary S. Calderone, pp. 98–110. New York: Association Press, 1974.

145   Gilligan, Carol et al. "Moral reasoning about sexual dilemmas: the development of an interview and scoring system." *Technical Report of the Commission on Obscenity and Pornography* 1:141–174, 1971.

146   Glass, J. Conrad, Jr. "Premarital sexual standards among church youth leaders: an exploratory study." *Journal for the Scientific Study of Religion* 11:361–367, Dec. 1972.

147   Kuhlen, Raymond G. and Nancy Bryant Houlihan. "Adolescent heterosexual interest in 1942–1963." *Child Development* 36(4):1049–1052, Dec. 1965.

148   Lantagne, Joseph E. "Interests of 4000 high school pupils in problems of marriage and parenthood." *Research Quarterly* 29(4):407–416, 1958.

149   Libby, Roger W. "Adolescent sexual attitudes and behavior." *Journal of Clinical Child Psychology* 3(3):36–42, Fall/Winter 1974.

150   Offer, Daniel. "Attitudes toward sexuality in a group of 1500 middle class teenagers." *Journal of Youth and Adolescence* 1(1):81–90, 1972.

151   Reiss, Ira L. *The Social Context of Premarital Sexual Permissiveness.* New York: Holt, Rinehart & Winston, 1967.

152   Schoof-Tams, Karin, Jürgen Schlaegel and Leonhard Walczak. "Differentiation of sexual morality between 11 and 16 years." *Archives of Sexual Behavior* 5(5):353–370, Sept. 1976.

153   Schwartz, Martin S. *A study of the attitudes, sex knowledge, and sources of sex information of 87 ninth grade lower class boys.* (Thesis—Columbia University.) Ann Arbor, MI: University Microfilms, 1968. (Order #69-9916)

154   Seventeen Magazine. *Dating, Mating and Sex: Seventeen In-Depth Study.* Triangle Publications, 1970.

155   Shipman, Gordon. "The psychodynamics of sex education." *The Family Coordinator* 17(1):3–12, Jan. 1968.

156   Sigusch, Volkmar and Gunter Schmidt. "Sexualpraxis und sexualmoral der schüler." *Sexualmedizin* 2(5):240–244, May 1973.

157   _____. "Teenage boys and girls in West Germany." *Journal of Sex Research* 9(2):107–123, May 1973.

158   Soares, Louise M. and Anthony T. Soares. "A study of students' sex attitudes and teachers' perceptions of students' sex attitudes." Paper presented at the Eastern Psychological Association Convention, Philadelphia, PA, Apr. 1969. 10p.

159   Starowicz, Zbigniew Lew. "Przemiany obyczaju seksualnego mlodżiezy." *Wiadomosci Lekarskie* 24(10):995–999, May 15, 1971.

160   Trenc, Pavle and Aleksadra Beluhan. "Ispitivanje stavova i aktivnosti u seksualnom zivotu srednjoskolske omladine u SR Hrvatskoj." *Arkhiv za Zastitu Majke i Djeteta* 17(6):269–320, Nov.–Dec. 1973.

161   Wallace, Jerry McLain. *Factors associated with the premarital sexual standards of North Carolina Baptist young people.* (Thesis—North Carolina State University at Raleigh.) Ann Arbor, MI: University Microfilms, 1971. (Order #72-17,739)

162   Wallace, Robert Clayton. *Sex education knowledge, verbal interaction and attitudes: an exploratory study in high school human biology classes.* (Thesis—University of Illinois.) Ann Arbor, MI: University Microfilms, 1972. (Order #71-14,979)

163 Walczak, Leonhard, Jürgen Schlaegel and Karin Schoof-Tams. "Sexualmoral jugendlicher; sexuelle sozialisation in vorpubertät, pubertät und früher adoleszence (II)." *Sexualmedizin* 4(5): 306–325, May 1975.

164 Wyman, Rachel. *Adolescents' attitudes toward sex as related to their perception of their parents.* (Thesis—New York University.) Ann Arbor, MI: University Microfilms, 1969. (Order #70-15,991)

SEX BEHAVIOR RESEARCH (ADOLESCENT)

165 Abernethy, Virginia. "Illegitimate conception among teenagers." *American Journal of Public Health* 64(7):662–665, July 1974.

166 Asayama, Shin'ichi. *Adolescent Sex Development and Adult Sex Behavior in Japan.* Tokyo: Japanese Association for Sex Education, 1974.

167 _____. "Comparison of sexual development of American and Japanese adolescents." *Psychologia* 1:129–131, 1957.

168 _____. "Statistical investigation of sexual development and behavior in Japanese students in 1974." *Journal of the Japanese Association for Sex Education.* 15p.

169 Berman, Myron. "Sex and the Jewish teenager." *Religious Education* 65(5):415–421, Sept.-Oct. 1970.

170 Berna, Jacques. "Das sexuelle verhalten der jugendlichen." *Psyche* 6(12):161–171, 1952–1953.

171 Biener, Kurt. "Baurenburschen und die sexualität." *Sexualmedizin* 5(3):180–184, Mar. 1976.

172 Broderick, Carlfred B. "Socio-sexual development in a suburban community." *Journal of Sex Research* 2(1):1–24, Apr. 1966.

173 Butman, Jean W. and Jane A. Kamm. *The Social, Psychological and Behavioral World of the Teen-Age Girl.* Ann Arbor: Institute for Social Research, 1965.

174 Clark, LeMon. "A report on the virginity of American unmarried women." *International Journal of Sexology* 4(3):166–169, Feb. 1951.

175 Cohen, Michael W. and Stanford B. Friedman. "Nonsexual motivation of adolescent sexual behavior." *Medical Aspects of Human Sexuality* 9(9):8–31, Sept. 1975.

176 Deutsch, Helene. *Selected Problems of Adolescence: With Special Emphasis on Group Formation.* Psychoanalytic Study of the Child Monograph No. 3. New York: International Universities Press, 1970.

177 Ehrmann, W.W. *Premarital Dating Behavior.* New York: Henry Holt, 1959.

178 Elias, James E. "Teenage sexual patterns." In: *An Examination of Risk-Taking Behavior of Youth,* pp. 10–14. Social Health Papers 5. New York: American Social Health Association, 1970.

179 Elias, James E. and Ronnie Elias. "The sexual world of the adolescent." *Counseling Psychologist* 5(1):92–97, 1975.

180 Elias, James E. and Paul H. Gebhard. "Sexuality and sexual learning in childhood." *Phi Delta Kappan* 50(7):401–405, Mar. 1969.

181 Eliasson, Rosmari. "Sexuelles debüt — und was dann; eine vergleichende studie über geschlechtsspezifisches verhalten." *Sexualmedizin* 4(7):429–434, July 1975.

182 Finkelstein, Ruth. "Program for the sexually active teenager." *Pediatric Clinics of North America* 19(3):791–794, Aug. 1972.

183 Gagnon, John H. "Religion, dating and the staging of socio-sexual experimentation in a college sample." Thesis, University of Chicago, 1969.

184 Garris, Lorrie, Allan Steckler and John R. McIntire. "Relationship between oral contraceptives and adolescent sexual behavior." *Journal of Sex Research* 12(2):135–146, May 1976.

185 Gianturco, Daniel T. and Harmon L. Smith. *The Promiscuous Teenager.* Springfield, IL: Charles C. Thomas, 1974.

186 Goldsmith, Sadja et al. "Teenagers, sex and contraception." *Family Planning Perspectives* 4(1):32–38, Jan. 1972.

187 Gray, Diana. "Turning out: a study of teenage prostitution." *Urban Life and Culture* 1(4):401–425, Jan. 1973.

188 Hornick, Edward J. "Sexuality in adolescents: a plea for celibacy." In: *Sexuality and Psychoanalysis,* ed. by Edward T. Adelson, pp. 238–241. New York: Brunner/Mazel, 1975.

189 Husslein, Adeline. "Geschlechtsverkehr, kontrazeption und aufklärung." *Sexualmedizin* 5(11):796–801, Nov. 1976.

190 Janus, Samuel. "Die neue moral an hochschulen; abhängigkeiten zwischen studiendauer, drogenmissbrauch und lebenseinstellung." *Sexualmedizin* 4(8):492–494, Aug. 1975.

191   Jones, Phillip H. "Pregnancy among high school students." *Health Services Reports* 88(2):187–192, Feb. 1973.

192   Kalogerakis, Michael G. "The effect on ego development of sexual experience in early adolescence." In: *Sexuality and Psychoanalysis,* ed. by Edward T. Adelson, pp. 242–250. New York: Brunner/Mazel, 1975.

193   Kisekka, Mere Nakateragga. *Heterosexual relationships in Uganda.* (Thesis—University of Missouri, Columbia.) Ann Arbor, MI: University Microfilms, 1973. (Order #74-18,570)

194   Klebanow, Sheila. "Developmental readiness and dependency in adolescent sexuality." In: *Sexuality and Psychoanalysis,* ed. by Edward T. Adelson, pp. 230–237. New York: Brunner/Mazel, 1975.

195   Launay, Cl. "Les inhibitions sexuelles chez l'adolescent." *Acta Paedo-Psychiatrica* 36(1):23–26, 1969.

196   Lawton, Shailer U. and Jules Archer. *Sexual Conduct of the Teen-Ager.* New York: Spectrolux Corp., 1951.

197   Lieberman, E. James. "From innocence to experience." Paper presented at 104th American Public Health Association Annual Meeting, Miami Beach, FL, Oct. 1976. 17p.

198   Martinson, Floyd M. *The Quality of Adolescent Sexual Experiences.* St. Peter, MN: Martinson, 1974. (Privately published. Avail. from The Book Mark, Gustavus Adolphus College, St. Peter, MN 56082.)

199   _____. "Sexual knowledge, values, and behavior patterns of adolescents." *Child Welfare* 47(7):405–410 passim, July 1968. (Also in *Human Sexuality and Social Work,* ed. by Harvey L. Gochros and LeRoy G. Schultz, pp. 21–30. New York: Association Press, 1972.)

200   Miller, Patricia Y. and William Simon. "Adolescent sexual behavior: context and change." *Social Problems* 22(1):58–76, Oct. 1974.

201   Money, John and Herman Musaph. *Handbook of Sexology.* Ed. by John Money and Herman Musaph, pp. 269–372. Amsterdam: Excerpta Medica, 1977.

202   Offer, Daniel. "Sexual behavior of a group of normal adolescents." *Medical Aspects of Human Sexuality* 5(9):40–49, Sept. 1971.

203   Offer, Daniel, Marcus David and Judith L. Offer. "A longitudinal study of normal adolescent boys." *American Journal of Psychiatry* 126(7):917–924, Jan. 1970.

204   Olsen, Gunnar Aagaard. "Sexual behavior and attitude in Greenland." Paper presented at the IV World Congress of Psychiatry, Madrid, 5–11 Sept., 1966. (Reprint in *Excerpta Medica International Congress Series* 150:3063–3066, 197?.)

205   Pondelicková, J. and Jiri Mellan. "Nase poznatky ze sexuologického prüzkumn mládezi." *Casopis Lekaru Ceskych (Prague)* 104(20):541–543, May 21, 1965.

206   Priester, Helen Moore. "The reported dating practices of one hundred and six high school seniors in an urban community." Masters thesis, Cornell University, 1941.

207   Ramsey, Glenn V. "Factors in the sex life of 291 boys." Thesis, Indiana University, 1941.

208   _____. "The sexual development of boys." *American Journal of Psychology* 56(2):217–234, Apr. 1943.

209   _____. "Sexual growth of negro and white boys." *Human Biology* 22(2):146–149, May 1950.

210   Reevy, W.R. "Adolescent Sexuality." In: *The Encyclopedia of Sexual Behavior,* ed. by Albert Ellis and Albert Abarbanel, pp. 52–67. New York: Hawthorn Books, 1961.

211   Rennert, Helmut. "Untersuchungen zur sexuellen entwicklung der jugend; eine statistische erhebung an medizinstudenten in halle." *Zeitschrift für ärztliche Fortbildung* 60(3):140–153, 1966.

212   Schlaegel, Jürgen, Karin Schoof-Tams and Leonhard Walczak. "Beziehungen zwischen jungen und mädchen; sexuelle sozialisation in vorpubertät, pubertät und früher adoleszenz (I)." *Sexualmedizin* 4(4):206–218, Apr. 1975.

213   Schmidt, Gunter and Volkmar Sigusch. "Changes in sexual behavior among young males and females between 1960–1970." *Archives of Sexual Behavior* 2(1):27–45, June 1972.

214   Schofield, Michael. *The Sexual Behavior of Young People.* Boston: Little, Brown, 1965.

215   Schwartz, Werner. "Jugendliche kindesväter." *Praxis der Kinderpsychologie und Kinderpsychiatrie* 18(3):103–109, Apr. 1969.

216   Sigusch, Volkmar. "Junge mädchen und die pille; bemerkungen zur hormonalen kontrazeption aus sexualwissenschaftlicher sicht." *Sexualmedizin* 3(6):288–297, June 1974.

217   Sigusch, Volkmar and Gunter Schmidt. *Schüler-sexualität: dokumentation der ergebnisse einer untersuchung an 16- und 17 jährigen schülern und schülerinnen.* Hamburg: Institut fur Sexualforschung, 1970.

218   Sorensen, Robert C. *Adolescent Sexuality in Contemporary America: Personal Values and Sexual Behavior Ages Thirteen to Ninteen.* New York: World Publishing Co., 1973.

219   Sprafke, Ulrike. "Sexualverhalten gefährdeter jugendlicher." *Dermatologische Monatsschrift* 155(8):554–568, 1969.

220   "Teenagers." *Journal of Sex Research* 2(1): whole issue, Apr. 1966.

221   Tekavcic, Bogdan. "The great difference in the sexual interests and the sexual behavior between girls and boys." In: Congrès International de Sexologie Médicale, Paris, 1974, *Papers,* pp. 641–664.

222   Toolan, James M. "Sexual behavior in high school and college students." In: *Sexuality and Psychoanalysis*, ed. by Edward T. Adelson, pp. 260–266. New York: Brunner/Mazel, 1975.

223   Undeutsch, Udo. "Die sexualität im jugendalter." *Stadium Generale* 3(8):433–454, July 1950.

224   Wagner, Nathaniel, Byron Fujita and Ronald J. Pion. "Sexual behavior in high school: data on a small sample." *Journal of Sex Research* 9(2):150–155, May 1973.

PREMARITAL SEX BEHAVIOR RESEARCH (ADOLESCENT)

225   Ball, John C. and Nell Logan. "Early sexual behavior of lower-class delinquent girls." *Journal of Criminal Law, Criminology and Police Science* 51(2):209–214, July–Aug. 1960.

226   Jessor, Shirley L. and Richard Jessor. "Transition from virginity to nonvirginity among youth: a social-psychological study over time." *Developmental Psychology* 11(4):473–484, July 1975.

227   Kantner, John F. and Melvin Zelnik. "Sexual experience of young unmarried women in the United States." *Family Planning Perspectives* 4(4):9–18, Oct. 1972.

228   Lewis, Robert A. "Parents and peers: socialization agents in the coital behavior of young adults." *Journal of Sex Research* 9(2):156–170, May 1973.

229   Lowry, Thomas P. "First coitus." *Medical Aspects of Human Sexuality* 3(5):91–97, May 1969.

230   _____. "Initial coital experiences: where and with whom." *Military Medicine* 129(10):966–967, Oct. 1964.

231   Miller, Warren B. "Sexuality, contraception, and pregnancy in a high-school population." *California Medicine* 119(2):14–21, Aug. 1973.

232   Reiss, Ira L. "Premarital sex as deviant behavior: an application of current approaches to deviance." *American Sociological Review* 35(1):78–87, Feb. 1970.

233   Vener, Arthur M. and Cyrus S. Stewart. "Adolescent sexual behavior in Middle America revisited: 1970–1973." *Journal of Marriage and the Family* 36(4):728–735, Nov. 1974.

234   Vener, Arthur, Cyrus S. Stewart and David L. Hager. "The sexual behavior of adolescents in Middle America: generational and American-British comparisons." *Journal of Marriage and the Family* 34(4):696–705, Nov. 1972.

235   Zelnik, Melvin and John F. Kantner. "The probability of premarital intercourse." *Social Science Research* 1(3):355–341, Sept. 1972.

236   _____. "Sexual and contraceptive experience of young unmarried women in the United States, 1976 and 1971." *Family Planning Perspectives* 9(2):55–71, Mar.–Apr. 1977.

237   _____. "Sexuality, contraception, and pregnancy among young unwed females in the United States." In: *Demographic and Social Aspects of Population Growth*, ed. by Charles F. Westoff and Robert Parke, Jr., pp. 357–374. Washington, DC: U.S. GPO, 1972.

COUNSELING

238   Brown, D.A. "Counseling the youthful homosexual." *School Counselor* 22(5):325–333, May 1975.

239   Gadpaille, Warren J. "Brief guide to office counseling: adolescent concerns about homosexuality." *Medical Aspects of Human Sexuality* 7(11):105 passim, Nov. 1973.

240   _____. "Brief guide to office counseling: counseling parents with sexually active young teenagers." *Medical Aspects of Human Sexuality* 8(7):127 passim, July 1974.

241   _____. "Brief guide to office counseling: a young adult with sexual fears." *Medical Aspects of Human Sexuality* 8(4):199–200, Apr. 1974.

242 Hofmann, Adele D. "Brief guide to office counseling: adolescent promiscuity." *Medical Aspects of Human Sexuality* 8(5):63–64, May 1974.

243 Wolfish, Martin G. "Adolescent sexuality: counseling, contraception, pregnancy." *Clinical Pediatrics* 12(4):244–247, Apr. 1973.

Sex Behavior Research (College Student)

244 Arafat, Ibtihaj Said and Donald Allen. "Birth control attitudes and practices of college women." Unpub. paper, United States, 1975. 14p.

245 Asayama, Shin'ichi. "Statistical investigation of sexual development and behavior in Japanese students in 1974." *Journal of the Japanese Association for Sex Education,* 15p.

246 Barker, William J. and Daniel Perlman. "Volunteer bias and personality traits in sexual standards research." *Archives of Sexual Behavior* 4(2):161–172, Mar. 1975.

247 Barták, Vladimir. "Changes in the sexual behavior of adolescents of Czechoslovakia and Germany." *Archives of Sexual Behavior* 1(2):181–184, 1971.

248 Belanger, Kathleen E. and Eleanor Bradley. "Two groups of university student women: sexual activity and the use of contraception." *Journal of the American College Health Association* 19:307–312, June 1971.

249 Bender, Stephen J. "Sex and the college student." *Journal of School Health* 43:278–280, May 1973.

250 Bergen, Marcelene Betsy. *Sexuality attitudes and behavior of selected university students.* (Dissertation—Kansas State University.) Ann Arbor, MI: University Microfilms, 1972. (Order #72-28,830)

251 Brady, John P. "The scalability of sexual experiences." *Psychological Record* 15(2):275–279, Apr. 1965.

252 Burgess, Jane Menzel. *The influence of family relationships on the sexual behavior of college students in Norway and in the United States.* (Thesis—University of Illinois at Urbana-Champaign.) Ann Arbor, MI: University Microfilms, 1972. (Order #73-9892)

253 Carpenter, George R. *Cross-cultural values as a factor in premarital intimacy.* (Thesis—Purdue University.) Ann Arbor, MI: University Microfilms, 1960. (Order #60-4158)

254 Collins, John K. "Reported sexual experiences of first-year university students." *Australian and New Zealand Journal of Sociology* 9(3):67–69, Oct. 1973.

255 DeLamater, John D. "Intimacy in a co-educational community." Unpub. paper, Dept. of Sociology, University of Wisconsin, 1971. 31p.

256 Elias, James E. "Current research—sex practices and attitudes on campus." Paper presented at Illinois State Deans Meeting, 1969. Mimeo. 13p.

257 Finger, Frank W. "Changes in sex practices and beliefs of male college students during 30 years." *Journal of Sex Research* 11(4):304–317, Nov. 1975.

258 _____. "Sex beliefs and practices among male college students." *Journal of Abnormal and Social Psychology* 42(1):57–67, Jan. 1947.

259 Freedman, Mervin B. *The College Experience.* Chapter 7: "Sex among College Students: A Contemporary Report," pp. 81–105; Chapter 8: "Sex and Society: Social and Historical Perspectives," pp. 107–129. San Francisco: Jossey-Bass, 1969.

260 Fröhlich, Hans H. and Hans Szewczyk. "Sexualerfahrungen von Berliner studenten—daten einer befragung." *Probleme und Ergebnisse der Psychologie* 32:17–36, 1970.

261 Gerson, Allan R. "Promiscuity as a function of the father-daughter relationship." *Psychological Reports* 34(3pt.1):1013–1014, Jan. 1974.

262 Giedt, F. Harold. "Changes in sexual behavior and attitudes following class study of the Kinsey Report." *Journal of Social Psychology* 33:131–141, 1951.

263 Greenberg, Jerrold S. "The masturbatory behavior of college students." *Psychology in the Schools* 9(4):427–432, Oct. 1972.

264 Hall, Patricia L. and Nathaniel N. Wagner. "Initial heterosexual experience in Sweden and the United States: a cross-cultural survey." *Proceedings of the 80th Annual Convention of the American Psychological Association* 7(1):293–294, 1972.

265 Herz, Sylvia. "Research study on behavioral patterns in sex and drug use on college campus." *Adolescence* 5(17):1–16, Spring 1970.

266 Hubin, P. "Biotype et psychologie sexuelle." *Revue de Médicine Psychosomatique* 6(1):39–45, 1964.

267 Hyams, Lyon et al. "Areas of sexuality producing anxiety in college women." *Medical Aspects of Human Sexuality* 10(3):96–99 passim, Mar. 1976.

268 Kanin, Eugene J. *Male sex aggression.* (Thesis—Indiana University.) Ann Arbor, MI: University Microfilms, 1964. (Order #65-3491)

269 King, Michael and Douglas Sobel. "Sex on the college campus: current attitudes and behavior." *Journal of College Student Personnel* 16:205–209, May 1975.

270 Kirkendall, Lester A. *Premarital Intercourse and Interpersonal Relationships.* New York: Julian Press, 1961.

271 Kirkpatrick, Clifford and Eugene J. Kanin. "Male sex aggression on a university campus." *American Sociological Review* 22(1):52–58, Feb. 1957.

272 Kisseka, Mere Nakateregga. "Sexual attitudes and behavior among students in Uganda." *Journal of Sex Research* 12(2):104–116, May 1976.

273 Langston, Robert D. "Sex guilt and sex behavior in college students." *Journal of Personality Assessment* 37(4):467–472, Oct. 1973.

274 _____. "Stereotyped sex role behavior and sex guilt." *Journal of Personality Assessment* 39(1):77–81, 1975.

275 Larsen, Knud S. "An investigation of sexual behavior among Norwegian college students: a motivation study." *Journal of Marriage and the Family* 33(1):219–227, Feb. 1971.

276 Lever, Janet and Pepper Schwartz. "Man and woman at Yale." *Sexual Behavior* 1(7):13–24, Oct. 1971.

277 Luckey, Eleanore B. and Gilbert Nass. "A comparison of sexual attitudes and behavior in an international sample." *Journal of Marriage and the Family* 31(2):364-379, May 1969.

278 Macklin, Eleanor D. "Cohabitation in college: going very steady." *Psychology Today* 8(6):53–59, Nov. 1974.

279 Manniche, Erik and Bjorn Holstein. "Huwelijk met de eerste seksuele partner?" *Tijdschrift voor Sociale Wetenschappen* 14(3):351–362, 1969.

280 Melikian, Levon H. and Terry Prothro. "Sexual behavior of university students in the Arab Near East." *Journal of Abnormal and Social Psychology* 49(1):59–64, Jan. 1954.

281 Miller, Howard and Warner Wilson. "Relation of sexual behaviors, values and conflict to avowed happiness and personal adjustment." *Psychological Reports* 23(3pt.2):1075–1086, 1968.

282 Monsour, Karem J. and Barbara Stewart. "Abortion and sexual behavior in college women." *American Journal of Orthopsychiatry* 43(5):804–814, Oct. 1973.

283 Mudd, John W. and Richard Siegel. "Sexuality—the experience and anxieties of medical students." *New England Journal of Medicine* 281(25):1397–1402, Dec. 18, 1969.

284 Murstein, Bernard I. "Sex drive, person perception, and marital choice." *Archives of Sexual Behavior* 3(4):331–348, July 1974.

285 Nutt, Roberta L. and William Sedlacek. "Freshman sexual attitudes and behavior." *Journal of College Student Personnel* 15:346–351, Sept. 1974.

286 Oswalt, Robert M. "Sexual and contraceptive behavior of college females." *Journal of American College Health Association* 22(5):392–394, June 1974.

287 Park, Georgia K. *The mixed dorm: its effect on student personality, social life and sex attitudes and behavior.* (Thesis—University of Minnesota.) Ann Arbor, MI: University Microfilms, 1972. (Order #72-27788)

288 Perlman, Daniel. "The sexual standards of Canadian university students." In: *Readings in Social Psychology, Focus on Canada,* ed. by D. Koulack and D. Perlman, pp. 139–160. Toronto: Wiley, 1973.

289 Peterman, Dan J. and Carl A. Ridley. "A comparison of cohabiting and noncohabiting college students." *Journal of Marriage and the Family* 36(2):344–354, May 1974.

290 Pocs, Ollie and Annette Godow. "Youth perception on parental sexuality: a correlate of their own sexual experience." Paper presented to National Council on Family Relations Annual Meeting, St. Louis, MO, Oct. 1974. 23p.

291 Reevy, William R. "Vestured genital apposition and coitus." Mimeo. 13p.

292 Robinson, Ira E. "Change in sexual behavior and attitudes of college students." *The Family Coordinator* 17(2):119–123, Apr. 1968.

293 Ross, Robert T. "Measures of the sex behavior of college males compared with Kinsey's results." *The Journal of Abnormal and Social Psychology* 45(4):753–755, Oct. 1950.

294 Schmidt, Gunter. "Male-female difference in sexual arousal and functioning." Paper presented at the Stony Brook Conference: A Research Workshop on Future Directions in Research in Human Sexuality, State University of New York, Stony Brook, June 5–9, 1974. (*Archives of Sexual Behavior* 4(4):353–365, July 1975.)

295 Schoenberg, B. *A Strange Breed of Cat (an Encounter in Human Sexuality).* Homewood, IL: ETC, 1975.

296 Servais, Jean-François and P. Hubin. "Étude des relations entre le biotype et la sexualité de l'homme jeune." *Revue de Médicine Psychosomatique* 6(1):29–45, 1964.

297 Simon, William and John Gagnon. "Beyond anxiety and fantasy: the coital experience of college youth." *Journal of Youth and Adolescence* 1(3):203–222, 1972.

298 Swensen, Clifford H. "Sexual behavior and psychopathology: a study of college men." *Journal of Clinical Psychology* 19(4):403–404, Oct. 1963.

299 Tebor, Irving B. *Selected attributes, interpersonal relationships, and aspects of psychosexual behavior of one hundred college freshman virgin men.* (Thesis—Oregon State University.) Ann Arbor, MI: University Microfilms, 1958. (Order #58-3825)

300 Van Wert, Johanna Rucker. "Sexual attitudes and behavior of students in midwestern samples from two universities." Master's thesis, Indiana University, 1976.

301 Vincent, Murray L. and Frank Stolling. "A survey of contraceptive practices and attitudes of unwed college students." *Journal of the American College Health Association* 21:257–263, Feb. 1973.

302 Warner, Marie Pichel. "Sex health for college students." *Journal of the American Medical Women's Association* 21(5):409–412, May 1966.

303 Wiechmann, Gerald H. and Altis L. Ellis. "A study of the effects of 'sex education' on premarital petting and coital behavior." In: *Sex Education; Rationale and Reaction,* ed. by Rex S. Rogers, pp. 265–270. London/New York: Cambridge University Press, 1974.

304 Wile, Ira S. "Report... concerning a pamphlet on sex hygiene." Report to the 1941 National Interfraternity Conference, Nov. 28, 1941. 13p.

305 Zuckerman, Marvin. "Scales for sex experience for males and females." *Journal of Consulting and Clinical Psychology* 41(1):27–29, Aug. 1973.

NONMARITAL SEX BEHAVIOR RESEARCH

306 Hobart, Charles W. "The social context of morality standards among anglophone Canadian students." *Journal of Comparative Family Studies* 5(1):26–40, Spring 1974.

307 Phillips, James K. *A study of the sexual attitudes, behavior patterns, and attitude-behavior pattern inconsistencies of graduate students.* (Thesis—University of Virginia.) Ann Arbor, MI: University Microfilms, 1969. (Order #69-0519)

PREMARITAL SEX BEHAVIOR RESEARCH

308 Baker, Judith and David Lefkowitz. "Sex on campus." *Journal of College Student Personnel* 12(5):332–335, Sept. 1971.

309 Bauman, Karl E. and Robert Wilson. "Sexual behavior of unmarried university students in 1968 and 1972." *Journal of Sex Research* 10(4):327–333, Nov. 1974.

310 Bell, Robert R. and Leonard Blumberg. "Courtship intimacy and religious background." *Marriage and Family Living* 21(4):356–360, Nov. 1959.

311 Bell, Robert R. and Jay Chaskes. "Premarital sexual experience among coeds, 1958 and 1968." *Journal of Marriage and the Family* 32(1):81–84, Feb. 1970.

312 Carns, Donald E. "Religiosity, premarital sexuality and the American college student: an empirical study." Dissertation, Indiana University, 1969.

313 Christensen, Harold T. and George R. Carpenter. "Timing patterns in the development of sexual intimacy: an attitudinal report on three modern western societies." *Marriage and Family Living* 24(1):30–35, Feb. 1962.

314 _____. "Value-behavior discrepancies regarding premarital coitus in three western cultures." *American Sociological Review* 27(1):66–74, Feb. 1962.

315 Christensen, Harold T. and Christina Gregg.

"Changing sex norms in America and Scandinavia." *Journal of Marriage and the Family* 32(4):616-627, Nov. 1970.

316 Clayton, Richard R. "Religious orthodoxy and premarital sex: research notes." *Social Forces* 47(4):469-474, June 1969.

317 Collins, John K. "Dating intimacy as a function of age, sex, and religion." *Australian Journal of Social Issues* 9(1):35-43, 1974.

318 D'Angelli, Judith F. and Herbert Cross. "Relationship of sex guilt and moral reasoning to premarital sex in college women and in couples." *Journal of Consulting and Clinical Psychology* 43(1):40-47, Feb. 1975.

319 Dedman, Jean. "The relationship between religious attitude and attitude toward premarital sex relations." *Marriage and Family Living* 21(2):171-176, May 1959.

320 Delcampo, Robert L. and Michael J. Sporakowski. "Premarital sexual permissiveness and contraceptive knowledge: a biracial comparison of college students." *Journal of Sex Research* 12(3):180-192, Aug. 1976.

321 Ehrmann, Winston W. "Premarital sexual behavior and sex codes of conduct with acquaintances, friends, and lovers." *Social Forces* 38(2):158-164, Dec. 1959.

322 Gregg, Christina F. *Premarital sexual attitudes and behavior in transition: 1958-1968.* (Thesis—Purdue University.) Ann Arbor, MI: University Microfilms, 1971. (Order #72-1865)

323 Hobart, Charles W. "Sexual permissiveness in young English and French Canadians." *Journal of Marriage and the Family* 34(2):292-304, May 1972.

324 Jedlicka, Davor. "Sequential analysis of perceived commitment to partners in premarital coitus." *Journal of Marriage and the Family* 37(2):385-390, May 1975.

325 Johnsen, Kathryn P. "A progress report on a study of the factors associated with the male's tendency to negatively stereotype the female." *Sociological Focus* 2(3):21-36, Spring 1969.

326 Kanin, Eugene J. "Some evidence bearing on the aim-inhibition hypothesis of love." *Sociological Quarterly* 33:210-217, Spring 1972.

327 Kelley, Robert K. "The premarital sexual revolution: comments on research." *The Family Coordinator* 21(3):334-336, July 1972.

328 Larsen, Knud S. "Premarital sex attitudes—a scale and some validity findings." *Journal of Social Psychology* 90:339-340, Aug. 1973.

329 Lehtinen, Marlene Warring. *Heterosexual behavior and attitudes of university students in relation to living arrangements.* (Thesis—Ohio State University.) Ann Arbor, MI: University Microfilms, 1972. (Order #73-2045)

330 Macklin, Eleanor D. "Heterosexual cohabitation among unmarried college students." *The Family Coordinator* 21(4):463-472, Oct. 1972.

331 Mosher, Donald L. and Herbert Cross. "Sex guilt and premarital sexual experiences of college students." *Journal of Consulting and Clinical Psychology* 36(1):27-32, Feb. 1971.

332 Packard, Vance. *The Sexual Wilderness; The Contemporary Upheaval in Male-Female Relationships.* New York: David McKay, 1968.

333 Podell, Lawrence and John C. Perkins. "A Guttman scale for sexual experience—a methodological note." *Journal of Abnormal and Social Psychology* 54(3):420-422, May 1957.

334 Reevy, William R. "Premarital petting behavior and marital happiness prediction." *Marriage and Family Living* 21(4):349-355, Nov. 1959.

335 Robinson, Ira and Karl King. "The premarital sexual revolution among college females." *The Family Coordinator* 21(2):189-194, Apr. 1972.

336 Rockwell, Kenneth et al. "Drugs and sex: scene of ambivalence." *Journal of the American College Health Association* 21(5):483-488, June 1973.

337 Silverman, Ira Jay. "A survey of cohabitation on two college campuses." *Archives of Sexual Behavior* 6(1):11-20, Jan. 1977.

338 Sorensen, Andrew A. et al. "Premarital sexual behavior and sociocultural factors of college students: a comparison of two eastern universities." *Journal of the American College Health Association* 24(3):169-174, Feb. 1976.

339 Spanier, Graham B. "Perceived parental sexual conservatism, religiosity, and premarital sexual behavior." *Sociological Focus* 9(3):285-298, Aug. 1976.

340 _____. "Perceived sex knowledge, exposure to eroticism and premarital sexual behavior: the impact of dating." *The Sociological Quarterly* 17:247-261, Spring 1976.

341 Teevan, James T., Jr. "Reference groups and

premarital sexual behavior." *Journal of Marriage and the Family* 34(2):283–291, May 1972.

342   Thomas, Lena B. *A study of the relationship between selected personal and religious background factors and the premarital sexual behavior of a sample of undergraduate students at the University of Maryland.* (Thesis—American University.) Ann Arbor, MI: University Microfilms, 1972. (Order #73-4673)

343   Vandiver, Richard Dale. "Premarital sexual permissiveness: some methodological and substantive issues." Paper presented at Midwest Sociological Society Meetings, Session 54, Omaha, NE, Apr. 5, 1974. 29p.

344   Venham, Lois. "Coeds and contraception: an examination of self-image and significant other influence." Paper presented at the National Council of Family Relations Annual Meeting, Oct. 1973. 26p.

345   Walsh, Robert H. and Mary Ferrell. "Selection of reference group, perceived reference group permissiveness, and personal permissiveness attitudes and behavior; a study of two consecutive panels (1967–1971; 1970–1974)." *Journal of Marriage and the Family* 38(3):495–507, Aug. 1976.

346   White, Henry E. "Premarital sexual behavior and attitudes of Chinese college youth in urbanized Hong Kong." Paper presented at the 37th Annual Meeting of the Southern Sociological Society, Atlanta, GA, Apr. 18–20, 1974. 15p.

PERSONALITY AND SEX BEHAVIOR

347   Abramson, Paul R. "The relationship of the frequency of masturbation to several aspects of personality and behavior." *Journal of Sex Research* 9(2):132–142, May 1973.

348   Clark, Lynn Fred. *Repressor-sensitizer personality styles and associated levels of verbal ability, social intelligence, sex knowledge, and quantitative ability (neutral content.)* (Thesis—University of Kansas.) Ann Arbor, MI: University Microfilms, 1968. (Order #67-10,131)

349   Eastman, William F. and Mary S. Fulghum. "Sexual problems and personality adjustment of college women." *Journal of the American College Health Association* 18:144–147, Dec. 18, 1969.

350   Galbraith, Gary G. and Robert Sturke. "Effects of stimulus sexuality, order of presentation, and sex guilt on free associative latencies." *Journal of Consulting and Clinical Psychology* 42(6):828–832, 1974.

351   Griffith, Mac and Eugene Walker. "Menstrual cycle phases and personality variables as related to response to erotic stimuli." *Archives of Sexual Behavior* 4(6):599–603, Nov. 1975.

352   Hunter, LaVerne. *Premarital sexual standards in a religiously conservative college.* (Thesis—University of Georgia.) Ann Arbor, MI: University Microfilms, 1971. (Order #72-34,092)

353   Janda, Louis H. "Effects of guilt, approachability of examiner, and stimulus relevance upon sexual responses to thematic apperception stimuli." *Journal of Consulting and Clinical Psychology* 43(3):369–374, June 1975.

354   Kilpatrick, Dean G. and Nelson Cauthen. "The relationship of ordinal position, dogmatism, and personal sexual attitudes." *Journal of Psychology* 73:115–120, 1969.

355   Lewis, Robert A. and Wesley R. Burr. "Premarital sexual intercourse and commitment among college students." Paper presented at 35th Annual Meeting of the Southern Sociological Society, 1971. 20p.

356   Mazer, Donald and Alvin R. Mahrer. "Developmental factors in masturbation: family background antecedents and later personality patterns." *Journal of Psychology* 79(1):21–27, Sept. 1971.

357   Mosher, Donald L. and Herbert Cross. "Sex guilt and premarital sexual experiences of college students." *Journal of Consulting and Clinical Psychology* 36(1):27–32, Feb. 1971.

358   Perlman, Daniel. "Self-esteem and sexual permissiveness." *Journal of Marriage and the Family* 36(3):470–473, Aug. 1974.

359   Raschke, Vernon J. *Religiosity and sexual permissiveness.* (Thesis—University of Minnesota.) Ann Arbor, MI: University Microfilms, 1972. (Order #73-1057)

360   Ray, Rose E. *Autonomic and self-report correlates of guilt responses to visual erotic stimuli.* (Thesis—Baylor University.) Ann Arbor, MI: University Microfilms, 1970. (Order #71-6033)

361   Staples, Robert. *A study of the influence of liberal-conservative attitudes on the premarital sexual standards of different racial, sex-role and social class groupings.* (Thesis—University of Minnesota.) Ann Arbor, MI: University Microfilms, 1971. (Order #72-14,378)

362   Sutker, Patricia B. and Dean Kilpatrick. "Personality, biographical, and racial correlates of sexual attitudes and behavior." *Proceedings of the 81st Annual Convention of the American Psychological Association, Montreal* 8:261–262, 1973.

363 Thomas, D.R. "Conservatism and premarital sexual experience." *British Journal of Social and Clinical Psychology* 114(2):195–196, June 1975.

364 Vandiver, Richard Dale. *Sources and interrelation of premarital sexual standards and general liberality-conservatism.* (Thesis—Southern Illinois University.) Ann Arbor, MI: University Microfilms, 1972. (Order #72-24,370)

365 Ward, Thomas J. "Cohabitation and drift: a conceptual model." Paper presented at the 1975 Annual Meeting of the Midwest Sociological Society, Chicago, IL: Apr. 9–12, 1975. 11p.

Sex Behavior (Aged)

BIBLIOGRAPHY

366 Berezin, Martin A. "Sex and old age: a review of the literature." *Journal of Geriatric Psychiatry* 2:131–149, 1968.

367 Birren, James E. and Julie L. Moore, eds. *Sexuality and Aging: A Selected Bibliography.* Los Angeles: Ethel Percy Andrus Gerontology Center, University of Southern California, 1975.

368 Wales, Jeffrey B. "Sexuality in middle and old age: a critical review of the literature." *Case Western Reserve Journal of Sociology* 6:82–105, May 1974.

AGING AND SEX BEHAVIOR

369 Amulree, Lord. "Sex and the elderly." *Practitioner* 172(1030):431–435, Apr. 1954.

370 Beigel, Hugo G. "Sex after 60: is it lechery?" *Osteopathic Physician* 44(1):68 passim, Jan. 1977.

371 Beigel, Hugo G., ed. Part IV: "Sex and Aging." In: *Advances in Sex Research*, pp. 129–158. New York: Harper & Row, 1963.

372 Berezin, Martin A. "Masturbation and old age." In: *Masturbation from Infancy to Senescence,* ed. by Irwin M. Marcus and John J. Francis, pp. 329–348. New York: International Universities Press, 1975.

373 Berman, Ellen M. and Harold I. Lief. "Sex and the aging process." In: *Sex and the Life Cycle,* ed. by Wilbur W. Oaks, Gerald A. Melchiode and Ilda Ficher, pp. 125–134. New York: Grune & Stratton, 1976.

374 Botwinick, Jack. *Aging and Behavior; A Comprehensive Integration of Research Findings.* New York: Springer, 1973.

375 Brenton, Myron. *Sex and Your Heart.* New York: Coward-McCann, 1968.

376 Burnside, Irene Mortenson, ed. *Sexuality and Aging.* Los Angeles: Ethel Percy Andrus Gerontology Center, University of Southern California, 1975.

377 Busse, Ewald W. "Sex after fifty (discussion follows)." In: *Sexuality and Psychoanalysis,* ed. by Edward T. Adelson, pp. 215–224. New York: Brunner/Mazel, 1975.

378 Busse, Ewald W. and Eric Pfeiffer. *Behavior and Adaptation in Late Life.* Boston: Little, Brown, 1970.

379 Butler, Robert and Myrna Lewis. *Sex after Sixty: A Guide for Men and Women in their Later Years.* New York: Harper & Row, 1976.

380 Calderone, Mary S. *Sexuality and the Later Years.* Pamphlet no. 10 in the series: Managing the Elderly Patient in Family Practice. Fort Washington, PA: McNeil Laboratories, 1975.

381 Chartham, Robert. *Sex and the Over-Fifties.* London: Leslie Frewin, 1969.

382 Cleveland, Martha. "Sex in marriage: at 40 and beyond." *Family Coordinator* 25(3):233–240, July 1976.

383 Comfort, Alexander. "Sexuality in old age." *Osteopathic Physician* 41(11):112–113 passim, Nov. 1974.

384 Daly, Michael Joseph. "Sexual attitudes in menopausal and postmenopausal women." *Medical Aspects of Human Sexuality* 2(5):48–53, May 1968.

385 De Beauvoir, Simone. *The Coming of Age.* New York: Putnam, 1972.

386 De Nicola, Pietro and Marino Peruzza. "Sex in the aged." *Journal of the American Geriatrics Society* 22(8):380–382, Aug. 1974.

387 Dean, Stanley R. "Geriatric sexuality: normal, needed, and neglected." *Geriatrics* 29:134–137, July 1974.

388 Dickinson, Peter A. *The Fires of Autumn; Sexual Activity in the Middle and Later Years.* New York: Drake, 1974.

389 Dresen, Sheila E. "The sexually active middle adult." *Journal of Nursing* 75(6):1001–1005, June 1975.

390   Felstein, Ivor. *Sex and the Longer Life.* London: Penguin, 1970.

391   Finkle, Alex L. "Emotional quality and physical quantity of sexual activity in aging males." *Journal of Geriatric Psychiatry* 6(1):70–79, 1973.

392   Francher, J. Scott and Janet Henkin. "The menopausal queen: adjustment to aging and the male homosexual." *American Journal of Orthopsychiatry* 43(4):670–674, July 1973.

393   Fry, William F. "Psychodynamics of sexual humor: sex and the elderly." *Medical Aspects of Human Sexuality* 10(2):140 passim, Feb. 1976.

394   Geller, Jack. "The role of sex hormones in problems of the mature years and beyond." *Journal of the American Geriatrics Society* 17(9):861–873, 1969.

395   Göppert, Hans. "Rückbildung und alter." In: *Die Sexualität des Menschen: Handbuch der medizinischen Sexualforschung,* pp. 34–55, 1968.

396   Hunt, Bernice and Morton Hunt. *Prime Time: A Guide to the Pleasures and Opportunities of the New Middle Age.* New York: Stein & Day, 1975.

397   Kaplan, Helen Singer and Clifford Sager. "Sexual patterns at different ages." *Medical Aspects of Human Sexuality* 5(6):10–23, June 1971.

398   Kassel, Victor. "Polygyny after 60." *Geriatrics* 21:214–218, Apr. 1966.

399   _____. "Sex in nursing homes." *Medical Aspects of Human Sexuality* 10(3):126–131, Mar. 1976.

400   Kaufman, Sherwin A. "Menopause and sex." *Sexual Behavior* 1(2):58–63, May 1971.

401   Kelly, James J. *Brothers and brothers: the gay man's adaptation to aging.* (Thesis—Brandeis University.) Ann Arbor, MI: University Microfilms, 1974. (Order #75-24,234)

402   _____. *Brothers and Brothers: The Gay Man's Adaptation to Aging (A Review of Research Findings and Social Policy Recommendations).* Waltham, MA: Brandeis University, Florence Heller School for Advanced Studies in Social Welfare, 1974.

403   Kent, Saul. "Impotence: the facts versus the fallacies." *Geriatrics* 30:164 passim, Apr. 1975.

404   Kuhn, Margaret E. "Sexual myths surrounding the aging." In: *Sex and the Life Cycle,* ed. by Wilbur W. Oaks, Gerald A. Melchiode and Ilda Ficher, pp. 117–124. New York: Grune & Stratton, 1976.

405   Leviton, Dan. "The significance of sexuality as a deterrent to suicide among the aged." *Omega* 4(2):163–174, Summer 1973.

406   Lief, Harold I. and Carlfred B. Broderick. "Interview: sex in older people." *Sexual Behavior* 1(7):72–74.

407   McCary, James Leslie. "Sexual advantages of middle-aged men." *Medical Aspects of Human Sexuality* 7(12):139–160, Dec. 1973.

408   Madorsky, Martin et al. "Effect on benign prostatic hypertrophy on sexual behavior." *Medical Aspects of Human Sexuality* 10(2):8 passim, Feb. 1976.

409   Mann, Carola H. "Sex and the mid-life crisis." Paper presented at meeting of the Eastern Association of Sex Therapists, New York, Mar. 1977. 10p.

410   Masters, William and Virginia Johnson. "Sexual inadequacy in the aging female." In: *Human Sexual Inadequacy,* pp. 335–350. Boston: Little, Brown, 1970.

411   _____. "Sexual inadequacy in the aging male." In: *Human Sexual Inadequacy,* pp. 316–334. Boston: Little, Brown, 1970.

412   Miller, Michael B., Herbert Bernstein and Harold Sharkey. "Family extrusion of the aged patient: family homeostasis and sexual conflict." *Gerontologist* 15(4):291–296, Aug. 1975.

413   Minnigerode, Fred A. "Age-status labeling in homosexual men." *Journal of Homosexuality* 1(3):273–276, Spring 1976.

414   Mozley, Paul D. "Woman's capacity for orgasm after menopause." *Medical Aspects of Human Sexuality* 9(8):104–105 passim, Aug. 1975.

415   Pearson, Manuel M. "Middle-aged male crisis." *Medical Aspects of Human Sexuality* 2(8):6–15, Aug. 1968.

416   Peterson, James A. and Barbara Payne. *Love in the Later Years: The Emotional, Physical, Sexual and Social Potential of the Elderly.* New York: Association Press, 1975.

417   Pfeiffer, Eric. "Sex and aging." *Sexual Behavior* 2(10):17–21, Oct. 1972.

418   _____. "Sex in old age." *North Carolina Journal of Mental Health* 4(1):34–42, 1970.

419 _____. "Sexuality in the aging individual." *Journal of the American Geriatrics Society* 22(11):481–484, Nov. 1974.

420 Prill, Hans-Joachim. "Die alternde vita sexualis." *Sexualmedizin* 6(2):85–90, Feb. 1977.

421 Raskind, Murray A. and Caroline E. Preston. "Brief guide to office counseling: sexual counseling of the elderly." *Medical Aspects of Human Sexuality* 9(5): 153–154, May 1975.

422 Reed, David M. "Sexual behavior in the separated, divorced, and widowed." In: *The Sexual Experience,* ed. by B.J. Sadock, M.I. Kaplan and A.M. Freedman, pp. 249–255. Baltimore: Williams & Wilkins, 1976.

423 Renshaw, Domeena C. "Sexuality and depression in adults and the elderly." *Medical Aspects of Human Sexuality* 9(9):40–62, Sept. 1975.

424 "Roundtable: sex after 50." *Medical Aspects of Human Sexuality* 2(1):41–47, Jan. 1968.

425 "Roundtable: sex and the menopause." *Medical Aspects of Human Sexuality* 4(11): 64–89, Nov. 1970.

426 Rubin, Herman H. and Benjamin W. Newman. *Active Sex after Sixty.* New York: Arco, 1969.

427 Rubin, Isadore. *Sexual Life after Sixty.* New York: Basic Books, 1965.

428 _____. *Sexual Life in the Later Years.* SIECUS Study Guide No. 12. New York: Sex Information and Education Council of the United States, 1970.

429 Schaffer, Ralph S. "Will you still need me when I'm 64?" In: *Out of the Closets; Voices of Gay Liberation,* ed. by Karla Jay and Allen Young, pp. 278–279. New York: Douglas, 1972.

430 Scheingold, Lee Dreisinger and Nathaniel N. Wagner. *Sound Sex and the Aging Heart: Sex in the Mid and Later Years with Special Reference to Cardiac Problems.* New York: Human Sciences Press, 1974.

431 Seidenberg, Robert. "Older man-younger woman marriages." *Medical Aspects of Human Sexuality* 9(11):7 passim, Nov. 1975.

432 Sontag, Susan. "The double standard of aging." *Saturday Review* 55:29–38, Sept. 23, 1972.

433 Sorg, David A. and Margaret B. Sorg. "Sexual satisfaction in maturing women." *Medical Aspects of Human Sexuality* 9(2):62 passim, Feb. 1975.

434 Stokes, Walter R. "Sexual function in the aging male." *Geriatrics* 6(5):304–308, Sept./Oct. 1951.

435 Sviland, Mary Ann P. "Helping elderly couples become sexually liberated: psychosocial issues." *Counseling Psychologist* 5(1):67–72, 1975.

436 Szewczyk, Hans. "Untersuchungen und nachuntersuchungen von alterssittlichkeitstätern." *Zeitschrift für Altersforschung* 26(3):307–315, 1971.

437 Tavris, Carol. "The sexual lives of women over 60." *Ms.* 6(1):62–65, July 1977.

438 Wasow, Mona. *Sexuality & Aging.* Illus. by Vivien Cohen. Madison, WI: Privately printed, 1976. (Pamphlet Order #300: Mona Wasow, 1120 Edgehill Dr., Madison, WI 53705).

439 Weinberg, Jack. "Sexuality in later life." *Medical Aspects of Human Sexuality* 5(4):216–227, Apr. 1971.

440 West, Norman D. "Sex in geriatrics: myth or miracle?" *Journal of the American Geriatric Society* 23(12):551-552, Dec. 1975.

441 Whiskin, Frederick E. "The geriatric sex offender." *Medical Aspects of Human Sexuality* 4(4):125–129, Apr. 1970.

442 Wikler, Revy and Peg Savage Grey. *Sex and the Senior Citizen.* New York: Frederick Fell, 1968.

SEX BEHAVIOR RESEARCH

443 Bowers, L.M., R.R. Cross and Frederick A. Lloyd. "Sexual function and urologic disease in the elderly male." *Journal of the American Geriatrics Society* 11(7): 647–652, July 1963.

444 Cameron, Paul. "Note on time spent thinking about sex." *Psychological Reports* 20(30)741–742, 1967.

445 Cameron, Paul and Henry Biber. "Sexual thoughts throughout the life-span." *The Gerontologist* :144–147, Summer 1973.

446 Cendron, H. and J. Vallery-Masson. "Les effets de l'âge sur l'activité sexuelle masculine; incidences de quelques facteurs dont le tabac." *Presse Médicale* 78(41):1795–1797, Oct. 3, 1970.

447 Christenson, Cornelia V. and Alan B. Johnson. "Sexual patterns in a group of older never-married women." *Journal of Geriatric Psychiatry* 6(1):80–98, 1973.

448 Edwards, Allan E. and June Rose Husted.

"Penile sensitivity, age, and sexual behavior." *Journal of Clinical Psychology* 30(3): 697–700, July 1976.

449 Ellis, William J. and John T. Grayhack. "Sexual function in aging males after orchiectomy and estrogen therapy." *Journal of Urology* 89(6):895–899, June 1963.

450 Finkle, Alex L. "Sex after prostatectomy." *Medical Aspects of Human Sexuality* 2(3):40–41, Mar. 1968.

451 Freeman, Joseph T. "Sexual capacities in the aging male." *Geriatrics* 16:37–43, Jan. 1961.

452 Gebhard, Paul H. "Normal and criminal sexual behavior at older ages." *Beiträge zur Sexualforschung* 41:83–87, 1967.

453 "Geriatric sexual relationships." In: *Handbook of Sexology,* ed. by John Money and Herman Musaph, pp. 809–860. Amsterdam: Excerpta Medica, 1977.

454 Hsu, Cheng-Jen and Pao-Hwei Chen. "Sexual activities in older males: I. Observation on the patients of Department of Internal Medicine, N.T.U.H." *Journal of the Formosa Medical Association* 64(3):129–133, Mar. 28, 1965.

455 Kahn, Edwin. *The sleep and other characteristics of the aged.* (Thesis—Yeshiva University.) Ann Arbor, MI: University Microfilms, 1968. (Order #68-17,170)

456 Kahn, Edwin and Charles Fisher. "REM sleep and sexuality in the aged." *Journal of Geriatric Psychiatry* 2(2):181–191, Spring 1969.

457 _____. "Some correlates of rapid eye movement sleep in the normal aged male." *Journal of Nervous and Mental Diseases* 148(5):495–505, 1969.

458 Karacan, Ismet et al. "Sleep related penile tumescence as a function of age." *American Journal of Psychiatry* 132(9):932–937, Sept. 1975.

459 Karacan, Ismet, Carolyn J. Hursch and Robert L. Williams. "Some characteristics of nocturnal penile tumescence in elderly males." *Journal of Gerontology* 27(1):39–45, 1972.

460 Kinsey, Alfred C. et al. *Sexual Behavior in the Human Male.* Philadelphia: W.B. Saunders, 1948.

461 _____. *Sexual Behavior in the Human Female.* Philadelphia: W.B. Saunders, 1953.

462 Martin, Clyde E. "Marital and sexual factors in relation to age, disease, and longevity." In: *Life History Research in Psychopathology,* vol. 4, ed. by R.D. Wirt and M. Roff, pp. 326–347. Minneapolis: University of Minnesota Press, 1975.

463 Masters, William and Virginia Johnson. "The geriatric sexual response." In: *Human Sexual Response,* pp. 221–270. Boston: Little, Brown, 1966.

464 Newman, Gustave and Claude R. Nichols. "Sexual activities and attitudes in older persons." *Journal of the American Medical Association* 173:33–35, May 7, 1960.

465 _____. "Sexual activities and attitudes in older persons." In: *Sexual Behavior and Personality Characteristics,* ed. by Manfred DeMartino, pp. 384–391. New York: Citadel Press, 1963.

466 Pearlman, Carl K. "Frequency of intercourse in males at different ages." *Medical Aspects of Human Sexuality* 6(11):92–113, Nov. 1972.

467 Pfeiffer, Eric and Glenn C. Davis. "Determinants of sexual behavior in middle and old age." *Journal of the American Geriatrics Society* 20(4):151–158, 1972.

468 Pfeiffer, Eric, Adriaan Verwoerdt and Hsioh-Shan Wang. "The natural history of sexual behavior in a biologically advantaged group of aged individuals." *Journal of Gerontology* 24:193–198, Apr. 1969.

469 _____. "Sexual behavior in aged men and women. I. Observations on 254 community volunteers." *Archives of General Psychiatry* 19:753–758, Dec. 1968.

470 Pfeiffer, Eric, Adriaan Verwoerdt and Glenn C. Davis. "Sexual behavior in middle life." *American Journal of Psychiatry* 128(10):1262–1267, Apr. 1972.

471 Pitt, Bruce. "Sexual behaviour in the elderly." In: *Psychosexual Problems: Psychotherapy, Counselling and Behaviour Modification,* ed. by Sidney Crown, pp. 297–303. London: Academic Press, 1976.

472 Raboch, Jan. "Der einfluss des alterns auf die symptomatik der funktionellen sexualstörungen." *Andrologie* 4(1):27–36, Oct. 1971.

473 _____. "Vliv veku na symptomatiku funkcnich sexuálnich poruch muze." *Ceskoslovenska Psychiatrie* 65(5):305–309, 1969.

474 Rubin, Isadore. "Sex over 65." In: *The Social Psychology of Sex,* ed. by Jacqueline P. Wiseman, pp. 226–228. New York: Harper & Row, 1976.

475 Schürch, Johannes. "Evolution des déviations sexuelles dans l'âge avancé: étude catamnestique." *Schweizer Archiv für Neurologie, Neurochirurgie, und Psychiatrie* 110(2):331–363, 1972.

476 Solnick, Robert L. et al. "Age and male erectile responsiveness." *Archives of Sexual Behavior* 6(1):1–9, Jan. 1977.

477 Verwoerdt, Adriaan, Eric Pfeiffer and Hsioh-Shan Wang. "Sexual behavior in senescence: I. Changes in sexual activity and interests of aging men and women." *Journal of Geriatric Psychiatry* 2(2):163–180, Spring 1969.

478 _____. "Sexual behavior in senescence: II. Patterns of sexual activity and interest." *Geriatrics* 24:137–154, Feb. 1969.

479 Wallin, Paul and Alexander L. Clark. "Religiosity, sexual gratification, and marital satisfaction in the middle years of marriage." *Social Forces* 42: 303–309, Mar. 1964.

480 Weinberg, Martin S. "The male homosexual: age-related variation in social and psychological characteristics." *Social Problems* 17(4):527–537, Spring 1970.

OTHER SOURCES OF INFORMATION

Andrus Gerontology Center
University of Southern California
3715 McClintock Ave., Los Angeles, CA 90007

National Institute on Aging
Dr. Robert N. Butler, Director
School of Psychiatry
Howard University, 2400 6th St. NW
Washington, DC 20001

Drugs and Sex Behavior

481 Adam, Kenneth S. and John G. Lohrenz. "Drug abuse, self abuse and the abuse of authority." *Canadian Psychiatric Association Journal* 15(1):79–81, 1970.

482 Alpert, Richard. "Drugs and sexual behavior." *Journal of Sex Research* 5(1): 50–56, Feb. 1969.

483 Althoff, Sally A. and Edward J. Nussel. "Social class trends in practices and attitudes of college students regarding sex, smoking, drinking and the use of drugs." *Journal of School Health* 41:390–394, Sept. 1971.

484 Arafat, Ibtihaj and Betty Yorburg. "Drug use and the sexual behavior of college women." *Journal of Sex Research* 9(1):21–29, Feb. 1973.

485 Bailly-Salin, P. et al. "Amours, délices et drogues. Quelques considérations sur le corps, la relation érotique et l'ascèse nirvanique sous l'influence toxicomaniaque." *Annales Médico-Psychologiques* 2(2):120–126, 1970.

486 Beaumont, G. "Untoward effects of drugs on sexuality." In: *Psychosexual Problems: Psychotherapy, Counselling and Behaviour Modification,* ed. by Sidney Crown, pp. 325–335. London: Academic Press, 1976.

487 Bell, Robert R. "Drugs." In: *Social Deviance: A Substantive Analysis,* pp. 191–225. Homewood, IL: Dorsey Press, 1971.

488 Bengesser, Gerhard. "Psychopharmakotherapie sexueller störungen." *Sexualmedizin* 5(6):424–427, June 1976.

489 Brady, John Paul. "Brevital-relaxation treatment of frigidity." *Behavior Research and Therapy* 4(2):71–77, 1966.

490 Cahn, L.A. "Influence of clopenthixol (Sordinol[R]) on the libido of the male." *Psychiatria, Neurologie, Neurochirurgia* 68(1):67–74, 1965.

491 Carter, Carol Sue and John M. Davis. "Effects of drugs on sexual arousal and performance." In: *Clinical Management of Sexual Disorders,* ed. by J. Meyer, pp. 195–205. Baltimore: Williams & Wilkins, 1976.

492 Chessick, Richard D. "The 'pharmacogenic orgasm' in the drug addict." *Archives of General Psychiatry* 3:545–556, Nov. 1960.

493 Clark, Jane S. et al. "Marriage and methadone: spouse behavior patterns in heroin addicts maintained on methadone." *Journal of Marriage and the Family* 34(3):496–502, Aug. 1972.

494 Cushman, Paul. "Sexual behavior in heroin addiction and methadone maintenance; correlation with plasma luteinizing hormone." *New York State Journal of Medicine* 72:1261–1265, June 1, 1972.

495 Dahlberg, Charles Clay. "Brief guide to office counseling: when patients ask about amyl nitrite as a sexual stimulant." *Medical Aspects of Human Sexuality* 10(7):137, July 1976.

496 _____. "Sexual behavior in the drug culture." *Medical Aspects of Human Sexuality* 5(4):64–71, Apr. 1971.

497 DeLeon, George and Harry Wexler. "Heroin

addiction: its relation to sexual behavior and sexual experience." *Journal of Abnormal Psychology* 81(1):36–38, Feb. 1973.

498   Densen-Gerber, Judianne. "Sexual behavior, abortion, and birth control in heroin addicts: legal and psychiatric considerations." *Contemporary Drug Problems* 1:783–793, Fall 1972.

499   Ditman, Keith S. "Inhibition of ejaculation by chlorprothixene." *American Journal of Psychiatry* 120:1004–1005, 1964.

500   Ellinwood, Everett H. and Kenneth Rockwell. "Effect of drug use on sexual behavior " (and commentaries). *Medical Aspects of Human Sexuality* 9(3):10–32, Mar. 1975.

501   Everett, Guy M. "Effects of amyl nitrite ('Poppers') on sexual experience." *Medical Aspects of Human Sexuality* 6(12):146–151, Dec. 1972.

502   _____. "Role of biogenic amines in the modulation of aggressive and sexual behavior in animals and man." In: *Sexual Behavior: Pharmacology and Biochemistry,* ed. by M. Sandler and G.L. Gessa, pp. 81–84. New York: Raven Press, 1975.

503   Ferguson, Patricia, Thomas Lennox and Dan J. Lettieri, eds. *Drugs and Sex: The Nonmedical Use of Drugs and Sexual Behavior.* Rockville, MD: National Institute on Drug Abuse, 1974. (Summaries of the major research findings of the last 15 years.)

504   Freedman, Alfred M. "Drugs and sexual behavior." In: *The Sexual Experience,* ed. by B.J. Sadock, H.I. Kaplan and A.M. Freedman, pp. 328–334. Baltimore: Williams & Wilkins, 1976.

505   Gallant, D.M. "The effect of alcohol and drug abuse on sexual behavior." *Medical Aspects of Human Sexuality* 2(1):30–36, Jan. 1968.

506   Gay, George R. " 'Sex-crazed dope fiends' — myth or reality?" *Drug Forum* 2(2):125–140, Winter 1973.

507   _____. "Sex in the 'drug culture.' " *Medical Aspects of Human Sexuality* 6(10):28–47, Oct. 1972.

508   Goode, Erich. "Drug use and sexual activity on a college campus." *American Journal of Psychiatry* 128(10):1272–1275, Apr. 1972.

509   Gossop, M.R., R.S. Stern and P. Connell. "Drug dependence and sexual dysfunction: a comparison of intravenous users of narcotics and oral users of amphetamines." *British Journal of Psychiatry* 124:431–434, May 1974.

510   Gottlieb, Adam. *Sex Drugs and Aphrodisiacs: Where to Obtain Them, How to Use Them, and Their Effects.* New York/San Francisco: High Times/Level, 1975.

511   Green, Michael and Sydney Berman. "Failure of ejaculation produced by dibenzyline." *Connecticut State Medical Journal* 18:30–33, 1954.

512   Greenberg, Harvey R. and Carlos Carrillo. "Thioridazine-induced inhibition of masturbatory ejaculation in an adolescent." *American Journal of Psychiatry* 124(7):991–993, 1968.

513   Greenblatt, David and Jan Koch-Weser. "Gynecomastia and impotence complications of spironolactone therapy." *Journal of the American Medical Association* 82, Jan. 1, 1973.

514   Henslin, James H. "Sex and drugs." Paper presented at 65th Annual Meeting of the American Sociological Assoc. 13p.

515   Herz, Sylvia. "Behavioral patterns in sex and drug use on the college campus." *Journal of the Medical Society of New Jersey* 67(1):3–6, Jan. 1970.

516   Hoch, Paul and Joseph Zubin, eds. *Problems of Addiction and Habituation. New York: Grune & Stratton, 1958.*

517   Hoffman, Martin. "Drug addiction and 'hypersexuality': related to modes of mastery." *Comprehensive Psychiatry* 5:262–270, Aug. 1964.

518   Hollister, Leo E. "Drugs and sexual behavior in man." *Life Sciences* 17(5):661–667, Sept. 1975.

519   Howard, Elliott J. "Sexual expenditure in patients with hypertensive disease." *Medical Aspects of Human Sexuality* 7(10):82–92, Oct. 1973.

520   Hushahn, Sigrid. *Genussverhalten und Sexualität; Ergebnisse einer Umfrage an 3666 Studenten Westdeutschlands.* Thesis, University of Hamburg, 1966.

521   Jarvik, Murray E. and Edward M. Brecher. "Drugs and sex: inhibition and enhancement effects." In: *Handbook of Sexology,* ed. by John Money and Herman Musaph, pp. 1095–1106. Amsterdam: Excerpta Medica, 1977.

522   Jones, Hardin B. and Helen C. Jones. *Sensual Drugs: Deprivation and Rehabilitation of the Mind.* Cambridge: Cambridge University Press, 1977.

523   Kaplan, Helen Singer. *The New Sex Therapy;*

Active Treatment of Sexual Dysfunctions. New York: Brunner/Mazel, 1974.

524 Kiev, Ari. "Depression and libido." *Medical Aspects of Human Sexuality* 3(11):35–45, Nov. 1969.

525 Kraft, Tom. "Drug addiction and personality disorder." *British Journal of Addiction* 64:403–408, 1970.

526 Latendresse, John D. "Masturbation and its relation to addiction." *Review of Existential Psychology and Psychiatry* 8(1):16–27, 1968.

527 Loewe, S. "Ejaculation induced by drug action." *Archives Internationales de Pharmacodynamie et de Thérapie* 60(1):37–47, Sept. 1938.

528 Maglin, Arthur. "Sex role differences in heroin addiction." *Social Casework* 55(3):160–167, Mar. 1974.

529 Mathis, James L. "Sexual aspects of heroin addiction." *Medical Aspects of Human Sexuality* 4(9):98–109, Sept. 1970.

530 Milman, Doris H. and Su Wen Huey. "Patterns of drug usage among university students: V. Heavy use of marihuana and alcohol by undergraduates." *Journal of the American College Health Association* 21(3):181–187, Feb. 1973.

531 Mintz, Jim. "Sexual problems of heroin addicts." *Archives of General Psychiatry* 31(5):700–703, Nov. 1974.

532 Money, John and Robert Yankowitz. "The sympathetic-inhibiting effects of the drug ismelin on human male eroticism, with a note on mellaril." *The Journal of Sex Research* 3(1):69–82, Feb. 1967.

533 Nyswander, Marie. *The Drug Addict as a Patient.* New York: Grune & Stratton, 1956.

534 Oaks, Wilbur W. "Sex and hypertension." *Medical Aspects of Human Sexuality* 6(11):128–137, Nov. 1972.

535 Ostow, Mortimer. "The libido plethora syndrome: a clinical study." *British Journal of Medicine and Psychology* 37:103–110, 1964.

536 Piemme, Thomas E. "Brief guides to office counseling: sex and illicit drugs." *Medical Aspects of Human Sexuality* 10(1):85–86, Jan. 1976.

537 Rockwell, Kenneth et al. "Drugs and sex: scene of ambivalence." *Journal of the American College Health Association* 21(5):483–488, June 1973.

538 "Roundtable: alcohol, drugs, and sex." *Medical Aspects of Human Sexuality* 4(2):18–34, Feb. 1970.

539 Sandler, Merton and G.L. Gessa, eds. *Sexual Behavior: Pharmacology and Biochemistry.* New York: Raven Press, 1975.

540 Servais, Jean-François and P. Hubin. "Étude psychopharmacologique de la méthyloestrénolone inhibiteur de la libido chez l'homme normal." *Acta Neurologica et Psychiatrica Belgica* 65:983–995, 1965.

541 Shader, Richard I. "Sexual dysfunction associated with mesoridazine besylate (Serentil)." *Psychopharmacologia* 27(3):293–294, 1972.

542 _____. "Sexual dysfunction associated with thioridazine hydrochloride." *Journal of the American Medical Association* 188(11):1007–1009, June 15, 1964.

543 Shader, Richard I. and Alberto DiMascio. "Endocrine effects of psychotropic drugs: VI. Male sexual function." *Connecticut Medicine* 32(11):847–848, Nov. 1968.

544 Springer, Alfred. "Ein beitrag zum problem des sexualverhaltens der jugendlichen drogenabhängigen." *Wien Zeitschrift für Nervenheilkunde* 31:139–155, 1973.

545 Story, Norman L. "Sexual dysfunction resulting from drug side effects." *Journal of Sex Research* 10(2):132–149, May 1974.

546 Suchman, Edward A. "The 'hang-loose' ethic and the spirit of drug use." In: *Studies in Human Sexual Behavior,* ed. by Ailon Shiloh, pp. 104–118. Springfield, IL: Charles C. Thomas, 1970.

547 Tobias, Jerry J. "The effects of drugs on the sexual activities of suburban youth." *Counseling and Values* 17(4):256–259, Spring 1973.

548 Vogt, Hermann J. "Medikamentöse bremsung und anregung des sexualtriebs." *Sexualmedizin* 5(4):253–256, Apr. 1976.

549 Wellisch, David K., George R. Gay and Roseann McEntee. "The Easy Rider syndrome: a pattern of hetero- and homosexual relationships in a heroin addict population." *Journal of Family Process* 9:425–430, 1970.

550 Witters, Weldon L. and Patricia Jones-Witters. *Drugs and Sex.* New York/London: Macmillan/Collier-Macmillan, 1975.

551 Witton, Kurt. "Sexual dysfunction secondary to mellaril." *Diseases of the Nervous System* 23:175, Mar. 1962.

552 Wolfe, Robert C. "Drug abuse and sex." *Sexual Behavior* 3(3):33–37, Mar. 1973.

553 Zuckerman, Marvin, Richard S. Neary and Barbara A. Brustman. "Sensation-seeking scale correlates in experience (smoking, drugs, alcohol, 'hallucinations' and sex) and preferences for complexity (designs)." *Proceedings of the Annual Convention of the APA,* 5(part 1):317–318, 1970.

ALCOHOL

554 Briddell, Dan W. and G.T. Wilson. "Effects of alcohol and expectancy set on male sexual arousal." *Journal of Abnormal Psychology* 85(2):225–234, Apr. 1976.

555 Burton, Genevieve and Howard M. Kaplan. "Sexual behavior and adjustment of married alcoholics." *Quarterly Journal of Studies on Alcohol* 29(3-A):603–609, 1968.

556 Daen, Phyllis. "The body image and sexual preferences of alcoholic, homosexual and heterosexual males." Unpub. doctoral dissertation, Adelphi College, 1960.

557 Deniker, Pierre, Daisy de Saugy and Martine Ropert. "The alcoholic and his wife." *Comprehensive Psychiatry* 5(6):374–383, Dec. 1964.

558 Dogliani, P. and V. Micheletti. "Sull'influsso della intossicazione alcoolica actua nell'incesto e nella zoofilia." *Rivista Sperimentale di Freniatria e Medicine* 82:485–499, 1958.

559 Ewing, John A. "Alcohol, sex and marriage." *Medical Aspects of Human Sexuality* 2(6):43 passim, June 1968.

560 Farkas, Gary M. and Raymond C. Rosen. "Effect of alcohol on elicited male sexual response." *Journal of Studies on Alcohol* 37(3):265–272, Mar. 1976.

561 Fox, Ruth. "Interview: a psychiatrist discusses drinking and sex." *Sexual Behavior* 1(2):67–69 passim, May 1971.

562 Gantt, W. Horsley. "Effect of alcohol on the sexual reflexes of normal and neurotic male dogs." *Psychosomatic Medicine* 14:174–181, Mar. 1952.

563 Hippler, Arthur E. "Patterns of sexual behavior: the Athabascans of interior Alaska." *Ethos* 2(1):47–68, Spring 1974.

564 Johnson, Harry J. *Executive Life-Styles; A Life Extension Institute Report on Alcohol, Sex and Health.* New York: Crowell, 1974.

565 Karpman, Benjamin. *The Alcoholic Woman.* Washington, DC: Linacre Press, 1948.

566 _____. *The Hangover.* Springfield, IL: Charles C. Thomas, 1957.

567 Lemere, Frederick and James W. Smith. "Alcohol-induced sexual impotence." *American Journal of Psychiatry* 130(2):212–213, Feb. 1973.

568 Levine, Jacob. "The sexual adjustment of alcoholics: a clinical study of a selected sample." *Quarterly Journal of Studies on Alcohol* 16:675–680, Dec. 1955.

569 McCaghy, Charles H. "Drinking and deviance disavowal: the case of child molesters." *Social Problems* 16(1)43–49, Summer 1968.

570 Man Thiel, David H. "Brief guide to office counseling: liver disease and sexual functioning." *Medical Aspects of Human Sexuality* 10(3):117–118, Mar. 1976.

571 Mendelsohn, Jack A. and Nancy Mello. "Alkohol, Aggression, Androgene; Alkoholabusus drosselt plasmatestosterone spiegel." *Sexualmedizin* 4(10):646–651, Oct. 1975.

572 Paredes, Alfonso. "Marital-sexual factors in alcoholism." *Medical Aspects of Human Sexuality* 7(4):98–115, Apr. 1973.

573 Parker, Frederick B. "A comparison of the sex temperament of alcoholics and moderate drinkers." *American Sociological Review* 24(3):366–374, June 1959.

574 _____. "Self-role strain and drinking disposition at a pre-alcoholic age level." *Journal of Social Psychology* 78(1):55–61, 1969.

575 Rada, Richard T. "Alcohol and rape (and commentaries)." *Medical Aspects of Human Sexuality* 9(3):48 passim, Mar. 1975.

576 Rosenblatt, Sidney, Milton Gross and Susan Chartoff. "Marital status and multiple psychiatric admissions for alcoholism." *Quarterly Journal of Studies on Alcohol* 30(2-A):445–447, 1969.

577 Schuckit, Marc A. "Sexual disturbance in the woman alcoholic." *Medical Aspects of Human Sexuality* 6(9):44–65, Sept. 1972.

578 Smith, James W. "Impotence in alcoholism." *Northwest Medicine* 71:523–524, July 1972.

579 Straus, Robert and Selden D. Bacon. *Drinking in College.* New Haven: Yale University Press, 1953.

580 Viamontes, Jorge A. "Brief guide to office

counseling: alcohol abuse and sexual dysfunction." *Medical Aspects of Human Sexuality* 8(11):185–186, Nov. 1974.

581 Virkkunen, M. "Incest offenses and alcoholism." *Medicine, Science and the Law* 14:124–128, Apr. 1974.

582 Westling, Achilles. "On the correlation of the consumption of alcoholic drinks with some sexual phenomenon of Finnish male students." *International Journal of Sexology* 7(3):109–115, Feb. 1954.

583 Wilson, G. Terence and David M. Lawson. "Effects of alcohol on sexual arousal in women." *Journal of Abnormal Psychology* 85(5):489–497, Oct. 1976.

584 _____. "Expectancies, alcohol, and sexual arousal in male social drinkers." *Journal of Abnormal Psychology* 85(6):587–594, Dec. 1976.

OTHER SOURCES OF INFORMATION

Rutgers Center of Alcohol Studies
New Brunswick, NJ 08093
Publish *Quarterly Journal of Studies on Alcohol;* can generate bibliographies by topics such as sex.

AMPHETAMINES

585 Bell, D.S. and W.H. Trethowan. "Amphetamine addiction and disturbed sexuality." *Archives of General Psychiatry* 4:74–78, Jan. 1961.

586 Gossop, M.R., R.S. Stern and P.H. Connell. "Drug dependence and sexual dysfunction: a comparison of intravenous users of narcotics and oral users of amphetamines." *British Journal of Psychiatry* 124:431–434, May 1974.

587 Greaves, George. "Sexual disturbances among chronic amphetamine users." *Journal of Nervous and Mental Disease* 155(5):363–365, 1972.

HALLUCINOGENIC DRUGS

588 Alpert, Richard. "Drugs and sexual behavior." *Journal of Sex Research* 5(1):50–56, Feb. 1969.

589 Furst, Peter T. and Michael D. Coe. "Ritual enemas." *Natural History* 86:88–91, Mar. 1977.

590 Guerra, Francisco. "Sex and drugs in the 16th century." *British Journal of Addiction* 69(3):269–289, Sept. 1974.

591 Kleber, Herbert. "Student use of hallucinogens." *Journal of the American College Health Association* 14:109–117, Dec. 1965.

592 La Barre, Weston. "Primitive psychotherapy in native American cultures: peyotism and confession." *Journal of Abnormal and Social Psychology* 42(3):294–309, July 1947.

593 Ludwig, Arnold M. and Jerome Levine. "Patterns of hallucinogenic drug abuse." *Journal of the American Medical Association* 191(2):92–96, Jan. 11, 1965.

594 Mann, Thaddeus. "Reproduction (I): sex, drugs and ethics." *Impact of Science on Society* 20(4):255–265, Oct./Dec. 1970.

595 Masters, R.E.L. "Sex, ecstasy and the psychedelic drugs." *Playboy* 14(11):94–96 passim, 223–227, Nov. 1967.

LSD

596 Alpert, Richard. "LSD and sexuality." *Psychedelic Review* 10:21–24, 1969.

597 Martin, A. Joyce. "The treatment of twelve male homosexuals with 'L.S.D.'" *Acta Psychotherapeutica et Psychosomatica* 10(5):394–402, 1962.

598 Thorne, Melvin G., Jr. and Barbara Sales. "Marital and LSD therapy with a transvestite and his wife." *Journal of Sex Research* 3(2):169–177, May 1967.

MARIJUANA

599 Amendt, Günter. "Haschisch und sexualität—eine empirische untersuchung uber die sexualität jugendlicher in der drogensubkultur." *Beiträge zur Sexualforschung* 53:1–124, 1974.

600 Burdsal, Charles et al. "A factor-analytic examination of sexual behaviors and attitudes and marihuana usage." *Journal of Clinical Psychology* 31:568–572, 1975.

601 Cohen, Sidney. "The sex-pot controversy." *Drug Abuse and Alcoholism Newsletter* 4(6):4p., July 1975.

602 Ewing, John A. "Students, sex and marijuana." *Medical Aspects of Human Sexuality* 6(2):101–117, Feb. 1972.

603 Goode, Erich. "Sex and marijuana." *Sexual Behavior* 2(5):45–51, May 1972.

604 Grilly, David M., D.P. Ferraro and Monique C. Braude. "Observations on the reproductive activi-

ty of chimpanzees following long-term exposure to marihuana." *Pharmacology* 11:304–307, 1974.

605 Koff, Wayne C. "Marijuana and sexual activity." *Journal of Sex Research* 10(3):194–204, Aug. 1974.

606 Kolansky, Harold and William T. Moore. "Effects of marihuana on adolescents and young adults." *Journal of the American Medical Association* 216(3):486–492, Apr. 19, 1971.

607 _____. "Marihuana use and autoerotic activity." In: *Masturbation from Infancy to Senescence,* ed. by Irwin M. Marcus and John J. Francis, pp. 439–458. New York: International Universities Press, 1975.

608 Kolodny, Robert C. et al. "Depression of plasma testosterone levels after chronic intensive marijuana use." *New England Journal of Medicine* 290:872–874, Apr. 18, 1974.

609 Lewis, Barbara. *The Sexual Power of Marijuana.* New York: Wyden, 1970.

610 Mendelson, Jack H. "Brief guide to office counseling: marihuana and sex." *Medical Aspects of Human Sexuality* 10(11):23–24, Nov. 1976.

611 Morley, J.E., P. Logie and A.D. Bensusan. "The subjective effects of dagga; including comparative studies with Britain and America." *South African Medical Journal* 47:1145–1149, July 7, 1973.

612 Robbins, Paul R. and Roland H. Tanck. "Psychological correlates of marijuana use: an exploratory study." *Psychological Reports* 33(3):703–706, Dec. 1973.

NICOTINE

613 Carney, Richard E., Herman Feldman and Wei P. Loh. "Sex chromatin, body-masculinity and smoking behavior." *Psychological Reports* 25(1):261–262, 1969.

614 Cendron, H. and J. Vallery-Masson. "Les effets de l'âge sur l'activité sexuelle masculine; incidences de quelques facteurs dont le tabac." *Presse Médicale* 78(41):1795–1797, Oct. 3, 1970.

615 Hofstätter, Dr. R. "Geschlechtsorgane und sexualfunktion." In: *Die Rauchende Frau, eine Klinische, Psychologische, und Soziale Studie.* Wien: Hölder-Pichler-Tempsky, A.G., 1924.

616 Landy, Eugene E. "Sex differences in some aspects of smoking behavior." *Psychological Reports* 20:575–580, Apr. 1967.

617 Mullan, J. "Personality of smokers: contribution to their characteristics from the sexological aspect." *Review of Czechoslovak Medicine* 17(1):19–24, 1971.

618 Ochsner, Alton. "Influence of smoking on sexuality and pregnancy." *Medical Aspects of Human Sexuality* 5(11):78–92, Nov. 1971.

619 Raboch, Jan and Jiri Mellan. "Smoking and fertility." *British Journal of Sexual Medicine* 2(4):35–37, Aug. 1975.

620 Schonfield, Jacob. "Differences in smoking, drinking and social behavior by race and delinquency status in adolescent males." *Adolescence* 1(4):367–380, 1966.

621 Sterling, Theodore D. and Diana Kobayashi. "A critical review of reports on the effects of smoking on sex and fertility." *Journal of Sex Research* 11(3):201–217, Aug. 1975.

622 Subak-Sharpe, Genell J. "Is your sex life going up in smoke?" *Today's Health* 52(8):50–53 passim, Aug. 1974.

L-DOPA

623 Ballivet, J., A. Marin and A. Gisselman. "Aspects de l'hypersexualité observée chez le parkinsonien lors traitement par la L-DOPA." *Annales Médico-Psychologiques* 2(4):515–522, Nov. 1973.

624 Benkert, Otto. "Biologisch-psychiatrischer ansatz zur therapie von potenzstörungen." *Andrologie* 5(3):235–243, Jan. 24, 1973.

625 Bowers, Malcolm B., Jr. and Melvin H. Van Woert. "Sexual behavior during L-DOPA treatment of Parkinson's Disease." *Medical Aspects of Human Sexuality* 6(7):88–98, July, 1972.

626 Bowers, Malcolm B., Jr., Melvin H. Van Woert and Linda Davis. "Sexual behavior during L-DOPA treatment for Parkinsonism." *American Journal of Psychiatry* 127(12):1691–1693, June 1971.

627 Keyes, D.M. et al. "L-DOPA effects on sexual behaviour: an experimental study." *Journal of Sex Research* 12(2):117–123, May 1976.

Special Groups

BIBLIOGRAPHIES

628 Griffith, Ernest R., Robert J. Timms and Michael A. Tomko, eds. *Sexual Problems of Pa-*

tients with Spinal Injuries: An Annotated Bibliography. Cincinnati: Dept. of Physical Medicine and Rehabilitation, College of Medicine, University of Cincinnati, Mar. 1973.

629 Institute for Sex Research, Information Service. *Diseases and Sex Behavior.* Bloomington, IN: 1976.

630 _____. *Ethnic Groups.* Bloomington, IN: 1976.

631 _____. *Mentally Ill.* Bloomington, IN: 1976.

632 _____. *Mentally Retarded.* Bloomington, IN: 1976.

633 _____. *Physically Handicapped and Sex Behavior.* Bloomington, IN: 1976.

634 _____. *Sex Behavior and Obesity.* Bloomington, IN: 1976.

635 _____. *Surgery and Sex Behavior.* Bloomington, IN: 1976.

636 Minnesota Council on Family Relations. *Family Life Literature and Films: An Annotated Bibliography and Supplement.* 1219 University Avenue, SE, Minneapolis, MN, 1974.

637 Rabin, Barry J. *Options' Resource Guide to Sexual Adjustment in Disability.* Long Beach, CA: Association for Sexual Adjustment in Disability, 1977.

638 Scarlett, Sharon, Cynthia Thurry and Irene Zupan, comps. *Psychological, Sexual, Social and Vocational Aspects of Spinal Cord Injury: A Selected Bibliography.* · Minneapolis: Minnesota Medical Rehabilitation Research and Training Center No. 2, July 1976. (Avail. from Dept. of Physical Medicine and Rehabilitation, Box 297, University of Minnesota.)

639 *A Selected Bibliography on Sexuality, Sex Education and Family Planning.* St. Paul: Planned Parenthood of Minnesota, 1976.

640 *Sex and the Handicapped: A Selected Bibliography (1927–1973).* Cleveland, OH: Veterans Administration Hospital, Apr. 1974. (Includes films.)

641 Staples, Robert. *The Black Family: A Bibliography.* Washington, DC: Howard University, 1972.

642 Swedish Central Committee for Rehabilitation. *Bibliography: Social and Sexual Intercourse.* Stockholm: 1972.

BLIND AND SEX BEHAVIOR

643 Foulke, Emerson. "Brief guides to office counseling: sex education and counseling for the blind." *Medical Aspects of Human Sexuality* 10(4):51–52, Apr. 1976.

644 Gillman, Arthur E. and Arlene R. Gordon. "Sexual behavior in the blind." *Medical Aspects of Human Sexuality* 7(6):49–60, June 1973.

645 Zacharias, Leona and Richard J. Wurtman. "Blindness and menarche." *Obstetrics and Gynecology* 33(5):603–608, May 1969.

OTHER SOURCES OF INFORMATION

SIECUS
84 Fifth Avenue, Suite 407,
New York, NY 10011

BRAIN DISEASES AND SEX BEHAVIOR

646 Blumer, Dietrich. "Changes of sexual behavior related to temporal lobe disorders in man." *Journal of Sex Research* 6(3):173–180, Aug. 1970.

647 Lesniak, Roman, A. Szymusik and R. Chrzanowski. "Multidirectional disorders of sexual drive in a case of brain tumor." *Forensic Science* 1:333–338, 1972.

648 Rosenblum, Jay A. "Human sexuality and the cerebral cortex." *Diseases of the Nervous System* 35(6):268–271, June 1974.

649 Saunders, M. and M. Rawson. "Sexuality in male epileptics." *Journal of the Neurological Sciences* 10:577–583, June 1970.

650 Taylor, David C. "Sexual behavior and temporal lobe epilepsy." *Archives of Neurology* 21(5):510–516, 1969.

651 Weinstein, Edwin A. "Sexual disturbances after brain injury." *Medical Aspects of Human Sexuality* 8(10):10–31, Oct. 1974.

652 Wiig, Elizabeth H. "Counseling the adult aphasic for sexual readjustment." *Rehabilitation Counseling Bulletin* 17(2):110–119, Dec. 1973.

COLON SURGERY AND SEX BEHAVIOR

653 Bernstein, William C. "Sexual dysfunction following radical surgery for cancer of rectum and sigmoid colon." *Medical Aspects of Human Sexuality* 6(3):156–163, Mar. 1972.

654 Binder, Donald P. *Sex, Courtship and the Single Ostomate.* Los Angeles: United Ostomy Association, 1973.

655 Dlin, Barney M. "Sex after ileostomy or colostomy." *Medical Aspects of Human Sexuality* 6(7):32–43, July 1972.

656 Lyons, Albert S. and Marlene Brockmeier. "Brief guide to office counseling: sex after ileostomy and colostomy." *Medical Aspects of Human Sexuality* 9(1):107–108, Jan. 1975.

657 Ward, E.J. "Sex and the ostomate." Paper presented at the Institute for Sex Research, Summer Program, Bloomington, IN, July 28, 1976. 5p.

658 Zinsser, Hans H. "Sex and surgical procedures in the male." In: *The Sexual Experience,* ed. by B.J. Sadock, H.I. Kaplan and A.M. Freedman, pp. 303–307. Baltimore: Williams & Wilkins, 1976.

OTHER SOURCES OF INFORMATION

United Ostomy Association
1111 Wilshire Blvd., Los Angeles, CA 90017

DIABETES AND SEX BEHAVIOR

659 Ellenberg, Max. "Impotence in diabetes: a neurologic rather than an endocrinologic problem." *Medical Aspects of Human Sexuality* 7(4):12–28, Apr. 1973.

660 Faerman, I. et al. "Impotence and diabetes: studies of androgenic function in diabetic impotent males." *Diabetes* 21:23–30, Jan. 1972.

661 Kolodny, Robert C. "Sexual dysfunction in diabetic females." *Medical Aspects of Human Sexuality* 6(4):98–107, Apr. 1972.

662 Mills, Lewis C. "Sexual disorders in the diabetic patient." In: *Sex and the Life Cycle,* ed. by Wilbur W. Oaks, Gerald A. Melchiode and Ilda Ficher, pp. 163–174. New York: Grune & Stratton, 1976.

DISEASES AND SEX BEHAVIOR

663 Abram, Harry S. et al. "Sexual functioning in patients with chronic renal failure." *Journal of Nervous and Mental Diseases* 160(3):220–226, Mar. 1975.

664 Burchell, R. Clay et al. "Viewpoints: what conditions require a patient to abstain from sexual activity?" *Medical Aspects of Human Sexuality* 10(9):54 passim, Sept. 1976.

665 Currey, H.L.F. "Osteoarthrosis of the hip joint and sexual activity." *Annals of the Rheumatic Diseases* 29:488–493, Sept. 1970.

666 Ford, Amasa B. and Alexander P. Orfirer. "Sexual behavior and the chronically ill patient." *Medical Aspects of Human Sexuality* 1(2):51–61, Oct. 1967.

667 Kass, Irving, Katherine Updegraff and Robert B. Muffley. "Sex in chronic obstructive pulmonary disease." *Medical Aspects of Human Sexuality* 6(2):33–42, Feb. 1972.

668 Luparello, Thomas J. "Asthma and sex." *Medical Aspects of Human Sexuality* 4(3):97–107, Mar. 1970.

669 Money, John. "Sexual problems of the chronically ill." In: *Sexual Problems—Diagnosis and Treatment in Medical Practice,* ed. by C.W. Wahl, pp. 266–287. New York: Free Press, 1967.

670 Rubin, Isadore. "Sexual adjustments in relation to pregnancy, illness, surgery, physical handicaps, and other unusual circumstances." In: *Human Sexuality in Medical Education and Practice,* ed. by Clark E. Vincent, pp. 532–551. Springfield, IL: Charles C. Thomas, 1968.

HEART DISEASE AND SEX BEHAVIOR

671 Brenton, Myron. *Sex and Your Heart.* New York: Coward-McCann, 1968.

672 Hellerstein, Herman K. "Sexual activity and the postcoronary patient." *Medical Aspects of Human Sexuality* 3(3):70–96, Mar. 1969.

673 Howard, Elliott J. "Sexual expenditure in patients with hypertensive disease." *Medical Aspects of Human Sexuality* 7(10):82–92, Oct. 1973.

674 Koller, Reuben et al. "Counseling the coronary patient on sexual activity." *Postgraduate Medicine* 51(4):133–136, Apr. 1972.

675 Lord, Jere W. "Peripheral vascular disorders and sexual function." *Medical Aspects of Human Sexuality* 7(9):34–43, Sept. 1973.

676 Scheingold, Lee Dreisinger and Nathaniel N. Wagner. *Sound Sex and the Aging Heart: Sex in the Mid and Later Years with Special Reference to Cardiac Problems.* New York: Human Sciences Press, 1974.

677 Wagner, Nathaniel N. "Sexual activity and the cardiac patient." In: *Human Sexuality: A Health Practitioner's Text,* ed. by Richard Green, pp. 173–179. Baltimore: Williams & Wilkins, 1975.

MASTECTOMY AND SEX BEHAVIOR

678 Byrd, Benjamin F. "Brief guide to office counseling: sex after mastectomy." *Medical Aspects of Human Sexuality* 9(4):53–54, Apr. 1975.

679 Ervin, Clinton V. "Psychologic adjustment to mastectomy." *Medical Aspects of Human Sexuality* 7(2):42–65, Feb. 1973.

680 Schain, Wendy S. "Psychosocial stages in breast cancer: implications for effective therapy." Paper presented at American Psychological Association, Sheraton Park Hotel, Washington, DC, Sept. 3, 1976. 23p.

681 Witkin, Mildred Hope. "Sex therapy and mastectomy." *Journal of Sex and Marital Therapy* 1(4):290–304, Summer 1975.

MENTALLY ILL AND SEX BEHAVIOR

682 Abernethy, Virginia and George L. Abernethy. "Risk for unwanted pregnancy among mentally ill adolescent girls." *American Journal of Orthopsychiatry* 44(3):442–449, Apr. 1974.

683 Arieti, Silvano. "Sexual conflict in psychotic disorders." In: *Sexual Problems: Diagnosis and Treatment in Medical Practice,* ed. by Charles William Wahl, pp. 228–237. New York: Free Press, 1967.

684 Axelrod, Terry, Eleanor O'Brien and Pauline Hines. "Agencies, hospital staff cooperate to develop sex education seminars." *Hospital and Community Psychiatry* 24(3):137 passim, Mar. 1973.

685 Barnett, Joseph. "Sex and the obsessive-compulsive person." *Medical Aspects of Human Sexuality* 5(2):35–45, Feb. 1971.

686 Beck, Aaron T. "Sexuality and depression." *Medical Aspects of Human Sexuality* 2(7):44 passim, July 1968.

687 Chrzanowski, Gerard. "Sex behavior as a clue to mental disease." *Medical Aspects of Human Sexuality* 5(3):200–209, Mar. 1971.

688 Erlenmeyer-Kimling, L. et al. "Changes in fertility rates of schizophrenic patients in New York State." *American Journal of Psychiatry* 125(7):88–99, Jan. 1969.

689 Eysenck, H.J. "Hysterical personality and sexual adjustment, attitudes and behavior." *Journal of Sex Research* 7(4):274–281, Nov. 1971.

690 Grunebaum, Henry U. and Virginia Abernethy. "Ethical issues in family planning for hospitalized psychiatric patients." *American Journal of Psychiatry* 132(3):236–240, Mar. 1975.

691 Kayton, Robert and Henry B. Biller. "Sex-role development and psychopathology in adult males." *Journal of Consulting and Clinical Psychology* 38(2):208–210, Apr. 1972.

692 Kempton, Winifred. *A Teacher's Guide to Sex Education for Persons with Learning Disabilities.* North Scituate, MA: Duxbury, 1975.

693 Leon, Sidney and Eileen D. Gambrill. "Behavior rehearsal as a method to increase heterosexual interaction." Unpub. paper, May 1972. 20p.

694 Levitt, Eugene E., Charles W. Perkins and Frank J. Connolly. "Sexual problems of psychiatric outpatients." *Journal of the Indiana State Medical Association* 67(5):343–345, May 1974.

695 Levy, Edwin Z. "Notes and comments on the sexual behavior of hospitalized adolescents." *Journal of National Association of Private Psychiatric Hospitals* 4(4):30–35, Winter 1972/73.

696 Nell, Renée. "Sex in a mental institution." *Journal of Sex Research* 4(4):303–312, Nov. 1968.

697 Paykel, Eugene S. and Myrna M. Weissman. "Marital and sexual dysfunction in depressed women." *Medical Aspects of Human Sexuality* 6(6):73–101, June 1972.

698 Phillips, Derek L. "Rejection of the mentally ill: the influence of behavior and sex." *American Sociological Review* 29(5):679–687, Oct. 1964.

699 Pinderhughes, Charles A., E. Barrabee Grace and L.J. Reyna. "Psychiatric disorders and sexual functioning." *American Journal of Psychiatry* 128(10):96–103, Apr. 1972.

700 Prosen, Harry. "Sexuality in females with 'hysteria.'" *American Journal of Psychiatry* 124(5):687–692, Nov. 1967.

701 Shulman, Bernard H. "Schizophrenia and sexual behavior." *Medical Aspects of Human Sexuality* 5(1):144–153, Jan. 1971.

702 Small, Iver F. and Joyce G. Small. "Sexual behavior and mental illness." In: *The Sexual Experience,* ed. by B.J. Sadock, H.I. Kaplan and A.M. Freedman, pp. 358–373. Baltimore: Williams & Wilkins, 1976.

703 Stine, Diane. "Sex education in a psychiatric hospital." *Journal of the National Association of Private Psychiatric Hospitals* 6(4):30–34, Winter 1974/75.

704 Tourney, Garfield and Lon M. Hatfield. "Androgen metabolism in schizophrenics, homosexuals and normal controls." *Biological Psychiatry* 6(1):23–36, 1973.

705 Tsuang, Ming T. "Hypersexuality in manic

patients." *Medical Aspects of Human Sexuality* 9(11):83 passim, Nov. 1975.

706   Turner, Edward T. "Attitudes of parents of deficient children toward their child's sexual behavior." *Journal of School Health* 40:548–550, Dec. 1970.

707   Wolfe, Stephen D. and W. Walter Menninger. "Fostering open communication about sexual concerns in a mental hospital." *Hospital and Community Psychiatry* 24(3):147–150, Mar. 1973.

MENTALLY RETARDED AND SEX BEHAVIOR

708   Abelson, Robert B. and Ronald C. Johnson. "Heterosexual and aggressive behaviors among institutionalized retardates." *Mental Retardation* 7(5):28–30, 1969.

709   Brantlinger, Ellen. "Sexuality: a special education for the mentally retarded." Bloomington, IN: Unpub. paper, 1976, 62p.

710   De La Cruz, Felix and Gerald D. LaVeck, eds. *Human Sexuality and the Mentally Retarded.* New York: Brunner/Mazel, 1973.

711   Fujita, Byron et al. "Sexuality, contraception and the mentally retarded." *Postgraduate Medicine* 47:193–197, May 1970.

712   Hall, Judy E. "Sexuality and the mentally retarded." In: *Human Sexuality: A Health Practitioner's Text,* ed. by Richard Green, pp. 181–195. Baltimore: Williams & Wilkins, 1975.

713   Hartman, Susan S. "Marriage education for mentally retarded adults." *Social Casework* 56(5):280–284, May 1975.

714   Kempton, Winifred and Rose Forman. *Updated Guide for Training in Sexuality and the Mentally Handicapped.* Philadelphia: Planned Parenthood of Southeastern Pennsylvania, 1976. (Avail. from P.P.S.P., 1220 Sansom St., Philadelphia, PA 19107.)

715   Meyerwitz, Joseph H. "Sex and the mentally retarded." *Medical Aspects of Human Sexuality* 5(11):94–118, Nov. 1971.

716   Rolett, Karin. *Organizing Community Resources in Sexuality Counseling and Family Planning for the Retarded: A Community Workers' Manual.* Chapel Hill, NC: Carolina Population Center, 1976.

717   Rosen, M. "Conditioning appropriate heterosexual behavior in mentally and socially handicapped populations." *Training School Bulletin*: 172–177, Feb. 4, 1970.

718   Thaller, Karl E. and Barbara D. Thaller, eds. *Sexuality and the Mentally Retarded.* Washington, DC: Office of Economic Opportunity, 1973. (Also Davis, V. Sue and William Q. Davis. *Sexuality and the Mentally Retarded. . .A Companion Monograph.* Washington, DC: Office of Economic Opportunity, 1974.) (Avail. from Planned Parenthood of Northern New York, Inc., Central Office, 161 Stone St., Annex, Watertown, NY 13601.)

OTHER SOURCES OF INFORMATION

Educational Division
Hallmark Films and Recordings
1511 E. North Ave., Baltimore, MD 21213

Ed. U. Press
760 Ostrom Ave., Syracuse, NY 13210

New Readers Press
Division of Laubach Literacy
Box 131, Syracuse, NY 11550

Planned Parenthood Association of Southeastern Pennsylvania
1220 Sansom St., Philadelphia, PA 19107

SIECUS
84 Fifth Ave., Suite 407, New York, NY 10011

NERVOUS SYSTEM IMPAIRMENT AND SEX BEHAVIOR

719   Geiger, Robert C. and Susan E. Knight. "Sexuality of people with cerebral palsy." *Medical Aspects of Human Sexuality* 9(3):70–83, Mar. 1975.

720   Horenstein, Sam. "Sexual dysfunction in neurological disease." *Medical Aspects of Human Sexuality* 10(4):6 passim, Apr. 1976.

721   McDowell, Fletcher H. "Sexual manifestations of neurologic disease." *Medical Aspects of Human Sexuality* 2(4):13–21, Apr. 1968.

722   Rosenblum, Jay A. "Human sexuality and the cerebral cortex." *Diseases of the Nervous System* 35(6):268–271, June 1974.

723   Smith, Bernard H. "Brief guides to office counseling: multiple sclerosis and sexual dysfunction." *Medical Aspects of Human Sexuality* 10(1):103–104, Jan. 1976.

724   Vas, C.J. "Sexual impotence and some autonomic disturbances in men with multiple sclerosis." *Acta Neurologica Scandinavica* 45:166–182, 1969.

725   Whitelaw, George P. and Reginald H. Smithwick. "Some secondary effects of sympathectomy: with particular reference to disturbance of sexual function." *New England Journal of Medicine* 245(4):121–130, July 26, 1951.

PARAPLEGICS AND SEX BEHAVIOR

726 Bregman, Susan. *Sexuality and the Spinal Cord Injured Woman.* Sister Kenny Institute, Office of Continuing Education, 1975. (Avail. from Dept. 188, Chicago Ave., Minneapolis, MN 55404.)

727 Cole, Theodore M. "Sexuality and the spinal cord injured." In: *Human Sexuality: A Health Practitioner's Text,* ed. by Richard Green, pp. 147–170. Baltimore: Williams & Wilkins, 1975.

728 Cole, Theodore M. and Maureen R. Stevens. "Rehabilitation professionals and sexual counseling for spinal cord injured adults." *Archives of Sexual Behavior* 4(6):631–638, Nov. 1975.

729 Comarr, A.E. "Sex among patients with spinal cord and/or cauda equina injuries." *Medical Aspects of Human Sexuality* 7(3):222–238, Mar. 1973.

730 Eisenberg, M.G. and L.C. Rustad. *Sex and the Spinal Cord Injured: Some Questions and Answers.* 2nd ed. Cleveland: Veterans Administration Hospital, 1975. (Avail. from Supt. of Docs., U.S. GPO, Washington, DC 20402. Stock #051-000-00081-1)

731 Enby, Gunnel. *Let There Be Love: Sex and the Handicapped.* New York: Taplinger, 1975.

732 Glass, Dorothea D. "Sexuality and the spinal cord injured patient." In: *Sex and the Life Cycle,* ed. by Wilbur W. Oaks, Gerald A. Melchiode and Ilda Ficher, pp. 179–190. New York: Grune & Stratton, 1976.

733 Gregory, Martha F. *Sexual Adjustment; a Guide for the Spinal Cord Injured.* Bloomington, IL: Accent Special Publications, 1974.

734 Jochheim, K.A. and H. Wahle. "A study on sexual function in 56 male patients with complete irreversible lesions of the spinal cord and cauda equina." *Paraplegia* 8(3):166–172, Nov. 1970.

735 Masham, Baroness Masham of Ilton. "The psychological and practical aspects of sex and marriage for the paraplegic." *Proceedings of the Royal Society of Medicine* 66:133–136, Feb. 1973.

736 Mooney, Thomas O., Theodore Cole and Richard Chilgren. *Sexual Options for Paraplegics and Quadriplegics.* Boston: Little, Brown, 1975.

737 Rabin, B.J. *The Sensuous Wheeler: Sexual Adjustment for the Spinal Cord Injured.* San Francisco: Multi-Media Resource Center, 1976.

738 *Sex: Rehabilitation's Stepchild.* Proceeding of the workshop, Continuing Education in the Treatment of Spinal Cord Injuries, Indianapolis, IN, June 23, 1973. Chicago: National Paraplegia Foundation, 1974.

OTHER SOURCES OF INFORMATION

National Paraplegia Foundation
333 North Michigan Ave., Chicago, IL 60601

Spinal Cord Injury Service
Rancho Los Amigos Hospital
7601 E. Imperial Hwy., Downey, CA 90242

Program in Human Sexuality
University of Minnesota Medical School
Research East Bldg.
2630 University Ave., S.E., Minneapolis, MN 55414

Spinal Cord Injury Service
Veterans Administration Hospital
10701 East Blvd., Cleveland, OH 44106

PHYSICALLY HANDICAPPED AND SEX BEHAVIOR

739 Albrecht, Gary L. "Sexual resocialization of the physically disabled: constraints on time and resources on the adult socialization process." Paper presented at 68th Annual Meeting of the American Sociological Association, N.Y., Aug. 27–30, 1973.

740 Anderson, Thomas P. and Theodore M. Cole. "Sexual counseling of the physically disabled." *Postgraduate Medicine* 58(1):117–123, July 1975.

741 Ayrault, Evelyn West. *Helping the Handicapped Teenager Mature.* New York: Association Press, 1971.

742 Griffith, Ernest R. and Roberta B. Trieschmann. "Treatment of sexual dysfunction in patients with physical disorders." In: *Clinical Management of Sexual Disorders,* ed. by J. Meyer, pp. 206–255. Baltimore: Williams & Wilkins, 1976.

743 Heslinga, K., A.M.C.M. Schellen and A. Verkuyl. *Not Made of Stone; the Sexual Problems of Handicapped People.* Springfield, IL: Charles C. Thomas, 1974.

744 Johnson, Warren R. *Sex Education and Counseling of Special Groups: The Mentally and Physically Handicapped, Ill and Elderly.* Springfield, IL: Charles C. Thomas, 1975.

745 Mourad, Mahmoud and Wu Shung Chiu. "Marital-sex adjustment of amputees." *Medical*

Aspects of Human Sexuality 8(2):47 passim, Feb. 1974.

746 Romano, Mary D. "Sexuality and the disabled female." *Accent on Living*:26–31, Winter 1973.

747 Sadoughi, Wanda, Martin Leshner and Herbert L. Fine. "Sexual adjustment in a chronically ill and physically disabled population: a pilot study." *Archives of Physical Medicine and Rehabilitation*:311–317, July 1971.

OTHER SOURCES OF INFORMATION:

> SIECUS
> 84 Fifth Ave., Suite 407, New York, NY 10011

> National Center on Educational Media and Materials for the Handicapped (NCEMMH)
> Ohio State University, College of Education
> Columbus, OH 43210

> Program in Human Sexuality
> University of Minnesota Medical School
> Research East Bldg.
> 2630 University Ave., Minneapolis, MN 55415

> Swedish Central Committee for Rehabilitation
> FACK
> S-161 03, Bromma 3, SWEDEN
> (Working-Group on Social and Sexual Intercourse for the Handicapped)

SEX BEHAVIOR AND OBESITY

748 Bruch, Hilde. "Obesity and sex." *Medical Aspects of Human Sexuality* 3(2):42–52, Feb. 1969.

749 Clarke, J. "Effects of obesity on sexual function." *British Journal of Sexual Medicine* 3(3):8–9, June 1976.

750 Friedman, Abraham I. *How Sex Can Keep You Slim.* Englewood Cliffs, NJ: Prentice-Hall, 1972.

751 Scheimann, Eugene and Paul G. Neimark. *Sex and the Overweight Woman.* New York: New American Library, 1970.

752 Schwartz, Ronald Alan. "The sexual behavior of obese women." (Thesis—Chicago Institute of Technology.) Ann Arbor, MI: University Microfilms, 1971. (Order #71-20,080)

SURGERY AND SEX BEHAVIOR

753 Bieber, Irving and Marvin G. Drellich. "Psychological adaptation to serious illness and organ ablation." In: *The Psychological Basis of Medical Practice,* ed. by Harold Lief et al., pp. 318–327. New York: Harper & Row, 1963.

754 Freeman, Walter. "Sexual behavior and fertility after frontal lobotomy." *Biological Psychiatry* 6(1):94–104, Feb. 1973.

755 Kerr, Charlotte H. "Obstetric trauma and subsequent sex relations." *Medical Aspects of Human Sexuality* 5(11):28–41, Nov. 1971.

756 Norcross, K. "Medical factors in sexual functioning; the effects of surgery on sexual functioning." *British Journal of Sexual Medicine* 1(8):28–29, Nov./Dec. 1974.

757 Pomeroy, Wardell B. "Psychosurgery and sexual behavior." In: *Studies in Topectomy,* ed. by Nolan D.L. Lewis, Carney Landis and H.E. King, pp. 150–171. New York: Grune & Stratton, 1956.

758 Rubin, Isadore. "Sexual adjustments in relation to pregnancy, illness, surgery, physical handicaps, and other unusual circumstances." In: *Human Sexuality in Medical Education and Practice,* ed. by Clark E. Vincent, pp. 532–551. Springfield, IL: Charles C. Thomas, 1968.

759 *Surgical Procedures: Impact on Sexuality.* (Filmstrip, 104 fr., color, 35mm w/record or cassette.) Human sexuality and nursing practice, no. 4. Costa Mesa, CA: Concept Media, Inc., 1975. (Avail. from Concept Media, Box 1893, Costa Mesa, CA 92626.)

760 Watts, G.T. "Sexual problems following major abdominal surgery." In: *Psychosexual Problems: Psychotherapy, Counselling and Behaviour Modification,* ed. by Sidney Crown, pp. 423–431. London: Academic Press, 1976.

UROGENITAL SURGERY AND SEX BEHAVIOR (FEMALE)

761 Abitbol, M. Maurice and James H. Davenport. "Sexual dysfunction after therapy for cervical carcinoma." *American Journal of Obstetrics and Gynecology* 119(2):181–189, May 15, 1974.

762 DiMusto, Juan Carlos. "Sexual activity after tubal ligation." *Medical Aspects of Human Sexuality* 7(6):174–187, June 1973.

763 Drellich, Marvin G. "Sex after hysterectomy." *Medical Aspects of Human Sexuality* 1(3):62–64, Nov. 1967.

764 Huffman, John W. "Brief guide to office counseling: hysterectomy—procedure and aftermath." *Medical Aspects of Human Sexuality* 9(11):123–124, Nov. 1975.

765 _____. "Sexual reactions after gynecologic surgery." *Medical Aspects of Human Sexuality* 3(11):48–57, Nov. 1969.

766 Mathis, James L. "The emotional impact of surgical sterilization of the female." *Journal of the Oklahoma Medical Association* 62:141–145, Apr. 1969.

767 Twombly, Gray Huntington. "Sex after radical gynecological surgery." *Journal of Sex Research* 4(4):275–281, Nov. 1968.

768 Weinberg, Paul C. "Psychosexual impact of treatment in female genital cancer." *Journal of Sex and Marital Therapy* 1(2):155–157, Winter 1974.

UROGENITAL SURGERY AND SEX BEHAVIOR (MALE)

769 Amelar, Richard D. and Lawrence Dubin. "Sex after major urologic surgery." *Journal of Sex Research* 4(4):265–274, Nov. 1968.

770 Ferber, Andrew S. et al. "Men with vasectomies: a study of medical, sexual, and psychological changes." *Psychosomatic Medicine* 29(4):354–366, July/Aug. 1967.

771 Finkle, Alex L. "Sex after prostatectomy." *Medical Aspects of Human Sexuality* 2(3):40–41, Mar. 1968.

772 Freund, Matthew and Joseph E. Davis. "A follow-up study of the effects of vasectomy on sexual behavior." *The Journal of Sex Research* 9(3):241–268, Aug. 1973.

773 Kakar, D.N. "Sexual problems related to vasectomy; suggested guidelines for future research." *The Journal of Family Welfare* 21(3):16–20, Mar. 1975.

774 Malin, Joseph M. "Sex after urologic surgery." *Medical Aspects of Human Sexuality* 7(10):245–264, Oct. 1973.

775 Wolfers, Helen. "Psychological aspects of vasectomy." *British Medical Journal* 4:297–300, 1970.

ETHNIC GROUPS

776 Bell, Alan P. "Black sexuality: fact & fancy." Paper presented to Focus: Black America Series, Indiana University, Bloomington, IN, Oct. 14, 1968. 12p.

777 Carrier, Joseph M. "Cultural factors affecting urban Mexican male homosexual behavior." *Archives of Sexual Behavior* 5(2):103–124, Mar. 1976.

778 Cooper, Jeff. "Free love in the far north: sex among the Eskimos." *Sexology* 41(1):39–42, Aug. 1974.

779 Hernton, Calvin C. "Social struggle and sexual conflict: black sexuality and the contemporary ideology of black power." In: *Sexuality: A Search for Perspective,* ed. by Donald L. Grummon and Andrew M. Barclay, pp. 126–139. New York: Van Nostrand Reinhold, 1971.

780 Lawrence, Charles R. "Color, class and culture: a minority view." In: *Sexuality: A Search for Perspective,* ed. by Donald L. Grummon and Andrew M. Barclay, pp. 109–125. New York: Van Nostrand Reinhold, 1971.

781 Rainwater, Lee. "Some aspects of lower class sexual behavior." *Medical Aspects of Human Sexuality* 2(2):15–25, Feb. 1968.

782 Reiss, Ira L. *The Social Context of Premarital Sexual Permissiveness.* New York: Holt, Rinehart & Winston, 1967.

783 Rosenberg, Bernard. "Sexual patterns in three ethnic subcultures of an American underclass." *Academy of Political and Social Sciences Annals* 376:61–75, Mar. 1968.

784 Seward, Georgene H. "Sex identity and the social order." *Journal of Nervous and Mental Diseases* 139:126–136, 1964.

785 Staples, Robert. "Black sexuality." In: *Sexuality and Human Values,* ed. by Mary Calderone, pp. 62–70. New York: Association Press, 1974.

786 _____. "Research on black sexuality: its implications for family life, sex education, and public policy." *The Family Coordinator:*183–188, Apr. 1972.

787 Sutker, Patricia and Richie S. Gilliard. "Personal sexual attitudes and behavior in blacks and whites." *Psychological Reports* 27(3):753–754, Dec. 1970.

788 Zelnik, Melvin and John Kantner. "Sexuality, contraception, and pregnancy among young unwed females in the United States." In: *Demographic and Social Aspects of Population Growth,* ed. by Charles F. Westoff and Robert Parke, Jr., pp. 357–374. Washington, DC: U.S. GPO, 1972.

SOCIAL CLASSES AND SEX BEHAVIOR

789   Ferdinand, Theodore N. "Sex behavior and the American class structure: a mosaic." *Medical Aspects of Human Sexuality* 3(1):34–46, Jan. 1969.

790   Ginzberg, Eli. "Sex and class behavior." In: *About the Kinsey Report; Observations by 11 Experts on "Sexual Behavior in the Human Male,"* ed. by Donald Porter Geddes and Enid Curie, pp. 131–145. New York: New American Library, 1948.

791   Hartnagel, Timothy Frank. *Sex identity, social class and juvenile deviance.* (Thesis—Indiana University.) Ann Arbor, MI: University Microfilms, 1968. (Order #69-4751)

792   Johnson, William Steven. *Social class and attitudes toward sexually oriented materials.* (Thesis—University of Southern California.) Ann Arbor, MI: University Microfilms, 1971. (Order #72-6070)

793   Jonas, Doris F. and A. David Jonas. *Sex & Status.* New York: Stein & Day, 1975.

794   Kerckhoff, Alan C. "Social class differences in sexual attitudes and behavior." *Medical Aspects of Human Sexuality* 8(11):10–31, Nov. 1974.

795   Pearlin, Leonard I. "Status inequality and stress in marriage." *American Sociological Review* 40(3):344–357, June 1975.

796   Reiss, Ira L. "Social class and premarital sexual permissiveness: a reexamination." *American Sociological Review* 30(5):747–756, Oct. 1965.

797   Rosenberg, Charles E. "Sexuality, class and role in 19th-century America." *American Quarterly* 25:131–153, May 1973.

798   Ruppel, Howard J., Jr. "Sex and social class." *Sexual Behavior* 3(2):14–18, Feb. 1973.

799   Strong, Ethelyn R. "Sexual development and behavior in varying socioeconomic groups." Paper presented at Institute for Sex Research Summer Program, Bloomington, IN, July 22, 1976. 19p.

SOCIAL CLASSES AND SEX BEHAVIOR— LOWER CLASS

800   Brown, Thomas Edwards. "Sex education and life in the Negro ghetto." *Pastoral Psychology* 19(184):9, May 1968.

801   Dryfoos, Joy G. "A formula for the 1970's: estimating the need for subsidized family planning services in the United States." *Family Planning Perspectives* 5(3):145–174, Summer 1973.

802   Fiasche, Angel. "Sex in the slums." *Medical Aspects of Human Sexuality* 7(9):88–97, Sept. 1973.

803   Harrison, Danny E. et al. "Premarital sexual standards of rural youth." *Journal of Sex Research* 10(4):266–277, Nov. 1974.

804   Kleinerman, Gerald et al. "Sex education in a ghetto school." *Journal of School Health* 41:29–33, Jan. 1971.

805   Rainwater, Lee. "Marital sexuality in four cultures of poverty." In: *Human Sexual Behavior,* ed. by Donald S. Marshall and Robert C. Suggs, pp. 187–205. New York: Basic Books, 1971.

806   Rubin, Lillian Breslow. *Worlds of Pain: Life in the Working-Class Family.* New York: Basic Books, 1976.

807   Schwartz, Martin S. "A report on the sex information knowledge of 87 lower class ninth grade boys." *The Family Coordinator* 18(4):361–371, Oct. 1969.

Sex Variations

Bisexuality

BIBLIOGRAPHIES

808   Parker, William. *Homosexuality: A Selective Bibliography of Over 3,000 Items. Supplement, 1970–1975.* Metuchen, NJ: Scarecrow Press, 1977.

809   Weinberg, Martin S. and Alan P. Bell, eds. *Homosexuality: An Annotated Bibliography.* New York: Harper & Row, 1972.

BISEXUALITY

810   Bieber, Irving et al. *Homosexuality; A Psychoanalytic Study.* New York: Basic Books, 1962.

811   "Bisexualidad." *Sexualmedica* (6):20–23, Apr. 1974.

812   Blair, Ralph Edward. "Counseling concerns and bisexual behavior." *Homosexual Counseling Journal* 1(2):26–30, Apr. 1974.

813   Bode, Janet. *View from Another Closet: Exploring Bisexuality in Women.* New York: Hawthorn Books, 1976.

814   Bon, Michel et al. "L'homosexualite: table ronde." *Cahiers de Sexologie Clinique* 2(1):65–89, 1976.

815   Caprio, Frank Samuel. "Bisexual conflicts and insomnia." *Journal of Clinical Psychopathology* 10(4):376–379, Oct. 1949.

816   Carroll, Jon. "Bisexual chic." *Oui* 3(2):48 passim, Feb. 1974.

817   Coons, Frederick W. "Ambisexuality as an alternative adaptation." *Journal of the American College Health Association* 21(2):142–144, Dec. 1972.

818   Duberman, Martin. "The bisexual debate." *New Times* :34 passim, June 28, 1974.

819   Falk, Ruth. *Women Loving: A Journey toward Becoming an Independent Woman.* New York: Random House, 1975.

820   Fast, Julius and Hal Wells. *Bisexual Living.* New York: M. Evans, 1975.

821   Ford, Clellan S. and Frank A. Beach. *Patterns of Sexual Behavior.* New York: Harper & Bros., 1951.

822   Freud, Sigmund. "Three essays on the theory of sexuality." In: *Readings in Human Sexuality,* ed. by Samuel T. Wilson, Richard L. Roe and Lucy E. Autrey, pp. 71–79. New York: West, 1975.

823   Karlen, Arno. *Sexuality and Homosexuality.* New York: W.W. Norton, 1971.

824   Kelly, Gary F. "Bisexuality and the youth culture." *Homosexual Counseling Journal* 1(2):16–25, Apr. 1974.

825   Marmor, Judd. *Sexual Inversion; The Multiple Roots of Homosexuality.* New York: Basic Books, 1965.

826   Mead, Margaret. "Bisexuality: what's it all about?" *Redbook* :29 passim, Jan. 1975.

827   Money, John and Anke A. Ehrhardt. *Man & Woman: Boy & Girl.* Baltimore: Johns Hopkins University Press, 1972.

828   Rado, Sandor. "A critical examination of the concept of bisexuality." In: *Sexual Inversion,* ed. by Judd Marmor, pp. 175–189. New York: Basic Books, 1965.

829   Richardson, Frank. *Napoleon: Bisexual Emperor.* New York: Horizon Press, 1973.

830   Spiers, Duane E. "The no-man's land of the bisexual." *Psychiatry* 22(3):6–11, 1976.

831   Stoller, Robert J. "The 'bedrock' of masculinity and femininity: bisexuality." In: *Psychoanalysis and Women: Contributions to New Theory and Therapy,* ed. by Jean Baker Miller, pp. 245–258. New York: Brunner/Mazel, 1973.

832   Stoller, Robert J. and Lawrence E. Newman. "The bisexual identity of transsexuals: two case examples." *Archives of Sexual Behavior* 1(1):17–28, 1971.

833   West, D.J. *Homosexuality.* Chicago: Aldine Publishing Co., 1968.

BISEXUALITY (FEMALE)

834   Smith-Rosenberg, Carroll. "The female world of love and ritual: relations between women in nineteenth-century America." *Signs: Journal of Women in Culture and Society* 1(1):1-29, Fall 1975.

835 Socarides, Charles W. "The historical development of theoretical and clinical concepts of overt female homosexuality." *Journal of the American Psychoanalytic Association* 21(2):386-414, Apr. 1963.

BISEXUALITY (MALE)

836 Matthews, Joan. "Bisexuality in the male." *Journal of Sex Research* 5(2):126-129, May 1969.

837 Myerson, Abraham and Rudolph Neustadt. "Bisexuality and male homosexuality: their biological and medical aspects." *Clinics* 1(4):932-957, Dec. 1942.

BISEXUALITY RESEARCH

838 Blumstein, Philip W. and Pepper Schwartz. "Bisexuality: some social psychological issues." Paper presented at American Sociological Association Annual Meeting, New York, Aug. 1976. 23p.

839 Goy, Robert W. and David A. Goldfoot. "Neuroendocrinology: animal models and problems of human sexuality (and discussion)." *Archives of Sexual Behavior* 4(4):405-420, July 1975.

840 Wolff, Charlotte. *Bisexuality: A Study.* London: Quartet Books, 1977.

BISEXUALITY RESEARCH (FEMALE)

841 Blumstein, Philip W. and Pepper Schwartz. "Bisexuality in women." *Archives of Sexual Behavior* 5(2):171-181, Mar. 1976.

842 _____. "Bisexual women." In: *The Social Psychology of Sex,* ed. by Jacqueline P. Wiseman, pp. 154-162. New York: Harper & Row, 1976.

843 _____. "Lesbianism and bisexuality." In: *Sexual Deviance and Sexual Deviants,* ed. by Erich Goode and Richard R. Troiden, pp. 278-295. New York: Morrow, 1974.

844 Sawyer, Ethel. "A study of a public lesbian community." Paper presented to the Sociology-Anthropology Department, George Washington University, Washington, DC, Sept. 1965. 46p.

845 Schäfer, Siegrid. "Sexual and social problems among lesbians." *Journal of Sex Research* 12(1):50-69, Feb. 1976.

846 Schäfer, Siegrid and Gunter Schmidt. *Weibliche Homosexualität: Dokumentation der Ergebnisse einer Untersuchung an homosexuellen und bisexuellen Frauen in der BRD.* Hamburg: Unveröffentliches ms., 1973.

BISEXUALITY RESEARCH (MALE)

847 Blumstein, Philip W. and Pepper Schwartz. "Bisexuality in men." *Urban Life* 5(3):339-358, Oct. 1976.

848 Churchill, W. *Homosexual Behavior among Males: A Cross-cultural and Cross-species Investigation.* New York: Hawthorn Books, 1967.

849 Freund, Kurt. "Male homosexuality: an analysis of the pattern." In: *Understanding Homosexuality; Its Biological and Psychological Bases,* ed. by J.A. Loraine, pp. 25-81. New York: American Elsevier, 1974.

850 Freund, Kurt and Ron Langevin. "Bisexuality in homosexual pedophilia." *Archives of Sexual Behavior* 5(5):415-423, Sept. 1976.

851 Humphreys, Laud. *The Tearoom Trade.* Chicago: Aldine Publishing Co., 1970.

852 Imieliński, Kazimierz. *Geneza Homo- i Biseksualizmu Środowiskowege, Teoria Orientacji Plciowej.* Warsaw: Polish State Medical Publishers, 1963.

853 Roesler, T. and Robert W. Deisher. "Youthful male homosexuality; homosexual experience and the process of developing homosexual identity in males aged 16-22 years." *Journal of the American Medical Association* 219(8):1018-1023, Feb. 1972.

854 Weinberg, Martin S. and Colin J. Williams. *Male Homosexuals; Their Problems and Adaptations.* New York: Oxford University Press, 1974. (Pap. ed.: New York: Penguin, 1975.)

BISEXUALITY STATISTICS

855 Hunt, Morton B. *Sexual Behavior in the 1970's.* Chicago: Playboy Press, 1974.

856 Kinsey, Alfred C. et al. *Sexual Behavior in the Human Female.* Philadelphia: W.B. Saunders, 1953.

857 _____. *Sexual Behavior in the Human Male.* Philadelphia: W.B. Saunders, 1948.

OTHER SOURCES OF INFORMATION

The Bisexual Center
Box 26227, San Francisco, CA 94126
Publication: *The Bi-Monthly: Newsletter of the Bisexual Center*

Bisexual Liberation Center
345 W. 85th St., Suite 46, New York, NY 10024
Publication: *Bisexual Expression*

Quaker Committee of Concern
c/o Bob Martin
600 W. 122nd St., New York, NY 10027

Homosexuality

BIBLIOGRAPHIES/REVIEWS OF THE LITERATURE

858   Acosta, Frank X. "Etiology and treatment of homosexuality: a review." *Archives of Sexual Behavior* 4(1):9–29, Jan. 1975.

859   American Library Association. Task Force on Gay Liberation. *A Gay Bibliography.* Philadelphia: 1975. (Frequently revised, includes audiovisuals; avail. from the Task Force, Box 2383, Philadelphia, PA 19103.)

860   Gonsiorek, John C. *Psychological Adjustment and Homosexuality.* (Journal Supplement Abstract Service, MS 1478.) Washington, DC: American Psychological Association, 1977.

861   "Guide to current literature." *Journal of Homosexuality.* 1(1), 1974. (Found in each issue.)

862   Mannion, Kristiann. *Female Homosexuality: A Comprehensive Review of Theory and Research.* (Journal Supplement Abstract Service, MS 1247.) Washington, DC: American Psychological Association, 1976.

863   Morin, Stephen F. *Annotated Bibliography of Research on Lesbianism and Male Homosexuality, 1967–74.* (Journal Supplement Abstract Service, MS 1191.) Washington, DC: American Psychological Association, 1976.

864   Parker, William. *Homosexuality: A Selective Bibliography of over 3,000 Items.* Metuchen, NJ: Scarecrow Press, 1971. (*Supplement, 1970–1975.* Scarecrow Press, 1977.)

865   Weinberg, Martin S. and Alan P. Bell, eds. *Homosexuality: An Annotated Bibliography.* New York: Harper & Row, 1972.

GENERAL/COLLECTIONS

866   Baskett, Edward E. *Entrapped.* Westport, CT: Lawrence Hill, 1976.

867   Boggan, E. Carrington et al. *The Rights of Gay People; The Basic ACLU Guide to a Gay Person's Rights.* An American Civil Liberties Union Handbook. New York: Avon, 1975.

868   Brown, Howard. *Familiar Faces, Hidden Lives: The Story of Homosexual Men in America Today.* New York: Harcourt Brace Jovanovich, 1976.

869   Bullough, Vern. *Sexual Variance in Society and History.* New York: Wiley, 1976.

870   Cory, Donald Webster. *The Homosexual in America.* New York: Greenberg, 1951.

871   _____. *Homosexuality: A Cross-Cultural Approach.* New York: Julian Press, 1956.

872   _____. *The Lesbian in America.* New York: Citadel Press, 1964.

873   Cory, Donald Webster and John P. Leroy. *The Homosexual and His Society; A View from Within.* New York: Citadel Press, 1963.

874   Ebert, Alan. *The Homosexuals.* New York: Macmillan, 1977.

875   Gibson, Gifford G. and Mary Jo Risher. *By Her Own Admission: A Lesbian Mother's Fight to Keep Her Son.* Garden City, NY: Doubleday, 1977.

876   Great Britain. Committee on Homosexual Offenses and Prostitution. *The Wolfenden Report.* New York: Stein & Day, 1963.

877   Green, Richard. "Homosexuality as a mental illness (with critical evaluations by six authors)." *International Journal of Psychiatry* 10(1):77–128, Mar. 1972.

878   Hyde, Harford Montgomery. *The Love that Dared Not Speak Its Name: A Candid History of Homosexuality in Britain.* Boston: Little, Brown, 1970.

879   Karlen, Arno. *Sexuality and Homosexuality.* New York: W.W. Norton, 1971.

880   Katz, Jonathan. *Gay American History: Lesbians and Gay Men in the U.S.A.: A Documentary.* New York: Crowell, 1976.

881   Katz, Jonathan, ed. *Homosexuality: Lesbians and Gay Men in Society, History and Literature.* Homosexuality Reprint Series of 56 titles. New York: Arno Press, 1975.

882   Klaich, Dolores. *Woman + Woman; Attitudes toward Lesbianism.* New York: Simon & Schuster, 1974.

883   Loraine, J.A., ed. *Understanding Homosexuality; Its Biological and Psychological Bases.* New York: American Elsevier, 1974.

884   McCaffrey, Joseph A., ed. *The Homosexual Dialectic.* Englewood Cliffs, NJ: Prentice-Hall, 1972.

885   Marmor, Judd and Richard Green. "Homosexual behavior." In: *Handbook of Sexology,* ed. by John Money and Herman Musaph, pp. 1051–1068. Amsterdam: Excerpta Medica, 1977.

886   Marmor, Judd. *Sexual Inversion: The Multiple Roots of Homosexuality.* New York: Basic Books, 1965.

887   Martin, Del and Phyllis Lyon. *Lesbian/Woman.* San Francisco: Glide Urban Center, 1972.

888   Miller, Merle. *On Being Different: What It Means to Be a Homosexual.* New York: Random House, 1971.

889   Rechy, John. *The Sexual Outlaw: A Documentary: A Non-fiction Account, with Commentaries, of Three Days and Nights in the Sexual Underground.* New York: Grove Press, 1977.

890   Rowse, Alfred Leslie. *Homosexuals in History: A Study of Ambivalence in Society, Literature and the Arts.* New York: Macmillan, 1977.

891   Ruitenbeek, Hendrik, ed. *The Problem of Homosexuality in Modern Society.* New York: E.P. Dutton, 1962.

892   Tripp, Clarence A. *The Homosexual Matrix.* New York: McGraw-Hill, 1975.

893   Weltge, Ralph W., ed. *The Same Sex; An Appraisal of Homosexuality.* Philadelphia: Pilgrim Press, 1969.

894   Wysor, Bettie. *The Lesbian Myth: Insights and Conversations.* New York: Random House, 1974.

RESEARCH

895   Altman, Dennis. *Homosexual: Oppression and Liberation.* New York: Outerbridge & Dienstfrey, 1971.

896   Bell, Alan P. and Martin S. Weinberg. *Homosexualities: A Study of Diversity among Men and Women.* New York: Simon & Schuster, 1978.

897   Bieber, Irving et al. *Homosexuality; A Psychoanalytic Study.* New York: Basic Books, 1962.

898   Churchill, Wainwright. *Homosexual Behavior Among Males: A Cross-cultural and Cross-species Investigation.* New York: Hawthorn Books, 1967.

899   Dannecker, Martin and Reimut Reiche. *Der gewöhnliche Homosexuelle: eine soziologische Untersuchung über männliche Homosexuelle in der Bundesrepublik.* Frankfurt am Main: Fischer, 1974.

900   Freedman, Mark. *Homosexuality and Psychological Functioning.* Belmont, CA: Brooks/Cole, 1971.

901   Hauser, Richard. *The Homosexual Society.* London: The Bodley Head, 1962.

902   Hoffman, Martin. *The Gay World; Male Homosexuality and the Social Creation of Evil.* New York: Basic Books, 1968.

903   Humphreys, Laud. *Tearoom Trade; Impersonal Sex in Public Places.* Chicago: Aldine Publishing Co., 1970.

904   Livingood, John M., ed. *National Institute of Mental Health Task Force on Homosexuality: Final Report and Background Papers.* DHEW Publication No. HSM-72-9116. Rockville, MD: NIMH, 1972. (Avail. from Supt. of Docs., U.S. GPO, Washington, DC 20402. Stock #1724-0244.)

905   Rosen, David H. *Lesbianism; A Study of Female Homosexuality.* Springfield, IL: Charles C. Thomas, 1974.

906   Saghir, Marcel T. and Eli Robins. *Male and Female Homosexuality: A Comprehensive Investigation.* Baltimore: Williams & Wilkins, 1973.

907   Schofield, Michael. *Sociological Aspects of Homosexuality: A Comparative Study of Three Types of Homosexuals.* Boston: Little, Brown, 1965.

908   Warren, Carol A.B. *Identity and Community in the Gay World.* New York: Wiley, 1974.

909   Weinberg, George. *Society and the Healthy Homosexual.* New York: St. Martin's Press, Feb. 1972.

910   Weinberg, Martin S. and Colin J. Williams. *Male Homosexuals: Their Problems and Adaptations.* New York: Oxford University Press, 1974. (Paper ed. with minor revisions: Penguin, 1975.)

911   West, D.J. *Homosexuality Re-Examined.* Minneapolis: University of Minnesota Press, 1977.

912   Williams, Colin J. and Martin S. Weinberg. *Homosexuals and the Military: A Study of Less Than Honorable Discharge.* New York: Harper & Row, 1971.

913   Wolff, Charlotte. *Love Between Women.* New York: St. Martin's Press, 1971.

STATISTICS

914 Hunt, Morton. *Sexual Behavior in the 1970's.* Chicago: Playboy Press, 1974.

915 Kinsey, Alfred C. et al. *Sexual Behavior in the Human Female.* Philadelphia: W.B. Saunders, 1953.

916 _____. *Sexual Behavior in the Human Male.* Philadelphia: W.B. Saunders. 1948.

917 Reid, John. "How 'gay' is New York?" *New York Magazine:* 72–79, Sept. 24, 1973.

ATTITUDES ON HOMOSEXUALITY RESEARCH

918 Dunbar, John, Marvin Brown and Donald M. Amoroso. "Some correlates of attitudes toward homosexuality." *Journal of Social Psychology* 89(2):271–279, Apr. 1973.

919 Levitt, Eugene E. and Albert D. Klassen. "Public attitudes toward homosexuality: part of the 1970 national survey by the Institute for Sex Research." *Journal of Homosexuality* 1(1):29–43, 1974.

920 MacDonald, A.P. and R.G. Games. "Some characteristics of those who hold positive and negative attitudes toward homosexuals." *Journal of Homosexuality* 1(1):9–27, Fall 1974.

921 Nyberg, Kenneth L. and Jon P. Alston. "Analysis of public attitudes toward homosexuality. *Journal of Homosexuality* 2(2):99–107, Winter 1976/77.

HOMOSEXUALITY THERAPY

922 Bell, Alan P. "The homosexual as patient." In: *Human Sexuality: A Health Practitioner's Text*, ed. by Richard Green, pp. 55–72. Baltimore: Williams & Wilkins, 1975.

923 Feldman, M.P. and M.J. MacCulloch. *Homosexual Behaviour: Therapy and Assessment.* Oxford, England: Pergamon Press, 1971.

924 Hatterer, Laurence J. *Changing Homosexuality in the Male.* New York: McGraw-Hill, 1970.

925 Jones, Clinton R. *Homosexuality and Counseling.* Philadelphia: Fortress Press, 1974.

926 Socarides, Charles W. *The Overt Homosexual.* New York: Grune & Stratton, 1968.

927 Symposium on Homosexuality and the Ethics of Behavioral Intervention, Ninth Annual Convention of the Association for Advancement of Behavior Therapy, San Francisco, Dec. 13, 1975.

"Papers . . . (and) invited responses." *Journal of Homosexuality* 2(3):195–259, Spring 1977.

RELIGIOUS ATTITUDES ON HOMOSEXUALITY

928 Bailey, Derrick Sherwin. *Homosexuality and the Western Christian Tradition.* London and New York: Longmans, Green, 1955.

929 Enroth, Ronald M. and Gerald E. Jamison. *The Gay Church.* Grand Rapids: W.B. Eerdmans, 1974.

930 Heron, Alastair, ed. *Toward a Quaker View of Sex: An Essay by a Group of Friends.* London: Friends Home Service Committee, 1963.

931 Jones, H. Kimball. *Toward a Christian Understanding of the Homosexual.* New York: Association Press, 1966.

932 McNeill, John J. *The Church and the Homosexual.* Kansas City: Sheed Andrews & McMeel, 1976.

933 Mickley, Richard R. *Christian Sexuality; A Reflection on Being Christian and Sexual.* 2nd ed. rev. with study guide. Los Angeles: The Universal Fellowship Press, 1976. (Avail. from the Universal Fellowship Press, Box 5570, Los Angeles, CA.)

934 Oberholtzer, W. Dwight, ed. *Is Gay Good? Ethics, Theology, and Homosexuality.* Philadelphia: Westminster Press, 1971.

935 Oraison, Marc. *The Homosexual Question.* New York: Harper & Row, 1977.

936 Perry, Troy D. as told to Charles Lucas. *The Lord Is My Shepherd and He Knows I'm Gay.* Los Angeles: Nash Publishing, 1972.

937 Pittenger, Norman. *Time for Consent: A Christian's Approach to Homosexuality.* London: S.C.M. Press, 1967.

GAY LIBERATION

938 Abbott, Sidney and Barbara Love. *Sappho Was a Right-On Woman.* New York: Stein & Day, 1972.

939 Bell, Arthur. *Dancing the Gay Lib Blues: A Year in the Homosexual Liberation Movement.* New York: Simon & Schuster, 1971.

940 Birkby, Phyllis et al., eds. *Amazon Expedition: A Lesbian Feminist Anthology.* Washington, NJ: Times Change Press, 1973. (Dist. by Monthly Review Press, New York, NY.)

941 Clarke, Lige and Jack Nichols. *I Have More*

Fun with You Than Anybody. New York: St. Martin's Press, 1972.

942   Fisher, Peter. *The Gay Mystique: The Myth and Reality of Male Homosexuality.* New York: Stein & Day, 1972.

943   Humphreys, Laud. *Out of the Closets: the Sociology of Homosexual Liberation.* Englewood Cliffs, NJ: Prentice-Hall, 1972.

944   Jay, Karla and Allen Young, eds. *After You're Out: Personal Experiences of Gay Men and Lesbian Women.* New York: Links, 1975.

945   _____. *Out of the Closets: Voices of Gay Liberation.* New York: Douglas, 1972.

946   Johnston, Jill. *Lesbian Nation: The Feminist Solution.* New York: Simon & Schuster, 1973.

947   Lauritsen, John and David Thorstad. *The Early Homosexual Rights Movement (1864–1935).* New York: Times Change Press, 1974.

948   Loovis, David. *Gay Spirit; A Guide to Becoming a Sensuous Homosexual.* New York: Strawberry Hill/Grove Press, 1974.

949   Martin, Del and Phyllis Lyon. *Lesbian Love and Liberation.* San Francisco: Multi Media Resource Center, 1973.

950   Richmond, Len and Gary Noguera, eds. *The Gay Liberation Book: Writings by and about Gay Men.* San Francisco: Ramparts Press, 1973.

951   Simpson, Ruth. *From the Closet to the Courts: The Lesbian Transition.* New York: Viking Press, 1976.

952   Teal, Don. *The Gay Militants.* New York: Stein & Day, 1971.

953   Tobin, Kay and Randy Wicker. *The Gay Crusaders.* New York: Paperback Library, 1972.

954   *The Universities and The Gay Experience; Proceedings of the Conference Sponsored by the Women and Men of the Gay Academic Union, Nov. 23 and 24, 1973.* New York: Gay Academic Union, 1974.

SEX EDUCATION ON HOMOSEXUALS

955   Calderwood, Deryck D. and Wasyl Szkodzinsky. *The Invisible Minority: The Homosexuals in Our Society.* (Multimedia kit.) Boston: Unitarian Universalist Association, 1972.

956   Clark, Don. *Loving Someone Gay.* Millbrae, CA: Celestial Arts, 1977.

957   Hunt, Morton. *Gay: What You Should Know about Homosexuality.* New York: Farrar, Straus & Giroux, 1977.

958   Loovis, David. *Straight Answers about Homosexuality for Straight Readers.* Englewood Cliffs, NJ: Prentice-Hall, 1977.

HOMOSEXUALITY IN LITERATURE

959   Crew, Louie and Rictor Norton, eds. "The homosexual imagination: a special issue." *College English* 36(3):whole issue, Nov. 1974.

960   Damon, Gene, Jan Watson and Robin Jordan, comps. *The Lesbian in Literature; A Bibliography.* Reno, NV: The Ladder, 1975.

961   Foster, Jeannette H. *Sex Variant Women in Literature: A Historical and Quantitative Survey.* 1956. Reprint. Baltimore: Diana Press, 1975.

962   Norton, Rictor. *The Homosexual Literary Tradition: An Interpretation.* Brooklyn, NY: Revisionist Press, 1974.

963   Young, Ian. *The Male Homosexual in Literature: A Bibliography.* Metuchen, NJ: Scarecrow Press, 1975.

PERIODICALS

The Advocate (bi-w.)
One Peninsula Place, Bldg. 1730, Suite 225
   San Mateo, CA 94402

Gai Saber (q.)
Gay Academic Union, Box 480 Lenox Hill
   Sta., New York, NY 10021

Gay Community News (w.)
22 Bromfield St., Boston, MA 02108

Homosexual Counseling Journal (q.)
Homosexual Community Counseling
   Center
30 E. 60th St., New York, NY 10022

Journal of Homosexuality (q.)
Haworth Press
149 Fifth Ave., New York, NY 10010

Lesbian Tide (bi-m.)
8855 Cattaraugus Ave., Los Angeles, CA
   90034

SexuaLaw Reporter (bi-m.)
1800 N. Highland Ave., Suite 106, Los Angeles, CA 90028

OTHER SOURCES OF INFORMATION

Center for Homosexual Education, Evaluation and Research

Department of Psychology,
San Francisco State University
San Francisco, CA 94132

Homosexual Community Counseling Center
30 E. 60th St., New York, NY 10023

National Gay Student Center
2115 S Street NW, Washington, DC 20008

National Gay Task Force
80 Fifth Ave., New York, NY 10011

Homosexual Information Center
3473½ Cahuenga Blvd., Hollywood, CA 90028

National Sex Forum
Research Library on Human Sexuality
1523 Franklin St., San Francisco, CA 94109

One, Inc.
2256 Venice Blvd., Los Angeles, CA 90006
(Has regional chapters)

Society for Individual Rights
83 Sixth St., San Francisco, CA 94103

Sadomasochism

GENERAL

964 Allen, Clifford. *A Textbook of Psychosexual Disorders.* 2nd ed. pp. 47–172. London: Oxford University Press, 1969.

965 Beyer, James C. and William F. Enos. "Obscure causes of death during sexual activity." *Medical Aspects of Human Sexuality* 11(9):81 passim, Sept. 1977.

966 Braun, Saul, ed. "S/M." In: *Catalog of Sexual Consciousness,* pp. 104–109. New York: Grove Press, 1975.

967 Callieri, Bruno and Aldo Semerari. "Contributo psicopatologico al problema della necrofilia." *Sessuologia* 7(1):1–21, Jan./Mar. 1966.

968 Coburn, Judith. "S & M." *New Times* 8(3):43 passim, Feb. 4, 1977.

969 Eisler, Robert. *Man into Wolf; an Anthropological Interpretation of Sadism, Masochism, and Lycanthropy.* London: Routledge & Kegan Paul, 1951.

970 Eulenburg, Albert. *Sadismus und Masochismus.* Wiesbaden: J.F. Bergmann, 1911. (Trans. by Harold Kent: *Algolagnia: The Psychology, Neurology and Physiology of Sadistic Love and Masochism.* New York: New Era Press, 1934.)

971 Ford, Clellan S. and Frank A. Beach. "Painful stimulation." In: *Patterns of Sexual Behavior,* pp. 55–67. New York: Harper & Bros., 1951.

972 Gebhard, Paul H. "Fetishism and sadomasochism." *Science and Psychoanalysis* 15:71–80, 1969.

973 Green, Gerald and Caroline Green. *S-M: The Last Taboo.* New York: Grove Press, 1973.

974 Grumley, Michael. *Hard Corps: Studies in Leather & Sadomasochism.* Photos. by Ed Gallucci. New York: E.P. Dutton, 1977.

975 Haft, Jay Stuart and H.B. Benjamin. "Foreign bodies in the rectum: some psychosexual aspects." *Medical Aspects of Human Sexuality* 7(8):74–95, Aug. 1973.

976 Hentig, Hans von. "Der biss." *Archiv für Kriminologie* 131:121–136, May/June 1963.

977 Heweston, John. "Society and the sexual life of children and adolescents: child murders." *Journal of Sex Education* 4(3):118–127, Dec. 1951/Jan. 1952.

978 Hunt, Morton. "Sadomasochism: incidence, frequency, techniques." In: *Sexual Behavior in the 1970's,* pp. 328–337. Chicago, Playboy Press, 1974.

979 Kinsey, Alfred C. et al. *Sexual Behavior in the Human Female.* Philadelphia: W.B. Saunders, 1953.

980 Klein, Henriette. "Masochism." *Medical Aspects of Human Sexuality* 6(11):33–53, Nov. 1972.

981 Krafft-Ebing, Richard von. *Psychopathia Sexualis. . .Eine Medicinisch-Gerichtliche Studie.* 11th ed. Stuttgart: Ferdinand Enke, 1901.

982 Leigh, L.H. "Sado-masochism, consent, and the reform of the criminal law." *Modern Law Review* 39:130–146, Mar. 1976.

983 Levitt, Eugene E. "Sadomasochism." *Sexual Behavior* 1(6): 69–80, Sept. 1971.

984 Ludovici, Anthony M. "Untapped reserves of sadism in modern men and women." *Journal of Sex Education* 1(3):95–100, Dec. 1948.

985 McLeish, John. "Sadism and masochism." *Medical World News* 93(4):363–367, 1960.

986 Otto, Herbert A. " 'The pornographic fringeland' on the American newsstand." *Journal of Human Relations* 12(3):375–390, 1964.

987 Randell, John B. "Sadism and masochism." In: *Sexual Variations,* pp. 95–102. London: Priory Press, 1973.

988 Rothman, G. *The Riddle of Cruelty.* New York: Philosophical Library, 1971.

989 Stekel, Wilhelm. *Sadism and Masochism.* New York: H. Liveright, 1939.

SADOMASOCHISM PSYCHOANALYSIS

990 Alby, Jean-Marc. "A propos d'un fantasme sadomasochique." *Revue Française de Psychanalyse* 35:277–285, Feb./Mar. 1971.

991 Baggally, W. "Hedonic conflict and the pleasure principle." *International Journal of Psycho-Analysis* 22(¾):280–300, 1941.

992 Bonaparte, Marie. "Some biophysical aspects of sadomasochism." *International Journal of Psycho-Analysis* 33(4):373–384, 1952.

993 Bromberg, Norbert. "Hitler's character and its development: further observations." *American Image* 28(4):289–303, Winter 1971.

994 Brown, Sidney and Marie Nyswander. "The treatment of masochistic adults." *American Journal of Orthopsychiatry* 26(2):351–364, Apr. 1956.

995 Friedenberg, F.S. "A contribution to the problem of sado-masochism." *Psychoanalytic Review* 43(1):91–96, Jan. 1956.

996 Garma, Angel. "Sadism and masochism in human conduct." *Journal of Clinical Psychopathology and Psychotherapy,* Pt. I—6(1):1–36, July 1944; Pt. II—6(2):355–390, Oct. 1944; Pt. III—6(3–4):493–508, Jan. 1945; Pt. IV—7(1):43–64, July 1945.

997 Gero, George. "Sadism, masochism, and aggression: their role in symptom-formation." *Psychoanalytic Quarterly* 31:31–42, 1962.

998 Hori, Akio. "Four cases of sexual perversion." *Kyushu Neuro-Psychiatry* 13(2):232–238, 1967.

999 Joseph, Edward D., ed. *Beating Fantasies: Regressive Ego Phenomena in Psychoanalysis.* The Kris Study Group of the N.Y. Psychoanalytic Institute, Monograph 1. New York: International Universities Press, 1965.

1000 Kamiat, Arnold H. "Male masochism and culture." *The Psychoanalytic Review* 23(1):84–91, Jan. 1936.

1001 Liss, Edward. "Learning: its sadistic and masochistic manifestations." *American Journal of Orthopsychiatry* 10:123–128, Jan. 1940.

1002 Lister, Milton. "The analysis of an unconscious beating fantasy in a woman." *International Journal of Psycho-Analysis* 38(1):22–31, 1957.

1003 McDougall, Joyce. "The anonymous spectator; a clinical study of sexual perversion." *Contemporary Psychoanalysis* 10(3):289–310, 1974.

1004 Novick, Jack and Kerry N. Novick. "Beating fantasies in children." *International Journal of Psycho-Analysis* 53(2):237–242, 1972.

1005 Rappaport, Ernest A. "Zoophily and zoerasty." *Psychoanalytic Quarterly* 37: 565–587, 1968.

1006 Sadger, J. "A contribution to the understanding of sado-masochism." *International Journal of Psycho-Analysis* 7(3–4):484–491, July/Oct. 1926.

1007 Schindler, Walter. "Betrachtungen über den sadomasochismus und dessen erscheinungsformen." *Zeitschrift für Psychotherapie und Medizinische Psychologie* 14:62–74, Mar. 1964.

1008 Stein, Conrad. "Inversion sadomasochique du complexe d'Oedipe et relation d'objet paranoïaque." *Revue Française de Psychanalyse* 24:301–332, May/June 1960.

1009 Stewart, Sidney. "Quelques aspects théoriques du fétichisme." *Interprétation* 2(2):83–103, Apr. 1968.

1010 Vanden Bergh, Richard L. and John F. Kelly. "Vampirism: a review with new observations." *Archives of General Psychiatry* 11:543–547, Nov. 1964.

1011 Weisman, Avery D. "Self-destruction and sexual perversion." In: *Essays in Self-Destruction,* ed. by E.S. Shneidman, pp. 265–299. New York: Science House, 1967.

HOMOSEXUAL SADOMASOCHISM

1012 Brody, Eugene B. "From schizophrenic to homosexual: a crisis in role and relating." *American Journal of Psychotherapy* 17:578–595, Oct. 1963.

1013 Cordova, Jeanne. "Towards a feminist expression of sado-masochism." *Lesbian Tide* 6(3):14–17, Nov./Dec. 1976.

1014 "Ein widerschein von liebeswirklichkeit; sadomasochistische annoncen in zeitschriften für homosexuelle." *Sexualmedizin* 3(11):585–588, Nov. 1974.

1015 Gregersen, Edgar. "The sadomasochistic scene." Paper presented at the American Anthropological Association Meeting, New Orleans, Nov. 1969. 5p.

1016 Klimmer, Rudolf. "Bericht über einen masochisten mit homosexuellem einschlag." *Zeitschrift für Ärztliche Fortbildung* 66(15): 782–785, 1972.

SADOMASOCHISM RESEARCH

1017 Kaunitz, Paul E. "Sadomasochistic marriages." *Medical Aspects of Human Sexuality* 11(2):66 passim, Feb. 1977.

1018 Mechler, Ulrich. *Sadistinnen und Masochisten. Part I and II.* Dachau, Germany: I. Prehm, 1959/1960.

1019 Spengler, Andreas. "Manifest sadomasochism of males: results of an empirical study." *Archives of Sexual Behavior* 6(6):441–456, Nov. 1977.

SADISM

1020 Berest, Joseph J. "Report on a case of sadism." *Journal of Sex Research* 6(3):210–219, Aug. 1970.

1021 "Die abschaffung der sünde." *Sexualmedizin* 6(5):425–428, May 1977.

1022 LeBeuf, Jacques and Paul LeFebvre. "Contribution à l'étude de la sado-nécrophilie." *Canadian Psychiatric Association Journal* 11:123–131, Apr. 1966.

1023 Mees, Hayden. "Case histories and short communications; sadistic fantasies modified by aversive conditioning and substitution: a case study." *Behavior Research and Therapy* 4(4):317–320, 1966.

1024 Revitch, Eugene. "Extreme manifestations of sexual aggression." *Welfare Reporter* 16(1):10–16, Jan. 1965.

1025 Riddell, William Renwick. "A case of supposed sadism." *Journal of the American Institute of Criminal Law and Criminology* 15(1):32–41, May 1924.

1026 Steg, Joseph. "Brief guide to office counseling: sadism." *Medical Aspects of Human Sexuality* 9(9):149–150, Sept. 1975.

1027 Verus. *Kinderprügeln und Sexualtrieb.* Leipzig: Walther Röhmann, 1904.

SADISM PSYCHOANALYSIS

1028 Cohen, Sydney. "The origin and function of sadistic behavior." *Journal of Contemporary Psychotherapy* 2(1):3–7, Summer 1969.

1029 Hori, Akio. "One case of sadism." *Acta Medica* 30(2):495–498, 1960.

1030 Karpman, Benjamin. "Felonious assault revealed as a symptom of abnormal sexuality; a contribution to the psychogenesis of psychopathic behavior." *Journal of Criminal Law and Criminology* 37(3):193–215, Sept.-Oct. 1946.

1031 Schreiber, Flora Rheta. *Sybil.* Chicago: Regnery, 1973.

1032 Socarides, Charles W. "The demonified mother: a study of voyeurism and sexual sadism." *The International Review of Psycho-Analysis* 1(½):187–195, 1974.

1033 Van Ophuijsen, J.H.W. "The sexual aim of sadism as manifested in acts of violence." *International Journal of Psycho-Analysis* 10(2–3):139–144, Apr./July 1921.

SADISM THERAPY

1034 Mees, Hayden L. "Case histories and short communications; sadistic fantasies modified by aversive conditioning and substitution: a case study." *Behavior Research & Therapy* 4(4):317–320, 1966.

MASOCHISM

1035 Appelbaum, Stephen A. "The masochistic character as a self-saboteur (with special reference to psychological testing." *Journal of Projective Techniques* 27(1):35–46, 1963.

1036 Ferber, Leon. "Beating fantasies." In: *Masturbation from Infancy to Senescence,* ed. by Irwin M. Marcus and John J. Francis, pp. 205–222. New York: International Universities Press, 1975.

1037 Kamait, Arnold H. "Male masochism and culture." *Psychoanalytic Review* 23(1):84–91, Jan. 1936.

1038 Marks, Isaac M., Stanley Rachman and Michael Gelder. "Methods for assessment of aversion treatment in fetishism with masochism." *Behaviour Research and Therapy* 3(4):253–258, Dec. 1965.

1039 Michaux, Leon, G. Rapaud and L. Moor. "Cinquante ans de mutilations monstrueuses chez un masochiste, fils de masochiste." *Presse Médicale* 68:655, 1960.

1040 Robertiello, Richard C. "Masochism and the female sexual role." *Journal of Sex Research* 6(1):56–58, Feb. 1970.

1041 Roche, Philip Q. "Masochistic motivations in criminal behavior." *Journal of Criminal Psychopathology* 4(3):431–444, Jan. 1943.

1042 Sack, Robert L. and Warren B. Miller. "Masochism: a clinical and theoretical overview." *Psychiatry* 38(3):244–257, Aug. 1975.

1043 Schindler, Walter. "The problem of masochism in individuals and nations." *International Journal of Sexology* 2(3):167–173, Feb. 1949.

MASOCHISM PSYCHOANALYSIS

1044 Barbara, Dominick A. "Masochism in love and sex." *American Journal of Psychoanalysis* 34(1):73–79, 1974.

1045 Bieber, Irving. "The meaning of masochism." *American Journal of Psychotherapy* 7(3):433–448, July 1953.

1046 Bonaparte, Marie. "Passivity, masochism and femininity." *International Journal of Psycho-Analysis* 16(3):325–333, July 1935.

1047 Eidelberg, Ludwig. "A contribution to the study of the masturbation phantasy." *The International Journal of Psycho-Analysis* 26(¾): 127–137, 1945.

1048 Fain, Michel. "Analyse du masochisme inadapté." *Revue Française de Psychanalyse* 32(1):145–149, Jan./Feb. 1968.

1049 Fenichel, Otto. "The clinical aspects of the need for punishment." *International Journal of Psycho-Analysis* 9:47–70, 1925.

1050 Finkelstein, J. "A propos de quelques conduites masochiques (Aperçus narcissiques)." *Revue Française de Psychanalyse* 26(1):67–86, Jan./Feb. 1962.

1051 Grunberger, Benjamin C. "Esquisse d'une théorie psychodynamique du masochisme." *Revue Française de Psychanalyse* 18:193–214, 1954.

1052 Horney, Karen. "The problem of feminine masochism." In: *Psychoanalysis and Women: Contributions to New Theory and Therapy*, ed. by Jean Baker Miller, pp. 17–32. New York: Brunner/Mazel, 1973.

1053 Keiser, Sylvan. "The fear of sexual passivity in the masochist." *International Journal of Psycho-Analysis* 30(2):162–171, 1949.

1054 Khan, Masud R. "Role of the 'collated internal object' in perversion-formation." *International Journal of Psycho-Analysis* 50(4):555–565, Oct. 1969.

1055 Lenzer, Gertrud. "On masochism: a contribution to the history of a phantasy and its theory." *Signs* 1(2):277–324, Winter 1975.

1056 Lewinsky, Hilde. "On some aspects of masochism." *International Journal of Psycho-Analysis* 25(3–4):150–155, 1944.

1057 Lihn, Henry. "Sexual masochism: a case report." *International Journal of Psycho-Analysis* 52(4):469–478, 1971.

1058 Loewenstein, Rudolph M. "A contribution to the psychoanalytic theory of masochism." *Journal of the American Psychoanalytic Association* 5(2):197–234, Apr. 1957.

1059 Nacht, Sacha. *Le Masochisme; Étude Psychanalytique.* 2nd ed. Paris: Librairie le Francois, 1948.

1060 Parkin, Alan. "On sexual enthrallment." *Journal of the American Psychoanalytic Association* 12(2):336–356, Apr. 1964.

1061 Reik, Theodor. *Masochism in Modern Man.* New York: Farrar & Rinehart, 1941.

MASOCHISM RESEARCH

1062 Brown, Judson S. "Theoretical note: a behavioral analysis of masochism." *Journal of Experimental Research in Personality* 1(1):65–70, Mar. 1965.

1063 Hauck, A. "Beitrage zur psychoendokrinologie des masochismus." *Acta Psychotherapeutica et Psychosomatica* 10(4):265–279, 1962.

1064 Kellerhals, Adolf. "Ein fall von masochismus." *Kriminalistik* 17(1):28–29, Jan. 1963.

1065 Shore, Miles F. et al. "Patterns of masochism: an empirical study." *British Journal of Medical Psychology* 44(1):59–66, Mar. 1971.

BONDAGE

1066 Edmondson, John S. "A case of sexual asphyxia without fatal termination." *British Journal of Psychiatry* 121(563):437–438, Oct. 1972.

1067 Leroy, Bernard. "Un singulier cas de perversion sexuelle; la passion des chaines." *Journal de Psychologie Normale et Pathologique* 5(4):1–16, July/Aug. 1908.

1068 Park, R.L. "Irving Klaw: the godfather of bondage." *Fetish Times Gazette* 1(1):18–21, 1976.

SEX HANGING

1069 Coe, John I. "Sexual asphyxias." *Life-Threatening Behavior* 4(3):171–175, Fall 1974.

1070 Edmondson, John S. "A case of sexual asphyxia without fatal termination." *British Journal of Psychiatry* 121(563):437–438, Oct. 1972.

1071 Ford, R. "Death by hanging of adolescent and young adult males." *Journal of Forensic Sciences* 2:171–176, 1957.

1072 Gregersen, Markil. "Autoerotische todesfälle." *Sexualmedizin* 4(11):690–697, Nov. 1975.

1073 Gwozdz, Feliks. "The sexual asphyxias: a review of current concepts and presentation of seven cases." *Forensic Science Gazette* 1(2):2–4, 1970.

1074 Henry, Russell Cole. " 'Sex' hangings in the female." *Medico-Legal Bulletin* 214:1–5, Feb. 1971.

1075 Hirschfeld, Magnus. "Report of a sex hanging." In: *Sexual Anomalies,* pp. 446–448. New York: Emerson Books, 1944.

1076 Kellerhals, Adolf. "Ein fall von masochismus." *Kriminalistic* 17(1):28–29, Jan. 1963.

1077 Litman, Robert E. and Charles Swearingen. "Bondage and suicide." *Archives of General Psychiatry* 27:80–85, 1972. (Reprinted with commentaries in *Medical Aspects of Human Sexuality* 7(11):164 passim, Nov. 1973.)

1078 Lukianowicz, Narcyz. "Symbolic self-strangulation in a transvestite schizophrenic." *Psychiatric Quarterly* 39(2):244–257, 1965.

1079 Petit, Germain et al. "Suicide ou mort accidentelle par pendaison chez un adolescent." *Médecine Légal et Dommage Corporel* 4:250–251, July/Sept. 1971.

1080 Resnick, H.L.P. "Erotized repetitive hangings: a form of self-destructive behavior." *American Journal of Psychotherapy* 26(1):4–21, Jan. 1972.

1081 Rupp, Joseph C. "The love bug." *Journal of Forensic Sciences* 18(3):259–262, July 1973.

1082 Schechter, Marshall D. "The recognition and treatment of suicide in children." In: *Clues to Suicide,* ed. by Edwin S. Schneidman and Norman L. Farberon, pp. 131–142. New York: McGraw-Hill, 1957.

1083 Shankel, L. Willard and Arthur C. Carr. "Transvestism and hanging episodes in a male adolescent." *Psychiatric Quarterly* 30:478–493, July 1956.

1084 Stearns, A. Warren. "Cases of probable suicide in young persons without obvious motivation." *Journal of the Maine Medical Association* 44(1):16–23, Jan. 1953.

1085 Usher, A. "Accidental hanging in relation to abnormal sexual practices." *Newcastle Medical Journal* 27:234, 1963.

1086 Weiman, W. "Todesfälle bei autoerotischer betätigung mit plastikbeutel." *Archiv für Kriminologie* 129(1–2):16–22, 1962.

1087 Weisman, Avery D. "Self-destruction and sexual perversion." In: *Essays in Self-Destruction,* ed. by E.S. Shneidman, pp. 265–299. New York: Science House, 1967.

OTHER SOURCES OF INFORMATION

The Eulenspiegel Society
Box 2783, New York, NY 10017

Transvestism

1088 Alpert, George, photog. *The Queens.* New York: Da Capo/Plenum Press, 1975.

1089 Baker, Roger. *Drag: A History of Female Impersonation on the Stage.* London: Triton Books, 1968.

1090 Beigel, Hugo G. "A weekend in Alice's Wonderland." *Journal of Sex Research* 5(2):108–122, May 1969.

1091 Beigel, Hugo G. and Robert Feldman. "The male transvestite's motivation in fiction, research, and reality." In: *Advances in Sex Research,* ed. by Hugo C. Beigel, pp. 198–210. New York: Harper & Row, 1963.

1092 Benjamin, Harry. *The Transsexual Phenomenon.* New York: Julian Press, 1966.

1093 Benjamin, Harry et al. "Transsexualism and transvestism—a symposium." *American Journal of Psychotherapy* 8(2):219–244, Apr. 1954.

1094 Brown, Daniel G. "Psychosexual disturbances: transvestism and sex-role inversion." *Marriage and Family Living* 22(3):218–227, Aug. 1960. (Also in: *The Encyclopedia of Sexual Behavior,* ed. by Albert Ellis and Albert Abarbanel, pp. 1012-1022. New York: Hawthorn, 1967.)

1095 Bruce, Virginia. "The expression of femininity in the male." *Journal of Sex Research* 3(2):129–139, May 1967.

1096 Buckner, H. Taylor. "The transvestic career path." *Psychiatry* 33(3):381–389, Aug. 1970.

1097 Bullough, Vern L. "Transvestites in the Middle Ages." American Journal of Sociology 79(6):1381–1394, May 1974.

1098 Burchard, Johann M. "Psychopathology of transvestism and transsexualism." *Journal of Sex Research* 1(1):39–43, Mar. 1965.

1099 Ford, Clellan S. and Frank A. Beach. *Patterns of Sexual Behavior,* pp. 130–131. New York: Harper & Bros., 1951.

1100 Forgy, Donald G. "The institution of berdache among the North American Plains Indians." *Journal of Sex Research* 11(1):1–15, Feb. 1975.

1101 Green, Richard. *Sexual Identity Conflict in Children and Adults.* New York: Basic Books, 1974.

1102 Green, Richard and John Money. *Transsexualism and Sex Reassignment.* Baltimore: Johns Hopkins Press, 1969.

1103 Hamburger, Christian, George K. Stürup and E. Dahl-Iversen. "Transvestism." In: *The Homosexuals,* ed. by A.M. Krich, pp. 293–308. New York: Citadel Press, 1954.

1104 Hirschfeld, Magnus. *Die Transvestiten.* Berlin: Alfred Pulvermacher & Co., 1910.

1105 Hofer, Gunter. "Transvestitismus." *Fortschritte der Neurologie, Psychiatrie und ihrer Grenzgebiete* 29(1):1–33, Jan. 1961.

1106 Johnson, Marcia. "Rapping with a street transvestite revolutionary." In: *Out of the Closets; Voices of Gay Liberation,* ed. by Karla Jay and Allen Young, pp. 112–120. New York: Douglas, 1972.

1107 Kinsey, Alfred C. et al. *Sexual Behavior in the Human Female,* pp. 451 passim. Philadelphia: W.B. Saunders, 1953.

1108 Kirkham, George L. and Edward Sagarin. "Cross-dressing." *Sexual Behavior* 2(4):53–59, Apr. 1972.

1109 Lawrence, Louise (Janet Thompson). "Transvestism: an empirical study." *International Journal of Sexology* 4(4):216–219, May 1951.

1110 Lukianowicz, Narcyz. "Survey of various aspects of transvestism in the light of our present knowledge." *Journal of Nervous and Mental Disease* 128(1):36–64, Jan. 1959. (104 citations)

1111 Money, John. "Cytogenetic and other aspects of transvestism and transsexualism." *Journal of Sex Research* 3(2):141–143, May 1967.

1112 Money, John and Patricia Tucker. *Sexual Signatures.* Boston: Little, Brown, 1975.

1113 Oppenheim, Garrett and Fae Robbin. *The Male Transvestite.* (A Confide cassette.) Tappan, New York: Confide (Personal Counseling Services, Box 56, Tappan, NY, 10983), 1974.

1114 Podolsky, Edward and Carlson Wade. *Transvestism Today.* New York: Epic, 1960.

1115 Prince, Virginia. *Understanding Cross Dressing.* Los Angeles: Chevalier, 1976.

1116 Raynor, Darrell G. *A Year Among the Girls.* New York: Lyle Stuart, 1966.

1117 Sagarin, Edward. *Odd Man In: Societies of Deviants in America.* Chicago: Quadrangle Books, 1969.

1118 Stoller, Robert J. "Pornography and perversion." *Archives of General Psychiatry* 22:490–499, June 1970.

1119 _____. "The term 'transvestism.' " *Archives of General Psychiatry* 24:230–237, Mar. 1971.

1120 _____. *Sex and Gender; On the Development of Masculinity and Femininity.* New York: Science House, 1968.

1121 Thompson, C.J.S. *The Mysteries of Sex: Women Who Posed as Men and Men Who Impersonated Women.* New York: Causeway, 1974.

1122 Wollman, Leo. "The effect of deviate behavior on marriage." *Osteopathic Physician* 41(5):111–115, May 1974.

ETIOLOGY

1123 Kockott, Götz. "Psychiatrische und lerntheoretische aspekte der transsexualität und des transvestitismus." *Der Nervenarzt* 41(8):387–391, Aug. 1970.

1124 Liakos, Aris. "Familial transvestism." *British Journal of Psychiatry* 113:49–51, 1967.

1125 Prince, Virginia. "Homosexuality, transvestism and transsexualism." *American Journal of Psychotherapy* 11(1):80–85, Jan. 1957.

1126 Spensley, James and James T. Barter. "The adolescent transvestite on a psychiatric service: family patterns." *Archives of Sexual Behavior* 1(4):347–356, 1971.

1127 Stoller, Robert J. "Transvestites' women." *American Journal of Psychiatry* 124(3):333–339, 1967.

1128 Wålinder, Jan. "Transvestism, definition and evidence in favor of occasional derivation from cerebral dysfunction." *International Journal of Neuropsychiatry* 1:567–573, Dec. 1965.

RESEARCH

1129 Bentler, Peter M. and Charles (Virginia) Prince. "Personality characteristics of male transvestites: III." *Journal of Abnormal Psychology* 74(2):140–143, Apr. 1969.

1130 _____. "Psychiatric symptomatology transvestites." *Journal of Clinical Psychology* 26(4):434–435, Oct. 1970.

1131 Bentler, Peter M., Richard W. Sherman and Charles (Virginia) Prince. "Personality characteristics of male transvestites." *Journal of Clinical Psychology* 26(3):287–291, July 1970.

1132 Brierley, Harry. "The heterosexual transvestite—a gender anomaly." Paper presented at the Annual Conference of the British Psychological Society, Bangor, 1974. 14p.

1133 Buckner, H. Taylor. "Deviant-group organizations." Unpub. master's thesis, University of California at Berkeley, 1964.

1134 Feinbloom, Deborah Heller. *Transvestites & Transsexuals: Mixed Views.* New York: Delacorte Press, 1976.

1135 Friend, Maurice R. et al. "Observations on the development of transvestism in boys." *American Journal of Orthopsychiatry* 24(3):563–575, July 1954.

1136 Goldfarb, Jack Harold. *The concept of sexual identity in normals and transvestites: its relationship to the body-image, self-concept and parental identification.* (Thesis—University of Southern California.) Ann Arbor, MI: University Microfilms, 1963. (Order #64-3098)

1137 Lukianowicz, Narcyz. "A rudimentary form of transvestism." *American Journal of Psychotherapy* 16:665–675, Oct. 1962.

1138 Money, John and Ernesto Pollitt. "Cytogenetic and psychosexual ambiguity; Klinefelter's syndrome and transvestism compared." *Archives of General Psychiatry* 11:589–595, Dec. 1964.

1139 Munroe, Robert L., John W.M. Whiting and David J. Hally. "Institutionalized male transvestism and sex distinctions." *American Anthropologist* 71(1):87–91, Feb. 1969.

1140 Prince, (Charles) Virginia and Peter M. Bentler. "Survey of 504 cases of transvestism." *Psychological Reports* 31(3):903–917, Dec. 1972.

1141 Randell, John B. "Transvestism and transsexualism; a study of 50 cases." *British Medical Journal* 5164:1448–1452, Dec. 1959.

1142 Rymph, David B. "Cross-sex behavior in an Isthmus Zapotec village." Paper presented at the 73rd Annual Meeting of the American Anthropological Assn., Mexico City, Nov. 19-24, 1974. 10p.

1143 Sabadini, G. and P.E. Turci. "Contributo al problema del travestitismo." *Revista Sperimentale di Freneatria; Medicina Legale delle Alienazioni Mentali* 94:105–123, Feb. 28, 1970.

1144 Taylor, A.J.W. and D.G. McLachlan. "Clinical and psychological observations on transvestism." *New Zealand Medical Journal* 61:496–506, Oct. 1962.

1145 _____. "Further observations and comments on transvestism." *New Zealand Medical Journal* 62(375):527–529, Nov. 1963.

THERAPY

1146 Bakwin, Harry. "Transvestism in children." *Journal of Pediatrics* 56(2):294–298, Feb. 1960.

1147 Barker, J.C. "Behavior therapy for transvestism: a comparison of pharmacological and electrical aversion techniques." *British Journal of Psychiatry* 111(472):262–278, 1965.

1148 Beigel, Hugo G. "Delayed reaction in the treatment of a transvestite." *British Journal of Medical Hypnotism* 15(4):2–6, 1964.

1149 _____. "Three transvestites under hypnosis." *Journal of Sex Research* 3(2):149–162, May 1967.

1150 Benjamin, Harry. "Transvestism and transsexualism in the male and female." *Journal of Sex Research* 3(2):107–127, May 1967.

1151 Clark, D.F. "A note on avoidance conditioning techniques in sexual disorder." *Behaviour Research and Therapy* 3:203–206, 1965.

1152 Dupont, Henry. "Social learning theory and the treatment of transvestite behavior in an eight-year old boy." *Psychotherapy: Theory, Research and Practice* 5(1):44–45, Winter 1968.

1153 Eyres, Alfred E. "Transvestism: employment of somatic therapy with subsequent improvement." *Diseases of the Nervous System* 21:52–53, Jan. 1960.

1154 Green, Richard. "Adults who want to change sex; adolescents who cross-dress; and children called 'sissy' and 'tomboy.'" In: *Human Sexuality: A Health Practitioner's Text,* ed. by Richard Green, pp. 83–95. Baltimore: Williams & Wilkins, 1975.

1155 Hora, Thomas. "The structural analysis of transvestitism." *Psychoanalytic Review* 40(3): 268–274, July 1953.

1156 Lambley, Peter. "Treatment of transvestism and subsequent coital problems." *Journal of Behavior Therapy and Experimental Psychiatry* 5(1):101–102, July 1974.

1157 Morgenstern, F.S., J.F. Pearce and W. Linford Rees. "Predicting the outcome of behaviour therapy by psychological tests." *Behaviour Research and Therapy* 2:191–200, 1965.

1158 Moss, Gene R., Richard T. Rada and James B. Appel. "Positive control as an alternative to aversion therapy." *Journal of Behavior Therapy and Experimental Psychiatry* 1(4):291–294, Dec. 1970.

1159 Pomeroy, Wardell B. "The diagnosis and treatment of transvestites and transsexuals." *Journal of Sex and Marital Therapy* 1(3):215–244, Spring 1975.

1160 Rekers, George A. et al. "Childhood gender identity change: operant control over sex-typed play and mannerisms." *Journal of Behavior Therapy and Experimental Psychiatry* 7(1):51–57, Mar. 1976.

1161 Serber, Michael. "Shame aversion therapy." *Journal of Behavior Therapy and Experimental Psychiatry* 1(3):213–215, Sept. 1970.

1162 Stoller, Robert J. "The treatment of transvestism and transsexualism." *Current Psychiatric Therapies* 6:92–104, 1966.

1163 Walker, Paul A. "Transvestites seek psychiatric help for wives, not selves." *Behavior Today* 7(28):6–7, July 12, 1976.

1164 Ward, Nicholas G. "Successful lithium treatment of transvestism associated with manic-depression." *Journal of Nervous and Mental Diseases* 161(3):204–206, Sept. 1975.

1165 Wollman, Leo. "Transvestism and hypnotism." *British Journal of Medical Hypnotism* 15(3):1–4, Spring 1964.

1166 Woody, Robert H. "Integrated aversion therapy and psychotherapy: two sexual deviation case studies." *Journal of Sex Research* 9(4):313–323, Nov. 1973.

LEGAL ASPECTS OF CROSS DRESSING

1167 Barnett, Walter. *Sexual Freedom and the Constitution.* Albuquerque: University of New Mexico Press, 1973.

1168 Boggan, E. Carrington et al. *The Rights of Gay People; The Basic ACLU Guide to A Gay Person's Rights.* An American Civil Liberties Union Handbook. New York: Avon, 1975.

1169 Bowman, Karl M. and Bernice Engle. "Medicolegal aspects of transvestism." *American Journal of Psychiatry* 113(7):583–588, Jan. 1957.

1170 Sherwin, Robert Veit. "The legal problem in transvestism." *American Journal of Psychotherapy* 8(2):243–244, Apr. 1954.

OTHER SOURCES OF INFORMATION

Chevalier Publications
Box 36091, Los Angeles, CA 90036
Transvestia (irreg. periodical); Phi Pi Epsilon (Foundation for Personality Expression) social organization; monographs, merchandise

International Alliance for Male Feminism
Box 623, Laurel, MD 20810
The Journal of Male Feminism (bi-m.) formerly *Hose and Heel*; hotline telephone service: 301/776-8832; membership directory

Outreach Foundation
102 Charles St., Suite 433, Boston, MA 02114
Outreach Newsletter (q.); reprint service; counseling service; nationwide workshops

Sexual Response Physiology

Coitus and Orgasm

SEXUAL RESPONSE PHYSIOLOGY

1171   Beach, Frank A. "Human sexuality in four perspectives." In: *Human Sexuality in Four Perspectives,* ed. by Frank A. Beach, pp. 1–21. Baltimore: Johns Hopkins University Press, 1977.

1172   Brecher, Ruth and Edward M. Brecher, eds. *An Analysis of Human Sexual Response.* Boston: Little, Brown, 1966.

1173   Diamond, Milton. "Sexual anatomy and physiology: clinical aspects." In: *Human Sexuality: A Health Practitioner's Text,* ed. by Richard Green, pp. 21–34. Baltimore: Williams & Wilkins, 1975.

1174   Fox, Cyril A. "Physiology of coitus." *Science Journal* 6(6):80–85, 1970.

1175   _____. "Recent studies in human coital physiology." *Clinics in Endocrinology and Metabolism* 2(3):527–543, Nov. 1973.

1176.   _____. "Some aspects and implications of coital physiology." *Journal of Sex and Marital Therapy* 2(3):205–213, Fall 1976.

1177   Fox, Cyril A. and Beatrice Fox. "Blood pressure and respiratory patterns during human coitus." *Journal of Reproduction and Fertility* 19:405–415, 1969.

1178   Geer, James H. "Genital measures: comments on their role in understanding human sexuality." *Journal of Sex and Marital Therapy* 2(3):165–172, Fall 1976.

1179   Humphrey, Tryphena and Davenport Hooker. "Human fetal reflexes elicited by genital stimulation." *Proceedings of the 8th International Congress of Neurology,* 2:587–590, 1961.

1180   Jovanic, U.J. "The recording of physiological evidence of genital arousal in human males and females." *Archives of Sexual Behavior* 1(4):309–320, 1971.

1181   Kaplan, Helen Singer. *The New Sex Therapy.* New York: Brunner/Mazel, 1974.

1182   MacLean, Paul D. "Brain mechanisms of elemental sexual functions." In: *The Sexual Experience,* ed. by B.J. Sadock, H.I. Kaplan and A.M. Freedman, pp. 119–127. Baltimore: Williams & Wilkins, 1976.

1183   Masters, William H. and Virginia E. Johnson. *Human Sexual Response.* Boston: Little, Brown, 1966.

1184   Sadock, Virginia A. "Sexual anatomy and physiology." In: *The Sexual Experience,* ed. by B.J. Sadock, H.I. Kaplan and A.M. Freedman, pp. 79–103. Baltimore: Williams & Wilkins, 1976.

1185   Sarrel, Philip M. "Sexual physiology and sexual functioning." *Postgraduate Medicine* 58(1):67–72, July 1975.

1186   Whalen, Richard E. "Brain mechanisms controlling sexual behavior." In: *Human Sexuality in Four Perspectives,* ed. by Frank A. Beach, pp. 215–246. Baltimore: Johns Hopkins University Press, 1977.

1187   Zuckerman, Marvin. "Physiological measures of sexual arousal in the human." In: *Technical Report of the Commission on Obscenity and Pornography.* vol. 1, pp. 61–101. Washington, DC: U.S. GPO, 1971. (Avail. from Supt. of Docs., U.S. GPO, Washington, DC 20402. Stock #5256-0002.)

SEXUAL RESPONSE PHYSIOLOGY (FEMALE)

1188   Benedek, Therese. "An investigation of the sexual cycle in women: methodological considerations." *Archives of General Psychiatry* 8:311–322, Apr. 1963.

1189   Daly, Michael J. "The clitoris as related to human sexuality." *Medical Aspects of Human Sexuality* 5(2):80–97, Feb. 1971.

1190   Debrovner, Charles H. "Vaginal lubrication." *Medical Aspects of Human Sexuality* 9(11):32 passim, Nov. 1975.

1191   De Hempel, Patricia Conrad. "Brief guide to office counseling: inadequate or overabundant vaginal lubrication." *Medical Aspects of Human Sexuality* 11(4):107–108, Apr. 1977.

1192   Fox, Cyril A., S.J. Meldrum and B.W. Watson. "Continuous measurement by radio-telemetry of vaginal pH during human coitus." *Journal of Reproduction and Fertility* 33(1):69–75, Apr. 1973.

1193   Grafenberg, Ernest. "The role of urethra in

female orgasm." *International Journal of Sexology* 3(3):145–148, Feb. 1950.

1194   Heiman, Julia R. "Women's sexual arousal." *Psychology Today* 8(11):91–94, Apr. 1975.

1195   Hoon, Emily Franck, Peter W. Hoon and John P. Wincze. "An inventory for the measurement of female sexual arousability: the SAI." *Archives of Sexual Behavior* 5(4):291–300, July 1976.

1196   Hoon, Peter W., John P. Wincze and Emily Franck Hoon. "A test of reciprocal inhibition: are anxiety and sexual arousal in women mutually inhibitory?" *Journal of Abnormal Psychology* 86(1):65–74, Feb. 1977.

1197   Kane, Francis J., Morris Lipton and John Ewing. "Hormonal influences in female sexual response." *Archives of General Psychiatry* 20(2):202–209, Feb. 1969.

1198   Kegel, Arnold. "Sexual functions of the pubococcygeus muscle." *Western Journal of Surgery, Obstetrics and Gynecology* 60:521–524, Oct. 1952.

1199   McCullough, Rita Colene. *Rhythms of sexual desire and sexual activity in the human female.* (Dissertation—University of Oregon.) Ann Arbor, MI: University Microfilms, 1973. (Order #74-6865)

1200   Masters, William H. and Virginia E. Johnson. "A pictorial review of the stages of sexual response in women." *Medical Aspects of Human Sexuality* 4(7):9 passim, July 1970.

1201   Stanley, Elizabeth. "Perspectives on the need for continuity of physical stimulation in female sexual arousal." *Medical Aspects of Human Sexuality* 8(2):98 passim, Feb. 1974.

1202   Wincze, John P., Peter W. Hoon and Emily Franck Hoon. "Sexual arousal in women: a comparison of cognitive and physiological responses by continuous measurement." *Archives of Sexual Behavior* 6(2):121–133, Mar. 1977.

SEXUAL RESPONSE PHYSIOLOGY (MALE)

1203   Bush, Irving M. and Nipank Shroff. "Answers to questions: anatomy of incomplete erection." *Medical Aspects of Human Sexuality* 7(12):63, Dec. 1973.

1204   Edwards, Allan E. and June R. Husted. "Penile sensitivity, age, and sexual behavior." *Journal of Clinical Psychology* 32(3):697–700, July 1976.

1205   Eeman, P.D. and Charles Berg. "Physiology of the orgasm and of psychoanalysis." *International Journal of Sexology* 3(2):92–98, Nov. 1949.

1206   Fox, Cyril A. et al. "Studies on the relationship between plasma testosterone levels and human sexual activity." *Journal of Endocrinology* 52:51–58, 1972.

1207   Ismail, A.A.A. "Relationship between plasma cortisol and human sexual activity." *Nature* 237(5353):288–289, June 2, 1972.

1208   Masters, William H. and Virginia E. Johnson. "A pictorial review of the stages of sexual response in men." *Medical Aspects of Human Sexuality* 6(9):78–83, Oct. 1972.

1209   Newman, Herbert F. "Vibratory sensitivity of the penis." *Fertility and Sterility* 21(11):791–793, Nov. 1970.

1210   Pirke, Karl M., Gotz Kockott and Franz Dittmar. "Psychosexual stimulation and plasma testosterone in man." *Archives of Sexual Behavior* 3(6):577–584, 1974.

1211   Rosen, Raymond C., David Shapiro and Gary E. Schwartz. "Voluntary control of penile tumescence." *Psychosomatic Medicine* 37(6):479–483, Nov./Dec. 1975.

1212   Schiavi, R.C. "Sex therapy and psychophysiological research." *American Journal of Psychiatry* 133(5):562–566, May 1976.

1213   Subrini, Louis and Pierre Assie. "L'érection: conceptions physiologiques nouvelles." *Cahiers de Sexologie Clinique* 2(4):367–374, 1976.

1214   Tordjman, Gilbert. "Les réactions physiologiques sexuelles de l'homme." *Cahiers de Sexologie Clinique* 1(3):263–270, May/June 1975.

1215   Weiss, Howard D. "Erection sustained after ejaculation." *Medical Aspects of Human Sexuality* 6(11):175, Nov. 1972.

1216   Zarcone, Vincent. "Heightened sexual interest and sleep disturbance." *Perceptual and Motor Skills* 39(3):1135–1141, Dec. 1974.

ORGASM RESEARCH

1217   Bunzl, Martin and Stephen Mullen. "A self-report investigation of two types of myotonic response during sexual orgasm." *Journal of Sex Research* 10(1):10–20, Feb. 1974.

1218   Cohen, Harvey, Raymond C. Rosen and Leonide Goldstein. "Electroencephalographic la-

terality changes during human sexual orgasm."
Archives of Sexual Behavior 5(3):189–199, May
1976.

1219   Fox, Cyril A. and Beatrice Fox. "A comparative study of coital physiology with special reference to the sexual climax." *Journal of Reproduction and Fertility* 24:319–336, 1971.

1220   Gagnon, John H. "Scripts and the coordination of sexual conduct." In: *Nebraska Symposium on Motivation,* ed. by James K. Cole and Richard Dienstbier, pp. 27–59. Lincoln: University of Nebraska Press, 1973.

1221   Hunt, Morton. *Sexual Behavior in the 1970's.* Chicago: Playboy Press, 1974.

1222   Proctor, E.B., N.N. Wagner and J.C. Butler. "The differentiation of male and female orgasm: an experimental study." In: *Perspectives on Human Sexuality; Psychological, Social and Cultural Research,* ed. by Nathaniel N. Wagner, pp. 115–132. New York: Behavioral Publications, 1974.

1223   Reich, Wilhelm. *The Discovery of the Orgone. Vol. 1: The Function of the Orgasm.* New York: Orgone Institute Press, 1942.

1224   Vance, Ellen Belle and Nathaniel N. Wagner. "Written descriptions of orgasm: a study of sex differences." *Archives of Sexual Behavior* 5(1):87–98, Jan. 1976.

1225   Whitman, Roy M. "Multiple orgasms." *Medical Aspects of Human Sexuality* 3(8):52–56, Aug. 1969.

ORGASM (FEMALE)

1226   Clark, Le Mon. "Is there a difference between a clitoral and a vaginal orgasm?" *Journal of Sex Research* 6(1):25–28, Feb. 1970.

1227   Cooper, Alan J. "Anatomy of the female orgasm: fact and fallacy." *British Journal of Sexual Medicine* 1(3):25–29, Jan./Feb. 1974.

1228   Elkan, Edward. "Evolution of female orgastic ability—a biological survey (Parts I–II)." *International Journal of Sexology* 2(1):1–13, Aug. 1948; 2(2):84–93, Nov. 1948.

1229   Fox, Cyril A. "Brief guide to office counseling: multiple climax—clarifying patients' concerns and misunderstanding." *Medical Aspects of Human Sexuality* 10(12):19–20, Dec. 1976.

1230   Kaplan, Helen Singer. "The classification of the female sexual dysfunctions." *Journal of Sex and Marital Therapy* 1(2):124–138, Winter 1974.

1231   Lief, Harold I. "What's new in sex research? Controversies over female orgasm." *Medical Aspects of Human Sexuality* 11(4):136–138, Apr. 1977.

1232   Marmor, Judd. "Some considerations concerning orgasm in the female." *Psychosomatic Medicine* 16(3):240–245, May/June 1954.

1233   Moore, Burness Evans. "Psychoanalytic reflections on the implications of recent physiological studies of female orgasm." *Journal of the American Psychoanalytic Association* 16(3):569–587, 1968.

1234   Robertiello, Richard C. "The 'clitoral' vs. 'vaginal' orgasm controversy and some of its ramifications." *Journal of Sex Research* 6(4):307–311, Nov. 1970.

1235   Shainess, Natalie. "Authentic feminine orgastic response." In: *Sexuality and Psychoanalysis,* ed. by E.T. Adelson, pp. 145–156. New York: Brunner/Mazel, 1975.

1236   _____. "Sexual problems of women." *Journal of Sex and Marital Therapy* 1(2):110–123, Winter 1974.

1237   Sherfey, Mary Jane. *The Nature and Evolution of Female Sexuality.* New York: Random House, 1972.

1238   _____. "Some biology of sexuality." *Journal of Sex and Marital Therapy* 1(2):97–109, Winter 1974.

1239   Shulman, Alix. "Organs and orgasms." In: *Women in Sexist Society,* ed. by V. Gornick and B.K. Moran, pp. 198–206. New York: Basic Books, 1971.

1240   Singer, Irving and Josephine Singer. "Periodicity of sexual desire in relation to time of ovulation in women." *Journal of Biosocial Science* 4:471–481, 1972.

1241   Wabrek, Alan J. and Carolyn J. Wabrek. "How emphasis on orgasm can make sex sexless." *Medical Aspects of Human Sexuality* 10(12):40–49, Dec. 1976.

ORGASM RESEARCH (FEMALE)

1242   Ard, Ben N., Jr. "Answers to questions: Percentages of women who experience orgasm." *Medical Aspects of Human Sexuality* 8(4):35–39, Apr. 1974.

1243   Butler, Carol A. "New data about female sexual response." *Journal of Sex and Marital Therapy* 2(1):40–46, Spring 1976.

1244 Clark, Alexander L. and Paul Wallin. "Women's sexual responsiveness and the duration and quality of their marriages." *American Journal of Sociology* 71(2):187–196, Sept. 1965.

1245 DeMartino, Manfred F. *Sex and the Intelligent Woman.* New York: Springer Publishing, 1974.

1246 Fisher, Seymour. *The Female Orgasm: Psychology, Physiology, Fantasy.* New York: Basic Books, 1973.

1247 _____. *Understanding the Female Orgasm.* New York: Basic Books, 1973.

1248 Gebhard, Paul H. "Factors in marital orgasm." *Medical Aspects of Human Sexuality* 2(7):22–25, July 1968.

1249 _____. "Postmarital coitus among widows and divorcees." In: *Divorce and After,* ed. by Paul Bohannan, pp. 82–96. New York: Doubleday, 1970.

1250 Hite, Shere. *The Hite Report: A Nationwide Study on Female Sexuality.* New York: Macmillan, 1976.

1251 Kinsey, Alfred C. et al. *Sexual Behavior in the Human Female.* Philadelphia: W.B. Saunders, 1953.

1252 Raboch, Jan. "Female sexual response and marital life." *Journal of Sex Research* 6(1):29–35, Feb. 1970.

1253 Schaefer, Leah Cahan. *Women and Sex.* New York: Pantheon Books, 1973.

1254 Shope, David F. "The orgastic responsiveness of selected college females." *Journal of Sex Research* 4(3):206–219, Aug. 1968.

1255 Singer, Josephine and I. Singer. "Types of female orgasm." *Journal of Sex Research* 8(4):255–267, Nov. 1972.

1256 Sorg, David A. and Margret B. Sorg. "Sexual satisfaction in maturing women." *Medical Aspects of Human Sexuality* 9(2):62 passim, Feb. 1975.

1257 Tavris, Carol and Susan Sadd. *The Redbook Report on Female Sexuality.* New York: Delacorte Press, 1977.

1258 Wallin, Paul and A.L. Clark. "A study of orgasm as a condition of women's enjoyment of coitus in the middle years of marriage." *Human Biology* 35(2):131–139, May 1963.

1259 Walshok, Mary. *Social correlates and sexual consequences of variations in gender role orientation: a national study of college students.* (Dissertation—Indiana University.) Ann Arbor, MI: University Microfilms, 1969. (Order #70-7515)

1260 Woodside, M. "Orgasm capacity among two hundred English working-class wives." *Marriage Hygiene* 1:133–137, 1948.

ORGASM (MALE)

1261 Donnelly, John D. "Brief guide to office counseling: retrograde ejaculation." *Medical Aspects of Human Sexuality* 9(1):51–52, Jan. 1975.

1262 Podolsky, Edward. "The nature of the orgasm." *Indian Medical Record* 73(2):1–2, Feb. 1953.

1263 Pomeroy, Wardell B. "The male orgasm: what every girl should know." *Cosmopolitan* 180(4):203–205, Apr. 1976.

ORGASM RESEARCH (MALE)

1264 Bostandzhiev, Todor P. and Ch. Merdzhanov. "Reofallografiia." In: *Problems of Contemporary Sexopathology,* ed. by A.A. Portnov, pp. 205–215. Moscow: RSFSR, Ministry of Public Health, 1972.

1265 Bunzl, Martin and Stephen Mullen. "A self-report investigation of two types of myotonic response during sexual orgasm." *Journal of Sex Research* 10(1):10–20, Feb. 1974.

1266 Kinsey, Alfred C. et al. *Sexual Behavior in the Human Male.* Philadelphia: W.B. Saunders, 1948.

1267 Money, John. "Components of eroticism in man: II. The orgasm and genital somesthia." *Journal of Nervous and Mental Disease* 132(4):289–297, Apr. 1961.

1268 Mosovich, Abraham and Alberto Tallaferro. "Studies on EEG and sex function orgasm." *Diseases of the Nervous System* 15(7):1–4, July 1954.

1269 Nadler, Ronald D. and Leonard A. Rosenblum. "Sexual behavior during successive ejaculations in Bonnet and Pigtail Macaques." *American Journal of Physical Anthropology* 38(2):217–220, Mar. 1973.

1270 Van Dis, Huib and Knut Larsson. "Seminal discharge following intracranial electrical stimulation." *Brain Research* 23(3):381–386, 1970.

Sex Counseling

Sex Counseling

COLLECTIONS

1271 "Brief guides to office counseling." These are short articles on problems that family physicians are likely to encounter among their patients. They appear as a regular feature of the journal *Medical Aspects of Human Sexuality*. Communication technique as well as basic factual information is discussed.

1272 *Education for Human Sexuality: The Professional's Role.* SIECUS Publications 4525 Packet II. New York: Human Sciences Press.

1273 *Medical Aspects of Human Sexuality; 750 Questions Answered by 500 Authorities.* Baltimore: Williams & Wilkins, 1975.

1274 "Sex counseling." *The Counseling Psychologist* 5(1):whole issue, 1975.

1275 "Symposium issue: sexuality and sexual health with self-test questions." *Postgraduate Medicine* 58(1):whole issue, July 1975.

COUNSELING

1276 Bowman, Henry. "Teacher as counselor in marriage education." *Marriage and Family Living* 9(1):1–8, Feb. 1947.

1277 Collins, Anne M. and William E. Sedlacek. "Counselor perceptions of sexual attitudes of female university students." *College Student Journal* 6(3):13–16, Sept./Oct. 1972.

1278 Cooper, Donna L. "Brief guide to office counseling: the intrauterine device." *Medical Aspects of Human Sexuality* 9(8):43–44, Aug. 1975.

1279 Farnsworth, Dana L. "Sexual morality and the dilemma of the colleges." *Medical Aspects of Human Sexuality* 4(10):64–94, Oct. 1970.

1280 Harrison, Don K. "Race as a counselor-client variable in counseling and psychotherapy: a review of the research." *Counseling Psychologist* 5(1):124–133, 1975.

1281 Horn, Robert E. "Psychosexual problems of the middle years." *Clinical Obstetrics and Gynecology* 13:746–755, Sept. 1970.

1282 Klemer, Richard H. "Problems of widowed, divorced and unmarried women." *Medical Aspects of Human Sexuality* 3(4):26–34, Apr. 1969.

1283 McKenney, Mary. "Divorce." *Booklegger Magazine* 1(2):13–17, Jan./Feb. 1974. (bibliography)

1284 Mayadas, Nazneen S. and Wayne D. Duehn. "Children in gay families: an investigation of services." *Homosexual Counseling Journal* 3(2):70–83 passim, Apr. 1976.

1285 Messinger, David. *Effects of counseling on development of masculine identity in adolescent boys.* (Thesis—Boston University School of Education.) Ann Arbor, MI: University Microfilms, 1971. (Order #71-26723)

1286 Pannor, Reuben. "Casework service for unmarried fathers." *Children* 10(2):65–70, Mar./Apr. 1963.

1287 Scheidlinger, Saul, Elmer L. Struening and Judith G. Rabkin. "Evaluation of a mental health consultation service in a ghetto area." *American Journal of Psychotherapy* 24(3):485–493, July 1970.

1288 Thompson, Andrew and Robert Zimmerman. "Goals of counseling: whose? when?" *Journal of Counseling Psychology* 16(2):121–125, Mar. 1969.

1289 Vincent, Clark E. "The physician as counselor in nonmarital and premarital pregnancies." *Medical Aspects of Human Sexuality* 1(2):28–38, Oct. 1967.

1290 Wright, Mary Ruth. "Psychological aspects of vasectomy counseling." *The Family Coordinator* 21(3):259–265, July 1972.

1291 Young, Barbara Ann. *The effects of sex, assigned therapist or peer role, topic intimacy, and expectations of partner compatibility on dyadic communication patterns.* (Thesis—University of Southern California.) Ann Arbor, MI: University Microfilms, 1969. (Order #69-13095)

SEX COUNSELING

1292 American Medical Association Committee on Human Sexuality. *Human Sexuality.* Chicago: American Medical Association, 1972.

1293 Babineau, Raymond and Allan J. Schwartz. "Reciprocity of sexual excitement." *Medical As-*

pects of Human Sexuality 10(7):123–125 passim, July 1976.

1294 Bradshaw, Barbara R. et al. *Counseling in Family Planning & Human Sexuality.* New York: Family Service Association of America, 1977.

1295 Burchell, R. Clay. "Brief guide to office counseling: instructing women in effective sexual techniques." *Medical Aspects of Human Sexuality* 9(4):89–90, Apr. 1975.

1296 Caplan, Harvey W. and Rebecca Black. "Unrealistic sexual expectations." *Medical Aspects of Human Sexuality* 8(8):8–36, Aug. 1974.

1297 Carlson, Noel R. and Diane A. Johnson. "Sexuality assertiveness training: a workshop for women." *Counseling Psychologist* 5(4):53–59, 1975.

1298 Clark, Thomas E. "Brief guide to office counseling: when a husband's sex desires exceed his wife's." *Medical Aspects of Human Sexuality* 8(1):79–80, Jan. 1974.

1299 Crown, Sidney, ed. *Psychosexual Problems: Psychotherapy, Counselling and Behaviour Modification.* London: Academic Press, 1976.

1300 Dormont, Paul. "Brief guide to office counseling: when patients inquire about their sexual 'normality.'" *Medical Aspects of Human Sexuality* 11(2):115–116, Feb. 1977.

1301 Dunn, Peter Bruce. "Brief guides to office counseling: sexual aversion to mate." *Medical Aspects of Human Sexuality* 10(4):77–78, Apr. 1976.

1302 Farmer, Ronald. "The effects of sex censorship in the home." Paper presented at Geigy Psychiatric Symposium on Liberation Movements and Psychiatry, Little Bay, N.S.W., Aug. 1973. 7p.

1303 Fox, Cyril A. "Brief guide to office counseling: multiple climax—clarifying patients' concerns and misunderstanding." *Medical Aspects of Human Sexuality* 10(12):19–20, Dec. 1976.

1304 Frank, E., Carol Anderson, and David J. Kupfer. "Profiles of couples seeking sex therapy and marital therapy." *American Journal of Psychiatry* 133(5):559–562, May 1976.

1305 Goldberg, Martin. "Roundtable: handling sexual refusals in marriage." *Medical Aspects of Human Sexuality* 10(6):30 passim, June 1976.

1306 Green, Richard, ed. *Human Sexuality: A Health Practitioner's Text.* Baltimore: Williams & Wilkins, 1975.

1307 Harbin, Henry. "Brief guide to office coun-seling: sexual conflicts arising from dominance or submission." *Medical Aspects of Human Sexuality* 9(11):97–98, Nov. 1975.

1308 Hartman, William E. and Marilyn A. Fithian. "You and sex counseling." *The Osteopathic Physician* 40(10):77–91 passim, Oct. 1973.

1309 Hawkins, Robert O. "Jealousy: a solvable problem." *Journal of Sex Education and Therapy* 2(1):35–38, Spring/Summer 1976.

1310 Israel, Spencer Leon. "Family-counseling role of the physician." *Journal of Marriage and the Family* 30(2):311–316, May 1968.

1311 Knapp, Jacquelyn J. "Some non-monogamous marriage styles and related attitudes and practices of marriage counselors." *The Family Coordinator* 24(4):505–514, Oct. 1975.

1312 Labby, Daniel H. "Brief guide to office counseling: when to refer sexual problems to a psychiatrist." *Medical Aspects of Human Sexuality* 9(12):79–80, Dec. 1975.

1313 Langmyhr, George. "Brief guide to office counseling: clitoral stimulation: do's and don'ts." *Medical Aspects of Human Sexuality* 9(8):51–52, Aug. 1975.

1314 Lansing, Cornelius. "Exploring sexual complaints." *Medical Aspects of Human Sexuality* 1(4):34–42, Dec. 1967.

1315 Lazarus, Arnold A. "Modes of treatment for sexual inadequacies." *Medical Aspects of Human Sexuality* 3(5):53–58, May 1969.

1316 Levitt, Eugene E. "Sexual counseling: what the busy physician can, and cannot, do." *Postgraduate Medicine* 58(1):91–97, July 1975.

1317 Lief, Harold I. "Sexual health services: training and treatment." *SIECUS Report* 2(2):1–3 passim, Nov. 1973.

1318 Livsey, Clara G. "Brief guide to office counseling: lack of vitality in the marital sexual relationship." *Medical Aspects of Human Sexuality* 9(8):49–50, Aug. 1975.

1319 McConnell, Lawrence G. "An examination of the counsellor's skills when counselling clients with sexual problems." *Family Coordinator* 25(2):183–188, Apr. 1976.

1320 Mace, David R. *Sexual Difficulties in Marriage.* Philadelphia: Fortress Press, 1972.

1321 McGuire, Linda S. "Meeting patients' needs regarding their sexuality." *Osteopathic Physician* 42(9):37–41, Sept. 1975.

1322 Masters, William H. and Virginia E. Johnson. "Counseling with sexually incompatible marriage partners." In: *Sex Education; Rationale and Reaction,* ed. by Rex S. Rogers, pp. 104–117. London/New York: Cambridge University Press, 1974.

1323 Mathis, James L. "Brief guide to office counseling: differentiating organic from functional impotence." *Medical Aspects of Human Sexuality* 9(8):61–62, Aug. 1975.

1324 Mead, Beverley T. "Brief guide to office counseling: low sexual drive in men." *Medical Aspects of Human Sexuality* 8(3):193–194, Mar. 1974.

1325 _____. "Brief guide to office counseling: marital discord and sex." *Medical Aspects of Human Sexuality* 8(12):29–30, Dec. 1974.

1326 Meyer, Jon K. *Clinical Management of Sexual Disorders.* Baltimore: Williams & Wilkins, 1976.

1327 Neiger, Stephen. *Overcoming Sexual Inadequacy.* (12 tape cassettes.) Chicago: Human Development Institute, 1973.

1328 Oliven, John F. *Clinical Sexuality; A Manual for the Physician and the Professions.* 3rd ed. Philadelphia: J.B. Lippincott, 1974.

1329 Peterson, James A. "The social context of sexual counseling." *The Counseling Psychologist* 5(1):114–120, 1975.

1330 Romano, Mary D. "Sexual counseling in groups." *Journal of Sex Research* 9(1):69–78, Feb. 1973.

1331 Rosen, Aaron, Wayne D. Duehn and Ronda S. Connaway. "Content classification and system for sexual counselling: method and application." *Journal of Sex and Marital Therapy* 1(1):53–62, Fall 1974.

1332 Sarembe, B. "Die Bevölderungsstruktur in der ehe- und sexualberatung." *Zeitschrift für Ärztliche Fortbildung (Jena)* 66(17):888–891, Sept. 1, 1972.

1333 Schoenberg, Mark. "Brief guide to office counseling: deviant sex drive." *Medical Aspects of Human Sexuality* 10(5):175–176, May 1976.

1334 Semmens, J.P. "Brief guide to office counseling: role of vaginal exercises in treatment of the sexually dysfunctional female." *Medical Aspects of Human Sexuality* 9(7):127–128, July 1975.

1335 Shainess, Natalie. "How 'sex experts' debase sex." *World of Research*:21–25, Jan. 2, 1973.

1336 Sigusch, Volkmar and Bernd Meyenburg. "Sexualberatung und sexualtherapie in der B.D.R." *Medizinische Welt* 25(16):711–715, Apr. 19, 1974.

1337 Skynner, A.C.R. "Sexual counselling techniques in general practice: part 1 (and) part 2." *British Journal of Sexual Medicine* 3(6):22–24, Dec. 1976; 4(1):23–24, Jan. 1977.

1338 Slovenko, Ralph. "Sex counseling and the law." *Medical Aspects of Human Sexuality* 3(1):47–58, Jan. 1969.

1339 Taylor, R.W. et al. "Psychological aspects of sexual medicine." *British Journal of Sexual Medicine* 3(3):21–26, June 1976.

1340 "A therapy program to enhance your sex life." *Behavior Today* 6(15):445–446, Apr. 14, 1975.

1341 Travis, Robert P. and Patricia Y. Travis. "Sexual restructuring." *Current Medical Dialog* 41(11):601–603 passim, Nov. 1974.

1342 Turner, Nathan W. "Brief guide to office counseling: overcoming poor sexual communication patterns." *Medical Aspects of Human Sexuality* 11(7):99–100, July 1977.

1343 Vincent, Clark E. "Sex and the young married." *Medical Aspects of Human Sexuality* 3(3):13–23, Mar. 1969.

1344 _____. *Sexual and Marital Health: The Physician as a Consultant.* New York: McGraw-Hill, 1973.

1345 Wabrek, Carolyn J. and Alan J. Wabrek. "Sexual counseling in a community hospital: a new program." *Connecticut Medicine* 38(5):253–254, May 1974.

1346 Waggoner, Raymond W. "Dealing with sexual problems—yours and your patient's." *Consultant* 15(1):21–22, Jan. 1975.

1347 Weber, Melva. "Sex counseling and the primary physician." *Medical World News*:35–49, Mar. 2, 1972.

1348 Wilson, Robert R. *Introduction to Sexual Counseling.* Chapel Hill, NC: Carolina Population Center, 1974.

1349 World Health Organization. *Education and Treatment in Human Sexuality: The Training of Health Professionals. Report of a WHO Meeting.* Technical Report Series: No. 572. Geneva: World Health Organization, 1975. (Avail. from Q Corporation, 49 Sheridan Ave., Albany, NY 12210.)

SEX COUNSELING (ADOLESCENT)

1350   Cogswell, Betty E. and Charles B. Arnold. "Organizational efforts to link adolescents to a sex information program." Paper presented at the American Sociological Association, 64th Meeting, San Francisco, Sept. 1, 1969. 12p.

1351   Gadpaille, Warren J. "Brief guide to office counseling: a teenager contemplating first coitus." *Medical Aspects of Human Sexuality* 9(3):181–182, Mar. 1975.

1352   Gellman, Robert. "Sexualité des adolescents." *Cahiers de Sexologie Clinique* 1(4):385–388 passim, 1975.

1353   Gianturco, Daniel T. and Harmon L. Smith. *The Promiscuous Teenager.* Springfield, IL: Charles C. Thomas, 1974.

1354   Gordon, Sol. *The Sexual Adolescent; Communicating with Teenagers about Sex.* North Scituate, MA: Duxbury Press, 1973.

1355   Hamelstein, Helaine. "Youth and their sexual problems." *Journal of Clinical Child Psychology* 3(3):31–33, Fall/Winter 1974.

1356   Kaplan, Jeffrey Gene. "Brief guide to office counseling: retarded sexual development in adolescence." *Medical Aspects of Human Sexuality* 9(8):47–48, Aug. 1975.

1357   Kappelman, Murray M. *Sex and the American Teenager.* New York: Reader's Digest Press, 1977.

1358   Kestenbaum, Clarice J. "Brief guide to office counseling: adolescent homosexual experiences. *Medical Aspects of Human Sexuality* 9(1):99–100, Jan. 1975.

1359   Kremer, Ellen B., David G. Zimpfer and Thorne T. Wiggers. "Homosexuality, counseling, and the adolescent male." *Personnel and Guidance Journal* 54(2):94–99, Oct. 1975.

1360   Nadelson, Carol C. "Brief guides to office counseling: telling a teenager about a sexual disorder." *Medical Aspects of Human Sexuality* 10(2):47–48, Feb. 1976.

1361   Sacks, Sylvia R. "Widening the perspectives on adolescent sex problems." *Adolescence* 1(1):79–90, Spring 1966.

SEX COUNSELING (COLLEGE STUDENT)

See also the heading PEER COUNSELING

1362   Bauer, Roger and Joan Stein. "Sex counseling on campus: short-term treatment techniques." *American Journal of Orthopsychiatry* 43(5):824–839, Oct. 1973.

1363   Coons, Frederick W. "Brief guide to office counseling: sex on campus: informing and advising a new student." *Medical Aspects of Human Sexuality* 8(9):25–26, Sept. 1974.

1364   Freeman, Harrop A. and Ruth S. Freeman. "Senior college women: sexual standards and activity. Part I. To whom does the college woman turn for sex counseling?" *Journal of the National Association of Women Deans and Counselors* 29(2):59–64, Winter 1966.

1365   Kaufman, Gershen. "Integrating one's sexuality: crisis and change." *International Journal of Group Psychotherapy* 23(4):445–464, Oct. 1973.

1366   Sarrel, Philip and Lorna J. Sarrel. "Birth control services and sex counseling at Yale." *Family Planning Perspectives* 3(3):33–36, July 1971.

1367   _____. "The college subculture." In: *Sexuality and Human Values,* ed. by Mary S. Calderone, pp. 71–84. New York: Association Press, 1974.

1368   _____. "A sex counselling service for college students." *American Journal of Public Health* 61(7):1341–1347, July 1971.

1369   Schwerner, Stephen A. "The counseling service and academic politics: a case for delivery of services." *Counseling Psychologist* 5(1):121–124, 1975.

1370   Wabrek, Alan J. and Harold I. Lief. "Medical school involvement in sex counseling for college students." *Journal of Medical Education* 47:740–741, Sept. 1972.

PREMARITAL COUNSELING

1371   Beukenkamp, Cornelius. "Anxiety activated by the idea of marriage as observed in group psychotherapy." *Mental Hygiene* 43(4):532–538, Oct. 1959.

1372   Biskind, Leonard H. "Sex and marriage." *International Journal of Sexology* 2(3):149–155, Feb. 1949.

1373   Brenton, Myron. "Profile of a sex-and-marriage clinic." *Sexual Behavior* 2(3):28–32, Mar. 1972.

1374   Chapman, J. Dudley. "Problems of the 'first night.'" *Osteopathic Physician* 37(8):69–72, May 1970.

1375 Dickinson, Robert Latou. "Premarital consultation." *Journal of the American Medical Association* 117:1687–1692, Nov. 1941.

1376 Dicks, Russel L. "Pre-marital counseling: the minister's responsibility." *Pastoral Psychology*:4p, Oct. 1950.

1377 Eastman, William F. and Clifford B. Reifler. "Marriage counseling in the student health service." *Journal of the American College Health Association* 17(4):289–295, Apr. 1969.

1378 Eastman, William F., Clifford B. Reifler and Myron B. Liptzin. "He loves me, he loves me not: student marital decisions." *Journal of the American College Health Association* 17(3):230–237, Feb. 1969.

1379 Ellis, Albert. "A rational approach to premarital counseling." *Psychological Reports* 8:333–338, 1961.

1380 Flowers, Charles E. "Changing concepts of the premarital examination." *Medical Aspects of Human Sexuality* 1(4):51–55, Dec. 1967.

1381 Greene, Bernard L. and Noel Lustig. " 'Contraindications' to marriage." *Medical Aspects of Human Sexuality* 2(3):4–11, Mar. 1968.

1382 Horejst, Charles R. "Small-group sex education for engaged couples." *Journal of Family Counseling* 2(2):23–27, Fall 1974.

1383 Landis, Judson T. "Danger signals in courtship." *Medical Aspects of Human Sexuality* 4(11):35–46, Nov. 1970.

1384 Lock, Frank. "Interview: a gynecologist's view of the general practitioner's role in sexual maladjustments due to emotional causes." *Medical Aspects of Human Sexuality* 1(2):62–64, Oct. 1967.

1385 Palazzetti, Piero. "La consulenza prematrimoniale nel quadro della pianificazione familiare (basi organizzative)." *Sessuologia* 15(2):57–60, Apr./June 1974.

1386 "Roundtable: how does premarital sex affect marriage?" *Medical Aspects of Human Sexuality* 2(11):14–21, Nov. 1968.

1387 Shonick, Helen. "Pre-marital counseling: three years' experience of a unique service." *Family Coordinator* 24(3):321–324, July 1975.

1388 Stokes, Walter R. and David R. Mace. "Premarital sexual behavior." *Marriage and Family Living* 15(3):234–249, Aug. 1953.

SEXUAL HISTORY TAKING

1389 Castelnuovo-Tedesco, Pietro. "Talking with patients about their sexual problems." *Medical Aspects of Human Sexuality* 2(6):21–28, June 1968.

1390 Chez, Ronald A. "Obtaining the sexual history in the female patient." *General Practitioner* 30(4):120–124, Oct. 1964.

1391 Green, Richard. "Taking a sexual history." In: *Human Sexuality: A Health Practitioner's Text,* ed. by Richard Green, pp. 9–19. Baltimore: Williams & Wilkins, 1975.

1392 Group for the Advancement of Psychiatry. Committee on Medical Education. *Assessment of Sexual Function: A Guide to Interviewing.* New York: Jason Aronson, 1974.

1393 Lief, Harold I. and Ellen M. Berman. "Sexual interviewing of the individual patient through the life cycle." In: *Sex and the Life Cycle,* ed. by Wilbur W. Oaks, Gerald A. Melchiode and Ilda Ficher, pp. 1–11. New York: Grune & Stratton, 1976.

1394 Marriage Council of Philadelphia. "Sexual performance evaluation." In: *Human Sexuality,* prepared by the American Medical Association Committee on Human Sexuality, pp. 159–166. Chicago: American Medical Association, 1972.

1395 Pomeroy, Wardell B. "The sex interview in counseling." In: *Sexuality and Human Values,* ed. by Mary S. Calderone, pp. 36–47. New York: Association Press, 1974.

1396 Schwartz, Ronald M. "Sexual history taking." *American College Health Association* 22(5):405–408, June 1974.

1397 Spark, Geraldine M. "Interviewing of couples with sexual problems." In: *Sex and the Life Cycle,* ed. by Wilbur W. Oaks, Gerald A. Melchiode and Ilda Ficher, pp. 13–17. New York: Grune & Stratton, 1976.

1398 "Viewpoints: in what types of presenting complaints should physicians inquire about sexual practices or take a sexual history?" *Medical Aspects of Human Sexuality* 7(6):34–44, June 1973.

PASTORAL COUNSELING

1399 Dicks, Russell. "Pre-marital counseling: the minister's responsibility." *Pastoral Psychology*:4p., Oct. 1950.

1400 Hennessy, Thomas C. and Andrew C. Varga. "A religious perspective on sexual counseling." *Counseling Psychologist* 5(1):111–114, 1975.

1401 Kennedy, Eugene M. "The new sexuality: here comes everybody." *Journal of Clinical Child Psychology* 3(3):56–59, Fall/Winter 1974.

1402 Larson, Richard F. "The clergyman's role in the therapeutic process: disagreement between clergymen and psychiatrists." *Psychiatry* 31(3):250–263, Aug. 1968.

1403 _____. "Clerical and psychiatric conceptions of the clergyman's role in the therapeutic setting." *Social Problems* 11(4):419–428, Spring 1964.

1404 Mace, David R. "The sexual revolution: its impact on pastoral care and counseling." *Journal of Pastoral Care* 25(4):220–232, Dec. 1971.

1405 Perkins, Worcester. "What contribution should the clergyman make to marriage counseling?" *Marriage and Family Living* 14(2):124–127, May 1952.

1406 Ratliff, Dale H. *Minor Sexual Deviance: Diagnosis and Pastoral Treatment.* Dubuque, IA: Kendall/Hunt, 1976.

1407 Stroup, Herbert W. and Norma Schweitzer Wood. *Sexuality and the Counseling Pastor.* Philadelphia: Fortress Press, 1974.

PEER COUNSELING

1408 Baldwin, Bruce A. and Robert R. Wilson. "A campus peer counseling program in human sexuality." *Journal of the American College Health Association* 22(5):399–404, June 1974.

1409 _____. "Peer services in human sexuality health education." *Crisis Intervention* 5(3):12–26, 1974.

1410 Bernier, Joseph J. "Peer counseling in human sexuality." Paper presented at the Annual Convention of the Southeastern Psychological Association, New Orleans, Apr. 8, 1973. 5p.

1411 Johnston, Cynthia D. "Sexuality and birth control: impact of outreach programming." *Personnel and Guidance Journal* 52(6):406–411, Feb. 1974.

1412 Mazur, Ronald M. *Training Peer Sex Educators.* Amherst: University of Massachusetts, University Health Services, 1976.

1413 _____. *What You Need to Know to Go PSE: Guidelines for In-Service Action.* Amherst: University of Massachusetts, University Health Services, Peer Sex Education Program, 1975.

1414 Weiss, Michael. "Unlearning." In: *Men and Masculinity,* ed. by J. Pleck and Jack Sawyer, pp. 162–170. Englewood Cliffs, NJ: Prentice-Hall, 1974.

1415 Welbourne, Ann. "A peer approach to adolescent sexual information and help." *Counseling Psychologist* 5(1):77–80, 1975.

TELEPHONE COUNSELING

1416 Carrera, Michael A. and Ann Welbourne. "Answering sex questions over the phone: a community based service." *Journal of Clinical Child Psychology* 3(3):46–48, Fall/Winter 1974.

1417 Hodges, Parker. "A day in the life of a telephone sex clinic." *Forum* 1(9):32–37, June 1972.

1418 Lester, David. "Telephone counseling and the masturbator: a dilemma." In: *Modern Sexuality,* ed. by Mary L. Gottesfeld, pp. 257–260. New York: Behavioral Publications, 1973.

1419 Preterm Institute. *Sex Counseling by Telephone.* Cambridge, MA: Schenkman, 1976.

1420 "Sex counseling over the telephone." *Sexual Behavior* 2(8):22–25, Aug. 1972.

1421 Vadies, Gene and Marilyn M. Machlowitz. "Hotlines: a new ally to family planning." *Journal of Clinical Child Psychology* 3(3):48–49, Fall/Winter 1974.

COUNSELORS SEX EDUCATION

1422 Brashear, Diane B. *The Social Worker as Sex Educator.* The Professional as Sex Educator series. Hempstead, NY: SIECUS, 1976. (Avail. from Human Sciences Press.)

1423 Brown, Asa J. "Affective openness: its relationship to sexuality and the counseling of adolescents." *Counseling and Values* 17(4):244–246, Summer 1973.

1424 Brown, D.A. "Counseling the youthful homosexual." *School Counselor* 22(5):325–333, May 1975.

1425 Carolina Population Center. *Sexual Counseling Skills Workshop: A Trainers' Handbook.* Chapel Hill: University of North Carolina, Carolina Population Center, 1977.

1426 Giroux, Roy and Ted Bicknell. "Human sexuality and the college student." *Counseling and Values* 17(4):241–243, Summer 1973.

1427 Kelly, Gary F. *The Guidance Counselor as Sex Educator.* The Professional as Sex Educator series. Hempstead, NY: SIECUS, 1976. (Avail. from Human Sciences Press.)

1428 _____. "Role-playing to develop sex counseling skills." *Journal of Sex Education and Therapy* 2(2):14–17, Fall/Winter 1976.

1429 Kirkendall, Lester A. "Males and sexual responsibility." Paper presented at the FCAA Western Area Conference, 1968. Chicago: Florence Crittenton Association of America, 1968. 6p.

1430 Kirkpatrick, J. Stephen. "Guidelines for counseling young people with sexual concerns." *Personnel and Guidance Journal* 54(3):144–148, Nov. 1975.

1431 Kriegman, George. "Homosexuality and the educator." *Journal of School Health* 39(5):305–311, May 1969.

1432 Landis, C.E., H.R. Miller and Richard P. Wettstone. "Sexual awareness training for counselors." *Teaching of Psychology* 2(1):33–36, Feb. 1975.

1433 McConnell, Lawrence G. "The counselor and his asexual client." *Canadian Counsellor* 8(3):207–210, June 1974.

1434 _____. "An examination of the counsellor's skills when counselling clients with sexual problems." *Family Coordinator* 25(2):183–188, Apr. 1976.

1435 _____. "The sexual value system." *Journal of Marriage and Family Counseling* 3(1):55–67, Jan. 1977.

1436 Mitchell, Marianne. *The Counselor and Sexuality.* Guidance Monograph Series VII: Special topics in counseling. Boston: Houghton Mifflin, 1973.

1437 Nash, Kermit B. "Group guidance and counseling programs: a vehicle for the introduction of sex education for adolescents in the public school." *Journal of School Health* 38(9):577–583, 1968.

1438 Nuehring, Elane M., Sara Beck Fein and Mary Tyler. "The gay college student; perspectives for mental health professionals." *Counseling Psychologist* 4(4):64–72, 1974.

1439 Pietrofesa, John J. "Human sexuality—an introduction." *Counseling and Values* 17(4):209–210, Summer 1973.

1440 _____. "Human sexuality and the school counselor." *Counseling and Values* 17(4):228–234, Summer 1973.

1441 _____. "The school counselor in sex education." *Personnel and Guidance Journal* :4p., Mar. 1976.

1442 Pietrofesa, John J. and Howard Splete. "Consultation: an effective dimension of childhood sexual development." *The School Counselor* 20(3):186–192, Jan. 1973.

1443 Schiller, Patricia. *Creative Approach to Sex Education and Counseling.* New York: Association Press, 1973.

1444 _____. "Pilot training project for professionals in a multidisciplinary approach for counseling." *Family Coordinator* 18(4):385–390, Oct. 1969.

1445 Stevens, Joanne. "Index of sexual knowledge needed by marriage counselors (a Delphi technique index)." Unpub. paper, University of Southern Mississippi, Hattiesburg, 1976. 11p.

1446 Szasz, George. "Teen-age sexual problems and the school counsellor." *School Guidance Worker* 28(1):5–10, Sept./Oct. 1972.

1447 Thomas, Jerril K. "Adolescent endocrinology for counselors of adolescents." *Adolescence* 8(31):395–406, Fall 1973.

OTHER SOURCES OF INFORMATION

American Association of Sex Educators, Counselors and Therapists
5010 Wisconsin Ave., NW, Suite 304, Washington, DC 20016

Sex Information and Education Council of the U.S. (SIECUS)
84 Fifth Ave., Suite 407, New York, NY, 10011

PERIODICALS

Medical Aspects of Human Sexuality
Hospital Publications, Inc.
609 Fifth Ave., New York, NY 10011

Sex Therapy

1448 Ard, Ben N. *Treating Psychosexual Dysfunction.* New York: Aronson, 1974.

1449 Arentewicz, Gerd and Gunter Schmidt. "Treatment of patients suffering from sexual function disturbances: problems and some results." Paper presented at the annual meeting of the International Academy of Sex Research, Hamburg, Aug. 2–4, 1976. 9p.

1450   Brenton, Myron. "Sex therapy for college students." *Sexual Behavior* 2(6):52–55, June 1972.

1451   Caplan, Ruth Thurlow. *Attitude change of couples involved in a sexual therapy program.* (Thesis—University of New Mexico.) Ann Arbor, MI: University Microfilms, 1973. (Order: #73-27,787)

1452   Congrès International de Sexologie Médicale. *Papers.* Textes réunis par Jacqueline Kahn-Nathan et France Reveillaud. Paris: Copédith, 1974. (Contributions in English and French.)

1453   Devanesan, Mona et al. "Changing attendance patterns to sex therapy programs as a function of location and personnel." *Journal of Sex & Marital Therapy* 2(4):309–314, Winter 1976.

1454   Ellis, Albert. "An informal history of sex therapy." *Counseling Psychologist* 5(1):9–13, 1975.

1455   Fordney-Settlage, Diane S. "Heterosexual dysfunction: evaluation of treatment procedures." *Archives of Sexual Behavior* 4(4):367–387, July 1975.

1456   Frank, E., Carol Anderson and David J. Kupfer. "Profiles of couples seeking sex therapy and marital therapy." *American Journal of Psychiatry* 133(5):559–562, May 1976.

1457   Gagnon, John H. "Sexual therapies." In: *Human Sexualities,* by John H. Gagnon, pp. 365–381. Glenview, IL: Scott, Foresman, 1977.

1458   Gittelson, Natalie. "The growing questions about sex therapy." *McCalls* 102(7):76 passim, Apr. 1975.

1459   Godlewski, Julian. "Analiza zawodowa i objawowo-lekarska 105 chorych Gabinetu Seksuologicznego Poradni TSM w Krakowie." In: *Problemy Seksuologii,* ed. by T. Bilikiewicz, v. 2, pp. 69–70. Warsaw: Panstwowy Zaklad Wydawnictw Lekarskich, 1965.

1460   Goldman, Martin and Avodah Offit. "Offit sexual therapy." *Reflections* 9(3):24–31, 1974.

1461   Harris, Gloria G. and Nathaniel N. Wagner. "Treatment of sexual dysfunction and casework techniques." In: *Modern Sexuality,* ed. by Mary L. Gottesfeld, pp. 244–250. New York: Behavioral Publications, 1973.

1462   Heiman, Julia, Leslie LoPiccolo and Joseph LoPiccolo. "What next? (How does one locate a therapist?)" In: *Becoming Orgasmic: A Sexual Growth Program for Women,* pp. 192–197. Englewood Cliffs, NJ: Prentice-Hall, 1976.

1463   Hodges, Parker. "A consumer guide to sex clinics." *Forum* 2(4):24–28 passim, Jan. 1973.

1464   Holden, Constance. "Sex therapy: making it as a science and an industry." *Science* 186:330–334, Oct. 25, 1974.

1465   Hoon, Emily Franck, Peter W. Hoon and John P. Wincze. "An inventory for the measurement of female sexual arousability: the SAI." *Archives of Sexual Behavior* 5(4):291–300, July 1976.

1466   Hotchner, Beverly. "The development of a sexuality center." *Journal of Sex Education and Therapy* 3(1):45–48, Spring/Summer 1977.

1467   Kaplan, Helen Singer. "Current thinking in sex therapy." *Medical Aspects of Human Sexuality* 8(10):89–95, Oct. 1974.

1468   _____. " 'Quack' sex therapy." *Medical Aspects of Human Sexuality* 11(2):32 passim, Feb. 1977.

1469   Kirsch, Irving and Brenda Smith. *Sex Therapy.* Chatsworth, CA: Books for Better Living, 1973.

1470   Koch, Joanne and Lew Koch. "A consumers guide to sex therapy for couples." *Psychology Today* 9(10):33–40, Mar. 1976.

1471   _____. "How to find a marriage counselor." *Psychology Today* 9(10):40 passim, Mar. 1976.

1472   _____. "Sex clinics." In: *The Marriage Savers,* pp. 113–157. New York: Coward, McCann & Geoghegan, 1976.

1473   _____. "Sex therapy: caveat emptor." *Psychology Today* 9(10):37, Mar. 1976.

1474   Kuriansky, Judith B. and Lawrence Sharpe. "Guidelines for evaluating sex therapy." *Journal of Sex & Marital Therapy* 2(4):303–308, Winter 1976.

1475   Lassen, Carol L. "Issues and dilemmas in sexual treatment." *Journal of Sex and Marital Therapy* 2(1):32–39, Spring 1976.

1476   Lazarus, Arnold A. "Modes of treatment for sexual inadequacies." *Medical Aspects of Human Sexuality* 3(5):53–58, May 1969.

1477   Levin, Robert J. " 'Most sex therapy clinics are frauds!' " *Physician's World* 3(1):17–21, Jan. 1975.

1478   Lief, Harold I. "Sexual health services: training and treatment." *SIECUS Report* 2(2):1–3 passim, Nov. 1973.

1479   Lowry, Thea Snyder and Thomas P. Lowry.

"Ethical considerations in sex therapy." *Journal of Marriage and Family Counseling* 1(3):229-236, July 1975.

1480 McCoy, Nancy Nichols and Peter A. D'Agostino. "Factor analysis of the Sexual Interaction Inventory." *Archives of Sexual Behavior* 6(1):25-35, Jan. 1977.

1481 McCrocklin, Michael T. "A perspective of sex and sex therapy." Paper presented to the Indiana Council on Family Relations, Feb. 19, 1974. 10p.

1482 McGrady, Patrick M., Jr. *The Love Doctors.* New York: Macmillan, 1972.

1483 Masters, William H. "Phony sex clinics—medicine's newest nightmare." *Today's Health* 52(11):22-26, Nov. 1974.

1484 Masters, William H., Virginia E. Johnson and Robert C. Kolodny, eds. *Ethical Issues in Sex Therapy and Research.* Boston: Little, Brown, 1977.

1485 Meyer, Jon K. "Training and accreditation for the treatment of sexual disorders." *American Journal of Psychiatry* 133(4):389-394, Apr. 1976.

1486 Meyer, Jon K., ed. *Clinical Management of Sexual Disorders.* Baltimore: Williams & Wilkins, 1976.

1487 Pasini, Willy. "Reflexions sur l'approche corporelle en sexologie." Paper presented at the International Congress of Sexology, Montreal, Canada, Oct. 1976. 6p.

1488 Peterson, James A. "The social context of sexual counseling." *Counseling Psychologist* 5(1):114-120, 1975.

1489 Pokrovskiı̆, N. Iû. "Iz opyta organizatsii seksologicheskoı̆ pomoshchi v Rostovskom Oblastnom Vrachebno-Fizkul'turnom Dispansere." *Zdravookhranenie Rossiiskoı̆ Federatsii* 15:25-27, Apr. 1971.

1490 Pomeroy, Wardell B. "Some thoughts on sex therapy for the private practitioner." In: Congrès International de Sexologie Médicale, Paris, 1974, *Papers,* pp. 185-187.

1491 Quinn, J.T. et al. "Experience of a clinic for sexual disorders." *Ulster Medical Journal* 42:187-191, 1973.

1492 Reed, David M. "Eight reasons for failure in sex therapy." *Medical Aspects of Human Sexuality* 10(5):134-139, May 1976.

1493 Renshaw, Domeena C. "Sex therapy in the 1970's." *Psychiatric Opinion* 12(5):6-11, May 1975.

1494 Sarembe, B. "Die bevülkerungsstruktur in der ehe- und sexualberatung." *Zeitschrift für Ärztliche Fortbildung (Jena)* 66(17):888-891, Sept. 1, 1972.

1495 Schoof, W. "Ein jahr sexologische poliklinik." In: *Ergebnisse zur Sexualforschung,* ed. by E. Schorsch and G. Schmidt, pp. 123-153. Köln: Wissenschafts-Verlag, 1975.

1496 Schultz, LeRoy G. "Ethical issues in treating sexual dysfunction." *Social Work* 20(2):126-128, Mar. 1975.

1497 _____. "A survey of social workers' attitudes and use of body and sex psychotherapies." *Clinical Social Work Journal* 3(2):90-99, 1975.

1498 Sigusch, Volkmar. "Bemerkungen zum verhältnis von ''sexualtherapie'' und gesellschaft." In: *Therapie sexueller Störungen,* ed. by Volkmar Sigusch, pp. 245-281. Stuttgart: Georg Thieme, 1975.

1499 Sigusch, Volkmar, ed. *Therapie sexueller Storungen.* Stuttgart: Georg Thieme, 1975.

1500 Sigusch, Volkmar and Bernd Meyenburg. "Sexualberatung und Sexualtherapie in der B.D.R." *Medizinische Welt* 25(16):711-715, Apr. 19, 1974.

1501 Vasil'chenko, G.S. "Structural analysis in the treatment of sexual disturbances." *Journal of Sex Research* 8(2):140-143, May 1972.

1502 Voznesenskiı̆, O.S. "O nekotorykh osobennostiakh lecheniia seksologicheskix bol'nykh v usloviiakh sanatoriia." In: *Problems of Contemporary Sexopathology,* ed. by A.A. Portnov, pp. 468-472. Moscow: Ministry of Public Health of RSFSR, 1972.

1503 Wolfe, Linda. "Take two aspirins and masturbate." *Playboy* 21(6):114-116 passim, June 1974.

BEHAVIOR THERAPY

1504 Annon, Jack S. *The Behavioral Treatment of Sexual Problems. Volume 1: Brief Therapy; Volume 2: Intensive Therapy.* Honolulu: Enabling Systems, 1974 and 1975. (Avail. from Multi Media Resource Center.)

1505 _____. "The PLISSIT model: a proposed conceptual scheme for the behavioral treatment of sexual problems." *Journal of Sex Education and Therapy* 2(1):1-15, Spring/Summer 1976.

1506 Arentewicz, Gerd et al. "Verhaltenstherapie sexueller funktionsstörungen: erfahrungen mit 23 paaren." In: *Ergebnisse zur Sexualforschung,* ed. by E. Schorsch and G. Schmidt, pp. 154–223. Köln: Wissenschafts-Verlag, 1975.

1507 Bancroft, John. "The Masters and Johnson approach in a NHS setting." *British Journal of Sexual Medicine* 1(8):6–10, Nov./Dec. 1974.

1508 Belliveau, Fred and Lin Richter. *Understanding Human Sexual Inadequacy.* New York: Bantam Books, 1970.

1509 Bianco, Fernando J. "Marital sexual dysfunction; presentation of a fundamental therapeutic program." In: Congres International de Sexologie Médicale, Paris 1974. *Papers,* pp. 523–526.

1510 Brady, John Paul. "Behavior therapy of sexual disorders." In: *The Sexual Experience,* ed. by B.J. Sadock, H.I. Kaplan and A.M. Freedman, pp. 457–463. Baltimore: Williams & Wilkins, 1976.

1511 Bruni, Ernest. "Psychotherapists as sex therapists." Paper presented at the American Psychological Association Alumni Meeting Symposium, Honolulu, Sept. 1972. 15p.

1512 Caird, William K. and John P. Wincze. *Sex Therapy; A Behavioral Approach.* Hagerstown, MD: Harper & Row, 1977.

1513 Caplan, Ruth Thurlow. *Attitude change of couples involved in a sexual therapy program.* (Thesis—University of New Mexico.) Ann Arbor, MI: University Microfilms, 1973. (Order #73-27,787)

1514 Dengrove, Edward. "Behavior therapy of the sexual disorders." *Journal of Sex Research* 3(1):49–61, Feb. 1967.

1515 Hartman, William E. and Marilyn A. Fithian. *Treatment of Sexual Dysfunction.* Long Beach, CA: Center for Marital and Sexual Studies, 1973.

1516 Horn, Patrice. "How to enhance healthy sexuality: behavior mod in the bedroom." *Psychology Today* 9(6):94–95, Nov. 1975.

1517 "An interview with Masters and Johnson on 'human sexual inadequacy.' " *Medical Aspects of Human Sexuality* 4(7):21–45, July 1970.

1518 Kaplan, Helen Singer. "Friction and fantasy: no-nonsense therapy for six sexual malfunctions." *Psychology Today* 8(5):77–86, Oct. 1974.

1519 _____. *The New Sex Therapy; Active Treatment of Sexual Dysfunctions.* New York: Brunner/Mazel, 1974.

1520 Kaplan, Helen Singer and Richard Kohl. "Adverse reactions to the rapid treatment of sexual problems." *Psychosomatics* 13(3):185–190, May/June 1972.

1521 Kroger, William S. "Learning a new way to reduce anxiety." *Osteopathic Physician* 41(3):80–91 passim, Mar. 1974.

1522 LoPiccolo, Joseph and Vinnie H. Miller. "Procedural outline sexual enrichment groups." *Counseling Psychologist* 5(1):46–49, 1975.

1523 _____. "A program for enhancing the sexual relationships of normal couples." *Counseling Psychologist* 5(1):41–45, 1975.

1524 Lobitz, W. Charles et al. "A closer look at simplistic behavior therapy for sexual dysfunction: two case studies." In: *Case Studies in Behavior Therapy,* ed. by H.J. Eysenck. London: Routledge & Kegan Paul, 1974. 56p.

1525 Lobitz, W. Charles and Joseph LoPiccolo. "New methods in the behavioral treatment of sexual dysfunction." *Journal of Behavior Therapy and Experimental Psychiatry* 3(4):265–271, Dec. 1972.

1526 McCarthy, Barry W. "A modification of Masters and Johnson sex therapy model in a clinical setting." *Psychotherapy: Theory, Research and Practice* 10(4):290–293, Winter 1973.

1527 Maddock, James W. "Initiation problems and time structuring in brief sex therapy." *Journal of Sex and Marital Therapy* 1(3):190–197, Spring 1975.

1528 Masters, William and Virginia Johnson. *Human Sexual Inadequacy.* Boston: Little, Brown, 1970.

1529 _____. "Principles of the new sex therapy." *American Journal of Psychiatry* 133(5):548–554, May 1976.

1530 Murphy, Christine V. and William L. Mikulas. "Behavioral features and deficiencies of the Masters and Johnson program." *Psychological Record* 24(2):221–227, Spring 1974.

1531 Nederlander, Caren E. Berman. "Sex education program for females incorporating graphic expression in the modification of sexual behavior." Unpub. doctoral dissertation, University of Michigan, 1976.

1532 Neiger, Stephen. *Overcoming Sexual Inadequacy.* (12 tape cassettes.) Chicago: Human Development Institute, 1973.

1533 Nims, Jerry P. "Imagery, shaping, and orgasm." *Journal of Sex and Marital Therapy* 1(3):198–203, Spring 1975.

1534 Pasini, Willy. "Evaluation critique des thérapies du couple." In: Congrès International de Sexologie Médicale, Paris, 1974, *Papers,* pp. 191–194.

1535 Powell, Leslie Charles et al. "Rapid treatment approach to human sexual inadequacy." *American Journal of Obstetrics and Gynecology* 119(1):89–97, May 1, 1974.

1536 Powers, Ann. "Flunking out at Masters and Johnson's." *Ms.* 2(11):83–87, May 1974.

1537 Prockaska, James O. and Robert Marzilli. "Modification of the Masters and Johnson approach to sexual problems." *Psychotherapy: Theory, Research and Practice* 10(4):294–296, Winter 1973.

1538 Robbins, Jhan and June Robbins. *An Analysis of Human Sexual Inadequacy.* New York: New American Library, 1970.

1539 Serber, Michael. "Videotape feedback in the treatment of couples with sexual dysfunction." *Archives of Sexual Behavior* 3(4):377–380, July 1974.

1540 Sharpe, Robert and V. Meyer. "Modification of 'cognitive sexual pain' by the spouse under supervision." *Behavior Therapy* 4(2):285–287, Mar. 1973.

1541 "A therapy program to enhance your sex life." *Behavior Today* 6(15):445–446, Apr. 14, 1975.

1542 Wish, Peter A. "The use of imagery-based techniques in the treatment of sexual dysfunction." *Counseling Psychologist* 5(1):52–55, 1975.

1543 Zwang, Gérard and Antoine Romieu. *Précis de Thérapeutique Sexologique: Traitement des Dysfonctionnements Érotiques du Couple.* Paris: Maloine, 1974.

DUAL-TEAM THERAPY

1544 Biggs, Mae and Richard Spitz. "Treating sexual dysfunction: the dual-sex therapy team." In: *Human Sexuality: A Health Practitioner's Text,* ed. by Richard Green, pp. 223–232. Baltimore: Williams & Wilkins, 1975.

1545 Golden, Joshua S. and Margaret A. Golden. "You know who and what's her name: the woman's role in sex therapy." *Journal of Sex and Marital Therapy* 2(1):6–16, Spring 1976.

1546 Sadock, Virginia A. and Benjamin Sadock. "Dual-sex therapy." In: *The Sexual Experience,* ed. by B.J. Sadock, H.I. Kaplan and A.M. Freedman, pp. 464–478. Baltimore: Williams & Wilkins, 1976.

1547 Sarrel, Philip M. and Lorna J. Sarrel. "The dual therapy approach to the treatment of sexual dysfunction (II)." In: Congrès International de Sexologie Médicale, Paris, 1974, *Papers,* pp. 195–196.

1548 Schumacher, Sallie. *The Therapeutic Foursome.* (Also: *The Use of Films in Desensitizing Sex Educators and Counselors,* by W. Cody Wilson.) (Audio-record.) Washington, DC: American Association of Sex Educators and Counselors, 1972.

1549 Waggoner, Raymond W., Emily Hartshorne Mudd and Marshall Shearer. "Training dual sex teams for rapid treatment of sexual dysfunction: a pilot program." *Psychiatric Annals* 3(5):61–67, May 1973.

1550 Zussman, Leon and Shirley Zussman. "Dual sex team therapy of the couple." Paper presented at the Department of Psychiatry, Payne Whitney Clinic, Cornell University Medical College, New York City, Nov. 16, 1972. 13p.

DESENSITIZATION

1551 Husted, June Rose. "Desensitization procedures in dealing with female sexual dysfunction." *Counseling Psychologist* 5(1):30–37, 1975.

1552 _____. *The effect of method of systematic desensitization and presence of sexual communication in the treatment of female sexual anxiety by counterconditioning.* (Thesis—University of California, Los Angeles.) Ann Arbor, MI: University Microfilms, 1972. (Order #72-20,446)

1553 Laughren, Thomas P. and David J. Kass. "Desensitization of sexual dysfunction: the present status." In: *Couples in Conflict,* ed. by Alan S. Gurman and David G. Rice, pp. 281–302. New York: Aronson, 1975.

1554 Obler, Martin. "Multivariate approaches to psychotherapy with sexual dysfunctions." *Counseling Psychologist* 5(1):55–60, 1975.

1555 _____. "Systematic desensitization in sexual disorders." *Journal of Behavior Therapy and Experimental Psychiatry* 4(2):93–101, June 1973.

1556 Wilson, W. Cody. *The Use of Films in Desensitizing Sex Educators and Counselors.* (Also: *The Therapeutic Foursome,* by Sallie Schumacher.) (Audiorecord.) Washington, DC: American Association of Sex Educators and Counselors, 1972.

GROUP THERAPY

1557 Barbach, Lonnie Garfield. "Group treatment of pre-orgasmic women." *Journal of Sex and Marital Therapy* 1(2):139–145, Winter 1974.

1558 Leiblum, Sandra, Raymond C. Rosen and Diane Pierce. "Group treatment format: mixed sexual dysfunctions." *Archives of Sexual Behavior* 5(4):313–322, July 1976.

1559 LoPiccolo, Joseph and Vinnie H. Miller. "Procedural outline sexual enrichment groups." *Counseling Psychologist* 5(1):46–49, 1975.

1560 _____. "A program for enhancing the sexual relationships of normal couples." *Counseling Psychologist* 5(1):41–45, 1975.

1561 Preterm Institute. *Exploring Human Sexuality.* Cambridge, MA: Schenkman, 1975.

1562 Sadock, Benjamin J. and Henry I. Spitz. "Group psychotherapy of sexual disorders." In: *The Sexual Experience,* ed. by Benjamin Sadock, H.I. Kaplan and A.M. Freedman, pp. 478–488. Baltimore: Williams & Wilkins, 1976.

1563 Stone, Abraham and Lena Levine. "Group therapy in sexual maladjustment." *American Journal of Psychiatry* 107(3):195–202, Sept. 1950.

1564 Zilbergeld, Bernie. "Group treatment of sexual dysfunction in men without partners." *Journal of Sex and Marital Therapy* 1(3):204–214, Spring 1975.

PSYCHOANALYTIC AND OTHER THERAPIES

1565 Bruni, Ernest. "Psychotherapists as sex therapists." Paper presented at American Psychological Association Alumni Meeting Symposium, Honolulu, Sept. 1972.

1566 Bryan, William J. "The effective uses of nudity in treating sexual problems." *Journal of the American Institute of Hypnosis* 13(2):71–78, Mar. 1972.

1567 Dengrove, Edward. "The mechanotherapy of sexual disorder." *Journal of Sex Research* 7(1):1–12, Feb. 1971.

1568 Ellis, Albert. "The rational-emotive approach to sex therapy." *Counseling Psychologist* 5(1):14–21, 1975.

1569 Kroger, William S. "Learning a new way to reduce anxiety." *Osteopathic Physician* 41(3):80–91 passim, Mar. 1974.

1570 Meyer, Jon K. "Psychodynamic treatment of the individual with a sexual disorder." In: *Clinical Management of Sexual Disorders,* ed. by J. Meyer, pp. 265–275. Baltimore: Williams & Wilkins, 1976.

1571 Milne, Hugo. "The role of the psychiatrist." In: *Psycho-Sexual Problems: Proceedings of the Congress held at the University of Bradford, 1974,* ed. by Hugo Milne and Shirley Hardy, pp. 65–80. Baltimore: University Park Press, 1975.

1572 O'Connor, John F. and Lenore O. Stern. "Results of treatment in functional sexual disorders." *New York State Journal of Medicine* 72:1927–1934, Aug. 1972.

1573 Sager, Clifford J. "The couples model in the treatment of sexual dysfunctions in the single person (discussion follows)." In: *Sexuality and Psychoanalysis,* pp. 124–140. New York: Brunner/Mazel, 1975.

1574 Segel, Harold J. "Psychotherapy vs. hypnotherapy in the treatment of sex problems." *American Journal of Clinical Hypnosis* 13(2):128–130, Oct. 1970.

1575 Wallnöfer, Heinrich. "Offenbarung in autogenen training; Konsequenzen aus tiefenpsychologischem blickwinkel." *Sexualmedizin* 4(6):362–364, June 1975.

LEGAL ASPECTS OF SEX THERAPY

1576 California. Senate. 1975–76. *Senate Bill No. 1184.* Introduced by Senator Zenovich. State of California, Office of the Attorney General, Department of Justice, Apr. 28, 1975. 11p.

1577 Leroy, David H. "The potential criminal liability of human sex clinics and their patients." *Saint Louis University Law Journal* 16:586–603, Summer 1972.

1578 Schultz, LeRoy G. "Avoiding legal problems in sex therapy." Paper presented at the 2nd Annual Conference of Sex Therapists and Counselors, University of Texas Medical School, Galveston, TX, Mar. 9, 1975. 9p.

1579 Sex and the Law. "Appendix IV." In: *Human Sexuality,* prep. by American Medical Association Committee on Human Sexuality, pp. 181–223. Chicago: American Medical Association, 1972.

1580 Slovenko, Ralph. "Sex counseling and the

law." *Medical Aspects of Human Sexuality* 3(1):47–58, Jan. 1969.

SEX THERAPISTS EDUCATION

1581 Ellis, Albert. "Certification for sex therapists." Paper presented at the International Congress of Sexology, Montreal, Canada, Oct. 1976. 11p.

1582 Freiberg, Patricia and Margaret W. Bridwell. "An interdisciplinary approach to female sexuality." *Counseling Psychologist* 5(1):106–111, 1975.

1583 Krohne, Eric C. "General guidelines for sex therapists." *Journal of Sex Education and Therapy* 2(2):32–33, Fall/Winter 1976.

1584 Lief, Harold I. "Sexual health services: training and treatment." *SIECUS Report* 2(2):1–3 passim, Nov. 1973.

1585 Money, John and Harvey Alexander. "AASEC sex therapist certification program." *Journal of Sex Education and Therapy* 1:44–47, Spring/Summer 1975.

1586 Schultz, Leroy G. "A survey of social workers' attitudes and use of body and sex psychotherapies." *Clinical Social Work Journal* 3(2):90–99, 1975.

1587 Sigusch, Volkmar and Bernd Meyenburg. "Sexualberatung und sexualtherapie in der B.D.R." *Medizinische Welt* 25(16):711–715, Apr. 19, 1974.

1588 World Health Organization. *Education and Treatment in Human Sexuality: The Training of Health Professionals. Report of a WHO Meeting.* Technical Report Series: No. 572. Geneva: World Health Organization, 1975. (Avail. from Q Corporation, 49 Sheridan Ave., Albany, NY 12210.)

SEX EDUCATION ADVICE

1589 Altman, Carole. *You Can Be Your Own Sex Therapist.* New York: Berkley/Putnam, 1976.

1590 Comfort, Alexander. *The Joy of Sex; A Cordon Bleu Guide of Lovemaking.* New York: Crown Publishers, 1972.

1591 Kaplan, Helen Singer. *The Illustrated Manual of Sex Therapy.* New York: Quadrangle/New York Times Book Co., 1975.

1592 Kass, David J. and Fred F. Stauss. *Sex Therapy at Home.* New York: Simon & Schuster, 1975.

1593 McCarthy, Barry W., Mary Ryan and Fred A. Johnson. *Sexual Awareness; A Practical Approach.* San Francisco: Boyd & Fraser Publishing/Scrimshaw Press, 1975.

1594 McCary, James Leslie. *Sexual Myths and Fallacies.* New York: Van Nostrand Reinhold, 1971.

1595 Nolte, Claude and Dorothy Nolte. *Wake Up in Bed, Together! A Handbook for Sexual Repatterning.* New York: Stein & Day, 1975.

1596 *SARguide for a Better Sex Life; A Self-Help Program for Personal Sexual Enrichment/Education Designed by the National Sex Forum.* San Francisco: Multi Media Resource Center, 1975.

SEX EDUCATION ADVICE (FEMALE)

1597 Barbach, Lonnie Garfield. *For Yourself: The Fulfillment of Female Sexuality.* Garden City, NY: Doubleday, 1975.

1598 Boston Women's Health Collective. *Our Bodies, Ourselves.* New York: Simon & Schuster, 1973.

1599 Dodson, Betty. *Liberating Masturbation.* New York: Bodysex Designs, 1974.

1600 Heiman, Julia, Leslie LoPiccolo and Joseph LoPiccolo. *Becoming Orgasmic: A Sexual Growth Program for Women.* Englewood Cliffs, NJ: Prentice-Hall, 1976.

1601 Smith, Carolyn, Toni Ayres and Maggie Rubenstein. *Getting in Touch; Self Sexuality for Women.* San Francisco: Multi Media Resource Center, 1972.

SEX EDUCATION ADVICE (MALE)

1602 Copelan, Rachel. *The Sexually Fulfilled Man.* New York: Weybright & Talley, 1972.

1603 McIlvenna, Ted. *When You Don't Make It. The Yes Book of Sex.* San Francisco: Multi Media Resource Center, 1973.

1604 McIlvenna, Ted and Herb Vandervoort. *You Can Last Longer. The Yes Book of Sex.* San Francisco: Multi Media Resource Center, 1972.

PERIODICALS

Journal of Sex & Marital Therapy
Human Sciences Press
72 Fifth Ave., New York, NY 10011

Journal of Sex Education and Therapy
American Association of Sex Educators,
Counselors & Therapists
5010 Wisconsin Ave., NW, Suite 304,
Washington, DC 20016

SIECUS Report
Human Sciences Press
72 Fifth Ave., New York, NY 10011

Therapist-Client Relationships and Surrogate Sex Partners

THERAPIST-CLIENT RELATIONSHIPS

1605 Arensberg, Frederick. "The analyst: a source of hope and hopelessness." *Voices* 6(3):49–51, 1970.

1606 Bieber, Toby. "A female therapist's view." *Psychiatric Opinion* 4(2):12–15, Apr. 1967.

1607 _____. "On treating male homosexuals." *Archives of General Psychiatry* 16(1):60–63, Jan. 1967.

1608 Brenton, Myron. "Phony sex therapists: how to spot them." *Sexology* 41(6):20–23, Jan. 1975.

1609 Butler, Sharon Elaine. *Sexual contact between therapists and patients.* (Dissertation—California School of Professional Psychology.) Ann Arbor, MI: University Microfilms, 1975. (Order #76-10,411)

1610 Chodoff, Paul. "Brief guide to office counseling: erotic undercurrents in the physician-patient relationship." *Medical Aspects of Human Sexuality* 8(5):181–182, May 1974.

1611 _____. "The seductive patient." *Medical Aspects of Human Sexuality* 2(2):52–55, Feb. 1968.

1612 Cohn, Ruth C. "The sexual fantasies of psychotherapists and their use in psychotherapy." *Journal of Sex Research* 2(3):219–226, Nov. 1966.

1613 D'Addario, Linda J. "Sexual relationships between female clients and male therapists." Unpub. doctoral dissertation, California School of Professional Psychology, 1977.

1614 Dahlberg, Charles Clay. "Sexual contact between patient and therapist." *Medical Aspects of Human Sexuality* 5(7):34–56, July 1971. (Also in: *Contemporary Psychoanalysis* 6(2), Spring 1970.)

1615 Dennis, Margaret H. "How to handle the sexually provocative patient." *Osteopathic Physician* 42(9):69 passim, Sept. 1975.

1616 Ellis, Albert. "To thine own therapeutic lust be true???; a rational-emotive approach to erotic feeling in the psychotherapy relationship." Paper read at the American Psychological Association Convention Symposium, Philadelphia, Aug. 31, 1963. 12p.

1617 Emde Boas, C. van. "Some reflections on sexual relations between physicians and patients." *Journal of Sex Research* 2(3):215–218, Nov. 1966.

1618 Feldman, Marvin J. "The use of obscene words in the therapeutic relationship." *American Journal of Psychoanalysis* 15(1):45–49, 1955.

1619 Fier, Betty. "Masters blasts MD's who rape patients." *Moneysworth,* 1 passim, Oct. 27, 1975.

1620 Fine, Reuben. "Erotic feelings in the psychotherapeutic relationship." *Psychoanalytic Review* 52:30–37, Spring 1965.

1621 _____. "A transference manifestation of male homosexuals." *Psychoanalysis and Psychoanalytic Review* 49(2):116–120, Spring 1961.

1622 Finney, Joseph C. "Therapist and patient after hours." *American Journal of Psychotherapy* 29(4):593–602, Oct. 1975.

1623 Freeman, Lucy and Julie Roy. *Betrayal: The True Story of the First Woman to Successfully Sue Her Psychiatrist for Using Sex in the Guise of Therapy.* New York: Stein & Day, 1976.

1624 Freeman, Nathan. "Sexuality in the therapeutic process: a round table discussion." *American Journal of Psychoanalysis* 18(1):1–27, 1958.

1625 Frick, Viola. "Sexuelle spannungen in der arzt-patient-beziehung." *Sexualmedizin* 5(4):262, Apr. 1976.

1626 Garfield, Sol L. "Values: an issue in psychotherapy: comments on a case study." *Journal of Abnormal Psychology* 83(2):202–203, Apr. 1974.

1627 Greenbank, R. "Management of sexual counter transference." *Journal of Sex Research* 1(3):233–238, Nov. 1965.

1628 Guze, Henry. "Sexual factors in the physician-patient relationship." *International Journal of Sexology* 5(1):14–19, Aug. 1951.

1629 Hare-Mustin, Rachel T. "Ethical considerations in the use of sexual contact in psychotherapy." *Psychotherapy: Theory, Research, and Practice* 11(4):308–310, Winter 1974.

1630 Hartland, John. "An alleged case of criminal assault on a married woman under hypnosis." *American Journal of Clinical Hypnosis* 16(3):188–198, Jan. 1974.

1631 Ishida, Yasuo. "Answers to questions: physician-patient sexual relations." *Medical Aspects of Human Sexuality* 8(10):103, Oct. 1974.

1632 Jones, J. David and Ila H. Gehman. "The taboo of virginity: resistances of male therapists and early adolescent girl patients in treatment." *Journal of the American Academy of Child Psychiatry* 10(2):351–357, Apr. 1971.

1633 Kardener, Sheldon H. "Sex and the physician-patient relationship." *American Journal of Psychiatry* 131(10):1134–1136, Oct. 1974.

1634 Kardener, Sheldon H., Marielle Fuller and Ivan N. Mensch. "A survey of physicians' attitudes and practices regarding erotic and nonerotic contact with patients." *American Journal of Psychiatry* 130(10)1077–1081, Oct. 1973.

1635 Kraft, Thomas. "Erotisierte übertragung in der verhaltenstherapie." *Zeitschrift für Psychosomatische Medizin und Psychoanalyse* 15(2):126–130, Apr./June 1969.

1636 Lehrman, N.S. "The analyst's sexual feelings: their appropriateness and their value." *American Journal of Psychotherapy* 14(3):545–549, July 1960.

1637 "Love thy analyst." *Time*:76, Mar. 24, 1975.

1638 Lowry, Thea Snyder and Thomas P. Lowry. "Ethical considerations in sex therapy." *Journal of Marriage and Family Counseling* 1(3):229–236, July 1975.

1639 McCartney, James L. "Overt transference." *Journal of Sex Research* 2(3):227–237, Nov. 1966.

1640 Mace, David R. "Delinquent sex and marriage counselors." *Sexual Behavior* 1(3):35–41, June 1971.

1641 Marmor, Judd. "Sexual acting-out in psychotherapy." *American Journal of Psychoanalysis* 32(1):3–8, 1972.

1642 Masters, William. "Phony sex clinics—medicine's newest nightmare." *Today's Health* 52(11):22–26, Nov. 1974.

1643 Masters, William and Virginia Johnson. *Human Sexual Inadequacy.* Boston: Little, Brown, 1970.

1644 _____. "Sex as a natural function—and the unethical therapist." In: *Sexuality and Human Values,* ed. by Mary S. Calderone, pp. 95–96. New York: Association Press, 1974.

1645 Mattsson, Ake. "The male therapist and the female adolescent patient." *Journal of the American Academy of Child Psychiatry* 9(4):707–721, Oct. 1970.

1646 Morgenthaler, Fritz. "Introduction to panel on disturbances of male and female identity as met with in psychoanalytic practice." *International Journal of Psycho-Analysis* 50:109–112, 1969.

1647 Mudd, John W. and Richard J. Siegel. "Sexuality—the experience and anxieties of medical students." *New England Journal of Medicine* 281(25):1397–1402, Dec. 18, 1969.

1648 Naiman, James. "Short term effects as indicators of the role of interpretations in psychoanalysis." *International Journal of Psycho-Analysis* 49(2–3):353–357, 1968.

1649 Perry, Judith Adams. "Physicians' erotic and nonerotic physical involvement with patients." *American Journal of Psychiatry* 25(3):233–240, July 1976.

1650 "Psychologists and malpractice insurance." *Science News*:169, Mar. 13, 1976.

1651 Robertiello, Richard C. "Iatrogenic psychiatric illness." *Journal of Contemporary Psychiatry* 7(1):3–8, Winter 1975.

1652 Rubenstein, Ben and Morton Levitt. "Therapeutic systems and moral assumptions." *International Review of Psycho-Analysis* 1:481–488, 1974.

1653 Scheflin, Albert E. "Quasi-courtship behavior in psychotherapy." *Psychiatry* 28(3):245–257, Aug. 1965.

1654 "Sex 'malpractice' costs MD $350,000. Psychiatrist's insurance balks at paying jury's award to ex-patient." *Medical World News*:37–40, May 5, 1975.

1655 Shepard, Martin. *The Love Treatment: Sexual Intimacy Between Patients and Psychotherapists.* New York: Wyden, 1971.

1656 _____. "The love treatment: the pros and cons of patient-therapist sex." *Forum* 1(7):18–25, Apr. 1972.

1657 Shochet, Bernard R. et al. "Dealing with the seductive patient." *Medical Aspects of Human Sexuality* 10(12):90–104, Dec. 1976.

1658 Shor, Joel and Jean Sanville. "Erotic provocations and dalliances in psychotherapeutic practice: some clinical cues for preventing and repairing therapist-patient collusions." *Clinical Social Work Journal* 2(2):83–95, Summer 1974.

1659   Siassi, Iradj and Mivart Thomas. "Physicians and the new sexual freedom." *American Journal of Psychiatry* 130(11): 1256–1257, Nov. 1973.

1660   Sloan, Don. "The seductive patient—a gynecologist's view." *Medical Aspects of Human Sexuality* 3(12):28–32, Dec. 1969.

1661   Stone, Alan A. "The legal implications of sexual activity between psychiatrist and patient." *American Journal of Psychiatry* 133(10):1138–1141, Oct. 1976.

1662   Strupp, Hans H. "Some observations on the fallacy of value-free psychotherapy and the empty organism: comments on a case study." *Journal of Abnormal Psychology* 83(2):199–201, Apr. 1974.

1663   Taylor, Barbie J. and Nathaniel N. Wagner. "Sex between therapist and clients: a review and analysis." *Professional Psychology*:593–601, Nov. 1976.

1664   Voth, Harold M. "Love affair between doctor and patient." *American Journal of Psychotherapy* 26:394–400, July 1972.

1665   Weisstein, Naomi. *Psychology Constructs the Female, or the Fantasy Life of the Male Psychologist.* (Pamphlet.) Boston: New England Free Press, 1970.

1666   Wollman, Leo. "The couple who took sex for granted." *Medical Economics* 1–7, Nov. 10, 1969.

SURROGATE SEX PARTNERS

1667   Apfelbau, Bernard. "The myth of the surrogate." Paper presented at the Society for the Scientific Study of Sex Conference, Beverly Hills, CA, Sept. 20, 1975. 6p.

1668   Cole, Martin. "The surrogate's role in sexual inadequacy." *British Journal of Sexual Medicine* 3(3):35–36, June 1976.

1669   Elias, Marilyn. "Stand-in for Eros." *Human Behavior* 6(3):17–23, Mar. 1977.

1670   Greene, Susan. "On the pressure to become a surrogate." Paper presented at the Society for the Scientific Study of Sex Conference, Beverly Hills, CA, Sept. 20, 1975. 5p.

1671   Jacobs, Marion, Linda A. Thompson and Patsy Truxaw. "The use of sexual surrogates in counseling." *The Counseling Psychologist* 5(1):73–77, 1975.

1672   Leroy, David H. "The potential criminal liability of human sex clinics and their patients." *St. Louis University Law Journal* 16:586–603, Summer 1972.

1673   Levine, Stephen B. "Current problems in diagnosis and treatment of psychological impotence." Paper presented at the Eastern Association for Sex Therapy, New York, Mar. 1977. 12p.

1674   Lowry, Thea Snyder and Thomas P. Lowry. "Ethical considerations in sex therapy." *Journal of Marriage and Family Counseling* 1(3):229–236, July 1975.

1675   Norcross, Keith. "The true evils of human sexuality." *British Journal of Sexual Medicine* 1(2):9–12, Nov./Dec. 1973.

1676   "Sex surrogates." In: *Catalog of Sexual Consciousness,* ed. by Saul Brown, pp. 135–137. New York: Grove Press, 1975.

1677   Symonds, Carolyn. "The life of a surrogate 'wife.'" *Forum* 2(12):33–37, Sept. 1973.

1678   "Trick or treatment?" *Time* 103(24):90, June 17, 1974.

1679   Waynberg, Jacques. "Vers une nouvelle thérapeutique des difficultés sexuelles." *Le Concours Médical* (Paris) 97(1):44–51, Jan. 4, 1975.

OTHER SOURCES OF INFORMATION

International Professional Surrogates Association (IPSA)
Box 5554, Santa Monica, CA 90405

American Association of Sex Educators, Counselors and Therapists (AASECT)
5010 Wisconsin Ave., Suite 304, Washington, DC 20016

Sex and Gender

Gender Role Identification

BIBLIOGRAPHIES

1680   "Annotated bibliography (of research in sex differences, 1966–1974)." In: *The Psychology of Sex Differences,* by Eleanor E. Maccoby and Carol Nagy Jacklin, pp. 395–627. Stanford, CA: Stanford University Press, 1974.

1681   Astin, Helen S., Allison Parelman and Anne Fisher. *Sex Roles: A Research Bibliography.* DHEW Publication No. (ADM) 75–166. Rockville, MD: National Institute of Mental Health, 1975. (456 annotations.) (Avail. from Supt. of Docs., U.S. GPO, Washington D.C. 20402.)

1682   Hochschild, Arlie Russell. "A review of sex role research." *American Journal of Sociology* 78(4):1011–1029, Jan. 1973.

1683   Oetzel, Roberta M. "Annotated bibliography (and) classified summary of research in sex differences." In: *The Development of Sex Differences,* by Eleanor E. Maccoby, pp. 223–351. Stanford, CA: Stanford University Press, 1966.

1684   Spiegel, Jeanne. *Sex Role Concepts; How Women and Men See Themselves and Each Other. A Selected Annotated Bibliography.* Washington, DC: Business and Professional Women's Foundation, 1969.

> Works cited in the annotated bibliographies listed above are *not* included in the following bibliography. Any literature search on sex roles or sex differences should begin with these five references.

GENDER ROLE IDENTIFICATION

1685   Adelson, Edward T., ed. *Sexuality and Psychoanalysis.* New York: Brunner/Mazel, 1975.

1686   Al-Hamdani, Muwaffak and Baha Abu-Laban. "Game involvement and sex-role socialization in Arab children." *International Journal of Comparative Sociology* 12(3):182–191, Sept. 1971.

1687   American Anthropological Association. "Sex roles in cross-cultural perspective." *American Ethnologist* 2(4):whole issue, Nov. 1975.

1688   Angrilli, Albert F. "The psychosexual identification of pre-school boys." *Journal of Genetic Psychology* 97:329–340, 1960.

1689   Auerbach, Aaron Gerald. *Antecedents of masculinity and femininity in young children.* (Thesis—Purdue University.) Ann Arbor, MI: University Microfilm, 1967. (Order #68-6276)

1690   Bates, John E. et al. "Gender role abnormalities in boys: an analysis of clinical ratings." *Journal of Abnormal Child Psychology* 2(1):1–16, 1974.

1691   Bates, John E. and Peter M. Bentler. "Play activities of normal and effeminate boys." *Developmental Psychology* 9(1):20–27, July 1973.

1692   Beach, Frank, ed. *Human Sexuality in Four Perspectives.* Baltimore: Johns Hopkins University Press, 1977.

1693   Beit-Hallahmi, Benjamin et al. "Grammatical gender and gender identity development: cross cultural and cross lingual implications." *American Journal of Orthopsychiatry* 44(3):424–431, Apr. 1974.

1694   Bell, Alan. "The Scylla and Charybdis of psychosexual development." *Journal of Sex Research* 5(2):86–89, May 1969.

1695   Bem, Sandra L. "The measurement of psychological androgyny." *Journal of Consulting and Clinical Psychology* 42(2):155–162, Apr. 1974.

1696   _____. "Sex role adaptability: one consequence of psychological androgyny." *Journal of Personality and Social Psychology* 31(4): 634–643, Apr. 1975.

1697   Bielefeld, Robert James. *The constructs of masculinity and femininity as measured by the personality inventory for children.* (Thesis—University of Minnesota.) Ann Arbor, MI: University Microfilms, 1971. (Order #72-14272)

1698   Bieliauskas, Vytautas J. and Richard H. Mikesell. "Masculinity-femininity and self concept." *Perceptual and Motor Skills* 34(1):163–167, 1972.

1699   Biller, Henry B. "Masculine development: an integrative review." *Merrill-Palmer Quarterly of Behavior and Development* 13(4):253–294, Oct. 1967.

1700   _____. "Sex-role uncertainty and psychopathology." *Journal of Individual Psychology* 29(1):24–25, May 1973.

1701   Biller, Henry B. and Donald A. Liebman. "Body-build, sex-role preference, and sex-role adoption in junior high school boys." *The Journal of Genetic Psychology* 118(1):81–86, Mar. 1971.

1702   Brogan, Donna and Nancy G. Kutner. "Measuring sex-role orientation: a narrative approach." *Journal of Marriage and the Family* 38(1):31–40, Feb. 1976.

1703   Brown, Daniel G. "Sex-role development in a changing culture." *Psychological Bulletin* 54(4):232–242, July 1958.

1704   Brown, Daniel G. and David B. Lynn. "Human sexual development: an outline of components and concepts." *Journal of Marriage and the Family* 28(2):155–162, May 1966.

1705   Brown, Fred. "Changes in sexual identification and role over a decade and their implications." *Journal of Psychology* 77:229–251, 1971.

1706   Buchanan, Barbara, Ian M. Thompson and R. Mark Kirk. "Gender identity problems in the sexually ambiguous child." *Missouri Medicine; Journal of the Missouri State Medical Association* 70(4):227–229, Apr. 1973.

1707   Bunge, Raymond G. et al. "Panel discussion: determination of sex and what to do about it." *Journal of Urology* 81(1):13–24, Jan. 1959.

1708   Burgess, Jane K. "Children in one-parent families." *Sexual Behavior* 3(1):9–13, Jan. 1973.

1709   Burns, Robert A. *The effect of father's absence on the development of the masculine identification of boys in residential treatment.* (Thesis—St. Johns University, NY.) Ann Arbor, MI: University Microfilms, 1971. (Order #72-2973)

1710   Constantinople, Anne. "Masculinity-femininity: an exception to a famous dictum?" *Psychological Bulletin* 80(5):389–407, Nov. 1973.

1711   Crook, John H. "Sexual selection, dimorphism, and social organization in the primates." In: *Sexual Selection and the Descent of Man,* ed. by Bernard Campbell, pp. 231–281. Chicago: Aldine Publishing Co., 1972.

1712   Davis, Ethelyn. "Some aspects of sex-role preference among adolescents." *Proceedings of the Southwestern Sociological Association* 15:137–145, 1965.

1713   Diamond, Milton. *Sexual Identity.* (Tape cassette.) Human Sexuality Series. New York: W.W. Norton, 1975.

1714   Domash, Leanne and Lawrence Balter. "Sex and psychological differentiation in preschoolers." *Journal of Genetic Psychology* 128:77–84, Mar. 1976.

1715   Duberman, Lucile. *Gender and Sex in Society.* New York: Praeger, 1975.

1716   Duryea, Walter R. "Sex-role preference in children: individual and group administration of the It scale for children." *Psychological Reports* 21(1):269–274, 1967.

1717   Ehrhardt, Anke A. "Androgens in prenatal development; behavior changes in nonhuman primates and men." *Advances in the Biosciences* 13:153–162, Jan. 1974.

1718   _____. "Maternalism in fetal hormonal and related syndromes." In: *Contemporary Sexual Behavior: Critical Issues in the 1970's,* ed. by Joseph Zubin and John Money, pp. 99–115. Baltimore: Johns Hopkins University Press, 1973.

1719   Ehrhardt, Anke A., Kathryn Evers and John Money. "Influence of androgen and some aspects of sexually dimorphic behavior in women with the late-treated adrenogenital syndrome." *Johns Hopkins Medical Journal* 123(3):115–122, Sept. 1968.

1720   Estep, Rhoda E., Martha Burt and Herman J. Milligan. "The socialization of sexual identity." *Journal of Marriage and the Family* 39(1):99–112, Feb. 1977.

1721   Falik, Leon A. "Sexuality and endocrine glands: embryonic sex differentiation." *Journal of Sex Research* 12(2):124–134, May 1976.

1722   Federman, Daniel D. "Genetic control of sexual difference." *Progress in Medical Genetics* 9:215–235, 1973.

1723   Fellows, Robert. "HTP and DCT indicators of sexual identification in children." *Journal of Projective Techniques and Personality Assessment* 33(4):376–379, 1969.

1724   Fisher, Gary M. "Relationship between diagnosis of neuropsychiatric disorder, sexual deviation, and the sex of the first-drawn figure." *Perceptual and Motor Skills* 9:47–50, 1959.

1725   Fitzgerald, Donald and Karlene Roberts. "Semantic profiles and psychosexual interests as indicators of identification." *Personnel and Guidance Journal* 44(8):802–806, 1966.

1726   Friedman, Richard C., Ralph M. Richart and Raymond L. Vande Wiele. *Sex Differences in Behavior.* New York: Wiley, 1974.

1727   Frueh, Terry and Paul E. McGhee. "Traditional sex role development and amount of time spent watching television." *Developmental Psychology* 11(1):109, Jan. 1975.

1728 Gadpaille, Warren J. "Innate masculine-feminine differences." *Medical Aspects of Human Sexuality* 7(2):141–157, Feb. 1973.

1729 _____. "Research into the physiology of maleness and femaleness; its contributions to the etiology and psychodynamics of homosexuality." *Archives of General Psychiatry* 26:193–206, Mar. 1972.

1730 Gagnon, John H. "The interaction of gender roles and sexual conduct: some preliminary considerations." Paper presented at the Conference on Sex and its Psychosocial Derivatives, Stanford University, CA, Jan. 28–30, 1977. 35p.

1731 Gardner, Richard A. "Women's Lib, sex role development, and children's play." *Medical Aspects of Human Sexuality* 7(8):50–72, Aug. 1973.

1732 Goldfarb, Jack Harold. *The concept of sexual identity in normals and transvestites: its relationship to the body-image, self-concept and parental identification.* (Thesis—University of Southern California.) Ann Arbor, MI: University Microfilms, 1963. (Order #64-3098)

1733 Goslin, David A., ed. *Handbook of Socialization Theory and Research.* Chicago: Rand McNally, 1969.

1734 Gray, Jeffrey A. and Anthony W. Buffery. "Sex differences in emotional and cognitive behaviour in mammals including man: adaptive and neural bases." *Acta Psychologica* 35(2):89–111, Mar. 1971.

1735 Green, Richard. *Sexual Identity Conflict in Children and Adults.* New York: Basic Books, 1974.

1736 _____. "Sexual identity: research strategies." *Archives of Sexual Behavior* 4(4):337–352, July 1975.

1737 Green, Richard and Marielle Fuller. "Family doll play and female identity in preadolescent males." *American Journal of Orthopsychiatry* 43(1):123–127, Jan. 1973.

1738 Green, R. and J. Money. "Effeminacy in a prepubertal boy: summary of eleven cases and recommendations for case management." *Pediatrics* 27(2):286–291, Feb. 1961.

1739 Gurwitz, Sharon B. and Kenneth A. Dodge. "Adults' evaluation of a child as a function of sex of adult and sex of child." *Journal of Personality and Social Psychology* 32(5):822–828, Nov. 1975.

1740 Hamblen, E.C. "The assignment of sex to an individual: some enigmas and some practical clinical criteria." *American Journal of Obstetrics and Gynecology* 74(6):1228–1244, Dec. 1957.

1741 Hammer, Signe, ed. *Women: Body and Culture. Essays on the Sexuality of Women in a Changing Society.* New York: Harper & Row, 1975.

1742 Hampson, Joan G. "Hermaphroditic genital appearance, rearing and eroticism in hyperadreno-corticism." *Bulletin of the Johns Hopkins Hospital* 96(6):265–273, June 1955.

1743 Hampson, John L. and Joan G. Hampson. The ontogenesis of sexual behavior in man. In: *Sex and Internal Secretions,* ed. by William C. Young, pp. 1401–1432. Baltimore: Williams & Wilkins, 1961.

1744 Harlow, Harry F. and M.K. Harlow. "The effect of rearing condition on behavior." In: *Sex Research: New Developments,* ed. by John Money, pp. 161–175. New York: Holt, Rinehart & Winston, 1965.

1745 Heilbrun, Alfred B. "Measurement of masculine and feminine sex role identities as independent dimensions." *Journal of Consulting and Clinical Psychology* 44(2):183–190, Apr. 1976.

1746 Heilbrun, Carolyn G. "Recognizing the androgynous human." In: *The Future of Sexual Relations,* ed. by Robert T. Francoeur and Anna K. Francoeur, pp. 131–139. Englewood Cliffs, NJ: Prentice-Hall, 1974.

1747 Hyde, Janet S. "Tomboyism: implications for theories of female development." Paper presented at Western Psychological Association meeting, San Francisco, Apr. 1974. 18p.

1748 Joffe, Carole. "Sex role socialization and the nursery school: as the twig is bent." *Journal of Marriage and the Family* 33(3):467–475, Aug. 1971.

1749 Josselyn, Irene M. "Sources of sexual identity." *Child & Family* 6(2):38–45, 1967.

1750 Kando, Thomas. "Role strain: a comparison of males, females, and transsexuals." *Journal of Marriage and the Family* 34(3):459–464, Aug. 1972.

1751 Katz, Jack L. "Biological and psychological roots of psychosexual identity." *Medical Aspects of Human Sexuality* 6(6):103–116, June 1972.

1752 Keller, R. "The problem of sexual differentiation and hermaphroditism." *Ciba Symposia* 2(3):471–477, June 1940.

1753   Kempf, Edward J. "Phylogeny of thermo-bi-dynamic bisexual differentiation." *Journal of Clinical Psychopathology and Psychotherapy* 7(1):1–34, July 1945.

1754   Kestenberg, Judith S. "Outside and inside, male and female." *Journal of the American Psychoanalytic Association* 16(3):457–520, July 1968.

1755   Kirkendall, Lester A. and Isadore Rubin. "Sexuality and the life cycle." In: *Sexuality and Man,* ed. by Mary S. Calderone, pp. 3–23. New York: Scribner, 1970.

1756   Kitahara, Michio. "Polygyny: insufficient father-son contact and son's masculine identity." *Archives of Sexual Behavior* 5(3):201–209, May 1976.

1757   Kleeman, James A. "The establishment of core gender identity in normal girls." *Archives of Sexual Behavior* 1(2):103–129, 1971.

1758   Kobasigawa, Akira. "Inhibitory and disinhibitory effects of models on sex-inappropriate behavior in children." *Psychologia: An International Journal of Psychology in the Orient* 11(1–2):86–96, 1968.

1759   Kohlberg, Lawrence. "A cognitive developmental analysis of children's sex-role concepts and attitudes." In: *The Development of Sex Differences,* ed. by Eleanor E. Maccoby, pp. 82–173. Stanford, CA: Stanford University Press, 1966.

1760   Kohlberg, Lawrence and Dorothy Z. Ullian. "Stages in the development of psychosexual concepts and attitudes." In: *Sex Differences in Behavior,* ed. by Richard C. Friedman, pp. 209–222. New York: Wiley, 1974.

1761   Kokonis, Nicholas D. "Choice of gender on the DAP and measures of sex role identification." *Perceptual and Motor Skills* 35:727–730, Dec. 1972.

1762   Kurland, Morton L. "Sexual difficulties due to stereotyped role playing." *Medical Aspects of Human Sexuality* 9(6):8–22, June 1975.

1763   La Barre, Weston. "Anthropological perspectives on sexuality." In: *Sexuality: a Search for Perspective,* ed. by Donald L. Grummon and Andrew M. Barclay, pp. 38–53. New York: Van Nostrand Reinhold, 1971.

1764   Lansky, Leonard M. "Some comments on Ward's (1968) 'Variance of sex-role preferences among boys and girls.' " *Psychological Reports* 23(2):649–650, 1968.

1765   Laws, Judith Long. "Exotica ≠ erotica: a plea for continuities in the study of human behavior and sexual behavior." Paper presented at American Psychological Association, Montreal, Canada, Aug. 29, 1973. 17p.

1766   Laws, Judith Long and Pepper Schwartz. *Sexual Scripts; The Social Construction of Female Sexuality.* Hinsdale, IL: Dryden Press, 1977.

1767   Lebovitz, Phil S. "Feminine behavior in boys: aspects of its outcome." *American Journal of Psychiatry* 128(10):1283–1289, Apr. 1972.

1768   LeLieuvre, Robert B. and Donald Wise. "Obviousness of two MF tests: a replication and extension." *Journal of Social Psychology* 93(1):143–144, June 1974.

1769   Lev-Ran, Arye. "Gender role differentiation in hermaphrodites." *Archives of Sexual Behavior* 3(5):391–424, Sept. 1974.

1770   Lewis, Michael. "Early sex differences in the human: studies on socioemotional development." *Archives of Sexual Behavior* 4(4):329–335, July 1975.

1771   Lief, Harold I. "Normal psychosexual functioning." In: *Human Behavior; Biological, Psychological, and Sociological,* ed. by Alfred M. Freedman and Harold I. Kaplan, pp. 505–518. New York: Atheneum, 1972.

1772   Lynn, David B. "The process of learning parental and sex-role identification." *Journal of Marriage and the Family* 28(4):466–470, Nov. 1966.

1773   Maccoby, Eleanor E., ed. *The Development of Sex Differences.* Stanford Studies in Psychology, V. Stanford, CA: Stanford University Press, 1966.

1774   Maccoby, Eleanor E. and Carol N. Jacklin. *The Psychology of Sex Differences.* Stanford, CA: Stanford University Press, 1974.

1775   MacLean, Paul D. "New findings relevant to the evolution of psychosexual functions of the brain." In: *Sex Research, New Developments,* ed. by John Money, pp. 197–218. New York: Holt, Rinehart & Winston, 1965.

1776   Marwell, Gerald. "Why ascription? Parts of a more or less formal theory of the functions and dysfunctions of sex roles." *American Sociological Review* 40(4):445–455, Aug. 1975.

1777   Masica, Daniel N., John Money and Anke A.

Ehrhardt. "Fetal feminization and female gender identity in the testicular feminizing syndrome of androgen insensitivity." *Archives of Sexual Behavior* 1(2):131–142, 1971.

1778   Mathis, James L. "The development of sexual identification." *Southern Medical Journal* 59:1282–1286, Nov. 1966.

1779   Mendelsohn, Robert A. "Sex development and adolescence." *Counseling and Values* 17(4):222–227, Summer 1973.

1780   Mikesell, Richard H. and Lawrence G. Calhoun. "Sex-role and need for approval in adolescents." *Child Study Journal* 2(1):35–37, 1971.

1781   Miller, Jean Baker, ed. *Psychoanalysis and Women: Contributions to New Theory and Therapy.* New York: Brunner/Mazel, 1973.

1782   Miller, Shirley Matile. "Effects of maternal employment on sex role perception, interests, and self-esteem in kindergarten girls." *Developmental Psychology* 11(3):405–406, May 1975.

1783   Mitchell, Leslie Howard. *Dominance and femininity as factors in the sex role adjustment of parents and children.* (Thesis—University of California, Berkeley.) Ann Arbor, MI: University Microfilms, 1965. (Order #66-3660)

1784   Money, John. "Ablatio penis: normal male infant sex-reassigned as a girl." *Archives of Sexual Behavior* 4(1):65–71, Jan. 1975.

1785   _____. "Determinants of human gender identity/role." In: *Handbook of Sexology,* ed. by John Money and Herman Musaph, pp. 57–79. Amsterdam: Excerpta Medica, 1977.

1786   _____. "Developmental differentiation of femininity and masculinity compared." In: *Man and Civilization: The Potential of Women,* ed. by S.M. Farber and R.H.L. Wilson, pp. 51–65. New York: McGraw-Hill, 1963.

1787   _____. "Gender role, gender identity, core gender identity: usage and definition of terms." *Journal of the American Academy of Psychoanalysis* 1(4):391–402, 1973.

1788   _____. "Psychosexual development in man." In: *The Encyclopedia of Mental Health,* pp. 1678–1709. New York: Franklin Watts, 1963.

1789   _____. "The sex instinct and human eroticism." *Journal of Sex Research* 1(1):3–16, Mar. 1965.

1790   _____. "Sexology: behavioral, cultural hormonal, neurological, genetic, etc." *Journal of Sex Research* 9(1):3–10, Feb. 1973.

1791   Money, John and Anke A. Ehrhardt. *Man and Woman; Boy and Girl: The Differentiation and Dimorphism of Gender Identity from Conception to Maturity.* Baltimore: Johns Hopkins University Press, 1972.

1792   Money, John and Patricia Tucker. *Sexual Signatures; On Being a Man or a Woman.* Boston: Little, Brown, 1975.

1793   Munroe, Robert L. and Ruth Monroe. "Male pregnancy symptoms and cross-sex identity in three societies." *Journal of Social Psychology* 84(1):11–25, June 1971.

1794   Mussen, Paul Henry. "Long-term consequents of masculinity of interests in adolescence." *Journal of Consulting Psychology* 26(5):435–440, 1962.

1795   _____. "Some antecedents and consequents of masculine sex-typing in adolescent boys." *Psychological Monographs* 75(2):1–24, 1961.

1796   Myrick, Robert D. "The counselor-consultant and the effeminate boy." *Personnel & Guidance Journal* 48(5):355–361, 1970.

1797   Nebraska Symposium on Motivation, 1973. *Papers.* Ed. by James K. Cole and Richard Dienstbier. Lincoln: University of Nebraska Press, 1974.

1798   Neubauer, Peter B. "Early sexual differences and development." In: *Sexuality and Psychoanalysis,* ed. by Edward T. Adelson, pp. 97–103. New York: Brunner/Mazel, 1975.

1799   Norris, A.S. and W.C. Keettel. "Change of sex role during adolescence: a case study." *American Journal of Obstetrics and Gynecology* 84(6):719–721, Sept. 15, 1962.

1800   Paluszny, Maria. "Sexual identity and role in children. How do these develop?" *Clinical Pediatrics* 13(2):154–158, Feb. 1974.

1801   Parker, Seymour, Joseph Birat and Janet Smith. "Father absence and cross sex identity: the puberty rites controversy revisited." *American Ethnologist* 2(4):687–705, Nov. 1975.

1802   Perry, David G. and Louise C. Perry. "Observational learning in children: effects of sex of model and subjects sex role behavior." *Journal of Personality and Social Psychology* 31(6):1083–1088, June 1975.

1803   Petras, John W. *Sex: Male; Gender: Mascu-*

line; Readings in Male Sexuality. Port Washington, NY: Alfred, 1975.

1804 Pleck, J. and Jack Sawyer, eds. *Men and Masculinity.* Englewood Cliffs, NJ: Prentice-Hall, 1974.

1805 Price, Dorothy. "In vitro studies of differentiation of the reproductive tract." *Philosophical Transactions of the Royal Society of London (Biological Science)* 259:133–139, 1970.

1806 Rado, Sandor. "A critical examination of the concept of bisexuality." *Psychosomatic Medicine* 2(4):459–467, Oct. 1940.

1807 Ramey, Estelle R. "Sex hormones and executive ability." *Annals of the New York Academy of Science* 208:237–245, Mar. 15, 1973.

1808 Rashevsky, Nicholas. "Contributions to the theory of organismic sets: why are there only two sexes?" *Bulletin of Mathematical Biophysics* 32:293–301, June 1970.

1809 Reed, Max R. and W. Asbjornsen. "Experimental alteration of the It scale in the study of sex-role preference." *Perceptual and Motor Skills* 26(1):15–24, 1968.

1810 Reinisch, June M. "Fetal hormones, the brain, and human sex differences: a heuristic, integrative review of the recent literature." *Archives of Sexual Behavior* 3(1):51–90, Jan. 1974.

1811 Reiss, Ira L. "Learning premarital sex roles." In: *The Family System in America,* pp. 110–127. New York: Holt, Rinehart & Winston, 1971.

1812 Rekers, George A. "Stimulus control over sex-typed play in cross-gender identified boys." *Journal of Experimental Child Psychology* 20:136–148, 1975.

1813 Rosen, Alexander C. "Brief report of MMPI characteristics of sexual deviation." *Psychological Reports* 35:73–74, 1974.

1814 Rosenberg, B.G. and Brian Sutton-Smith. *Sex and Identity.* New York: Holt, Rinehart & Winston, 1972.

1815 Ross, Michael W. "Relationship between sex role and sex orientation in homosexual men." *New Zealand Psychologist* 4(1):25–29, Apr. 1975.

1816 Rutherford, Eldred Eugene. *Familial antecedents of sex role development in young children.* (Thesis—University of California, Berkeley.) Ann Arbor, MI: University Microfilms, 1964. (Order #64-13,090)

1817 Rutter, Michael "Normal psychosexual development." *Journal of Child Psychology and Psychiatry* 11:259–283, 1971.

1818 Ryle, A. and M. Lunghi. "Parental and sex-role identification of students measured with a repertory grid technique." *British Journal of Social and Clinical Psychology* 11:149–161, June 1972.

1819 Sagarin, Edward. "Sex rearing and sexual orientation: the reconciliation of apparently contradictory data." *Journal of Sex Research* 11(4):329–334, Nov. 1975.

1820 Sannito, Thomas et al. "A test of female sex identification: the Thorne femininity study." *Journal of Clinical Psychology* 28(4):531–539, Oct. 1972.

1821 Schonfeld, William A. "Body-image disturbances in adolescents with inappropriate sexual development." *American Journal of Orthopsychiatry* 34(3):493–502, Apr. 1964.

1822 Searl, M.N. "A note on the relation between physical and psychical differences in boys and girls." *International Journal of Psycho-Analysis* 19(1):50–62, Jan. 1938.

1823 Seidman, Jerome M. *The Adolescent—A Book of Readings.* New York: Holt, Rinehart & Winston, 1960.

1824 Shainess, Natalie. "The formation of gender identity." *Journal of Sex Research* 5(2):75–85, May 1969.

1825 Shemberg, K.M. and D.B. Leventhal. "Masculinity-femininity and need for social approval." *Journal of Projective Techniques and Personality Assessment* 32(6):575–577, 1968.

1826 Sher, Monroe A. and Leonard M. Lansky. "The It scale for children: effects of variations in the sex-specificity of the It figure." *Merrill-Palmer Quarterly* 14(4):322–330, 1968.

1827 Shuttleworth, Frank Kayley. "A biosocial and developmental theory of male and female sexuality." *Marriage and Family Living* 21(2):163–170, May 1959.

1828 Singer, June. *Androgyny: Toward a New Theory of Sexuality.* Garden City, NY: Anchor, 1976.

1829 Staples, Robert. "Male-female sexual variations: functions of biology or culture." *Journal of Sex Research* 9(1):11–20, Feb. 1973.

1830 Steinmann, Anne and Anthony P. Jurich.

"The effects of a sex education course on the sex role perceptions of junior high school students." *Family Coordinator* 24(1):27–31, Jan. 1975.

1831 Stoller, Robert J. *Sex and Gender; On the Development of Masculinity and Femininity.* New York: Science House, 1968.

1832 Stranan, Robert F. "Remarks on Bem's measurement of psychological androgyny: alternative methods and a supplementary analysis." *Journal of Consulting and Clinical Psychology* 43(4):568–571, Aug. 1975.

1833 Strodtbeck, Fred L. and Paul G. Creelan. "The interaction linkage between family size, intelligence, and sex-role identity." *Journal of Marriage and the Family* 30(2):301–307, May 1968.

1834 Sullivan, Kathleen A. "Feminine identity development of the adolescent girl: a review of literature." *Maternal-Child Nursing Journal* 2(3):221–228, Fall 1973.

1835 Summers, Darryl L. and Donald W. Felker. "Use of the It scale for children in assessing the sex-role preference in pre-school Negro children." *Developmental Psychology* 2(3):330–334, May 1970.

1836 Suomi, S.J., G.P. Sackett and Harry F. Harlow. "Development of sex preference in rhesus monkeys." *Developmental Psychology* 3(3):326–336, Nov. 1970.

1837 Thomas, Paula Jean. *Sub-cultural differences in sex role preference patterns.* (Thesis—Western Reserve University.) Ann Arbor, MI: University Microfilms, 1965. (Order #66-3046)

1838 Tobach, Ethel. "Some evolutionary aspects of human gender." *American Journal of Orthopsychiatry* 41(5):710–715, Oct. 1971.

1839 Tolor, Alexander. "Children's figure drawings and changing attitudes toward sex roles." *Psychological Reports* 34(2):343–349, Apr. 1974.

1840 Troiden, Richard R. "Androgyny: a neglected dimension of homosexuality." Paper presented at the North Central Sociological Association, Columbus, OH, May 4–6, 1975, 21p.

1841 Uddenberg, Nils. "Mother-father and daughter-male relationships: a comparison." *Archives of Sexual Behavior* 5(1):69–79, Jan. 1976.

1842 Urberg, Kathryn A. and Gisela Labouvie-Uief. "Conceptualizations of sex roles: a life span developmental study." *Developmental Psychology* 12(1):15–23, Jan. 1976.

1843 Vroegh, Karen. "Lack of sex-role differentiation in preschoolers' figure drawings." *Journal of Projective Techniques & Personality Assessment* 34(1):83–40, 1970.

1844 _____. "Masculinity and femininity in the preschool years." *Child Development* 39(4):1253–1257, 1968.

1845 Wahrman, Ralph and Meredith D. Pugh. "Sex, non-conformity and influence." *Sociometry* 37(1):137–147, Mar. 1974.

1846 Walshok, Mary Lindenstein. *The social correlates and sexual consequences of variations in gender role orientation: a national study of college students.* (Thesis—Indiana University.) Ann Arbor, MI: University Microfilms, 1969. (Order #70-7515)

1847 Walzer, Stanley et al. "Genetics, cytogenetics, sex reversal and behavior." In: *Handbook of Sexology,* ed. by John Money and Herman Musaph, pp. 87–173. Amsterdam: Excerpta Medica, 1977.

1848 Westman, Jack C. "Traumatic phallic amputation during infancy." *Archives of Sexual Behavior* 4(1):53–63, Jan. 1975.

1849 Whitam, Frederick L. "Childhood indicators of male homosexuality." *Archives of Sexual Behavior* 6(2):89–96, Mar. 1977.

1850 Williams, John E. "Awareness and expression of sex stereotypes in young children." *Developmental Psychology* 11(5):635–642, Sept. 1975.

1851 Williams, Juanita H. *Psychology of Women: Behavior in a Biosocial Context.* New York: W.W. Norton, 1977.

1852 Wiseman, Jacqueline P., ed. *The Social Psychology of Sex.* New York: Harper & Row, 1976.

1853 Wright, Derek. "A sociological portrait: sex differences." *New Society* 18(474):825–827, Oct. 28, 1971.

1854 Yachnes, Eleanor. "Some mythical aspects of masculinity." *Medical Aspects of Human Sexuality* 7(9):200–210, Sept. 1973.

1855 Yorburg, Betty. *Sexual Identity; Sex Roles and Social Change.* New York: Wiley, 1974.

1856 Young, George H. and Claud A. Bramblett. "Gender and environment as determinants of behavior in infant common baboons (Papio cynocephalus)." *Archives of Sexual Behavior* 6(5):365–385, Sept. 1977.

1857 Zuger, Bernard. "Sex identity: nature or

nurture?" *Medical World News (Psychiatry):* 33–34, 1973.

Hormones and Sex Behavior

ENCYCLOPEDIA

1858   Money, John and Herman Musaph, eds. *Handbook of Sexology.* Amsterdam: Excerpta Medica, 1977.

ENDOCRINOLOGY

1859   Birnbaum, Michael D. and Bernard A. Eskin. "Psychosexual aspects of endocrine disorders." *Medical Aspects of Human Sexuality* 7(1):134–149, Jan. 1973.

1860   *Brain and Behavior. Vol. 3: The Brain and Gonadal Function.* Proceedings of the Third Conference on Brain and Behavior, UCLA, 1963. UCLA Forum in Medical Sciences, no. 3. Berkeley/Los Angeles: University of California Press, 1966.

1861   Burrows, Harold. *Biological Actions of Sex Hormones.* 2nd ed. Cambridge, Eng.: Cambridge University Press, 1949.

1862   Diamond, Milton, ed. *Perspectives in Reproduction and Sexual Behavior.* Bloomington: Indiana University Press, 1968.

1863   Dingman, Joseph F. "Endocrine aspects of impotence." *Medical Aspects of Human Sexuality* 3(4):57–66, Apr. 1969.

1864   "Endokrinologischer wettstreit: trotz wissensexplosion eine fülle ofener fragen." *Sexualmedizin* 5(10):736–739, Oct. 1976.

1865   Lief, Harold I., Joseph F. Dingman and Melvin P. Bishop. "Psychoendocrinologic studies in a male with cyclic changes in sexuality." *Psychosomatic Medicine* 24(4):357–368, July/Aug. 1962.

1866   Michael, R.P. and Doris Zumpe. "Environmental and endocrine factors influencing annual changes in sexual potency in primates." *Psychoneuroendocrinology* 1(3):303–313, 1976.

1867   Pleissner, K. "Anatomische und physiologische grundlagen weiblicher sexualstörungen." *Zeitschrift für Ärztliche Fortbildung* 65(13):682–686, July 1, 1971.

1868   Young, William C., ed. *Sex and Internal Secretions.* 3rd ed. Baltimore: Williams & Wilkins, 1961.

SEX HORMONES

1869   Barden, Tom P. "The role of prostaglandins in reproductive physiology." *Ohio State Medical Journal* 66:1008–1012, Oct. 1970.

1870   Bardwick, Judith M. "The sex hormones, the central nervous system and affect variability in humans." In: *Women in Therapy,* ed. by V. Franks and V. Burtle, pp. 27–50. New York: Brunner/Mazel, 1974.

1871   Boyar, Robert M. et al. "Twenty-four hour patterns of plasma luteinizing hormone and follicle-stimulating hormone in sexual precocity." *New England Journal of Medicine* 289:282–286, Aug. 9, 1973.

1872   Brotherton, Janet and A.W. Harcus. "The effect of oral cyproterone acetate on urinary FSH and LH levels in adult males being treated for hypersexuality." *Journal of Reproduction and Fertility* 33(2):356–357, May 1973.

1873   Carlson, Lars A., Lars-Göran Ekelund and Lars Orö. "Clinical, metabolic and cardiovascular effects of different prostaglandins in man." *Acta Medica Scandinavica* 188:553–559, Dec. 1970.

1874   Carter, Carol Sue, ed. *Hormones and Sexual Behavior.* Benchmark Papers in Animal Behavior, v. 1. Stroudsburg, PA: Dowden, Hutchinson & Ross, 1974.

1875   Charney, Charles W. "Castration in the male." *Medical Aspects of Human Sexuality* 4(5):80–83, May 1970.

1876   Cooper, Alan J. and A.A.A. Ismail. "A pilot study of Mesterolone in impotence." *Psychopharmacologia* 26:379–386, 1972.

1877   Curtis, R.F. et al. "Identification of primate sexual pheromones and the properties of synthetic attractants." *Nature* 232(5310):396–398, Aug. 6, 1971.

1878   Davidson, Julian M. et al. "Relative thresholds of behavioral and somatic responses to estrogen." *Physiology and Behavior* 3:227–229, 1968.

1879   Diamond, Milton. "Vaginal stimulation and progesterone in relation to pregnancy and parturition." *Biology of Reproduction* 6(2):281–287, Apr. 1972.

1880   Dorfman, Ralph I., Enrico Forchielli and Marcel Gut. "Androgen biosynthesis and related studies." *Recent Progress in Hormone Research* 19:251–273, 1973.

1881   Gupta, Derek. "Inhärente tendenz zur

weiblichkeit; hormone und die kontrolle der männlichen sexualfunktion." *Sexualmedizin* 3(2):68–74, Feb. 1974.

1882 Kupperman, Herbert S. "Sex hormones." In: *Encyclopedia of Sexual Behavior,* ed. by Albert Ellis and Albert Abarbanel, pp. 494–502. New York: Hawthorne Books, 1967.

1883 Kyger, Kent and Warren W. Webb. "Progesterone levels and psychological state in normal women." *American Journal of Obstetrics and Gynecology* 113:759–762, July 15, 1972.

1884 Levine, Lenore S. et al. "Androgen production in boys with sexual precocity and congenital adrenal hyperplasia." *Metabolism* 21(5):457–464, May 1972.

1885 Lincoln, G.A. "Luteinising hormone and testosterone in man." *Nature* 252(5480):232–233, Nov. 15, 1974.

1886 Michael, R.P. and Doris Zumpe. "Environmental and endocrine factors influencing annual changes in sexual potency in primates." *Psychoneuroendocrinology* 1(3):303–313, 1976.

1887 "Potentiale der Männlichkeit." *Sexualmedizin* 5(5):366–372, May 1976.

1888 Schiavi, R.C. et al. "Luteinizing hormone and testosterone during nocturnal sleep: relation to penile tumescent cycles." *Archives of Sexual Behavior* 6(2):97–104, Mar. 1977.

1889 Seneca, Harry and Edward Henderson. "Human spermhormone." *Journal of the American Geriatrics Society* 22(4):145–148, Apr. 1974.

1890 Sokolov, Jacque J., Ronald T. Harris and Michael R. Hecker. "Isolation of substances from human vaginal secretions previously shown to be sex attractant pheromones in higher primates." *Archives of Sexual Behavior* 5(4):269–274, July 1976.

1891 Tourney, Garfield and Lon M. Hatfield. "Plasma androgens in male schizophrenics." *Archives of General Psychiatry* 27:53–55, Dec. 1972.

1892 Weaver, Robert G. "Scrotum and testes." *Medical Aspects of Human Sexuality* 4(10):124–143, Oct. 1970.

1893 Wood, Clive. "Hormones after vasectomy." *British Journal of Sexual Medicine* 3(4):13, Aug. 1976.

HORMONES AND SEX DIFFERENTIATION

1894 Beach, Frank A. "Hormonal modification of sexually dimorphic behavior." *Psychoneuroendocrinology* 1(1):3–23, July 1975.

1895 Diamond, Milton. "Human sexual development: biological foundations for social development." In: *Human Sexuality in Four Perspectives,* ed. by Frank A. Beach, pp. 22–61. Baltimore: Johns Hopkins University Press, 1977.

1896 Dörner, Günter. *Hormones and Brain Differentiation.* New York: Elsevier, 1976.

1897 Ehrhardt, Anke A. "Androgens in prenatal development; behavior changes in nonhuman primates and men." *Advances in the Biosciences* 13:153–162, Jan. 1974.

1898 _____. "Maternalism in fetal hormonal and related syndromes." In: *Contemporary Sexual Behavior: Critical Issues in the 1970's,* ed. by Joseph Zubin and John Money, pp. 99–115. Baltimore: Johns Hopkins University Press, 1973.

1899 _____. *Zur Wirkung fötaler hormone auf Intelligenz und geschlechtsspezifisches Verhalten.* (Dissertation—Universität Düsseldorf.) Düsseldorf: Gahmig-Druck, 1969.

1900 Erwin, J. and Brian Anderson. "Agonistic behavior of pregnant female monkeys (Macaca nemestrina): possible influences of fetal gonadal hormones." *Psychological Reports* 36(3):699–702, June 1975.

1901 Hohlweg, W. "Die bedeutung der von fötalen gonaden sezernierten sexualhormone für die ausbildung des geschlechtsspezifischen genitalapparates und für die determination eines heterosexuellen oder homosexuellen sexualverhaltens." *Wiener Medizinische Wochenschrift* 121(51/52):927–932, Dec. 24, 1971.

1902 Hutt, Corinne. "Sex differences in human development." *Human Development* 15(3):153–170, 1972.

1903 Hyyppä, Markku. "The role of the hypothalamus in hormonal sex differentiation." *Revue Romaine de Physiologie* 5(4):289–299, 1968.

1904 Money, John and Anke A. Ehrhardt. "Fetal hormones and the brain: effect on sexual dimorphism of behavior—a review." *Archives of Sexual Behavior* 1(3):241–262, 1971.

1905 _____. "Gender dimorphic behavior and fetal sex hormones." *Recent Progress in Hormone Research* 28:735–754, 1972.

1906 _____. *Man & Woman: Boy & Girl: The Differentiation and Dimorphism of Gender Identi-*

ty from Conception to Maturity. Baltimore: Johns Hopkins University Press, 1972.

1907   Pinch, Lewis, Thomas Aceto and Heino F. Meyer-Bahlburg. "Cryptorchidism: a pediatric review." *Urologic Clinics of North America* 1(3):573–592, Oct. 1974.

1908   Reinisch, June M. "Effects of prenatal hormone exposure on psychological development in humans and animals: with a note on the state of the field." In: *Hormones, Behavior and Psychopathology,* ed. by Edward J. Sachar, pp. 69–94. New York: Raven Press, 1976.

1909   _____. "Fetal hormones, the brain, and human sex differences: a heuristic, integrative review of the recent literature." *Archives of Sexual Behavior* 3(1):51–90, Jan. 1974.

1910   Reinisch, June M. and William G. Karow. "Prenatal exposure to synthetic progestins and estrogens: effects on human development." *Archives of Sexual Behavior* 6(4):257–288, July 1977.

1911   Walker, Paul A. and John Money. "Prenatal androgenization of females." *Hormones* 3:119–128, 1972.

1912   Ward, Ingeborg L. "Prenatal stress feminizes and demasculinizes the behavior of males." *Science* 175:82–84, Jan. 7, 1972.

1913   Yalom, Irvin D., Richard Green and Norman Fisk. "Prenatal exposure to female hormones." *Archives of General Psychiatry* 28:554–561, Apr. 1973.

PUBERTY

1914   Adams, Paul L. "Delayed sexual maturation in boys." *Medical Aspects of Human Sexuality* 6(4):34–63, Apr. 1972.

1915   Aldama Magnet, Javier De et al. "Patología puberal femenina." *Sexualmedica* (13):57–63, Feb. 1975.

1916   Birnbaum, Michael D. and Bernard A. Eskin. "Psychosexual aspects of endocrine disorders." *Medical Aspects of Human Sexuality* 7(1):134–149, Jan. 1973.

1917   Ehrhardt, Anke A. and Heino F.L. Meyer-Bahlburg. "Psychological correlates of abnormal pubertal development." *Clinics in Endocrinology and Metabolism* 4(1):207–221, Mar. 1975.

1918   Israel, Spencer Leon. "Normal puberty and adolescence." *Annals of the New York Academy of Sciences* 142(3):773–778, 1967.

1919   Knorr, Deitrich et al. "Plasma testosterone in male puberty." *Endocrinologica* 75:181–194, 1974.

1920   Krause, Walter. "Die pubertas tarde des knaben; lokalisation der störung mit hilfe klinisch-endokriner tests." *Sexualmedizin* 5(11):778–781, Nov. 1976.

1921   Michael, R.P. and Margo Wilson. "Changes in the sexual behavior of male rhesus monkeys (M. mulatta) at puberty. Comparisons with the behavior of adults." *Folia Primatologica* 19:384–403, May 1973.

1922   Root, Allen W. "Endocrinology of puberty II. Aberrations of sexual maturation." *Journal of Pediatrics* 83(2):187–200, Aug. 1973.

1923   Schonfeld, William A. "Body-image disturbances in adolescents with inappropriate sexual development." *American Journal of Orthopsychiatry* 34(3):493–502, Apr. 1964.

1924   Teja, Jagdish S. "Periodic psychosis of puberty: a longitudinal case study." *Journal of Nervous and Mental Disease* 162(1):52–57, Jan. 1976.

MENSTRUAL CYCLE

1925   Auger, Jeanine Ann Roose. *A psychophysiological study of the normal menstrual cycle and of some possible effects of oral contraceptives.* (Dissertation—University of California, Los Angeles.) Ann Arbor, MI: University Microfilms, 1967. (Order #67-17,356)

1926   Corfman, Philip A. "Coordinated studies of the effects of oral contraceptives." *Contraception* 9(2):109–122, Feb. 1974.

1927   Diamond, Milton, Leonard Diamond and Marian Mast. "Visual sensitivity and sexual arousal levels during the menstrual cycle." *Journal of Nervous and Mental Disease* 155(3):170–176, 1972.

1928   Luschen, Mary E. and David M. Pierce. "Effect of the menstrual cycle on mood and sexual arousability." *Journal of Sex Research* 8(1):41–47, Feb. 1972.

1929   Melges, Frederick T. and David A. Hamburg. "Psychological effects of hormonal changes in women." In: *Human Sexuality in Four Perspectives,* ed. by Frank A. Beach, pp. 269–295. Baltimore: Johns Hopkins University Press, 1977.

1930   Mitani, Yasushi. "The effect of the atomic bomb on human menstruation." *International Journal of Fertility* 1(3):281–292, Apr./June 1956.

1931   Moos, Rudolf H. et al. "Fluctuations in

symptoms and moods during the menstrual cycle." *Journal of Psychosomatic Research* 13(1):37–44, 1969.

1932 Persky, Harold et al. "Reproductive hormone levels and sexual behavior of young couples during the menstrual cycle." Paper presented at International Congress of Sexology, Montreal, Canada, Oct. 1976. 30p.

1933 "Roundtable: sex and the menstrual cycle." *Medical Aspects of Human Sexuality* 2(7):12–17, July 1968.

1934 Singer, Irving and Josephine Singer. "Periodicity of sexual desire in relation to time of ovulation in women." *Journal of Biosocial Science* 4:471–481, 1972.

1935 Wineman, E.W. "Autonomic balance changes during the human menstrual cycle." *Psychophysiology* 8(1):1–6, Jan. 1971.

CLIMACTERIC

1936 Geller, Jack. "The role of sex hormones in problems of the mature years and beyond." *Journal of the American Geriatrics Society* 17(9):861–873, 1969.

1937 Greenblatt, Robert B., Moshe Oettinger and Clorinda S.S. Bohler. "Estrogen-androgen levels in aging men and women: therapeutic considerations." *Journal of the American Geriatrics Society* 24(4):173–178, 1976.

1938 McKinlay, Sonja M. and John B. McKinlay. "Selected studies of the menopause." *Journal of Biosocial Science* 5(4):533–555, Oct. 1973.

1939 Sturgis, Somers H. "Hormone therapy in the menopause: indications and contraindications." *Medical Aspects of Human Sexuality* 3(5):69–75, May 1969.

HORMONES AND BEHAVIOR

1940 Beach, Frank A. "Behavioral endocrinology: an emerging discipline." *American Scientist* 63(2):178–187, Mar./Apr. 1975.

1941 Beumont, Pierre Joseph Victor. "Behavioural changes after treatment with testosterone: case report." *Psychological Medicine* 2(1):70–72, Feb. 1972.

1942 Beumont, Pierre Joseph Victor and C.J. Beardwood. "The occurrence of the syndrome of anorexia nervosa in male subjects." *Psychological Medicine* 2(3):216–231, Aug. 1972.

1943 Daniels, George E. "Approaches to a bio-logical basis of human behavior." *Diseases of the Nervous System* 32(4):227–240, Apr. 1971.

1944 Dotson, Louis E., Leon S. Robertson and Barry Tuchfeld. "Plasma alcohol, smoking, hormone concentrations and self-reported aggression: a study in a social-drinking situation." *Journal of Studies on Alcohol* 36(5):578–586, May 1975.

1945 Friedman, Richard C., R.M. Richart and R.L. Vande Wiele, eds. *Sex Differences in Behavior.* New York: Wiley, 1974.

1946 Gray, Jeffrey A. "Sex differences in emotional behaviour in mammals including man: endocrine bases." *Acta Psychologica* 35(1):29–46, Jan. 1971.

1947 Joslyn, Wallace Danforth. "Androgen-induced social dominance in infant female rhesus monkeys." *Journal of Child Psychology and Psychiatry and Allied Disciplines* 14(2):137–145, June 1973.

1948 Kling, Arthur, Gene Borowitz and Rosalind D. Cartwright. "Plasma levels of 17-Hydroxy-corticosteroids during sexual arousal in man." *Journal of Psychosomatic Research* 16:215–221, 1972.

1949 Levine, Seymour, ed. *Hormones and Behavior.* New York: Academic Press, 1972.

1950 Lunde, Donald T. and David A. Hamburg. "Techniques for assessing the effects of sex hormones on affect, arousal, and aggression in humans." *Recent Progress in Hormone Research* 28:627–663, 1972.

1951 Meyer-Bahlburg, Heino F.L. et al. "Aggressiveness and testosterone measures in man." *Psychosomatic Medicine* 36(3):269–274, May/June 1974.

1952 Rose, Robert M. and John W. Holaday. "Plasma testosterone, dominance rank and aggressive behaviour in male rhesus monkeys." *Nature* 231(5302):366–368, June 11, 1971.

HORMONES AND SEX BEHAVIOR

1953 Bahr, Robert. *The Virility Factor: Masculinity through Testosterone, the Male Sex Hormone.* New York: Putnam, 1976.

1954 Barclay, Andrew M. "Biopsychological perspectives on sexuality." In: *Sexuality: a Search for Perspective,* ed. by Donald L. Grummon and Andrew M. Barclay, pp. 54–66. New York: Van Nostrand Reinhold, 1971.

1955 Beach, Frank A. "Hormonal control of sex-related behavior." In: *Human Sexuality in Four Perspectives,* ed. by Frank A. Beach, pp. 247–267. Baltimore: Johns Hopkins University Press, 1977.

1956 Benkert, Otto et al. "Sexual impotence: studies of the hypothalamic-pituitary-thyroid axis and the effect of oral thyrotropin-releasing factor." *Archives of Sexual Behavior* 5(4):275–281, July 1976.

1957 Cherlin, Richard S. and Gerald B. Appel. "Brief guide to office counseling: sexual function in Addison's disease." *Medical Aspects of Human Sexuality* 11(3):129–130, Mar. 1977.

1958 Christensen, L.W. and Lynwood G. Clemens. "Possible involvement of cyclic AMP in regulation of masculine sexual behaviour by testosterone." *Journal of Endocrinology* 61:153–161, 1974.

1959 Connell, Elizabeth B. et al. *Hormones, Sex and Happiness.* Chicago: Cowles, 1971.

1960 Cooper, Alan J. "The place of testosterone in male sexuality." *British Journal of Sexual Medicine* 1(6):6–10, Aug./Sept. 1974.

1961 Davidson, Julian M. "Hormones and sexual behavior in the male." *Hospital Practice* 10(9):126–137, Sept. 1975.

1962 Dmowski, W. Paul, Manuel Luna and Antonio Scommegna. "Hormonal aspects of female sexual response." *Medical Aspects of Human Sexuality* 8(6):92–113, June 1974.

1963 Eaton, G. Gray and John A. Resko. "Ovarian hormones and sexual behavior in Macaca nemestrina." *Journal of Comparative and Physiological Psychology* 86(5):919–925, May 1974.

1964 Falik, Leon A. "Sexuality and endocrine glands: embryonic sex differentiation." *Journal of Sex Research* 12(2):124–134, May 1976.

1965 Felstein, Ivor. "Case history." *British Journal of Sexual Medicine* 3(2):38, Apr. 1976.

1966 Ferin, J. and P. Veldekens. "Déterminisme hormonal du désir sexuel chez la femme." In: Congrès International de Sexologie Médicale, Paris, 1974, *Papers,* pp. 45–52.

1967 Fox, Cyril A. "Physical and hormonal mechanisms of human coitus with special reference to the sexual climax." Unpub. doctoral dissertation, University of Cambridge (England), 1970.

1968 Gessa, Gian Luigi. "Role of brain monoamines in male sexual behavior." *Life Sciences* 14(3):425–436, Feb. 1974.

1969 Gessa, Gian Luigi and A. Tagliamonte. "Evidence that brain serotonin inhibits and that brain dopamine stimulates copulatory behavior in males." In: Congrès International de Sexologie Médicale, Paris, 1974, *Papers,* pp. 501–502.

1970 Green, Richard. "Biologic studies." In: *Sexual Identity Conflict in Children and Adults,* pp. 29–41. New York: Basic Books, 1974.

1971 Greenblatt, Robert B. "Psychogenic and endocrine aspects of sexual behavior." *Osteopathic Physician* 41(11):102 passim, Nov. 1974.

1972 Hart, Benjamin L. "Gonadal androgen and sociosexual behavior of male mammals: a comparative analysis." *Psychological Bulletin* 81(7):383–400, July 1974.

1973 Hupin, P. and Jean-François Servais. "Comparaison des effets inhibiteurs de la methyloestrénolone et du 6-alpha-methyl-lynestrénol sur la libido de l'homme normal." *Acta Neurologica et Psychiatrica Belgica* 68(8):407–415, 1968.

1974 Janowsky, David S., William E. Fann and John M. Davis. "Monoamines and ovarian hormone-linked sexual and emotional changes: a review." *Archives of Sexual Behavior* 1(3):205–218, 1971.

1975 Kane, Francis J., Morris A. Lipton and John A. Ewing. "Hormonal influences in female sexual response." *Archives of General Psychiatry* 20(2):202–209, Feb. 1969.

1976 Kaplan, Helen Singer. "Hormones and sex." In: *The New Sex Therapy,* pp. 46–61. New York: Brunner/Mazel, 1974.

1977 Kennedy, B.J. "Effect of massive doses of sex hormones on libido." *Medical Aspects of Human Sexuality* 7(3):67–78, Mar. 1973.

1978 Kinsey, Alfred C. et al. "Hormonal factors in sexual response." In: *Sexual Behavior in the Human Female,* pp. 714–761. Philadelphia: W.B. Saunders, 1953.

1979 Kraemer, Helena et al. "Orgasmic frequency and plasma testosterone levels in normal human males." *Archives of Sexual Behavior* 5(2):125–132, Mar. 1976.

1980 Legros, J.J. "Influence des hormones sexuelles sur le comportement humain." *Revue Médicale de Liège* 29(3):65–72, Feb. 1974.

1981 Legros, J.J. et al. "FSH, LH and testosterone blood level in patients with psychogenic impotence." *Endocrinologia Experimentalis* 7:59–63, 1973.

1982 Levine, Seymour. "Sexual motivation." In: *The Chemistry of Mood, Motivation, and Memory,* ed. by J.L. McGaugh. New York: Plenum, 1972.

1983 Lunde, Donald T. "Sex hormones, mood, and behavior (discussion follows)." In: *Sexuality and Psychoanalysis,* ed. by Edward T. Adelson, pp. 13–35. New York: Brunner/Mazel, 1975.

1984 Luttge, William G. "The role of gonadal hormones in the sexual behavior of the rhesus monkey and human: a literature survey." *Archives of Sexual Behavior* 1(1):61–88, 1971.

1985 Melges, Frederick T. and David A. Hamburg. "Psychological effects of hormonal changes in women." In: *Human Sexuality in Four Perspectives,* ed. by Frank A. Beach, pp. 269–295. Baltimore: Johns Hopkins University Press, 1977.

1986 Meuser, Wolfgang and Eberhard Nieschlag. "Stimme und hormone." *Sexualmedizin* 6(7):560–566, July 1977.

1987 Meyer-Bahlburg, Heino F.L. "Sex hormones and male homosexuality in comparative perspective." *Archives of Sexual Behavior* 6(4):297–325, July 1977. (A comprehensive review of the question. Includes a bibliography with 94 citations.)

1988 Money, John and Tom Mazur. "Liebe geht durch die nase; sexuelle stimulation durch vaginale pheromone." *Sexualmedizin* 3(6):304, June 1974.

1989 Pirke, Karl M. "Endokrinologie der sexuellen reaktion." *Sexualmedizin* 6(1):40–42, Jan. 1977.

1990 Pirke, Karl M., Götz Kockott and Franz Dittmar. "Psychosexual stimulation and plasma testosterone in man." *Archives of Sexual Behavior* 3(6):577–584, Nov. 1974.

1991 Raboch, Jan and L. Stárka. "Coital activity of men and the levels of plasmatic testosterone." *Journal of Sex Research* 8(3):219–224, Aug. 1972.

1992 Rada, Richard T., Donald Richard Laws and Robert Kellner. "Plasma testosterone levels in the rapist." *Psychosomatic Medicine* 30(4):257–268, July/Aug. 1976.

1993 Reichlin, Seymour. "Relationship of the pituitary gland to human sexual behavior." *Medical Aspects of Human Sexuality* 5(2):146–154, Feb. 1971.

1994 Sandler, Merton and G.L. Gessa, eds. *Sexual Behavior: Pharmacology and Biochemistry.* New York: Raven Press, 1975.

1995 Schiavi, R.C. and Daniel White. "Androgens and male sexual function: a review of human studies." *Journal of Sex and Marital Therapy* 2(3):214–228, Fall 1976.

1996 Schmidt, Gunter. "Sexuelle motivation und kontrolle; zur manipulierbarkeit sexueller lernprozesse." *Sexualmedizin* 3(2):60–65, Feb. 1974.

1997 Selenkow, Herbert A. "Thyroid hormones and human reproduction." *Medical Aspects of Human Sexuality* 2(9):26–36, Sept. 1968.

1998 Signoret, J.P. "Hormones et comportement sexuel des mammifères." In: Congrès International de Sexologie Médicale, Paris, 1974, *Papers,* pp. 17–44.

1999 Signoret, J.P. and J.C. Thiery. "Bases neurophysiologiques et endocriniennes de l'activité sexuelle." *Le Concours Médical, Paris* 97(1):79–94, Jan. 4, 1975.

2000 Soulairac, André and Marie-Louise Soulairac. "Rôle de l'hypothalamus dans la sexualité des mammifères." In: Congrès International de Sexologie Médicale, Paris, 1974, *Papers,* pp. 1–16.

2001 Spitz, Cathy J., Alice R. Gold and David B. Adams. "Cognitive and hormonal factors affecting coital frequency." *Archives of Sexual Behavior* 4(3):249–263, May 1975.

Transexualism

2002 Benjamin, Harry. *The Transsexual Phenomenon.* New York: Julian Press, 1966. (Paperback ed.: Warner Paperback Library.)

2003 Driscoll, James Patrick. "The transsexuals." Unpub. master's thesis, San Francisco State College, 1969.

2004 Erickson Educational Foundation. *Counseling the Transsexual; Guidelines for Transsexuals; Information on Transsexualism for Law Enforcement Officers; Medical Management of the Transsexual; Religious Aspects of Transsexualism.* (Pamphlets, avail. from the Janus Information Facility, University of Texas Medical Branch, Galveston, TX 77550.)

2005 Feinbloom, Deborah H. *Transvestites &*

Transsexuals; Mixed Views. New York: Delacorte, 1976.

2006 Green, Richard. Sexual Identity Conflict in Children and Adults. New York: Basic Books, 1974.

2007 Jones, Clinton R. The Way Of a Transsexual: The Hardest Decisions. (A Confide Interview Cassette.) Tappan, NY: Confide-Personal Counseling Services, 1975.

2008 Kando, Thomas. Sex Change; The Achievement of Gender Identity among Feminized Transsexuals. Springfield, IL: Charles C. Thomas, 1973.

2009 MacDonald Allen, D.G. The Janus Sex: The Androgynous Challenge. Hicksville, NY: Exposition, 1975.

2010 Money, John and Patricia Tucker. Sexual Signatures: On Being a Man or a Woman. Boston: Little, Brown, 1975.

2011 Stoller, Robert J. Sex and Gender; On the Development of Masculinity and Femininity. New York: Science House, 1968.

2012 Sulcov, Mark B. "Transsexualism: its social reality." Unpub. doctoral dissertation, Indiana University, 1973.

2013 Wålinder, Jan. Transsexualism; A Study of Forty-three Cases. Reports from the Psychiatric Research Centre, St. Jörgen's Hospital, University of Göteborg, Sweden, 2. Göteborg: Akademiförlaget-Gumperts, 1967.

COLLECTIONS

2014 "Gender." Journal of Sex Research 5(2):whole issue, May 1969.

2015 Green, Richard and John Money, eds. Transsexualism and Sex Reassignment. Baltimore: Johns Hopkins University Press, 1969.

2016 Laub, Donald R. and Patrick Gandy, eds. Proceedings of the Second Interdisciplinary Symposium on Gender Dysphoria Syndrome (Stanford University School of Medicine, Feb. 2-4, 1973.) Stanford, CA: Division of Reconstructive and Rehabilitation Surgery, Stanford University Medical Center.

2017 Meyer, Jon K., ed. "Symposium on Sex Assignment and Reassignment: Intersex and Gender Identity Disorders." Clinics in Plastic Surgery 1(2):whole issue, Apr. 1974.

2018 "Operations for change of sex." Journal of Nervous and Mental Disease 147(5):whole issue, Nov. 1968.

2019 "Selected proceedings of the First International Congress on Gender Identity, London, England, July 1969." Archives of Sexual Behavior 1(2):145-173, 1971.

2020 "Transvestism—Transsexualism." Journal of Sex Research 3(2):whole issue, May 1967.

TRANSEXUALISM RESEARCH

2021 Barr, Ronald F. "Responses to erotic stimuli of transsexual and homosexual males." British Journal of Psychiatry 123(576):579-585, Nov. 1973.

2022 Finney, Joseph C. et al. "A study of transsexuals seeking gender reassignment." American Journal of Psychiatry 132(9):962-964, Sept. 1975.

2023 Hamburger, Christian. "The desire for change of sex as shown by personal letters from 465 men and women." Acta Endocrinologica 14(4):361-375, 1953.

2024 Hoenig, J. and J.C. Kenna. "The prevalence of transsexualism in England and Wales." British Journal of Psychiatry 124(579):181-190, Feb. 1974.

2025 Kando, Thomas. "Passing and stigma management: the case of the transsexual (a comparison of males, females, and transsexuals)." Sociological Quarterly 13(4):475-483, Fall 1972.

2026 _____. "Role strain: a comparison of males, females, and transsexuals." Journal of Marriage and the Family 34(3):459-464, Aug. 1972.

2027 Krippner, Stanley, Harry Benjamin and Virginia Allen. "Case History Data from 392 Male and 71 Female Transsexuals." Journal of the American Society of Psychosomatic Dentistry and Medicine. Monograph Supplement, no. 1., Oct. 1973.

2028 Langevin, Ron, Daniel Paitich and Betty Steiner. "The clinical profile of male transsexuals living as females vs. those living as males." Archives of Sexual Behavior 6(2):143-154, Mar. 1977.

2029 Lindgren, Thomas W. and Ira B. Pauly. "A body image scale for evaluation of transsexuals." Archives of Sexual Behavior 4(6):639-656, Nov. 1975.

2030 Meyer, Jon K. "Clinical variants among applicants for sex reassignment." Archives of Sexual Behavior 3(6):527-558, Nov. 1974.

2031 Meyer, Jon K., Norman J. Knorr and Dietrich Blumer. "Characterization of a self-designated transsexual population." *Archives of Sexual Behavior* 1(3):219–230, 1971.

2032 Money, John and David Block. "Speech, sexuality and the temporal lobe: an analysis of spontaneous speech of thirteen male transsexuals." *Journal of Sex Research* 7(1):35–41, Feb. 1971.

2033 Pauly, Ira B. "Female transsexualism: Part I and II." *Archives of Sexual Behavior* 3(6):487–507 passim, Nov. 1974.

2034 Roback, Howard Byron et al. "Comparative psychiatric status of male applicants for sexual reassignment surgery, Jejunoileal bypass surgery and psychiatric outpatient treatment." *Journal of Sex Research* 12(4): 315–320, Nov. 1976.

2035 _____. "Psychopathology in female sex-change applicants and two help-seeking controls." *Journal of Abnormal Psychology* 85(4):430–432, Aug. 1976.

2036 Sabalis, Robert F. et al. "The three sisters: transsexual male siblings." *American Journal of Psychiatry* 131(8):907–909, Aug. 1974.

2037 Stinson, Byron. "A study of twelve applicants for transsexual surgery." *Ohio State Medical Journal* 68:245–249, Mar. 1972.

2038 Stoller, Robert J. and Lawrence E. Newman. "The bisexual identity of transsexuals: two case examples." *Archives of Sexual Behavior* 1(1):17–28, 1971.

2039 Vietze, G. "Zur pathogenese des trans-sexualismus: literatur und fallbericht." *Psychiatrie, Neurologie und Medizinische Psychologie* 22(3):81–91, 1970.

2040 Wålinder, Jan. "Incidence and sex ratio of transsexualism in Sweden." *British Journal of Psychiatry* 119(549):195–196, Aug. 1971.

2041 Wojdowski, Pat and Irving B. Tebor. "Social and emotional tensions during Transsexual passing." *Journal of Sex Research* 12(3):193–205, Aug. 1976.

TRANSEXUALISM ETIOLOGY

2042 Baker, Howard J. "Male transsexualism: confirmation of a hypothesis?" *Archives of General Psychiatry* 32(12):1587–1588, Dec. 1975.

2043 Hoenig, J. and J.C. Kenna. "The nosological position of transsexualism." *Archives of Sexual Behavior* 3(3):273–287, May 1974.

2044 Leader, Elaine. "Transsexualism: a study of

cross-gender identity disorder." *Clinical Social Work Journal* 3(3):155–166, Fall 1975.

2045 Philbert, M. "Male transsexualism: an endocrine study. Translated and condensed from Le transsexualisme male: étude endocrinienne à propos d'une observation." *Archives of Sexual Behavior* 1(1):91–93, 1971.

2046 Weitzman, Elliott L., Charles A. Shamoian and Nikolas Golosow. "Family dynamics in male transsexualism." *Psychosomatic Medicine* 33(4):289–300, July 1971.

TRANSEXUAL TREATMENT

2047 Baker, Howard J. and Richard Green. "Treatment of transsexualism." *Current Psychiatric Therapies* 10:88–99, 1970.

2048 Barlow, David H., Gene G. Abel and Edward B. Blanchard. "Gender identity change in a transsexual: an exorcism." *Archives of Sexual Behavior* 6(5):387–395, Sept. 1977.

2049 De Betz, Barbara. "Brief guide to office counseling: gender disorders: homosexuality, transvestism, transsexualism and hermaphroditism." *Medical Aspects of Human Sexuality* 9(4):87–88, Apr. 1975.

2050 Forester, B.M. and Hillel Isaiah Swiller. "Transsexualism: a review of syndrome and presentation of possible successful therapeutic approach." *International Journal of Group Psychotherapy* 22(3):343–351, July 1972.

2051 Newman, Lawrence E. "Transsexualism in adolescence; problems in evaluation and treatment." *Archives of General Psychiatry* 23(2):112–121, Aug. 1970.

2052 Newman, Lawrence E. and Robert J. Stoller. "Nontranssexual men who seek sex reassignment." *American Journal of Psychiatry* 131(4):437–441, Apr. 1974.

2053 Pomeroy, Wardell. "The diagnosis and treatment of transvestites and transsexuals." *Journal of Sex and Marital Therapy* 1(3):215–224, Spring 1975.

2054 Steiner, Betty, Andrew Zajac and Johann W. Mohr. "A gender identity project; the organization of a multidisciplinary study." *Canadian Psychiatric Association Journal* 19(1):7–12, Feb. 1974.

2055 Wollman, Leo. *The Way of a Transsexual: How the Doctor Can Help.* (A Confide Interview Cassette.) Tappan, NY: Confide-Personal Counseling Services, 1975.

TRANSEXUAL SURGERY

2056 Benjamin, Harry. "Should surgery be performed on transexuals?" *American Journal of Psychotherapy* 25(1):74–82, 1971.

2057 Block, Norman L. and Arthur N. Tessler. "Transsexualism and surgical procedures." *Medical Aspects of Human Sexuality* 7(2):158 passim, Feb. 1973.

2058 Jones, Howard W., John Money and Jon K. Meyer. "An appraisal of the role of the gynecologist in the treatment of male transsexualism." *Current Medical Dialog* 40(5):379–385, May 1973.

2059 Noe, Joel M., Donald R. Laub and Werner Schulz. "The external male genitalia: the interplay of surgery and mechanical prostheses." In: *Clinical Management of Sexual Disorders,* ed. by J. Meyer, pp. 252–264. Baltimore: Williams & Wilkins, 1976.

2060 Ryan, James J. "Surgical intervention in the treatment of sexual disorders." In: *Clinical Management of Sexual Disorders,* ed. by J. Meyer, pp. 226–251. Baltimore: Williams & Wilkins, 1976.

2061 Strait, Joyce and Hilke Faber. "The transsexual patient after surgery." *American Journal of Nursing* 73:462–463, Mar. 1973.

TRANSEXUAL SURGERY AND ADJUSTMENT

2062 Bentler, Peter M. "A typology of transsexualism: gender identity theory and data." *Archives of Sexual Behavior* 5(6):567–584, Nov. 1976.

2063 McKee, Embry A. "Transsexualism: a selective review." *Southern Medical Journal* 69(2):185–187, Feb. 1976.

2064 Money, John and George Wolff. "Sex reassignment: male to female to male." *Archives of Sexual Behavior* 2(3):245–250, June 1973.

2065 Money, John, Florence Clarke and Tom Mazur. "Families of seven male-to-female transsexuals after 5–7 years: sociological sexology." *Archives of Sexual Behavior* 4(2):187–198, Mar. 1975.

2066 Stürup, Georg K. "Male transsexuals: a long-term followup after sex reassignment operations." *Acta Psychiatria Scandinivica* 53(1):51–63, Jan. 1976.

LEGAL ASPECTS OF SEX REASSIGNMENT

2067 Boggan, E. Carrington et al. *The Rights of Gay People; The Basic ACLU Guide to a Gay Person's Rights.* An American Civil Liberties Union Handbook. New York: Avon, 1975.

2068 Brent, Golda Gail. "Some legal problems of the postoperative transsexual." *Journal of Family Law* 12(3):405–422, 1972/1973.

2069 Crovitz, Elaine. "Treatment of the transsexual and medicolegal issues." *Forensic Science* 7(1):1–8, Jan./Feb. 1976.

2070 Hawley, Donna Lea. "The legal problems of sex determination." *Alberta Law Review* 15:122–141, 1977.

2071 Holloway, John P. "Transsexuals: legal considerations." *Archives of Sexual Behavior* 3(1):33–50, Jan. 1974.

2072 Kennedy, Ian McColl. "Transsexualism and single sex marriage." *Anglo-American Law Review* 2:112–138, Jan./Mar. 1973.

2073 Kouri, Robert P. "Comments on transsexualism in the province of Quebec." *Revue de Droit, Université de Sherbrooke* 4:168–183, 1973.

2074 Lentz, William D. "Constitutional law: marriage rights — homosexuals and transsexuals." *Akron Law Review* 8(2):369–374, Winter 1975.

2075 Meyers, David W. *The Human Body and the Law; A Medico-Legal Study.* Chicago: Aldine Publishing Co., 1970.

2076 Presser, Carole Smith. "Legal problems attendant to sex reassignment surgery." *Journal of Legal Medicine* 5(4):17–24, Apr. 1977.

2077 Schroeder, Leila O. "Renaissance for the transsexual: a new birth certificate." *Journal of Forensic Sciences* 18(3):237–245, July 1973.

2078 Smith, Douglas K. "Transsexualism, sex reassignment surgery and the law." *Cornell Law Review* 56:963–1009, 1971.

2079 Strauss, S.A. "Transsexualism and the law." *Comparative and International Law Journal of Southern Africa* 3:348–359, Nov. 1970.

2080 Wålinder, Jan and Inga Thuwe. "A law concerning sex reassignment of transsexuals in Sweden." *Archives of Sexual Behavior* 5(3):255–258, May 1976.

2081 Wetherbee, R. Michael. "Transsexuals rights under, and problems with, the law." *Sexual Law Reporter* 3(1):1 passim, Jan./Feb. 1977.

BIOGRAPHIES OF TRANSEXUALS

2082 Conn, Canary. *Canary; The Story of a Transsexual.* Los Angeles: Nash, 1974.

2083 Dianna. *Behold, I Am a Woman,* by Dianna as told to Felicity Cochrane. New York: Pyramid Communications, 1972.

2084 Fry, Jane. *Being Different: The Autobiography of Jane Fry.* Collected, compiled and edited, with introduction and conclusion, by Robert Bogdan. New York: Wiley, 1974.

2085 Jorgensen, Christine. *Christine Jorgensen: A Personal Biography.* Intro. by Harry Benjamin. New York: Paul S. Eriksson, 1967.

2086 Martino, Mario with Harriett. *Emergence: A Transsexual Autobiography.* New York: Crown, 1977.

2087 Morris, Jan. *Conundrum.* New York: Harcourt Brace Jovanovich, 1974.

2088 Reese, Tamara. *"Reborn"; A Factual Life Story of a Transition from Male to Female.* Los Angeles: Irene Lipman, 1955.

2089 Sinclair, Abby. *I Was Male.* (Including a comprehensive analysis of the sex-change phenomenon by George Griffith and Carlson Wade.) Chicago: Novel Books, 1965.

PERIODICALS

Renaissance
Box 11341, Santa Ana, CA 92711

OTHER SOURCES OF INFORMATION

The Janus Information Facility
University of Texas Medical Branch
Galveston, TX 77550
(Supersedes Erickson Educational Foundation; distributes informational material; provides professional referrals.)

Marriage

Marital Sex Behavior Research

2090 Ard, Ben N. "Premarital sexual experience: a longitudinal study." *Journal of Sex Research* 10(1):32–39, Feb. 1974.

2091 _____. "Sex in lasting marriages: a longitudinal study." *Journal of Sex Research* 13(4):274–285, Nov. 1977.

2092 Bell, Robert R. "Changing aspects of marital sexuality." In: *Sexuality Today and Tomorrow,* ed. by Sol Gordon and Roger W. Libby, pp. 213–218. North Scituate, MA: Duxbury Press, 1976.

2093 _____. "Female sexual satisfaction as related to levels of education." *Sexual Behavior* 1(8):8–14, Nov. 1971.

2094 _____. "Religious involvement and marital sex in Australia and the United States." *Journal of Comparative Family Studies* 5(2):109–116, Aug. 1974.

2095 Bell, Robert R. and Phyllis L. Bell. "Sexual satisfaction among married women." *Medical Aspects of Human Sexuality* 6(12):136–144, Dec. 1972.

2096 Bell, Robert R. and Janet Connelly. "Noncoital sex in marriage." Paper presented at the National Council on Family Relations Annual Meeting, Oct. 1973. 15p.

2097 Burgess, Ernest W. and Paul Wallin. *Engagement and Marriage.* Philadelphia: J.B. Lippincott, 1953.

2098 Clark, Alexander L. *A study of factors associated with wives' sexual responsiveness.* (Dissertation—Stanford University.) Ann Arbor, MI: University Microfilms, 1960. (Order #60-6723)

2099 Clark, Alexander L. and Paul Wallin. "Women's sexual responsiveness and the duration and quality of their marriages." *American Journal of Sociology* 71(2):187–196, Sept. 1965.

2100 Cuber, John F. and Peggy B. Harroff. *The Significant Americans; A Study of Sexual Behavior Among the Affluent.* New York: Appleton-Century, 1965.

2101 Davis, Katharine B. "A study of the sex life

of the normal married woman." *The Social Hygiene Bulletin* 8(12):9–13, June 1921.

2102   DeYoung, Gerrit E. et al. "A causal model of effects of personality and marital role factors upon diary-reported sexual behavior." *Proceedings of the 81st Annual Convention of the American Psychological Association, Montreal.* 8:355–356, 1973.

2103   Edwards, John N. and Alan Booth. "The cessation of marital intercourse." *American Journal of Psychiatry* 133(11):1333–1336, Nov. 1976.

2104   Ellis, Albert. "Female sexual response and marital relations." *Social Problems* 1(4):152–155, Apr. 1954.

2105   Freund, Matthew and Joseph E. Davis. "A follow-up study of the effects of vasectomy on sexual behavior." *Journal of Sex Research* 9(3):241–268, Aug. 1973.

2106   Gebhard, Paul H. "Factors in marital orgasm." *Medical Aspects of Human Sexuality* 2(7):22–25, July 1968.

2107   Gorer, Geoffrey. *Sex and Marriage in England Today: A Study of the Views and Experience of the Under-45s.* London: Nelson, 1971.

2108   Gross, Leonard, ed. *Sexual Issues in Marriage; A Contemporary Perspective.* Holliswood, NY: Spectrum, 1975.

2109   Hamblin, Robert L. and Robert O. Blood. "Pre-marital experience and the wife's sexual adjustment." *Social Problems* 4(2):122–130, Oct. 1956.

2110   Hamilton, G.V. *A Research in Marriage.* New York: Albert & Charles Boni, 1929.

2111   Hunt, Morton. *Sexual Behavior in the 1970's.* Chicago: Playboy Press, 1974. (Paperback ed.: Dell Publishing Co., 1975)

2112   King, Charles E. "The sex factor in marital adjustment." *Marriage and Family Living* 16(3):237–240, Aug. 1954.

2113   Kinsey, Alfred C. et al. *Sexual Behavior in the Human Female.* Philadelphia: W.B. Saunders, 1953.

2114   _____. *Sexual Behavior in the Human Male.* Philadelphia: W.B. Saunders, 1948.

2115   Lief, Harold I. "The role of sex in marriage." *Medical Aspects of Human Sexuality* 10(10):42 passim, Oct. 1976.

2116   LoPiccolo, Joseph and Jeffrey C. Steger. "The sexual interaction inventory: a new instrument for assessment of sexual dysfunction." *Archives of Sexual Behavior* 3(6):585–595, Nov. 1974.

2117   Mowrer, Harriet R. "Sex and marital adjustment: a critique of Kinsey's approach." *Social Problems* 1(4):147–152, Apr. 1954.

2118   Reevy, William R. "Petting experience and marital success: a review and statement." *Journal of Sex Research* 8(1):48–60, Feb. 1972.

2119   Rogawski, Alexander S. "How children affect the marital sexual relationship." *Medical Aspects of Human Sexuality* 10(6):48 passim, June 1976.

2120   "Sexual performance evaluation." In: *Sex Education in Medicine,* ed. by H.I. Lief and A. Karlen, pp. 123–132. New York: Spectrum, 1976.

2121   Shope, David F. and Carlfred B. Broderick. "Level of sexual experience and predicted adjustment in marriage." *Journal of Marriage and the Family* 29(3): 424–427, Aug. 1967.

2122   Thomason, Bruce. *Differential non-sexual and sexual behavior in the marital adjustment of Penn. State alumni: a comparison of well adjusted (happy) and poorly adjusted (unhappy) marriages of Penn. State alumni in respect to certain non-sexual and sexual factors.* (Dissertation—Pennsylvania State College.) Ann Arbor, MI: University Microfilms, 1951. (Order #3312)

2123   _____. "Extent of spousal agreement on certain nonsexual and sexual aspects of marital adjustment." *Marriage and Family Living* 17(4):332–337, Nov. 1955.

2124   Vincent, Clark E. "Historical and theoretical perspectives: sex, love and commitment revisited." *Journal of Sex and Marital Therapy* 2(4):265–272, Winter 1976.

2125   Wallin, Paul and Alexander L. Clark. "Religiosity, sexual gratification, and marital satisfaction in the middle years of marriage." *Social Forces* 42:303–309, Mar. 1964.

2126   _____. "A study of orgasm as a condition of women's enjoyment of coitus in the middle years of marriage." *Human Biology* 35(2):131–139, May 1963.

COITAL FREQUENCY

2127   Barrett, J.C. "An analysis of coital patterns." *Journal of Biosocial Science* 2(4):351–357, Oct. 1970.

2128 Broderick, Carlfred B. "Guidelines in diagnosing marriages." *Osteopathic Physician* 41(5):59–69, May 1974.

2129 Burgoyne, David S. "Factors affecting coital frequency." *Medical Aspects of Human Sexuality* 8(4):143 passim, Apr. 1974.

2130 Clark, Alexander L. and Paul Wallin. "The accuracy of husbands' and wives' reports of the frequency of marital coitus." *Population Studies* 18(2):165–173, Nov. 1964.

2131 Edwards, John N. and Alan Booth. "Sexual behavior in and out of marriage: an assessment of correlates." *Journal of Marriage and the Family* 38(1):73–81, Feb. 1976.

2132 Fink, Paul Jay. "Concern about variations in coital frequency." *Medical Aspects of Human Sexuality* 8(6):171–172, June 1974.

2133 Finkle, A.L. et al. "Sexual potency in aging males. I. Frequency of coitus among clinic patients." *Journal of the American Medical Association* 170(12):113–115, July 18, 1959.

2134 Gould, Ketayun H. "Comments (on anthropology and population problems)." *Current Anthropology* 13(2):249–250, Apr. 1972.

2135 Gupta, Anima Sen and David B. Lynn. "A study of sexual behavior in females." *Journal of Sex Research* 8(3):207–218. Aug. 1972.

2136 Harvey, O.L. "A note on the frequency of human coitus." *American Journal of Sociology* 38(1):64–70, July 1932.

2137 James, William H. "Coital rates and the pill." *Nature* 234:555–556, Dec. 31, 1971.

2138 _____. "Comments: the reliability of the reporting of coital frequency." *Journal of Sex Research* 12(3):247–248, Aug. 1976.

2139 _____. "The distribution of coitus within the human intermenstruum." *Journal of Biosocial Science* 3:159–171, 1971.

2140 _____. "Marital coital rates, spouses' ages, family size and social class." *Journal of Sex Research* 10(3):205–218, Aug. 1974.

2141 Jensen, Gordon D. and Mina-May Brown Robbins. "Brief guide to office counseling: frequency of marital coitus." *Medical Aspects of Human Sexuality* 9(4):95–96, Apr. 1975.

2142 Levinger, George. "Husbands and wives estimates of coital frequency." *Medical Aspects of Human Sexuality* 4(9):42 passim, Sept. 1970.

2143 _____. "Systematic distortion in spouses' reports of preferred and actual sexual behavior." *Sociometry* 29:291–299, Sept. 1966.

2144 Martin, J. David. "A note on a mathematical 'theory' of coital frequency in marriage." *Journal of Sex Research* 6(4):326–331, Nov. 1970.

2145 Martin, Peter A. "Male-female differences in desired frequency of intercourse." *Medical Aspects of Human Sexuality* 9(11):108 passim, Nov. 1975.

2146 Morris, Naomi M. "The frequency of sexual intercourse during pregnancy." *Archives of Sexual Behavior* 4(5):501–507, Sept. 1975.

2147 Mudd, Emily (Hartshorne), Marvin Stein and Howard E. Mitchell. "Paired reports of sexual behavior of husbands and wives in conflicted marriages." *Comprehensive Psychiatry* 2:149–156, June 1961.

2148 Nag, Moni. "Sex, culture, and human fertility: India and the United States." *Current Anthropology* 13(2):231–237, Apr. 1972.

2149 Pearl, Raymond. "Pregnancy rates and coitus rates." *Human Biology* 12(4):545–558, Dec. 1940.

2150 Pearlman, Carl K. "Frequency of intercourse in males at different ages." *Medical Aspects of Human Sexuality* 6(11):92–113, Nov. 1972.

2151 Reed, David M. "What is the norm for sexual relations in marriage?" *Medical Aspects of Human Sexuality* 1(3):6–9, Nov. 1967.

2152 Salzman, Leon. "Relationship of coital frequency to sexual satisfaction." *Medical Aspects of Human Sexuality* 3(9):6 passim, Sept. 1969.

2153 Spitz, Cathy J., Alice R. Gold and David B. Adams. "Cognitive and hormonal factors affecting coital frequency." *Archives of Sexual Behavior* 4(3):249–263, May 1975.

2154 Udry, J. Richard and Naomi M. Morris. "Distribution of coitus in the menstrual cycle." Paper presented at the Population Association of America Meeting, Cincinnati, OH, Apr. 1967. 13p.

2155 _____. "Frequency of intercourse by day of the week." *Journal of Sex Research* 6(3):229–234, Aug. 1970.

2156 _____. "Seasonality of coitus and seasonality of birth." *Demography* 4(2):673–679, 1967.

2157 Wallin, Paul and Alexander L. Clark. "Cultural norms and husbands' and wives' reports of their marital partners' preferred frequency of coitus relative to their own." *Sociometry* 21(3):247–254, Sept. 1958.

2158 ———. "Marital satisfaction and husbands' and wives' perception of similarity in their preferred frequency of coitus." *Journal of Abnormal and Social Psychology* 57(3):370–373, Nov. 1958.

2159 Westoff, Charles F. "Coital frequency and contraception." *Family Planning Perspectives* 6(3):136–144, Summer 1974.

2160 Wilson, W. Cody. "The distribution of selected sexual attitudes and behaviors among the adult population of the United States." *Journal of Sex Research* 11(1):46–64, Feb. 1975.

OTHER SOURCES OF INFORMATION

Office of Population Research
Princeton University
21 Prospect Ave., Princeton, NJ 08540
(National survey conducted every five
    years includes question on coital fre-
    quency.)

Trial Marriage

2161 Arafat, Ibtihaj Said and Betty Yorburg. "On living together without marriage." *Journal of Sex Research* 9(2):97–106, May 1973.

2162 Belgum, David. *Why Marry? Since You Don't Need a License to Love.* Minneapolis: Augsburg Publishing House, 1972.

2163 Berger, Miriam E. "Trial marriage: harnessing the trend constructively." *The Family Coordinator* 20(1):38–43, Jan. 1971.

2164 Blaine, Graham B. et al. "Does living together before marriage make for a better marriage? *Medical Aspects of Human Sexuality* 9(1):32 passim, Jan. 1975.

2165 Blaine, William L. and John Bishop. *Practical Guide for the Unmarried Couple.* New York: Sun River/Two Continents, 1976.

2166 Bower, Donald W. and Victor A. Christopherson. "University student cohabitation: a regional comparison of selected attitudes and behavior." *Journal of Marriage and the Family* 39(3):447–452, Aug. 1977.

2167 Catlin, Nancy, James W. Croake and James F. Keller. "MMPI profiles of cohabiting college students." *Psychological Reports* 38(2):407–410, Apr. 1976.

2168 Clayton, Richard Reid and Harwin L. Voss. "Shacking up: cohabitation in the 1970's." *Journal of Marriage and the Family* 39(2):273–283, May 1977.

2169 Danziger, Carl and Mathew Greenwald. *Alternatives: A Look at Unmarried Couples and Communes.* New York: Institute of Life Insurance Research Services, (1973?).

2170 English, D. Ailene and Harold Osborne. "Non-marital student cohabitation: a study of attitudes and behavior relating to alternate family life styles." Paper presented at the 39th Annual Meeting of the Southwestern Sociological Association, TX, Apr. 7–12, 1976. 32p.

2171 Garza, Joseph M. "Living together and the double-funnel theory of courtship." Edited revision of a paper presented at the 4th Annual Sociological Research Symposium, Virginia Commonwealth University, Richmond, Feb. 28–Mar. 2, 1974.

2172 Henze, Lura F. and John W. Hudson. "Personal and family characteristics of cohabiting and noncohabiting college students." *Journal of Marriage and the Family* 36(4):722–726, Nov. 1974.

2173 Johnson, Michael P. "Commitment: a conceptual structure and empirical application." *Sociological Quarterly* 14:395–406, Summer 1973.

2174 ———. "Courtship and commitment: a study of cohabitation on a university campus." Unpub. master's thesis, University of Iowa, 1969.

2175 Katz, Barbara J. "Without this ring." In: *Readings in Human Sexuality,* ed. by Samuel T. Wilson, Richard L. Roe and Lucy E. Autrey, pp. 177–181. New York: West, 1975.

2176 Kieffer, Carolynne Marie. "Consensual cohabitation: a descriptive study of the relationships and socio-cultural characteristics of eighty couples in settings of two Florida universities." Unpub. master's thesis, Florida State University, 1972.

2177 King, Morgan D. *The Cohabitation Handbook; Living Together and the Law.* Berkeley, CA: Ten Speed Press, 1975.

2178 Lyness, Judith L., Milton E. Lipetz and Keith E. Davis. "Living together: an alternative to marriage." *Journal of Marriage and the Family* 34(2):305–311, May 1972.

2179 McCreary-Juhasz, Anne. "Changing patterns of premarital sexual behavior." *Intellect* 104(2374):511–514, Apr. 1976.

2180 Macklin, Eleanor D. "Cohabitation in college: going very steady." *Psychology Today* 8(6):53–59, Nov. 1974.

2181 _____. "Heterosexual cohabitation among unmarried college students." *The Family Coordinator* 21(4):463–472, Oct. 1972.

2182 _____. "Unmarried heterosexual cohabitation on the university campus." In: *The Social Psychology of Sex,* ed. by Jacqueline P. Wiseman, pp. 108–142. New York: Harper & Row, 1976.

2183 Massey, Carmen and Ralph Warner. *Sex, Living Together, and the Law; a Legal Guide for Unmarried Couples (and Groups).* Berkeley, CA: Courtyard Books/Nolo Press, 1974.

2184 Michielutte, Robert et al. "Consensual and legal marital unions in Costa Rica." *International Journal of Comparative Sociology* 14(1–2):119–128, Mar./June 1973.

2185 Montgomery, Jason. "Commitment and cohabitation cohesion." Paper presented at the Annual Meeting of the National Council on Family Relations, Oct. 1973. 10p.

2186 Morrison, James L. and Scott M. Anderson. "College student cohabitation." *College Student Journal* 7(4):14–19, Nov. 1973.

2187 Nielson, Patrick A. "In re Cary: a judicial recognition of illicit cohabitation." *Hastings Law Journal* 25:1226–1247, Apr. 1974.

2188 Peterman, Dan J., Carl A. Ridley and Scott M. Anderson. "A comparison of cohabiting and noncohabiting college students." *Journal of Marriage and the Family* 36(2):344–354, May 1974.

2189 Rodman, Hyman. "Marital relationships in a Trinidad village." *Marriage and Family Living* 23(2):166–170, May 1961.

2190 Silverman, Ira Jay. "A survey of cohabitation on two college campuses." *Archives of Sexual Behavior* 6(1):11–20, Jan. 1977.

2191 Smith, Patrick B. and Ko Kimmel. "Student-parent reactions to off-campus cohabitation." *Journal of College Student Personnel* 11(3):188–193, May 1970.

2192 Stanton, Elaine. "Swinging as a way of life." *The Humanist* 34(2):18–20, Mar./Apr. 1974.

2193 Stevens, Doris. "Alternatives to the family." Paper presented at the 39th Annual Meeting of the Southwestern Sociological Association, TX, Apr. 7–12, 1976. 65p.

2194 Thorman, George. "Cohabitation: a report on the married-unmarried lifestyle." *Futurist* 7(5):250–253, Dec. 1973.

2195 _____. "Living together unmarried; a study of thirty couples at the University of Texas." *The Humanist* 34(2):15–18, Mar./Apr. 1974.

2196 Trost, Jan. "Attitudes to and occurrence of cohabitation without marriage." Paper presented at the 6th World Congress of Social Psychiatry, Yugoslavia, Oct. 4–10, 1976. 15p.

2197 _____. "Married and unmarried cohabitation: the case of Sweden, with some comparisons." *Journal of Marriage and the Family* 37(3):677–682, Aug. 1975.

2198 _____. "A renewed social institution: cohabitation without marriage." Paper presented at the 4th World Congress for Rural Sociology, Poland, Aug. 9–13, 1976. 17p.

2199 _____. "Various forms of cohabitation and their relationship to psychical and social criteria of adaptation." Paper presented at the 3rd International Stress Symposium, Stockholm, May 1972. 28p.

2200 United States Department of Commerce. Bureau of the Census. "Marital status and living arrangements: March 1976." *Current Population Reports.* Series P-20(306):1–62, Jan. 1977. (Avail. from Supt. of Docs., U.S. GPO, Washington, DC 20402.)

2201 Van Deusen, Edmund L. *Contract Cohabitation; an Alternative to Marriage.* New York: Grove Press, 1974.

2202 Ward, Thomas J. "Cohabitation and drift: a conceptual model." Paper presented at the Annual Meeting of the Midwest Sociological Society, Chicago, Apr. 9–12, 1975. 11p.

2203 Whitehurst, Robert N. "The double standard and male dominance in non-marital living arrangements: a preliminary statement." Paper presented at the Annual Meeting of the American Orthopsychiatric Association, NY, Mar. 1969. 16p.

2204 _____. "Sex: in and out of marriage." *The Humanist* 30(1):27–28, Jan./Feb. 1970.

OTHER SOURCES OF INFORMATION

Institute on the Family and the Bureaucratic Society
Marvin B. Sussman, Dir.
Case Western Reserve University
Cleveland, OH 44106

Extramarital Sex Behavior

2205 Bellville, Titus P. "A psychiatrist looks at infidelity." *Medical Aspects of Human Sexuality* 1(3):65–69, Nov. 1967.

2206 Broderick, Carlfred B. "Brief guide to office counseling: extramarital sexual involvement." *Medical Aspects of Human Sexuality* 9(9):93–94, Sept. 1975.

2207 Cuber, John F. and Peggy G. Harroff. "Other involvements." In: *The Social Psychology of Sex,* ed. by Jacqueline P. Wiseman, pp. 83–96. New York: Harper & Row, 1976.

2208 Cuber, John F. with Peggy B. Harroff. *The Significant Americans; A Study of Sexual Behavior among the Affluent.* New York: Appleton-Century-Crofts, 1965.

2209 Edwards, John N. "Extramarital involvement: fact and theory." *Journal of Sex Research* 9(3):210–224, Aug. 1973.

2210 Ellis, Albert. "Healthy and disturbed reasons for having extramarital relations." *Journal of Human Relations* 16(4):490–501, 1968.

2211 English, Oliver Spurgeon. "Values in psychotherapy: the affair." *Voices: The Art and Science of Psychotherapy* 3(4):9–14, Winter 1968.

2212 Feder, Irwin. "Wife-swapping and troilism: sexual gambits for the married couple." In: *Free Sex: A Delusion,* ed. by Norman Hill, pp. 141–162. New York: Popular Library, 1971.

2213 Ford, Clelland and Frank A. Beach. *Patterns of Sexual Behavior,* pp. 114–118. New York: Harper-Hoeber, 1951.

2214 Goldberg, Martin. "Brief guides to office counseling: infidelity." *Medical Aspects of Human Sexuality* 10(2):161–162, Feb. 1976.

2215 Goody, Jack. "A comparative approach to incest and adultery." *British Journal of Sociology* 7(4):286–305, Dec. 1956.

2216 Greene, Bernard L., Ronald R. Lee and Noel Lustig. "Conscious and unconscious factors in marital infidelity." *Medical Aspects of Human Sexuality* 8(9):87–111, Sept. 1974.

2217 Greenwald, Harold. "Dialogue: sexual fidelity in marriage." *Sexual Behavior* 2(10):29–32, Oct. 1972.

2218 ———. "Sex away from home." *Sexual Behavior* 1(6):8–14, Sept. 1971.

2219 Harper, Robert A. "Extramarital sex rela-

tions." In: *The Encyclopedia of Sexual Behavior* ed. by Albert Ellis and Albert Abarbanel, pp. 384–391. New York: Hawthorn Books, 1967.

2220 Hunt, Morton M. *The Affair; a Portrait of Extra-Marital Love in Contemporary America.* New York: World Publishing Co., 1969.

2221 Issacharoff, Amnon. "Brief guide to office counseling: conflict over desire for extramarital or group sex." *Medical Aspects of Human Sexuality* 9(7):133–134, July 1975.

2222 Lawrence, Raymond. "Towards a more flexible monogamy." In: *The Future of Sexual Relations,* ed. by Robert T. Francoeur and Anna K. Francoeur, pp. 66–74. Englewood Cliffs, NJ: Prentice-Hall, 1974.

2223 Libby, Roger W. and Robert N. Whitehurst, eds. *Renovating Marriage.* Danville, CA: Consensus, 1973.

2224 Masters, William H. and Virginia E. Johnson with Robert J. Levin. *The Pleasure Bond; a New Look at Sexuality and Commitment.* Boston: Little, Brown, 1974.

2225 Mead, Beverly T. et al. "What impact does adultery generally have on a marriage?" *Medical Aspects of Human Sexuality* 9(10):122–142, Oct. 1975.

2226 Neubeck, Gerhard. "The dimensions of the 'extra' in extramarital relations." In: *Marital Counseling; Psychology, Ideology, Science,* comp. and ed. by Hirsch Lazaar Silverman, pp. 136–147. Springfield, IL: Charles C. Thomas, 1967.

2227 Neubeck, Gerhard, ed. *Extramarital Relations.* Englewood Cliffs, NJ: Prentice-Hall, 1969.

2228 Pauly, Ira B. "Premarital and extramarital intercourse." In: *The Sexual Experience,* ed. by B.J. Sadock, H.I. Kaplan and A.M. Freedman, pp. 256–267. Baltimore: Williams & Wilkins, 1976.

2229 Peterson, James A. "The office wife." In: *Sexual Issues in Marriage; a Contemporary Perspective,* ed. by Leonard Gross, pp. 199–213. New York: Spectrum, 1975.

2230 "Roundtable: marital infidelity." *Medical Aspects of Human Sexuality* 7(10):162–191, Oct. 1973.

2231 "Roundtable: The significance of extramarital sex relations." *Medical Aspects of Human Sexuality* 3(10):33–47, Oct. 1969.

2232 Saul, Leon J. *Fidelity and Infidelity; and*

What Makes or Breaks a Marriage. Philadelphia: J.B. Lippincott, 1967.

2233 Sprey, Jetse. "Extramarital relationships." *Sexual Behavior* 2(8):34–40, Aug. 1972.

2234 Strean, Herbert S. "The extramarital affair: a psychoanalytic view." *Psychoanalytic Review* 63(1):101–113, Spring 1976.

2235 "Viewpoints: should a husband or wife confess infidelity?" *Medical Aspects of Human Sexuality* 4(5):8–15, May 1970.

2236 Viewpoints: what is the chief cause of marital infidelity?" *Medical Aspects of Human Sexuality* 8(1):90–110, Jan. 1974.

2237 Vincent, Clark E. "The physician as counselor in postmarital and extramarital pregnancies." *Medical Aspects of Human Sexuality* 1(3):34–41, Nov. 1967.

2238 Whitehurst, Robert N. "Violence potential in extramarital sexual response." *Journal of Marriage and the Family* 33(4):683–691, Nov. 1971.

2239 Wolf, Alexander. "The problem of infidelity." Paper presented at the Society of Medical Psychoanalysis — Psychoanalytic Symposium on Marriage, Mar. 6, 1965. 33p.

EXTRAMARITAL SEX BEHAVIOR (FEMALE)

2240 Bromberg, Norbert. "Polygamous women." In: *Sexual Behavior and the Law,* ed. by Ralph Slovenko, pp. 341–355. Springfield, IL: Charles C. Thomas, 1965.

2241 Framo, James L. "Husbands' reactions to wives' infidelity." *Medical Aspects of Human Sexuality* 9(5):78–104, May 1975.

2242 Garfield District Staff of the Family Service Association, Cleveland, Ohio. "Infidelity in women as a manifestation of character disorder." *Smith College Study in Social Work* 32(3):180–198, June 1962.

2243 Hirt, Stefanie and Donald McClean. "Women and extra-marital relationships." *International Journal of Sexology* 4(2):98–103, Nov. 1950.

2244 Salzman, Leon. "Female infidelity." *Medical Aspects of Human Sexuality* 6(2):118–136, Feb. 1972.

2245 Weisberg, Miriam. "Discussion: role of the spouse in infidelity." *Smith College Study in Social Work* 32(3):199–204, June 1962.

2246 Wolfe, Linda. *Playing Around; Women and Extramarital Sex.* New York: Morrow, 1975.

EXTRAMARITAL SEX BEHAVIOR (MALE)

2247 Feldman, Sandor S. "The attraction of 'the other woman.'" *Journal of the Hillside Hospital* 13(1):3–17, Jan. 1964.

2248 Weisberg, Miriam and Murray A. Goldstone. "Early treatment of infidelity in the neurotic." *Social Casework* 51:358–367, June 1970.

EXTRAMARITAL SEX BEHAVIOR RESEARCH

2249 Bell, Robert R. "Extramarital sexual behavior." In: *Social Deviance: a Substantive Analysis,* pp. 63–87. Homewood, IL: Dorsey Press, 1971.

2250 Edwards, John N. and Alan Booth. "Sexual behavior in and out of marriage: an assessment of correlates." *Journal of Marriage and the Family* 38(1):73–81, Feb. 1976.

2251 Franck, Roberte. *L'Infidelité conjugale, ses raisons, ses causes, ses drames.* Paris: Société Générale d'Editions, 1969.

2252 Hunt, Morton. *Sexual Behavior in the 1970's.* Chicago: Playboy Press, 1974. (Chapter 5.)

2253 Johnson, Ralph E. "Extramarital sexual intercourse: a methodological note." *Journal of Marriage and the Family* 32(2):279–282, May 1970.

2254 _____. *Marital patterns during the middle years.* (Dissertation—University of Minnesota.) Ann Arbor, MI: University Microfilms, 1968. (Order #69-6822)

2255 _____. "Some correlates of extramarital coitus." *Journal of Marriage and the Family* 32(3):449–456, Aug. 1970.

2256 Magar, Edward Magar. *Adultery and Its Compatibility with Marriage.* Monona, WI: Nefertiti Publishers, 1972.

2257 Myers, Lonny. "Extramarital sex: is the neglect of its positive aspects justified?" In: *Sex and the Life Cycle,* ed. by Wilbur W. Oaks, Gerald A. Melchiode and Ilda Ficher, pp. 105–115. New York: Grune & Stratton, 1976.

2258 Neubeck, Gerhard and Vera M. Schletzer. "A study of extra-marital relationships." *Marriage and Family Living* 24(3):279–281, Aug. 1962.

2259 Singh, B. Krishna, Bonnie L. Walton and J. Sherwood Williams. "Extramarital sexual permissiveness: conditions and contingencies." *Journal of Marriage and the Family* 38(4):701–712, Nov. 1976.

EXTRAMARITAL SEX BEHAVIOR RESEARCH (FEMALE)

2260 Bell, Robert R. and Dorthyann Peltz. "Extramarital sex among women." *Medical Aspects of Human Sexuality* 8(3):10–40, Mar. 1974.

2261 Bell, Robert R., Stanley H. Turner and Lawrence Rosen. "A multivariate analysis of female extramarital coitus." *Journal of Marriage and the Family* 37(2):375–384, May 1975.

2262 Kinsey, Alfred C. et al. *Sexual Behavior in the Human Female.* Philadelphia: W.B. Saunders, 1953. (Chapter 10)

2263 Maykovich, Minako K. "Attitudes versus behavior in extramarital sexual relations." *Journal of Marriage and the Family* 38(4):693–699, Nov. 1976.

2264 Vincent, Clark E. "Illicit pregnancies among married and divorced females." In: *Deviancy and the Family,* ed. by C.D. Bryant and J.G. Wells, pp. 379–389. Philadelphia: Davis, 1973.

EXTRAMARITAL SEX BEHAVIOR RESEARCH (MALE)

2265 Kinsey, Alfred C. et al. *Sexual Behavior in the Human Male.* Philadelphia: W.B. Saunders, 1948. (Chapter 19)

2266 Pietropinto, Anthony and Jacqueline Simenauer. *Beyond the Male Myth.* New York: Times Books, 1977. (Chapter 11)

COMARITAL SEX BEHAVIOR

2267 Bartell, Gilbert D. *Group Sex; A Scientist's Eyewitness Report on the American Way of Swinging.* New York: Wyden, 1971.

2268 _____. "Group sex among the Mid-Americans." *Journal of Sex Research* 6(2): 113–130, May 1970.

2269 Bell, Robert R. and Lillian Silvan. " 'Swinging'—the sexual exchange of marriage partners." Paper presented at the Annual Meeting of the Society for the Study of Social Problems, Washington, DC, 1970. 18p.

2270 Breedlove, William and Jerrye Breedlove. *Swap Clubs; A Study in Contemporary Sexual Mores.* Los Angeles: Sherbourne Press, 1964.

2271 Carneiro, Robert. "Extra-marital sex freedom among the Kuikura Indians of Mato Grosso." *Revista do Museu Pauliste, N.S.* 10:135–142, 1956/1958.

2272 Cole, Charles Lee and Graham B. Spanier. "Comarital mate-sharing and family stability." *Journal of Sex Research* 10(1):21–31, Feb. 1974.

2273 _____. "Introduction into mate-swapping: a review." *Family Process* 12(3):279–290, Sept. 1973.

2274 Constantine, Larry, Joan Constantine and Sheldon K. Edelman. "Counseling implications of comarital and multilateral relations." *The Family Coordinator* 21(3):267–273, July 1972.

2275 Dean, Michael Leigh. "Institutionalized comarital mate sharing: appraisal of an emerging life style in North America." 1975 revision of a paper presented at the 1973 Annual Meeting of the Midwest Sociological Society. 43p.

2276 Denfield, Duane. "Dropouts from swinging." *The Family Coordinator* 23(1):45–49, Jan. 1974.

2277 Denfield, Duane and Michael Gordon. "The sociology of mate swapping; or the family that swings together clings together." *Journal of Sex Research* 6(2):85–100, May 1970.

2278 Ellis, Albert. *The Civilized Couple's Guide to Extramarital Adventure.* New York: Wyden, 1972.

2279 Fang, Betty. "Swinging: in retrospect." *Journal of Sex Research* 12(3):220–237, Aug. 1976.

2280 Freilich, Morris and Lewis A. Coser. "Structured imbalances of gratification: the case of the Caribbean mating system." *British Journal of Sociology* 23:1–19, Mar. 1972.

2281 Harris, Sarah. "Before we began to swing." In: *Deviancy and the Family,* ed. by C.D. Bryant and J.G. Wells, pp. 283–294. Philadelphia: Davis, 1973.

2282 Henshel, Anne-Marie. "Swinging: a study of decision making in marriage." *American Journal of Sociology* 78(4):885–891, Jan. 1973.

2283 Knapp, Jacquelyn J. "An exploratory study of seventeen sexually open marriages." *Journal of Sex Research* 12(3):206–219, Aug. 1976.

2284 Lobell, John and Mimi Lobell. *The Complete Handbook for a Sexually Free Marriage.* New York: Pinnacle, 1975.

2285 Myers, Lonny and Hunter Leggitt. *Adultery & Other Private Matters: Your Right to Personal Freedom in Marriage.* Chicago: Nelson Hall, 1975.

2286 O'Neill, Nena. *The Marriage Premise.* New York: M. Evans, 1977.

2287 O'Neill, Nena and George O'Neill. *Open Marriage; a New Life Style for Couples.* New York: M. Evans, 1972.

2288 Ramey, James W. "Intimate groups and networks: frequent consequence of sexually open marriage." *The Family Coordinator* 24(4):515–530, Oct. 1975.

2289 Rubenstein, Paul and Herbert Margolis. *The Groupsex Tapes.* New York: David McKay, 1971.

2290 Schupp, Cherie Evelyn. *An analysis of some social-psychological factors which operate in the functioning relationship of married couples who exchange mates for the purpose of sexual experience.* (Dissertation—United States International University.) Ann Arbor, MI: University Microfilms, 1970. (Order #70-22,535)

2291 Smith, James R. and Lynn G. Smith. "Co-marital sex and the sexual freedom movement." *Journal of Sex Research* 6(2):131–142, May 1970.

2292 Smith, James R. and Lynn G. Smith, eds. *Beyond Monogamy; Recent Studies of Sexual Alternatives in Marriage.* Baltimore: Johns Hopkins University Press, 1974.

2293 Symonds, Carolyn. "The utopian aspects of sexual mate swapping: in theory and practice." Paper presented at the Annual Meeting of the Society for the Study of Social Problems, 1970, Washington, DC. 11p.

2294 Varni, Charles A. "An exploratory study of spouse swapping." Paper presented at the Meeting of the Pacific Sociological Association, Honolulu, 1971. 18p.

2295 Walshok, Mary Lindenstein. "The emergence of middle-class deviant subcultures: the case of swingers." *Social Problems* 18(4):488–495, Spring 1971.

2296 Ziskin, Jay and Mae Ziskin. "Co-marital sex agreements: an emerging issue in sexual counseling." *Counseling Psychologist* 5(1):81–84, 1975.

2297 _____. *The Extra-Marital Sex Contract.* Los Angeles: Nash Publishing, 1973.

ATTITUDES ON EXTRAMARITAL SEX BEHAVIOR

2298 Callahan, Sidney Cornelia. "The emancipation of women and the sexual revolution." In: *Sexuality: a Search for Perspective,* ed. by Donald L. Grummon and Andrew M. Barclay, pp. 213–225. New York: Van Nostrand Reinhold, 1971.

2299 Ellis, Albert. "Sex without guilt." In: *Sexuality: a Search for Perspective,* ed. by Donald L. Grummon and Andrew M. Barclay, pp. 226–244. New York: Van Nostrand Reinhold, 1971.

2300 Ellis, Albert and Donald Bloch. *The Pros and Cons of Extramarital Sexual Relationships.* (Tape cassette.) Claremont, CA: American Association of Marriage and Family Counselors, 1976.

2301 Elliston, Frederick. "In defense of promiscuity." In: *Philosophy and Sex,* ed. by R. Baker and F. Elliston, pp. 222–243. Buffalo, NY: Prometheus Books, 1975.

2302 English, Oliver Spurgeon and Melvin S. Heller. "Debate: Is marital infidelity justified?" *Sexual Behavior* 1(1):26–35, Apr. 1971.

2303 Framo, James L. et al. "How does an affair affect a marriage?" *Sexual Behavior* 2(9):46–51, Sept. 1972.

2304 Fry, William F. "Psychodynamics of sexual humor: a look at adultery." *Medical Aspects of Human Sexuality* 9(4):32–41, Apr. 1975.

2305 Reiss, Ira L. "Heterosexual relationships of patients: premarital, marital and extramarital." In: *Human Sexuality: a Health Practitioner's Text,* ed. by Richard Green, pp. 37–52. Baltimore: Williams & Wilkins, 1975.

2306 Stern, Herold S. "The concept of chastity in biblical society." *Journal of Sex Research* 2(2):89–97, July 1966.

2307 Wasserstrom, Richard. "Is adultery immoral?" In: *Philosophy and Sex,* ed. by R. Baker and F. Elliston, pp. 207–221. Buffalo, NY: Prometheus Books, 1975.

ATTITUDES ON EXTRAMARITAL SEX BEHAVIOR RESEARCH

2308 Alston, Jon P. "Attitudes of white Protestants and Catholics toward nonmarital sex." *Journal for the Scientific Study of Religion* 13(1):73–74, Mar. 1974.

2309 _____. "Attitudes toward extramarital and homosexual relations." *Journal for the Scientific Study of Religion* 13(4):479–481, Dec. 1974.

2310 Broderick, Carlfred B. "The case for sexual fidelity (commentary follows)." *Medical Aspects of Human Sexuality* 10(9):16 passim, Sept. 1976.

2311 Christensen, Harold T. "Attitudes toward marital fidelity: a nine-culture sampling of university student opinion." *Journal of Comparative Family Studies* 4(2):197–214, Fall 1973.

2312 Christensen, Harold T. "A cross-cultural comparison of attitudes toward marital infidelity." *International Journal of Comparative Sociology* 3(1):124–137, Sept. 1962.

2313 Christensen, Harold T. and Christina F. Gregg. "Changing sex norms in America and Scandinavia." *Journal of Marriage and the Family* 32(4):616–627, Nov. 1970.

2314 Edwards, Maxine and Nick Stinnett. "Perceptions of college students concerning alternate life styles." *Journal of Psychology* 87(1):143–156, May 1974.

2315 Huang, Lucy Jen and Wilbert M. Leonard. "The marriage contract and attitudes toward sex roles: a synopsis of some findings." Paper presented at the 39th Annual Meeting of the Midwest Sociological Society, St. Louis, MO, Apr. 7–12, 1976. 6p.

2316 Johnson, Ralph E. "Attitudes toward extramarital relationships." *Medical Aspects of Human Sexuality* 6(4):168–191, Apr. 1972.

2317 Jones, Arthur Hosking. "Sex, educational and religious influences on moral judgments relative to the family." *American Sociological Review* 8(4):405–411, Aug. 1943.

2318 Knapp, Jacquelyn J. "Some non-monogamous marriage styles and related attitudes and practices of marriage counselors." *The Family Coordinator* 24(4):505–514, Oct. 1975.

2319 Levitt, Eugene E. and Albert D. Klassen. "Public attitudes toward sexual behaviors: the latest investigation of the Institute for Sex Research." Paper presented at the Annual Convention of the American Orthopsychiatric Association, New York City, 1973. 24p.

2320 Maykovich, Minako K. "Attitudes versus behavior in extramarital sexual relations." *Journal of Marriage and the Family* 38(4):693–699, Nov. 1976.

2321 Pauly, Ira B. and Steven G. Goldstein. "Physicians' attitudes toward premarital and extramarital intercourse." *Medical Aspects of Human Sexuality* 5(1):32–45, Jan. 1971.

2322 Rodman, Hyman, F.R. Nichols and Patricia Voydanoff. "Lower-class attitudes toward 'deviant' family patterns: a cross-cultural study." *Journal of Marriage and the Family* 32(2):315–321, May 1969.

2323 Sponaugle, G.C. "Correlates of attitudes toward extramarital sexual relations." Paper presented at the Midwest Sociological Society, St. Louis, MO, Apr. 24, 1976. 27p.

2324 Stratton, John R. "Sexual permissiveness and self-evaluation: a question of substance and a question of method." *Journal of Marriage and the Family* 29(3):434–441, Aug. 1967.

Sex Education

Sex Education

CURRICULA

2325 American School Health Association, Committee on Health Guidance in Sex Education. "Growth patterns and sex education: a suggested program for kindergarten through grade twelve." *Journal of School Health* 37(5a): whole issue, May 1967.

2326 Broderick, Carlfred B. and Jessie Bernard, eds. *The Individual, Sex and Society: A SIECUS Handbook for Teachers and Counselors.* Baltimore: Johns Hopkins University Press, 1969.

2327 Burke, Susan, ed. *Responsible Parenthood and Sex Education.* London: International Planned Parenthood Federation, 1970.

2328 Burt, John J. and Linda Brower Meeks. *Education for Sexuality: Concepts and Programs for Teaching.* 2nd ed. Philadelphia: W.B. Saunders, 1975.

2329 Butts, June Dobbs. "Sex education in Bermuda: curriculum development and community implementation." *Journal of Research and Development in Education* 10(1):42–49, Fall 1976.

2330 Diamond, Milton. "Human sexuality: mass

sex education student and community reaction." *Journal of Sex Education and Therapy* 2(2):1-11, Fall/Winter 1976.

2331 Educational Research Council of America and The Westlake City Public School System, Ohio. *Education in Human Sexuality* (for Primary Grades through High School—Student Books and Teacher Manuals). Cleveland: Educational Research Council of America, 1972.

2332 *Family Life Education Curriculum Guide.* California Youth Authority, 1974. (Avail. from State of California Documents Section, Box 20191, Sacramento, CA 95820.)

2333 Hinton, Gertrude D.M. *Teaching Sex Education; A Guide for Teachers.* Palo Alto, CA: Fearon Publishers, 1969.

2334 Miller, Mary Susan and Patricia J. Schiller. *A Teacher's Round Table on Sex Education.* Boston: National Association of Independent Schools, 1977.

2335 Morrison, Eleanor S. and Mila U. Price. *Values in Sexuality; A New Approach to Sex Education.* New York: Hart, 1974.

2336 Schiller, Patricia. *Creative Approach to Sex Education and Counseling.* New York: Association Press, 1973.

2337 Stayton, William R. and Nathan W. Turner. "An innovative model for training professionals in human sexuality." *Journal of Sex Education and Therapy* 2(2):49-52, Fall/Winter 1976.

2338 United Nations Educational, Scientific and Cultural Organization. *Health Education, Sex Education and Education for Home and Family Life.* Hamburg: Institute for Education, 1965.

2339 Whisnant, Billie and June Talarico. "Sex education in public health work." *Overview* 2(1):18-22, Spring 1973.

CHILD

2340 Barrett, Ann and Bonnie Bean. "A short course on sexuality for ten-to-twelve-year olds." In: *Sexual Behaviour in Canada: Patterns and Problems,* ed. by Benjamin Schlesinger, pp. 253-263. Toronto: University of Toronto Press, 1977.

ADOLESCENTS

2341 Cogswell, Betty E. and Charles B. Arnold. "Organizational efforts to link adolescents to a sex information program." Paper presented at the American Sociological Association 64th Meeting, San Francisco, Sept. 1, 1969. 12p.

2342 Fodor, John T. "A conceptual approach to curriculum development in venereal disease education." *Journal of School Health* 43(5):303-306, May 1973.

2343 Hoyman, Howard S. "Our most explosive sex education issue: birth control." *Journal of School Health* 39(7):458-469, Sept. 1969.

2344 Kelly, Gary F. "Group guidance on sex education." *Personnel and Guidance Journal* 49(10):809-814, June 1971.

COLLEGE STUDENTS

2345 Amdur, Millard J. et al. "Issues in developing a multi-disciplinary sex education program in a public university." *Journal of the American College Health Association* 22(5):364-369, June 1974.

2346 Baldwin, Bruce A. and Robert R. Wilson. "Peer services in human sexuality health education." *Crisis Intervention* 5(3):12-26, 1974.

2347 Coplin, Haskell R. "Model for a non-credit lecture series in human sexuality." *Teaching of Psychology* 2(1):28-31, Feb. 1975.

2348 Gebhard, Paul H. "Preparation for a course on human sexuality." *Teaching of Psychology* 2(1):31-33, Feb. 1975.

2349 Gochros, Havey L. "Introducing human sexuality into the graduate social work curriculum." *Social Work Education Reporter* 18(3):47-50, Sept./Oct. 1970.

2350 Landis, C.E., H.R. Miller and Richard P. Wettstone. "Sexual awareness training for counselors." *Teaching of Psychology* 2(1):33-36, Feb. 1975.

2351 Mazur, Ronald M., prog. dir. *Training Peer Sex Educators.* Amherst: University Health Services, University of Massachusetts, 1976.

2352 Powell, Marion G. and Benjamin Schlesinger. "A course on human sexuality for Canadian graduate social work students." In: *Sexual Behavior in Canada: Patterns and Problems,* ed. by Benjamin Schlesinger, pp. 270-278. Toronto: University of Toronto Press, 1977.

2353 Sarrel, Philip and Haskell R. Coplin. "A course in human sexuality for the college student." *American Journal of Public Health* 61(5):1030-1037, May 1971.

PARENTS

2354 Heagarty, Margaret, Geraldine Glass and Helen King. "Sex and the preschool child." *American Journal of Nursing* 74(8):1479–1482, Aug. 1974.

2355 Miller, H.R. and E.M. King. "Sex education for parents using behavior rehearsal." *Journal of Family Counseling* 2(2):28–31, 1974.

2356 Rosenberg, Pearl and Lois M. Rosenberg. "A group experience in sex education for the family." *International Journal of Group Psychotherapy* 26(2):235–241, Apr. 1976.

2357 _____. "Sex education for adolescents and their families." *Journal of Sex and Marital Therapy* 2(1):53–67, Spring 1976.

2358 Rosner, Aria C. "An exemplary awareness program for parents." *Journal of School Health* 43(6):396–397, June 1973.

2359 Snegroff, Stanley. "A community school program designed to improve knowledge and communication between parents and their children regarding pubescent sexuality." *Journal of Sex Education and Therapy* 2(2):41–44, Fall/Winter 1976.

2360 Woody, Jane Divita. "Contemporary sex education: attitudes and implications for child-rearing." *Journal of School Health* 43(4):241–246, Apr. 1973.

SEX EDUCATION MATERIALS

2361 "Bibliography of religious publications on sexuality and sex education." *SIECUS Report* 5(3):8–9, Jan. 1977. (Avail. from SIECUS; enclose stamped, self-addressed, legal size envelope.)

2362 "Human sexuality: books for everyone." *SIECUS Report* 4(3):7–10, Jan. 1976. (Avail. from SIECUS; enclose stamped, self-addressed, legal size envelope.)

2363 Minnesota Council on Family Relations. *Family Life Literature and Films: An Annotated Bibliography, 1972* (and) *1974 Supplement.* Minneapolis: Minnesota Council on Family Relations, 1972/1974.

2364 Singer, Laura and Judith Buskin. *Sex Education on Films: A Guide to Visual Aids and Programs.* New York: Teacher's College Press, 1971.

SEX EDUCATION MATERIALS (CHILD)

2365 Andry, Andrew C. and Steven Schepp. *How Babies are Made.* New York: Time-Life Books, 1968.

2366 De Schweinitz, Karl. *Growing Up: How We Become Alive, Are Born and Grow.* 4th ed. New York: P.F. Collier, 1974.

2367 Follett Family Life Education Program. Six titles: *Families Live Together; The World of Living Things; How New Life Begins; Living Things and Their Young; How We are Born; Man and Woman.* Chicago: Follett, 1969.

2368 Gordon, Sol and Judith Gordon. *Did the Sun Shine Before You Were Born?* New York: Third Press, 1974.

2369 Gruenberg, Sidonie M. *The Wonderful Story of How You Were Born.* rev. ed. New York: Doubleday, 1973.

2370. Johnson, Eric W. and Corinne B. Johnson. *Love and Sex and Growing Up.* Philadelphia: J.B. Lippincott, 1970.

2371 Knudsen, Per Holm. *The True Story of How Babies are Made.* Chicago: Childrens Press, 1973.

2372 Mayle, Peter. *Where Did I Come From?* Secaucus, NJ: Lyle Stuart, 1973.

2373 Sheffield, Margaret. *Where Do Babies Come From?* New York: Knopf, 1973.

SEX EDUCATION MATERIALS (EARLY ADOLESCENT)

2374 Calderwood, Deryck D. "Criteria for the selection of books on sex education for adolescent youth." *Family Life Coordinator* 15(4): 175–176, Oct. 1966.

2375 Gordon, Sol. *Facts about Sex for Today's Youth.* rev. ed. New York: John Day, 1973.

2376 Johnson, Eric W. *Love and Sex in Plain Language.* 3rd rev. ed. New York: J.B. Lippincott, 1977.

2377 _____. *Sex: Telling It Straight.* Philadelphia: J.B. Lippincott, 1970.

2378 Pomeroy, Wardell B. *Boys and Sex.* New York: Delacorte Press, 1968.

2379 _____. *Girls and Sex.* New York: Delacorte Press, 1969.

SEX EDUCATION MATERIALS (ADOLESCENT)

2380 Bohannan, Paul. *Love, Sex and Being Human.* Garden City, NY: Doubleday, 1969.

2381 Calderwood, Deryck. *About Your Sexuality.* (Multimedia kit.) Boston: Beacon Press, 1971.

2382 Fiore, Evelyn and Richard S. Ward. *Sex Facts for Teenagers.* New York: Ace Books, 1971.

2383 Hamilton, Eleanor. *Sex before Marriage.* New York: Meredith Press, 1969.

2384 Hettlinger, Richard. *Growing Up with Sex.* New York: Seabury Press, 1971.

2385 Kelly, Gary F. *Learning about Sex: The Contemporary Guide for Young Adults.* Woodbury, NY: Barron's Educational Series, 1976.

2386 Mazur, Ronald M. *Commonsense Sex; A Basis for Discussion and Reappraisal.* Boston: Beacon Press, 1973.

2387 Miller, Benjamin F., Edward B. Rosenberg and Benjamin L. Stockowski. *Masculinity and Femininity* (and) *Instructor's Manual.* Boston: Houghton Mifflin, 1971.

2388 Southard, Helen. *Sex before Twenty: New Answers for Young People.* rev. ed. New York: E.P. Dutton, 1971.

SEX EDUCATION MATERIALS (COLLEGE STUDENT)

2389 Byrne, Donn and Lois A. Byrne, eds. *Exploring Human Sexuality.* New York: Crowell, 1977.

2390 DeLora, Joann S. and Carol A.B. Warren. *Understanding Sexual Interaction* (and) *Instructor's Manual.* Boston: Houghton Mifflin, 1977.

2391 Diamond, Milton. *Human Sexuality.* (30 audiocassettes.) New York: Jeffrey Norton, 1975. (Also avail. as 30 videocassettes or videotapes from The Public Television Library, 475 l'Enfant Plaza, SW, Washington, DC 20024. *Study Guide to Human Sexuality, A TV Course by Dr. Milton Diamond* by Lleni Jeffrey and John Blakemore is avail. from Dr. Blakemore, Monterey Peninsula College, Monterey, CA 93940.)

2392 *Focus: Human Sexuality: An Annual Editions Reader* (and) *Instructor's Guide.* Guilford, CT: Annual Editions, 1976 (etc.).

2393 Gagnon, John H. *Human Sexualities.* Glenview, IL: Scott, Foresman, 1977.

2394 Green, Richard, ed. *Human Sexuality: A Health Practitioner's Text.* Baltimore: Williams & Wilkins, 1975.

2395 Hettlinger, Richard, ed. *Human Sexuality: A Psychosocial Perspective.* rev. ed. Belmont, CA: Wadsworth Publishing, 1975.

2396 Katchadourian, Herant A. and Donald T. Lunde. *Fundamentals of Human Sexuality.* 2nd ed. New York: Holt, Rinehart & Winston, 1975. (Brief version published as *Biological Aspects of Human Sexuality.*)

2397 Lief, Harold I. and Arno Karlen, eds. *Sex Education in Medicine.* New York: Spectrum, 1976.

2398 McCary, James Leslie. *Teaching Human Sexuality; A Guide for Instructors.* New York: Van Nostrand, 1973. (Designed for use with *Human Sexuality* 2nd ed. or *Human Sexuality; a Brief Edition.*)

2399 McCary, James Leslie and Donna R. Copeland, eds. *Modern View of Human Sexual Behavior.* Chicago: Science Research Associates, 1976.

2400 Morrison, Eleanor S. and Vera Borosage, eds. *Human Sexuality: Contemporary Perspectives.* 2nd ed. Palos Altos, CA: Mayfield Publishing, 1977.

2401 Sadock, Benjamin J., Harold I. Kaplan and Alfred M. Freedman, eds. *The Sexual Experience.* Baltimore: Williams & Wilkins, 1976.

2402 Shope, David F. *Interpersonal Sexuality.* Philadelphia: W.B. Saunders, 1975.

2403 Steen, Edwin Benzel and James H. Price. *Human Sex and Sexuality; With a Dictionary of Sexual Terms.* New York: Wiley, 1977.

2404 Wilson, Samuel T. et al., eds. *Human Sexuality; A Text with Readings* (and) *Instructor's Manual.* St. Paul, MN: West, 1977.

2405 Wiseman, Jacqueline P., ed. *The Social Psychology of Sex.* New York: Harper & Row, 1976.

SEX EDUCATION MATERIALS (PARENTS)

2406 Gordon, Sol. *Let's Make Sex a Household Word; A Guide for Parents and Children.* New York: John Day, 1975.

2407 _____. *The Sexual Adolescent; Communicating with Teenagers about Sex.* North Scituate, MA: Duxbury Press, 1973.

2408 Gordon, Sol and Irving R. Dickman. *Sex Education: The Parents' Role.* Public Affairs Pamphlet, no. 549. New York: Public Affairs Committee, 1977.

2409 Johnson, Warren R. and Edwin G. Belzer. *Human Sexual Behavior and Sex Education.* 3rd ed. Philadelphia: Lea & Febiger, 1973.

2410 Kappelman, Murray M. *Sex and the American Teenager: The Problems of Adolescent Sexuality — And How to Cope with Them in Today's*

Changing World. New York: Reader's Digest Press, 1977.

2411 Katchadourian, Herant A. *Human Sexuality: Sense and Nonsense.* San Francisco: W.H. Freeman, 1974.

2412 McCary, James Leslie. *A Complete Sex Education for Parents, Teenagers, and Young Adults.* New York: Van Nostrand Reinhold, 1973.

2413 _____. *Sexual Myths and Fallacies.* New York: Schocken Books. 1973.

2414 Pomeroy, Wardell B. *Your Child and Sex: A Guide for Parents.* New York: Delacorte Press, 1974.

2415 Rubin, Isadore and Lester A. Kirkendall, eds. *Sex in the Childhood Years.* New York: Association Press, 1970.

2416 Scanzoni, Letha. *Sex Is A Parent Affair.* Glendale, CA: Regal Books, 1973.

2417 SIECUS. *Sexuality and Man.* (12 study guides.) New York: Scribner, 1970.

OTHER SOURCES OF INFORMATION

American Association for Health, Physical Education & Recreation
National Education Association
1201 16th St., NW, Washington, DC 20036
(For information on current and projected programs in sex education in schools)

American Association of Sex Educators, Counselors and Therapists
5010 Wisconsin Ave., NW, Suite 304, Washington, DC 20016
(Publish the *Journal of Sex Education and Therapy*)

Institute for Family Research and Education
760 Ostrom Ave., Syracuse, NY 13210
(Program development and training; materials)

SIECUS (Sex Information and Education Council of the United States)
84 Fifth Ave., Suite 407, New York, NY 10011
(Publish *SIECUS Report;* bibliographies; study guides. Publications avail. from Human Sciences Press, 72 Fifth Ave., New York, NY 10011)

Youth and Student Affairs
Planned Parenthood Federation
810 Seventh Ave., New York, NY 10019
(Publish *A Guide to Sexuality Handbooks;* other materials)

Sex Education Research

2418 Bidgood, Frederick. "The effects of sex education: a summary of the literature." *SIECUS Report* 1(4):11 passim, Mar. 1973.

2419 Bloch, Doris. *Attitudes and practices of mothers in the sex education of their daughters.* (Dissertation—University of California, Berkeley.) Ann Arbor, MI: University Microfilms, 1970. (Order #71-15,701)

2420 Brody, Eugene B., Frank Otte and Janet La Granade. "Early sex education in relationship to later coital and reproductive behavior: evidence from Jamaican women." *American Journal of Psychiatry* 133(8):969–972, Aug. 1976.

2421 Burke, Susan, ed. *Responsible Parenthood and Sex Education.* Proceedings of a Working Group held in Tunisia. London: International Planned Parenthood Federation, 1970.

2422 Carrera, Michael A., guest ed. "Sex education." *Journal of Research and Development in Education* 10(1):whole issue, Fall 1976.

2423 Carton, Jacqueline and John Carton. "Evaluation of a sex education program for children and their parents: attitude and interactional changes." *The Family Coordinator* 20(4):377–386, Oct. 1971.

2424 Dearth, Paul B. "Viable sex education in the schools: expectations of students, parents, and experts." *The Journal of School Health* 44(4):190–193, Apr. 1974

2425 Diamond, Milton. "Human sexuality: mass sex education student and community reaction." *Journal of Sex Education and Therapy* 2(2):1–11, Fall/Winter 1976.

2426 Gendel, Evalyn S. and Pauline B. Green. "Sex education controversy—a boost to new and better programs." *Journal of School Health* 41(1):24–28, Jan. 1971.

2427 Haims, Lawrence J. *Sex Education and the Public Schools; A Multidimensional Study for the 1970s.* Lexington, MA: Lexington Books, 1973.

2428 Harter, Carl L. and Vestal W. Parrish. "Maternal preference of socialization agent for sex education." *Journal of Marriage and the Family* 30(3):418–426, Aug. 1968.

2429 International Planned Parenthood Federation. Europe Region. *A Survey on the Status of Sex Education in European Member Countries.* London: International Planned Parenthood Federation, 1975.

2430 Joseph, P.J. "The need for sex education—a study of venereal disease patients." *Journal of Family Welfare* 19(3):91–99, Mar. 1973.

2431 Kellogg, Edmund H., David K. Kline and Jan Stepán. *The World's Laws and Practices on Population and Sexuality Education.* Law and Population Monograph Series, no. 25. Medford, MA: Fletcher School of Law and Diplomacy, Tufts University, 1975.

2432 Kirkendall, Lester A. and Greg J. Miles. "Sex education research." *Review of Educational Research* 38(5):528–544, Dec. 1968.

2433 Libby, Roger W., Allan C. Acock and David Payne. "Configurations of parental preferences concerning sources of sex education for adolescents." *Adolescence* 9(33):73–80, Spring 1974.

2434 Machen, Robert B. *The effect of ten hours of instruction in sex education on anxiety related to sex concepts.* (Dissertation—American University.) Ann Arbor, MI: University Microfilms, 1970. (Order #71-8618)

2435 O'Rourke, Thomas W. and Diane M. O'Rourke. "The current status of family life and sex education in the public schools of Illinois: a rebuttal." *Journal of School Health* 43(6):404–405, June 1973.

2436 Quality Educational Development, Inc. "Sex education programs in the public schools of the United States." In: *Technical Report of the Commission on Obscenity and Pornography,* 5, pp. 295–338. Washington, D.C.: U.S. GPO, 1971. (Avail. from Supt. of Docs., U.S. GPO, Washington, DC 20402. Stock #5256-0006.)

2437 Ranney, Brooks. "Sex education and family planning advice by South Dakota doctors." *Medical Aspects of Human Sexuality* 6(8):25–33, Aug. 1972.

2438 Rogers, Rex S., ed. *Sex Education: Rationale and Reaction.* London/New York: Cambridge University Press, 1974.

2439 Shatin, Leo and J.A. Southworth. "Sex knowledge, intelligence and sexual adjustment." *The Journal of Social Psychology* 54:219–233, 1961.

2440 Stewart, Clarence Milton. *A model for structuring sex-education workshops in the United States of America.* (Dissertation—American University.) Ann Arbor, MI: University Microfilms, 1971. (Order #72-9155)

2441 Stuve, Gilbert Edmund. *Use of the "citizen's committee" as an educational policy device in the area of public controversy: a study of sex education advisory committees in selected Detroit suburbs.* (Dissertation—Wayne State University.) Ann Arbor, MI: University Microfilms, 1972. (Order #73-12,604)

2442 Young, Marjorie A.C. *Review of Research and Studies Related to the Health Education Aspects of Family Planning (1967 to 1971); Studies Related to School and College Programs of Family Life Education.* Health Education Monograph no. 33. San Francisco: Society for Public Health Education, 1973.

CHILD

2443 Coates, Edward Eugene. "Some apparent effects of the acquisition of factual human reproductive information upon selected attitudes of upper elementary students." Unpub. doctoral dissertation, University of Tennessee, 1970.

2444 Moore, James E. and Diane Kendall. "Children's concepts of reproduction." *Journal of Sex Research* 7(1):42–61, Feb. 1971.

2445 Paonessa, John J. and Mary W. Paonessa. "The preparation of boys for puberty." *Social Casework* 52(1):39–44, Jan. 1971.

2446 Ramsey, Glen V. "Sex information of younger boys." *American Journal of Orthopsychiatry* 13(2):347–352, Apr. 1943.

2447 Rogers, Rex S. "The effects of televised sex education at the primary school level." In: *Sex Education; Rationale and Reaction,* ed. by Rex S. Rogers, pp. 251–264. London/New York: Cambridge University Press, 1974.

2448 Thornburg, Hershel D. "Educating the preadolescent about sex." *The Family Coordinator* 23(1):35–39, Jan. 1974.

ADOLESCENT

2449 Anderson, J. Harold. "Sex education in North Carolina." *Western Carolina University Journal of Education* 6(1):20–22, Spring 1974.

2450 Baker, Luther G. and James B. Darcy. "Survey of family life and sex education programs in Washington secondary schools and development of guidelines for statewide coordinated programs." *The Family Coordinator* 19(3):228–233, July 1970.

2451 Bloom, Jean Louise. *An investigation of the effect of presenting a sex education course to high school students who have been removed from the regular classroom situation because of severe emotional or physical problems.* (Dissertation—New York University.) Ann Arbor, MI: University Microfilms, 1968. (Order #69-11,738)

2452 Bracher, Marjory. "The Martinson report: implications for sex education." *Journal of School Health* 37(10):491–496, 1967.

2453 Calderwood, Deryck. *Adolescent appraisals and opinions concerning their sex education in selected institutions.* (Dissertation—Oregon State University.) Ann Arbor, MI: University Microfilms, 1970. (Order #71-2465)

2454 Carter, Mary. "Knowledge about sexual matters in delinquent girls." *British Journal of Psychiatry* 115(519):221–224, 1969.

2455 Cheetham, R.W.S., H. Sibisi and R.J. Cheetham. "Psychiatric problems encountered in urban Zulu adolescents with specific reference to changes in sex education." *Australian and New Zealand Journal of Psychiatry* 8(1):41–48, Mar. 1974.

2456 Cogswell, Betty E. "Communication with adolescents; a study of sex information sessions." *Sociological Symposium* 6:1–17, Spring 1971.

2457 Dickinson, George E. "Sex information sources of black and white adolescents in a Southern community." *Sociological Symposium* 6:19–22, Spring 1971.

2458 Diprizio, Chrisann. *The effects of a program of sex education on the attitudes of junior high school students and their parents.* Unpub. doctoral dissertation, Northwestern University, 1974.

2459 Donohue, John Earl. *Sources of sexuality concept formation among high school students.* (Dissertation—University of Denver.) Ann Arbor, MI: University Microfilms, 1971. (Order #71-17142)

2460 Elias, James E. "Sex education, sex research and the adolescent." Paper presented to the National Science Teachers Association Meeting, Evansville, IN, Apr. 25, 1969. 11p.

2461 Fox, David J., Anne Steinmann and Stuart M. Losen. "The impact of sex education on the sex role perceptions of junior high school stu-

dents." *International Mental Health Research Newsletter* 16(1):13–14, Spring 1974.

2462 Gohagan, John Kenneth. *A Policy Analysis of the Potential Effects of Education on Adolescent and Post-adolescent Fertility: A Bayesian Approach.* Center for Population Studies, no. 9. Cambridge, MA: Harvard University, 1973.

2463 Greenberg, Jerrold S. "A study of personality change associated with the conducting of a high school unit in homosexuality." *Journal of School Health* 45(7):394–398, Sept. 1975.

2464 Hikel, James Steven. *A qualitative study of teenagers' talk about sex: implications for sex education.* (Dissertation—University of Montana.) Ann Arbor, MI: University Microfilms, 1972. (Order #72-33,058)

2465 Hoch, Loren Lee. "Attitude change as a function of sex education in a high school general biology class." Unpub. doctoral dissertation, Indiana University, 1968.

2466 House, Elizabeth A. and Sadja Goldsmith. "Planned parenthood services for the young teenager." *Family Planning Perspectives* 4(2):27–31, Apr. 1972.

2467 Hughey, James Broadus, Jr. *A study of a team teaching program in sexuality education.* (Dissertation—Colorado State College.) Ann Arbor, MI: University Microfilms, 1969. (Order #69-19,219)

2468 Johnson, Greg. "Kids, sex, and the Bible Belt high school." *Social Welfare in Appalachia* 8:5–7, 1976.

2469 Kravetz, James H. and Sidney A. Smith. "Sex education: too little—too late." *Fertility and Sterility* 24(3):202–207, Mar. 1973.

2470 Lee, Margie. "Background factors related to sex information and attitudes." *Journal of Educational Psychology* 42:467–485, Dec. 1952.

2471 Mandel, Nathan G. "Family life education in a rural community: a brief program." *Journal of Marriage and the Family* 28(4):526–527, Nov. 1966.

2472 Meerdink, Robert C. *The accuracy and sources of information concerning sex concepts of junior high school students, and their self-ratings of their knowledge of the concepts.* (Dissertation—University of South Dakota.) Ann Arbor, MI: University Microfilms, 1970. (Order #71-1148)

2473 Reichelt, Paul A. and Harriet H. Werley. "A sex information program for sexually active teenagers." *Journal of School Health* 45(2):100–107, Feb. 1975.

2474 _____. "Sex knowledge of teenagers and the effect of an educational rap session." *Journal of Research and Development in Education* 10(1):13–22, Fall 1976.

2475 Rubin, Isadore. *A critical evaluation of certain selected operational principles of sex education for the adolescent.* (Dissertation—New York University.) Ann Arbor, MI: University Microfilms, 1963. (Order #63-6677)

2476 Schwartz, Martin Sidney. *A study of the attitudes, sex knowledge, and sources of sex information of 87 ninth grade lower class boys.* (Dissertation—Columbia University.) Ann Arbor, MI: University Microfilms, 1968. (Order #69-9916)

2477 Soares, Louise H. and Anthony T. Soares. "A study of students' sex attitudes and teachers' perceptions of students' sex attitudes." Paper presented at the Eastern Psychological Association Convention, Philadelphia, Apr. 1969. 10p.

2478 Thornburg, Hershel D. "A comparative study of sex information sources." *Journal of School Health* 42(2):88–91, Feb. 1972.

2479 Wallace, Robert Clayton. *Sex education knowledge, verbal interaction and attitudes: an exploratory study in high school biology classes.* (Dissertation—University of Illinois at Urbana-Champaign.) Ann Arbor, MI: University Microfilms, 1970. (Order #71-14,979)

COLLEGE STUDENT

2480 Anderson, Carla Lee. "What are psychology departments doing about sex education?" *Teaching of Psychology* 2(1):24–27, Feb. 1975.

2481 Belzer, Edwin G. and E. Bernard Daly. "A quasi-experimental determination of the effects of a university course, 'Human sexuality and educating about it,' on opinions about selected premarital heterosexual behaviors." *Journal of Sex Education and Therapy* 2(1):52–62, Spring/Summer 1976.

2482 Cantor, Joanne R., Herminia Alfonso and Dolf Zillmann. "The persuasive effectiveness of the peer appeal and a communicator's first-hand experience." *Communication Research* 3(3):293–310, July 1976.

2483 Herold, Edward S. et al. "Human sexuality: a student taught course." *The Family Coordinator* 22(2):183–186, Apr. 1973.

2484 Hurster, Madeline. "Findings of the ACHA Family Life/Sex Education Study." *Journal of the American College Health Association* 19(2):116–120, Dec. 1970.

2485 McCreary-Juhasz, Anne. "How accurate are student evaluations of the extent of their knowledge of human sexuality." *Journal of School Health* 37(8):409–412, Oct. 1967.

2486 Mazur, Ronald M., prog. dir. *Training Peer Sex Educators.* Amherst: University Health Services, University of Massachusetts, 1976.

2487 Olson, David H. and Arthur E. Gravatt. "Attitude change in a functional marriage course." *The Family Coordinator* 17(2):99–104, Apr. 1968.

2488 Price, Quentin L. *Influence of sex and family life education on student attitude toward traditional family ideology and sex knowledge.* (Dissertation—United States International University.) Ann Arbor, MI: University Microfilms, 1969. (Order #71-7881)

2489 Redfering, David L. and Ralph M. Roberts. "Personality correlates and the effects of a Human Sexuality course on sexual attitudes and information retention of college students." *Journal of Sex Education and Therapy* 2(2):34–40, Fall/Winter 1976.

2490 Rees, Bill and Steve Zimmerman. "Effects of formal sex education on the sexual behaviors and attitudes of college students." *Journal of the American College Health Association* 22(5):370–371, June 1974.

2491 Schwartz, Allan J. *Human sexuality and community mental health on campus: evaluating procedures used to screen and select undergraduate leaders for human sexuality discussion groups.* (Dissertation—University of Rochester.) Ann Arbor, MI: University Microfilms, 1973. (Order #73-25,849)

2492 Sheppard, Samona. "A survey of college-based courses in human sexuality." *Journal of the American College Health Association* 23:14–18, Oct. 1974.

2493 Spanier, Graham B. "Sexual socialization and premarital sexual behavior: an empirical investigation of the impact of formal and informal sex education." Unpub. doctoral dissertation, Northwestern University, 1973.

2494 Sunseri, A.J., J.H. Sunder and D. Jucha. "Initial sources of sex information: percentage and rank order." *College Student Journal* 7(4):20–23, Nov. 1973.

2495 Thornburg, Hershel D. "Age and first sources of sex information as reported by 88 college women." *Journal of School Health* 40(3):156–158, Mar. 1970.

2496 Vennewitz, Peter Jan. "A study to determine the effects of a college human sexuality course upon student sex knowledge and attitudes toward selected sexual topics." Unpub. doctoral dissertation, Oregon State University, 1975.

2497 Watts, Parris René. "Comparison of knowledge gain and attitude change among three methods of teaching sex education in university personal health classes." Unpub. doctoral dissertation, Indiana University, 1974.

2498 Wiechmann, Gerald H. and Altis L. Ellis. "A study of the effects of 'sex education' on premarital petting and coital behavior." *The Family Coordinator* 18(3):231–234, July 1969.

2499 Wright, Mary Ruth and James L. McCary. "Positive effects of sex education on emotional patterns of behavior." *Journal of Sex Research* 5(3):162–169, Aug. 1969.

2500 Zuckerman, Marvin, Richard Tushup and Stephen Finner. "Sexual attitudes and experience: attitude and personality correlates and changes produced by a course in sexuality." *Journal of Consulting and Clinical Psychology* 44(1):7–19, Feb. 1976.

PROFESSIONAL GROUPS

2501 Carolina Population Center. State Services Office. *Report of the Pilot Training Workshop in Human Sexuality and Sexual Counseling.* Chapel Hill, NC: Carolina Population Center, 1975.

2502 Coombs, Robert H. "Sex attitudes of physicians and marriage counselors." *The Family Coordinator* 20(3):269–277, July 1971.

2503 Doyle, Averil Marie. *Effect of graduate training in human sexuality on the counselor's ability to deal with sexually related problems in the counseling setting.* (Dissertation—University of Missouri, Kansas City.) Ann Arbor, MI: University Microfilms, 1975. (Order #76-11,484)

2504 McCreary-Juhasz, Anne M. "Sex knowledge of prospective teachers and graduate nurses." *Canadian Nurse:* 48–50, July 1967.

2505 Mace, David R., R.H.O. Bannerman and J. Burton, eds. *The Teaching of Human Sexuality in Schools for Health Professionals.* Public Health Papers, no. 57. Geneva: World Health Organization, 1974. (Avail. from Q Corporation, 49 Sheridan Ave., Albany, NY 12210.)

2506 Maddock, James W. "Sex education in professional schools." *Journal of Research and Development in Education* 10(1):73–79, Fall 1976.

2507 Stayton, William R. and Nathan W. Turner. "An innovative model for training professionals in human sexuality." *Journal of Sex Education and Therapy* 2(2): 49–52, Fall/Winter 1976.

DOCTORS

2508 Alzate, Heli. "Los conocimientos sexuales de los medicos." *Revista Colombiana de Obstetricia y Gynecología* (Bogotá, Colombia) 24(5): 323–328, Sept./Oct. 1973.

2509 Chapman, J. Dudley and Jack Leahy. "D.O.'s and their sexual practices and attitudes." *Osteopathic Physician* 41(11):56 passim, Nov. 1974.

2510 Crawley, Lawrence Q., James L. Malfetti and F.E. Bartholomew. "Sex education for school physicians: follow-up of an in-service training course." *Family Coordinator* 23(4):359–364, Oct. 1974.

2511 _____. "Sex education for school physicians: report on an in-service training course." *Journal of School Health* 42(1):25–31, Jan. 1972.

2512 Herndon, C.N. and E.M. Nash. "Premarriage and marriage counseling: a study of practices of North Carolina physicians." *Journal of the American Medical Association* 180:395–401, 1962.

2513 Pauly, Ira B. "Influence of training and attitudes on sexual counseling in medical practice." *Medical Aspects of Human Sexuality* 6(3):84–117, Mar. 1972.

2514 Pauly, Ira B. and Steven Goldstein. "Physician's ability to treat sexual problems." *Medical Aspects of Human Sexuality* 4(10):24–49, Oct. 1970.

2515 _____. "Physicians' perception of their education in human sexuality." *Journal of Medical Education* 45(10):745–753, Oct. 1970.

2516 Sadock, Virginia A. and Harold I. Kaplan. "Comprehensive sex therapy training: a new approach." *American Journal of Psychiatry* 32(8):858–860, Aug. 1975.

2517 Wan, Livia S. et al. "Continuing education in family planning for practicing physicians." *American Journal of Public Health* 64(1):32–36, Jan. 1974.

MEDICAL STUDENTS

2518 Alzate, Heli. "A course in human sexuality in a Colombian medical school." *Journal of Medical Education* 49:438–443, May 1974.

2519 Cade, Jerry D. and William F. Jessee. "Sex education in American medical schools." *Journal of Medical Education* 46(1):64–68, Jan. 1971.

2520 Chez, Ronald A. "Movies of human sexual response as learning aids for medical students." *Journal of Medical Education* 46:9977–9981, Nov. 1971.

2521 Engel, Illona M., Phillip J. Resnik and Stephen B. Levine. "The use of programmed patients and videotapes in teaching medical students to take a sexual history." *Journal of Medical Education* 51(5):425–427, May 1976.

2522 Garrard, Judith, Aldona Vaitkus and Richard A. Chilgren. "Evaluation of a course in human sexuality." *Journal of Medical Education* 47:772–778, Oct. 1972.

2523 Golden, Joshua S. and Edward H. Liston. "Medical sex education: the world of illusion and the practical realities." *Journal of Medical Education* 47:761–771, Oct. 1972.

2524 Hoch, Zwi, Hadassa Kubat and J.M. Brandes. "Results of the Sex Knowledge and Attitude Test of medical students in Israel." Paper presented at the International Congress of Sexology, Montreal, Canada, Oct. 1976. 30p.

2525 Lief, Harold I. and Arno Karlen. *Sex Education in Medicine.* New York: Spectrum Publications, 1976.

2526 Lippard, Vernon W., ed. *Macy Conference on Family Planning, Demography and Human Sexuality in Medical Education.* New York: Josiah Macy Jr. Foundation, 1971.

2527 Marcotte, David B. et al. "The effect of a spaced sex education course on medical students' sexual knowledge and attitudes." *Medical Education* 10:117–121, 1976.

2528 Rosenberg, Pearl and Richard A. Chilgren. "Sex education discussion groups in a medical setting." *International Journal of Group Psychotherapy* 23(1):23–41, Jan. 1973.

2529 Tyler, Edward A. "Introducing a sex education course into the medical curriculum." *Journal of Medical Education* 45:1025–1031, Dec. 1970.

2530 Woods, Sherwyn M. "Sexual problems of medical students." *Medical Aspects of Human Sexuality* 6(2):66–85, Feb. 1972.

2531 Woods, Sherwyn M. and Joseph Natterson. "Sexual attitudes of medical students: some implications for medical education." *American Journal of Psychiatry* 124(3):323–332, Sept. 1967.

NURSES

2532 Ellis, Albert and Earl W. Fuller. "The sex, love and marriage questions of senior nursing students." *Journal of Social Psychology* 31:209–216, 1950.

2533 Harper, Mary W., Betty R. Marcom and Victor D. Wall. "Abortion: do attitudes of nursing personnel affect the patient's perception of care?" *Nursing Research* 21(4):327–331, July/Aug. 1972.

2534 Houser, Carolyn et al. "The teaching of fertility regulation in basic schools of nursing in the United States." *American Journal of Public Health* 59(6):982–995, June 1969.

2535 Kessler, Kenneth and Theodore Weiss. "Ward staff problems with abortion." *Psychiatry in Medicine* 5(2):97–103, 1974.

2536 McDermott, John F. and Walter F. Char. "Abortion repeal in Hawaii: an unexpected crisis in patient care." *American Journal of Orthopsychiatry* 41(4):620–626, July 1971.

2537 Mandetta, Anne F. "Learning about human sexuality—a course model." *Nursing Outlook* 22(8):525–527, Aug. 1974.

2538 Mims, Fern. *An interdisciplinary course in human sexuality for medical and nursing students.* (Doctoral dissertation—University of Cincinnati.) Ann Arbor, MI: University Microfilms, 1974. (Order #74-8457)

2539 Mims, Fern, Rosalee Yeaworth and Stephen Hornstein. "Effectiveness of an interdisciplinary course in human sexuality." *Nursing Research* 23(3):248–252, May/June 1974.

2540 Payne, Tyana. "Sexuality of nurses: correlations of knowledge, attitudes and behavior." *Nursing Research* 25(4):286–292, July/Aug. 1976.

2541 Quirk, Barbara. "The nurse's role in advising patients on coitus during pregnancy." *Nursing Clinics of North America* 8:501–507, Sept. 1973.

2542 Walker, Edith G. "Study of sexuality in the nursing curriculum." *Nursing Forum* 10(1):18–30, 1971.

TEACHERS

2543 Battista, Anna. *An exploration of factors associated with the effectiveness of training* *health education teachers: an evaluation of New York University's experienced teacher fellowship program in sex education for the elementary school.* (Dissertation—New York University.) Ann Arbor, MI: University Microfilms, 1972. (Order #72-26584)

2544   Bender, Stephen J. "The human reproduction knowledge of prospective elementary teachers." *Education Quest* 14:9–10, 1970.

2545   Benjamin, Ruby R. "Programs in sex education: use of clinics in a community hospital for training graduate students." *The Family Coordinator* 20(4):341–348, Oct. 1971.

2546   Bennett, Virginia D.C., Peter Taylor and Susan Ford. "An experimental course in sex education for teachers." *Mental Hygiene* 53(4):625–631, Oct. 1969.

2547   Carrera, Michael A. *Guidelines for the preparation of high school teachers of sex education.* (Doctoral dissertation—Columbia University.) Ann Arbor, MI: University Microfilms, 1970. (Order #70-26,768)

2548   _____. "Training the sex educator: guidelines for teacher training institutions." *American Journal of Public Health* 62(2):233–243, 1972.

2549   Fretz, Bruce R. and Warren R. Johnson. "Influence of intensive workshop on teachers' sex information and attitudes toward sex education." *Research Quarterly of the American Association for Health, Physical Education and Recreation* 42:156–163, May 1971.

2550   Giacquinta, Joseph B. "Status, risk, and receptivity to innovations in complex organizations: a study of the responses of four groups of educators to the proposed introduction of sex education in elementary school." *Sociology of Education* 48:38–58, Winter 1975.

2551   Hobbs, George William. *An investigation of certain factors related to self-concept, sexual knowledge and attitude toward sex education of a group of elementary teachers.* (Dissertation—North Texas University.) Ann Arbor, MI: University Microfilms, 1970. (Order #71-553)

2552   Kent, Rosemary M., James R. Abernathy and Robert C. Middour. "Teacher readiness for roles in family life education: an exploratory study." *American Journal of Public Health* 61(3):586–599, Mar. 1971.

2553   McCreary-Juhasz, Anne. "Characteristics essential to teachers in sex education." *Journal of School Health* 40(1):17–19, Jan. 1970.

2554   Malfetti, James L. and Arline M. Rubin. "Sex education: who is teaching the teachers?" *The Family Coordinator* 17(2):110–117, Apr. 1968.

2555   Mizokawa, Donald Tsuneo. "Assessment of sex knowledge of beginning teachers." Unpub. master's thesis, University of Hawaii, 1969.

2556   Plonsky, Carolyn Giffen. "A scale to measure elementary school teachers' attitudes toward contraceptive education." Unpub. doctoral dissertation, Teachers College, Columbia University, 1975.

2557   Rausher, Shirley R. "An analysis of attitudes toward sexism of teacher-education stuents." *Journal of Sex Education and Therapy* 2(2):18–22, Fall/Winter, 1976.

2558   Ready, Jerry Lee. *An attitudinal survey of teachers of family life and sex education in the Public Schools of Illinois.* (Dissertation—University of Iowa.) Ann Arbor, MI: University Microfilms, 1972. (Order #72-26,727)

2559   Reed, Charles E. "An analysis of the perceptions of high school principals in public and Catholic schools relative to the importance of sex education in the curriculum." *Journal of School Health* 43(3):198–200, Mar. 1973.

2560   Rubin, Arline M. *Sex attitudes of female sex educators.* (Dissertation—Columbia University.) Ann Arbor, MI: University Microfilms, 1970. (Order #72-4183)

2561   Stewart, Clarence Milton. *A model for structuring sex-education workshops in the United States of America.* (Dissertation—American University.) Ann Arbor, MI: University Microfilms, 1971. (Order #72-9155)

SOCIAL WORKERS

2562   Abramowitz, Naomi R. "Human sexuality in the social work curriculum." *The Family Coordinator* 20(4):349–354, Oct. 1971.

2563   Carrera, Michael A. and Gary Rosenberg. "Inservice education in human sexuality for social work practitioners." In: *Modern Sexuality,* ed. by Mary L. Gottesfeld, pp. 261–267. New York: Behavioral Publications, 1973.

2564   Castor, Jane and Pamela Sue Hudson. "Social work attitudes toward referral to Planned Parenthood." *Social Service Review* 45(3):302–309, Sept. 1971.

2565 Gochros, Harvey L. and Jean S. Gochros. *The Sexually Oppressed.* New York: Association Press, 1977.

2566 Lassen, Carol L. "Issues and dilemmas in sexual treatment." *Journal of Sex and Marital Therapy* 2(1):32–39, Spring 1976.

2567 Valentich, Mary and James Gripton. "Teaching human sexuality to social work students." *Family Coordinator* 24(3):273–280, July 1975.

2568 Young, Rhodes C., Jane Castor and Pamela Sue Hudson. "Attitude clusters in birth control counseling by social workers." *American Journal of Public Health* 61(9):1832–1839, Sept. 1971.

Sex and Society

Anthropological Perspectives on Human Sexuality

2569 Aberle, David F. et al. "The incest taboo and mating patterns of animals." *American Anthropologist* 65(2):253–265, Apr. 1963.

2570 Anderson, Robert T. and Gallatin Anderson. "Sexual behavior and urbanization in a Danish village." *Southwestern Journal of Anthropology* 16(2):93–109, 1960.

2571 Beach, Frank A. "Cross-species comparisons and the human heritage." *Archives of Sexual Behavior* 5(5):469–485, Sept. 1976.

2572 _____. "Human sexuality in four perspectives." In: *Human Sexuality in Four Perspectives,* ed. by Frank A. Beach, pp. 1–21. Baltimore: Johns Hopkins University Press, 1977.

2573 Beard, Alice. "The quarter is our turf: a study of the interface between gay and straight economy." Paper presented at the American Anthropological Association 73rd Annual Meeting, Mexico City, Nov. 19–24, 1974. 33p.

2574 Beidelman, Thomas O. "The filth of incest: a text and comments on Kaguru notions of sexuality, alimentation and aggression." *Cahiers d'Études Africaines* 12(1):164–173, 1972.

2575 Benedict, Ruth. "Sex in primitive society." *American Journal of Orthopsychiatry* 9:570–573, July 1939.

2576 Berndt, Ronald M. and Catherine H. Berndt. *Sexual Behavior in Western Arnhem Land.* Viking Fund Publications in Anthropology, no. 16. New York: Wenner-Gren Foundation for Anthropological Research, 1951.

2577 Bick, Mario. "Blind man's bluff: the anthropologist confronts sexual antagonism." Paper presented at the 70th Annual Meeting of the American Anthropological Association, New York, Nov. 1971. 9p.

2578 Bock, E. Wilbur and Sugiyama Iutaka. "Social status, mobility and premarital pregnancy: a case of Brazil." *Journal of Marriage and the Family* 32(2):284–292, May 1970.

2579 Bonte, Monique. *Aspects Traditionnels et Coutumiers de la Sexualité au Rwanda.* Hraflex Books Descriptive Ethnography Series, no. FO42-001. New Haven: Human Relations Area Files, 1973.

2580 Broude, Gwen J. "Norms of premarital sexual behavior: a cross-cultural study." *Ethos* 3(3):381–402, Fall 1975.

2581 Broude, Gwen J. and Sarah J. Greene. "Cross-cultural codes on twenty sexual attitudes and practices." *Ethnology* 15(4):409–429, Oct. 1976.

2582 Bryk, Felix. *Neger-eros; Ethnologische Studien über das Sexualleben bei Negern.* Berlin/Köln: A. Marcus & E. Weber, 1928.

2583 Burton, Roger V. "Folk theory and the incest taboo." *Ethos* 1(4):504–516, Winter 1973.

2584 Campbell, Bernard, ed. *Sexual Selection and the Descent of Man, 1871–1971.* Chicago: Aldine Publishing Co., 1972.

2585 Caputo, G. Craig. *A cross-cultural analysis of sexual restrictions and cultural complexity.* (Dissertation—Yale University.) Ann Arbor, MI: University Microfilms, 1973. (Order #74-10,339)

2586 Carrier, Joseph Michel. "Cultural factors affecting urban Mexican male homosexual behavior." Paper presented at the American Anthropological Association 73rd Annual Meeting, Mexico City, Nov. 19–24, 1974. 46p.

2587 Chard, Chester S. "Sternberg's materials on the sexual life of the Gilyak." *Anthropological Papers of the University of Alaska* 10(1):13–23, Dec. 1961.

2588 Churchill, Wainwright. *Homosexual Behavior among Males: A Cross-Cultural and Cross Species Investigation.* New York: Hawthorn Books, 1967.

2589 Cohen, Yehudi A. "Ends and means in political control: state organization and the punishment of adultery, incest, and violation of celibacy." *American Anthropologist* 71(4):658–687, Aug. 1969.

2590 "Cross-cultural family research." *Journal of Marriage and the Family* 31(2):whole issue, May 1969.

2591 Danielsson, Bengt. *Love in the South Seas.* London: G. Allen & Unwin, 1956.

2592 Davenport, William. "Sexual patterns and their regulation in a society of the southeast Pacific." In: *Sex and Behavior,* ed. by Frank A. Beach. New York: Wiley, 1965.

2593 Devereux, George. "Institutionalized homosexuality of the Mohave Indians." *Human Biology* 9:498–527, 1937.

2594 _____. "Sexual life of the Mohave Indians; an interpretation in terms of social psychology." Unpub. doctoral dissertation, University of California at Berkeley, 1936.

2595 _____. "The significance of the external female genitalia and of female orgasm for the male." *Journal of the American Psychoanalytic Association* 6(2):278–286, Apr. 1958.

2596 Dorjahn, Vernon R. "Fertility, polygyny and their interrelations in Temne society." *American Anthropologist* 60(5):838–860, Oct. 1958.

2597 DuBois, Cora. *The People of Alor.* Minneapolis: University of Minnesota Press, 1944.

2598 Dubois, Jean Claude. "Transsexualisme et anthropologie culturelle." *Gynecologia Pratique* 20(6):431–440, 1969.

2599 Edgerton, Robert B. "Pokot intersexuality: an East African example of the resolution of sexual incongruity." *American Anthropologist* 66(6):1288–1299, Dec. 1964.

2600 Eichler, Margrit. "Power and sexual fear in primitive societies." *Journal of Marriage and the Family* 37(4):917–926, Nov. 1975.

2601 Elwin, Verrier. *The Muria and Their Ghotul.* Bombay: Oxford University Press, 1947.

2602 Ember, Melvin. "On the origin and extension of the incest taboo." *Behavior Science Research* 10(4):249–281, 1975.

2603 Evans-Pritchard, E.E. "Sexual inversion among the Azande." *American Anthropologist* 72(6):1428–1434, Dec. 1970.

2604 _____. "Some notes on Azande sex habits." *American Anthropologist* 75(1): 171–176, Feb. 1973.

2605 Fehlinger, Hans. *Sexual Life of Primitive People.* New York: United Book Guild, 1945.

2606 Fischer, Ann. "Reproduction in Truk." *Ethnology* 2(4):526–540, Oct. 1963.

2607 Flynn, Charles. "Sexuality and insult behavior." *Journal of Sex Research* 12(1):1–13, Feb. 1976.

2608 Ford, Clellan S. *A Comparative Study of Human Reproduction.* Yale University Publications in Anthropology, no. 32. New Haven: Yale University Press, 1945.

2609 _____. "Sex offenses: an anthropological perspective." *Law and Contemporary Problems* 25(2):225–243, Spring 1960.

2610 Ford, Clellan S. and Frank A. Beach. *Patterns of Sexual Behavior.* New York: Harper & Bros., 1951.

2611 Freilich, Morris. "Serial polygyny, Negro peasants, and model analysis." *American Anthropologist* 63(5):955–975, Oct. 1961.

2612 Freire-Maia, N. "Inbreeding and celibacy." *Human Heredity* 20(4):383–387, 1970.

2613 Fry, Peter. "Male homosexuality and Afro-Brazilian possession cults (1)." Paper presented at the American Anthropological Association 73rd Annual Meeting, Mexico City, Nov. 19–24, 1974. 51p.

2614 Ghiselin, Michael T. *The Economy of Nature and the Evolution of Sex.* Berkeley: University of California Press, 1974.

2615 Gladwin, Thomas and Seymour Sarason. *Truk: Man in Paradise.* Viking Fund Publications in

Anthropology, no. 20. New York: Wenner-Gren Foundation for Anthropological Research, 1953.

2616 Goodland, Roger. *A Bibliography of Sex Rites and Customs; An Annotated Record of Books, Articles, and Illustrations in All Languages.* London: George Routledge & Sons, 1931. (Reprint ed.: Boston: Longwood Press, 1977.)

2617 Goody, Jack. "A comparative approach to incest and adultery." *British Journal of Sociology* 7(4):286–305, Dec. 1956.

2618 Gorer, Geoffrey. *Himalayan Village.* London: Michael Joseph, 1938.

2619 Hallowell, A. "Psychosexual adjustment, personality, and the good life in a nonliterate culture." In: *Psychosexual Development in Health and Disease,* ed. by Paul H. Hoch and Joseph Zubin, pp. 102–123. New York: Grune & Stratton, 1949.

2620 Heider, Karl G. "Anthropological models of incest laws in the United States." *American Anthropologist* 71(4):693–701, Aug. 1969.

2621 _____. "Dani sexuality: a low energy system." *Man* 11(N.S.):188–201, 1976.

2622 Heiser, Charles B. "The penis gourd of New Guinea." *Annals of the Association of American Geographers* 63(3):312–318, Sept. 1973.

2623 Hennigh, Lawrence. "Control of incest in Eskimo folktales." *Journal of American Folklore* 79(312):356–369, Apr./June, 1966.

2624 Henry, Jules. "The social function of child sexuality in Pilagá Indian culture." In: *Psychosexual Development in Health and Disease,* ed. by Paul H. Hoch and Joseph Zubin, pp. 91–101. New York: Grune & Stratton, 1949.

2625 Heweston, John. "Society and the sexual life of children and adolescents: child murders." *Journal of Sex Education* 4(3):118–127, Dec. 1951/Jan. 1952.

2626 Hippler, Arthur E. "Patterns of sexual behavior: the Athabascans of interior Alaska." *Ethos* 2(1):47–68, Spring 1974.

2627 Honigmann, John J. "An anthropological approach to sex." *Social Problems* 2(4):7–15, July 1954.

2628 _____. "A cultural theory of obscenity." *Journal of Criminal Psychopathology* 5(4):715–733, Apr. 1944.

2629 Howard, Alan and Irwin Howard. "Pre-mari-

tal sex and social control among the Rotumans." *American Anthropologist* 66(2):266–283, Apr. 1964.

2630 Hsu, Francis L.K. "Sex crime and personality: a study in comparative cultural patterns." *American Scholar*:57–66, Winter 1951/1952.

2631 _____. "Suppression versus repression; a limited psychological interpretation of four cultures." *Psychiatry* 12(3):223–242, Aug. 1949.

2632 Jensen, Gordon D. "Cross-cultural studies and animal studies of sex." In: *The Sexual Experience,* ed. by B.J. Sadock, H.I. Kaplan and A.M. Freedman, pp. 289–302. Baltimore: Williams & Wilkins, 1976.

2633 Jones, Louis Thomas. *Love — Indian Style.* San Antonio: Naylor, 1973.

2634 Karsch-Haack, Ferdinand. *Das gleichgeschlechtliche Leben der Naturvölker.* München: Ernst Reinhardt, 1911.

2635 Kehoe, Alice B. "The function of ceremonial sexual intercourse among the northern Plains Indians." *Plains Anthropologist* 15(48):99–103, 1970.

2636 Kisekka, Mere Nakateregga. *Heterosexual relationships in Uganda.* (Dissertation—University of Missouri.) Ann Arbor, MI: University Microfilms, 1973. (Order #74-18,570)

2637 Kortmulder, K. "An ethnological theory of the incest taboo and exogamy." *Current Anthropology* 9(5):437–449, Dec. 1968.

2638 LaBarre, Weston. "Anthropological perspectives on sexuality." In: *Sexuality: A Search for Perspective,* ed. by Donald L. Grummon and Andrew M. Barclay, pp. 38–53. New York: Van Nostrand Reinhold, 1971.

2639 _____. "Obscenity: an anthropological appraisal." *Law and Contemporary Problems* 20(4):533–543, Fall 1955.

2640 Lagercrantz, Sture. *Penis Sheat(h)s and Their Distribution in Africa.* Uppsala: Uppsala University, 1976.

2641 Laubscher, Barend J. *Sex, Custom and Psychopathology; A Study of South African Pagan Natives.* New York: Robert M. McBride, 1938.

2642 Lee, Richard Borshay. "Male-female residence arrangements and political power in human hunter-gatherers." *Archives of Sexual Behavior* 3(2):167–173, Mar. 1974.

2643 Leibowitz, Lila. "Desmond Morris is wrong

about breasts, buttocks, and body hair." *Psychology Today* 3(9):16 passim, Feb. 1970.

2644   LeVine, Robert A. "Gusii sex offenses: a study in social control." *American Anthropologist* 61(6):965–990, Dec. 1959.

2645   Lindenbaum, Shirley. "Sorcerers, ghosts, and polluting women: an analysis of religious belief and population control." *Ethnology* 11(3):241–253, July 1972.

2646   Longmore, Laura. *The Dispossessed: A Study of the Sex Life of Bantu Women in Urban Areas in and Around Johannesburg.* London: J. Cape, 1959.

2647   Malinowski, Bronislaw. *Sex and Repression in Savage Society.* New York: Harcourt, Brace & Co., 1927.

2648   _____. *Sexual Life of Savages in North-Western Melanesia.* New York: Harcourt, Brace & World, 1962 (c. 1929).

2649   Marshall, Donald S. and Robert C. Suggs, eds. *Human Sexual Behavior; Variations in the Ethnographic Spectrum.* New York: Basic Books, 1971.

2650   Mayer, Karl Herbert. *The Mushroom Stones of Mesoamerica.* Ramona, CA: Acoma Books, 1977.

2651   Mead, Margaret. *From the South Seas; Studies of Adolescence and Sex in Primitive Societies.* New York: Morrow, 1939.

2652   _____. *Male and Female: A Study of Sexes in the Changing World.* New York: Morrow, 1949.

2653   _____. "Psychologic weaning: childhood and adolescence." In: *Psychosexual Development in Health and Disease,* ed. by Paul H. Hoch and Joseph Zubin, pp. 124–135. New York: Grune & Stratton, 1949.

2654   Meggitt, M.J. "Male-female relationships in the highlands of Australian New Guinea." *American Anthropologist* 66(4):204–224, Aug. 1964.

2655   Meigs, Anna S. "Male pregnancy and the reduction of sexual opposition in a New Guinea Highlands society." *Ethnology* 15(4):393–407, Oct. 1976.

2656   Messenger, John C. "Sex and repression in Inis Beag." In: *Sexual Deviance and Sexual Deviants,* ed. by E. Goode and R. Troiden, pp. 38–44. New York: Morrow, 1974.

2657   Michael, Richard P. and John H. Crook,

eds. *Comparative Ecology and Behaviour of Primates; Proceedings of a Conference Held at the Zoological Society, London, Nov. 1971.* London/New York: Academic Press, 1973.

2658   Milner, Richard B. "The trickster, the bad nigga, and the new urban ethnography: an initial report and editorial code." *Urban Life and Culture* 1(1):109–117, Apr. 1972.

2659   Money, John. "Sex training and traditions in Arnhem Land." *British Journal of Medical Psychology* 43:383–399, Dec. 1970.

2660   Montagu, M.F. Ashley. *Coming into Being among the Australian Aborigines.* London: George Routledge & Sons, 1937.

2661   _____. "Man—and human nature." *American Journal of Psychiatry* 112(6):401–410, Dec. 1955.

2662   Montague, Susan P. "Copulation in Kakuwaga." *Man* 8(2):304–305, June 1973.

2663   Murdock, George P. "The social regulation of sexual behavior." In: *Psychosexual Development in Health and Disease,* ed. by Paul H. Hoch and Joseph Zubin, pp. 256–266. New York: Grune & Stratton, 1949.

2664   Nag, Moni. *Factors Affecting Human Fertility in Nonindustrial Societies; A Cross-Cultural Study.* Yale University Publications in Anthropology, no. 66. New Haven: Department of Anthropology, Yale University, 1962.

2665   Nemecek, Ottokar. *Virginity; Pre-Nuptial Rites and Rituals.* New York: Philosophical Library, 1958.

2666   Newman, Graeme. *Comparative Deviance: Perception and Law in Six Cultures.* New York: Elsevier, 1976.

2667   Nimmo, H. Arlo. "Bajau sex and reproduction." *Ethnology* 9(3):251–262, July 1970.

2668   Opler, Marvin K. "Anthropological and cross-cultural aspects of homosexuality." In: *Sexual Inversion,* ed. by Judd Marmor, pp. 108–123. New York: Basic Books, 1965.

2669   _____. "Cross-cultural aspects of kissing." *Medical Aspects of Human Sexuality* 3(2):11–21, Feb. 1969.

2670   Orr, Douglass W. "Anthropological and historical notes on the female sexual role." *Journal of the American Psychoanalytic Association* 16(3):601–612, July 1968.

2671 Ortner, Sherry B. "Sherpa purity." *American Anthropologist* 75(1):49-63, Feb. 1973.

2672 Pinard, Leo William. *Heterosexual relations in the Central Visayas.* (Dissertation—University of Notre Dame.) Ann Arbor, MI: University Microfilms, 1972. (Order #72-16,271)

2673 "Primitive and ancient societies." In: *Encyclopedia of Sexual Behavior,* ed. by Albert Ellis and Albert Abarbanel, p. 22. New York: Hawthorn Books, 1967.

2674 Rabin, Albert I. "Some psychosexual differences between kibbutz and non-kibbutz Israeli boys." *Journal of Projective Techniques* 22:328-332, Sept. 1958.

2675 Ram, Bali and G. Edward Ebanks. "Stability of unions and fertility in Barbados." *Social Biology* 20(2):143-150, June 1973.

2676 Róheim, Géza. "Ceremonial prostitution in Duau (Normandy Island)." *Journal of Clinical Psychopathology* 7(4):753-764, Apr. 1946.

2677 _____. "The primal horde and incest in central Australia." *Journal of Criminal Psychopathology* 3(3):454-560, Jan. 1952.

2678 Rosenblatt, Paul C. "Communication in the practice of love magic." *Social Forces* 49(3):482-487, Mar. 1971.

2679 Rosenblatt, Paul C. and Walter J. Hillabrant. "Divorce for childlessness and the regulation of adultery." *Journal of Sex Research* 8(2):117-127, May 1972.

2680 Rosenblatt, Paul C., Stephen S. Fugita and Kenneth V. McDowell. "Wealth transfer and restrictions on sexual relations during betrothal." *Ethnology* 8(3):319-328, 1969.

2681 Rymph, David B. "Cross-sex behavior in an Isthmus Zapotec village." Paper presented at the American Anthropological Association 73rd Annual Meeting, Mexico City, Nov. 19-24, 1974. 10p.

2682 Schapera, Isaac. *Married Life in an African Tribe.* New York: Sheridan House, 1941.

2683 Schneider, Jane. "Of vigilance and virgins: honor, shame and access to resources in Mediterranean societies." *Ethnology* 10(1):1-24, Jan. 1971.

2684 Scott, William Henry. "Social and religious culture of the Kalingas of Madukayan." *Southwestern Journal of Anthropology* 16(2):174-190, Summer 1960.

2685 Seligman, Brenda Z. and E.E. Evans-Prit-chard. "The problem of incest and exogamy: a restatement." *American Anthropologist* 52(3):305-316, July/Sept. 1950.

2686 Slater, Mariam K. *The Caribbean Family: Legitimacy in Martinique.* New York: St. Martin's Press, 1977.

2687 _____. "Ecological factors in the origin of incest." *American Anthropologist* 61(6):1042-1059, Dec. 1959.

2688 Smith, Alfred G. "The extension of incest taboos in the Woleai, Micronesia." *American Anthropologist* 62(4):643-647, Aug. 1960.

2689 Sonenschein, David. "Anthropology and sex research." Paper presented at the Central States Anthropological Society Meeting, Detroit, May 2-5, 1968. 10p.

2690 _____. "Homosexuality as a subject of anthropological inquiry." *Anthropological Quarterly* 39(2):73-82, Apr. 1966.

2691 Stephens, William N. "A cross-cultural study of menstrual taboos." *Genetic Psychology Monographs* 64:385-416, 1961.

2692 _____. "A cross-cultural study of modesty." *Behavior Science Notes* 7(1):1-28, 1972.

2693 Suggs, Robert. *Marquesan Sexual Behavior.* New York: Harcourt, Brace & World, 1966.

2694 Swartz, Marc C. "Sexuality and aggression on Romonum, Truk." *American Anthropologist* 60(3):467-486, June 1958.

2695 Sykes, A.J.M. "Joking relationships in an industrial setting." *American Anthropologist* 68(1):188-193, Feb. 1966.

2696 Tobach, Ethel. "Some evolutionary aspects of human gender." *American Journal of Orthopsychiatry* 41(5):710-715, Oct. 1971.

2697 Trager, George L. "A scheme for the cultural analysis of sex." *Southwestern Journal of Anthropology* 18(2):114-118, Summer 1962.

2698 Tuteur, Werner. "Child molesters and men who expose themselves—an anthropological approach." *Journal of Forensic Sciences* 8(4):515-525, Oct. 1963.

2699 Watson, Lawrence C. "Marriage and sexual adjustment in Guajiro society." *Ethnology* 12(2):153-161, Apr. 1973.

2700 Webster, Paula. "The politics of rape in primitive society." Paper presented at the American Anthropological Association 75th Annual Meeting, Washington, DC, 1976. 11p.

2701   Weil, Peter M. "Staff of life: food and fertility in West African society." *Africa* 46(2):182–195, 1976.

2702   Weiss, Jerome. "The gemblakan: kept boys among the Javanese of Ponorogo." Paper presented at the American Anthropological Association 73rd Annual Meeting, Mexico City, Nov. 19–24, 1974. 55p.

2703   Westermarck, Edward A. *The History of Human Marriage.* 5th rev. ed. New York: Allerton, 1922.

2704   White, Leslie A. "Definition and prohibition of incest." *American Anthropologist* 50(3): 416–435, July/Sept. 1948.

2705   Whiting, John W.M. and Beatrice B. Whiting. "Aloofness and intimacy of husbands and wives: a cross-cultural study." *Ethos* 3(2):183–207, Summer 1975.

2706   Williams, George C. and Jeffrey B. Mitton. "Why reproduce sexually?" *Journal of Theoretical Biology* 39:545–554, June 1973.

2707   Wintrob, Ronald M. "Sexual guilt and culturally sanctioned delusions in Liberia, West Africa." *American Journal of Psychiatry* 125(1):89–95, 1968.

2708   Wolf, Arthur P. "Childhood association and sexual attraction." *American Anthropologist* 73(3):503–515, June 1970.

2709   Wortis, Joseph. "Sex taboos, sex offenders and the law." *American Journal of Orthopsychiatry* 9:554–564, July 1939.

OTHER SOURCES OF INFORMATION

Human Relations Area Files
Box 2054, Yale Station, New Haven, CT 06520
(Complete copies of the Human Relations Area Files are located in libraries throughout the world. A listing of these libraries can be obtained from HRAF.)

Sex Attitudes Research

2710   Abramson, Paul R. and Donald L. Mosher. "Development of a measure of negative attitudes toward masturbation." *Journal of Consulting and Clinical Psychology* 43(4):485–490, 1975.

2711   Athanasiou, Robert. "French and American sexuality." *Psychology Today* 6(2):55–56 passim, July 1972.

2712   _____. "A review of public attitudes on sexual issues." In: *Contemporary Sexual Behavior: Critical Issues in the 1970s,* ed. by Joseph Zubin and John Money, pp. 361–390. Baltimore: Johns Hopkins University Press, 1973.

2713   Athanasiou, Robert, Philip Shaver and Carol Tavris. "Sex." *Psychology Today* 4(2):39–52, July 1970.

2714   Barfield, Marguerite Durham. *A study of relationships between sex information scores and selected personality variables, religious commitment, and biographical variables.* (Dissertation— University of Houston.) Ann Arbor, MI: University Microfilms, 1971. (Order #72-2263)

2715   Barker, Elizabeth Dunning. *The perception of sexual symbolism.* (Dissertation—Columbia University.) Ann Arbor, MI: University Microfilms, 1957. (Order #21,627)

2716   Bauman, Karl E. "Volunteer bias in a study of sexual knowledge, attitudes and behavior." *Journal of Marriage and the Family* 35(1):27–31, Feb. 1973.

2717   Bayer, Alan E. "Sexual permissiveness and correlates as determined through interaction analyses." *Journal of Marriage and the Family* 39(1):29–40, Feb. 1977.

2718   Bechtel, H. Kenneth and Thomas D. McDonald. "Stereotypes and intolerance of deviants." Rev. version of paper presented at the 39th Annual Meeting of the Midwest Sociological Society, Chicago, Apr. 9–12, 1975. 22p.

2719   Berry, David F. and Philip A. Marks. "Anti-homosexual prejudice as a function of attitude toward own sexuality." *Proceedings of the 77th Annual Convention of the American Psychological Association* 4(2):573–574, 1969.

2720   Blake, Dean Moishe. "Measuring attitude toward homosexuals: a brief scale for educational and evaluative purposes: a technical manual." Unpub. master's thesis, University of Iowa, 1974.

2721   Bower, Donald W. and Victor A. Christopherson. "University student cohabitation: a regional comparison of selected attitudes and behavior." *Journal of Marriage and the Family* 39(3):447–452, Aug. 1977.

2722   Cameron, Paul and Patt Fleming. "Self-reported degree of pleasure associated with sexual activity across the adult life-span." Paper presented at the Midwestern Psychological Association Meeting, Chicago, May 1, 1975. 6p.

2723   Christensen, Harold T. "Normative theory derived from cross-cultural family research." *Journal of Marriage and the Family* 31(2):209–222, May 1969.

2724   _____. "Scandinavian and American sex norms: some comparisons, with sociological implications." *The Journal of Social Issues* 22(2):60–75, Apr. 1966.

2725   Christensen, Harold T. and George R. Carpenter. "Value-behavior discrepancies regarding premarital coitus in three western cultures." *American Sociological Review* 27(1):66–74, Feb. 1962.

2726   Clayton, Richard Reid. "Premarital sexual intercourse: a substantive test of the contingent consistency model." *Journal of Marriage and the Family* 34(2):273–281, May 1972.

2727   Collins, Anne M. and William E. Sedlacek. "Counselor perceptions of sexual attitudes of female university students." *College Student Journal* 6(3):13–16, Sept./Oct. 1972.

2728   Conley, John A. and Thomas W. O'Rourke. "Attitudes of college students toward selected issues in human sexuality." *Journal of School Health* 43:286–292, May 1973.

2729   Croake, James W. and Barbara E. James. "A four year comparison of premarital sexual attitudes." *Journal of Sex Research* 9(2):91–96, May 1973.

2730   Curran, James P. "Convergence toward a single sexual standard?" *Social Behavior and Personality* 3(2):189–195, 1975.

2731   Dargitz, Robert Earl. "The propensity to sanction selected forms of deviant sexual behavior." Unpub. doctoral dissertation, Indiana University, 1976.

2732   Edwards, Maxine and Nick Stinnett. "Perceptions of college students concerning alternate life styles." *Journal of Psychology* 87(1):143–156, May 1974.

2733   Erskine, Hazel Gaudet. "The polls: morality." *Public Opinion Quarterly* 30(4):669–680, Winter 1966.

2734   _____. "The polls: more on morality and sex." *Public Opinion Quarterly* 31(1):116–128, Spring 1967.

2735   Eysenck, Hans J. "Personality and attitudes to sex: a factorial study." *Personality: An International Journal* 1(4):355–376, Winter 1970.

2736   Eysenck, S.B.G. and H.J. Eysenck. "Attitudes to sex, personality and lie scale scores." *Perceptual and Motor Skills* 33(1):216–218, Aug. 1971.

2737   Farley, Frank H. et al. "Sex, politics and personality: a multi-dimensional study of college students." *Archives of Sexual Behavior* 6(2):105–120, Mar. 1977.

2738   Farrell, Ronald A. *Societal reaction to homosexuals: toward a generalized theory of deviance.* (Dissertation—University of Cincinnati.) Ann Arbor, MI: University Microfilms, 1972. (Order #72-31,729)

2739   Fennessey, Alice. *An exploration of the domain of attitudes toward homosexuality.* (Dissertation—Columbia University.) Ann Arbor, MI: University Microfilms, 1975. (Order #77-0136)

2740   Fretz, Bruce R. "Assessing attitudes towards sexual behaviors." *Counseling Psychologist* 5(1):100–106, 1975.

2741   Gordon, Michael. "From an unfortunate necessity to a cult of mutual orgasm: sex in American marital education literature, 1830–1940." In: *Studies in the Sociology of Sex,* ed. by James M. Henslin, pp. 53–77. New York: Appleton-Century-Crofts, 1971.

2742   Gorsuch, Richard and Roger A. Smith. "Changes in college students' evaluation of moral behavior: 1969 versus 1939, 1949, and 1958." *Journal of Personality and Social Psychology* 24(3):381–391, Dec. 1972.

2743   Grummon, Donald, Andrew M. Barclay and Nancy K. Hammond, eds. *Sexuality: A Search for Perspective.* New York: Van Nostrand Reinhold, 1971.

2744   Hammersmith, Sue Kiefer and Martin S. Weinberg. "Homosexual identity: commitment, adjustment, and significant others." *Sociometry* 36(1):56–79, Mar. 1973.

2745   Hassell, Julie and Edward Smith. "Female homosexuals' concepts of self, men, and women." *Journal of Personality Assessment* 39(2):154–159, Mar. 1975.

2746   Hassellund, Hans. "On some sociosexual sex differences." *Journal of Sex Research* 7(4):263–273, Nov. 1971.

2747 Haynes, Stephen N. and Jerome L. Oziel. "Homosexuality: behaviors and attitudes." *Archives of Sexual Behavior* 5(4):283–289, July 1976.

2748 Hunt, Morton. *Sexual Behavior in the 1970's.* Chicago: Playboy Press, 1974.

2749 Israel, Joachim and Rosmari Eliasson. "Consumption, society, sex roles and sexual behavior." *Acta Sociologica* 14(1/2):68–82, 1971.

2750 Jenkins, David Price. *Demographic variations in societal response to homosexuality.* (Dissertation—State University of New York at Albany.) Ann Arbor, MI: University Microfilms, 1976. (Order #76-16,840)

2751 Johnson, Ralph Aulden. *Knowledge of and attitude toward sexuality as variables in satisfactory and dissatisfactory marital relationships.* (Dissertation—University of Utah.) Ann Arbor, MI: University Microfilms, 1972. (Order #73-1590)

2752 Jurich, Anthony P. *Variables affecting the selection of premarital sexual standards.* (Dissertation—Pennsylvania State University.) Ann Arbor, MI: University Microfilms, 1972. (Order #73-13,996)

2753 Kilpatrick, Dean G. et al. "Dogmatism and personal sexual attitudes." *Psychological Reports* 23:1105–1106, Dec. 1968.

2754 King, Karl, Jack O. Balswick and Ira E. Robinson. "The continuing premarital sexual revolution among college females." *Journal of Marriage and the Family* 39(3):455–459, Aug. 1977.

2755 Kinsey, Alfred C. et al. *Sexual Behavior in the Human Female.* Philadelphia: W.B. Saunders, 1953.

2756 ———. *Sexual Behavior in the Human Male.* Philadelphia: W.B. Saunders, 1948.

2757 Kirkpatrick, R. George. "Collective consciousness and mass hysteria: collective behavior and anti-pornography crusades in Durkheimian perspective." *Human Relations* 28(1):63–84, Feb. 1975.

2758 LaTorre, Ronald A. and Karen Kear. "Attitudes toward sex in the aged." *Archives of Sexual Behavior* 6(3):203–213, May 1977.

2759 Levitt, Eugene E. and Albert D. Klassen. "Public attitudes toward sexual behavior: the latest investigation of the Institute for Sex Research." Paper presented at the Annual Meeting of the American Orthopsychiatric Association, New York, June 1, 1973. 8p.

2760 LoPiccolo, Joseph. "Mothers and daughters: perceived and real differences in sexual values." *Journal of Sex Research* 9(2):171–177, May 1973.

2761 Lowman, Annelle Zerbe. "The effect of assertive training for women on sexual satisfaction." Unpub. master's thesis, Indiana University, 1976.

2762 Marcotte, David B., Dean G. Kilpatrick and A. Willis. "The Sheppe and Hain study revisited: professional students and their knowledge and attitudes about human sexuality." *Medical Education* 11:201–204, 1977.

2763 Miller, Warren B. "Sexual attitude questionnaire: an instrument for measuring two psychological dimensions of sexuality relevant to population growth." Paper presented at the Family and Fertility Conference sponsored by the Center for Population Research, National Institute for Child Health and Human Development, Bethesda, MD, June 13–16, 1973. 15p.

2764 Miller, William R. and Harold I. Lief. "Masturbatory attitudes, knowledge, and experience: data from the Sex Knowledge and Attitude Test (SKAT)." *Archives of Sexual Behavior* 5(5):447–467, Sept. 1976.

2765 Mirande, Alfred M. and Elizabeth L. Hammer. "Love, sex, permissiveness, and abortion: a test of alternative models." *Archives of Sexual Behavior* 5(6):553–566, Nov. 1976.

2766 Neeley, Roy E., Jr. *Sexual knowledge and permissiveness among unmarried mothers.* (Dissertation—Florida State University.) Ann Arbor, MI: University Microfilms, 1971. (Order #72-13,545)

2767 "Newsline: sexuality—properly viewed, everything is lewd." *Psychology Today* 7(4):17–18, Sept. 1973.

2768 Ogren, David John. *Sexual guilt, behavior, attitudes, and information.* (Dissertation—University of Houston.) Ann Arbor, MI: University Microfilms, 1974. (Order #75-8246)

2769 O'Neill, William, ed. *The American Sexual Dilemma.* New York: Holt, Rinehart & Winston, 1972.

2770 Pietropinto, Anthony and Jacqueline Simenauer. *Beyond the Male Myth.* New York: Times Books, 1977.

2771 Pocs, Ollie and Annette G. Godow. "The shock of recognizing parents as sexual beings."

Paper presented at the Midwest Sociological Society Annual Meeting, Omaha, Apr. 3–6, 1974. 23p.

2772   Ranker, Jess Elwood. *Attitudes toward sex in marriage and patterns of erotic behavior in dating and courtship before marriage.* (Dissertation—University of Southern California.) Ann Arbor, MI: University Microfilms, 1967. (Order #67-10,772)

2773   Reevy, William R. *Marital prediction scores of college women relative to behavior and attitudes.* (Dissertation—Pennsylvania State University.) Ann Arbor, MI: University Microfilms, 1954. (Order #11,832)

2774   Rettig, Salomon and Benjamin Pasamanick. "Changes in moral values over three decades 1929–1958." *Social Problems* 6(4):320–328, Spring 1959.

2775   Scully, Diana and Pauline B. Bart. "A funny thing happened on the way to the orifice: women in gynecology textbooks." *American Journal of Sociology* 78(4):1045–1050, Jan. 1973.

2776   Smigel, Erwin O. and Rita Seiden. "The decline and fall of the double standard." *Annals of the American Academy of Political and Social Science* 376:6–17, Mar. 1968.

2777   Smith, Alma Dell et al. "Male student professionals: their attitudes toward women, sex, and change." *Psychological Reports* 39:143–148, 1976.

2778   Sutker, Patricia B. and Rickie S. Gilliard. "Personal sexual attitudes and behavior in blacks and whites." *Psychological Reports* 27(3):753–754, Dec. 1970.

2779   Thornburg, Hershel D. *An analysis of the attitudes of ministerial students in post-baccalaureate schools of religion toward sex as measured by the Sex Attitude Inventory.* (Dissertation—University of Oklahoma.) Ann Arbor, MI: University Microfilms, 1968. (Order #68-6961)

2780   Thorne, Frederick C. and Thomas D. Haupt. "The objective measurement of sex attitudes and behavior in adult males." *Journal of Clinical Psychology* 22(4):395–403, 1966.

2781   Troyer, Beverly Jayne. *The influence of personal factors on attitudes of college students toward human sexuality and sexual decision-making situations in a selected Minnesota college.* (Dissertation—University of Minnesota.) Ann Arbor, MI: University Microfilms, 1971. (Order #71-28,320)

2782   Vacalis, T. Demetri, Robert D. Langston and Elaine Malchanov. "The relationship between sex guilt and self-actualization and the implica-

tions for sex education." *Journal of Sex Education and Therapy* 3(1):14–18, Spring/Summer 1977.

2783   Vandiver, Richard Dale. *Sources and interrelation of premarital sexual standards and general liberality-conservatism.* (Dissertation—Southern Illinois University.) Ann Arbor, MI: University Microfilms, 1972. (Order #72-24,370)

2784   Walsh, Robert H. *A survey of parents and their own children's sexual attitudes.* (Dissertation—University of Iowa.) Ann Arbor, MI: University Microfilms, 1970. (Order #70-15,654)

2785   Weaver, Herbert B. and Abe Arkoff. "Measurement of attitudes concerning sexual permissiveness." *Social Science* 40(3):163–170, June 1965.

2786   Weinberg, Martin S. *Sex, modesty, and deviants.* (Dissertation—Northwestern University.) Ann Arbor, MI: University Microfilms, 1965. (Order #65-12,1436)

2787   White, Alice M., Leonard Fichtenbaum and John Dollard. "Measured relationships between sexual motivation and anxiety." *Journal of Counseling Psychology* 14(6):544–549, Nov. 1967.

2788   Wiechmann, Gerald Helmut. *A multiple factor analysis of premarital sex attitudes of college undergraduates.* (Dissertation—Southern Illinois University.) Ann Arbor, MI: University Microfilms, 1965. (Order #66-1093)

2789   Wilson, W. Cody. "The distribution of selected attitudes and behaviors among the adult population of the United States." *Journal of Sex Research* 11(1):46–64, Feb. 1975.

2790   Wise, Gordon L., Alan L. King and J. Paul Merenski. "Reactions to sexy ads vary with age." *Journal of Advertising Research* 14(4):11–16, Aug. 1974.

ATTITUDES ON NONMARITAL SEX BEHAVIOR RESEARCH

2791   Alston, Jon P. "Review of the polls. Attitudes of white Protestants and Catholics toward nonmarital sex." *Journal for the Scientific Study of Religion* 13(1):73–74, Mar. 1974.

2792   _____. "Review of the polls. Attitudes toward extramarital and homosexual relations." *Journal for the Scientific Study of Religion* 13(4):479–481, Dec. 1974.

2793   Bauman, Karl E. and Robert R. Wilson. "Premarital sexual attitudes of unmarried university students: 1968 vs. 1972." *Archives of Sexual Behavior* 5(1):29-37, Jan. 1976.

2794 Bell, Robert R. and Jack V. Buerkle. "Mother and daughter attitudes to premarital sexual behavior." *Marriage and Family Living* 23(4):390-392, Nov. 1961.

2795 Berger, David G. and Morton G. Wenger. "The ideology of virginity." *Journal of Marriage and the Family* 35(4):666-676, Nov. 1973.

2796 Cardwell, Jerry D. "The relationship between religious commitment and premarital sexual permissiveness: a five dimensional analysis." *Sociological Analysis* 30:72-80, Summer 1969.

2797 Carns, Donald E. "Talking about sex: notes on first coitus and the double sexual standard." *Journal of Marriage and the Family* 35(4):677-688, Nov. 1973.

2798 Christensen, Harold T. "Attitudes toward marital infidelity: a nine-culture sampling of university student opinion." *Journal of Comparative Family Studies* 4(2):197-214, Fall 1973.

2799 Clayton, Richard Reid. "Premarital sexual intercourse: a substantive test of the contingent consistency model." *Journal of Marriage and the Family* 34(2):273-281, May 1972.

2800 Collins, John K., Judith R. Kennedy and Ronald D. Francis. "Insights into a dating partner's expectations of how behavior should ensue during the courtship process." *Journal of Marriage and the Family* 38(2):373-378, May 1976.

2801 Croaks, James W. and Barbara E. James. "Attitudes toward premarital sexual behavior as a function of behavioral commitment." *College Student Journal* 6(3):36-41, Sept./Oct. 1972.

2802 Driscoll, Richard H. and Keith E. Davis. "Sexual restraints: a comparison of perceived and self-reported reasons for college students." *Journal of Sex Research* 7(4):253-262, Nov. 1971.

2803 Eliasson, Rosmari. "Doppelmoral und lebensrollen; die einstellungen in einer sexualliberalen gesellschaft." *Sexualmedizin* 3(12):624-628, Dec. 1974.

2804 Eysenck, H.J. "Personality, premarital sexual permissiveness, and assortive mating." *Journal of Sex Research* 10(1):47-51, Feb. 1974.

2805 Gottheil, Edward and Abraham Freedman. "Sexual beliefs and behavior of single male medical students." *Journal of the American Medical Association* 212(8):1327-1332, May 25, 1970.

2806 Heltsley, Mary E. and Carlfred B. Broderick. "Religiosity and premarital sexual permissiveness: reexamination of Reiss's traditionalism proposition." *Journal of Marriage and the Family* 31(3):441-443, Aug. 1969.

2807 Holmes, Ronald Michael. *Premarital sexual permissiveness of two-year college students and four-year college students and its implications for student personnel workers.* (Dissertation—Indiana University.) Ann Arbor, MI: University Microfilms, 1972. (Order # 71-10,828)

2808 Johnson, Clara L. "Attitudes toward premarital sex and family planning for single-never-pregnant teenage girls." *Adolescence* 9(34):255-262, Summer 1974.

2809 Korber, George William. *Parental standards of adolescent sexual behavior: a study of values in conflict.* (Dissertation—Stanford University.) Ann Arbor, MI: University Microfilms, 1952. (Order # 4677)

2810 Larsen, Knud S. "Premarital sex attitudes—a scale and some validity findings." *Journal of Social Psychology* 90:339-340, Aug. 1973.

2811 Lester, David. "Adolescent suicide and premarital sexual behavior." *Journal of Social Psychology* 82(1):131-132, Oct. 1970.

2812 McMahon, Judith Wantland. *Sex guilt, reported heterosexual behavior, and attitudes toward premarital permissiveness among women.* (Dissertation—Washington University.) Ann Arbor, MI: University Microfilms, 1972. (Order # 73-5050)

2813 Middendorp. C.P., W. Brinkman and W. Koomen. "Determinants of premarital sexual permissiveness: a secondary analysis." *Journal of Marriage and the Family* 32(3):369-379, Aug. 1970.

2814 Nyberg, Kenneth Langeland. *Homosexual and homoerotic behavior differences in men and women.* (Dissertation—University of Utah.) Ann Arbor, MI: University Microfilms, 1973. (Order # 73-32,032)

2815 Reiss, Ira L. "Double standard in premarital sexual intercourse: a neglected concept." *Social Forces* 34(3):224-230, Mar. 1956.

2816 _____. "An integrative and summary study of premarital sex." In: *The Family System in America,* pp. 151-181. New York: Holt, Rinehart & Winston, 1971.

2817 _____. "Premarital sexual permissiveness among Negroes and whites." *American Sociological Review* 29(5):688-698, Oct. 1964.

2818 _____. "The scaling of premarital sexual permissiveness." *Journal of Marriage and the Family* 26(2):188–198, May 1964.

2819 _____. *The Social Context of Premarital Sexual Permissiveness.* New York: Holt, Rinehart & Winston, 1967.

2820 Reiss, Ira L. and Brent C. Miller. *A Theoretical Analysis of Heterosexual Permissiveness.* Minnesota Family Study Center Technical Report, no. 11. Minneapolis: University of Minnesota Department of Sociology, 1974.

2821 Rodman, Hyman, F.R. Nichols and Patricia Voydanoff. "Lower-class attitudes toward 'deviant' family patterns: a cross-cultural study." *Journal of Marriage and the Family* 31(2):315–321, May 1969.

2822 Ruppel, Howard J., Jr. "Religiosity and premarital sexual permissiveness: a response to the Reiss-Heltsley and Broderick debate." *Journal of Marriage and the Family* 32(4):647–655, Nov. 1970.

2823 Schalmo, Gail B. and Bernard H. Levin. "Presence of the double standard in a college population." *Psychological Reports* 34:227–230, Feb. 1974.

2824 Snyder, Eldon E. and Elmer Spreitzer. "Attitudes of the aged toward nontraditional sexual behavior." *Archives of Sexual Behavior* 5(3):249–254, May 1976.

2825 Steffensmeier, Darrell and Renee Steffensmeier. "Sex differences in reactions to homosexuals: research continuities and further developments." *Journal of Sex Research* 10(1):52–67, Feb. 1974.

2826 Stratton, John R. and Stephan P. Spitzer. "Sexual permissiveness and self-evaluation: a question of substance and a question of method." *Journal of Marriage and the Family* 29(3):434–441, Aug. 1967.

2827 Walsh, Robert H. "The generation gap in sexual beliefs." *Sexual Behavior* 2(1):4–10, Jan. 1972.

2828 Wells, James Gipson. *The structure and change of premarital sex norms.* (Dissertation—Florida State University.) Ann Arbor, MI: University Microfilms, 1969. (Order # 70-11,174)

2829 Zelnik, Melvin and John F. Kantner. "Sexual and contraceptive experience of young unmarried women in the United States, 1976 and 1971." *Family Planning Perspectives* 9(2):55–71, Mar./Apr. 1977.

Sex Ethics

2830 Baker, Robert and Frederick Elliston, eds. *Philosophy & Sex.* Buffalo: Prometheus Books, 1975.

2831 Baker, Sidney J. "The place of sexology in philosophy." *International Journal of Sexology* 2(3):174–177, Feb. 1949.

2832 Calderone, Mary S., ed. *Sexuality and Human Values.* New York: Association Press, 1974.

2833 Christensen, Harold T. "Cultural relativism and premarital sex norms: research basis for moral decision." *Annals of the New York Academy of Science* 184:265–273, June 7, 1971.

2834 Comfort, Alexander. *Barbarism and Sexual Freedom; Lectures on the Sociology of Sex from the Standpoint of Anarchism.* London: Freedom Press, 1948.

2835 Ellis, Albert. *Sex Without Guilt.* New York: Lyle Stuart, 1958.

2836 Ellis, Havelock. *Little Essays of Love and Virtue.* Garden City, NY: Doubleday, Doran & Co., 1930.

2837 Folsom, Joseph K. "Kinsey's challenge to ethics and religion." *Social Problems* 1(4):164–168, Apr. 1954.

2838 Francoeur, Robert T. and Anna K. Francoeur, eds. *The Future of Sexual Relations.* Englewood Cliffs, NJ: Prentice-Hall, 1974.

2839 Girodias, Maurice. "The erotic society." *Encounter* 26(2):52–58, Feb. 1966.

2840 Golod, S.I. "Sociological problems of sexual morality." *Soviet Review* 11(2):127–142, Summer 1970.

2841 Grummon, Donald L. and Andrew M. Barclay, eds. *Sexuality: A Search for Perspective.* New York: Van Nostrand Reinhold, 1971.

2842 Guyon, René. *The Ethics of Sexual Acts.* New York: Knopf, 1948.

2843 Hefner, Hugh M. *The Playboy Philosophy, Part I-IV.* Chicago: Playboy Magazine, 1962–1965.

2844 Howard, Clifford. *Sex and Religion: A Study of Their Relationship and Its Bearing upon Civilization.* London: Williams & Norgate, 1925. (Reprint ed.: New York: AMS Press, 1975.)

2845 Johnson, Warren R. and Bruce R. Fretz.

"What is sexual 'normality'?" *Sexual Behavior* 1(3):68–77, June 1971.

2846   Jurich, Anthony P. and Julie A. Jurich. "The effect of cognitive moral development upon the selection of premarital sexual standards." *Journal of Marriage and the Family* 36(4):736–741, Nov. 1974.

2847   Kinsey, Alfred C. et al. *Sexual Behavior in the Human Male,* pp. 465–487. Philadelphia: W.B. Saunders, 1948.

2848   Kirkendall, Lester A. "The cutting edge of human sexuality." *Journal of Sex Education and Therapy* 1:15–28, Spring/Summer 1975.

2849   _____. "A new bill of sexual rights and responsibilities." *Humanist* 36:4–6, Jan./Feb. 1976.

2850   Kirkendall, Lester A. and Peter B. Anderson. "Authentic selfhood: basis for tomorrow's sexual morality." *Pastoral Psychology* 21(208):19–32, Nov. 1970.

2851   Lamson, Herbert D. "The ethics of sexual acts — a critical study." *International Journal of Sexology* 3(1):38–41, Aug. 1949.

2852   Morrison, Eleanor S. and Mila U. Price. *Values in Sexuality.* New York: Hart Publishing Co., 1974.

2853   Paul, Leslie. *Eros Rediscovered: Restoring Sex to Humanity.* New York: Association Press, 1970.

2854   Poffenberger, Thomas et al. "Premarital sexual behavior: a symposium." *Marriage and Family Living* 24(3):254–278, Aug. 1962.

2855   Reich, Wilhelm. *The Invasion of Compulsory Sex-Morality.* New York: Farrar, Straus & Giroux, 1971.

2856   Richardson, Herbert W. *Nun, Witch, Playmate: The Americanization of Sex.* New York: Harper & Row, 1971.

2857   Rist, Ray C., ed. *The Pornography Controversy: Changing Moral Standards in American Life.* New Brunswick, NJ: Transaction, 1975.

2858   Roy, Rustum and Della Roy. *Honest Sex.* New York: New American Library, 1968.

2859   Russell, Bertrand R. *Marriage and Morals.* New York: H. Liveright, 1929.

2860   Savramis, Demosthenes. *The Satanizing of Women; Religion Versus Sexuality.* Garden City, NY: Doubleday, 1974.

2861   Schofield, Michael. *Promiscuity.* London: Gollancz, 1976.

2862   Smith, F. Joseph and Erling Eng, eds. *Facets of Eros; Phenomenological Essays.* The Hague: Nijhoff, 1972.

2863   Sporken, Paul, section coordinator. "Religion, ideology and sex." In: *Handbook of Sexology,* ed. by John Money and H. Musaph, pp. 1313–1351. Amsterdam: Elsevier/North Holland, 1977.

2864   Swedenborg, Emanuel. *Conjugal Love and Its Chaste Delights; Also, Adulterous Love and Its Sinful Pleasures.* New York: American Swedenborg Printing & Publishing Society, 1871.

2865   Watts, Alan Wilson. *Nature, Man, and Woman.* New York: Pantheon, 1958.

2866   Wilson, John. *Logic and Sexual Morality.* Baltimore: Penguin Books, 1965.

2867   Wilson, Robert Anton. "Modern attitudes toward sex." In: *The Encyclopedia of Sexual Behavior,* ed. by Albert Ellis and Albert Abarbanel, pp. 186–192. New York: Hawthorn Books, 1967.

2868   Wiseman, Jacqueline P., ed. *The Social Psychology of Sex.* New York: Harper & Row, 1976.

2869   Wood, Frederic C. *Sex and the New Morality.* New York: Association Press, 1968.

JUDAIC

2870   Borowitz, Eugene B. *Choosing a Sex Ethic: A Jewish Inquiry.* New York: Schocken Books, 1970.

2871   Epstein, Louis M. *Sex Laws and Customs in Judaism.* rev. ed. New York: Ktav Publishing House, 1968.

2872   Feldman, David Michael. *Birth Control in Jewish Law: Marital Relations, Contraception and Abortion as Set Forth in the Classic Texts of Jewish Law.* New York: New York University Press, 1968.

2873   Gittelsohn, Roland B. *Consecrated unto Me; A Jewish View of Love and Marriage.* New York: Union of American Hebrew Congregations, 1966; (and supplement) *Love, Sex and Marriage; A Jewish View.* New York: Union of American Hebrew Congregations, 1976.

2874   Gordis, Robert. *Love and Sex: A Modern Jewish Perspective.* New York: Farrar, Straus & Giroux, 1978.

2875   Rosner, Fred. *Sex Ethics in the Writings of Moses Maimonides.* New York: Bloch, 1974.

CATHOLIC

2876   Bertocci, Peter Anthony. *Sex, Love and The Person.* New York: Sheed & Ward, 1967.

2877   Clemens, Alphonse H. "Catholicism and sex." In: *The Encyclopedia of Sexual Behavior,* ed. by Albert Ellis and Albert Abarbanel, pp. 228–234, New York: Hawthorn Books, 1967.

2878   Gaffney, Louis. "Psychological reflections on marital love and contraception." *Journal of Religion and Health* 10(1):11–22, Jan. 1971.

2879   Ginder, Richard. *Binding with Briars; Sex and Sin in the Catholic Church.* Englewood Cliffs, NJ: Prentice-Hall, 1975.

2880   Goergen, Donald. *The Sexual Celibate.* New York: Seabury Press, 1974.

2881   Keane, Philip S. *Sexual Morality: A Catholic Perspective.* New York: Paulist Press, 1977.

2882   Kosnik, Anthony et al. *Human Sexuality; New Directions in American Catholic Thought: A Study Commissioned by the Catholic Theological Society of America.* New York: Paulist Press, 1977.

2883   McNeill, John. *The Church and the Homosexual.* Kansas City: Sheed Andrews & McMeel, 1976.

2884   Ryan, Mary Perkins and John Julian Ryan. *Love and Sexuality; A Christian Approach.* New York: Holt, Rinehart & Winston, 1967.

2885   Steinmetz, Urban G. *The Sexual Christian.* St. Meinrad, IN: Abbey Press, 1972.

2886   Taylor, Michael J., ed. *Sex: Thoughts for Contemporary Christians.* Garden City, NY: Doubleday, 1972.

2887   Toon, Mark. *The Philosophy of Sex According to St. Thomas Aquinas.* Philosophical Studies no. 156. Abstract series no. 12. Washington: Catholic University of America Press, 1954.

2888   Valente, Michael F. *Sex: The Radical View of a Catholic Theologian.* New York: Bruce Publishing, 1970.

2889   Valentini, Norberto and Clara di Meglio. *Sex and the Confessional.* New York: Stein & Day, 1974.

2890   Woods, Richard. *Another Kind of Love: Homosexuality and Spirituality.* Chicago: Thomas More, 1977.

PROTESTANT

2891   Babbage, Stuart Barton. *Sex and Sanity: A Christian View of Sexual Morality.* Philadelphia: Westminster Press, 1967.

2892   Bailey, Derrick Sherwin. *Common Sense about Sexual Ethics: A Christian View.* New York: Macmillan, 1962.

2893   Barnhouse, Ruth Tiffany and Urban T. Holmes III, eds. *Male and Female: Christian Approaches to Sexuality.* New York: Seabury Press, 1976.

2894   Barr, O. Sydney. *The Christian New Morality; A Biblical Study of Situation Ethics.* New York: Oxford University Press, 1969.

2895   Clemons, James T. "Toward a Christian affirmation of human sexuality." *Religion in Life* 43:425–435, Winter 1974.

2896   Cole, William Graham. "Protestantism and sex." In: *The Encyclopedia of Sexual Behavior,* ed. by Albert Ellis and Albert Abarbanel, pp. 883–888. New York: Hawthorn Books, 1967.

2897   Drakeford, John W. *A Christian View of Homosexuality.* Nashville: Broadman, 1977.

2898   Ferm, Deane William. *Responsible Sexuality—Now.* New York: Seabury Press, 1971.

2899   Fletcher, Joseph. *Moral Responsibility; Situation Ethics at Work.* Philadelphia: Westminster Press, 1967.

2900   Graham, LeRoy Stoney. *An examination and analysis of the relevance of the Christian ethic of sex with respect to premarital sexual intercourse; an inquiry based on the thought of Reinhold Niebuhr and Emil Brunner in view of the findings of Alfred Kinsey and Margaret Mead.* (Dissertation—Drew University.) Ann Arbor, MI: University Microfilms, 1965. (Order #65-11,327)

2901   Hiltner, Seward. *Sex and the Christian Life.* New York: Association Press, 1957.

2902   Holmes, Urban T., III et al. *The Sexual Person: The Church's Role in Human Sexual Development.* New York: Seabury Press, 1970.

2903   Lutheran Church, Missouri Synod, Family Life Research Committee. *Sex and the Church: A Sociological, Historical, and Theological Investigation of Sex Attitudes,* ed. by Oscar E. Feucht. Marriage and Family Research Series v. 5. St. Louis: Concordia, 1961.

2904   Mace, David R. *The Christian Response to*

the Sexual Revolution. Nashville: Abingdon Press, 1970.

2905   Mazur, Ronald Michael. *Commonsense Sex; A Basis for Discussion and Reappraisal.* Boston: Beacon Press, 1968.

2906   "Perspectives on sex." *Church and Society* 40(4):whole issue, Mar./Apr. 1970.

2907   Piper, Otto A. *The Biblical View of Sex and Marriage.* New York: Scribner, 1960.

2908   Pittenger, W. Norman. *Making Sexuality Human.* Philadelphia: Pilgrim Press, 1970.

2909   Sapp, Stephen. *Sexuality, the Bible, and Science.* Philadelphia: Fortress Press, 1977.

2910   Thielicke, Helmut. *The Ethics of Sex.* New York: Harper & Row, 1964.

2911   *Towards a Quaker View of Sex; An Essay by a Group of Friends.* rev. ed. London: Friends Home Service Committee, 1964.

2912   Unsworth, Richard P. *Dignity and Exploitation; Christian Reflections on Images of Sex in the 1970s.* New York: Advisory Council on Church and Society, United Presbyterian Church in the U.S.A., 1974.

2913   Williams, T.M. *See No Evil: Christian Attitudes toward Sex in Art and Entertainment.* Grand Rapids, MI: Zondervan, 1976.

2914   Wessler, Martin F. *Christian View of Sex Education: A Manual for Church Leaders.* Ed. by W.J. Fields. Sex Education Series. St. Louis: Concordia, 1967.

2915   Wynn, John Charles, ed. *Sexual Ethics and Christian Responsibility; Some Divergent Views.* New York: Association Press, 1970.

Changing Roles of Men and Women

2916   Badaracco, Marie R., Robert E. Gould and Louis Landman. "Recent trends toward unisex: a panel." *American Journal of Psychoanalysis* 34(1):17–31, 1974.

2917   Baker, Robert and Frederick Elliston, eds. *Philosophy and Sex.* Buffalo, NY: Prometheus Books, 1975.

2918   Barnhouse, Ruth Tiffany and Urban Tigner Holmes, III, eds. *Male and Female: Christian Approaches to Sexuality.* New York: Seabury Press, 1976.

2919   Bell, Robert R. "Sex as a weapon and changing social roles." *Medical Aspects of Human Sexuality* 4(6):99–111, June 1970.

2920   Bianchi, Eugene C. and Rosemary R. Ruether. *From Machismo to Mutuality: Essays on Sexism and Woman-Man Liberation.* New York: Paulist Press, 1976.

2921   Bruck, Connie and Sandra Bem. "Professing androgyny." *Human Behavior* 6(10):22–31, Oct. 1977.

2922   Dreitzel, Hans Peter, ed. *Family, Marriage, and the Struggle of the Sexes.* New York: Macmillan, 1972.

2923   Eslinger, Kenneth N. *Sex role, mobility orientation, and the control of romantic love.* (Dissertation—Ohio State University.) Ann Arbor, MI: University Microfilms, 1971. (Order #72-15,205)

2924   Fabian, Judith Janaro. "The role of the therapist in the process of sexual emancipation." *Psychiatric Opinion* 10(4):31–33, Aug. 1973.

2925   Filene, Peter Gabriel. *Him/Her/Self: Sex Roles in Modern America.* New York: Harcourt Brace Jovanovich, 1975.

2926   Francoeur, Anna K. and Robert T. Francoeur, eds. *The Future of Sexual Relations.* Englewood Cliffs, NJ: Prentice-Hall, 1974.

2927   Garside, Christine. "Women's liberation movement: some effects upon women, men, and children." In: *Configurations: Biological and Cultural Factors in Sexuality and Family Life,* ed. by Raymond Prince and Dorothy Barrier, pp. 103–111. Lexington, MA: Heath, 1974.

2928   Gebhard, Paul H. "Stressor aspects of societal attitudes to sex roles and relationships." Paper presented at the 3rd International Symposium on Society, Stress, and Disease, Stockholm, May 29–June 3, 1972. 11p.

2929   Ginsberg, George L. "Effects on men of increased sexual freedom for women." *Medical Aspects of Human Sexuality* 7(2):66–89, Feb. 1973.

2930   Gordon, Sol and Roger W. Libby, eds. *Sexuality Today and Tomorrow: Contemporary Issues in Human Sexuality.* North Scituate, MA: Duxbury Press, 1976.

2931   Gould, Robert E. "Socio-cultural roles of the male and female." In: *The Sexual Experience,* ed. by B.J. Sadock, H.I. Kaplan and A.M. Freedman, pp. 280–289. Baltimore: Williams & Wilkins, 1976.

2932   Gould, Robert E. et al. "Do men like women to be sexually assertive?" *Medical Aspects of Human Sexuality* 11(3):36 passim, Mar. 1977.

2933   Grambs, Jean D. and Walter B. Waetjen. *Sex: Does It Make a Difference? Sex Roles in the Modern World.* North Scituate, MA: Duxbury Press, 1975.

2934   Greenfield, Sidney M. "On the critique of romantic love: some sociological consequences of proposed alternatives." In: *Symposium on Love,* ed. by Mary Ellen Curtin, pp. 53–67. New York: Behavioral Publications, 1973.

2935   Halleck, Seymour. "Sex and power." *Medical Aspects of Human Sexuality* 3(10):8–24, Oct. 1969.

2936   Herman, Sondra R. "Sex-roles and sexual attitudes in Sweden: the new phase." *The Massachusetts Review* 13(1–2):45–64, Winter/Spring 1972.

2937   Hettlinger, Richard F. "The new sexuality." In: *Modern Views of Human Sexual Behavior,* ed. by J.L. McCary and D.R. Copeland, pp. 397–409. Chicago: Science Research Associates, 1976.

2938   Johnson, Flora. "Victoria waives the rules: sex, marriage and feminism in the nineteenth century." In: *Our National Passion: 200 Years of Sex in America,* ed. by S. Barnes, S. Frank and T. Horwitz, pp. 59–77. Chicago: Follett Publishing, 1976.

2939   Lindbeck, Violette S. "The cost of sexual apartheid." In: *Sexuality: A Search for Perspective,* ed. by D.L. Grummon and A.M. Barclay, pp. 91–108. New York: Van Nostrand Reinhold, 1971.

2940   Nash, James L. "Vasectomy as a vehicle for prevention of family disorders." *Fertility and Sterility* 24(8):640–643, Aug. 1973.

2941   O'Neill, William L., ed. *The American Sexual Dilemma.* New York: Holt, Rinehart & Winston, 1972.

2942   Osofsky, Joy D. and Howard J. Osofsky. "Androgyny as a life style." *The Family Coordinator* 21(4):411–418, Oct. 1972.

2943   Robertiello, Richard C. "After the sexual revolution and the women's liberation movement." *Journal of Contemporary Psychotherapy* 5(1):31–34, Winter 1972.

2944   Scanzoni, Letha and John Scanzoni. *Men, Women, and Change: A Sociology of Marriage and Family.* New York: McGraw-Hill, 1976.

2945   Tavris, Carol and Carole Offir. *The Longest War; Sex Differences in Perspective.* New York: Harcourt Brace Jovanovich, 1977.

2946   Vincent, Clark E. "Implications of changes in male-female role expectations for interpreting M-F scores." *Journal of Marriage and the Family* 28(2):196–199, May 1966.

MEN

2947   Balswick, Jack O. and Charles W. Peek. "The inexpressive male and family relationships during early adulthood." *Sociological Symposium* 4:1–12, Spring 1970.

2948   Brenton, Myron. *The American Male.* New York: Coward-McCann, 1966.

2949   Brown, Fred. "Changes in sexual identification and role over a decade and their implications." *Journal of Psychology* 77:229–251, 1971.

2950   Dufresne, Meri Jill Mendelsohn. *Differential reactions of males to three different female sex roles.* (Dissertation—University of Connecticut.) Ann Arbor, MI: University Microfilms, 1971. (Order #72-14,228)

2951   Farrell, Warren T. *The Liberated Man; Beyond Masculinity: Freeing Men and Their Relationships with Women.* New York: Random House, 1974.

2952   Goldberg, Herb. "The psychological pressures on the American male." *Human Behavior* 2(4):73–75, Apr. 1973.

2953   Greenson, Ralph R. "On sexual apathy in the male." *Medical Aspects of Human Sexuality* 3(8):25–34, Aug. 1969.

2954   Hacker, Helen Mayer. "The new burdens of masculinity." *Marriage and Family Living* 19(3):227–233, Aug. 1957.

2955   Luce, Ralph A. "From hero to robot: masculinity in America—stereotype and reality." *Psychoanalytic Review* 54(4):53–74, Winter 1967.

2956   Mead, Beverley T. et al. "Is there a need for 'men's liberation'?" *Medical Aspects of Human Sexuality* 10(7):36 passim, July 1976.

2957   Naffziger, Claudeen Cline and Ken Naffziger. "Development of sex role stereotypes." *The Family Coordinator* 23(3):251–258, July 1974.

2958   Nichols, Jack. *Men's Liberation; A New Definition of Masculinity.* New York: Penguin, 1975.

2959   Petras, John W., ed. *Sex: Male/Gender:*

Masculine; Readings in Male Sexuality. Port Washington, NY: Alfred Publishing Co., 1975.

2960   Pleck, Joseph H. and Jack Sawyer, eds., *Men and Masculinity.* Englewood Cliffs, NJ: Prentice-Hall, 1974.

2961   Rudy, Arthur J. and Robert Peller. "Men's liberation." *Medical Aspects of Human Sexuality* 6(9):84–93, Sept. 1972.

2962   Rueger, Russ. "Seeking freedom from the male myth." *Human Behavior* 2(4):75–77, Apr. 1973.

2963   Steinmann, Anne and David J. Fox. *The Male Dilemma; How to Survive the Sexual Revolution.* New York: J. Aronson, 1974.

2964   Steinmetz, Suzanne K. "Male liberation—destroying the stereotypes." Paper presented at the National Council on Family Relations Annual Meeting, Oct. 1973. 27p.

2965   Stevens, Barbara. "The sexually oppressed male." *Psychotherapy: Theory, Research and Practice* 11(1):16–21, Spring 1974.

2966   Tavris, Carol. "Men and women report their views on masculinity." *Psychology Today* 10(8):34 passim, Jan. 1977.

2967   "Viewpoints: what's happened to masculinity in the United States?" *Medical Aspects of Human Sexuality* 2(6):36–42, June 1968.

WOMEN

2968   Ardener, Shirley G. "Sexual insult and female militancy." *Man* (Journal of the Royal Anthropological Institute) 8(3):423–440, Sept. 1973.

2969   Aring, Charles D. "Man versus women: a historical and cultural framework." *Annals of Internal Medicine* 73(6):1025–1031, Dec. 1970.

2970   Bernard, Jessie. "The second sex and the cichlid effect." *Journal of the National Association of Women Deans and Counselors* 31:8–17, Fall 1967.

2971   Brashear, Diane B. and Kathleen Willis. "Claiming our own: a model for women's growth." *Journal of Marriage and Family Counseling* 2(3):251–258, July 1976.

2972   Callahan, Sidney Cornelia. "The emancipation of women and the sexual revolution." In: *Sexuality: A Search for Perspective,* ed. by Donald L. Grummon and Andrew M. Barclay, pp. 213–225. New York: Van Nostrand Reinhold, 1971.

2973   Chilman, Catherine S. "Some psychosocial aspects of female sexuality." *The Family Coordinator* 23(2):123–131, Apr. 1974.

2974   Clavan, Sylvia. "Changing female sexual behavior and future family structure." *Pacific Sociological Review* 15(3):295–308, July 1972.

2975   Dempewolff, Judith Ann. "Development and validation of a feminism scale." *Psychological Reports* 34(2):651–657, Apr. 1974.

2976   Dorn, Dean S. "Idealized sex roles among young people." *Journal of Human Relations* 18(1):789–797, First Quarter 1970.

2977   Easley, Eleanor B. "The dilemma of women in our culture: gynecologic repercussions. Part II." *American Journal of Obstetrics and Gynecology* 110(6):858–864, July 15, 1971.

2978   _____. "Gynecologic repercussions of the modern social scene." *American Journal of Obstetrics and Gynecology* 72(6):1261–1267, Dec. 1956.

2979   Ehrlich, Carol. "The male sociologist's burden: the place of women in marriage and family texts." *Journal of Marriage and the Family* 33(3):421–430, Aug. 1971.

2980   Gaffney, Louis. "Psychological reflections on marital love and contraception." *Journal of Religion and Health* 10(1):11–22, Jan. 1971.

2981   Gochros, Jean S. "Women — minority in transition." In: *The Sexually Oppressed,* ed. by H.L. Gochros and J.S. Gochros, pp. 71–83, New York: Association Press, 1977.

2982   Grant, Annette. "The new feminist literature: a critique." *Sexual Behavior* 2(9):15–18, Sept. 1972.

2983   Grunebaum, Henry U. "Thoughts on love, sex, and commitment." *Journal of Sex and Marital Therapy* 2(4):277–283, Winter 1976.

2984   Guber, Selma. "Should women be sexually aggressive?" *Sexual Behavior* 2(9):30-32, Sept. 1972.

2985   Gunther, Max. "Wives who run away." In: *Deviancy and the Family,* ed. by C.D. Bryant and J.G. Wells, pp. 79–85. Philadelphia: Davis, 1973.

2986   Hammer, Signe, ed. *Women: Body and Culture; Essays on the Sexuality of Women in a Changing Society.* New York: Harper & Row, 1975.

2987   Heidensohn, Frances. "The deviance of women: a critique and an enquiry." *British Journal of Sociology* 19(2):160–175, 1968.

2988 Humphrey, Frederick G. "Changing roles for women: implications for marriage counselors." *Journal of Marriage and Family Counseling* 1(3):219–227, July 1975.

2989 Iven, Donna. "Sex roles in sexual behavior: an historical perspective." Paper presented at the Annual Meeting of the Midwest Sociological Association, Omaha, Apr. 3–6, 1974. 26p.

2990 Johnson, Paula and Jacqueline D. Goodchilds. "Pornography, sexuality, and social psychology." *Journal of Social Issues* 29(3):231–238, 1973.

2991 Kallan, Richard A. and Robert D. Brooks. "The playmate of the month: naked but nice." *Journal of Popular Culture* 8:328–336, Fall 1974.

2992 Lazar, Gerald M. "Brief guide to office counseling: when women get the 'seven year itch.'" *Medical Aspects of Human Sexuality* 9(11):93–94, Nov. 1975.

2993 Linnér, Birgitta. "What does equality between the sexes imply?" *American Journal of Orthopsychiatry* 41(5):747–756, Oct. 1971.

2994 Lipman-Blumen, Jean and Ann R. Tickamyer. "Sex roles in transition: a ten-year perspective." *Annual Review of Sociology* 1:297–337, 1975.

2995 Liss-Levinson, Nechama, Emily Coleman and Laura Brown. "A program of sexual assertiveness training for women." *Counseling Psychologist* 5(4):74–78, 1975.

2996 Mazur, Ronald M. "The double standard." *Sexual Behavior* 2(11):42–48, Nov. 1972.

2997 Miller, Jean Baker, ed. *Psychoanalysis and Women: Contributions to New Theory and Therapy.* New York: Brunner/Mazel, 1973.

2998 Presser, Harriet B. "The timing of the first birth, female roles, and black fertility." *Milbank Memorial Fund Quarterly* 49(3 part 1):329–361, July 1971.

2999 Rice, Joy K. and David G. Rice. "Implications of the women's liberation movement for psychotherapy." *American Journal of Psychiatry* 130(2):191–196, Feb. 1973.

3000 Schwab, John J. "Antipathy to marriage." *Sexual Behavior* 2(8):41–49, Aug. 1972.

3001 _____. "The difficulties of being wife, mistress, and mother." *Medical Aspects of Human Sexuality* 8(5):146–160, May 1974.

3002 Shor, Joel. "Female sexuality: aspects and

prospects." *Psychoanalysis: Journal of Psychoanalytic Psychology* 2(3):3–32, Winter 1954.

3003 Simon, Rita James. *The Contemporary Woman and Crime.* Crime and Delinquency Issues: A Monograph Series. Rockville, MD: Center for Studies of Crime and Delinquency, National Institute of Mental Health, 1975. (DHEW Publication No. ADM-75-161 avail. from Supt. of Docs., U.S. GPO, Washington, DC 20402.)

3004 Sprey, Jetse. "On the origin of sex roles." *Sociological Focus* 5(2):1–8, Winter 1971/1972.

3005 Steinmetz, Suzanne K. "The sexual context of social research." *American Sociologist* 9(3):111–116, Aug. 1974.

3006 Stemple, Diane and Jane E. Tyler. "Sexism in advertising." *The American Journal of Psychoanalysis* 34:271–273, 1974.

3007 Stokes, Walter R. "Inadequacy of female orgasm as a problem in marriage counseling." *Journal of Sex Research* 4(3):225–233, Aug. 1968.

3008 Stoll, Clarice Stasz. "The sociology of sex roles: essay review." *The Sociological Quarterly* 13:419–425, Summer 1972.

3009 Stuart, Martha and William T. Liu. *The Emerging Woman: The Impact of Family Planning.* Boston: Little, Brown, 1970.

3010 Suyin, Han. "The changing status of women, literacy and education and family planning." *Journal of Sex Research* 3(4):275–283, Nov. 1967.

3011 "Viewpoints: has women's liberation become a cause of marital and sexual strife?" *Medical Aspects of Human Sexuality* 5(9):12–19, Sept. 1971.

3012 Whirley, Marilyn Peddicord and Susan B. Poulsen. "Assertiveness and sexual satisfaction in employed professional women." *Journal of Marriage and the Family* 37(3):573–581, Aug. 1975.

3013 Yorburg, Betty. "Sexual identity in America." In: *Modern Views of Human Sexual Behavior,* ed. by J. McCary and D. Copeland, pp. 17–35. Chicago: Science Research Associates, 1976.

STATUS OF WOMEN

3014 Bardwick, Judith M. *The Psychology of Women: A Study of Bio-Cultural Conflicts.* New York: Harper & Row, 1971.

3015 Barker-Benfield, G.J. *The Horrors of the Half-Known Life: Male Attitudes toward Women* and Sexuality in Nineteenth-Century America. New York: Harper & Row, 1976.

3016 Beauvoir, Simone de. *Le deuxième Sexe.* Paris: Gallimard, 1949.

3017 Berger, Arthur. "Sex and the serpent on Madison Avenue." *Human Behavior* 2(6):73–76, June 1973.

3018 Bernard, Jessie. *The Future of Motherhood.* New York: Dial Press, 1974.

3019 Bullough, Vern L. and Bonnie Bullough. *The Subordinate Sex; A History of Attitudes toward Women.* Urbana: University of Illinois Press, 1973.

3020 Bullough, Vern L. and Martha Voght. "Women, menstruation, and nineteenth-century medicine." *Bulletin of the History of Medicine* 47(1):66–82, Jan./Feb. 1973.

3021 Burnham, John. "The progressive era revolution in American attitudes toward sex." *Journal of American History* 59(4):885–908, Mar. 1973.

3022 Calderone, Mary Steichen. "It's society that is changing sexuality." *Center Magazine* 5(4):58–68, July/Aug. 1972.

3023 Carter, Luther J. "New feminism: potent force in birth-control policy." *Science* 167(3922): 1234–1236, Feb. 1970.

3024 Chesler, Phyllis. "Women as psychiatric and psychotherapeutic patients." *Journal of Marriage and the Family* 33(4):746–759, Nov. 1971.

3025 Cohen, Martin. "You've come a long way, baby. . .or have you?" *Sexual Behavior* 2(6):49–51, June 1972.

3026 Coleman, James S. "Female status and premarital sexual codes." *American Journal of Sociology* 72(2):217, Sept. 1966.

3027 Compton, Ariel S. "Who's hysterical?" *Journal of Sex and Marital Therapy* 1(2):158–174, Winter 1974.

3028 Decter, Midge. *The New Chastity and Other Arguments against Women's Liberation.* New York: Coward, McCann & Geoghegan, 1972.

3029 Degler, Carl N. and Clelia Duel Mosher. "What ought to be and what was: women's sexuality in the nineteenth century." *American Historical Review* 79(5):1467–1490, Dec. 1974.

3030 Ferrell, Mary Z., William L. Tolone and Robert H. Walsh. "Maturational and societal changes in the sexual double-standard: a panel analysis (1967–1971; 1970–1974)." *Journal of Marriage and the Family* 39(2):255–271, May 1977.

3031 Firestone, Shulamith. *The Dialectic of Sex.* New York: Morrow, 1970.

3032 Frankfort, Ellen. *Vaginal Politics.* New York: Quadrangle Books, 1972.

3033 Friedan, Betty. *The Feminine Mystique.* New York: W.W. Norton, 1963.

3034 Gordon, Linda. *Woman's Body, Woman's Right: A Social History of Birth Control in America.* New York: Grossman, 1976.

3035 Gornick, Vivian and Barbara K. Moran, eds. *Woman in Sexist Society.* New York: Basic Books, 1971.

3036 Greenbaum, Henry. "The psychological impact of the sex revolution." In: *Sexuality and Psychoanalysis,* ed. by E.T. Adelson, pp. 291–305. New York: Brunner/Mazel, 1975.

3037 Greer, Germaine. *The Female Eunuch.* New York: McGraw-Hill, 1971.

3038 Haller, John S. and Robin M. Haller. *The Physician and Sexuality in Victorian America.* Urbana: University of Illinois Press, 1974.

3039 Henley, Nancy M. "Power, sex and nonverbal communication." *Berkeley Journal of Sociology* 18:1–26, 1973/1974.

3040 Howell, Mary C. "Brief guide to office counseling: the 'sexual revolution' and the feminist movement." *Medical Aspects of Human Sexuality* 9(2):175–176, Feb. 1975.

3041 Hunt, Janet G. and Larry L. Hunt. "The sexual mystique: a common dimension of racial and sexual stratification." *Sociology and Social Research* 59(3):231–242, Apr. 1975.

3042 Kellogg, Edmund H. "Reform of laws affecting population growth: recent developments." *Journal of International Law and Economics* 10(1):1–36, 1975.

3043 Ladner, Joyce A. *Tomorrow's Tomorrow: The Black Woman.* Garden City, NY: Doubleday, 1971.

3044 Laws, Judith Long and Pepper Schwartz. *Sexual Scripts: The Social Construction of Female Sexuality.* Hinsdale, IL: Dryden, 1977.

3045 Ludwig, Edward G. and David L. Larson. "Sex liberalization and liberation of the female: implications for romantic love." *Sociological Focus* 7(1):14–23, Winter 1973/1974.

3046   Madison, Jan and Rosalyn Meadow. "A one-day intensive sexuality workshop for women." *Journal of Sex Education and Therapy* 3(1):38–41, Spring/Summer 1977.

3047   Martin, Del. *Battered Wives.* San Francisco: Glide Urban Center, 1976.

3048   Mason, Karen Oppenheim and Larry Bumpass. "U.S. women's sex-role ideology, 1970." *American Journal of Sociology* 80(5):1212–1219, Mar. 1975.

3049   Meade, Marion. "Does rock degrade women?" *Sexual Behavior* 1(5):28–29, Aug. 1971.

3050   Muller, Charlotte. "Feminism, society and fertility control." *Family Planning Perspectives* 6(2):68–72, Spring 1974.

3051   Myron, Nancy and Charlotte Bunch, eds. *Lesbianism and the Women's Movement.* Baltimore: Diana Press, 1975.

3052   Neubardt, Selig B. "Women's liberation and the male gynecologist." *Medical Aspects of Human Sexuality* 8(10):158–199, Oct. 1974.

3053   Nietzke, Ann. "Hostility on the laugh track." *Human Behavior* 3(5):64–70, May 1974.

3054   O'Connell, Barbara E. "Women's reactions to 'wolf-whistles' and lewd remarks." *Medical Aspects of Human Sexuality* 11(10):59 passim, Oct. 1977.

3055   O'Faolain, Julia and Lauro Martines, eds. *Not in God's Image.* New York: Harper & Row, 1973.

3056   Peterson, Gail Beaton. "Sexism in the treatment of sexual dysfunction." *The Family Coordinator* 22(4):397–404, Oct. 1973.

3057   Rossi, Lee D. "The whore vs. the girl-next-door: stereotypes of women in *Playboy, Penthouse* and *Oui." Journal of Popular Culture* 9:90–94, Summer 1975.

3058   Sacks, Michael Paul. "Sexual equality and Soviet women." *Society* 14(5):48–51, July/Aug. 1977.

3059   Shear, Marie. "Freemeat talks back: explicit sex — liberation or exploitation?" *Journal of Communication* 26:38–39, Winter 1976.

3060   Sherfey, Mary Jane. *The Nature and Evolution of Female Sexuality.* New York: Random House, 1972.

3061   Shorter, Edward. "Female emancipation, birth control, and fertility in European history." *The American Historical Review* 78(3):605–640, June 1973.

3062   Smith-Rosenberg, Caroll and Charles Rosenberg. "The female animal: medical and biological views of woman and her role in nineteenth-century America." *Journal of American History* 60:332–356, Sept. 1973.

3063   Symonds, Alexandra. "The psychology of the female liberation movement." *Medical Aspects of Human Sexuality* 5(4):24–33, Apr. 1971.

PERIODICALS

Sex Roles; A Journal of Research
Plenum Publishing Corp.
227 W. 17th St., New York, NY 10011

Signs; Journal of Women in Culture and Society
The University of Chicago Press
5801 Ellis Ave., Chicago, IL 60637

OTHER SOURCES OF INFORMATION

International Planned Parenthood Federation
111 Fourth Ave., New York, NY 10003

Women's History Research Center
2325 Oak, Berkeley, CA 94708

Legal Aspects of Sex Behavior

Child Victims

3064   Amir, Menachem. "The role of the victim in sex offenses." In: *Sexual Behaviors: Social, Clinical, and Legal Aspects,* ed. by H.L.P. Resnick and Marvin E. Wolfgang, pp. 131–167. Boston: Little, Brown, 1972.

3065   Ausloos, Guy. "Les attentats à la pudeur: revue de la littérature et commentaires." *Bulletin du Centre Médico-Social de Pro Familia* (Lausanne) 13:13–30, Nov. 1976.

3066   Bakan, David. "Slaughter of the innocents." *Journal of Clinical Child Psychology* 2(3):10–12, Fall 1973.

3067   Beigel, Hugo G. "Children who seduce adults." *Sexology* 40(7):30–34, Feb. 1974.

3068   Bender, Lauretta and Abram Blau. "The reaction of children to sexual relations with adults." *American Journal of Orthopsychiatry* 7:500–518, 1937.

3069   Bender, Lauretta and Alvin E. Grugett. "A follow-up report on children who had atypical sexual experience." *American Journal of Orthopsychiatry* 22:825–837, 1952.

3070   Brant, Renee S.T. and Veronica B. Tisza. "The sexually misused child." *American Journal of Orthopsychiatry* 47(1):80–90, Jan. 1977.

3071   Brunold, Heinz. "Observations after sexual traumata suffered in childhood." *Excerpta Criminologica* (Netherlands) 4(1):5–8, Jan./Feb. 1964.

3072   Burgess, Ann Wolbert, Lynda Lytle Holmstrom and Maureen McCausland. "Child sexual assault by family member: decisions following disclosure." Paper presented at the 28th Annual Meeting of the American Association of Psychiatric Services for Children, San Francisco, Nov. 1976. 21p.

3073   Burton, Lindy. *Vulnerable Children: Three Studies of Children in Conflict: Accident Involved Children, Sexually Assaulted Children, and Children with Asthma,* pp. 87–169. New York: Schocken Books, 1968.

3074   Capraro, Vincent J. "Sexual assault of female children." *Annals of the New York Academy of Sciences* 142(3):817–819, May 10, 1967.

3075   Chaneles, Sol. "Child victims of sex offenses." *Federal Probation* 31(2):52–56, June 1967.

3076   Chaneles, Sol and Donald Brieland. *Sexual Abuse of Children: Implications for Casework.* Denver: American Humane Association, Children's Division, 1967.

3077   DeFrancis, Vincent. "Protecting the child victim of sex crimes committed by adults." *Federal Probation* 35(3):15–20, Sept. 1971.

3078   _____. *Protecting the Child Victim of Sex Crimes Committed by Adults: Final Report.* Denver: American Humane Association, CHILDREN'S Division, 1969.

3079   Eaton, Antoinette Parisi and Earl Vastbinder. "The sexually molested child; a plan of management." *Clinical Pediatrics* 8(8):438–441, Aug. 1969.

3080   Elonen, Anna S. and Sara B. Zwarensteyn. "Sexual trauma in young blind children." *New Outlook for the Blind* 69(10):440–442, Dec. 1975.

3081   Finch, Stuart M. "Adult seduction of the child: effects on the child." *Medical Aspects of Human Sexuality* 7(3):170–187, Mar. 1973.

3082   _____. "Sexual activity of children with other children and adults." *Clinical Pediatrics* 6(1):1–2, Jan. 1967.

3083   Flammang, C.J. "Interviewing child victims of sex offenders." In: *Rape Victimology,* ed. by LeRoy G. Schultz, pp. 245–256. Springfield, IL: Charles C. Thomas, 1975.

3084   Gagnon, John H. "Female child victims of sex offenses." *Social Problems* 13(2):176–192, Fall 1965. (Also: Shiloh, Ailon, ed. *Studies in Human Sex Behavior: The American Scene.* Springfield, IL: Charles C. Thomas, 1970.)

3085   Gagnon, John H. and William Simon. "Sexual encounters between adults and children." In: *Sexuality and Man,* SIECUS, pp. 83–98. New York: Scribner, 1970.

3086   Gibbens, T.C.N. and Joyce Prince. *Child Victims of Sex Offences.* London: Institute for the Study and Treatment of Delinquency, Oct. 1963.

3087 Goldberg, Jacob Alter and Rosamond Goldberg. *Girls on City Streets: A Study of 1400 Cases of Rape.* New York: Foundation Books, 1940.

3088 Grimm, H. "Eine statistische betrachtung über kinder und jugendliche als gegenstand von pressemeldungen über sexuelle delikte." *Ärztliche Jugendkunde* 53(3/4):81–84, 1961.

3089 Hayman, Charles R. et al. "Sexual assault on women and children in the District of Columbia." *Public Health Reports* 83(12):1021–1028, Dec. 1968.

3090 Hogan, Walter L. "Brief guide to office counseling: the raped child." *Medical Aspects of Human Sexuality* 8(11):129–130, Nov. 1974.

3091 Kainz, Anna. "Kinder als opfer strafbarer handlungen." *Kriminalistik* 21(11):605–608, 1967.

3092 Katzman, Marshall. "Early sexual trauma." *Sexual Behavior* 2(2):13–17, Feb. 1972.

3093 Kaufman, Irving, Alice L. Peck and Consuelo Taquiri. "The family constellation and overt incestuous relations between father and daughter." *American Journal of Orthopsychiatry* 24(2):266–279, Apr. 1954.

3094 Kiefer, C. Raymond. "Brief guide to office counseling: sexual molestation of a child." *Medical Aspects of Human Sexuality* 7(12):127–128, Dec. 1973.

3095 Kinsey, Alfred C. et al. *Sexual Behavior of the Human Female,* pp. 116–122. Philadelphia: W.B. Saunders, 1953.

3096 Landis, Judson T. "Experiences of 500 children with adult sexual deviation." *Psychiatric Quarterly Supplement* 30(1):91–109, 1956.

3097 Libai, David. "The protection of the child victim of a sexual offense." In: *Rape Victimology,* ed. by LeRoy G. Schultz, pp. 277–335. Springfield, IL: Charles C. Thomas, 1975.

3098 MacDonald, John M. *Rape: Offenders and Their Victims,* pp. 111–131. Springfield, IL: Charles C. Thomas, 1971.

3099 Miller, Patricia Y. "Blaming the victim of child molestation: an empirical analysis." Unpub. doctoral dissertation, Northwestern University, 1976.

3100 Mohr, Johann W. "A child has been molested." *Medical Aspects of Human Sexuality* 2(11):43–50, Nov. 1968.

3101 Oliven, John F. "The child as victim of sexual aggression." In: *Clinical Sexuality,* 3rd ed. pp. 55–71. Philadelphia: J.B. Lippincott, 1974.

3102 Peters, Joseph J. "Children who are victims of sexual assault and the psychology of offenders." *American Journal of Psychotherapy* 30(3):398–421, July 1976.

3103 Potrykus, Dagmar and Manfred Wöbcke. *Sexualität zwishen Kindern und Erwachsenen.* Munich: Goldmann, 1974.

3104 Radzinowicz, L., ed. *Sexual Offenses; A Report of the Cambridge (University) Department of Criminal Science,* pp. 83–112. London: Macmillan, 1957.

3105 Reifen, David. "Protection of children involved in sexual offenses: a new method of investigation in Israel." *Journal of Criminal Law, Criminology and Police Science* 49(3):222–229, Sept./Oct. 1958.

3106 Robinson, Henry A., Dale B. Sherrod and Courtney N. Malcarney. "Review of child molestation and alleged rape cases." *American Journal of Obstetrics and Gynecology* 110:405–406, June 1, 1971.

3107 Roth, Edwin I. "Emergency treatment of raped children." *Medical Aspects of Human Sexuality* 6(8):85 passim, Aug. 1972.

3108 Saperstein, Avalie. "Child rape victims and their families." In: *Rape Victimology,* ed. by LeRoy G. Schultz, pp. 274–276. Springfield, IL: Charles C. Thomas, 1975.

3109 Schultz, LeRoy G. "The child sex victim: social psychological and legal perspectives." *Child Welfare* 52(3):147–157, Mar. 1973.

3110 _____. "Psychotherapeutic and legal approaches to the sexually victimized child." *International Journal of Child Psychotherapy* 1(4):115–128, 1972.

3111 _____. "Sexual victims." In: *The Sexually Oppressed,* ed. by H.L. Gochros and J.S. Gochros, pp. 110–125. New York: Association Press, 1977.

3112 Scrignar, C.B. "Sex and the under-aged girl." *Medical Aspects of Human Sexuality* 2(12):34 passim, Dec. 1968.

3113 Smith, Quentin Ted and Sarah B. Vinson. "Child rape experience at Grady Hospital." Paper presented at the 28th Annual Meeting of the American Association of Psychiatric Services for Children, San Francisco, Nov. 1976. 17p.

3114 Splane, R.B. "Helping the child who is a

victim of sex offences." *Canadian Welfare* 36:272–273, Nov. 15, 1960.

3115 Stokes, R.E. "A research approach to sexual offences involving children." *Canadian Journal of Corrections* 6(1):87–94, 1964.

3116 Tormes, Yvonne M. *Child Victims of Incest.* Denver: American Humane Association, Children's Division, 1968.

3117 Virkkunen, Matti. "Victim-precipitated pedophilia offences." *British Journal of Criminology* 15(2):175–180, Apr. 1975.

3118 Walter, Emil J. "Psychological danger spots." *International Journal of Sexology* 3(3):172–175, Feb. 1950.

3119 Walters, David R. *Physical and Sexual Abuse of Children: Causes and Treatment.* Bloomington: Indiana University Press, 1975.

3120 Weeks, Ruth B. "Brief guide to office counseling: counseling parents of sexually abused children." *Medical Aspects of Human Sexuality* 10(8):43–44, Aug. 1976.

3121 Weiss, Joseph et al. "A study of girl sex victims." *Psychiatric Quarterly* 29:1–27, Jan. 1955.

OTHER SOURCES OF INFORMATION

American Humane Association
Children's Division
Box 1266, Denver, CO 80201

Child Sexual Abuse Treatment Program
Santa Clara County Juvenile Probation Dept.
840 Guadalupe Pkwy., San Jose, CA 95110

Incest

3122 Abernethy, Virginia. "Dominance and sexual behavior: a hypothesis." *American Journal of Psychiatry* 131(7):813–817, July 1974.

3123 Bagley, Christopher. "Incest behavior and incest taboo." *Social Problems* 16(4):505–519, Spring 1969.

3124 Bardis, Panos D. "Marriage and family customs in ancient Egypt: an interdisciplinary study: part II." *Social Science* 42(2):104–119, Apr. 1967.

3125 Barry, Maurice J., Jr. "Incest." In: *Sexual Behavior and the Law,* ed. by Ralph Slovenko, pp. 521–538. Springfield, IL: Charles C. Thomas, 1965.

3126 Caspari, Ernst. "Sexual selection in human evolution." In: *Sexual Selection and the Descent of Man,* ed. by Bernard Campbell, pp. 332–356. Chicago: Aldine Publishing Co., 1972.

3127 Cavallin, Hector. "Incest." *Sexual Behavior* 3(2):19–22, Feb. 1973.

3128 Cormier, Bruno M. and Paul Boulanger. "Life cycle and episodic recidivism." *Canadian Psychiatric Association Journal* 18(4):283–287, Aug. 1973.

3129 Coult, Allan D. "Causality and cross-sex prohibitions." *American Anthropologist* 65(2):266–277, Apr. 1963.

3130 Devroye, A. "L'inceste: revue de données bibliographiques." *Acta Psychiatrica Belgica* 73(6):661–712, Nov. 1973.

3131 Dubreuil, Guy. "Les bases psychoculturelles du tabou de l'inceste." *Canadian Psychiatric Association Journal* 7(5):218–234, Oct. 1962.

3132 Durkheim, Emile. *Incest; The Nature and Origin of the Taboo* (together with *The Origins and the Development of the Incest Taboo by Albert Ellis*). New York: Lyle Stuart, 1963. (Durkheim's work originally appeared as "La prohibition de l'inceste et ses origines." in *L'Annee Sociologique,* v. 1, 1897.)

3133 Eskildsen, Gustavo Alfredo. "The origin and persistence of the incest taboo and its relation to the genesis and evolution of human society: a critique of existing theories and a new hypothesis." Unpub. master's thesis, Indiana University, 1971.

3134 Fox, J.R. "Sibling incest." *British Journal of Sociology* 13(2):128–150, June 1962.

3135 Fox, Robin. "Alliance and constraint: sexual selection and the evolution of human kinship systems." In: *Sexual Selection and the Descent of Man,* ed. by Bernard Campbell, pp. 282–331. Chicago: Aldine Publishing Co., 1972.

3136 Hentig, Hans von. "Blutschadefälle muttersohn." *Monatsschrift für Kriminologie und Strafrechtsreform* 45(1/2):15–19, 1962.

3137 Layman, William A. "Pseudo incest." *Comprehensive Psychiatry* 13(4):385–389, July/Aug. 1972.

3138 Lester, David. "Incest." *Journal of Sex Research* 8(4):268–285, Nov. 1972.

3139 Lindzey, Gardner. "Some remarks concerning incest, the incest taboo, and psychoanalytic theory." *American Psychologist* 22(12):1051–1059, Dec. 1967.

3140   McCary, James L. "Nymphomania: a case history." *Medical Aspects of Human Sexuality* 6(11):192–210, Nov. 1972.

3141   Machotka, Pavel, Frank S. Pittman and Kalman Flomenhaft. "Incest as a family affair." *Family Process* 6(1):98–116, Mar. 1967.

3142   Masters, R.E.L. *Patterns of Incest: A Psycho-social Study of Incest.* New York: Julian Press, 1963.

3143   Messer, Alfred A. "The 'Phaedra complex.'" *Archives of General Psychiatry* 21:213–218, Aug. 1969.

3144   Middleton, Russell. "Brother-sister and father-daughter marriage in ancient Egypt." *American Sociological Review* 27(5):603–611, Oct. 1962.

3145   Parker, Seymour. "The precultural basis of the incest taboo: toward a biosocial theory." *American Anthropologist* 78(2):285–305, June 1976.

3146   Parsons, Talcott. "The incest taboo in relation to social structure and the socialization process of the child." *British Journal of Sociology* 5(2):101–117, June 1954.

3147   Raybin, James B. "Homosexual incest." *Journal of Nervous and Mental Disease* 148(2):105–110, Feb. 1969.

3148   Santiago, Luciano P.R. *The Children of Oedipus; Brother-Sister Incest in Psychiatry, Literature, History and Mythology.* Roslyn Heights, NY: Libra, 1973.

3149   Schwartzman, John. "The individual, incest, and exogamy." *Psychiatry* 27:171–180, May 1974.

3150   Sidler, Nikolaus. *Zur Universalität des Inzesttabu; Eine Kritische Untersuchung der These und der Einwände.* Soziologische gegenwartsfragen nr. 36. Stuttgart: Ferdinand Enke, 1971.

3151   Slotkin, J.S. "On a possible lack of incest regulations in old Iran." *American Anthropologist* 49(4):612–617, Oct./Dec. 1947.

3152   Spillman, Emil V. "Treatment of sexual problems in the South—differences in the diagnosis and therapy based on geographical location." *Journal of the American Institute of Hypnosis* 13(1):5–10, Jan. 1972.

3153   Vestergaard, Emma. "Fader-datter incest." *Nordisk Tidsskrift for Kriminalvidenskab* 48:159–188, 1960.

3154   Weber, Ellen. "Incest — sexual abuse begins at home." *Ms.* 5(10):64–67, Apr. 1977.

3155   Young, Frank W. "Incest taboos and social solidarity." *American Journal of Sociology* 72(6):589–600, 1967.

INCEST RESEARCH

3156   Bigras, Julien et al. "En deçà et delà de l'inceste chez l'adolescente." *Canadian Psychiatric Association Journal* 11(3):189–204, June 1966.

3157   Bischof, Norbert. "The biological foundations of the incest taboo." *Social Science Information* 11(6):7–36, Dec. 1972.

3158   Cavallin, H. "Incestuous fathers: a clinical report." *American Journal of Psychiatry* 122(10):1132–1138, Apr. 1966.

3159   DeVos, George A. "Affective dissonance and primary socialization: implications for a theory of incest avoidance." *Ethos* 3(2):165–182, Summer 1975.

3160   Ferracuti, Franco. "Incest between father and daughter." In: *Sexual Behaviors: Social, Clinical, and Legal Aspects,* ed. by H.L.P. Resnick and Marvin E. Wolfgang, pp. 169–183. Boston: Little, Brown, 1972.

3161   Forston, Raymon C. and Jack E. Dison. "A description and appraisal of theories of incest." Paper presented at the 39th Annual Meeting of the Southwestern Sociological Association, TX, Apr. 7–12, 1976. 14p.

3162   Gebhard, Paul H. et al. *Sex Offenders: An Analysis of Types.* New York: Harper-Hoeber, 1965.

3163   Gligor, Alyce Mapp. *Incest and sexual delinquency: a comparative analysis of two forms of sexual behavior in minor females.* (Dissertation—Western Reserve University.) Ann Arbor, MI: University Microfilms, 1966. (Order #67-4588)

3164   Greaves, Thomas. "Explaining incest rules." *Cornell Journal of Social Relations* 1(2):39–50, 1966.

3165   Guggisberg, Michel. "Inceste et perversion (à propos de 17 cas)." *Schweizer Archiv für Neurologie, Neurochirurgie und Psychiatrie* 94(1):208–210, 1964.

3166   Hentig, Hans von and Theodor Viernstein.

Untersuchungen über den Inzest. Heidelberg: Carl Winters, 1925.

3167   Hunt, Morton. *Sexual Behavior in the 1970's,* pp. 337–351. Chicago: Playboy Press, 1974.

3168   Kaufman, Irving, Alice L. Peck and Consuelo Taquiri. "The family constellation and overt incestuous relations between father and daughter." *American Journal of Orthopsychiatry* 24(2):266–279, Apr. 1954.

3169   Kinberg, Olof, Gunnar Inghe and Svend Riemer. *Incestproblemet i Sverige.* Stockholm: Natur och Kultur, 1943.

3170   Kunter, M. "Sozialanthropologische aspekte des vater-tochter-inzestes." *Das öffentliche Gesundheitswesen* 34:48–51, Feb. 1972.

3171   Larson, Carl A. "Genetic-hygienic impairment through incestuous matings." *Eugenics Quarterly* 3(2):104–105, June 1956.

3172   Lukianowicz, Narcyz. "Incest. I: paternal incest. II: other types of incest." *British Journal of Psychiatry* 120:301–313, Mar. 1972.

3173   Lutier, J. "Rôle des facteurs culturels et psychosociaux dans les délits incestueux au milieu rural." *Annales de Médicine Légale* 41(1):80–83, 1961.

3174   MacLean, Charles J. and Morton S. Adams. "A method for the study of incest." *Annals of Human Genetics* 36:323–332, 1973.

3175   Magal, V. and H.Z. Winnik. "Role of incest in family structure." *Israel Annals of Psychiatry and Related Disciplines* 6(2):173–189, Dec. 1968.

3176   Maisch, Herbert. *Incest.* New York: Stein & Day, 1972. (First published in German in 1968 as *Inzest.*)

3177   Martin, James O. "A psychological investigation of convicted incest offenders by means of two projective techniques." Unpub. doctoral dissertation, Michigan State University, 1958.

3178   Molnar, G. and P. Cameron. "Incest syndromes: observations in a general hospital psychiatric unit." *Canadian Psychiatric Association Journal* 20(5):373–377, Aug. 1975.

3179   Poznanski, Elva and Peter Blos. "Incest." *Medical Aspects of Human Sexuality* 9(10):46 passim, Oct. 1975.

3180   Rennert, Helmut. "Zur problematik des inzest." *Deutsche Zeitschrift für die Gesamte Gerichtliche Medizin* 48:50–57, 1958.

3181   Rhinehart, John W. "Genesis of overt incest." *Comprehensive Psychiatry* 2(6):338–349, Dec. 1961.

3182   Riemer, Svend. "A research note on incest." *American Journal of Sociology* 45:566–575, Jan. 1940.

3183   Sade, Donald Stone. "Inhibition of son-mother mating among free-ranging Rhesus monkeys." In: *Science and Psychoanalysis: Vol. 12, Animal and Human,* ed. by J.H. Masserman, pp. 18–38. New York: Grune & Stratton, 1968.

3184   Sagarin, Edward. "Incest: problems of definition and frequency." *Journal of Sex Research* 13(2):126–135, May 1977.

3185   Salvini, Alessandro. "Considerazioni interdisciplinari sull'incesto." *Sessuologia* 14(4): 33–39, Oct./Dec. 1973.

3186   Scheurell, Robert P. and Irwin D. Rinder. "Social networks and deviance: a study of lower class incest, wife beating, and nonsupport offenders." *The Wisconsin Sociologist* 10(2/3): 56–73, Spring/Summer 1973.

3187   Segner, Leslie Louise. *Two studies of the incest taboo: I. Sexual activity of mice (mus musculus) as a function of familiarity: II. A cross-cultural investigation of the correlates of incest in myth.* (Dissertation—University of Texas at Austin.) Ann Arbor, MI: University Microfilms, 1968. (Order #68-10,886)

3188   Shepher, Joseph. *Self-imposed incest avoidance and exogamy in second generation kibbutz adults.* (Dissertation—Rutgers University.) Ann Arbor, MI: University Microfilms, 1971. (Order #72-871)

3189   Szabo, Denis. "Problèmes de socialisation et d'integration socio-culturelles: contribution à l'étiologie de l'inceste." *Canadian Psychiatric Association Journal* 7(5):235–249, Oct. 1962.

3190   Traver, Harold Henry. *The theory and practice of incest.* (Dissertation—University of California at Santa Barbara.) Ann Arbor, MI: University Microfilms, 1973. (Order #74-7152)

3191   Tuteur, Werner. "Further observations on incestuous fathers." *Psychiatric Annals* 2(9): 77–87, Sept. 1972.

3192   Vayda, Andrew P. "Love in Polynesian atolls." *Man* 61:204–205, Dec. 1961.

3193   Weinberg, Samuel Kirson. "Incest." In: *Problems of Sex Behavior,* ed. by Edward Sagarin and Donal E.F. MacNamara, pp. 167–202. New York: Crowell, 1968.

3194 _____. *Incest Behavior.* New York: Citadel Press, 1955.

3195 Weiner, Irving B. "Father-daughter incest: a clinical report." *Psychiatric Quarterly* 36:607–632, Oct. 1962.

INCEST PSYCHOANALYSIS

3196 Barry, Maurice J. and Adelaide M. Johnson. "The incest barrier." *Psychoanalytic Quarterly* 27:485–500, 1958.

3197 Carruthers, E.A. "Net of incest." *Yale Review* 63:211–227, Winter 1974.

3198 Ferrari, Marcello. "Contributo alla conoscenza della psicodinamica dell'incesto." *Ospedale Psichiatrico* 35:253–264, Apr./Sept. 1967.

3199 Frances, Vera and Allen Frances. "Incest taboo and family structure." *Family Process* 15(2):235–244, June 1976.

3200 Gordon, Lillian. "Incest as revenge against the pre-oedipal mother." *Psychoanalytic Review* 42(3):284–292, July 1955.

3201 Henderson, D. James. "Incest: a synthesis of data." *Canadian Psychiatric Association Journal* 17:299–314, Aug. 1972.

3202 Kahn, Eugen. "On incest and Freud's Oedipus complex." *Confinia Psychiatrica* 8(2):89–101, 1965.

3203 Raphling, David L., Bob L. Carpenter and Allen Davis. "Incest: a genealogical study." *Archives of General Psychiatry* 16(4):505–511, Apr. 1967.

3204 Rascovsky, Arnaldo and Matilde Rascovsky. "The prohibition of incest, filicide and the sociocultural process." *The International Journal of Psychoanalysis* 53(2):271–276, 1972.

3205 Schechner, Richard. "Incest and culture: a reflection on Claude Lévi-Strauss." *Psychoanalytic Review* 58(4):563–572, 1971.

3206 Schneck, Jerome M. "Zooerasty and incest fantasy." *The International Journal of Clinical and Experimental Hypnosis* 22(4):299–302, Oct. 1974.

3207 Scott, W. Clifford M. "Psychodynamics of father daughter incest—discussion." *Canadian Psychiatric Association Journal* 7(5):250–252, Oct. 1962.

3208 Seidenberg, Robert. "The sexual basis of social prejudice." *Psychoanalytic Review* 39(1):90–95, Jan. 1952.

3209 Stein, Robert. *Incest and Human Love; The Betrayal of the Soul in Psychotherapy.* New York: Joseph Okpaku, 1973.

3210 Weich, Martin J. "The terms 'mother' and 'father' as a defense against incest." *Journal of the American Psychoanalytic Association* 16(4):783–791, 1968.

INCEST THERAPY

3211 Cormier, Bruno M., Miriam Kennedy and Jadwiga Sangowicz. "Psychodynamics of father daughter incest." *Canadian Psychiatric Association Journal* 7(5):203–217, Oct. 1962.

3212 Edwards, Neil B. "Case conference: assertive training in a case of homosexual pedophilia." *Journal of Behavior Therapy and Experimental Psychiatry* 3(1):55–63, Mar. 1972.

3213 Eist, Harold I. and Adeline U. Mandel. "Family treatment of ongoing incest behavior." *Family Process* 7(2):216–232, 1968.

3214 Greene, Nancy R. "A view of family pathology involving child molest (sic) — from a juvenile probation perspective." Paper presented at the American Society of Criminology, Toronto, Oct. 30–Nov. 2, 1975. 12p.

3215 Harbert, Terry L. et al. "Measurement and modification of incestuous behavior: a case study." *Psychological Reports* 34:79–86, Feb. 1974.

3216 Hersko, Marvin et al. "Incest: a three-way process." *Corrective Psychiatry* 7(1):22–31, Jan./Mar. 1961.

3217 Kennedy, Miriam and Bruno M. Cormier. "Father-daughter incest—treatment of the family." *Laval Medical* 40:946–950, Nov. 1969.

3218 Langsley, Donald G., Michael N. Schwartz and Robert H. Fairbairn. "Father-son incest." *Comprehensive Psychiatry* 9(3):218–226, May 1968.

3219 Pittman, Frank S. "Brief guides to office counseling: counseling incestuous families." *Medical Aspects of Human Sexuality* 10(4):54–58, Apr. 1976.

INCEST VICTIMOLOGY

3220 Adams, Morton S., Ruth T. Davidson and Phyllis Cornell. "Adoptive risks of the children of incest — a preliminary report." *Child Welfare* 46:137-142, Mar. 1967.

3221 Benward, Jean and Judianne Densen-Gerber. "Incest as a causative factor in antisocial behavior: an exploratory study." *Contemporary Drug Problems* 4:323-340, Fall 1975.

3222 Canepa, Giacomo and Tullio Bandini. "Studio criminologico sulla personalita delle vittime di incesto." *Zacchia: Archivo di Medicina Legale Sociale e Criminologia* 5:75-104, Jan./Mar. 1969.

3223 Dingman, Jocelyn. "Incest: the cover-up crime." In: *Sexual Behavior in Canada: Patterns and Problems,* ed. by Benjamin Schlesinger, pp. 211-220. Toronto: University of Toronto Press, 1977.

3224 Greenland, Cyril. "Incest." *British Journal of Delinquency* 9(1):62-64, July 1958.

3225 *Incest: The Victim Nobody Believes.* (16mm film.) J. Gary Mitchell Film Co., 2000 Bridgeway, Sausolito, CA 94965.

3226 Nau, Elizabeth. "La personalité des victimes d'incest." *Acta Medicinae Legalis et Socialis* 19:195-198, Apr./June 1966.

3227 Phillip, Erhard. "La personalité des délinquants d'inceste." *Acta Medicinae Legalis et Socialis* 19:213-219, Apr./June 1966.

3228 Pirnay-Dufrasne, Régine. "Relation incestueuse dans une famille nombreuse." *Acta Psychiatrica Belgica* 73(6):713-724, Nov. 1973.

3229 Pomeroy, Wardell B. "A new look at incest." *Forum* 6(2):8-13, Nov. 1976.

3230 Schachter, M. and S. Cotte. "Étude médico-psychologique et sociale psychiatrique de l'inceste, dans la perspective pédopsychiatrique." *Acta Paedopsychiatrica* (Basel) 27(4):139-146, June 1960.

3231 Seemanová, Eva. "A study of children of incestuous matings." *Human Heredity* 21(2):108-128, 1971.

3232 Sloane, Paul and Eva Karpinsky. "Effects of incest on the participants." *American Journal of Orthopsychiatry* 12:666-673, Oct. 1942.

3233 Tormes, Yvonne M. *Child Victims of Incest.* Denver: The American Humane Association, Children's Division, 1968.

3234 Yorukoglu, Atalay and John P. Kemph. "Children not severely damaged by incest with a parent." *Journal of the American Academy of Child Psychiatry* 5(1):111-124, Jan. 1966.

LEGAL ASPECTS OF INCEST

3235 Berest, Joseph J. "Medico-legal aspects of incest." *Journal of Sex Research* 4(3):195-205, Aug. 1968.

3236 Giannini, Maria Cristina. "L'incesto (note di legislazione comparata)." *Sessuologia* 8(1):29-48, Jan./Mar. 1967.

3237 Hall Williams, J.E. "The neglect of incest: a criminologist's view." *Medicine, Science, and the Law* 14(1):64-67, Jan. 1974.

3238 Hentig, Hans von. "Inzest in der geschwisterreihe." *Archiv für Kriminologie* 129(1/2):6-12, Jan./Feb. 1962.

3239 Hughes, Graham. "The crime of incest." *Journal of Criminal Law, Criminology and Police Science* 55(3):322-331, Sept. 1964.

3240 Papertain, Gérard. "Complexe du Rubicon; l'inceste dans quelque sociétés antiques." *Confinia Psychiatrica* 15(2):116-124, 1972.

Pedophilia

3241 Caprio, Frank S. and Donald R. Brenner. "Pedophilia." In: *Sexual Behavior; Psycho-Legal Aspects,* pp. 204-216. New York: Citadel Press, 1961.

3242 McCaghy, Charles H. "Child molesting." *Sexual Behavior* 1(5):16-24, Aug. 1971.

3243 Mohr, Johann W. "The pedophilias: their clinical, social and legal implications." *Canadian Psychiatric Association Journal* 7(5):255-260, Oct. 1962.

3244 Shoor, Mervyn, Mary Helen Speed and Claudia Bartelt. "Syndrome of the adolescent child molester." *American Journal of Psychiatry* 122:783-789, Jan. 1966.

3245 Swanson, David W. "Who violates children sexually?" *Medical Aspects of Human Sexuality* 5(2):184-197, Feb. 1971.

3246 Walter, Emil J. "Psychological danger spots." *International Journal of Sexology* 3(3):172-175, Feb. 1950.

3247 Whiskin, Frederick E. "The geriatric sex offender." *Geriatrics* 22(10):168-172, Oct. 1967.

RESEARCH

3248 Atwood, Robert William. *A study of pedophilia.* (Dissertation—Brigham Young University.) Ann Arbor, MI: University Microfilms, 1969. (Order #70-4713)

3249 Atwood, Robert William and Robert J. Howell. "Pupillometric and personality test score differences of female aggressing pedophiliacs and normals." *Psychonomic Science* 22(2):115–116, Jan. 1971.

3250 Bell, Alan P. and Calvin S. Hall. *The Personality of a Child Molester: An Analysis of Dreams.* Chicago: Aldine Publishing Co., 1971.

3251 Bernard, F. "An enquiry among a group of pedophiles." *Journal of Sex Research* 11(3): 242–255, Aug. 1975.

3252 Calmas, Wilfred Earl. *Fantasies of the mother-son relationship of the rapist and the pedophile.* (Dissertation—Boston University.) Ann Arbor, MI: University Microfilms, 1965. (Order #65-11,211)

3253 Fisher, Gary M. "Psychological needs of heterosexual pedophiliacs." *Diseases of the Nervous System* 30(6):419–421, June 1969.

3254 Fitch, J.H. "Men convicted of sexual offences against children; a descriptive follow-up study." *British Journal of Criminology* 3(1):18–37, July 1962.

3255 Freund, Kurt. "Diagnosing heterosexual pedophilia by means of a test for sexual interest." *Behaviour Research and Therapy* 3:229–234, Dec. 1965.

3256 _____. "Erotic preference in pedophilia." *Behaviour Research and Therapy* 5:339–348, 1967.

3257 _____. "The female child as a surrogate object." *Archives of Sexual Behavior* 2(2):119–133, Dec. 1972.

3258 Frisbie, Louis V., Frank J. Vanasek and Harvey F. Dingman. "The self and the ideal self: methodological study of pedophiles." *Psychological Reports* 20(3):699–706, 1967.

3259 Gebhard, Paul H. et al. "Child molestation." In: *Problems of Sex Behavior,* ed. by Edward Sagarin and Donal E.F. MacNamara, pp. 241–267. New York: Crowell, 1968.

3260 _____. *Sex Offenders; An Analysis of Types.* New York: Harper-Hoeber, 1958.

3261 Gebhard, Paul H. and John H. Gagnon. "Male sex offenders against very young children." *The American Journal of Psychiatry* 121(6):576–579, Dec. 1964.

3262 Glueck, Bernard C. "Psychodynamic patterns in the sex offender." *Psychiatric Quarterly* 28(1):1–21, Jan. 1954.

3263 Goldstein, Michael, et al. "Experience with pornography: rapists, pedophiles, homosexuals, transsexuals, and controls." *Archives of Sexual Behavior* 1(1):1–15, 1971.

3264 Groth, Aloysius Nicholas. *A differential classification of pedophiles determined by the nature of their object-relations.* (Dissertation—Boston University.) Ann Arbor, MI: University Microfilms, 1971. (Order #72-25,281)

3265 McCaghy, Charles H. *Child molesters: a study of their careers as deviants.* (Dissertation—University of Wisconsin.) Ann Arbor, MI: University Microfilms, 1966. (Order #66-9938)

3266 _____. "Child molesters: a study of their careers as deviants." In: *Criminal Behavior Systems: A Typology,* ed. by Marshall B. Clinard and Richard Quinney, pp. 75–88, New York: Holt, Rinehart & Winston, 1967.

3267 McCreary, Charles P. "Personality differences among child molesters." *Journal of Personality Assessments* 39(6):591–593, Dec. 1975.

3268 McGeorge, John. "Sexual assaults on children." *Medicine, Science and the Law* 414:245–253, 1964.

3269 Mohr, Johann W., R.E. Turner and M.B. Jerry. *Pedophilia and Exhibitionism, A Handbook.* Toronto: University of Toronto Press, 1964.

3270 Mulcock, Donald. "A study of 100 non-selected cases of sexual assaults on children." *International Journal of Sexology* 7(3):125–128, Feb. 1954.

3271 Nedoma, Karel et al. "Sexual behavior and its development in pedophilic men." *Archives of Sexual Behavior* 1(3):267–271, 1971.

3272 Peters, Joseph J. "Children who are victims of sexual assault and the psychology of offenders." *American Journal of Psychotherapy* 30(3):398–421, July 1976.

3273 Quinsey, Vernon L. et al. "Penile circumference, skin conductance, and ranking responses of child molesters and 'normals' to sexual and nonsexual visual stimuli." *Behavior Therapy* 6(2):213–219, Mar. 1975.

3274 Revitch, Eugene and Rosalee G. Weiss.

"The pedophiliac offender." *Diseases of the Nervous System* 23(2):73-78, Feb. 1962.

3275   Seghorn, Theoharis. *Adequacy of ego functioning in rapists and pedophiles.* (Dissertation—Boston University.) Ann Arbor, MI: University Microfilms, 1970. (Order #70-22,413)

3276   Stricker, George. "Stimulus properties of the Blacky to a sample of pedophiles." *Journal of General Psychology* 77(1):35-39, 1967.

3277   _____. "Stimulus properties of the Rorschach to a sample of pedophiles." *Journal of Projective Techniques and Personality Assessment* 28(2):241-244, June 1964.

3278   Swanson, David W. "Adult sexual abuse of children: the man and circumstances." *Diseases of the Nervous System* 29(10):677-683, Oct. 1968.

3279   Vanasek, Frank J., Louise V. Frisbie and Harvey F. Dingman. "Patterns of affective responses in two groups of pedophiles." *Psychological Reports* 22:659-668, Apr. 1968.

3280   Virkkunen, M. "Victim-precipitated pedophilia offences." *British Journal of Criminology* 15(2):175-180, Apr. 1975.

3281   Walters, David R. *Physical and Sexual Abuse of Children: Causes and Treatment.* Bloomington: Indiana University Press, 1975.

HOMOSEXUAL PEDOPHILIA

3282   Brongersma, E. *Das verfemte Geschlecht: Dokumentation über Knabenliebe.* Munich: Lichtenberg, 1970. (First published in Amsterdam in 1961 under the title *Pedofilie*.)

3283   Fisher, Gary M. and Leisla M. Howell. "Psychological needs of homosexual pedophiliacs." *Diseases of the Nervous System* 31:623-625, Sept. 1970.

3284   Freund, Kurt and Ron Langevin. "Bisexuality in homosexual pedophilia." *Archives of Sexual Behavior* 5(5):415-423, Sept. 1976.

3285   Glueck, Bernard C. "Psychodynamic patterns in the homosexual sex offender (and discussion)." *American Journal of Psychiatry* 112(8):584-590, Feb. 1956.

3286   Jersild, Jens. *De Paedofile; Borneelskere (with Summaries in English).* Copenhagen: Nyt Nordisk Forlag Arnold Busck, 1964. (English ed.: *The Normal Homosexual Male versus the Boy Molester,* 1967.)

3287   Roeder, Fritz Douglas and D. Müller. "The stereotaxic treatment of paedophilic homosexuality." *German Medical Monthly* 14(6):265-271, June 1969.

3288   Rossman, G. Parker. "Literature on pederasty." *Journal of Sex Research* 9(4):307-312, Nov. 1973.

3289   _____. *Sexual Experience Between Men and Boys: Exploring the Pederast Underground.* New York: Association Press, 1976.

3290   Serber, Michael and Claudia G. Keith. "The Atascadero project: model of a sexual retraining program for incarcerated homosexual pedophiles." *Journal of Homosexuality* 1(1):86-97, Fall 1974.

3291   Taylor, Brian. "Motives for guilt-free pederasty: some literary considerations." *Sociological Review* 24(1)N.S.:97-114, Feb. 1976.

3292   Wyss, Rudolf. *Unzucht mit Kindern; Untersuchungen zur Frage der sogenannten Pädophilie.* Monographien aus dem Gesamtgebiete der Neurologie und Psychiatrie heft 121. Berlin: Springer-Verlag, 1967.

PEDOPHILIA PSYCHOANALYSIS

3293   Allen, Clifford. "The problem of John Ruskin: a psychosexological analysis." *International Journal of Sexology* 4(1):7-14, Aug. 1950.

3294   Kraemer, William, ed. *The Forbidden Love: The Normal and Abnormal Love of Children.* London: Sheldon, 1976.

3295   Shoor, Mervyn, Mary Helen Speed and Claudia Bartelt. "Syndrome of the adolescent child molester." *American Journal of Psychiatry* 122:783-789, Jan. 1966.

3296   Socarides, Charles W. "Meaning and content of a pedophiliac perversion." *Journal of the American Psychoanalytic Association* 7(1):84-94, 1959.

PEDOPHILIA THERAPY

3297   Dingman, Harvey F., Louise V. Frisbie and Frank J. Vanasek. "Erosion of morale in resocialization of pedophiles." *Psychological Reports* 23(3):792-794, 1968.

3298   Gigeroff, Alex K., Johann W. Mohr and Edward R. Turner. "Sex offenders on probation: heterosexual pedophiles." *Federal Probation* 32(4):17-21, Dec. 1968.

3299   Mohr, Johann W. and R. Turner. "Sexual

deviations. Part IV. Pedophilia." *Applied Therapeutics* 9(4):362–365, Apr. 1967.

3300 Peters, Joseph J. and Robert L. Sadoff. "Clinical observations on child molesters." *Medical Aspects of Human Sexuality* 4(11):20–32, Nov. 1970.

3301 Roeder, Fritz Douglas, D. Müller and H. Orthner. "The stereotaxic treatment of pedophilic homosexuality and other sexual deviations." In: *Psychosurgery,* ed. by E. Hitchcock, L. Laitinen and K. Vaernet, pp. 87–111. Springfield, IL: Charles C. Thomas, 1972.

PEDOPHILIA PSYCHOTHERAPY

3302 Hartman, Valdemar. "Group psychotherapy with sexually deviant offenders (pedophiles)—the peer group as an instrument of mutual control." *Journal of Sex Research* (1):45–57, Mar. 1965.

3303 _____. "Notes on group psychotherapy with pedophiles." *Canadian Psychiatric Association Journal* 10(4):283–289, July/Aug. 1965.

3304 Kurland, Morton L. "Pedophilia erotica." *Journal of Nervous and Mental Disease* 131: 394–403, 1960.

3305 Resnik, H.L.P. and Joseph J. Peters. "Outpatient group therapy with convicted pedophiles." *International Journal of Group Psychotherapy* 17(2):151–158, Apr. 1968.

PEDOPHILIA BEHAVIOR THERAPY

3306 Bancroft, John, H. Gwynne Jones and B.R. Pullan. "A simple transducer for measuring penile erection, with comments on its use in the treatment of sexual disorders." *Behavior Research and Therapy* 4:239–241, 1966.

3307 Davison, Gerald C., Robert J. Kohlenberg and G. Terence Wilson. "Goals and strategies in behavioral treatment of homosexual pedophilia: comments on a case study." *Journal of Abnormal Psychology* 83(2):196–198, Apr. 1974.

PEDOPHILIA AVERSION THERAPY

3308 Kohlenberg, Robert J. "Treatment of a homosexual pedophiliac using in vivo desensitization: a case study." *Journal of Abnormal Psychology* 83(2):192–195, Apr. 1974.

3309 Laws, Donald Richard and A.W. Pawlowski. "An automated fading procedure to alter responsiveness in pedophiles." *Journal of Homosexuality* 1(2):149–163, Winter 1974/1975.

3310 Quinsey, Vernon L. "Methodological issues in evaluating the effectiveness of aversion therapies for institutionalized child molesters." *Canadian Psychologist* 14(4):350–361, Oct. 1973.

3311 Quinsey, Vernon L., Sidney G. Bergersen and Cary M. Steinman. "Changes in physiological and verbal responses of child molesters during aversion therapy." *Canadian Journal of Behavioral Science* 8(2):202–212, Apr. 1976.

3312 Rosenthal, Ted L. "Response-contingent versus fixed punishment in aversion conditioning of pedophilia: a case study." *Journal of Nervous and Mental Disease* 156(6):440–443, 1973.

Prostitution

BIBLIOGRAPHY

3313 Bullough, Vern et al. *A Bibliography of Prostitution.* New York: Garland, 1977.

PROSTITUTION

3314 Anderson, Mauriça. "Hookers, arise!" *Human Behavior* 4(1):40–42, Jan. 1975.

3315 Benjamin, Harry. "Prostitution." In: *The Encyclopedia of Sexual Behavior,* ed. by Albert Ellis and Albert Abarbanel, pp. 869–882. New York: Hawthorn Books, 1961.

3316 Benjamin, Harry and Albert Ellis. "An objective examination of prostitution." *International Journal of Sexology* 8(2):100–105, Nov. 1954.

3317 Benjamin, Harry and R.E.L. Masters. *Prostitution and Morality.* New York: Julian Press, 1964.

3318 Bess, Barbara and Samuel Janus. "Prostitution." In: *The Sexual Experience,* ed. by B.J. Sadock, H.I. Kaplan and A.M. Freedman, pp. 594–610. Baltimore: Williams & Wilkins, 1976.

3319 Critchfield, Richard. "Sex in the third world." *Human Behavior* 6(4):40–47, Apr. 1977.

3320 Davis, Kingsley. "The sociology of prostitution." *American Sociological Review* 2(5):744–755, Oct. 1937.

3321 Devereux, George. "The Mohave Indian Kamalo:y." *Journal of Clinical Psychopathology* 9(3):433–457, July 1948.

3322 Esselstyn, T.C. "Prostitution in the United States." *Annals of the American Academy of Political and Social Science* 376:123–135, Mar. 1968.

3323   Forrest, David V. "The American soldier and the Vietnamese women." *Sexual Behavior* 2(5):8–15, May 1972.

3324   Fry, Monroe. *Sex, Vice, and Business.* New York: Ballantine, 1959.

3325   Fry, William F. "Psychodynamics of sexual humor: prostitution." *Medical Aspects of Human Sexuality* 10(11):74 passim, Nov. 1976.

3326   Gagnon, John H. "Prostitution." In: *International Encyclopedia of the Social Sciences,* ed. by David L. Sills, v. 12, pp. 592–598. New York: Macmillan, 1968.

3327   Gebhard, Paul H. "Prostitution." In: *Encyclopaedia Britannica.* 15th ed. Chicago: Encyclopaedia Britannica. 1974.

3328   Harris, Sarah. *They Sell Sex; the Call Girl and Big Business.* Greenwich, CT: Fawcett, 1960.

3329   Hong, Lawrence K., William Darrough and Robert W. Duff. "The sensuous rip-off: consumer fraud turns blue." *Urban Life and Culture* 3(4):464–470, Jan. 1975.

3330   Iga, Mamoru. "Sociocultural factors in Japanese prostitution and the 'Prostitution Prevention Law.'" *Journal of Sex Research* 4(2):127–146, May 1968.

3331   Kumar, Pramod. "Prostitution: a sociopsychological analysis." *Indian Journal of Social Work* 21(4):425–430, Mar. 1961.

3332   Lemert, Edwin M. "Prostitution." In: *Problems of Sex Behavior,* ed. by Edward Sagarin and Donal E.F. MacNamara, pp. 68–109. New York: Crowell, 1968.

3333   MacMillan, Jackie. "Rape and prostitution." *Victimology* 1(3):414–420, Fall 1976.

3334   Millet, Kate. *The Prostitution Papers.* New York: Avon, 1973.

3335   Niemoeller, Adolf Frederick. *The Business Side of the Oldest Business; a Survey of the Organization, Management, and Earnings of Prostitution from Antiquity.* Girard, KS: Haldeman-Julius, 1945.

3336   Putnam, Samuel. "Prostitution." In: *Encyclopaedia Sexualis,* ed. by Victor Robinson, pp. 640–670. New York: Dingwall-Rock, 1936.

3337   Reckless, Walter C. "A sociologist looks at prostitution." *Federal Probation* 7(2):12–16, Apr./June 1943.

3338   Riegel, Robert E. "Changing American attitudes toward prostitution (1800–1920)." *Journal of the History of Ideas* 29:437–452, July 1968.

3339   Sandford, Jeremy. *Prostitutes: Portraits of People in the Sexploitation Business.* London: Secker & Warburg, 1975.

3340   Sheehy, Gail. "The economics of prostitution: who profits? who pays?" In: *Sexual Deviance and Sexual Deviants,* ed. by E. Goode and R. Troiden, pp. 110–123. New York: Morrow, 1974. (Also in *Ms.*, June 1973, pp. 59 passim.)

3341   _____. *Hustling; Prostitution in Our Wide-Open Society.* New York: Delacorte Press, 1973.

3342   Stearn, Jess. *Sisters of the Night; the Startling Story of Prostitution in New York Today.* New York: Julian Messner, 1956.

3343   Stein, Martha L. "Prostitution." In: *Handbook of Sexology,* ed. by John Money and Herman Musaph, pp. 1069–1085. Amsterdam: Excerpta Medica, 1977.

3344   Thornton, Robert Y. "Organized crime in the field of prostitution." *Journal of Criminal Law, Criminology and Police Science* 46(6):775–779, Mar./Apr. 1956.

3345   "Viewpoints: Is prostitution still a significant health problem?" *Medical Aspects of Human Sexuality* 2(10):39–46, Oct. 1968.

3346   Whittaker, Peter. *The American Way of Sex.* New York: Berkley Publishing, 1974.

3347   Wigfield, Arthur S. "Sex, marriage and the partial eclipse of prostitution." *Gazzetta Sanitaria* 22(1):31–36, 1973.

3348   Winick, Charles. "Interview with a prostitution investigator." *Sexual Behavior* 2(11):17–21, Nov. 1972.

3349   Winick, Charles and Paul M. Kinsie. *The Lively Commerce: Prostitution in the United States.* Chicago: Quadrangle Books, 1971.

3350   _____. "Prostitution." *Sexual Behavior* 3(1):33–43, Jan. 1973.

3351   Winslow, Robert W. and Virginia Winslow. *Deviant Reality: Alternative World Views.* Boston: Allyn & Bacon, 1974.

PROSTITUTION HISTORY

3352   American Social Health Association. "Milestones in the march against commercialized prostitution in the United States." *Journal of Social Hygiene* 22(9):431–438, Dec. 1936.

3353 Amos, Sheldon. *A Comparative Survey of Laws in Force for the Prohibition, Regulation, and Licensing of Vice in England and Other Countries; with an Appendix Giving the Text of Laws and Police Regulations as They Now Exist in England, in British Dependencies, in the Chief Towns of Continental Europe, and in Other Parts of the World. . .* London: Stevens & Sons, 1877.

3354 Banes, Sally. "Prostitution in the U.S." In: *Our National Passion: 200 Years of Sex in America,* ed. by S. Banes, S. Frank and T. Horwitz, pp. 101–119. Chicago: Follett, 1976.

3355 Bellocq, E.J. *Storyville Portraits: Photographs from the New Orleans Red-Light District, Circa 1912.* New York: Museum of Modern Art, 1970.

3356 Brundage, James A. "Prostitution in the medieval canon law." *Signs* 1(4):825–845, Summer 1976.

3357 Bullough, Vern L. "The American brothel." *Medical Aspects of Human Sexuality* 7(4):198–211, Apr. 1973.

3358 _____. *The History of Prostitution.* New Hyde Park, NY: University Books, 1964.

3359 _____. "History of prostitution in the United States." *Medical Aspects of Human Sexuality* 4(9):64–76, Sept. 1970.

3360 Burford, E.J. *Bawds and Lodgings: A History of the London Bankside Brothels, c. 100–1675.* London: Owen, 1976.

3361 _____. *The Orrible Synne: A Look at London Lechery from Roman to Cromwellian Times.* London: Calder & Boyars, 1973.

3362 Burnham, John. "Medical inspection of prostitutes in America in the nineteenth century: the St. Louis experiment and its sequel." *Bulletin of the History of Medicine* 45(3):203–218, May/June 1971.

3363 Davis, Burke. "Sex in the Civil War." In: *Our Incredible Civil War,* pp. 101–108. New York: Ballantine, 1974.

3364 Evans, R.J. "Prostitution, state and society in Imperial Germany." *Past and Present* 70:106–129, Feb. 1976.

3365 Flexner, Abraham. *Prostitution in Europe.* New York: Century, 1914.

3366 Gould, George and R.E. Dickerson. *Digest of State and Federal Laws Dealing with Prostitution and Other Sex Offenses.* Ed. by Bascom Johnson. New York: The American Social Hygiene Association, 1942.

3367 Hall, Gladys Mary. *Prostitution in the Modern World.* New York: Emerson Books, 1936.

3368 Harding, T. Swan. "The endless war on 'vice'." *Medical Record*:1–3, Apr. 20, 1938.

3369 Henriques, L. Fernando. *Prostitution and Society: v. 1—Primitive, Classical and Oriental; v. 2—Prostitution in Europe and the New World; v. 3—Modern Sexuality.* London: Macgibbon & Kee, 1962, 1963, 1968.

3370 Holmes, Kay Ann. "Reflections by gaslight: prostitution in another age." *Issues in Criminology* 7(1):83–101, Winter 1972.

3371 Hoover, John Edgar. "White slave traffic." *Journal of Criminal Law and Criminology* 24(2):475–482, July/Aug. 1933.

3372 Johnson, Bascom. "Prostitution in the United States. Parts I–III." *The Commentator,* Mar./Apr./May 1937.

3373 Johnson, Claudia D. "That guilty third tier: prostitution in nineteenth-century American theaters." *American Quarterly* 27:575–584, Dec. 1975.

3374 LaCroix, Paul. *History of Prostitution Among All the Peoples of the World, from the Most Remote Antiquity to the Present Day.* 3 vols. Chicago: P. Covici, 1926. (Translation of *Histoire de la Prostitution chez Tous les Peuples du Monde . . .* Bruxelles: Rozez, 1861.)

3375 Martin, Cy. *Whiskey and Wild Women; an Amusing Account of the Saloons and Bawds of the Old West.* New York: Hart, 1974.

3376 New York Society for the Suppression of Vice. *Annual Reports,* 1875–1948.

3377 Patil, B.R. "The Devadasis." *Indian Journal of Social Work* 35(4):377–389, Jan. 1975.

3378 Peake, Richard Henry. *The stage prostitute in the English dramatic tradition from 1558 to 1625.* (Dissertation—University of Georgia.) Ann Arbor, MI: University Microfilms, 1966. (Order #67-3580)

3379 Pivar, David J. *Purity Crusade: Sexual Morality and Social Control, 1868–1900.* Contributions in American History, no. 23. Westport, CT: Greenwood Press, 1973.

3380 Ploss, Herman Heinrich, Max Bartels and Paul Bartels. "Prostitution." In: *Woman; an Historical, Gynaecological and Anthropological Com-*

pendium, vol. 2, pp. 78–116. London: Heinemann, 1935. (Vol. 3 contains references cited.)

3381   Powell, Aaron Macy. *State Regulation of Vice. Regulation Efforts in America. The Geneva Congress.* New York: Wood & Holbrook, 1878.

3382   *The Prostitute and the Social Reformer; Commercial Vice in the Progressive Era.* New York: Arno, 1974.

3383   *Prostitution in the Victorian Age; Debates on the Issue from 19th Century Critical Journals.* Intro. by Keith Nield. Westmead, Hants, England: Gregg International, 1973.

3384   Roby, Pamela A. *Politics and prostitution: a case study of the formulation, enforcement and judicial administration of the New York State penal laws on prostitution, 1870–1970.* (Dissertation—New York University.) Ann Arbor, MI: University Microfilms, 1971. (Order #72-3118)

3385   Rose, Al. *Storyville, New Orleans: Being an Authentic, Illustrated Account of the Notorious Red-Light District.* University, AL: University of Alabama, 1974.

3386   Sanger, William W. *The History of Prostitution.* New York: Medical Publishing, 1898.

3387   Simons, G.L. *A Place for Pleasure: The History of the Brothel.* London: Harwood-Smart, 1975.

3388   Wagner, Roland Richard. *Virtue against vice: a study of moral reformers and prostitution in the Progressive Era.* (Dissertation—University of Wisconsin.) Ann Arbor, MI: University Microfilms, 1971. (Order #71-28,372)

3389   Woolston, Howard Brown. *Prostitution in the United States.* New York: Century, 1921.

PROSTITUTION RESEARCH

3390   Atkinson, Maxine and Jacqueline Boles. "Prostitution as an ecology of confidence games: the scripted behavior of prostitutes and vice officers." Paper presented at the 39th Annual Meeting of the Southern Sociological Society, Miami, Apr. 7–12, 1976. 21p.

3391   Barrera Caraza, Estanislao. "Prostitución en Xalapa; estudio de algunos aspectos socioeconomicos." Unpub. master's thesis, Universidad Veracruzana at Jalapa, Mexico, 1974.

3392   Bell, Robert R. "Prostitution." In: *Social Deviance: A Substantive Analysis,* pp. 226–247. Homewood, IL: Dorsey Press, 1971.

3393   British Social Biology Council. *Women of the Streets: A Sociological Study of the Common Prostitute,* ed. by C.H. Rolph. London: Secker & Warburg, 1955.

3394   Bryan, James H. "Apprenticeships in prostitution." *Social Problems* 12(3):287–297, Winter 1965. (Also in *Studies in Human Sexual Behavior, The American Scene,* ed. by A. Shiloh, pp. 420–433. Springfield, IL: Charles C. Thomas, 1970.)

3395   _____. "Occupational ideologies and individual attitudes of call girls." *Social Problems* 13(4):441–450, Spring 1966.

3396   Bryant, Clifton D. and Eddie C. Palmer. "Massage parlors and 'hand whores'. Some sociological observations." *Journal of Sex Research* 11(3):227–241, Aug. 1975.

3397   Bullough, Vern L. "Problems and methods for research in prostitution and the behavioral sciences." *Journal of History of Behavior Sciences* 1(3):244–251, July 1965. (Also in *Studies in Human Sexual Behavior, the American Scene,* ed. by Ailon Shiloh, pp. 14–23. Springfield, IL: Charles C. Thomas, 1970.)

3398   Gallo, Maria Teresa de and Heli Alzate. "Brothel prostitution in Colombia." *Archives of Sexual Behavior* 5(1):1–7, Jan. 1976.

3399   Gamboa, Victor and H.J. Feenstra. "Deviant stereotypes: call girls, male homosexuals, and lesbians." *Philippine Sociological Review* 17(3–4):136–148, July–Oct. 1969.

3400   Gebhard, Paul H. "Misconceptions about female prostitutes." *Medical Aspects of Human Sexuality* 3(3):24–30, Mar. 1969.

3401   Greenwald, Harold. *The Call Girl; A Social and Psychoanalytic Study.* New York: Ballantine, 1958.

3402   Heyl, Barbara Sherman. "The madam as teacher: the training of house prostitutes." *Social Problems* 24(5):545–555, June 1977.

3403   Hijmans, A. *Vrow en man in de prostitutie; een sociologisch-psychologische studie.* Gravenhage: Van Keulen, 1956.

3404   Hilton, Diana Gray. "Turning out: a study of teenage prostitution." Unpub. master's thesis, University of Washington, 1971.

3405   Hironimus, Helen. "Survey of 100 May Act violators committed to the federal reformatory for women." *Federal Probation* 7(2):31–34, Apr./June 1943.

3406   Hong, Lawrence K., William Darrough and

Robert W. Duff. "The sensuous rip-off: consumer fraud turns blue." *Urban Life and Culture* 3(4):464–470, Jan. 1975.

3407 James, Jennifer. *Ethnographic semantic approaches to the study of an urban subculture: streetwalkers.* (Dissertation—University of Washington.) Ann Arbor, MI: University Microfilms, 1972. (Order #72-28611)

3408 Janus, Samuel and Barbara Bess. "Wann Prostituierte umkehren." *Sexualmedizin* 5(5):335–337, May 1976.

3409 Kagan, Herman. *Prostitution and sexual promiscuity among adolescent female offenders.* (Dissertation—University of Arizona.) Ann Arbor, MI: University Microfilms, 1969. (Order #69-18329)

3410 Karp, David A. *Public sexuality and hiding behavior: a study of the Times Square sexual community.* (Dissertation—New York University.) Ann Arbor, MI: University Microfilms, 1971. (Order #72-13374)

3411 Khalaf, Samir. "Correlates of prostitution: some popular errors and misconceptions." *Journal of Sex Research* 4(2):147–162, May 1968.

3412 _____. *Prostitution in a Changing Society; a Sociological Survey of Legal Prostitution in Beirut.* Beirut: Khayats, 1965.

3413 Pomeroy, Wardell B. "Some aspects of prostitution." *Journal of Sex Research* 1(3):177–187, Nov. 1965.

3414 Primov, George and Carolynne Kieffer. "The Peruvian brothels as sexual dispensary and social arena." *Archives of Sexual Behavior* 6(3):245–253, May 1977.

3415 Raboch, Jan and Iva Sípová. "Warum prostitution ewig ist; serrüttetes familienmilieu begünstigt dirnenhafte verhaltensweisen." *Sexualmedizin* 4(2):71–72, Feb. 1975.

3416 Roebuck, Julian and Wolfgang Frese. "The after-hours club: an illegal social organization and its client system." *Urban Life* 5(2):131–164, July 1976.

3417 _____. *The Rendezvous: A Case Study of an After-Hours Club.* New York: Free Press, 1976.

3418 Roebuck, Julian and Patrick McNamara. "Ficheras and free-lancers: prostitution in a Mexican border city." *Archives of Sexual Behavior* 2(3):231–244, June 1973.

3419 Rosenblum, Karen E. "Female deviance and the female sex role: a preliminary investigation." *British Journal of Sociology* 26(2):169–185, June 1975.

3420 Sepúlveda Niño, Saturnino. *La Prostitución en Columbia.* Bogotá: Tercer Mundo, 1974.

3421 Shoham, Shlomo and Giora Rahav. "Social stigma and prostitution." *British Journal of Criminology* 8(4):402–412, 1968.

3422 Stuckey, Johanna. "A feminist looks at prostitution." In: *Sexual Behaviour in Canada: Patterns and Problems,* ed. by Benjamin Schlesinger, pp. 221–234. Toronto: University of Toronto Press, 1977.

3423 Tappan, Paul W. *Delinquent Girls in Court.* New York: Columbia University Press, 1947.

3424 Van Waters, Miriam. "Study and treatment of persons charged with prostitution." *Federal Probation* 7(2):27–30, Apr./June 1943.

3425 Vorenberg, Elizabeth and James Vorenberg. " 'The biggest pimp of all': prostitution and some facts of life." *Atlantic* 239(1):27–38, Jan. 1977.

3426 Wei, Yu and Amos Wong. "A study of 500 prostitutes in Shanghai." *International Journal of Sexology* 2(4):234–238, May 1949.

PROSTITUTION INTERVIEW SCHEDULES

3427 Barrera Caraza, Estanislao. "Analisis de la prostitución en Xalapa. Datos sobre eltipo de construccion de la vivienda. . . ." In: "Prostitución en Xalapa; estudio de algunos aspectos socioeconomicos," pp. 262–267. Unpub. master's thesis, Universidad Veracruzana at Jalapa, Mexico, 1974.

3428 Hilton, Diana G. "Interview schedule." In: "Turning out: a study of teenage prostitution," pp. 203–210. Unpub. master's thesis, University of Washington, 1971.

3429 Khalaf, Samir. "Interview schedule." In: *Prostitution in a Changing Society,* pp. 115–126. Beirut: Khayats, 1965.

CLIENTS OF PROSTITUTES

3430 Barber, R.N. "Prostitution and the increasing number of convictions for rape in Queensland." *Australian and New Zealand Journal of Criminology* 2(3):169–174, 1969.

3431 Beckerman, Wilfred. "Sex and the falling rate of profit." *New Statesman* 86:83–84, July 20, 1973.

3432 Benjamin, Harry. "Prostitution re-assessed II (Response)." *International Journal of Sexology* 5(1):37–39, Aug. 1951.

3433 "Clients of prostitutes." *British Medical Journal* 5219:1794–1795, Dec. 17, 1960; 5219:1957, Dec. 31, 1960.

3434 Denfield, Duane and Michael Gordon. "The sociology of mate swapping; or the family that swings together clings together." *Journal of Sex Research* 6(2):85–100, May 1970. (Also in *Beyond Monogamy; Recent Studies of Sexual Alternatives in Marriage,* ed. by James R. Smith and Lynn G. Smith, pp. 68–83. Baltimore: Johns Hopkins University Press, 1974.)

3435 Ellis, Albert. "Why married men visit prostitutes." *Sexology* 25(6):344–347, Jan. 1959.

3436 Gibbens, T.C.N. and M. Silberman. "The clients of prostitutes." *British Journal of Venereal Diseases* 36(2):113–117, June 1960.

3437 Janus, Samuel, Barbara Bess and Carol Saltus. *A Sexual Profile of Men in Power.* Englewood Cliffs, NJ: Prentice-Hall, 1977.

3438 Karpf, Maurice J. "The effects of prostitution on marital sex adjustment." *Marriage and Family Living* 15(1):65–71, Feb. 1953.

3439 Kirkendall, Lester A. "Circumstances associated with teenage boys' use of prostitution." *Marriage and Family Living* 22(2):145–149, May 1960.

3440 Sagarin, Edward. "Cabbie, where's the action?" *Sexual Behavior* 1(8):56–62, Nov. 1971.

3441 Scarlet, Iain. *The Professionals: Prostitutes and their Clients.* London: Sidgwick & Jackson, 1972.

3442 Simpson, Mary and Thomas R. Schill. "Patrons of massage parlors: some facts and figures." *Archives of Sexual Behavior* 6(6):521–525, Nov. 1977.

3443 Stein, Martha. *Lovers, Friends, Slaves ... The Nine Male Sexual Types, Their Psycho-Sexual Transactions with Call Girls.* New York: Berkley, 1974.

3444 Stewart, George Lee. "On first being a john." *Urban Life and Culture* 1(3):255–274, Oct. 1972.

3445 "Viewpoints: why do married men visit prostitutes?" *Medical Aspects of Human Sexuality* 4(7):80 passim, July 1970.

3446 Whitehead, J.A. and Denise Winn. "Sexual deviants and the prostitute." *British Journal of Sexual Medicine* 2(6):15–16, Dec. 1975.

3447 Winick, Charles. "Prostitutes' clients' perception of the prostitutes and of themselves." *International Journal of Social Psychiatry* 8(4):289–297, 1962.

INCIDENCE OF CONTACTS WITH PROSTITUTES

3448 Athanasiou, Robert, Phillip Shaver and Carol Tavris. "Sex: A *Psychology Today* report on ... questions about sexual attitudes and practices." *Psychology Today*:39–52, July 1970.

3449 Eddy, George Sherwood. *Sex and Youth.* Garden City, NY: Doubleday, Doran, 1928.

3450 Gebhard, Paul H. et al. *Sex Offenders; an Analysis of Types.* New York: Harper, 1965.

3451 Gottheil, Edward and Abraham Freedman. "Sexual beliefs and behavior of single male medical students." *Journal of the American Medical Association* 212:1327–1332, May 25, 1970.

3452 Hunt, Morton. *Sexual Behavior in the 1970's,* pp. 143–145 passim. New York: Dell, 1974.

3453 Kinsey, Alfred C. et al. "Intercourse with prostitutes." In: *Sexual Behavior in the Human Male,* pp. 595–609. Philadelphia: W.B. Saunders, 1948.

3454 Lowry, Thomas P. "Initial coital experiences: where and with whom." *Military Medicine* 129:966–967, Oct. 1964.

3455 Packard, Vance. *The Sexual Wilderness,* pp. 163–164. New York: David McKay, 1968.

3456 Reitman, Ben L. "Pimps." In: *Encyclopaedia Sexualis,* ed. by Victor Robinson, pp. 605–613. New York: Dingwall-Rock, 1936.

PIMPS

3457 Binderman, Murray B., Dennis Wepman and Ronald B. Newman. "A portrait of 'the life.'" *Urban Life* 4(2):213–225, July 1975.

3458 Bryan, James H. "Apprenticeships in prostitution." *Social Problems* 12(3):287–297, Winter 1965.

3459 Finmore, Rhoda Lee. *Immoral Earnings or Mr. Martin's Profession.* London: M.H. Publications, 1951.

3460 Hartsuiker, Jan Frederik. *De Souteneur in het Nederlandse Recht.* The Netherlands: Drukkerij de Kroon-Ijsselstein, 1964.

3461 James, Jennifer. "Prostitute-pimp relationships." *Medical Aspects of Human Sexuality* 7(11):147–163, Nov. 1973.

3462 Milner, Richard B. "The trickster, the bad nigga, and the new urban ethnography: an initial report and editorial code." *Urban Life and Culture* 1(1):109–117, Apr. 1972.

3463 Ostwald, Hans Otto August. *Das Erotische Berlin.* Berlin/Leipzig: Hermann Seemann Nachfolger, 1905.

3464 Powis, David. "Males living on the earnings of prostitution." *Police Journal* 37(10):463-469, Oct. 1964.

3465 Reitman, Ben Lewis. *The Second Oldest Profession: A Study of the Prostitute's "Business Manager".* New York: Vanguard Press, 1931.

3466 Sheehy, Gail. *Hustling: Prostitution in Our Wide-open Society.* New York: Delacorte Press, 1973.

3467 Wepman, Dennis, Ronald B. Newman and Murray B. Binderman. *The Life: the Lore and Folk Poetry of the Black Hustler.* Folklore and Folklife series. Philadelphia: University of Pennsylvania Press, 1976.

3468 Winick, Charles and Paul M. Kinsie. *The Lively Commerce: Prostitution in the United States.* Chicago: Quadrangle, 1971.

BROTHELS

3469 Bellocq, E.J. *Storyville Portraits: Photographs from the New Orleans Red-Light District, Circa 1912.* New York: Museum of Modern Art, 1970.

3470 Brassaï, Gyula Halasz. *The Secret Paris of the 1930's.* New York: Pantheon, 1976.

3471 Bryant, Clifton D. and C. Eddie Palmer. "Massage parlors and 'hand whores'. Some sociological observations." *Journal of Sex Behavior* 11(3):227–241, Aug. 1975.

3472 Bullough, Vern L. "The American brothel." *Medical Aspects of Human Sexuality* 7(4):198–211, Apr. 1973.

3473 Castle, Robert M. "Ash Meadows: a fly-in brothel." In: *Deviance,* ed. by Jerry Jacobs, pp. 41–51. Palo Alto, CA: National Press Books, 1974.

3474 Engle, Robert. *Brothels of Nevada . . . Official Guide to Legal Prostitution in Nevada with Houses & Girls Fully Rated & Described.* Los Angeles: Melrose Square, 1973.

3475 Green, Robin. "Joe Conforte, crusading pimp: a concerned citizen's fight to keep prostitutes off the streets of Nevada." In: *The Sex Industry,* ed. by G.P. Csicsery, pp. 38–58. New York: New American Library, 1973.

3476 Hurwood, Bernhardt J. *The Girls, the Massage, and Everything.* Greenwich, CT: Fawcett, 1973.

3477 Kleinman, Larry. "A massage parlor survey/New York." In: *The Sex Industry,* ed. by G.P. Csicsery, pp. 81–93. New York: New American Library, 1973.

3478 _____. *Sex Parlor.* New York: New American Library, 1973.

3479 Kroll, Eric. *Sex Objects: An American Documentary.* Danbury, NH: Addison House, 1977.

3480 Mankoff, Allan H. *Mankoff's Lusty Europe: The First All-Purpose European Guide to Sex, Love, and Romance.* New York: Viking Press, 1972.

3481 Pomeroy, Wardell B. "Massage parlors: a healthy set outlet? Yes! says a famous doctor." *Sexology* 41(4):28–30, Nov. 1974.

3482 Rasmussen, Paul K. and Lauren L. Kuhn. "The new masseuse: play for pay." *Urban Life* 5(3):271–292, Oct. 1976.

3483 Semper Idem (pseud.). *The "Blue Book"; a Bibliographical Attempt to Describe the Guide Books to the Houses of Ill Fame in New Orleans as They Were Published There.* (New Orleans?) Privately Printed, 1936.

3484 Simons, G.L. *A Place for Pleasure. The History of the Brothel.* London: Harwood-Smart, 1975.

3485 Stewart, George Lee. "On first being a john." *Urban Life and Culture* 1(3):255–274, Oct. 1972.

3486 Thornton, Robert Y. "Organized crime in the field of prostitution." *Journal of Criminal Law, Criminology and Police Science* 46(6):775–779, Mar./Apr. 1956.

3487 Van Gelder, Lindsy. "She's pretty: that's all the massage parlors ask." In: *The Sex Industry,* ed. by G.P. Csicsery, pp. 94–104. New York: New American Library, 1973.

3488 Velarde, Albert J. "Becoming prostituted: the decline of the massage parlour profession and the masseuse." *British Journal of Criminology* 15(3):251–263, July 1975.

3489 Velarde, Albert J. and Mark Warlick. "Massage parlors: the sensuality business." *Society* 2(1):63–64, Nov./Dec. 1973.

3490 Vogliotti, Gabriel R. *The Girls of Nevada.* Secaucus, NJ: Citadel Press, 1975.

3491 Whittaker, Peter. *The American Way of Sex.* Toronto: Longman Canada, 1974.

HOMOSEXUAL PROSTITUTION

3492 Benjamin, Harry and R.E.L. Masters. "Homosexual prostitution." In: *Prostitution and Morality; a Definitive Report on the Prostitute in Contemporary Society and an Analysis of the Causes and Effects of the Suppression of Prostitution,* pp. 286–337. New York: Julian Press, 1964.

3493 Bloch, Iwan. "Die männliche prostitution im altertum." In: *Prostitution,* 387–427. Berlin: L. Marcus, 1912.

3494 Butts, William Marlin. "Boy prostitutes of the metropolis." *Journal of Clinical Psychopathology* 8(4):673–681, Apr. 1947.

3495 Carrier, Joseph Michel. "Cultural factors affecting urban Mexican male homosexual behavior." *Archives of Sexual Behavior* 5(2):103–124, Mar. 1976.

3496 Caukins, Sivan E. and Neil R. Coombs. "The psychodynamics of male prostitution." *American Journal of Psychotherapy* 30(3):441–451, July 1976.

3497 Coombs, Neil R. "Male prostitution: a psychosocial view of behavior." *American Journal of Orthopsychiatry* 44(5):782–789, 1974.

3498 Craft, Michael. "Boy prostitutes and their fate." *British Journal of Psychiatry* 112(492): 1111–1114, 1966.

3499 Deisher, Robert, V. Eisner and Stephen I. Sulzbacher. "The young male prostitute." *Pediatrics* 43(6):936–941, 1969.

3500 Drew, Dennis and Jonathan Drake. *Boys for Sale: A Sociological Study of Boy Prostitution.* New York: Brown Book Co., 1969.

3501 Ehrhardt, Helmut. "Über homosexuelle verhaltensweisen als straftatbestand." *Münchener Medizinische Wochenschrift* 107:178–181, Jan. 22, 1965.

3502 Esselstyn, T.C. "Prostitution in the United States." *Annals of the American Academy of Political and Social Science* 376:123–135, Mar. 1968.

3503 Gandy, Patrick. "Hamburger hustlers."

Paper presented at American Anthropological Association Meeting, Nov. 29, 1971. 10p.

3504 Gandy, Patrick and Robert Deisher. "Young male prostitutes—the physician's role in social rehabilitation." *Journal of the American Medical Association* 212(10):1661–1666, June 8, 1970.

3505 Ginsburg, Kenneth N. "The 'meat-rack': a study of the male homosexual prostitute." *American Journal of Psychotherapy* 21(2):170–185, 1967.

3506 Giza, Jerzy St. "Zur problematik der homosexuellen prostitution in Polen." *Archiv für Kriminologie* 133(5–6):146–156, 1964.

3507 Hansen, Edward, M. Forrester and F. Bird. *The Tenderloin Ghetto: The Young Reject in Our Society.* San Francisco: Glide Urban Center, 1966.

3508 Harris, Mervyn. *The Dilly Boys.* Rockville, MD: New Perspectives, 1973.

3509 Hauser, Richard. "The homosexual prostitute." In: *The Homosexual Society,* pp. 44–50. London: The Bodley Head, 1962.

3510 Hoffman, Martin. "The male prostitute." *Sexual Behavior* 2(8):16–21, Aug. 1972.

3511 Hyde, Harford Montgomery. *The Cleveland Street Scandal.* New York: Coward, McCann & Geoghegan, 1976.

3512 Jersild, Jens. *Boy Prostitution.* Copenhagen: G.E.C. Gad, 1956.

3513 _____. "Homosexual prostitution." In: *The Normal Homosexual Male Versus the Boy Molester,* pp. 79–84. Copenhagen: Arnold Busck, 1967.

3514 Laserstein, Botho. *Strichjunge Karl; ein internationaler kriminalistischer Tatsachenbericht aus dem Reich der Liebe, die ihren Namen nicht nennt.* Hamburg: Christian Hansen Schmidt, 1954.

3515 Lloyd, Robin. *For Money or Love: Boy Prostitution in America.* New York: Vanguard, 1976.

3516 MacNamara, Donal E.J. "Male prostitution in an American city: a pathological or socio-economic phenomenon?" Paper presented at the American Orthopsychiatric Association Meeting, New York, Mar. 18, 1965. 8p.

3517 Palmieri, Vincenzo Mario and Franco Ferracutti. "L'omosessualità come problema criminologico e penitenziario." *Sessuologia* 6(3): 114–134, July/Sept. 1965.

3518 Panajian, Avedis. *A psychological study of*

male prostitutes. (Dissertation—United States International University.) Ann Arbor, MI: University Microfilms, 1974. (Order #74-10,372)

3519 Pittman, David J. "The male house of prostitution." *Trans-Action* 8(5/6):21-27, Mar./Apr. 1971. (Also in *The Sex Industry,* ed. by G.P. Csicsery, pp. 22-37. New York: New American Library, 1973.)

3520 Raven, Simon. "Boys will be boys." *Encounter* 86:19-24, Nov. 1960.

3521 Reiss, Albert J., Jr. "The social integration of queers and peers." *Social Problems* 9(2):102-120, Fall 1961.

3522 Ross, H. Laurence. "The 'hustler' in Chicago." *Journal of Student Research* 1(1):13-19, 1959.

3523 Russell, Donald H. "On the psychopathology of boy prostitutes." *International Journal of Offender Therapy* 15(1):49-52, 1971.

3524 Schachter, M. and S. Cotte. "Étude de la prostitution juvénile à la lumière du test de Rorschach." *Archives de Neurologie* 1:1-15, Jan. 1951.

3525 Simpson, Colin, Lewis Chester and David Leitch. *The Cleveland Street Affair.* Boston: Little, Brown, 1976.

3526 Thornton, Nathaniel. "Some aspects of male prostitution." *Journal of Sex Education* 2(1):3-8, Aug./Sept. 1949.

3527 Viqueira Hinojosa, Antonio. "Cases of international proxenetism in Spain." *International Criminal Police Review* 189:175-178, June/July 1965.

3528 Weiss, Jerome. "The gemblakan: kept boys among the Javanese of Ponorogo." Paper presented to the annual meeting of the American Anthropological Association, Mexico City, Nov. 19-24, 1974. 55p.

3529 Whittaker, Peter. *The American Way of Sex.* New York: Putnam, 1974.

3530 Zuanazzi, Gianfrancesco and L. Bonuzzi. "Antisocialità minorile, prostituzione maschile, omosessualità." *Sessuologia* 6(3):164-166, July/Sept. 1965.

LEGAL ASPECTS OF PROSTITUTION

3531 American Law Institute. *Model Penal Code: Article 207, Sexual Offenses and Offenses Against the Family. Council Draft No. 10.* Submitted to the Council of the American Law Institute for discussion at the meetings Mar. 15-17, 1956. Philadelphia: 1956.

3532 Babcock, Barbara Allen et al, eds. "Women and the criminal law." In: *Sex Discrimination and the Law: Causes and Remedies,* pp. 819-941. Boston: Little, Brown, 1975.

3533 Benjamin, Harry. "Prostitution reassessed." *International Journal of Sexology* 4(3):154-160, Feb. 1951.

3534 Chesser, Eustace. *Live and Let Live; the Moral of the Wolfenden Report.* London: Heinemann, 1958.

3535 Cheverie, Evelyn. "Victimless crime laws." *North Carolina Central Law Journal* 6:258-274, Spring 1975.

3536 *Federal Probation* 7(2):whole issue, Apr./June 1943.

3537 Great Britain. Committee on Homosexual Offenses and Prostitution. *The Wolfenden Report.* (Authorized American edition.) New York: Stein & Day, 1963.

3538 Haft, Marilyn. "Hustling for rights." *Civil Liberties Review* 1(2):8-26, Winter/Spring 1974.

3539 _____. "Sexual Privacy." Paper presented at ACLU Biennial Conference, University of Wisconsin, Milwaukee, June 13-16, 1974. 14p.

3540 James, Jennifer. "The law and commercialized sex." Paper presented at SIECUS Conference, "Sex: The Law and the Citizen," New York City, Oct. 26, 1973. 11p.

3541 James, Jennifer et al. *The Politics of Prostitution; Resources for Legal Change.* Seattle: Social Research Associates, 1975. (Avail. from The Politics of Prostitution, 335 N.E. 53rd St., Seattle, WA 98105.)

3542 James, Thomas E. *Prostitution and the Law.* London: Heinemann, 1951.

3543 Jennings, M. Anne. "The victim as criminal: a consideration of California's prostitution law." *California Law Review* 64:1235-1284, Sept. 1976.

3544 Kelleher, Maureen E. "Anatomy of a law: politics and prostitution in the big city." Paper presented at the Society for the Study of Social Problems Convention, U.S., Aug. 1976. 34p.

3545 Lindsay, Mary K. "Prostitution: delinquency's time bomb." *Crime and Delinquency* 16(2):151-157, Apr. 1970.

3546 "1972 Supreme Court appeal dismissal of established massage laws' validity." *Criminal Law Reporter* 17(23):2474, Sept. 10, 1975.

3547 Roby, Pamela A. "Politics and Prostitution; a case study of the revision, enforcement and administration of the New York penal laws on prostitution." *Criminology* 9(4):425–447, Feb. 1972.

3548 Ròsenbleet, Charles and Barbara J. Pariente. "The prostitution of the criminal law." *American Criminal Law Review* 11:373–427, Winter 1973.

3549 Sagarin, Edward and Donal E.J. MacNamara. "The problem of entrapment." *Crime and Delinquency* 16:363–378, Oct. 1970.

3550 St. James, Margo. "Prostitutes as political prisoners." *Realist* (95):9, Dec. 1972.

3551 Schwartz, Louis B. "Morals offences and the model penal code." *Columbia Law Review* 63:669–686, 1963.

3552 Schwartz, Neil M. "Pandering — successful procurement not necessary for conviction of completed crime." *Santa Clara Lawyer* 14:180–188, Fall 1973.

3553 Shanahan, Louise. "The threat of legalized prostitution." *Marriage* 53(10):54–59, Oct. 1971.

3554 Sherwin, Robert Veit and Charles Winick. "Debate: should prostitution be legalized?" *Sexual Behavior* 2(1):66–73, Jan. 1972.

3555 "Solicitation for prostitution: privacy, free speech and equal protection." *Yale Review of Law and Social Action*:144–165, Winter 1973.

3556 Titus, Herbert W. "The perils of decriminalization." *Center Report* (Center for the Study of Democratic Institutions) 7(1):3–5, Feb. 1974.

3557 United States. Federal Security Agency. National Advisory Police Committee. *Techniques of Law Enforcement Against Prostitution.* Washington, DC: U.S. GPO, 1943.

3558 "Viewpoints: should prostitution be legalized?" *Medical Aspects of Human Sexuality* 8(4):54–83, Apr. 1974.

3559 Wilson, Paul. *The Sexual Dilemma; Abortion, Homosexuality, Prostitution and the Criminal Threshold.* St. Lucia, Queensland: University of Queensland Press, 1971.

3560 Women Endorsing Decriminalization. "Prostitution: a non-victim crime?" *Issues in Criminology* 8(2):137–162, Fall 1973.

PERIODICALS

SexuaLaw Reporter (bi-m.)
1800 N. Highland Ave., Suite 106, Los Angeles, CA 90028

Sex Problems Court Digest (m.)
1860 Broadway, New York, NY 10023

OTHER SOURCES OF INFORMATION

Fédération Abolitionniste Internationale
28, place Saint-Georges, 75009, Paris, France
Revue Abolitionniste (irreg.)

COYOTE: A Loose Woman's Organization
Box 26354, San Francisco, CA 94126

Rape

BIBLIOGRAPHIES

3561 Chappell, Duncan, Gilbert Geis and Faith Fogarty. "Forcible rape: bibliography." *Journal of Criminal Law & Criminology* 65(2):248–263, June 1974.

3562 Fogarty, Faith. "A selective bibliography. In: *Forcible Rape: The Crime, the Victim, and the Offender,* ed. by D. Chappell, R. Geis and G. Geis, pp. 356–382. New York: Columbia University Press, 1977.

3563 Kemmer, Elizabeth Jane. *Rape and Rape-Related Issues; An Annotated Bibliography.* Garland Reference Library of Social Science, v. 39. New York: Garland Publishing, 1977.

3564 Kenton, Charlotte. *Rape: January 1970 through June 1973. 64 Citations.* Literature Search, no. 73-24. Bethesda, MD: National Library of Medicine, 1973.

3565 Walker, Marcia J., ed. *Toward the Prevention of Rape; A Partially Annotated Bibliography.* Center for Correctional Psychology Report, no. 27. University, AL: University of Alabama, Department of Psychology, Jan. 1975.

GENERAL

3566 Amir, Menachem. "Forcible rape." *Sexual Behavior* 1(8):24–36, Nov. 1971.

3567 Astor, Gerald. *The Charge is Rape.* Chicago: Playboy Press, 1974.

3568 Brownmiller, Susan. *Against our Will; Men, Women and Rape.* New York: Simon & Schuster, 1975.

3569 Connell, Noreen and Cassandra Wilson,

eds. *Rape: The First Sourcebook for Women, by New York Radical Feminists.* New York: New American Library, 1974.

3570 Evrard, John R. "Rape: the medical, social, and legal implications." *American Journal of Obstetrics and Gynecology* 111:197–199, Sept. 15, 1971.

3571 Gager, Nancy and Cathleen Schurr. *Sexual Assault: Confronting Rape in America.* New York: Grosset & Dunlap, 1976.

3572 Goldner, Norman S. "Rape as a heinous but understudied offense." *Journal of Criminal Law, Criminology and Police Science* 63(3):402–407, Sept. 1972.

3573 Goode, Erich and Richard R. Troiden, eds. "Rape." In: *Sexual Deviance and Sexual Deviants,* pp. 297–353. New York: Morrow, 1974.

3574 Hayman, Charles R. et al. "Roundtable: Rape and its consequences." *Medical Aspects of Human Sexuality* 6(2):12 passim, Feb. 1972.

3575 Horos, Carol V. *Rape. . .with a Nationwide Directory of U.S. Rape Crisis Centers Compiled by The Center for Women Policy Studies.* New Canaan, CT: Tobey Publishing, 1974.

3576 Inglis, Amirah. *The White Women's Protection Ordinance; Sexual Anxiety and Politics in Papua.* Brighton, U.K.: Sussex University Press, 1975.

3577 MacKellar, Jean S. and Menachem Amir. *Rape: The Bait and the Trap: A Balanced, Humane, Up-to-Date Analysis of its Causes and Control.* New York: Crown, 1975.

3578 Menen, Aubrey. "The rapes of Bangladesh." *Reflections* 8(5):6–14, 1973.

3579 Parks, R.D. "Six men tell why: 'I am a rapist.' " *Sexology* 40(6):11–15, Jan. 1974.

3580 Pearson, Pat (Hendricks). " 'Go ahead, rape her, she'll love it,' the media tells American males." Paper presented at the Fourth Annual Conference of the Popular Culture Association, Milwaukee, May 2–4, 1974. 20p.

3581 Pekkanen, John. *Victims: An Account of a Rape.* New York: Dial, 1976.

3582 Puppe, George et al. *The Hymen; a Medico-Legal Study in Rape.* New York: Physicians & Surgeons Press, 1935.

3583 Rada, Richard T. "Commonly asked questions about the rapist." *Medical Aspects of Human Sexuality* 11(1):47–56, Jan. 1977.

3584 Rogers, Kenneth P. *For One Sweet Grape; the Extraordinary Memoir of a Convicted Rapist-Murderer.* Chicago: Playboy Press, 1974.

3585 Schiff, Arthur F. "Rape." *Medical Aspects of Human Sexuality* 6(5):76 passim, May 1972.

3586 Shaffer, Helen B. "Crime of rape." *Editorial Research Reports*:43–60, Jan. 19, 1972.

3587 Storaska, Frederic. *How to Say No to a Rapist and Survive.* New York: Random House, 1975.

3588 "Viewpoints: castration for rapists." *Medical Aspects of Human Sexuality* 7(2):12–27, Feb. 1973.

3589 Winslow, Robert W. and Virginia Winslow. "Forcible rape." In: *Deviant Reality; Alternative World Views,* pp. 297–313. Boston: Allyn & Bacon, 1974.

3590 Zuspan, Frederick P. et al. "Alleged rape: an invitational symposium." *Journal of Reproductive Medicine* 12(4):133–152, Apr. 1974.

RESEARCH

3591 Abbott, Daniel J. and James M. Calonico. "Black man, white woman—the maintenance of a myth: rape and the press in New Orleans." In: *Crime and Delinquency: Dimensions of Deviance,* ed. by Marc Reidel and Terence P. Thornberry, pp. 141–153. New York: Praeger, 1974.

3592 Amir, Menachem. "Alcohol and forcible rape." *British Journal of Addiction* 62:219–232, 1967.

3593 _____. *Patterns in Forcible Rape.* Chicago: University of Chicago Press, 1971.

3594 _____. *Patterns in forcible rape: with special reference to Philadelphia, Pennsylvania, 1958 and 1960.* (Dissertation—University of Pennsylvania.) Ann Arbor, MI: University Microfilms, 1965. (Order #66-4597)

3595 Barclay, Andrew M. and Ralph N. Haber. "The relation of aggressive to sexual motivation." *Journal of Personality* 33(3):462–475, Sept. 1965.

3596 Brodyaga, Lisa et al. *Rape and Its Victims: A Report for Citizens, Health Facilities and Criminal Justice Agencies.* Washington, DC: National Institute of Law Enforcement and Criminal Justice, 1975.

3597 Burgess, Ann Wolbert and Lynda Lytle Holmstrom. "Accountability: a right of the rape victim." Paper presented at the American Orthopsychiatric Association, San Francisco, Apr. 11, 1974. 10p.

3598 _____. *Rape: Victims of Crisis.* Bowie, MD: Robert J. Brady, 1974.

3599 Calhoun, Lawrence G., James W. Selby and Louise Warring. "Social perception of victims' causal role in rape — exploratory examination of four factors." *Human Relations* 29(6):517–526, June 1976.

3600 Calmas, Wilfred Earl. *Fantasies of the mother-son relationship of the rapist and the pedophile.* (Dissertation—Boston University.) Ann Arbor, MI: University Microfilms, 1965. (Order #65-11,211)

3601 Chappell, Duncan, Robley Geis and Gilbert Geis, eds. *Forcible Rape: The Crime, the Victim, and the Offender.* New York: Columbia University Press, 1977.

3602 Clark, Lorenne M.G. and Debra J. Lewis. *Rape: The Price of Coercive Sexuality.* Toronto: The Women's Press, 1977.

3603 Cohen, Murray L. and Theoharis Seghorn. "Profile of the rapist." *Psychiatric Spectator* 6:17–20, 1971.

3604 Dost, Oskar P. *Psychologie der Notzucht; Untersuchung—Verfolgung—Vorbeugung.* Hamburg: Kriminalistik, 1963.

3605 Gebhard, Paul H. et al. *Sex Offenders; An Analysis of Types.* New York: Harper & Row, 1965.

3606 Geller, Sheldon H. "Female sexual offences: effects of the 1974 Toronto transit strike." Paper presented at the Canadian Psychological Association Convention, Quebec City, June 1975. 14p.

3607 Goldstein, Michael J. and Harold S. Kant. *Pornography and Sexual Deviance.* Berkeley: University of California Press, 1973.

3608 Hammer, Emanuel F. "A comparison of H-T-P's of rapists and pedophiles." *Journal of Projective Techniques* 18(3):346–354, 1954.

3609 Hayman, Charles R. et al. "Rape in the District of Columbia." *American Journal of Obstetrics and Gynecology* 113(1):91–97, May 1, 1972.

3610 Heiple, Phil and Ivan Jankovic. "Rape in Yugoslavia." Paper presented at the American Sociological Association Meeting, New York, Sept. 3, 1976. 37p.

3611 Kanin, Eugene J. "Male aggression in dating-courtship relations." *American Journal of Sociology* 63(2):197–204, Sept. 1957.

3612 Karacan, Ismet et al. "Nocturnal penile tumescence and sleep of convicted rapists and other prisoners." *Archives of Sexual Behavior* 3(1):19–26, Jan. 1974.

3613 Kercher, Glen A. *An investigation of the responses of convicted rapists to erotic stimuli.* (Dissertation—Baylor University.) Ann Arbor, MI: University Microfilms, 1970. (Order #71-17,407)

3614 Lester, David. "Rape and social structure." *Psychological Reports* 35:146, 1974.

3615 Ludovici, Anthony M. "Criminal assaults on young women in England and Wales." *International Journal of Sexology* 8(2):83–88, Nov. 1954.

3616 MacDonald, John M. *Rape: Offenders and Their Victims.* Springfield, IL: Charles C. Thomas, 1971.

3617 McGuire, Linda S. and Michael Stern. "Survey of incidence of and physicians' attitudes toward sexual assault." *Public Health Reports* 91(2):103–109, Mar./Apr. 1976.

3618 Medea, Andra and Kathleen Thompson. *Against Rape.* New York: Farrar, Straus & Giroux, 1974.

3619 Ng, Allan Y. "The pattern of rape in Singapore." *Singapore Medical Journal* 15(7):49–50, Mar. 1974.

3620 Palm, Rose and David Abrahamsen. "A Rorschach study of the wives of sex offenders." *Journal of Nervous and Mental Disease* 119(2):167–172, Feb. 1954.

3621 Perdue, William C. and David Lester. "Personality characteristics of rapists." *Perceptual and Motor Skills* 35:514, 1972.

3622 Rada, Richard T., Donald Richard Laws and Robert Kellner. "Plasma testosterone levels in the rapist." *Psychosomatic Medicine* 30(4):257–268, July/Aug. 1976.

3623 Ruff, Carol F., Donald I. Templer and Joyce L. Ayers. "The intelligence of rapists." *Archives of Sexual Behavior* 5(4):327–329, July 1976.

3624 Schiff, Arthur F. "Rape in foreign countries." *Medical Trial Technique Quarterly* 20:66–74, Summer 1973.

3625 _____. "Rape in other countries." *Medicine, Science and the Law* 11:139–143, July 1971.

3626 _____. "A statistical evaluation of rape." *Forensic Science* 2:339–349, Aug. 1973.

3627   Schultz, LeRoy G., ed. *Rape Victimology.* Springfield, IL: Charles C. Thomas, 1975.

3628   Seghorn, Theoharis. *Adequacy of ego functioning in rapists and pedophiles.* (Dissertation—Boston University.) Ann Arbor, MI: University Microfilms, 1970. (Order #70-22,413)

3629   Stürup, Georg K. "Treatment of sexual offenders in Herstedvester, Denmark; the rapists." *Acta Psychiatrica Scandinavica* 44(supplement 204):1–63, 1968.

3630   Walker, Marcia J. and Stanley L. Brodsky, eds. *Sexual Assault: The Victim and the Rapist.* Lexington, MA: Heath, 1976.

3631   Wille, Warren S. "Case study of a rapist: an analysis of the causation of criminal behavior." *Corrective Psychiatry* 7(1):10–21, Jan./Mar. 1961.

HOMOSEXUAL RAPE

3632   Bell, Robert R. "Prisons." In: *Social Deviance: A Substantive Analysis,* pp. 320–353. Homewood, IL: Dorsey Press, 1971.

3633   Berger, Richard S. "Criminal law: escape from prison, defenses, duress, homosexual attacks." *Akron Law Review* 8(2):352–359, Winter 1975.

3634   Carroll, Leo. "Race and sexual assault in a maximum security prison." Paper presented at the Annual Meeting of the Society for the Study of Social Problems, Montreal, Aug. 1974. 36p.

3635   Danziger, Peter L. "Sexual assaults and forced homosexual relationships in prison: cruel and unusual punishment." *Albany Law Review* 36(2):428–438, 1971.

3636   Davis, Alan J. "Sexual assaults in the Philadelphia prison system and sheriff's vans." *Transaction*:8–16, Dec. 1968.

3637   Kerrigan, J. and J. Tamura. "The people vs. Marsha Lovercomp." *California Reporter* 118:823–833, Dec. 1974.

3638   Kuby, Lolette. "Rape: the double standard." *Aphra* 5(1):31–35, Winter 1973/1974.

3639   Miller, Judi. "When men are rape victims." *Sexology* 43(4):51–56, Nov. 1976.

3640   Ragan, James Arthur. "Duress—defense to escape—substantial threats of homosexual attack may support the defense of duress in a prosecution for prison escape." *American Journal of Criminal Law* 3(3):331–340, Winter 1975.

3641   Sagarin, Edward. "Prison homosexuality and its effects on post-prison sexual behavior." *Psychiatry* 39(3):245–257, Aug. 1976.

3642   Scacco, Anthony M. *Rape in Prison.* Springfield, IL: Charles C. Thomas, 1975.

3643   Weiss, Carl and David James Friar. *Terror in the Prisons; Homosexual Rape and Why Society Condones It.* Indianapolis: Bobbs-Merrill, 1974.

VICTIMOLOGY

3644   Amir, Menachem. "Victim precipitated forcible rape." *Journal of Criminal Law, Criminology and Police Science* 58(4):493–502, Dec. 1967.

3645   Burgess, Ann Wolbert and Lynda Lytle Holmstrom. "Coping behavior of the rape victim." *American Journal of Psychiatry* 133(4):413–418, Apr. 1976.

3646   Curtis, Lynn A. "Victim precipitation and violent crime." *Social Problems* 21(4):594–605, Apr. 1974.

3647   Feinman, Saul. "Attribution of fault to rape victims." Paper presented at the 39th Annual Meeting of the Midwest Sociological Society, St. Louis, April 7–12, 1976. 56p.

3648   Geis, Gilbert. "Group sexual assaults." *Medical Aspects of Human Sexuality* 5(5):101–113, May 1971.

3649   Jones, Cathaleene and Elliot Aronson. "Attribution of fault to a rape victim as a function of respectability of the victim." *Journal of Personality and Social Psychology* 26(3):415–419, June 1973.

3650   Kuby, Lolette. "Rape: the double standard." *Aphra* 5(1):31–35, Winter 1973–1974.

3651   Landau, Sybil. "Rape: the victim as defendant." *Trial* 10(4):19–22, July/Aug. 1974.

3652   Lynch, W. Ware. *Rape! One Victim's Story; a Documentary.* Chicago: Follett, 1974.

3653   MacDonald, John Marshall. "False accusations of rape." *Medical Aspects of Human Sexuality* 7(5):170 passim, May 1973.

3654   Mathiasen, Sally Ellis. "The rape victim: a victim of society and the law." *Willamette Law Journal* 11:36–55, Winter 1974.

3655   Mendelsohn, B. "The origin of the doctrine of victimology." *Excerpta Criminologica* (Netherlands) 3(3):239–244, May/June 1963.

3656   Metzger, Deena. "It is always the woman

who is raped." *American Journal of Psychiatry* 133(4):405–408, Apr. 1976.

3657   Mundy, Jean. "Rape—for women only." Paper presented at the American Psychological Association Convention, New Orleans, Sept. 1, 1974. 4p.

3658   Notman, Malkah T. and Carol C. Nadelson. "The rape victim: psychodynamic considerations." *American Journal of Psychiatry* 133(4): 408–413, Apr. 1976.

3659   Peters, Joseph J. "The Philadelphia rape victim study." Paper presented at the First International Symposium on Victimology, Jerusalem, Sept. 2–6, 1973. 23p.

3660   Russell, Diana E.H. *The Politics of Rape; The Victim's Perspective.* New York: Stein & Day, 1975.

3661   Scarpitti, Frank R. and Ellen Scarpitti. "Victims of rape." *Society* 14(5):29–32, July/Aug. 1977.

3662   Sebba, Leslie and Sorel Cahan. "Sex offences—the genuine and the doubted victim." Paper presented at the 1st International Symposium on Victimology, Jerusalem, Sept. 2–6, 1973. 23p.

3663   Sutherland, Sandra and Donald Scherl. "Patterns of response among victims of rape." *American Journal of Orthopsychiatry* 40(3): 503–511, Apr. 1970.

3664   Weis, Kurt and Sandra S. Borges. "Victimology and rape: the case of the legitimate victim." *Issues in Criminology* 8(2):71–115, Fall 1973.

LEGAL ASPECTS

3665   Aitken, Janet. "Rape prosecutions." *Women Lawyers Journal* 60(4):192–198, Fall 1974.

3666   Bohmer, Carol and Audrey Blumberg. "Twice traumatized: the rape victim and the court." *Judicature* 58(8):390–399, Mar. 1975.

3667   Chappell, Duncan. "Forcible rape and the criminal justice system; surveying present practices and projecting future trends." *Crime and Delinquency* 22(2):125–136, Apr. 1976.

3668   "Complainant credibility in sexual offense cases: a survey of character testimony and psychiatric experts." *Journal of Criminal Law and Criminology* 64(1):67–75, 1973.

3669   Cottell, Louis C. "Rape: the ultimate invasion of privacy." *FBI Law Enforcement Bulletin* 43(5):2–6, 1974.

3670   Johnson, Edwinna Gayle. "Evidence—rape trials—victim's prior sexual history." *Baylor Law Review* 27:362–369, Spring 1975.

3671   Landau, Sybil. "Rape: the victim as defendant." *Trial* 10(4):19–22, July/Aug. 1974.

3672   LeGrand, Camille E. "Rape and rape law: sexism in society and law." *California Law Review* 61:919–941, May 1973.

3673   Mathiasen, Sally E. "The rape victim: a victim of society and the law." *Willamette Law Journal* 11:36–55, Winter 1974.

3674   Ploscowe, Morris. "Rape." In: *Problems of Sex Behavior,* ed. by Edward Sagarin and Donal E.F. MacNamara, pp. 203–240. New York: Crowell, 1968.

3675   Schwartz, Barry. "The effect in Philadelphia of Pennsylvania's increased penalties for rape and attempted rape." *Journal of Criminal Law, Criminology and Police Science* 59(4): 509–515, 1968.

3676   Sherwin, Robert Veit. "Sexual expression and the law: the law of rape." *International Journal of Sexology* 4(4):206–210, May 1951.

3677   Shopper, Moisy. "Psychiatric and legal aspects of statutory rape, pregnancy and abortion in juveniles." *Journal of Psychiatry & Law* 1(3): 275–295, Fall 1973.

3678   Slovenko, Ralph. "Statutory rape." *Medical Aspects of Human Sexuality* (3):155 passim, Mar. 1971.

3679   Smith, Cyril J. "History of rape and rape laws." *Women Lawyers Journal* 60(4):188–191 passim, Fall 1974.

3680   Viano, Emilio C. "Rape and the law in the United States: an historical and sociological analysis." *International Journal of Criminology and Penology* 2:317–328, 1974.

VICTIM EXAMINATION, TREATMENT AND COUNSELING

3681   American College of Obstetricians and Gynecologists. "Medical procedures in cases of suspected rape." *Medical Aspects of Human Sexuality* 7(9):65–71, Sept. 1973.

3682   _____. "Prevention of pregnancy in cases of suspected rape: modification of A.C.O.G. recommendations." *Medical Aspects of Human Sexuality* 7(12):166, Dec. 1973.

3683   Bard, Morton and Katherine Ellison. "Crisis

intervention and investigation of forcible rape." *The Police Chief* 41(5):68–74, May 1974.

3684 Blanchard, Edward B. and Gene G. Abel. "An experimental case study of the biofeedback treatment of a rape induced psychophysiological cardiovascular disorder." *Behavior Therapy* 7(1):113–119, Jan. 1976.

3685 Breen, James L., Earl Greenwald and Caterine A. Gregori. "The molested young female; evaluation and therapy of alleged rape." *Pediatric Clinics of North America* 19(3):717–725, Aug. 1972.

3686 Burgess, Ann Wolbert and Lynda Lytle Holmstrom. "Crisis and counseling requests of rape victims." *Nursing Research* 23(3):196–202, May/June 1974.

3687 _____. "The rape victim in the emergency room." *American Journal of Nursing* 73(10): 1741–1745, Oct. 1973.

3688 DeMasi, Andrew D. "Management of the rape victim." *The Osteopathic Physician* 41(1): 97–100, Jan. 1974.

3689 Enos, William F., James C. Beyer and Geoffrey Thomas Mann. "The medical examination of cases of rape." *Journal of Forensic Science* 17(1):50–56, Jan. 1972.

3690 Evans, Hanna I. and Nicole B. Sperekas. "Community assistance for rape victims." *Journal of Community Psychology* 4(4):378–381, Oct. 1976.

3691 Fox, Sandra Sutherland and Donald J. Scherl. "Crisis intervention with victims of rape." *Social Work* 17(1):37–42, Jan. 1972.

3692 Geis, Gilbert, Duncan Chappell and Fay G. Cohen. *Hospital Care for Rape Victims: Results of a Nationwide Study.* Forcible Rape Series, no. 1. Seattle: Battelle Human Affairs Research Centers, Mar. 1975.

3693 Hardgrove, Grace. "An interagency service network to meet needs of rape victims." *Social Casework* 57(4):245–253, Apr. 1976.

3694 Hayman, Charles R. "A public health program for sexually assaulted females." *Public Health Reports* 82(6):497–504, June 1967.

3695 Hayman, Charles R. and Charlene Lanza. "Sexual assault on women and girls." *American Journal of Obstetrics and Gynecology* 109(3): 480–486, Feb. 1971.

3696 _____. "Victimology of sexual assault." *Medical Aspects of Human Sexuality* 5(10):152 passim, Oct. 1971.

3697 Hilberman, Elaine. *The Rape Victim.* Washington, DC: American Psychiatric Association, 1976.

3698 Lanza, Charlene. "Nursing support for the victim of sexual assault." *Quarterly Review; Official Organ of the District of Columbia Nurses Association* 39(2):9–10, Summer 1971.

3699 McCombie, Sharon L. "Characteristics of rape victims seen in crisis intervention." *Studies in Social Work* 46(2):137–158, Mar. 1976.

3700 McCombie, Sharon L. et al. "Development of a medical center rape crisis intervention program." *American Journal of Psychiatry* 133(4): 418–421, Apr. 1976.

3701 McCubbin, Jack H. and Daniel E. Scott. "Brief guide to office counseling: Treating the victim of rape." *Medical Aspects of Human Sexuality* 8(7):51–52, July 1974.

3702 Massey, Joe B., Celso-Ramón Garcia and John P. Emich. "Management of sexually assaulted females." *Obstetrics and Gynecology* 38(1):29–36, July 1971.

3703 Nadelson, Carol C. and Malkah T. Notman. "Emotional repercussions of rape." *Medical Aspects of Human Sexuality* 11(3):16 passim, Mar. 1977.

3704 Oliven, John F. "Forcible intercourse (rape)." In: *Clinical Sexuality* 3rd ed., pp. 259–269. Philadelphia: J.B. Lippincott, 1974.

3705 Rife, Dwight W. "Scientific evidence in rape cases." *Journal of Criminal Law and Criminology* 31(2):232–235, July/Aug. 1940.

3706 Robinson, G. Erlick, James Oldham and Marlaina Sniderman. "The establishment of a rape crisis centre." In: *Sexual Behaviour in Canada: Patterns and Problems,* ed. by Benjamin Schlesinger, pp. 195–200. Toronto: University of Toronto Press, 1977.

3707 Root, Irving, Wendell Ogden and Wayne Scott. "The medical investigation of alleged rape." *Western Journal of Medicine* 120(4):329–333, Apr. 1974.

3708 Rosenfeld, David L. and Celso-Ramón García. "Brief guide to office counseling: Injuries incurred during rape." *Medical Aspects of Human Sexuality* 10(3):77–78, Mar. 1976.

3709 Schultz, LeRoy G. "The emotional aftermath of rape: social work implications." *Journal of Humanics* 2(2):23–26, 1975.

3710 _____. "Interviewing the sex offender's victim." *Journal of Criminal Law, Criminology and Police Science* 50(5):448–452, Jan./Feb. 1960.

3711 _____. "Sexual victims." In: *The Sexually Oppressed,* ed. by H.L. Gochros and J.S. Gochros, pp. 110–125. New York: Association Press, 1977.

3712 Williams, Cindy Cook and Reg Arthur Williams. "Rape: a plea for help in the emergency room." *Nursing Forum* 12(4):389–401, 1973.

OTHER SOURCES OF INFORMATION

National Center for the Prevention and Control of Rape
National Institute of Mental Health
5600 Fishers Lane, Rockville, MD 20852

Rape Research Group
Center for Correctional Psychology
University of Alabama
Department of Psychology
University, AL 35486

Women Organized Against Rape
Box 17374, Philadelphia, PA 19105

Sex Offenses

BIBLIOGRAPHIES

3713 Macindoe, Ian. *Therapeutic Treatments for Sex Offenders.* (A review of the literature.) Reports from the Research Laboratories, no. PR-71-3. Minneapolis: Department of Psychiatry, University of Minnesota, Apr. 20, 1971.

3714 Munroe, Allan R., comp. *Research in Sexual Deviation and Sexual Offenses: A Bibliography.* Ottawa: Canadian Criminology & Corrections Association, May 1974.

SEX OFFENDERS

3715 Cohen, Murray L. and Richard J. Boucher. "Misunderstandings about sex criminals." *Sexual Behavior* 2(3):57–62, Mar. 1972.

3716 Kozol, Harry L. "Myths about the sex offender." *Medical Aspects of Human Sexuality* 5(6):51–62, June 1971.

3717 Littner, Ner. "The psychology of the sex offender: causes, treatment, prognosis." *Police Law Quarterly* 3:5–31, Jan. 1974.

3718 Sadoff, Robert L. "Anonymous sexual offenders." *Medical Aspects of Human Sexuality* 6(3):118–123, Mar. 1972.

3719 _____. "Myths regarding the sex criminal." *Medical Aspects of Human Sexuality* 3(7):64–74, July 1969.

3720 Whiskin, Frederick E. "The geriatric sex offender." *Medical Aspects of Human Sexuality* 4(4):125–129, Apr. 1970.

RESEARCH

3721 Carroll, James L. and Gerald B. Fuller. "An MMPI comparision of three groups of criminals." *Journal of Clinical Psychology* 27(2):240–242, Apr. 1971.

3722 Cook, Royer F., Robert H. Fosen and Asher Pacht. "Pornography and the sex offender: patterns of previous exposure and arousal effects of pornographic stimuli." *Journal of Applied Psychology* 55(6):503–511, Dec. 1971.

3723 Ellis, Albert and Ralph Brancale. *The Psychology of Sex Offenders.* Springfield, IL: Charles C. Thomas, 1956.

3724 Frisbie, Louise V. *Another Look at Sex Offenders in California.* Mental Health Research Monograph, no. 12. Sacramento: Department of Mental Hygiene, State of California, 1969.

3725 Gebhard, Paul H. "A comparison of white-black offender groups." In: *Sexual Behaviors: Social, Clinical and Legal Aspects,* ed. by H.L.P. Resnick and M.E. Wolfgang, pp. 89–130. Boston: Little, Brown, 1972.

3726 Gebhard, Paul H. et al. *Sex Offenders; an Analysis of Types.* New York: Harper & Row, 1965.

3727 Glueck, Bernard C., Jr., dir. *Final Report: Research Project for the Study and Treatment of Persons Convicted of Crimes Involving Sexual Aberrations, June 1952 to June 1955.* Albany: New York State Department of Corrections and New York State Department of Mental Hygiene, 1956.

3728 Goldstein, Michael et al. "Experience with pornography: rapists, pedophiles, homosexuals, transsexuals, and controls." *Archives of Sexual Behavior* 1(1):1–15, 1971.

3729 Goldstein, Michael and Harold S. Kant. *Pornography and Sexual Deviance.* Berkeley: University of California Press, 1973.

3730 Grunhut, Max, Rudolf Sieverts and Jacob M. Van Bemmelen. *Sexual Crime Today.* The Hague: Martinus, 1960.

3731 Hausman, William, chairman. "Report on Sex Offenders; A Sociological, Psychiatric, and Psychological Study, Nov. 1, 1972" (and) "The

Task Force on Anti-Social Behaviors being an Addendum to the Report . . ., January 14, 1974." Unpub. papers, Department of Psychiatry, University of Minnesota.

3732   Henn, Fritz A., Marijan Herjanic and Robert H. Vanderpearl. "Forensic psychiatry: profiles of two types of sex offenders." *American Journal of Psychiatry* 133(6):694–696, June 1976.

3733   Karpman, Benjamin. *The Sex Offender and His Offenses: Etiology, Pathology, Psychodynamics and Treatment.* New York: Julian Press, 1954.

3734   Kirk, Stuart A. "The sex offenses of blacks and whites." *Archives of Sexual Behavior* 4(3):295–302, May 1975.

3735   Kupperstein, Lenore. "An analysis of sex offenses committed in Philadelphia during 1962 . . . sponsored and distributed by The Pennsylvania Prison Society." Unpub. bachelor of arts dissertation, University of Pennsylvania, 1963.

3736   Lopez, Thomas W. *Emotional expression in the adult sex offender.* (Dissertation—Boston University.) Ann Arbor, MI: University Microfilms, 1970. (Order #70-23,127)

3737   Nelsen, R. Owen. *A Study of the role of sex offenders' marriages in the commission of their sex offenses.* (Dissertation—University of Minnesota.) Ann Arbor, MI: University Microfilms, 1973. (Order #74-10,555)

3738   Pacht, Asher R. and James E. Cowden. "An exploratory study of five hundred sex offenders." *Criminal Justice and Behavior* 1(1):13–20, Mar. 1974.

3739   Radzinowicz, Leon, ed. *Sexual Offences; a Report of the Cambridge Department of Criminal Science.* London: Macmillan, 1957.

3740   Resnik, H.L.P. and Marvin E. Wolfgang, eds. *Sexual Behaviors: Social, Clinical, and Legal Aspects.* Boston: Little, Brown, 1972.

3741   Roberts, Robert E., Laurence Abrams and John R. Finch. "'Delinquent' sex behavior among adolescents." *Medical Aspects of Human Sexuality* 7(1):162 passim, Jan. 1973.

3742   Roberts, Robert E., George W. McBee and Moody C. Bettis. "Youthful sex offenders: an epidemiologic comparison of types." *Journal of Sex Research* 5(1):29–40, Feb. 1969.

3743   Tinklenberg, Jared R. and Kenneth M. Woodrow. "Drug use among youthful assaultive and sex offenders." *Aggression* 52:209–224, 1974.

3744   Vuocolo, Alfred Bernard. *The administration of the New Jersey sex offender program.* (Dissertation—New York University.) Ann Arbor, MI: University Microfilms, 1967. (Order #67-10,994)

3745   Yaffe, Maurice and T.G. Tennent. "Pornography: a psychological appraisal." *British Journal of Hospital Medicine* 10:379–386, Mar. 1973.

EXHIBITIONISM

3746   Blank, Leonard. "The impulse to look and to show." *Journal of Sex Research* 3(3):223–228, Aug. 1967.

3747   Davis, Sharon Kantorowski and Phillip W. Davis. "Meanings and process in erotic offensiveness: an expose of exposees." *Urban Life* 5(3):377–396, Oct. 1976.

3748   Hackett, Thomas P. "Brief guide to office counseling: encounters by women or children with exhibitionists." *Medical Aspects of Human Sexuality* 9(3):139–140, Mar. 1975.

3749   Halleck, Seymour. "Brief guide to office counseling: voyeurism and exhibitionism in adolescence." *Medical Aspects of Human Sexuality* 9(5):75–76, May 1975.

3750   Karpman, Benjamin. "The psychopathology of exhibitionism; review of the literature." *Journal of Clinical Psychopathology* 9(2):179–225, Apr. 1948.

3751   Macdonald, John M. *Indecent Exposure.* Springfield, IL: Charles C. Thomas, 1973.

3752   Mohr, Johann W., R.E. Turner and M.B. Jerry. *Pedophilia and Exhibitionism; a Handbook.* Toronto: University of Toronto Press, 1964.

3753   Paitich, Daniel. *Attitudes toward parents in male homosexuals and exhibitionists.* (Dissertation—University of Toronto.) Ann Arbor, MI: University Microfilms, 1964. (Order #64-11,275)

3754   Rickles, Nathan King. *Exhibitionism.* Philadelphia: J.B. Lippincott, 1950.

3755   Smukler, Arthur J. and Douglas Schiebel. "Personality characteristics of exhibitionists." *Diseases of the Nervous System* 36(11):600–603, Nov. 1975.

3756   Spitz, Herman H. *A clinical investigation of certain personality characteristics of 20 adult male exhibitionists.* (Dissertation—New York University.) Ann Arbor, MI: University Microfilms, 1955. (Order #13,640)

3757   Wagner, Edwin E. "Projective test data

from two contrasted groups of exhibitionists."
Perceptual and Motor Skills 39(1 pt. 1):131–140,
Aug. 1974.

3758   Zechnick, Robert. "Exhibitionism: genesis,
dynamics, and treatment." *Psychiatric Quarterly*
45(1):70–75, 1971.

VOYEURISM

3759   Allen, David W. *The Fear of Looking; or
Scopophilic-Exhibitionistic Conflicts.* Charlottes-
ville: University Press of Virginia, 1974.

3760   Feigelmann, William. "Peeping: the pattern
of voyeurism among construction workers."
Urban Life and Culture 3(1):35–49, Apr. 1974.

3761   Hamilton, James W. "Voyeurism: some
clinical and theoretical considerations." *American Journal of Psychotherapy* 26:277–287, Apr.
1972.

3762   Kutchinsky, Berl. "Deviance and crimi-
nality: the case of voyeur in a peeper's paradise."
Diseases of the Nervous System 37(3):145–151,
Mar. 1976.

3763   Sagarin, Edward. "Power to the peephole."
Sexual Behavior 3(2):2–7, Feb. 1973.

3764   Smith, R. Spencer. "Voyeurism: a review of
literature." *Archives of Sexual Behavior* 5(6):
585–608, Nov. 1976.

SEX PSYCHOPATHS

3765   Bowman, Karl M. and Bernice Engle. "Certain aspects of sex psychopath laws." *American
Journal of Psychiatry* 114(8):690–697, Feb. 1958.

3766   Canada. *Royal Commission on the Criminal Law Relating to Criminal Sexual Psychopaths.*
(Cat. No. Z1-1954/6.) Ottawa: The Queen's Printer
and Controller of Stationery, 1958.

3767   DiFuria, Giulio and Hayden L. Mees.
"Dangerous to be at large—a constructive cri-
tique of Washington's sexual psychopath law."
Washington Law Review 38(3):531–537, Fall 1963.

3768   Dix, George E. "Differential processing of
abnormal sex offenders: utilization of California's
mentally disordered sex offender program." *Journal of Criminal Law and Criminology* 67(2):
233–243, June 1976.

3769   Group for the Advancement of Psychiatry.
Committee on Psychiatry and Law. *Psychiatry and
Sex Psychopath Legislation: the 30s to the 80s.*
GAP Publication, no. 98. New York: Group for the
Advancement of Psychiatry, 1977.

3770   Jacobs, Daniel. "Psychiatric examinations
in the determination of sexual dangerousness in
Massachusetts." *New England Law Review*
10:85–103, Fall 1974.

3771   Koocher, Gerald P. "American 'sex psychopath' laws: injustice in practice." *International
Journal of Offender Therapy* 17(2):148–151, 1973.

3772   Marcus, Eric H. "Psychiatric evaluation of
the 'sexual psychopath'." *Medical Trial Technique
Quarterly* (Mundelein) 17:83–88, Sept. 1970.

3773   Meeks, Wilson M. "Criminal sexual
psychopaths and sexually dangerous persons."
*Corrective Psychiatry and Journal of Social Ther-
apy* 9(1):22–27, First Quarter 1963.

3774   Morrow, William R. and Donald B. Peterson. "Follow-up of discharged psychiatric offenders—'not guilty by reason of insanity' and 'criminal sexual psychopaths.'" *Journal of Criminal
Law, Criminology and Police Science* 57(1):31–34,
1966.

3775   Rees, Jim. "'Voluntary' castration of mentally disordered sex offenders." *Criminal Law
Bulletin* 13:30–48, Jan./Feb. 1977.

3776   Sidley, Nathan T. and Francis J. Stolarz. "A
proposed 'dangerous sex offender' law." *American Journal of Psychiatry* 130(7):765–768, July
1973.

3777   Smith, Charles E. "Recognizing and sentencing the exceptional and dangerous offender."
Federal Probation 35(4):3–12, Dec. 1971.

3778   Sullivan, Peter. "Commitment of sexual
psychopaths and the requirements of procedural
due process." *Fordham Law Review* 44:923–949,
Apr. 1976.

3779   Sutherland, Edwin H. "The diffusion of sex-
ual psychopath laws." In: *Crime and Justice in
Society,* ed. by Richard Quinney, pp. 88–97.
Boston: Little, Brown, 1969.

3780   Swanson, Alan. "Sexual psychopath stat-
utes: summary and analysis." *Journal of Criminal
Law, Criminology and Police Science* 51(2):
215–235, July/Aug. 1960.

3781   Swigert, Victoria Lynn, Ronald A. Farrell
and William C. Yoels. "Sexual homicide: social,
psychological, and legal aspects." *Archives of
Sexual Behavior* 5(5):391–401, Sept. 1976.

THERAPY

3782   Bancroft, John. "The control of deviant
sexual behaviour by drugs: 1. Behavioural

changes following oestrogens and anti-androgens." *British Journal of Psychiatry* 125:310–315, Sept. 1974.

3783 Barnett, Ola Johnson. *The use of nonprofessionals in the rehabilitation of mentally disordered sex offenders.* (Dissertation—University of California at Los Angeles.) Ann Arbor, MI: University Microfilms, 1971. (Order #71-22,998)

3784 Beit-Hallahmi, Benjamin. "Treating the sex offender." *Crime and Delinquency* 20(1):33–37, Jan. 1974.

3785 Bromberg, Walter and Girard H. Franklin. "The treatment of sexual deviates with group psychodrama." *Group Psychotherapy* 4:274–289, Mar. 1952.

3786 Cabeen, Charles W. "Factors related to improvement of sex offenders in therapy." Unpub. doctoral dissertation, University of California at Los Angeles, 1955.

3787 Cabeen, Charles W. and James C. Coleman. "The selection of sex-offender patients for group psychotherapy." *International Journal of Group Psychotherapy* 12(3):326–334, July 1962.

3788 Cohen, Murray L. and Harry L. Kozol. "Evaluation for parole at a sex offender treatment center." *Federal Probation* 30(3):50–55, Sept. 1966.

3789 Costell, Ronald M. and Irvin Yalom. "Institutional group therapy." *International Psychiatry Clinics* 8(4):119–144, 1972.

3790 DiFuria, Giulio and Hayden L. Mees. "Legal and psychiatric problems in the care and treatment of sexual offenders (a national survey)." *American Journal of Psychiatry* 120:980–985, Apr. 1964.

3791 Fensterheim, Herbert. "Behavior therapy of the sexual variations." *Journal of Sex and Marital Therapy* 1(1):16–28, Fall 1974.

3792 Ferracuti, Franco and R. Bartilotti. "Technical and legal aspects in the pharmacologic treatment of sex offenders." In: *Sexual Behavior: Pharmacology and Biochemistry,* ed. by M. Sandler and G.L. Gessa, pp. 205–208. New York: Raven Press, 1975.

3793 Freese, Amorette Lee. "Group therapy with exhibitionists and voyeurs." *Social Work* 17(2):44–52, Mar. 1972.

3794 Gigeroff, Alex K., Johann W. Mohr and R. Edward Turner. "Sex offenders on probation: an overview." *Federal Probation* 33(2):22–26, June 1969.

3795 Group for the Advancement of Psychiatry. Committee on Psychiatry and Law. *Psychiatry and Sex Psychopath Legislation: the 30s to the 80s.* GAP Publication, no. 98. New York: Group for the Advancement of Psychiatry, 1977.

3796 Guttmacher, Manfred S. *Sex Offenses: The Problem, Causes and Prevention.* New York: W.W. Norton, 1951.

3797 Hauptmann, Walter. "Zum derzeitigen stand der somatischen behandlungsmethoden bei abnormen sexualdelinquenten." *Monatsschrift für Kriminologie und Strafrechtsreform* 56(1):1–14, Feb. 1973.

3798 Kerr, Nora. "Special handling for sex offenders." *Perspectives in Psychiatric Care* 10(4):160–162, 1972.

3799 Laws, Donald Richard and Michael Serber. "Measurement and evaluation of assertive training with sexual offenders." In: *The Crumbling Walls: Treatment and Counseling of Prisoners,* ed. by R.J. Hosford and S. Moss, pp. 165–172. Champaign: University of Illinois Press, 1975.

3800 MacDonald, George J. *Treatment Program for the Sexual Offender.* A series of reports, 1968–1974. Fort Steilacoom, WA: Western State Hospital.

3801 McGrath, P.G. "Sexual offenders." In: *Psycho-Sexual Problems; Proceedings of the Congress Held at the University of Bradford, 1974,* ed. by Hugo Milne and Shirley Hardy, pp. 169–175. Baltimore: University Park Press, 1975.

3802 MacKay, Dougal. "Modification of sexual behaviour." In: *Psychosexual Problems: Psychotherapy, Counselling and Behaviour Modification,* ed. by Sidney Crown, pp. 85–132. London: Academic Press, 1976.

3803 Maclay, W.S., M. Remy and Johann W. Mohr. "Psychiatric treatment as an alternative to imprisonment; a seminar held at Hart House, University of Toronto, June 1st and 2nd, 1961." *Criminal Law Quarterly* 4(3):296–328, Jan. 1962.

3804 Mohr, Johann W. "Evaluation of treatment." *International Psychiatry Clinics* 8(4):227–242, 1972.

3805 Mueller, D., Fritz Douglas Roeder and H. Orthner. "Further results of stereotaxis in the human hypothalamus in sexual deviations; first use of this operation in addiction to drugs." *Neurochirurgia* 16:113–126, July 1973.

3806 Pacht, Asher R., Seymour Halleck and John

C. Ehrmann. "Diagnosis and treatment of the sexual offender: a nine-year study." *American Journal Psychiatry* 118(9):802–808, Mar. 1962.

3807   Peters, Joseph J. and Robert L. Sadoff. "Psychiatric services for sex offenders on probation." *Federal Probation* 35(3):33–37, Sept. 1971.

3808   Roberts, Leigh M. and Asher R. Pacht. "Termination of inpatient treatment for sex deviates: psychiatric, social and legal factors." *The American Journal of Psychiatry* 121(9):873–880, Mar. 1965.

3809   Roether, Hermann A. and Joseph J. Peters. "Cohesiveness and hostility in group psychotherapy." *American Journal of Psychiatry* 128(8):1014–1017, Feb. 1972.

3810   Rooth, F. Graham and I.M. Marks. "Persistent exhibitionism: short-term response to aversion, self-regulation, and relaxation treatments." *Archives of Sexual Behavior* 3(3):227–248, May 1974.

3811   Schmideberg, Melitta. "Reality therapy with offenders." *British Journal of Criminology* 5(2):168–182, Apr. 1965.

3812   Shorkey, Clayton T. and Sam A. Cangelosi. *Modification of Sexual Behavior: Summary and Annotated Bibliography.* Journal Supplement Abstract Service MS. 1114. Washington, DC: American Psychological Association, 1975.

3813   Symposium on Sex Offenders. *International Journal of Offender Therapy and Comparative Criminology* 16(2):whole issue, 1972.

3814   Tennent, Gavin and James Cass. "The control of deviant sexual behavior by drugs: a double-blind controlled study of Benperiodol, Chlorpromazine, and Placebo." *Archives of Sexual Behavior* 3(3):261–271, May 1974.

3815   Turner, R. Edward. "The group treatment of sexual deviations." *Canadian Journal of Corrections* 3(4):485–491, Oct. 1961.

RECIDIVISM

3816   Cormier, Bruno M. and Paul Boulanger. "Life cycle and episodic recidivism." *Canadian Psychiatric Association Journal* 18(4):283–287, Aug. 1973.

3817   Cutter, Fred. "Recidivism in sexual psychopaths: some impressions." *Psychological Newsletter* 10:28–32, 1958.

3818   Dix, George E. "Differential processing of abnormal sex offenders: utilization of California's mentally disordered sex offender program." *Journal of Criminal Law and Criminology* 67(2):233–243, June 1976.

3819   Frisbie, Louise V. "Treated sex offenders who reverted to sexually deviant behavior." *Federal Probation* 29(2):52–57, June 1965.

3820   Frisbie, Louise V. and Ernest H. Dondis. *Recidivism Among Treated Sex Offenders.* Mental Health Research Monograph, no. 5. Sacramento: Department of Mental Hygiene, State of California, 1965.

3821   Glueck, Bernard C., Jr., dir. *Final Report: Research Project for the Study and Treatment of Persons Convicted of Crimes Involving Sexual Aberrations, June 1952 to June 1955.* Albany: New York State Department of Correction and New York State Department of Mental Hygiene, 1956.

3822   Gray, K.G. and Johann W. Mohr. "Follow-up of male sexual offenders." In: *Sexual Behavior and the Law,* ed. by Ralph Slovenko, pp. 742–756. Springfield, IL: Charles C. Thomas, 1965.

3823   Kraus, J. "Judicial labels as a typology of offences committed by male juveniles." *British Journal of Criminology*:269–274, July 1973.

3824   Lidberg, Lars. "Återfall i sexualkriminalitet efter kastration." *Nordisk Psykiatrisk Tidsskrift* 28:387–391, 1968.

3825   Mohr, Johann W. "The contribution of research to the selection of appropriate alternatives for sexual offenders." In: *Psychiatric Treatment as an Alternative to Imprisonment,* pp. 317–328. Toronto: Canada Law Book Company, 1962.

3826   Morrow, William R. and Donald B. Peterson. "Follow-up of discharged psychiatric offenders—'not guilty by reason of insanity' and 'criminal sexual psychopaths.' " *Journal of Criminal Law, Criminology and Police Science* 57(1):31–34, 1966.

3827   Radzinowicz, Leon, ed. *Sexual Offences; a Report of the Cambridge Department of Criminal Science.* London: Macmillan, 1957.

3828   Witter, Hermann. "A psychiatric-psychological study of German recidivists." *International Journal of Offender Therapy* 12(2):79–83, 1968.

LEGAL ASPECTS

3829   Black, James Allen. *The sentencing of sex offenders.* (Dissertation—State University of Iowa.) Ann Arbor, MI: University Microfilms, 1966. (Order #66-7191)

3830 Bohmer, Carol. "Judicial use of psychiatric reports in the sentencing of sex offenders." *Journal of Psychiatry and Law* 1(2):223–242, Summer 1973.

3831 Drzazga, John. *Sex Crimes and Their Legal Aspects.* Springfield, IL: Charles C. Thomas, 1960.

3832 Eckert, William G. "Forensic aspects of sex crimes and problems." *Inform* 3(4):3–8, Oct. 1971.

3833 Enos, William F. and James C. Beyer. "Sex crimes." In: *Medicolegal Investigation of Death,* ed. by W.U. Spitz and R.S. Fisher, pp. 373–384, Springfield, IL: Charles C. Thomas, 1973.

3834 Gagnon, John. "Sexual offenses and offenders." In: *Human Sexualities,* pp. 295–319. Glenview, IL: Scott, Foresman, 1977.

3835 Gigeroff, Alex K. *Sexual Deviations in the Criminal Law.* Clarke Institute of Psychiatry Monograph Series, no. 2. Toronto: University of Toronto Press, 1968.

3836 Helpern, Milton and Donal E.J. MacNamara. "Interview; sexual crimes and the medical examiner." *Medical Aspects of Human Sexuality* 8(4):161 passim, Apr. 1974.

3837 Macdonald, John Marshall. *Psychiatry and the Criminal; A Guide to Psychiatric Examinations for the Criminal Courts.* Springfield, IL: Charles C. Thomas, 1958.

3838 MacNamara, Donal E.J. "Police and sex: an interview with a criminologist." *Sexual Behavior* 1(4):24–31, July 1971.

3839 MacNamara, Donal E.J. and Edward Sagarin. *Sex, Crime, and the Law.* New York: Free Press, 1977.

3840 Morosco, B. Anthony. *The Prosecution and Defense of Sex Crimes.* New York: Bender, 1977.

3841 Ploscowe, Morris. *Sex and the Law.* rev. ed. New York: Ace Books, 1962.

3842 Reiss, Albert J., Jr. "Sex offenses: the marginal status of the adolescent." *Law and Contemporary Problems* 25(2):309–333, Spring 1960.

3843 Sadoff, Robert L. "Sex and the law." In: *The Sexual Experience,* ed. by B.J. Sadock, H.I. Kaplan and A.M. Freedman, pp. 567–595. Baltimore: Williams & Wilkins, 1976.

3844 Sherwin, Robert Veit. "Law and sex." In: *Handbook of Sexology,* ed. by John Money and Herman Musaph, pp. 1121–1133. Amsterdam: Excerpta Medica, 1977.

3845 _____. *Sex and the Statutory Law.* New York: Oceana Publications, 1949.

3846 Tappan, Paul W. "Sentences for sex criminals." *Journal of Criminal Law, Criminology, and Police Science* 42(3):332–337, Sept./Oct. 1951.

3847 _____. "Some myths about the sex offender." *Federal Probation* 19(2):7–12, June 1955.

PERIODICALS

Sex Problems Court Digest
1860 Broadway, Suite 1110, New York, NY 10023

SexuaLaw Reporter
1800 N. Highland Ave., Suite 106, Los Angeles, CA 90028

TSA News (a newsletter concerning the evaluation and treatment of sexual aggressives)
University of Tennessee Center for the Prevention and Control of Rape
865 Poplar Avenue, 4-E, Memphis, TN 38104

OTHER SOURCES OF INFORMATION

Canadian Criminology & Corrections Association
55 Parkdale Ave., Ottawa, Canada

INFORM; The International Reference Organization in Forensic Medicine and Sciences (Newsletter; bibliographies; reference service)
Dr. William G. Eckert
Dept. of Pathology, St. Francis Hospital
929 N. St. Francis, Wichita, KA 67214

Erotica

Erotica

LITERATURE REVIEWS

3848 Money, John and Robert Athanasiou. "Pornography: review and bibliographic annotations." *American Journal of Obstetrics and Gynecology* 115(1):130–146, Jan. 1973.

3849 Moos, Rudolf H. "The effects of pornography: a review of the findings of the Obscenity and Pornography Commission." *Comments on Contemporary Psychiatry* 1(4):123–131, Jan. 1972.

3850– *Technical Report of the Commission on Ob-*
3853 *scenity and Pornography.* v. 1. Washington, DC: U.S. GPO, 1971. (Avail. from Supt. of Docs., U.S. GPO, Washington, DC 20402. Stock #5256-002.):

>   **3850** Cairns, Robert B., J.C.N. Paul and J. Wishner. Psychological assumptions in sex censorship: an evaluative review of recent research (1961–1968), pp. 5–21.

>   **3851** Mann, Jay. Experimental induction of human sexual arousal, pp. 23–60.

>   **3852** Zuckerman, Marvin. Physiological measures of sexual arousal in the human, pp. 61–101.

>   **3853** Kupperstein, Lenore. The role of pornography in the etiology of juvenile delinquency: a review of the research literature, pp. 103–111.

3854 Yaffé, Maurice. "Research survey and bibliography." In: *Pornography: The Longford Report,* pp. 460–507. London: Coronet Books, 1972.

3855 Yaffé, Maurice and T.G. Tennent. "Pornography: a psychological appraisal." *British Journal of Hospital Medicine* 10:379–386, Mar. 1973.

COMMISSION REPORTS

3856 Longford, Frank Pakenham, 7th Earl of, chairman. *Pornography: The Longford Report.* London: Coronet Books, 1972.

3857 *The Report of the Commission on Obscenity and Pornography.* Washington, DC: U.S. GPO, Sept. 1970. (Avail. from Supt. of Docs., U.S. GPO, Washington, DC 20402. Stock #052-056-00001-2.) (Paperback ed.: Bantam, 1970.)

3858 *Technical Report of the Commission on Obscenity and Pornography.* v. 1–9. Washington, DC: U.S. GPO, 1971–1972. (Avail. from Supt. of Docs., U.S. GPO, Washington, DC 20402. Stock #5256-0002 through #5256-0010.)

RESEARCH

3859 Amoroso, Donald M. and Marvin Brown. "Problems in studying the effects of erotic materials." *Journal of Sex Research* 9(3):187–195, Aug. 1973.

3860 Athanasiou, Robert and Phillip Shaver. "Correlates of heterosexuals' reactions to pornography." *Journal of Sex Research* 7(4):298–311, Nov. 1971.

3861 Bell, Robert R. "Pornography." In: *Social Deviance: A Substantive Analysis,* pp. 144–170. Homewood, IL: Dorsey Press, 1971.

3862 Byrne, Donn, Jeffrey D. Fisher and John Lamberth. "Evaluations of erotica: facts or feelings?" *Journal of Personality and Social Psychology* 29(1):111–116, Jan. 1974.

3863 Gordon, Michael and Robert R. Bell. "Medium and hard-core pornography: a comparative analysis." *Journal of Sex Research* 5(4):260–268, Nov. 1969.

3864 Higgins, John W. and Marshall B. Katzman. "Determinants in the judgment of obscenity." *American Journal of Psychiatry* 125(12): 1733–1738, 1969.

3865 Houston, Judith A. *Capturing policies of pornographic pictorial representations by normative judgment analysis.* (Dissertation—University of Northern Colorado.) Ann Arbor, MI: University Microfilms, 1973. (Order #74-9755)

3866 Houston, Judith A. and Samuel R. Houston. "Identifying pornographic materials with judgment analysis." *Journal of Psychology* 88:277–287, 1974.

3867 Johnson, William Steven. *Social class and attitudes toward sexually oriented materials.* (Dissertation—University of Southern California.) Ann Arbor, MI: University Microfilms, 1971. (Order #72-6070)

3868 Kinsey, Alfred C. et al. *Sexual Behavior in*

the Human Female, pp. 669–672. Philadelphia: W.B. Saunders, 1953.

3869   Knowles, Lyle and Houshang Poorkaj. "Attitudes and behavior on viewing sexual activities in public places." *Sociology and Social Research* 58(2):130–135, Jan. 1974.

3870   Levitt, Eugene E. "Pornography: some new perspectives on an old problem." *Journal of Sex Research* 5(4):247–259, Nov. 1969.

3871   Love, Robert E., Lloyd R. Sloan and Michael J. Schmidt. "Viewing pornography and sex guilt: the priggish, the prudent, and the profligate." *Journal of Consulting and Clinical Psychology* 44(4):624–629, Aug. 1976.

3872   Merritt, C. Gary, Joel E. Gerstl and Leonard A. LoSciuto. "Age and perceived effects of erotica—pornography: a national sample study." *Archives of Sexual Behavior* 4(6):605–621, Nov. 1975.

3873   Reed, John P. and Robin S. Reed. "P.R.U.D.E.S. (Pornography research using direct erotic stimuli)." *Journal of Sex Research* 8(3):237–246, Aug. 1972.

3874   Rosen, Lawrence and Stanley H. Turner. "Exposure to pornography: an exploratory study." *Journal of Sex Research* 5(4):235–246, Nov. 1969.

3875   Smith, Don D. "The social content of pornography." *Journal of Communication* 26(1):16–24, Winter 1976.

3876   Stauffer, John and Richard Frost. "Male and female interest in sexually-oriented magazines." *Journal of Communication* 26:25–30, Winter 1976.

3877   Wallace, Douglas H. *Pornography: evaluational reactions and some attitudinal correlates.* (Dissertation—Wayne State University.) Ann Arbor, MI: University Microfilms, 1971. (Order #71-29,807)

3878   Wallace, Douglas H. and Gerald Wehmer. "Evaluation of visual erotica by sexual liberals and conservatives." *Journal of Sex Research* 8(2):147–153, May 1972.

3879   Wilson, W. Cody. "American experience with pornography." In: *Social Change and Human Behavior: Mental Health Challenges of the Seventies,* ed. by George V. Coelho, pp. 111–136. Rockville, MD: National Institute of Mental Health, 1972.

3880   Wilson, W. Cody and Michael J. Goldstein,

eds. "Pornography: attitudes, use, and effects." *Journal of Social Issues* 29(3):whole issue, 1973.

3881   Zuckerman, Marvin. "Research on pornography." In: *Sex and the Life Cycle,* ed. by W.W. Oaks, G.A. Melchiode and I. Ficher, pp. 147–161. New York: Grune & Stratton, 1976.

PHYSIOLOGICAL AND PSYCHOLOGICAL RESPONSE TO VISUAL STIMULI

3882   Adamson, John D. et al. "Physiological responses to sexual and unpleasant film stimuli." *Journal of Psychosomatic Research* 16:153–162, 1972.

3883   Bahm, Robert Michael. *The influence of non-sexual cues, sexual explicitness and sex guilt on female's erotic response to literature.* (Dissertation—University of Massachusetts.) Ann Arbor, MI: University Microfilms, 1972. (Order #73-5524)

3884   Barclay, Andrew M. "Linking sexual and aggressive motives: contributions of 'irrelevant' arousals." *Journal of Personality* 39(4):481–492, Dec. 1971.

3885   Barclay, Andrew M. and Douglas M. Little. "Urinary acid phosphatase secretion under different arousal conditions." *Psychophysiology* 9(1):69–77, Jan. 1972.

3886   Bernick, Niles, Arthur Kling and Gene Borowitz. "Physiologic differentiation of sexual arousal and anxiety." *Psychosomatic Medicine* 33(4):341–352, July/Aug. 1971.

3887   Boylin, Eugene Robert. *The relationship among personality variables, forms of erotic stimuli, and measures of sexual responsivity of males and females.* (Dissertation—Southern Illinois University.) Ann Arbor, MI: University Microfilms, 1971. (Order #72-10,236)

3888   Brown, Marvin et al. "Factors affecting viewing time of pornography." *Journal of Social Psychology* 90:124–135, 1973.

3889   Brown, Walter A. and George Heninger. "Cortisol, growth hormone, free fatty acids, and experimentally evoked affective arousal." *American Journal of Psychiatry* 132(11):1172–1175, Nov. 1975.

3890   Byrne, Donn and John Sheffield. "Response to sexually arousing stimuli as a function of repressing and sensitizing defenses." *Journal of Abnormal Psychology* 70(2):114–118, Apr. 1965.

3891   Cantor, Joanne R., Dolf Zillman and Bryant Jennings. "Enhancement of experienced sexual arousal in response to erotic stimuli through misattribution of unrelated residual excitation." *Journal of Personality and Social Psychology* 32(1):69–75, July 1975.

3892 Cattell, Raymond B., George F. Kawash and Gerrit E. DeYoung. "Validation of objective measures of ergic tension: response of the sex erg to visual stimuli." *Journal of Experimental Research in Personality* 6(1):76–83, 1972.

3893 Colson, Charles E. *Content, tolerance level, and perceived internal response in the ascription of social deviance.* (Dissertation—University of Illinois.) Ann Arbor: University Microfilms, 1971. (Order #72-06898)

3894 _____. "The evaluation of pornography: effects of attitude and perceived physiological reaction." *Archives of Sexual Behavior* 3(4):307–323, July 1974.

3895 Donnerstein, Edward, Marcia Donnerstein and Ronald Evans. "Erotic stimuli and aggression: facilitation or inhibition." *Journal of Personality and Social Psychology* 32(2):237–244, Aug. 1975.

3896 Englar, Ronald C. and C. Eugene Walker. "Male and female reactions to erotic literature." *Psychological Reports* 32(2):481–482, Apr. 1973.

3897 Firth, Diana and Norman Worrall. "Electrodermal response to sexual materials." *Perceptual and Motor Skills* 41:60–62, 1975.

3898 Freund, Kurt and Ronald M. Costell. "The structure of erotic preference in the nondeviant male." *Behavior Research and Therapy* 8:15–20, Feb. 1970.

3899 Gebhard, Paul H. "Sex differences in sexual response." *Archives of Sexual Behavior* 2(3):201–203, June 1973.

3900 Geer, James H., Patricia Morokoff and Pamela Greenwood. "Sexual arousal in women: the development of a measurement device for vaginal blood volume." *Archives of Sexual Behavior* 3(6):559–564, Nov. 1974.

3901 Griffitt, William. "Response to erotica and the projection of response to erotica in the opposite sex." *Journal of Experimental Research in Personality* 6(4)330–338, Apr. 1973.

3902 Griffitt, William, James May and Russell Veitch. "Sexual stimulation and interpersonal behavior: heterosexual evaluative responses, visual behavior and physical proximity." *Journal of Personality and Social Psychology* 30(3):367–377, Sept. 1974.

3903 Hamel, Robert F. "Female subjective and pupillary reaction to nude male and female figures." *Journal of Psychology* 87(2):171–175, 1974.

3904 Hamrick, Narecia D. "Physiological and verbal responses to erotic visual stimuli in a female population." *Behavioral Engineering* 2(1):9–16, Summer/Fall 1974.

3905 Hare, Robert. "Anxiety (APQ) and autonomic responses to affective visual stimulation." *Journal of Experimental Research in Personality* 5(3):233–241, Sept. 1971.

3906 Hare, Robert et al. "Autonomic responses to affective visual stimulation." *Psychophysiology* 7(3):408–417, 1971.

3907 Heiman, Julia R. *Responses to erotica: an exploration of physiological and psychological correlates of human sexual response.* (Dissertation—State University of New York at Stony Brook.) Ann Arbor, MI: University Microfilms, 1975. (Order #75-24,648)

3908 Hirschman, Richard. "Cross-modal effects of anticipatory bogus heart rate feedback in a negative emotional context." *Journal of Personality and Social Psychology* 31(1):13–19, Jan. 1975.

3909 Hoon, Peter W., John P. Wincze and Emily Franck Hoon. "A test of reciprocal inhibition: are anxiety and sexual arousal in women mutually inhibitory?" *Journal of Abnormal Psychology* 86(1):65–74, Feb. 1977.

3910 Keir, Richard George. *Sex, individual differences, and film effects on responses to sexual films.* (Dissertation—University of Connecticut.) Ann Arbor, MI: University Microfilms, 1972. (Order #73-9854)

3911 Kolársky, Ales and Jaroslav Madlafousek. "Variability of stimulus effect in the course of phallometric testing." *Archives of Sexual Behavior* 6(2):135–142, Mar. 1977.

3912 Lehman, Robert E. "The disinhibiting effects of visual material in treating orgasmically dysfunctional women." *Behavioral Engineering* 1(2):1–3, Fall/Winter 1973/1974.

3913 Levitt, Eugene E. and Roger K. Hinesley. "Some factors in the valences of erotic visual stimuli." *Journal of Sex Research* 3(1):63–68, Feb. 1967.

3914 McConaghy, Nathaniel. "Penile volume responses to moving and still pictures of male and female nudes." *Archives of Sexual Behavior* 3(6):565–570, Nov. 1974.

3915 Mosher, Donald L. *The development and validation of a sentence completion measure of guilt.* (Dissertation—Ohio State University.) Ann Arbor, MI: University Microfilms, 1961. (Order #61-5110)

3916 _____. "Sex differences, sex experience, sex guilt, and explicitly sexual films." *Journal of Social Issues* 29(3):95–112, 1973.

3917 Osborn, Candice A. and Robert H. Pollack. "The effects of two types of erotic literature on physiological and verbal measures of female sexual arousal." *Journal of Sex Research* 13(4):250–256, Nov. 1977.

3918 Pirke, Karl M., Götz Kockott and Franz Dittmar. "Psychosexual stimulation and plasma testosterone in man." *Archives of Sexual Behavior* 3(6):577–584, Nov. 1974.

3919 Ray, Rose E. and William D. Thompson. "Autonomic correlates of female guilt responses to erotic visual stimuli." *Psychological Reports* 34:1299–1306, 1974.

3920 Ray, Rose E. and C. Eugene Walker. "Biographical and self-report correlates of female guilt responses to visual erotic stimuli." *Journal of Consulting Psychology* 41(1):93–96, Aug. 1973.

3921 Sandford, Donald A. "Patterns of sexual arousal in heterosexual males." *Journal of Sex Research* 10(2):150–155, May 1974.

3922 Schmidt, Gunter, Volkmar Sigusch and Ulrich Meyberg. "Psychosexual stimulation in men: emotional reactions, changes of sex behavior, and measures of conservative attitudes." *Journal of Sex Research* 5(3):199–217, Aug. 1969.

3923 Schmidt. Gunter, Volkmar Sigusch and Siegrid Schäfer. "Responses to reading erotic stories: male-female differences." *Archives of Sexual Behavior* 2(3):181–199, June 1973.

3924 Steele, Daniel G. *Female responsiveness to erotic films and its relation to attitudes, sexual knowledge and selected demographic variables.* (Dissertation—Baylor University.) Ann Arbor, MI: University Microfilms, 1973. (Order #73-19,137)

3925 Steele, Daniel G. and C. Eugene Walker. "Female responsiveness to erotica and the 'ideal' erotic film from a feminine perspective." *Journal of Nervous and Mental Disease* 162(4):266–273, Apr. 1976.

3926 Stephan, Walter G., Ellen Berscheid and Elaine Walster. "Sexual arousal and heterosexual perception." *Journal of Personality and Social Psychology* 20(1):93–101, Oct. 1971.

3927 Thompson, Joseph J. and Paul W. Dexon. "A power function between ratings of pornographic stimuli and psychophysical responses in young normal adult women." *Perceptual and Motor Skills* 38(3, pt.2):1236–1238, June 1974.

3928 Wallace, Douglas H. and Gerald Wehmer. "Pornography and attitude change." *Journal of Sex Research* 7(2):116–125, May 1971.

3929 Wincze, John P., Peter W. Hoon and Emily Franck Hoon. "Sexual arousal in women: a comparison of cognitive and physiological responses by continuous measurement." *Archives of Sexual Behavior* 6(2):121–133, Mar. 1977.

BEHAVIORAL EFFECT OF EROTICA RESEARCH

3930 Baron, Robert A. "The aggression-inhibiting influence of heightened sexual arousal." *Journal of Personality and Social Psychology* 30(3):318–322, Sept. 1974.

3931 Berkowitz, Leonard. "Stimulus/response: sex and violence: we can't have it both ways." *Psychology Today* 5(7):14 passim, Dec. 1971.

3932 Brown, Marvin, Donald M. Amoroso and Edward E. Ware. "Behavioral effects of viewing pornography." *Journal of Social Psychology* 98:235–245, 1976.

3933 Ernst, Jan-Peter et al. "Reaktionen auf sexual-aggresive filme." In: *Ergebnisse zur Sexualforschung,* ed. by E. Schorsch and G. Schmidt, pp. 272–298. Köln: Wissenschafts Verlag, 1975.

3934 Geen, Russell G., John J. Rabosky and Roger Pigg. "Awareness of arousal and its relation to aggression." *British Journal of Social and Clinical Psychology* 11(2):115–121, June 1972.

3935 Goldstein, Michael and Harold S. Kant. *Pornography and Sexual Deviance.* Berkeley: University of California Press, 1973.

3936 Jaffe, Yoram et al. "Sexual arousal and behavioral aggression." *Journal of Personality and Social Psychology* 30(6):759–764, Dec. 1974.

3937 Katz, Harvey Alan. *The effects of previous exposure to pornographic film, sexual instrumentality, and guilt on male verbal aggression against women.* (Dissertation—University of Connecticut.) Ann Arbor, MI: University Microfilms, 1970. (Order #71-18,418)

3938 Kutchinsky, Berl. "The effect of easy availability of pornography on the incidence of sex crimes: the Danish experience." *Journal of Social Issues* 29(3):163–181, 1973.

3939 Mann, Jay. "The effects of erotica." *Sexual Behavior* 3(2):23–29, Feb. 1973.

3940 _____. "Satiation of the transient stimulating effect of erotic films." *Journal of Personality and Social Psychology* 30(6):729–735, Dec. 1974.

3941 Meyer, Timothy P. "The effects of sexually arousing and violent films on aggressive behavior." *Journal of Sex Research* 8(4):324–331, Nov. 1972.

3942 Reifler, Clifford B. et al. "Pornography: an experimental study of effects." *American Journal of Psychiatry* 128(5):575–582, Nov. 1971.

3943 Rosene, James Melvin. *The effects of violent and sexually arousing film content: an experimental study.* (Dissertation—Ohio University.) Ann Arbor, MI: University Microfilms, 1971. (Order #72-13,691)

3944 Sachs, Donald H. and Karen G. Duffy. "Effect of modeling on sexual imagery." *Archives of Sexual Behavior* 5(4):301–311, July 1976.

3945 Wills, Gary. "Measuring the impact of erotica." *Psychology Today* 11(3):30 passim, Aug. 1977.

3946 Zillman, Dolf. *Emotional arousal as a factor in communication-mediated aggressive behavior.* (Dissertation—University of Pennsylvania.) Ann Arbor, MI: University Microfilms, 1969. (Order #70-16, 232)

CONSUMERS

3947 Karp, David A. "Hiding in pornographic bookstores: a reconsideration of the nature of urban anonymity." *Urban Life and Culture* 1(4):427–451, Jan. 1973.

3948 _____. *Public sexuality and hiding behavior: a study of the Times Square sexual community.* (Dissertation—New York University.) Ann Arbor, MI: University Microfilms, 1971. (Order #72-13,374)

3949 Lewittes, Don J. and William L. Simmons. "Impression management of sexually motivated behavior." *Journal of Social Psychology* 96:39–44, 1975.

3950 Nawy, Harold. "In the pursuit of happiness?: Consumers of erotica in San Francisco." *Journal of Social Issues* 29(3):147–161, 1973.

3951 Siebenand, Paul Alcuin. *The beginnings of gay cinema in Los Angeles: the industry and the audience.* (Dissertation—University of Southern California.) Ann Arbor, MI: University Microfilms, 1975. (Order #76-5257)

3952 Sonenschein, David. "Dynamics in the uses of erotica." *Adolescence* 7(26):233–244, Summer 1972.

3953 Zellinger, David A. et al. "A commodity theory analysis of the effects of age restrictions upon pornographic materials." *Journal of Applied Psychology* 60(1):94–99, 1975.

INDUSTRY

3954 Brady, John. "Nude journalism." *Journal of Popular Culture* 9:153–161, Summer 1975.

3955 Csicsery, George Paul, ed. *The Sex Industry.* New York: New American Library, 1973.

3956 Hamalian, Leo. "Nobody knows my names: Samuel Roth and the underside of modern letters." *Journal of Modern Literature* 3:889–921, Apr. 1974.

3957 Morthland, John. "Porn films—an in-depth report." *Take One* 4(4):11–17, Mar./Apr. 1973.

3958 Schindler, Gordon, ed. *A Report on Denmark's Legalized Pornography.* Torrence, CA: Banner, 1969.

3959 See, Carolyn. *Blue Money: Pornography and the Pornographers—An Intimate Look at the Two-Billion-Dollar Fantasy Industry.* New York: David McKay, 1974.

3960 Slade, Joseph W. "Recent trends in pornographic films." *Society*:77–84, Sept./Oct. 1975.

3961 Waring, E.M. and J.J. Jeffries. "The conscience of a pornographer." *Journal of Sex Research* 10(1):40–46, Feb. 1974.

CENSORSHIP: DISCUSSION, HISTORY, AND RESEARCH

3962 Boyer, Paul S. *Purity in Print; the Vice-Society Movement and Book Censorship in America.* New York: Scribner, 1968.

3963 Busha, Charles H., ed. *An Intellectual Freedom Primer.* Littleton, CO: Libraries Unlimited, 1977.

3964 Carmen, Ira H. *Movies, Censorship, and the Law.* Ann Arbor: University of Michigan Press, 1966.

3965 Cline, Victor B., ed. *Where Do You Draw the*

Line?: An Exploration into Media Violence, Pornography, and Censorship. Provo, UT: Brigham Young University Press, 1974.

3966 Clor, Harry M. *Obscenity and Public Morality; Censorship in a Liberal Society.* Chicago: University of Chicago Press, 1969.

3967 Clor, Harry M. and Richard F. Hettlinger. "Debate: should there be censorship of pornography?" *Sexual Behavior* 1(9):66–73, Dec. 1971.

3968 Daily, Jay E. *The Anatomy of Censorship.* New York: M. Dekker, 1973.

3969 Downs, Robert Bingham, ed. *The First Freedom; Liberty and Justice in the World of Books and Reading.* Chicago: American Library Association, 1960.

3970 Ernst, Morris Leopold and Alan U. Schwartz. *Censorship: The Search for the Obscene.* New York: Macmillan, 1964.

3971 Facey, Paul W. *The Legion of Decency: a sociological analysis of the emergence and development of a social pressure group.* (Dissertation—Fordham University, 1945.) New York: Arno Press Dissertations on Film Series, 1974.

3972 Gallagher, Neil. *How to Stop the Porno Plague.* Minneapolis: Bethany Fellowship, 1977.

3973 Holbrook, David, ed. *The Case against Pornography.* LaSalle, IL: Library Press, 1972.

3974 Hughes, Douglas A., ed. *Perspectives on Pornography.* New York: St. Martin's Press, 1970.

3975 Hutchison, Earl Ray, Sr. *Henry Miller and Tropic of Cancer, from Paris to Wisconsin—on the censorship trail.* (Dissertation—University of Wisconsin.) Ann Arbor, MI: University Microfilms, 1966. (Order #67-9005)

3976 Kilpatrick, James Jackson. *The Smut Peddlers.* Garden City, NY: Doubleday, 1960.

3977 Kuh, Richard H. *Foolish Figleaves! Pornography In and Out of Court.* New York: Macmillan, 1967.

3978 Leach, Michael. *I Know It When I See It: Pornography, Violence, and Public Sensitivity.* Philadelphia: Westminster, 1975.

3979 Lewis, Felice Flanery. *Literature, Obscenity, & Law.* Carbondale, IL: Southern Illinois University Press, 1976.

3980 Loth, David. *The Erotic in Literature; A Historical Survey of Pornography as Delightful as It Is Indiscreet.* New York: Julian Messner, 1961.

3981 McCoy, Ralph E. *Freedom of the Press; An Annotated Bibliography.* Carbondale, IL: Southern Illinois University Press, 1968.

3982 Norwick, Kenneth P. *Lobbying for Freedom: A Citizen's Guide to Fighting Censorship at the State Level.* New York: St. Martin's Press, 1975.

3983 Oboler, Eli M. *The Fear of the Word: Censorship and Sex.* Metuchen, NJ: Scarecrow Press, 1974.

3984 Pope, Michael. *Sex and the Undecided Librarian: A Study of Librarians' Opinions on Sexually Oriented Literature.* Metuchen, NJ: Scarecrow Press, 1974.

3985 Rist, Ray C., ed. *The Pornography Controversy: Changing Moral Standards in American Life.* New Brunswick, NJ: Transaction, 1975.

3986 Rodgers, Harrell R. "Censorship campaigns in eighteen cities." *American Politics Quarterly* 2(4):371–392, Oct. 1974.

3987 Somerville, Don Smith. *A study of local regulations and group actions on the circulation of newsstand publications.* (Dissertation—University of Illinois.) Ann Arbor, MI: University Microfilms, 1956. (Order #18,199)

3988 Tribe, David. *Questions of Censorship.* New York: St. Martin's Press, 1973.

3989 Zurcher, Louis A. and R. George Kirkpatrick. *Citizens for Decency: Antipornography Crusades as Status Defense.* Austin: University of Texas Press, 1976.

LEGAL ASPECTS OF OBSCENITY

3990 Barnett, Walter. "Corruption of morals: the underlying issue of the Pornography Commission Report." *Law and the Social Order* (2):189–243, 1971.

3991 Bosmajian, Haig A., ed. *Obscenity and Freedom of Expression.* New York: Burt Franklin, 1976.

3992 Cairns, Robert B., James C.N. Paul and Julius Wishner. "Sex censorship: the assumptions of anti-obscenity laws and the empirical evidence." *Minnesota Law Review* 46(6):1009–1042, May 1962.

3993 Carmen, Ira Harris. *State and local motion picture censorship and constitutional liberties with special emphasis on the communal acceptance of Supreme Court decision-making.* (Dissertation—University of Michigan.) Ann Arbor, MI: University Microfilms, 1964. (Order #65-5280)

3994   De Grazia, Edward. *Censorship Landmarks.* New York: R.R. Bowker, 1969.

3995   Fox, Richard G. "Obscenity." *Alberta Law Review* 12(2):172–235, 1974.

3996   Friedman, Leon, ed. *Obscenity; the Complete Oral Arguments before the Supreme Court in the Major Obscenity Cases.* New York: Chelsea House Publishers, 1970.

3997   Hunsaker, David M. "The 1973 obscenity-pornography decisions: analysis, impact, and legislative alternatives." *San Diego Law Review* 11:906–956, 1974.

3998   Jeffries, John Allison. *Legal censorship of obscene publications: search for a censoring standard.* (Dissertation—Indiana University.) Ann Arbor, MI: University Microfilms, 1968. (Order #69-7690)

3999   Kim, Chin. "Constitution and obscenity: Japan and the U.S.A." *American Journal of Comparative Law* 23:255–283, Spring 1975.

4000   Kronhausen, Eberhard and Phyllis Kronhausen. *Pornography and the Law; the Psychology of Erotic Realism and Pornography.* 2nd ed. New York: Ballantine, 1964.

4001   Lipton, Morris A. "Pornography." In: *The Sexual Experience,* ed. by B.J. Sadock, H.I. Kaplan and A.M. Freedman, pp. 584–593. Baltimore: Williams & Wilkins, 1976.

4002   Lockhart, William B. and Robert C. McClure. "Literature, the law of obscenity, and the constitution." *Minnesota Law Review* 38(4):295–395, Mar. 1954.

4003   Neef, Marian and Stuart Nagel. "Judicial behavior in pornography cases." *Journal of Urban Law* 52(1):1–23, Aug. 1964.

4004   Norwick, Kenneth P. *Pornography: the Issues and the Law.* Public Affairs Pamphlet, no. 477. New York: Public Affairs Committee, 1972.

4005   Pilpel, Harriet F. "Obscenity and the Constitution; the good and bad news about the latest Supreme Court ruling—and some suggestions for publishers to take to courthouse or statehouse." *Publishers Weekly* 204:24–27, Dec. 10, 1973.

4006   Reed, John P. and Robin S. Reed. "Consensus and dissensus in pornography definitions: a content analysis." *International Behavioural Scientist* 5(3):1–12, Sept. 1973.

4007   Richards, David A.J. "Free speech and obscenity law: toward a moral theory of the first amendment." *University of Pennsylvania Law Review* 123(1):45–91, Nov. 1974.

4008   Schauer, Frederick F. *The Law of Obscenity.* Washington, DC: Bureau of National Affairs, 1976.

4009   Shugrue, Richard E. and Patricia Zieg. "An atlas for obscenity: exploring community standards." *Creighton Law Review* 7(2):157–181, 1973/1974.

4010   Stevens, Kenneth R. "United States v. 31 photographs: Dr. Alfred Kinsey and obscenity law." *Indiana Magazine of History* 71(4):299–318, Dec. 1975.

4011   Sunderland, Lane V. *The Court, the Congress and the President's Commission.* Domestic Affairs Study 27. Washington, DC: American Enterprise Institute for Public Policy Research, 1975.

OTHER SOURCES OF INFORMATION

American Civil Liberties Union
22 E. 40th St., New York, NY 10016
(publish *Civil Liberties*)

First Amendment Lawyers Association
1737 Chestnut St., Suite 1200, Philadelphia, PA 19103

American Library Association
Office for Intellectual Freedom
50 E. Huron St., Chicago, IL 60611
(publish *Newsletter on Intellectual Freedom*)

Morality in Media
487 Park Ave., New York, NY 10022
(publish *MM Newsletter*)

Sex In The Arts

4012   Brusendorff, Ove and Poul Henningsen. *A History of Eroticism.* 6 vols. New York: Lyle Stuart, 1963–1966.

4013   *Erotic Art of China: A Unique Collection of Chinese Prints and Poems Devoted to the Art of Love.* New York: Crown, 1977.

4014   Gagnon, John H. "Erotic environment." In: *Human Sexualities,* pp. 341–363. Glenview, IL: Scott, Foresman, 1977.

4015   Ginzburg, Ralph. *An Unhurried View of Erotica.* New York: Helmsman Press, 1958.

4016 Klaf, Franklin S. and Bernhardt J. Hurwood. *A Psychiatrist Looks at Erotica.* New York: Ace Books, 1964.

4017 Laemmel, Klaus. "Sex and the arts." In: *The Sexual Experience,* ed. by Alfred M. Freedman, Harold I. Kaplan and Benjamin J. Sadock, pp. 527–566. Baltimore: Williams & Wilkins, 1976.

4018 Lesoualc'h, Theo. *Érotique du Japon.* Bibliothèque Internationale d'Érotologie, no. 19. Paris: J.J. Pauvert, 1968.

4019 Lo Duca, Giuseppe. *Histoire de l'Érotisme.* Paris: J.J. Pauvert, 1959.

4020 McDermott, John Francis and Kendall B. Taft. *Sex in the Arts; A Symposium.* New York/London: Harper, 1932.

4021 Peckham, Morse. *Art and Pornography: an Experiment in Explanation.* Institute for Sex Research Studies in Sex and Society, no. 2. New York: Basic Books, 1969.

4022 Surieu, Robert. *Sarv-é Naz; an Essay on Love and the Representation of Erotic Themes in Ancient Iran.* Geneva: Nagel, 1967.

4023 Webb, Peter. *The Erotic Arts.* London: Secker & Warburg, 1975.

SEX IN ART

4024 Amaya, Mario. "Flesh and filigree." *Artnews* 68(8):24 passim, Dec. 1969.

4025 Anand, Mulk Raj. *Kama Kala; Some Notes on the Philosophical Basis of Hindu Erotic Sculpture.* Geneva: Nagel, 1958.

4026 Benayoun, Robert. *Érotique du Surréalisme.* Bibliothèque Internationale d'Érotologie, no. 14. Paris: J.J. Pauvert, 1965.

4027 Beurdeley, Michel and Kristofer Schipper. *Chinese Erotic Art.* Rutland, VT: Tuttle, 1969.

4028 Bowie, Theodore et al. *Studies in Erotic Art.* Institute for Sex Research Studies in Sex and Society, no. 3. New York: Basic Books, 1970.

4029 Burland, Cottie. *Erotic Antiques or Love is an Antic Thing.* Galashiels, Scotland: Lyle, 1974.

4030 Estren, Mark James. *A History of Underground Comics.* San Francisco: Straight Arrow, 1974.

4031 Evans, Tom and Mary Anne Evans. *Shunga: The Art of Love in Japan.* New York: Paddington, 1975.

4032 Feininger, Andreas and J. Bon. *Maids, Madonnas & Witches; Women in Sculpture from Prehistoric Times to Picasso.* Trans. by Joan Bradley. New York: Abrams, 1961.

4033 Flegon, A. *Eroticism in Russian Art.* London: Flegon, 1976.

4034 Fuchs, Eduard. *Geschichte der Erotischen Kunst.* 3 vols. Munchen: A. Langen, 1922–26.

4035 Gauthier, Xavière. *Surréalisme et Sexualité.* Paris: Gallimard, 1971.

4036 Gerdts, William H. *The Great American Nude: A History in Art.* New York: Praeger, 1974.

4037 Gip, Bernard. *Les Passions de la Grande Catherine.* Paris: L'Or du Temps, 1970.

4038 Grant, Michael and Antonia Mulas. *Eros in Pompeii: The Secret Rooms of the National Museum of Naples.* New York: Morrow, 1975.

4039 Grosbois, Charles. *Shunga; Images of Spring; Essay on Erotic Elements in Japanese Art.* Geneva: Nagel, 1964.

4040 Hess, Thomas B. and Linda Nochlin. *Woman as Sex Object: Studies in Erotic Art, 1730–1970.* New York: Newsweek, 1972.

4041 Kahmen, Volker. *Erotic Art Today.* Greenwich, CT: New York Graphic Society, 1971.

4042 Kronhausen, Phyllis and Eberhard Kronhausen. *Erotic Art; a Survey of Erotic Fact and Fancy in the Fine Arts.* New York: Grove Press, 1969.

4043 _____. *Erotic Art 2.* New York: Grove Press, 1970.

4044 _____. *Erotische Exlibris.* Hamburg: Gala Verlag, 1970.

4045 Lal, Kanwar. *The Cult of Desire.* New Hyde Park, NY: University Books, 1967.

4046 Larco Hoyle, Rafael. *Checan; Essay on Erotic Elements in Peruvian Art.* Geneva: Nagel, 1965.

4047 Levine, Nancy Bruning, ed. *Hardcore Crafts.* New York: Ballantine, 1976.

4048 Lucie-Smith, Edward. *Eroticism in Western Art.* New York: Praeger, 1972.

4049 Marcadé, Jean. *Eros Kalos; Essay on Erotic Elements in Greek Art.* Geneva: Nagel, 1962.

4050 _____. *Roma Amor; Essay on Erotic Elements in Etruscan and Roman Art.* Geneva: Nagel, 1961.

4051 Melville, Robert and Simon Wilson. *Erotic Art of the West; with a Short History of Western Erotic Art.* New York: Putnam, 1973.

4052 Ouellette, William and Barbara Jones. *Erotic Postcards.* New York: Excalibur, 1977.

4053 Rawson, Philip. *The Art of Tantra.* Greenwich, CT: New York Graphic Society, 1973.

4054 _____. *Erotic Art of the East; The Sexual Theme in Oriental Painting and Sculpture.* New York: Putnam, 1968.

4055 _____, ed. *Primitive Erotic Art.* New York: Putnam, 1973.

4056 Smith, Bradley. *Erotic Art of the Masters; the 18th, 19th, & 20th Centuries.* Secaucus, NJ: Lyle Stuart, 1974.

4057 Villeneuve, Roland. *Le Diable; Érotologie de Satan.* Bibliothèque Internationale d'Érotologie, no. 10. Paris: J.J. Pauvert, 1963.

4058 _____. *Fétichisme et Amour.* Paris: Éditions Azur/Claude Offenstadt, 1968.

4059 _____. *Le Musée de la Bestialité.* Paris: Éditions Azur/Claude Offenstadt, 1969.

4060 Vorberg, Gaston. *Ars Erotica Veterum: Ein Beitrag zum Geschlechtsleben des Altertums.* Stuttgart: J. Püttmann, 1926.

4061 Waas, Emil. *Erotische Graphik von der Antike bis Heute.* Bonn: Verlag der Europäischen Bücherei, H.M. Hieronimi, 1966.

4062 Witkowski, Gustave Joseph. *L'Art Profane à l'Église, Ses Licences Symboliques, Satiriques et Fantaisistes.* Paris: J. Schemit, 1908.

SEX IN LITERATURE BIBLIOGRAPHIES

4063 Deakin, Terence J. *Catalogi Librorum Eroticorum; a Critical Bibliography of Erotic Bibliographies and Book-Catalogues.* London: Cecil & Amelia Woolf, 1964.

4064 Dixon, Rebecca. "Bibliographical control of erotica." In: *An Intellectual Freedom Primer,* ed. by Charles H. Busha. Littleton, CO: Libraries Unlimited, 1977.

4065 Parker, William. *Homosexuality: A Selective Bibliography of over 3,000 Items.* Metuchen, NJ: Scarecrow Press, 1971. (*Supplement, 1970-1975.* Scarecrow Press, 1977.)

4066 Reisner, Robert George. *Show Me the Good Parts; the Reader's Guide to Sex in Literature.* New York: Citadel Press, 1964.

SEX IN LITERATURE

4067 Atkins, John. *Sex in Literature.* London: Calder & Boyars, 1970.

4068 Blei, Franz. *Formen der Liebe.* Berlin/Wien: Trianon, 1930.

4069 Bunce, Fredrick W. *The parallel forms of erotic painting and poetry in the 16th century French court.* (Doctoral dissertation—Ohio University.) Ann Arbor, MI: University Microfilms, 1974. (Order #74-7633)

4070 Burnham, John. "American historians and the subject of sex." *Societas* 2(4):307–316, Fall 1972.

4071 Calverton, V.F. *Sex Expression in Literature.* New York: Boni & Liveright, 1926.

4072 De, Sushil Kumar. *Ancient Indian Erotics and Erotic Literature.* Calcutta: Firma K.L. Mukhopadhyay, 1959.

4073 Englisch, Paul. *Geschichte der Erotischen Literatur.* 2nd ed. Stuttgart: J. Püttmann, 1932.

4074 "Eros and literature." *Mosaic; a Journal for the Comparative Study of Literature and Ideas* 1(2):whole issue, Jan. 1968.

4075 Foster, Jeannette Howard. *Sex Variant Women in Literature; a Historical and Quantitative Survey.* 1956. Reprint. Baltimore: Diana Press, 1975.

4076 Foxon, David F. *Libertine Literature in England, 1660-1745.* New Hyde Park, NY: University Books, 1966.

4077 Frantz, David O. " 'Lewd priapians' and Renaissance pornography." *Studies in English Literature* 12(1):157–172, Winter 1972.

4078 Glicksberg, Charles I. *The Sexual Revolution in Modern American Literature.* The Hague: Nijhoff, 1971.

4079 Goldfarb, Russell M. *Sexual Repression and Victorian Literature.* Lewisburg, PA: Bucknell University Press, 1970.

4080 Haworth, H.E. " 'The virtuous romantics'—indecency, indelicacy, pornography and obscenity in Romantic poetry." *Papers on Language and Literature* 10:287–306, Summer 1974.

4081 Henderson, Jeffrey. *The Maculate Muse: Obscene Language in Attic Comedy.* New Haven/London: Yale University Press, 1975.

4082 Humana, Charles and Wang Wu. *The Ying-Yang.* London: Tandem, 1971.

4083 Hurwood, Bernhardt J. *The Golden Age of Erotica.* Los Angeles: Sherbourne Press, 1965.

4084 Hyde, Harford Montgomery. *A History of Pornography.* New York: Farrar, Straus & Giroux, 1965.

4085 Ivker, Barry. *An Anthology and Analysis of 17th and 18th Century French Libertine Fiction.* Monograph Publishing on Demand: Sponsor Series. Institute for Sex Research Studies in Sex and Society, no. 5. Ann Arbor, MI: University Microfilms, 1977.

4086 _____. *Sexual perversion in eighteenth-century English and French fiction.* (Doctoral dissertation—Indiana University.) Ann Arbor, MI: University Microfilms, 1968. (Order #68-15,443)

4087 Kiell, Norman. *Varieties of Sexual Experience: Psychosexuality in Literature.* New York: International Universities, 1976.

4088 Kronhausen, Phyllis and Eberhard Kronhausen. *Erotic Fantasies; a Study of the Sexual Imagination.* New York: Grove Press, 1970.

4089 Kunkel, Francis Leo. *Passion and the Passion: Sex and Religion in Modern Literature.* Philadelphia: Westminster, 1975.

4090 Legman, Gershon. *The Horn Book; Studies in Erotic Folklore and Bibliography.* New Hyde Park, NY: University Books, 1964.

4091 Marchand, Henry L. *The French Pornographers.* New York: Book Awards, 1965.

4092 Marcus, Steven. *The Other Victorians; a Study of Sexuality and Pornography in Mid-Nineteenth-Century England.* Institute for Sex Research Studies in Sex and Society, no. 1. New York: Basic Books, 1966.

4093 Michelson, Peter. *The Aesthetics of Pornography.* New York: Herder & Herder, 1971.

4094 Moravia, Alberto. "Eroticism in literature." In: *Perspectives on Pornography,* ed. by Douglas A. Hughes, pp. 1–3. New York: St. Martin's Press, 1970.

4095 Mordell, Albert. *The Erotic Motive in Literature.* 1919. Reprint. New York: Octagon Books, 1976.

4096 Perkins, Michael. *The Secret Record: Modern Erotic Literature.* New York: Morrow, 1976.

4097 Praz, Mario. *The Romantic Agony.* Trans. from the Italian by Angus Davidson. 2nd ed. London: Geoffrey Cumberlege, Oxford University Press, 1951.

4098 Purdy, Strother. "On the psychology of erotic literature." In: *Modern Views of Human Sexual Behavior,* ed. by J. McCary and D. Copeland, pp. 346–352. Chicago: Science Research Associates, 1976.

4099 Saba Sardi, Francesco. *Sesso e Mito; Storia e Testi della Letteratura Erotica.* Milano: Sugar Editore, 1960.

4100 Sisk, John P. "The promise of dirty words." *American Scholar* 44:385–404, Summer 1975.

4101 Sontag, Susan. "The pornographic imagination." In: *Perspectives on Pornography,* ed. by Douglas A. Hughes, pp. 131–169. New York: St. Martin's Press, 1970.

4102 Stern, Bernhard. *Illustrierte Geschichte der Erotischen Literatur aller Zeiten und Völker.* Vienna: Privatdruck des Verlages C.W. Stern, 1908.

4103 Waldemar, Charles. *Spielarten der Liebe; Erotische Elemente in Modernen Roman.* Flensburg: C. Stephenson, 1961.

4104 Waldrop, Bernard Keith. *Aesthetic uses of obscenity in literature.* (Doctoral dissertation—University of Michigan.) Ann Arbor, MI: University Microfilms, 1964. (Order #65-5954)

4105 Waniek, Marilyn Nelson. "The space where sex should be: towards a definition of the Black American literary tradition." *Studies in Black Literature* 6:7–13, Fall 1975.

4106 Wedeck, Harry E. *Dictionary of Erotic Literature.* New York: Philosophical Library, 1962.

4107 Young, Wayland. *Eros Denied; Sex in Western Society.* New York: Grove Press, 1964.

SEX IN CINEMA

4108 Atkins, Thomas R., ed. *Sexuality in the Movies.* Bloomington, IN: Indiana University Press, 1975.

4109 Coulteray, Georges de. *Le Sadisme au Cinéma.* Paris: Le Terrain Vague, 1964.

4110 Evans, Walter. "Monster movies: a sexual theory." *Journal of Popular Film* 2:353–365, Fall 1965.

4111 Farber, Stephen. "Images of adolescence." *Sexual Behavior* 2(8):9–15, Aug. 1972.

4112 _____. "Sex in contemporary movies: the new Puritanism." *Sexual Behavior* 1(9):17–23, Dec. 1971.

4113   Geduld, Harry. "I, a curious moviegoer: some reflections on eroticism in the movies." *Humanist* 30:40, May/June 1970.

4114   Haskell, Molly. *From Reverence to Rape; the Treatment of Women in the Movies.* New York: Holt, Rinehart & Winston, 1974.

4115   Hoffman, Frank A. "Prolegomena to a study of traditional elements in the erotic film." *Journal of American Folklore* 78(308):143–148, Apr./June 1965.

4116   Jones, G. William. "Eroticism and the art of film." *Library Journal* 96(20):3809–3810, Nov. 15, 1971.

4117   Knight, Arthur. "Sex in cinema." *Playboy* 16(11), Nov. 1969 (annually in the Nov. issue)–24(11), Nov. 1977. (1969–1972 articles were co-authored with Hollis Alpert.)

4118   Knight, Arthur and Hollis Alpert. "The history of sex in cinema." *Playboy* 12(4), Apr. 1965 (20 articles in scattered issues)–16(1), Jan. 1969.

4119   Kyrou, Ado. *Amour Érotisme et Cinéma.* Paris: Le Terrain Vague, 1957.

4120   Lo Duca, Giuseppe. *L'Érotisme au Cinéma.* 3 vols. Paris: J.J. Pauvert, 1957–62. (*Supplément,* 1968).

4121   Mellen, Joan. "Lesbianism in the movies." *Sexual Behavior* 2(5):36–44, May 1972.

4122   _____. *Women and Their Sexuality in the New Film.* New York: Horizon Press, 1973.

4123   Phillips, Gene D. "Homosexuality in the movies." *Sexual Behavior* 1(2):18 passim, May 1971.

4124   Tyler, Parker. *A Pictorial History of Sex in Films.* Secaucus, NJ: Citadel Press, 1974.

4125   _____. *Screening the Sexes; Homosexuality in the Movies.* New York: Holt, Rinehart & Winston, 1972.

4126   Walker, Alexander. *The Celluloid Sacrifice: Aspects of Sex in the Movies.* London: Joseph, 1966.

4127   Wead, George. "Sex and the silent comedian." *Sexual Behavior* 2(12):10–16, Dec. 1972.

4128   Weightman, John. "Modalities of sex." *Encounter* 38:32–35, Mar. 1972.

4129   Wortley, Richard. *Erotic Movies.* New York: Crescent, 1975.

SEX IN THEATER

4130   DeStrulle, Arlene. "Sexual fantasy theatre." *Drama Review* 20:64–74, Mar. 1976.

4131   Durandeau, André. "Théâtre érotique." *Cahiers de Sexologie Clinique* 2(1):99–103, 1976.

4132   Elsom, John. *Erotic Theatre.* New York: Taplinger, 1973.

4133   "Homosexuality in the theatre." *Canadian Theatre Review* 12:6–41, Fall 1976.

4134   Peake, Richard Henry. *The stage prostitute in the English dramatic tradition from 1558 to 1625.* (Doctoral dissertation—University of Georgia.) Ann Arbor, MI: University Microfilms, 1966. (Order #67-3580)

4135   Rabenalt, Arthur Maria. *Mimus Eroticus.* 5 vols. Hamburg: Verlag fur Kulturforschung, 1965–1967.

4136   Weightman, John. "Centre 69?" *Encounter* 37:27–29, Oct. 1971.

SEX IN PHOTOGRAPHS

4137   Aratow, Paul. *100 Years of Erotica: A Photographic Portfolio of Mainstream American Subculture from 1845–1945.* San Francisco: Straight Arrow, 1973.

4138   Gabor, Mark. *The Pin-Up: A Modest History.* New York: Universal Books, 1972.

4139   Jay, Bill. "The erotic dawn of photography." *Image* 1(4):40–46, 1972.

4140   Lacey, Peter. *The History of the Nude in Photography.* New York: Bantam Books, 1964.

4141   Ovenden, Graham and Peter Mendes. *Victorian Erotic Photography.* New York/London: St. Martin's Press/Academy, 1973.

4142   Seufert, Reinhard. *The Porno-Photographia.* Los Angeles: Argyle, 1968.

4143   Stoctay, G.G. *America's Erotic Past: 1868–1940.* San Diego: Greenleaf Classics, 1973.

SEX IN MUSIC AND DANCE

4144   Berger, Morroe and La Meri. *A Curious and Wonderful Gymnastic.* Brooklyn: Dance Perspectives, 1961.

4145   Carey, James T. "Changing courtship patterns in the popular song." *American Journal of Sociology* 74(6):720–731, May 1969.

4146 Cray, Ed. *The Erotic Muse.* New York: Oak Publications, 1969.

4147 Damase, Jacques. *Les Folies du Music-Hall; Histoire du Music-Hall à Paris de 1914 à Nos Jours.* Paris: Éditions "Spectacles," 1960.

4148 Goldberg, Herb. "Rock music and sex." *Sexual Behavior* 1(5):25–31, Aug. 1971.

4149 Howard, Walter and Irongard Auras. *Musique et Sexualité.* Bibliothèque Internationale de Musicologie. Paris: Presses Universitaires de France, 1957.

4150 Leaf, Earl. *Isles of Rhythm.* New York: A.S. Barnes, 1948.

4151 MacDougal, Duncan. "Music and sex." In: *Encyclopedia of Sexual Behavior* 2nd ed., ed. by Albert Ellis and Albert Abarbanel, pp. 746–756. New York: Hawthorn Books, 1967.

4152 Winick, Charles. "Popular music and sex." *Medical Aspects of Human Sexuality* 4(10):148–157, Oct. 1970.

4153 _____. "Sex and dancing." *Medical Aspects of Human Sexuality* 4(9):122–132, Sept. 1970.

4154 Wortley, Richard. *A Pictorial History of Striptease; 100 Years of Undressing to Music.* Secaucus, NJ: Chartwell Books, 1976.

Research

Sex Research Methodology

4155 Back, Kurt W. and J.M. Stycos. *The Survey under Unusual Conditions.* Society for Applied Anthropology Monograph, no. 1. Ithaca, NY: Cornell University, 1959.

4156 Barker, William J. and D. Perlman. "Volunteer bias and personality traits in sexual standards research." *Archives of Sexual Behavior* 4(2):161–172, Mar. 1975.

4157 Caird, William and John P. Wincze. "Assessment of sexual dysfunction, male and female." In: *Sex Therapy: A Behavioral Approach,* pp. 48–72. Hagerstown, MD: Harper & Row, 1977.

4158 Clark, Alexander L. and Paul Wallin. "The accuracy of husbands' and wives' reports of the frequency of marital coitus." *Population Studies* 18(2):165–173, Nov. 1964.

4159 Cogswell, Betty E. "Communication with adolescents; a study of sex information sessions." *Sociological Symposium* 6:1–17, Spring 1971.

4160 Cogswell, Betty E. and Jane Schoultz. "Say it your own way — tell it like it is: new data collection strategies." *Research Preview* 17(2):6–10, Nov. 1970.

4161 Diamant, Louis. "Attitude, personality, and behavior in volunteers and nonvolunteers for sexual research." *Proceedings of the Annual Convention of the APA* 5(pt. 1):423–424, 1970.

4162 Engel, James F. and Hugh G. Whales. "Spoken versus pictured questions on taboo topics." *Journal of Advertising Research* 2(1):11–17, Mar. 1962.

4163 Gebhard, Paul H. "Securing sensitive personal information by interviews." In: *Selections from the Fifth and Sixth National Colloquia on Oral History,* ed. by P. Olch and F. Pogue, pp. 63–79. New York: Oral History Association, 1972.

4164 Geer, James H. "Genital measures: comments on their role in understanding human sexuality." *Journal of Sex and Marital Therapy* 2(3):165–172, Fall 1976.

4165 Hampe, Gary D. and Howard J. Ruppel, Jr. "The measurement of premarital sexual permissiveness: a comparison of two Guttman scales," and "Rejoin(d)er" by Harold T. Christensen. *Journal of Marriage and the Family* 36(3):451–468, Aug. 1974.

4166 Higginbotham, Howard N. and Gary M. Farkas. "Basic and applied research in human sexuality: current limitations and future directions in sex therapy." In: *Handbook of Behavior Therapy with Sexual Problems,* ed. by Joel Fisher and

Harvey L. Gochros, pp. 223–250. New York: Pergamon Press, 1977.

4167 James, William H. "The reliability of the reporting of coital frequency." *Journal of Sex Research* 7(4):312–314, Nov. 1971.

4168 Johnson, Weldon T. and J.D. Delamater. "Response effects in sex surveys." *The Public Opinion Quarterly* 40:165–181, Summer 1976.

4169 Kaats, Gilbert R. and Keith E. Davis. "Effects of volunteer biases in studies of sexual behavior and attitudes." *Journal of Sex Research* 7(1):26–34, Feb. 1971.

4170 Kinsey, Alfred C. et al. *Sexual Behavior in the Human Male.* Philadelphia: W.B. Saunders, 1948. (Chapters 2–3.)

4171 Knudsen, Dean D., H. Pope and D.P. Irish. "Response differences to questions on sexual standards: an interview-questionnaire comparison." *The Public Opinion Quarterly* 31(290–297), Summer 1967.

4172 Mehan, Hugh and Houston Wood. *The Reality of Ethnomethodology.* New York: Wiley, 1975.

4173 Robinson, John P. and Phillip R. Shaver. *Measures of Social Psychological Attitudes.* rev. ed. Ann Arbor: University of Michigan, Institute for Social Research, 1973.

4174 Rokeach, Milton. *Beliefs, Attitudes, and Values: A Theory of Organization and Change.* San Francisco: Jossey-Bass, 1976.

4175 Sagarin, Edward. "Typologies of sexual behavior." *Journal of Sex Research* 7(4):282–288, Nov. 1971.

4176 Shaw, Marvin E. and J.M. Wright. *Scales for the Measurement of Attitudes.* New York: McGraw-Hill, 1967.

4177 Straus, Murray A. *Family Measurement Techniques: Abstracts of Published Instruments 1935-1965.* Minneapolis: University of Minnesota Press, 1969.

4178 Udry, J. Richard and Naomi M. Morris. "A method for validation of reported sexual data." *Journal of Marriage and the Family* 29(3):442–446, Aug. 1967.

4179 U.S. National Institute of Mental Health. Conference on Methodologic Issues in Sex Research. *Papers.* Rockville, MD, Nov. 17–19, 1977. (Publication projected by the U.S. Government Printing Office.)

4180 Weinberg, Martin S. "Homosexual samples: differences and similarities." *Journal of Sex Research* 6(4):312–325, Nov. 1970.

4181 Weinberg, Martin S. and Colin Williams. "Fieldwork among deviants: Social relations with subjects and others." In: *Research on Deviance,* ed. by Jack D. Douglas, pp. 163–186. New York: Random House, 1972.

PUBLISHED QUESTIONNAIRES AND INTERVIEW SCHEDULES

DATING

4182 Bardis, Panos D. "A Dating Scale; a technique for the quantitative measurement of liberalism concerning selected aspects of dating." *Social Science* 37(1):44–47, Jan. 1962.

4183 Ehrmann, Winston. *Premarital Dating Behavior.* New York: Henry Holt, 1959.

4184 Herold, Edward S. "A dating adjustment scale for college students." *Adolescence* 8(29):51–60, Spring 1973.

LOVE

4185 Rubin, Zick. "Measurement of romantic love." *Journal of Personality and Social Psychology* 16(2):265–273, Oct. 1970.

SELF/BODY IMAGE

4186 Berscheid, Ellen, Elaine Walster and George Bohrnstedt. "Body image: the happy American body: a survey report." *Psychology Today* 7(6):119–131, Nov. 1973.

4187 Kurtz, Richard M. "Body attitude and physical health." *Journal of Clinical Psychology* 26(2):149–151, Apr. 1970.

4188 Offer, Daniel. *The Psychological World of the Teen-ager: A Study of Normal Adolescent Boys,* pp. 227–261. New York: Basic Books, 1969.

4189 Olasov, Joseph Tigler. *Bodily experience and sexual responsivity in women.* (Dissertation—University of Tennessee.) Ann Arbor, MI: University Microfilms, 1975. (Order #76-11,076)

4190 Rosenberg, Morris. *Society and the Adolescent Self-Image,* pp. 305–319. Princeton, NJ: Princeton University Press, 1965.

SEX BEHAVIOR AND ATTITUDES (ADOLESCENT)

4191 Reiss, Ira L. *The Social Context of Premari-*

tal Sexual Permissiveness, pp. 183–194. New York: Holt, Rinehart & Winston, 1967.

4192 Schiller, Patricia. "Sex attitude sample inventory for adolescents." In: *Creative Approach to Sex Education and Counseling,* pp. 214–220. New York: Association Press, 1973.

4193 Sorensen, Robert C. "Survey questionnaires: male and female." In: *Adolescent Sexuality in Contemporary America: Personal Values and Sexual Behavior,* pp. 473–549. New York: World Publishing Co., 1972.

4194 Vener, Arthur M. and Cyrus S. Stewart. "Adolescent sexual behavior in Middle America revisited: 1970–1973." *Journal of Marriage and the Family* 36(4):728–735, Nov. 1974.

SEX KNOWLEDGE / ATTITUDE / EXPERIENCE

4195 Eysenck, H.J. *Sex and Personality.* Austin: University of Texas Press, 1976.

4196 Fretz, Bruce R. "Assessing attitudes towards sexual behaviors." *The Counseling Psychologist* 5(1):100–106, 1975.

4197 Harbison, J.J.M. et al. "A questionnaire measure of sexual interest." *Archives of Sexual Behavior* 3(4):357–366, July 1974.

4198 Lief, Harold I. and David M. Reed. *Sex Knowlege and Attitude Test (SKAT)* (1972). (Avail. from Center for the Study of Sex Education in Medicine, University of Pennsylvania, 2025 Chestnut St., Philadelphia, PA 19104.)

4199 McHugh, Gelolo. *The Sex Attitudes Survey and Profile* (1976), The Sex Knowledge Inventory — Form X (1968), *The Sex Knowledge Inventory — Form Y* (1977). (Avail. from Family Life Publications, Box 427, Saluda, NC 28773.)

4200 Reiss, Ira L. *The Social Context of Premarital Sexual Permissiveness,* pp. 183–233. New York: Holt, Rinehart & Winston, 1967.

POPULAR PRESS

4201 Athanasiou, Robert and Robert Shaver. "A research questionnaire on sex." *Psychology Today* 3(2):64–69, July 1969; (Results) 4(2):39–52, July 1970.

4202 Hite, Shere. *The Hite Report: A Nationwide Study on Female Sexuality.* New York: Macmillan, 1976.

4203 Pietropinto, Anthony and Jacqueline Simenauer. *Beyond the Male Myth; What Women Want to Know about Men's Sexuality: A Nationwide Survey.* New York: Times Books, 1977.

4204 Tavris, Carol and Susan Sadd. *The Redbook Report on Female Sexuality.* New York: Delacorte Press, 1977.

WOMEN

4205 Fisher, Seymour. *The Female Orgasm: Psychology, Physiology, Fantasy,* pp. 447–474. New York: Basic Books, 1973.

4206 Hoon, Emily F., P.W. Hoon and J. Wincze. "An inventory for the measurement of female sexual arousability: the SAI." *Archives of Sexual Behavior* 5(4):291–300, July 1976.

4207 Newton, Niles. *Maternal Emotions: A Study of Women's Feelings toward Menstruation, Pregnancy, Childbirth, Breast Feeding, Infant Care, and Other Aspects of Their Femininity,* pp. 105–112. New York: Paul B. Hoeber, 1955.

SCALES

4208 Bentler, Peter M. "Heterosexual behavior assessment. I. Males; II. Females." *Behavior Research and Therapy* 6:21–25, 27–30, 1968.

4209 Brady, John Paul and Eugene E. Levitt. "The scalability of sexual experiences." *The Psychological Record* 15(2):275–279, Apr. 1965.

4210 Christensen, Harold T. and George R. Carpenter. "Value-behavior discrepancies regarding premarital coitus in three western cultures." *American Sociological Review* 27(1):66–74, Feb. 1962.

4211 Freund, Kurt et al. "Extension of the general identity scale for males." *Archives of Sexual Behavior* 6(6):507–519, Nov. 1977.

4212 Joe, Victor C. "A test of the Zuckerman heterosexual scales." *Journal of Personality Assessment* 39(3):271–273, 1975.

4213 Larsen, Knud S. "Premarital sex attitudes—a scale and some validity findings." *Journal of Social Psychology* 90:339–340, Aug. 1973.

4214 Marcotte, David B. and Constance Logan. "Medical sex education: allowing attitude alteration." *Archives of Sexual Behavior* 6(2):155–162, Mar. 1977.

4215 Paitich, D. et al. "The Clarke SHQ: a clinical sex history questionnaire for males." *Archives of Sexual Behavior* 6(5):421–436, Sept. 1977.

4216 Podell, Lawrence and J.C. Perkins. "A Guttman scale for sexual experience: a methodological note." *Journal of Abnormal and Social Psychology* 54(3):420–422, May 1957.

4217 Reiss, Ira L. "The premarital sexual permissiveness scales." In: *The Social Context of Premarital Sexual Permissiveness,* pp. 15–37. New York: Holt, Rinehart & Winston, 1967.

4218 Thorne, Frederick C. "Scales for rating sexual experience." *Journal of Clinical Psychology* 22(4):404–407, 1966.

4219 Zuckerman, Marvin. "Scales for sex experience for males and females." *Journal of Consulting and Clinical Psychology* 41(1):27–29, Aug. 1973.

PSYCHOLOGICAL TESTS

"MMPI"

4220 Beutler, Larry E. et al. "MMPI and MIT discriminators of biogenic and psychogenic impotence." *Journal of Consulting and Clinical Psychology* 43(6):899–903, 1975.

4221 Butcher, James. *MMPI: Research Developments and Clinical Applications.* New York: McGraw-Hill, 1969.

4222 Lanchar, David. *The MMPI: Clinical Assessment & Automated Interpretation.* Los Angeles: Western Psychological Services, 1974.

4223 *Minnesota Multiphasic Personality Inventory.* (Avail. from Psychological Corp., 304 E. 45th St., New York, NY 10017.)

"Thorne Sex Inventory"

4224 Thorne, Frederick C. *The Integration Level Test Series.* (Avail. from Clinical Psychology Publishing Co., 4 Conant Square, Brandon, VT 05733.)

4225 Thorne, Frederick C., Thomas D. Haupt and Robert M. Allen. *Psychological Clinic from the University of Miami: Objective Studies of Adult Male Sexuality Utilizing the Sex Inventory.* Monograph Supplement, no. 21. Brandon, VT: Journal of Clinical Psychology, Oct. 1966.

SEX GUILT

4226 Galbraith, Gary G. "The Mosher sex-guilt scale and the Thorne Sex Inventory: intercorrelations." *Journal of Clinical Psychology* 25(3): 292–294, July 1969.

4227 Mosher, Donald L. "The development and multitrait multimethod matrix analysis of three measures of three aspects of guilt." *Journal of*

Consulting and Clinical Psychology 32(6):690–695, 1968.

MF SCALES

"Review of Major M-F Tests"

4228 Constantinople, Anne. "Masculinity-femininity: an exception to a famous dictum?" *Psychological Bulletin* 80(5):389–407, Nov. 1973.

"Adjective Check List M-F Scale"

4229 Heilbrun, Alfred B. "Measurement of masculine and feminine sex role identities as independent dimensions." *Journal of Consulting and Clinical Psychology* 44(2):183–190, Apr. 1976.

"Bem Sex-Role Inventory"

4230 Bem, Sandra L. "The measurement of psychological androgyny." *Journal of Consulting and Clinical Psychology* 42(2):155–162, Apr. 1974.

4231 Strahan, Robert F. "Remarks on Bem's measurement of psychological androgyny: alternative methods and a supplementary analysis." *Journal of Consulting and Clinical Psychology* 43(4):568–571, Aug. 1975.

" 'CPI' Femininity Scale"

4232 Gough, Harrison G. "A cross-cultural analysis of the CPI femininity scale." *Journal of Consulting Psychology* 30(2):136–141, 1966.

"Sex Role Orientation"

4233 Brogan, Donna and Nancy G. Kutner. "Measuring sex-role orientation: a normative approach." *Journal of Marriage and the Family* 38(1):31–40, Feb. 1976.

"Sex Role Survey"

4234 MacDonald, A.P., Jr. "Identification and measurement of multidimensional attitudes toward equality between the sexes." *Journal of Homosexuality* 1(2):165–182, Winter 1974/1975. (*Sex Role Survey* avail. from the Center for the Study of Human Sexuality, 4105 Medical Pkwy., Suite 205, Austin, TX 78756.)

SEXUAL ORIENTATION

"Sexual Orientation Method"

4235 Feldman, Martin P. and M.J. MacCulloch. *Homosexual Behavior: Therapy and Assessment,* pp. 55–64. New York: Pergamon Press, 1971.

4236 Feldman, Martin P., V. Mellor and J.M. Pinschof. "The application of anticipatory avoidance learning to the treatment of homosexuality:

III. The Sexual Orientation Method." *Behavior Research and Therapy* 4:289–299, 1966.

4237 Sambrooks, Jean E. and M.J. MacCulloch. "A modification of the Sexual Orientation Method and an automated technique for presentation and scoring." *British Journal of Social and Clinical Psychology* 12(2):163–174, June 1973.

4238 Woodward, Roger. "A comparison of two scoring systems for the Sexual Orientation Method." *British Journal of Social and Clinical Psychology* 12(4):411–414, Nov. 1973.

"Kinsey Scale"

4239 Kinsey, Alfred C. et al. *Sexual Behavior in the Human Male,* pp. 636–650. Philadelphia: W.B. Saunders, 1948.

HOMOSEXUALITY QUESTIONNAIRE

4240 Weinberg, Martin S. and Colin J. Williams. *Male Homosexuals: Their Problems and Adaptations,* pp. 293–306. New York: Oxford University Press, 1974.

"Attitudes on Homosexuality"

4241 Blake, Dean Moishe. "Measuring attitude toward homosexuals: a brief scale for educational purposes: a technical manual." Unpub. master's thesis, University of Iowa, 1974.

4242 Brown, Marvin and Donald M. Amoroso. "Attitudes toward homosexuality among West Indian male and female college students." *Journal of Social Psychology* 97(2):163–168, Dec. 1975.

4243 Lumby, Malcolm E. "Homophobia: the quest for a valid scale." *Journal of Homosexuality* 2(1):39–47, Fall 1976.

4244 MacDonald, A.P., Jr. and Richard G. Games. "Some characteristics of those who hold positive and negative attitudes toward homosexuals." *Journal of Homosexuality* 1(1):9–27, Fall 1974. (*Attitudes toward Homosexuality Scales, Forms G (General), M (Male), & L (Female),* avail. from the Center for the Study of Human Sexuality, 4105 Medical Pkwy., Suite 205, Austin, TX 78756.)

OTHER SOURCES OF QUESTIONNAIRES AND INTERVIEW SCHEDULES

Consulting Psychologists Press
577 College Ave., Palo Alto, CA 94306

Enabling Systems
Villa Professional Plaza at Eaton Square, 444 Hobron Lane, Suite 311, Honolulu, HI 96815

Western Psychological Services
12031 Wilshire Blvd., Los Angeles, CA 90025

Family Life Publications
Box 427, Saluda, NC 28773

Psychological Corporation
304 E. 45th St., New York, NY 10017

Ethical Issues in Sex Research

4245 Alexander, Leo. "Limitations in experimental research on human beings." *Lex et Scientia* 3(1):8–24, Jan./Mar. 1966.

4246 _____. "Protection of privacy in behavioral research." *Lex et Scientia* 4(1):34–38, Jan./Mar. 1967.

4247 Barber, Bernard. "Research on research on human subjects: problems of access to a powerful profession." *Social Problems* 21(1):103–112, Summer 1973.

4248 Becker, Howard S. and Irving L. Horowitz. "Radical politics and sociological research: observations of methodology and ideology." *American Journal of Sociology* 78(1):48–66, July 1972.

4249 Bowman, Claude C. "Hidden valuations in the interpretation of sexual and family relationships." *American Sociological Review* 11(5):536–544, Oct. 1946.

4250 Butler, Robert N. "Privileged communication and confidentiality in research." *Archives of General Psychiatry* 8(2):139–141, Feb. 1963.

4251 Davison, Gerald C. "Homosexuality: the ethical challenge." *Journal of Consulting and Clinical Psychology* 44(2):157–162, 1976.

4252 Denzin, Norman K. and Kai T. Erikson. "On the ethics of disguised observation." *Social Problems* 15(4):502–506, Spring 1968.

4253 "Ethical issues." *Archives of Sexual Behavior* 4(4):459–465, July 1975.

4254 Feinbloom, Deborah. "Ethical implications of fieldwork." In: *Transvestites & Transsexuals: Mixed Views,* pp. 255–269. New York: Delacorte Press, 1976.

4255 Galliher, John F. "The protection of human subjects: a reexamination of the professional code of ethics." *American Sociologist* 8(3):93–100, Aug. 1973.

4256 Hendel, Samuel and Robert Bard. "Should

there be a researcher's privilege?" *AAUP Bulletin* 59(4):398–401, Winter 1973.

4257   Hershey, Nathan and Robert D. Miller. *Human Experimentation and the Law.* Germantown, MD: Aspen Systems Corporation, 1976.

4258   Kolodny, Robert C. *(Proceedings of the) Ethics Congress, Jan. 25–27, 1978, sponsored by the Reproductive Biology Research Foundation, St. Louis, MO.* Boston: Little, Brown, 1979 (in press).

4259   Masters, William H., Virginia E. Johnson and Robert C. Kolodny, eds. *Ethical Issues in Sex Therapy and Research.* Boston: Little, Brown, 1977.

4260   Nejelshi, Paul and Kurt Finsterbusch. "The prosecutor and the researcher: present and prospective variations in the Supreme Court's Branzburg decision." *Social Problems* 21(1):3–21, Summer 1973.

4261   Rainwater, Lee and David Pittman. "Ethical problems in studying a politically sensitive and deviant community." *Social Problems* 14(4):357–366, Spring 1967.

4262   Rubin, Zick and Cynthia Mitchell. "Couples research as couples counseling; some unintended effects of studying close relationships." *American Psychologist* 31(1):17–25, Jan. 1976.

4263   Sagarin, Edward. "Ideology as a factor in the consideration of deviance." *Journal of Sex Research* 4(2):84–94, May 1968.

4264   _____. "The research setting and the right not to be researched." *Social Problems* 21(1):52–65, Summer 1973.

4265   Sorensen, Robert C. *Adolescent Sexuality in Contemporary America,* pp. 13–27. New York: World Publishing Co., 1973.

4266   Standridge, Linda Williams. "Experimentation on humans in biomedical research: implications for the industry of recent legislation and cases." *Women Lawyers Journal* 63:88–95, Summer 1977.

4267   U.S. Department of Health, Education and Welfare. *The Institutional Guide to DHEW Policy on Protection of Human Subjects.* Washington, DC: DHEW, 1971.

OTHER SOURCES OF INFORMATION

National Commission for the Protection of Human Subjects of Biomedical and Behavioral Research
5333 Westbard Ave., Bethesda, MD 20016

III. INDEXES

Author Index

The numbers refer to individual citations.

Abbott, Daniel J., 3591
Abbott, Sidney, 938
Abel, Gene G., 2048, 3684
Abelson, Robert B., 708
Aberle, David F., 2569
Abernathy, James R., 2552
Abernethy, George L., 682
Abernethy, Virginia, 165, 682, 690, 3122
Abitbol, M. Maurice, 761
Abrahamsen, David, 3620
Abram, Harry S., 663
Abramowitz, Naomi R., 2562
Abrams, Laurence, 3741
Abramson, Paul R., 347, 2710
Abu-Laban, Baha, 1686
Aceto, Thomas, 1907
Acock, Allan C., 2433
Acosta, Frank X., 858
Adam, Kenneth S., 481
Adams, David B., 2001, 2153
Adams, Morton S., 3174, 3220
Adams, Paul L., 90, 1914
Adamson, John D., 3882
Adelson, Edward T., 1685
Aitken, Janet, 3665
Albrecht, Gary L., 739
Alby, Jean-Marc, 990
Aldama Magnet, Javier De, 1915
Alexander, Harvey, 1585
Alexander, Leo, 4245, 4246
Alfonso, Herminia, 2482
Al-Hamdani, Muwaffak, 1686
Allen, Clifford, 964, 3293
Allen, David W., 3759
Allen, Donald, 244
Allen, Robert M., 4225
Allen, Virginia, 2027
Alpert, George, 1088
Alpert, Hollis, 4118
Alpert, Richard, 482, 588, 596
Alston, Jon P., 921, 2308, 2309, 2791, 2792
Althoff, Sally A., 483
Altman, Carole, 1589
Altman, Dennis, 895
Alzate, Helí, 2508, 2518, 3398
Amaya, Mario, 4024
Amdur, Millard J., 2345
Amelar, Richard D., 769
Amendt, Günter, 599
Amir, Menachem, 3064, 3566, 3577, 3592–3594, 3644
Amoroso, Donald M., 918, 3859, 3932, 4242
Amos, Sheldon, 3353
Amulree, Lord, 369

Anand, Mulk Raj, 4025
Anderson, Brian, 1900
Anderson, Carla Lee, 2480
Anderson, Carol, 1304, 1456
Anderson, Gallatin, 2570
Anderson, J. Harold, 2449
Anderson, Mauriça, 3314
Anderson, Peter B., 2850
Anderson, Robert T., 2570
Anderson, Scott M., 2186, 2188
Anderson, Thomas P., 740
Andry, Andrew C., 2365
Angrilli, Albert F., 91, 1688
Annon, Jack S., 1504, 1505
Apfelbau, Bernard, 1667
Appel, Gerald B., 1957
Appel, James B., 1158
Appelbaum, Stephen A., 1035
Arafat, Ibtihaj Said, 244, 484, 2161
Aratow, Paul, 4137
Archer, Jules, 196
Ard, Ben N., Jr., 1242, 1448, 2090, 2091
Ardener, Shirley G., 2968
Arensberg, Frederick, 1605
Arentewicz, Gerd, 1449, 1506
Arieti, Silvano, 683
Aring, Charles D., 2969
Arkin, E.A., 92, 93
Arkoff, Abe, 2785
Arnold, Charles B., 1350, 2341
Aronson, Elliot, 3649
Asayama, Shin'ichi, 166–168, 245
Asbjornsen, W., 1809
Assie, Pierre, 1213
Astin, Helen S., 1681
Astor, Gerald, 3567
Athanasiou, Robert, 2711–2713, 3448, 3848, 3860, 4201
Atkins, John, 4067
Atkins, Thomas R., 4108
Atkinson, Maxine, 3390
Atwood, Robert William, 3248, 3249
Auerbach, Aaron Gerald, 1689
Auger, Jeanine Ann Roose, 1925
Auras, Irongard, 4149
Ausloos, Guy, 3065
Axelrod, Terry, 684
Ayers, Joyce L., 3623
Ayrault, Evelyn West, 741
Ayres, Toni, 1601

Babbage, Stuart Barton, 2891
Babcock, Barbara Allen, 3532
Babineau, Raymond, 1293
Back, Kurt W., 4155
Bacon, Selden D., 579
Badaracco, Marie R., 2916
Baggally, W., 991

Bagley, Christopher, 3123
Bahm, Robert Michael, 3883
Bahr, Robert, 1953
Bailey, Derrick Sherwin, 928, 2892
Bailly-Salin, P., 485
Baizerman, Michael, 135
Bakan, David, 3066
Baker, Howard J., 2042, 2047
Baker, Judith, 308
Baker, Luther G., 2450
Baker, Robert, 2830, 2917
Baker, Roger, 1089
Baker, Sidney J., 2831
Bakwin, Harry, 70, 1146
Baldwin, Bruce A., 1408, 1409, 2346
Balistrieri, James, 117
Ball, John C., 225
Ballivet, J., 623
Balswick, Jack O., 2754, 2947
Balter, Lawrence, 1714
Bancroft, John, 1507, 3306, 3782
Bandini, Tullio, 3222
Banes, Sally, 3354
Bannerman, R.H.O., 2505
Barbach, Lonnie Garfield, 1557, 1597
Barbara, Dominick A., 1044
Barber, Bernard, 4247
Barber, R.N., 3430
Barclay, Andrew M., 1954, 2743, 2841, 3595, 3884, 3885
Bard, Morton, 3683
Bard, Robert, 4256
Barden, Tom P., 1869
Bardis, Panos D., 3124, 4182
Bardwick, Judith M., 1870, 3014
Barfield, Marguerite Durham, 2714
Barker, Elizabeth Dunning, 2715
Barker, J.C., 1147
Barker, William J., 246, 4156
Barker-Benfield, G.J., 3015
Barlow, David H., 2048
Barnett, Joseph, 685
Barnett, Ola Johnson, 3783
Barnett, Walter, 8, 1167, 3990
Barnhouse, Ruth Tiffany, 2893, 2918
Baron, Robert A., 3930
Barr, O. Sydney, 2894
Barr, Ronald F., 2021
Barrera Caraza, Estanislao, 3391, 3427
Barrett, Ann, 2340
Barrett, J.C., 2127
Barry, Maurice J., Jr., 3125, 3196
Bart, Pauline B., 2775
Barták, Vladimir, 247
Bartell, Gilbert D., 2267, 2268
Bartels, Max, 3380
Bartels, Paul, 3380
Bartelt, Claudia, 3244, 3295

Barter, James T., 1126
Bartholomew, F.E., 2510, 2511
Bartilotti, R., 3792
Baskett, Edward E., 866
Bates, John E., 1690, 1691
Battista, Anna, 2543
Bauer, Roger, 1362
Bauman, Karl E., 309, 2716, 2793
Bayer, Alan E., 2717
Beach, Frank A., 35, 75, 821, 971, 1099, 1171, 1692, 1894, 1940, 1955, 2213, 2571, 2572
Bean, Bonnie, 2340
Beard, Alice, 2573
Beardwood, C.J., 1942
Beasley, Ruth, 4
Beaumont, G., 486
Beaumont, Pierre Joseph Victor, 1942
Bechtel, H. Kenneth, 2718
Beck, Aaron T., 686
Becker, Howard S., 4248
Beckerman, Wilfred, 3431
Beidelman, Thomas O., 2574
Beigel, Hugo G., 370, 371, 1090, 1091, 1148, 1149, 3067
Beit-Hallahmi, Benjamin, 1693, 3784
Belanger, Kathleen E., 248
Belgum, David, 2162
Bell, Alan P., 776, 809, 865, 896, 922, 1694, 3250
Bell, Arthur, 939
Bell, D.S., 585
Bell, Phyllis L., 2095
Bell, Robert R., 9, 36, 310, 311, 487, 2092-2095, 2249, 2260, 2261, 2269, 2794, 2919, 3392, 3632, 3861, 3863
Belliveau, Fred, 1508
Bellocq, E.G., 3355, 3469
Bellville, Titus P., 2205
Beluhan, Aleksadra, 160
Belzer, Edwin G., 2409, 2481
Bem, Sandra L., 1695, 1696, 2921, 4230
Benayoun, Robert, 4026
Bender, Lauretta, 3068, 3069
Bender, Stephen J., 249, 2544
Bene, Eva, 140
Benedek, Therese, 1188
Benedict, Ruth, 2575
Bengesser, Gerhard, 488
Benjamin, H.B., 975
Benjamin, Harry, 1092, 1093, 1150, 2002, 2027, 2056, 3315-3317, 3432, 3492, 3533
Benjamin, Ruby R., 2545
Benkert, Otto, 624, 1956
Bennett, Virginia D.C., 2546
Bensusan, A.D., 611
Bentler, Peter M., 1129-1131, 1140, 1691, 2062, 4208
Benward, Jean, 3221
Berest, Joseph J., 1020, 3235
Berezin, Martin A., 366, 372
Berg, Charles, 1205
Bergen, Marcelene Betsy, 250

Berger, Arthur, 3017
Berger, David G., 2795
Berger, Miriam E., 2163
Berger, Morroe, 4144
Berger, Richard S., 3633
Bergersen, Sidney G., 3311
Berkowitz, Leonard, 3931
Berman, Ellen M., 373, 1393
Berman, Myron, 169
Berman, Sydney, 511
Berna, Jacques, 170
Bernard, F., 3251
Bernard, Jessie, 2326, 2970, 3018
Berndt, Catherine H., 2576
Berndt, Ronald M., 2576
Bernick, Niles, 3886
Bernier, Joseph J., 1410
Bernstein, Herbert, 412
Bernstein, William C., 653
Berry, David F., 2719
Berscheid, Ellen, 3926, 4186
Bertocci, Peter Anthony, 2876
Bess, Barbara, 3318, 3408, 3437
Bettis, Moody C., 3742
Beukenkamp, Cornelius, 1371
Beurdeley, Michel, 4027
Beutler, Larry E., 4220
Beyer, James C., 965, 3689, 3833
Bianchi, Eugene C., 2920
Bianco, Fernando J., 1509
Biber, Henry, 445
Bick, Mario, 2577
Bicknell, Ted, 1426
Bidgood, Frederick, 2418
Bieber, Irving, 753, 810, 897, 1045
Bieber, Toby, 1606, 1607
Bielefeld, Robert James, 1697
Bieliauskas, Vytautas J., 1698
Biener, Kurt, 171
Biggs, Mae, 1544
Bigras, Julien, 3156
Biller, Henry B., 691, 1699, 1700, 1701
Binder, Donald P., 654
Binderman, Murray B., 3457, 3467
Birat, Joseph, 1801
Bird, F., 3507
Birkby, Phyllis, 940
Birnbaum, Michael D., 1859, 1916
Birren, James E., 367, 476
Bischof, Norbert, 3157
Bishop, John, 2165
Bishop, Melvin P., 1865
Biskind, Leonard H., 1372
Black, James Allen, 3829
Black, Rebecca, 1296
Blaine, Graham B., 2164
Blaine, William L., 2165
Blair, Ralph Edward, 812
Blake, Dean Moishe, 2720, 4241
Blanchard, Edward B., 2048, 3684
Blank, Leonard, 3746
Blau, Abram, 3068
Blei, Franz, 4068
Bloch, Donald, 2300
Bloch, Doris, 2419
Bloch, Iwan, 3493

Block, David, 2032
Block, Norman L., 2057
Blood, Robert O., 2109
Bloom, Jean Louise, 2451
Blos, Peter, 3179
Blumberg, Audrey, 3666
Blumberg, Leonard, 310
Blumer, Dietrich, 646, 2031
Blumstein, Philip W., 838, 841-843, 847
Bock, E. Wilbur, 2578
Bode, Janet, 813
Boggan, E. Carrington, 867, 1168, 2067
Bohannan, Paul, 2380
Bohler, Clorinda S.S., 1937
Bohmer, Carol, 3666, 3830
Bohrnstedt, George, 4186
Boles, Jacqueline, 3390
Bon, J., 4032
Bon, Michel, 814
Bonaparte, Marie, 992, 1046
Bonte, Monique, 2579
Bonuzzi, L., 3530
Booth, Alan, 2103, 2131, 2250
Borges, Sandra S., 3664
Borosage, Vera, 56, 2400
Borowitz, Eugene B., 2870
Borowitz, Gene, 1948, 3886
Bosmajian, Haig A., 3991
Bostandzhiev, Todor P., 1264
Botwinick, Jack, 374
Boucher, Richard J., 3715
Boulanger, Paul, 3128, 3816
Bower, Donald W., 2166, 2721
Bowers, L.M., 443
Bowers, Malcolm B., Jr., 625, 626
Bowie, Theodore, 4028
Bowman, Claude C., 4249
Bowman, Henry, 1276
Bowman, Karl M., 1169, 3765
Boyar, Robert M., 1871
Boyer, Paul S., 3962
Boylin, Eugene Robert, 3887
Bracher, Marjory, 2452
Bradley, Eleanor, 248
Bradshaw, Barbara R., 1294
Brady, John P., 251, 489, 1510, 3954, 4209
Bramblett, Claud A., 1856
Brancale, Ralph, 3723
Brandes, J.M., 2524
Brant, Renee S.T., 3070
Brantlinger, Ellen, 709
Brashear, Diane B., 1422, 2971
Brassaï, Gyula Halasz, 3470
Braude, Monique C., 604
Braun, Saul, 37, 966
Brecher, Edward M., 60, 521, 1172
Brecher, Ruth, 1172
Breedlove, Jerrye, 2270
Breedlove, William, 2270
Breen, James L., 3685
Bregman, Susan, 726
Breiner, S.J., 94
Brenner, Donald R., 3241
Brent, Golda Gail, 2068

Brenton, Myron, 375, 671, 1373, 1450, 1608, 2948
Briddell, Dan W., 554
Bridwell, Margaret W., 1582
Brieland, Donald, 3076
Brierley, Harry, 1132
Brinkman, W., 2813
Brockmeier, Marlene, 656
Broderick, Carlfred B., 71, 95, 96, 172, 406, 2121, 2128, 2206, 2310, 2326, 2806
Brodsky, Stanley L., 3630
Brody, Eugene B., 1012, 2420
Brodyaga, Lisa, 3596
Brogan, Donna, 1702, 4233
Bromberg, Norbert, 993, 2240
Bromberg, Walter, 3785
Brongersma, E., 3282
Brooks, Robert D., 2991
Brotherton, Janet, 1872
Broude, Gwen J., 2580, 2581
Brown, Asa J., 1423
Brown, D.A., 238, 1424
Brown, Daniel G., 1094, 1703, 1704
Brown, Fred, 1705, 2949
Brown, Howard, 868
Brown, Judson S., 1062
Brown, Laura, 2995
Brown, Marvin, 918, 3859, 3888, 3932, 4242
Brown, Sidney, 994
Brown, Thomas Edwards, 800
Brown, Walter A., 3889
Brownmiller, Susan, 3568
Bruce, Virginia, 1095
Bruch, Hilde, 748
Bruck, Connie, 2921
Brundage, James A., 3356
Bruni, Ernest, 1511, 1565
Brunold, Heinz, 3071
Brunswick, Ann F., 141
Brusendorff, Ove, 4012
Brustman, Barbara A., 553
Bryan, James H., 3394, 3395, 3458
Bryan, William J., 1566
Bryant, Clifton D., 3396, 3471
Bryk, Felix, 2582
Buchanan, Barbara, 1706
Buckner, H. Taylor, 1096, 1133
Buerkle, Jack V., 2794
Buffery, Anthony W., 1734
Bullough, Bonnie, 3019
Bullough, Vern L., 10, 869, 1097, 3019, 2020, 3313, 3357-3359, 3397, 3472
Bumpass, Larry, 3048
Bunce, Frederick W., 4069
Bunch, Charlotte, 3051
Bunge, Raymond G., 1707
Bunzl, Martin, 1217, 1265
Burchard, Johann M., 1098
Burchell, R. Clay, 664, 1295
Burdsal, Charles, 600
Burford, E.J., 3360, 3361
Burgess, Ann Wolbert, 3072, 3596, 3597, 3645, 3686, 3687
Burgess, Ernest W., 2097

Burgess, Jane K., 1708
Burgess, Jane Menzel, 252
Burgoyne, David S., 2129
Burke, Susan, 2327, 2421
Burland, Cottie, 4029
Burnham, John, 3021, 3362, 4070
Burns, Robert A., 1709
Burnside, Irene Mortenson, 376
Burr, Wesley R., 355
Burrows, Harold, 1861
Burt, John J., 2328
Burt, Martha, 1720
Burton, Genevieve, 555
Burton, J., 2505
Burton, Lindy, 3073
Burton, Roger V., 2583
Bush, Irving M., 1203
Busha, Charles H., 3963
Buskin, Judith, 2364
Busse, Ewald W., 377, 378
Butcher, James, 4221
Butler, Carol A., 1243
Butler, J.C., 1222
Butler, Robert N., 379, 4250
Butler, Sharon Elaine, 1609
Butman, Jean W., 173
Butts, June Dobbs, 2329
Butts, William Marlin, 3494
Byrd, Benjamin F., 678
Byrne, Donn, 2389, 3862, 3890
Byrne, Lois A., 2389

Cabeen, Charles W., 3786, 3787
Cade, Jerry D., 2519
Cahan, Sorel, 3662
Cahn, L.A., 490
Caird, William K., 1512, 4157
Cairns, Robert B., 3850, 3992
Calderone, Mary S., 38, 380, 2832, 3022
Calderwood, Deryck D., 142, 955, 2374, 2381, 2453
Calhoun, Lawrence G., 1780, 3599
Callahan, Sidney Cornelia, 2298, 2972
Callieri, Bruno, 967
Calmas, Wilfred Earl, 3252, 3600
Calonico, James M., 3591
Calverton, V.F., 4071
Cameron, P., 3178
Cameron, Paul, 444, 445, 2722
Campbell, Bernard, 2584
Canepa, Giacomo, 3222
Cangelosi, Sam A., 3812
Cantor, Joanne R., 2482, 3891
Capes, Mary, 72, 97
Caplan, Harvey W., 1296
Caplan, Ruth Thurlow, 1451, 1513
Capraro, Vincent J., 3074
Caprio, Frank Samuel, 815, 3241
Caputo, G. Craig, 2585
Cardwell, Jerry D., 2796
Carey, James T., 4145
Carlson, Lars A., 1873
Carlson, Noel R., 1297
Carmen, Ira H., 3964, 3993
Carneiro, Robert, 2271

Carney, Richard E., 613
Carns, Donald E., 312, 2797
Carpenter, Bob L., 3203
Carpenter, George R., 253, 313, 314, 2725, 4210
Carr, Arthur C., 1083
Carrera, Michael A., 1416, 2422, 2547, 2548, 2563
Carrier, Joseph M., 777, 2586, 3495
Carrillo, Carlos, 512
Carroll, James L., 3721
Carroll, Jon, 816
Carroll, Leo, 3634
Carruthers, E.A., 3197
Carter, Carol Sue, 39, 491, 1874
Carter Luther J., 3023
Carter, Mary, 2454
Carton, Jacqueline, 2423
Carton, John 2423
Cartwright, Rosalind D., 1948
Caspari, Ernst, 3126
Cass, James, 3814
Castelnuovo-Tedesco, Pietro, 1389
Castle, Robert M., 3473
Castor, Jane, 2564, 2568
Catlin, Nancy, 2167
Cattell, Raymond B., 3892
Caukins, Sivan E., 3496
Cauthen, Nelson, 354
Cavallin, Hector, 3127, 3158
Cendron, H., 446, 614
Chaneles, Sol, 3075, 3076
Chapman, J. Dudley, 1374, 2509
Chappell, Duncan, 3561, 3601, 3667, 3692
Char, Walter, F., 2536
Chard, Chester S., 2587
Charney, Charles W., 1875
Chartham, Robert, 381
Chartoff, Susan, 576
Chaskes, Jay, 311
Cheetham, R.J., 2455
Cheetham, R.W.S., 2455
Chen, Pao-Hwei, 454
Cherlin, Richard S., 1957
Chesler, Phyllis, 3024
Chesser, Eustace, 3534
Chessick, Richard D., 492
Chester, Lewis, 3525
Cheverie, Evelyn, 3535
Chez, Ronald A., 1390, 2520
Chilgren, Richard A., 736, 2522, 2528
Chilman, Catherine S., 2973
Chiu, Wu Shung, 745
Chodoff, Paul, 1610, 1611
Christensen, Harold T., 313-315, 2311-2312, 2723-2725, 2798, 2833, 4210
Christensen, L.W., 1958
Christenson, Cornelia V., 16, 447
Christopherson, Victor A., 2166, 2721
Chrzanowski, Gerard, 687
Chrzanowski, R., 647
Churchill, Wainwright, 848, 898, 2588

Clark, Alexander L., 479, 1244, 1252, 2098, 2099, 2125, 2126, 2130, 2157, 2158, 4158
Clark, D.F., 1151
Clark, Don, 956
Clark, Jane S., 493
Clark, LeMon, 174, 1226
Clark, Lorenne M.G., 3602
Clark, Lynn Fred, 348
Clark, Thomas E., 1298
Clarke, Florence, 2065
Clarke, J., 749
Clarke, Lige, 941
Clavan, Sylvia, 2974
Clayton, Richard R., 316, 2168, 2726, 2799
Clemens, Alphonse H., 2877
Clemens, Lynwood G., 1958
Clemons, James T., 2895
Cleveland, Martha, 382
Cline, Victor B., 3965
Clor, Harry M., 3966, 3967
Coates, Edward Eugene, 2443
Coburn, Judith, 968
Coe, John I., 1069
Coe, Michael D., 589
Cogswell, Betty E., 1350, 2341, 2456, 4159, 4160
Cohen, Fay G., 3692
Cohen, Harvey, 1218
Cohen, Martin, 3025
Cohen, Michael W., 175
Cohen, Murray L., 3603, 3715, 3788
Cohen, Sidney, 601, 1028
Cohen, Yehudi A., 2589
Cohn, Ruth C., 1612
Cole, Charles Lee, 2272, 2273
Cole, James K., 1797
Cole, Martin, 1668
Cole, Theodore M., 727, 728, 736, 740
Cole, William Graham, 2896
Coleman, Emily, 2995
Coleman, James C., 3787
Coleman, James S., 3026
Collins, Anne M., 1277, 2727
Collins, John K., 254, 317, 2800
Colson, Charles E., 3893, 3894
Comarr, A.E., 729
Comfort, Alexander, 383, 1590, 2834
Compton, Ariel S., 3027
Conley, John A., 2728
Conn, Canary, 2082
Conn, Jacob H., 98-104
Connaway, Ronda S., 1331
Connell, Elizabeth B., 1959
Connell, Noreen, 3569
Connell, P.H., 509, 586
Connelly, Janet, 2096
Connolly, Frank J., 694
Constantine, Joan, 2274
Constantine, Larry, 2274
Constantinople, Anne, 1710, 4228
Cook, Royer F., 3722
Coombs, Neil R., 3496, 3497
Coombs, Robert H., 2502
Coons, Frederick W., 817, 1363

Cooper, Alan J., 1227, 1876, 1960
Cooper, Donna L., 1278
Cooper, Jeff, 778
Copelan, Rachel, 1602
Copeland, Donna R., 52, 2399
Coplin, Haskell R., 2347, 2353
Cordova, Jeanne, 1013
Corfman, Philip A., 1926
Cormier, Bruno M., 3128, 3211, 3217, 3816
Cornell, Phyllis, 3220
Cory, Donald Webster, 870-873,
Coser, Lewis A., 2280
Costell, Ronald M., 3789, 3898
Cotte, S., 3230, 3524
Cottell, Louis C., 3669
Coult, Allan D., 3129
Coulteray, Georges de, 4109
Cowden, James E., 3738
Craft, Michael, 3498
Crawley, Lawrence Q., 2510, 2511
Cray, Ed, 4146
Creelan, Paul G., 1833
Crew, Louie, 959
Cristante, Francesca, 143
Critchfield, Richard, 3319
Croake, James W., 2167, 2729, 2801
Crook, John H., 1711, 2657
Cross, Herbert, 318, 331, 357
Cross, R.R., 443
Crovitz, Elaine, 2069
Crown, Sidney, 1299
Csicery, George Paul, 3955
Cuber, John F., 11, 2100, 2207, 2208
Curran, James P., 2730
Currey, H.L.F., 655
Curtis, Lynn A., 3646
Curtis, R.F. 1877
Cushman, Paul, 494
Cutter, Fred, 3817

D'Addario, Linda J., 1613
Daen, Phyllis, 556
D'Agostino, Peter A., 1480
Dahlberg, Charles Clay, 495, 496, 1614
Dahl-Iversen, E., 1103
Daily, Jay E., 3968
Daly, E. Bernard, 2481
Daly, Michael J., 384, 1189
Damase, Jacques, 4147
Damon, Gene, 960
D'Angelli, Judith F., 318
Daniels, George E., 1943
Danielsson, Bengt, 2591
Dannecker, Martin, 899
Danziger, Carl, 2169
Danziger, Peter L., 3635
Darcy, James B., 2450
Dargitz, Robert Earl, 2731
Darrough, William, 3320, 3406
Davenport, James H., 761
Davenport, William, 2592
David, Marcus, 203
Davidson, Julian M., 1878, 1961
Davidson, Ruth T., 3220
Davis, Alan J., 3636

Davis, Allen, 3203
Davis, Burke, 3363
Davis, Ethelyn, 1712
Davis, Glenn C., 467, 470
Davis, John M., 491, 1974
Davis, Joseph E., 772, 2105
Davis, Katharine B., 2101
Davis, Keith E., 2178, 2802, 4169
Davis, Kingsley, 3329
Davis, Linda, 626
Davis, Phillip W., 3747
Davis, Sharon Kantorowski, 3747
Davison, Gerald C., 3307, 4251
De, Sushil Kumar, 4072
Deakin, Terence J., 4063
Dean, Michael Leigh, 2275
Dean, Stanley R., 387
Dearth, Paul B., 2424
De Beauvoir, Simone, 386, 3016
De Betz, Barbara, 2049
Debrovner, Charles H., 1190
Decter, Midge, 3028
Dedman, Jean, 319
DeFrancis, Vincent, 3077, 3078
Degler, Carl N., 3029
De Grazia, Edward, 3994
De Hempel, Patricia Conrad, 1191
Deisher, Robert W., 853, 3499, 3504
De La Cruz, Felix, 710
DeLamater, John D., 255, 4168
Delcampo, Robert L., 320
DeLeon, George, 497
DeLora, Joann S., 2390
DeMartino, Manfred F., 1245
DeMasi, Andrew D., 3688
Dempewolff, Judith Ann, 2975
Denfield, Duane, 2276, 2277, 3434
Dengrove, Edward, 1514, 1567
De Nicola, Pietro, 385
Deniker, Pierre, 557
Dennis, Margaret H., 1615
Densen-Gerber, Judianne, 498, 3221
Denzin, Norman K., 4252
De Saugy, Daisy, 557
De Schweinitz, Karl, 2366
DeStrulle, Arlene, 4130
Deutsch, Helene, 176
Devanesan, Mona, 1453
Devereux, George, 2593-2595, 3321
DeVos, George A., 3159
Devroye, A., 3130
Dexon, Paul W., 3927
DeYoung, Gerrit E., 2102, 3892
Diamant, Louis, 4161
Diamond, Leonard, 1927
Diamond, Milton, 40, 1173, 1713, 1862, 1879, 1895, 1927, 2330, 2391, 2425
Dickerson, R.E., 3366
Dickinson, George E., 2457
Dickinson, Peter A., 388
Dickinson, Robert Latou, 12, 1375
Dickman, Irving R., 2408
Dicks, Russel L., 1376, 1399
Dienstbier, Richard, 1797
DiFuria, Giulio, 3767, 3790
DiMascio, Alberto, 541

Di Meglio, Clara, 2889
DiMusto, Juan Carlos, 762
Dingman, Harvey F., 3258, 3279, 3297
Dingman, Jocelyn, 3223
Dingman, Joseph F., 1863, 1865
Diprizio, Chrisann, 2458
Dison, Jack E., 3161
Ditman, Keith S., 499
Dittmar, Franz, 1210, 1990, 3918
Dix, George E., 3768, 3818
Dixon, Rebecca, 4064
Dlin, Barney M., 655
Dmowski, W. Paul, 1962
Dodge, Kenneth A., 1739
Dodson, Betty, 1599
Dogliani, P., 558
Dollard, John, 2787
Domash, Leanne, 1714
Dondis, Ernest H., 3820
Donnelly, John D., 1261
Donnerstein, Edward, 3895
Donnerstein, Marcia, 3895
Donohue, John Earl, 2459
Dorfman, Ralph I., 1880
Dorjahn, Vernon R., 2596
Dormont, Paul, 1300
Dorn, Dean S., 2976
Dörner, Günter, 1896
Dost, Oskar P., 3604
Dotson, Louis E., 1944
Downs, Robert Bingham, 3969
Doyle, Averil Marie, 2503
Drake, Jonathan, 3500
Drakeford, John W., 2897
Dreitzel, Hans Peter, 2922
Drellich, Marvin G., 753, 763
Dresen, Sheila E., 389
Drew, Dennis, 3500
Driscoll, James Patrick, 2003
Driscoll, Richard H., 2802
Dryfoos, Joy G., 801
Drzazga, John, 3831
Duberman, Lucile, 1715
Duberman, Martin, 818
Dubin, Lawrence, 769
DuBois, Cora, 2597
Dubois, Jean Claude, 2598
Dubreuil, Guy, 3131
Duehn, Wayne D., 1284, 1331
Duff, Robert W., 3329, 3406
Duffy, Karen G., 3944
Dufresne, Meri Jill Mendelsohn, 2950
Dunbar, John, 918
Dunn, Peter Bruce, 1301
DuPont, Henry, 1152
Durandeau, André, 4131
Durkheim, Emile, 3132
Duryea, Walter R., 1716

Easley, Eleanor B., 2977, 2978
Eastman, William F., 349, 1377, 1378
Eaton, Antoinette Parisi, 3079
Eaton, G. Gray, 1963
Ebanks, G. Edward, 2675
Ebert, Alan, 874

Eckert, William G., 3832
Eckstein, Rudolf, 105
Eddy, George Sherwood, 3449
Edelman, Sheldon K., 2274
Edgerton, Robert B., 2599
Edmondson, John S., 1066, 1070
Edwards, Allan E., 448, 1204
Edwards, J.B., 106
Edwards, John N., 41, 2103, 2131, 2209, 2250
Edwards, Maxine, 2314, 2732
Edwards, Neil B., 3212
Eeman, P.D., 1205
Ehrhardt, Anke A., 827, 1717-1719, 1777, 1791, 1897-1899, 1904-1906, 1917
Ehrhardt, Helmut, 3501
Ehrlich, Carol, 2979
Ehrmann, John C., 3806
Ehrmann, Winston W., 177, 321, 4183
Eichler, Margrit, 2600
Eidelberg, Ludwig, 1047
Eidletz, Elizabeth M., 53
Eisenberg, M.G., 730
Eisler, Robert, 969
Eisner, V., 3499
Eist, Harold I., 3213
Ekelund, Lars-Göran, 1873
Elias, James E., 84, 178-180, 256, 2460
Elias, Marilyn, 1669
Elias, Ronnie, 179
Eliasson, Rosmari, 181, 2749, 2803
Elkan, Edward, 1228
Ellenberg, Max, 659
Ellinwood, Everett H., 500
Ellis, Albert, 5, 303, 1379, 1454, 1568, 1581, 1616, 2104, 2210, 2278, 2299, 2300, 2532, 2835, 3316, 3435, 3723
Ellis, Altis L., 2498
Ellis, Havelock, 2836
Ellis, William J., 449
Ellison, Katherine, 3683
Elliston, Frederick, 2301, 2830, 2917
Elonen, Anna S., 3080
Elsom, John, 4132
Elwin, Verrier, 2601
Ember, Melvin, 2602
Emde Boas, C. Van, 1617
Emich, John P., 3702
Enby, Gunnel, 731
Eng, Erling, 2862
Engel, Illona M., 2521
Engel, James F., 4162
Englar, Ronald C., 3896
Engle, Bernice, 1169, 3765
Engle, Robert, 3474
Englisch, Paul, 4073
English, D. Ailene, 2170
English, Oliver Spurgeon, 2211, 2302
Enos, William F., 965, 3689, 3833
Enroth, Ronald M., 929
Epstein, Louis M., 2871
Erikson, Kai T., 4252

Erlenmeyer-Kimling, L., 688
Ernst, Jan-Peter, 3933
Ernst, Morris Leopold, 3790
Erskine, Hazel Gaudet, 2733, 2734
Ervin, Clinton V., 679
Erwin, Jr., 1900
Eskildsen, Gustavo Alfredo, 3133
Eskin, Bernard A., 1859, 1916
Eslinger, Kenneth N., 2923
Esselstyn, T.C., 3322, 3502
Estep, Rhoda E., 1720
Estren, Mark James, 4030
Eulenburg, Albert, 970
Evans, Hannah I., 3690
Evans, May Anne, 4031
Evans, R.J., 3364
Evans, Ronald, 3895
Evans, Tom, 4031
Evans, Walter, 4110
Evans-Pritchard, E.E., 2603, 2604, 2685
Everett, Guy M., 501, 502
Evers, Kathryn, 1719
Evrard, John R., 3570
Ewing, John A., 559, 602, 1197, 1975
Eyres, Alfred E., 1153
Eysenck, H.J., 13, 689, 2735, 2736, 2804, 4195
Eysenck, S.B.G., 2736

Faber, Hilke, 2061
Fabian, Judith Janaro, 2924
Facey, Paul W., 3971
Faerman, I., 660
Fain, Michel, 1048
Fairbairn, Robert H., 3218
Falik, Leon A., 1721, 1964
Falk, Ruth, 819
Fang, Betty, 2279
Fann, William E., 1974
Farber, Stephen, 4111, 4112
Farkas, Gary M., 560, 4166
Farley, Frank H., 2737
Farmer, Ronald, 1302
Farnsworth, Dana L., 1279
Farrell, Ronald A., 2738, 3781
Farrell, Warren T., 2951
Fast, Julius, 820
Feder, Irwin, 2212
Federman, Daniel D., 1722
Feenstra, H.J., 3399
Fehlinger, Hans, 2605
Feigelmann, William, 3760
Fein, Sara Beck, 1438
Feinbloom, Deborah Heller, 1134, 2005, 4254
Feininger, Andreas, 4032
Feinman, Saul, 3647
Feldman, David Michael, 2872
Feldman, Herman, 613
Feldman, M.P., 923, 4235, 4236
Feldman, Marvin J., 1618
Feldman, Robert, 1091
Feldman, Sandor S., 2247
Felker, Donald W., 1835
Fellows, Robert, 1723
Felstein, Ivor, 390, 1965

Fenichel, Otto, 1049
Fennessey, Alice, 2739
Fensterheim, Herbert, 3791
Ferber, Andrew S., 770
Ferber, Leon, 1036
Ferdinand, Theodore N., 789
Ferguson, Patricia, 503
Ferin, J., 1966
Ferm, Deane William, 2898
Ferracuti, Franco, 3160, 3517, 3792
Ferrari, Marcello, 3198
Ferraro, D.P., 604
Ferrell, Mary Z., 345, 3030
Fiasche, Angel, 802
Ficher, Ilda, 57
Fichtenbaum, Leonard, 2787
Fields, W.J., 2914
Fier, Betty, 1619
Filene, Peter Gabriel, 2925
Finch, John R., 3741
Finch, Stuart M., 73, 74, 3081, 3082
Fine, Herbert L., 747
Fine, Reuben, 1620, 1621
Finger, Frank W., 257, 258
Fink, Paul Jay, 2132
Finkelstein, J., 1050
Finkelstein, Ruth, 182
Finkle, Alex L., 391, 450, 771, 2133
Finmore, Rhoda Lee, 3459
Finner, Stephen, 2500
Finney, Joseph C., 1622, 2022
Finsterbusch, Kurt, 4260
Fiore, Evelyn, 2382
Firestone, Shulamith, 3031
Firth, Diana, 3897
Fisher, Anne, 1682, 2606
Fisher, Charles, 456, 457
Fisher, Gary M., 1724, 3253, 3283
Fisher, Jeffrey D., 3862
Fisher, Peter, 942
Fisher, Seymour, 1246, 1247, 4205
Fisk, Norman, 1913
Fitch, J.H., 3254
Fithian, Marilyn A., 1308, 1515
Fitzgerald, Donald, 1725
Flammang, C.J., 3083
Flegon, A., 4033
Fleming, Patt, 2722
Fletcher, Joseph, 2899
Flexner, Abraham, 3365
Flomenhaft, Kalman, 3141
Flowers, Charles E., 1380
Flynn, Charles, 2607
Fodor, John T., 2342
Fogarty Faith, 3561. 3562
Folsom, Joseph K., 2837
Forchielli, Enrico, 1880
Ford, Amasa B., 666
Ford, Clellan S., 75, 821, 971, 1099, 2213, 2608-2609
Ford, R., 1071
Ford, Susan, 2546
Fordney-Settlage, Diane S., 1455
Forester, B.M., 2050
Forgy, Donald G., 1100
Forman, Rose, 714
Forrest, David V., 3323

Forrester, M., 3507
Forston, Raymon C., 3161
Fosen, Robert H., 3722
Foster, Jeannette H., 961, 4075
Foulke, Emerson, 643
Fox, Beatrice, 1177, 1219
Fox, Cyril A., 1174-1177, 1192, 1206, 1219, 1229, 1303, 1967
Fox, David J., 2461, 2963
Fox, J.R., 3134
Fox, Richard G., 3995
Fox, Robin, 3135
Fox, Ruth, 561
Fox, Sandra Sutherland, 3691
Foxon, David F., 4076
Framo, James L., 2241, 2303
Frances, Allen, 3199
Frances, vera, 3199
Francher, J. Scott, 392
Francis, Ronald D., 2800
Franck, Roberte, 2251
Francoeur, Anna K., 2838, 2926
Francoeur, Robert T., 2838, 2926
Frank, E. 1457, 1304
Frankfort, Ellen, 3032
Franklin, Girard H., 3785
Frantz, David O., 4077
Freedman, Abraham, 2805, 3451
Freedman, Alfred M., 61, 504, 2401
Freedman, Mark, 900
Freedman, Mervin B., 259
Freeman, Harrop A., 1364
Freeman, Joseph T., 451
Freeman, Lucy, 14, 77, 1623
Freeman, Nathan, 1624
Freeman, Ruth S., 1364
Freeman, Walter, 754
Freese, Amorette Lee, 3793
Freiberg, Patricia, 1582
Freilich, Morris, 2280, 2611
Freire-Maia, N., 2612
Frese, Wolfgang, 3416, 3417
Fretz, Bruce R., 2549, 2740, 2845, 4196
Freud, Sigmund, 822
Freund, Kurt, 849, 850, 3255-3257, 3284, 3898, 4211
Freund, Matthew, 772, 2105
Friar, David James, 3643
Frick, Viola, 1625
Friedan, Betty, 3033
Friedenberg, F.S., 995
Friedman, Abraham I., 750
Friedman, Leon, 3996
Friedman, Richard C., 1726, 1945
Friedman, Stanford B., 175
Friend, Maurice R., 1135
Frisbie, Louis V., 3258, 3279, 3297, 3724, 3819, 3820
Fröhlich, Hans H., 260
Frost, Richard, 3876
Frueh, Terry, 1727
Fry, Jane, 2084
Fry, Monroe, 3324
Fry, Peter, 2613
Fry, William F., Jr., 107, 393, 2304, 3325

Fuchs, Eduard, 4034
Fugita, Stephen S., 2680
Fujita, Byron, 224, 711
Fulghum, Mary S., 349
Fuller, Earl W., 2532
Fuller, Gerald B., 3721
Fuller, Marielle, 1634, 1737
Furst, Peter T., 589

Gabor, Mark, 4138
Gadpaille, Warren J., 14, 76, 77, 239-241, 1351, 1728, 1729
Gaffney, Louis, 2878, 2980
Gager, Nancy, 3571
Gagnon, John H., 15, 42, 108, 183, 297, 1221, 1457, 1730, 2393, 3084, 3085, 3261, 3326, 3834, 4014
Galbraith, Gary G., 350, 4226
Gallagher, Neil, 3972
Gallant, D.M., 505
Galliher, John F., 4255
Gallo, Maria Teresa de, 3398
Gamboa, Victor 3399
Gambrill, Eileen D., 693
Games, Richard G., 920, 4244
Gandy, Patrick, 2016, 3503, 3504
Gantt, W. Horsley, 562
García, Celso-Ramón, 3702, 3708
Gardner, Richard A., 109, 1731
Garfield, Sol L., 1626
Garma, Angel, 996
Garrard, Judith, 2522
Garris, Lorrie, 184
Garside, Christine, 2927
Garza, Joseph M., 2171
Gauthier, Xavière, 4035
Gay, George R., 506, 507, 549
Gebhard, Paul H., 16, 21, 22, 43, 84, 86, 180, 452, 972, 1248, 1249, 1251, 2106, 2113, 2348, 2928, 3162, 3259-3260, 3327, 3400, 3450, 3605, 3725, 3726, 3899, 4163
Geduld, Harry, 4113
Geen, Russell G., 3934
Geer, James H., 1178, 3900, 4164
Gehman, Ila H., 1632
Geiger, Robert C., 719
Geis, Gilbert, 3561, 3601, 3648, 3692
Geis, Robley, 3601
Gelder, Michael, 1038
Geller, Jack, 394, 1936
Geller, Sheldon H., 3606
Gellman, Robert, 1352
Gendel, Evalyn S., 2426
Gerdts, William H., 4036
Gero, George, 997
Gerson, Allan R., 261
Gerstl, Joel E., 3872
Gessa, G.L., 539, 1968, 1969, 1994
Ghiselin, Michael T., 2614
Giacquinta, Joseph B., 2550
Giannini, Maria Cristina, 3236
Gianturco, Daniel T., 185, 1353
Gibbens, T.C.N., 3086, 3436
Gibson, Gifford G., 875
Giedt, F. Harold, 262
Giese, Hans, 43

Gigeroff, Alex K., 3298, 3794, 3835
Gilliard, Richie S., 787, 2778
Gilligan, Carol, 144, 145
Gillman, Arthur E., 644
Ginder, Richard, 2879
Ginsberg, George L., 2929
Ginsburg, Kenneth N., 3505
Ginzberg, Eli, 790
Ginzburg, Ralph, 4015
Gip, Bernard, 4037
Girodias, Maurice, 2839
Giroux, Roy, 1426
Gisselman, A., 623
Gittelsohn, Roland B., 2873
Gittelson, Natalie, 1458
Giza, Jerzy St., 3506
Gladwin, Thomas, 2615
Glass, Dorothea D., 732
Glass, Geraldine, 110, 2354
Glass, J. Conrad, Jr., 146
Glicksberg, Charles I., 4078
Gligor, Alyce Mapp, 3163
Glueck, Bernard C., 3262, 3285,
    3727, 3821
Gochros, Harvey L., 44, 2349, 2565
Gochros, Jean S., 2565, 2981
Godlewski, Julian, 1459
Godow, Annette, 290, 2771
Goergen, Donald, 2880
Gohagan, John Kenneth, 2462
Gold, Alice R., 2001, 2153
Goldberg, Herb, 2952, 4148
Goldberg, Jacob Alter, 3087
Goldberg, Martin, 1305, 2214
Goldberg, Rosamond, 3087
Golden, Joshua S., 1545, 2523
Golden, Margaret A., 1545
Goldfarb, Jack Harold, 1136, 1732
Goldfarb, Russell M., 4079
Goldfoot, David A., 839
Goldman, Martin, 1460
Goldner, Norman S., 3572
Goldsmith, Sadja, 186, 2466
Goldstein, Leonide, 1218
Goldstein, Michael, 3263, 3607,
    3728, 3729, 3880, 3935
Goldstein, Steven G., 2321, 2514,
    2515
Goldstone, Murray A., 2248
Golod, S.I., 2840
Golosow, Nikolas, 2046
Gonsiorek, John C., 860
Goodchilds, Jacqueline D., 2990
Goode, Erich, 508, 603, 3573
Goodland, Roger, 2616
Goody, Jack, 2215, 2617
Göppert, Hans, 395
Gordis, Robert, 2874
Gordon, Arlene R., 644
Gordon, Judith, 2368
Gordon, Lillian, 3200
Gordon, Linda, 3034
Gordon, Michael, 36, 2277, 2741,
    3434, 3863
Gordon, Sol, 45, 1354, 2368, 2375,
    2406-2407, 2930
Gorer, Goeffrey, 17, 2107, 2618

Gornick, Vivian, 3035
Gorsuch, Richard, 2742
Goslin, David A., 1733
Gossop, M.R., 509, 586
Gottheil, Edward, 2805, 3451
Gottlieb, Adam, 510
Gough, Harrison G., 4232
Gould, George, 3366
Gould, Ketayun H., 2134
Gould, Robert E., 2916, 2931, 2932
Goy, Robert W., 839
Grace, E. Barrabee, 699
Grafenberg, Ernest, 1193
Graham, LeRoy Stoney, 2900
Grambs, Jean D., 2933
Grant, Annette, 2982
Grant, Michael, 4038
Gravatt, Arthur E., 2487
Gray, Diana, 187
Gray, Jeffrey A., 1734, 1946
Gray, K.G., 3822
Grayhack, John T., 449
Greaves, George, 587
Greaves, Thomas, 3164
Green, Caroline, 973
Green, Gerald, 973
Green, Michael, 511
Green, Pauline B., 2426
Green, Richard, 60, 85, 885, 877,
    1101, 1102, 1154, 1306, 1391,
    1735-1738, 1913, 1970, 2006,
    2015, 2047, 2394
Green, Robin, 3475
Greenbank, R., 1627
Greenbaum, Henry, 3036
Greenberg, Harvey R., 512
Greenberg, Jerrold S., 263, 2463
Greenblatt, David, 513
Greenblatt, Robert B., 1937, 1971
Greene, Bernard L., 1381, 2216
Greene, Nancy R., 3214
Greene, Sarah J., 2581
Greene, Susan, 1670
Greenfield, Sidney M., 2934
Greenland, Cyril, 3224
Greenson, Ralph R., 2953
Greenwald, Earl, 3685
Greenwald, Harold, 2217, 2218, 3401
Greenwald, Mathew, 2169
Greenwood, Pamela, 3900
Greer, Germaine, 3037
Gregersen, Edgar, 1015
Gregersen, Markil, 1072
Gregg, Christina F., 315, 322, 2313
Gregori, Caterine A., 3685
Gregory, Martha F., 733
Grey, Peg Savage, 442
Griffith, Ernest R., 638, 742
Griffith, Mac, 351
Griffitt, William, 3901, 3902
Grilly, David M., 604
Grimm, H., 78, 3088
Gripton, James, 2567
Grosbois, Charles, 4039
Gross, Leonard, 46, 2108
Gross, Milton, 576
Groth, Aloysius Nicholas, 3264

Gruenberg, Sidonie M., 2369
Grugett, Alvin E., 3069
Grumley, Michael, 974
Grummon, Donald, 2743, 2841
Grunberger, Benjamin C., 1051
Grunebaum, Henru Y., 690, 2983
Grunhut, Max. 3730
Guber, Selma, 2985
Guerra, Francisco, 590
Guggisberg, Michel, 3165
Gunther, Max. 2984
Gupta, Anima Sen, 2135
Gupta, Derek, 1881
Gurwitz, Sharon B., 1739
Gut, Marcel, 1880
Guttmacher, Manfred S., 3796
Guyon, René, 2842
Guze, Henry, 1628
Gwozdz, Feliks, 1073

Haber, Ralph N., 3595
Hacker, Helen Mayer, 2954
Hackett, Thomas P., 3748
Haft, Jay Stuart, 975
Haft, Marilyn, 3538, 3539
Hager, David L., 234
Haims, Lawrence J., 2427
Hall, Calvin S., 3250
Hall, Gladys Mary, 3367
Hall, Judy E., 712
Hall, Patricia L., 264
Hall Williams, J.E., 3237
Halleck, Seymour, 2935, 3749, 3806
Haller, John S., 3038
Haller, Robin M., 3038
Hallowell, A., 2619
Hally, David J., 1139
Halverson, H.M., 79
Hamalian, Leo, 3956
Hamblen, E.C., 1740
Hamblin, Robert L., 2109
Hamburg, David A., 1929, 1950, 1985
Hamburger, Christian, 1103, 2023
Hamel, Robert F., 3903
Hamelstein, Helaine, 1355
Hamilton, Eleanor, 2383
Hamilton, G.V., 2110
Hamilton, James W., 3761
Hammer, Elizabeth L., 2765
Hammer, Emanuel F., 3608
Hammer, Signe, 1741, 2986
Hammersmith, Sue Kiefer, 2744
Hammond, Nancy K., 2743
Hampe, Gary D., 4165
Hampson, Joan G., 1742, 1743
Hampson, John L., 1743
Hamrick, Narecia D., 3904
Hansen, Edward, 3507
Harbert, Terry L., 3215
Harbin, Henry, 1307
Harbison, J.J.M., 4197
Harcus, A.W., 1872
Hardgrove, Grace, 3693
Harding, T. Swan, 3368
Hare, Robert, 3905, 3906
Hare-Mustin, Rachel T., 1629
Harlow, Harry F., 1744, 1836

Harlow, M.K., 1744
Harper, Mary W., 2533
Harper, Robert A., 2219
Harris, Gloria G., 1461
Harris, Mervyn, 3508
Harris, Ronald T., 1890
Harris, Sarah, 2281, 3328
Harrison, Danny E., 803
Harrison, Don K., 1280
Harroff, Peggy B., 11, 2100, 2207, 2208
Hart, Benjamin L., 1972
Hart, Gavin, 18
Harter, Carl L., 2428
Hartland, John, 1630
Hartman, Susan S., 713
Hartman, Valdemar, 3302, 3303
Hartman, William E., 1308, 1515
Hartnagel, Timothy Frank, 791
Hartsuiker, Jan Frederik, 3460
Harvey, O.L., 2136
Haskell, Molly, 4114
Hassell, Julie, 2745
Hassellund, Hans, 2746
Hatfield, Lon M., 704, 1891
Hatterer, Laurence J., 924
Hauck, A., 1063
Haupt, Thomas D., 2780, 4225
Hauptmann, Walter, 3797
Hauser, Richard, 901, 3509
Hausman, William, 3731
Hawkins, Robert O., 1309
Hawley, Donna Lea, 2070
Haworth, H.E., 4080
Hayman, Charles R., 3089, 3574, 3609, 3694-3696
Haynes, Stephen N., 2747
Heagarty, Margaret, 110, 2354
Hecker, Michael R., 1890
Hefner, Hugh M., 2843
Heidensohn, Frances, 2987
Heider, Karl G., 2620, 2621
Heilbrun, Alfred B., 1745, 4229
Heilbrun, Carolyn G., 1746
Heiman, Julia R., 1194, 1462, 1600, 3907
Heiple, Phil, 3610
Heiser, Charles B., 2622
Heller, Melvin S., 2302
Hellerstein, Herman K., 672
Helpern, Milton, 3836
Heltsley, Mary E., 2806
Hendel, Samuel, 4256
Henderson, D. James, 3201
Henderson, Edward, 1889
Henderson, Jeffrey, 4081
Heninger, George, 3889
Henkin, Janet, 392
Henley, Nancy M., 3039
Henn, Fritz A., 3732
Hennessy, Thomas C., 1400
Hennigh, Lawrence, 2623
Henningsen, Poul, 4012
Henriques, L. Fernando, 3369
Henry, Jules, 2624
Henry, Russell Cole, 1074

Henshel, Anne-Marie, 2282
Henslin, James H., 514
Henslin, James M., 47
Hentig, Hans von, 976, 3136, 3166, 3238
Henze, Lura F., 2172
Herjanic, Marijan, 3732
Herman, Sondra R., 2936
Herndon, C.N., 2512
Hernton, Calvin C., 779
Herold, Edward S., 2483, 4185
Heron, Alastair, 930
Hershey, Nathan, 4257
Hersko, Marvin, 3216
Herz, Sulvia, 265, 515
Heslinga, K., 743
Hess, Thomas B., 4040
Hettlinger, Richard, 2384, 2395, 2937, 3967
Heweston, John, 977, 2625
Heyl, Barbara Sherman, 3402
Higginbotham, Howard N., 4166
Higgins, John W., 3864
Hijmans, A., 3403
Hikel, James Steven, 2464
Hilberman, Elaine, 3697
Hillabrant, Walter J., 2679
Hiltner, Seward, 2901
Hilton, Diana Gray, 3404, 3428
Hines, Pauline, 684
Hinesley, Roger K., 3913
Hinton, Gertrude D.M., 2333
Hippler, Arthur E., 563, 2626
Hironimus, Helen, 3405
Hirschfeld, Magnus, 1075, 1104
Hirschman, Richard, 3908
Hirt, Stefanie, 2243
Hite, Shere, 19, 1250, 4202
Hobart, Charles W., 306, 323
Hobbs, George William, 2551
Hoch, Loren Lee, 2465
Hoch, Paul H., 111, 516
Hoch, Zwi, 2524
Hochschild, Arlie Russell, 1682
Hodges, Parker, 1417, 1463
Hoenig, J., 2024, 2043
Hofer, Gunter, 1105
Hoffman, Frank A., 4115
Hoffman, Martin, 517, 902, 3510
Hofmann, Adele D., 242
Hofstatter, Dr. R., 615
Hogan, Walter L., 3090
Hohlweg, W., 1901
Holaday, John W., 1952
Holbrook, David, 3973
Holden, Constance, 1464
Hollister, Leo E., 518
Holloway, John P., 2071
Holmes, Kay Ann, 3370
Holmes, Ronald Michael, 2807
Holmes III, Urban T., 2893, 2902, 2918
Holmstrom, Lynda Lytle, 3072, 3597, 3598, 3645, 3686, 3687
Holstein, Bjorn, 279
Hong, Lawrence K., 3329, 3406
Honigmann, John J., 2627, 2628

Hooker, Davenport, 1179
Hoon, Emily Franck, 1195, 1196, 1202, 1465, 3909, 3929, 4206
Hoon, Peter W., 1195, 1196, 1202, 1465, 3909, 3929, 4206
Hoover, John Edgar, 3371
Hora, Thomas, 1155
Horejst, Charles R., 1382
Horenstein, Sam, 720
Hori, Akio, 998, 1029
Horn, Patrice, 1516
Horn, Robert E., 1281
Horney, Karen, 1052
Hornick, Edward J., 188
Hornstein, Stephen, 2539
Horos, Carol V., 3575
Horowitz, Irving L., 4248
Hotchner, Beverly, 1466
Houlihan, Nancy Bryant, 147
House, Elizabeth A., 2466
Houser, Carolyn, 2534
Houston, Judith A., 3865, 3866
Houston, Samuel R., 3866
Howard, Alan, 2629
Howard, Clifford, 2844
Howard, Elliott J., 519, 673
Howard, Irwin, 2629
Howard, Walter, 4149
Howell, Leisla M., 3283
Howell, Mary C., 3040
Howell, Robert J., 3249
Hoyman, Howard S., 2344
Hsu, Cheng-Jen, 454
Hsu, Francis L.K., 2630, 2631
Huang, Lucy Jen, 2315
Hubin, P., 266, 296, 540
Hudson, John W., 2172
Hudson, Pamela Sue, 2564, 2568
Huey, Su Wen, 530
Huey, William P., 90
Huffman, John W., 764, 765
Hughes, Douglas A., 3974
Hughes, Graham, 3239

Jacobs, Daniel, 3770
Jacobs, Marion, 1671
Jaffe, Yoram, 3936
James, Barbara E., 2729, 2801
James, Jennifer, 3407, 3461, 3540, 3541
James, Thomas E., 3542
James, William H., 2137-2140, 4167
Jamison, Gerald E., 929
Janda, Louis H., 353
Jankovic, Ivan, 3610
Janowsky, David S., 1974
Janus, Samuel, 190, 3318, 3408, 3437
Jarvik, Murray E., 521
Jay, Bill, 4139
Jay, Karla, 944, 945
Jedlicka, Davor, 324
Jeffries, J.J., 3961
Jeffries, John Allison, 3998
Jenkins, David Price, 2750
Jennings, Bryant, 3891
Jennings, M. Anne, 3543

Jennsen, Gordon D., 2141, 2632
Jerry, M.B., 3269, 3752
Jersild, Jens, 3286, 3512, 3513
Jessee, William F., 2519
Jessor, Richard, 226
Jessor, Shirley L., 226
Jochheim, K.A., 734
Joe, Victor C., 4212
Joffe, Carole, 1748
Johnsen, Kathryn P., 325
Johnson, Adelaide M., 3196
Johnson, Alan B., 447
Johnson, Bascom, 3372
Johnson, Clara L., 2808
Johnson, Claudia D., 3373
Johnson, Corinne B., 2370
Johnson, Diane A., 1297
Johnson, Edwinna Gayle, 3670
Johnson, Eric W., 2370, 2376, 2377
Johnson, Flora, 2938
Johnson, Fred A., 1593
Johnson, Greg, 2468
Johnson, Harry J., 564
Johnson, Marcia, 1106
Johnson, Michael P., 2173, 2174
Johnson, Paula, 2990
Johnson, Ralph Aulden, 2751
Johnson, Ralph E., 2253-2255, 2316
Johnson, Ronald C., 708
Johnson, Virginia E., 24, 410, 411,
    463, 476, 1183, 1200, 1208, 1322,
    1484, 1528, 1529, 1643, 1644,
    2224, 4259
Johnson, Warren R., 80, 744, 2409,
    2549, 2845
Johnson, Weldon T., 4168
Johnson, William Steven, 792, 3867
Johnston, Cynthia D., 1411
Johnston, Jill, 946
Jonas, A. David, 793
Jonas, Doris F., 793
Jones, Arthur Hosking, 2317
Jones, Barbara, 4052
Jones, Cathaleene, 3649
Jones, Clinton R., 925, 2007
Jones, G. William, 4116
Jones, H. Gwynne, 3306
Jones, H. Kimball, 931
Jones, Hardin B., 522
Jones, Helen C., 522
Jones, Howard W., 2058
Jones, J. David, 1632
Jones, Louis Thomas, 2633
Jones, Phillip H., 191
Jones-Witters, Patricia, 550
Jordan, Robin, 960
Jorgensen, Christine, 2085
Joseph, Edward D., 999
Joseph, P.J., 2430
Joslyn, Wallace Danforth, 1947
Josselyn, Irene M., 1749
Jovanic, U.J., 1180
Jucha, D., 2494
Jurich, Anthony P., 1830, 2752, 2846
Jurich, Julie A., 2846

Kaats, Gilbert R., 4169

Kagan, Herman, 3409
Kahmen, Volker, 4041
Kahn, Edwin, 455-457
Kahn, Eugen, 3202
Kainz, Anna, 3091
Kakar, D.N., 773
Kallan, Richard A., 2991
Kalogerakis, Michael G., 192
Kamiat, Arnold H., 1000, 1037
Kamm, Jane A., 173
Kando, Thomas, 1750, 2008, 2025,
    2026
Kane, Francis J., 1197, 1975
Kanin, Eugene J., 268, 271, 326, 3611
Kanner, Leo, 104
Kant, Harold S., 3263, 3607, 3729,
    3935
Kantner, John F., 227, 235-237, 788,
    2829
Kaplan, Harold I., 61, 2401, 2516
Kaplan, Helen Singer, 397, 523,
    1181, 1230, 1467, 1468,
    1518-1520, 1591, 1976
Kaplan, Howard M., 555
Kaplan, Jeffrey Gene, 1356
Kappelman, Murray M., 1357, 2409
Karacan, Ismet, 458, 459, 3612
Kardener, Sheldon H., 1633, 1634
Karlen, Arno, 823, 879, 2397, 2525
Karow, William G., 1910
Karp, David A., 3410, 3947, 3948
Karpf, Maurice J., 3438
Karpinsky, Eva, 3234
Karpman, Benjamin, 565, 566, 1030,
    3733, 3750
Karsch-Haack, Ferdinand, 2634
Kass, David J., 1553, 1592
Kass, Irving, 667
Kassel, Victor, 398, 399
Katchadourian, Herant A., 2396,
    2411
Katz, Barbara J., 2175
Katz, Harvey Alan, 3937
Katz, Jack L., 1751
Katz, Jonathan, 880, 811
Katzman, Marshall, 3092, 3864
Kaufman, Gershen, 1365
Kaufman, Irving, 3093, 3168
Kaufman, Sherwin A., 400
Kaunitz, Paul E., 1017
Kawash, George F., 3892
Kayton, Robert, 691
Keane, Philip S., 2881
Kear, Karen, 2758
Keettel, W.C., 1799
Kegel, Arnold, 1198
Kehoe, Alice B., 2635
Keir, Richard George, 3910
Keiser, Sylvan, 1053
Keith, Claudia G., 3290
Kelleher, Maureen E., 3544
Keller, James F., 2167
Keller, R., 1752
Kellerhals, Adolf, 1064, 1076
Kelley, Robert K., 327
Kellner, Robert, 1992, 3622
Kellogg, Edmund H., 2431, 3042

Kelly, Gary F., 824, 1427, 1428, 2344,
    2385
Kelly, James J., 401, 402
Kelly, John F., 1010
Kemmer, Elizabeth Jane, 3653
Kempf, Edward J., 1753
Kemph, John P., 3232
Kempton, Winifred, 692, 714
Kendall, Diane, 2444
Kenna, J.C., 2024, 2043
Kennedy, B.J., 1977
Kennedy, Eugene M., 1401
Kennedy, Ian McColl, 2072
Kennedy, Judith R., 2800
Kennedy, Miriam, 3211, 3217
Kent, Rosemary R., 2552
Kent, Saul, 403
Kenton, Charlotte, 3564
Kercher, Glen A., 3613
Kerckhoff, Alan C., 794
Kerr, Charlotte H., 755
Kerr, Nora, 3798
Kerrigan, J., 3637
Kerscher, Karl-Heinz Ignatz, 112
Kessler, Kenneth, 2535
Kestenbaum, Clarice J., 1358
Kestenberg, Judith S., 1754
Keyes, D.M., 627
Khalaf, Samir, 3411, 3412, 3429
Khan, Masud R., 1054
Kiefer, C. Raymond, 3094
Kieffer, Carolynne Marie, 2176, 3414
Kiell, Norman, 4087
Kiev, Ari, 524
Kilpatrick, Dean G., 354, 362, 2753,
    2762
Kilpatrick, James Jackson, 3976
Kim, Chin, 3999
Kimmel, Ko, 2191
Kinberg, Olof, 3169
King, Alan L., 2790
King, Charles E., 2112
King, E.M., 2355
King, Helen, 110, 2354
King, Karl, 335, 2754
King, Michael, 269
King, Morgan D., 2177
Kinsey, Alfred C., 21, 22, 86, 87, 856,
    857, 915, 916, 979, 1107, 1251,
    1266, 1978, 2113, 2114, 2262,
    2265, 2755, 2756, 2847, 3095,
    3453, 3868, 4170, 4239
Kinsie, Paul M., 3349, 3350, 3468
Kirk, Stuart A., 3734
Kirk, R. Mark, 1706
Kirkendall, Lester A., 49, 270, 1429,
    1755, 2415, 2432, 2848, 2850, 3439
Kirkham, George L., 1108
Kirkpatrick, Clifford, 271
Kirkpatrick, J. Stephen, 1430
Kirkpatrick, R. George, 2757, 3989
Kirsch, Irving, 1469
Kisekka, Mere Nakateragga, 193,
    272, 2636
Kitahara, Michio, 1756
Klaf, Franklin S., 4016
Klaich, Dolores, 882

Klassen, Albert D., 919, 2759, 2319
Klebanow, Sheila, 194
Kleber, Herbert, 591
Kleeman, James, A. 1757
Klein, Henriette, 980
Kleinerman, Gerald, 804
Kleinman, Larry, 3477, 3478
Klemer, Richard H., 1282
Klimmer, Rudolf, 1016
Kline, David K., 2431
Kling, Arthur, 1948, 3886
Knapp, Jacquelyn J., 1311, 2283, 2318
Knight, Arthur, 4117, 4118
Knight, Susan E., 719
Knorr, Deitrich, 1919
Knorr, Norman J., 2031
Knowles, Lyle, 3869
Knudsen, Dean D., 4171
Knudsen, Per Holm, 2371
Kobasigawa, Akira, 1758
Kobayashi, Diana, 621
Koch, Joanne, 1470–1473
Koch, Lew, 1470–1473
Koch-Weser, Jan, 513
Kockott, Götz, 1123, 1210, 1990, 3918
Koff, Wayne C., 605
Kohl, Richard, 1520
Kohlberg, Lawrence, 1759, 1760
Kohlenberg, Robert J., 3307, 3308
Kokonis, Nicholas D., 1761
Kolansky, Harold, 606, 607
Kolářský, Aleš, 3911
Koller, Reuben, 674
Kolodny, Robert C., 608, 661, 1484, 4258, 4259
Koocher, Gerald P., 3771
Koomen, W., 2813
Korber, George William, 2808
Korner, Anneliese F., 113
Kortmulder, K., 2637
Kosnik, Anthony, 2882
Kouri, Robert P., 2073
Kozol, Harry L., 3716, 3788
Kraemer, Helena, 1979
Kraemer, William, 3294
Krafft-Ebing, Richard von, 981
Kraft, Tomas, 525, 1635
Kraus, J., 3823
Krause, Walter, 1920
Kravetz, James H., 2469
Kreitler, Hans, 114
Kreitler, Shulamith, 114
Kremer, Ellen B., 1359
Kriegman, George, 1431
Krippner, Stanley, 2027
Kroger, William S., 1521, 1569
Krohne, Eric C., 1583
Kroll, Eric, 3479
Kronhausen, Eberhard, 4000, 4042–4044, 4088
Kronhausen, Phyllis, 4000, 4042–4044, 4088
Kubat, Hadassa, 2524
Kuby, Lolette, 3638, 3650
Kuh, Richard H., 3977

Kuhlen, Raymond G., 147
Kuhn, Lauren L., 3482
Kuhn, Margaret E., 404
Kumar, Pramod, 3331
Kunkel, Francis Leo, 4089
Kunter, M., 3170
Kupfer, David J., 1304, 1456
Kupperman, Herbert S., 1882
Kupperstein, Lenore, 3735, 3853
Kuriansky, Judith B., 1474
Kurland, Morton L., 1762, 3304
Kurtz, Richard M., 4187
Kutchinsky, Berl, 3762, 3938
Kutner, Nancy G., 1702, 4233
Kyger, Kent, 1883
Kyrou, Ado, 4119

La Barre, Weston, 592, 1763, 2638, 2639
Labby, Daniel H., 1312
Labouvie-Uief, Gisela, 1842
Lacey, Peter, 4140
LaCroix, Paul, 3374
Ladner, Joyce A., 3043
Laemmel, Klaus, 4017
Lagercrantz, Sture, 2640
La Granade, Janet, 2420
Lal, Kanwar, 4045
Lamberth, John, 3862
Lambley, Peter, 1156
Lamson, Herbert D., 2851
Lanchar, David, 4222
Landau, Sybil, 3651, 3671
Landis, C.E., 1432, 2350
Landis, Judson T., 1383, 3096
Landman, Louis, 2916
Lando, Pier Luigi, 115
Landreth, Catherine, 116
Landy, Eugene E., 616
Langevin, Ron, 850, 2028, 3284
Langmyhr, George, 1313
Langsley, Donald G., 3218
Langston, Robert D., 273, 274, 2782
Lansing, Cornelius, 1314
Lansky, Leonard M., 1764, 1826
Lantagne, Joseph E., 148
Lanza, Charlene, 3695, 3696, 3698
Larco Hoyle, Rafael, 4046
Larsen, Knud S., 275, 328, 2810, 4213
Larson, Carl A., 3171
Larson, David L., 3045
Larson, Richard F., 1402, 1403
Larsson, Knut, 1270
Laserstein, Botho, 3514
Lassen, Carol L., 1475, 2566
Latendresse, John D., 526
LaTorre, Ronald A., 2758
Laub, Donald R., 2016, 2059
Laubscher, Barend J., 2641
Laughren, Thomas P., 1553
Launay, Cl, 195
Lauritsen, John, 947
LaVeck, Gerald D., 710
Lawrence, Charles R., 780
Lawrence, Raymond, 2222

Laws, Donald Richard, 1992, 3309, 3622, 3799
Laws, Judith Long, 1765, 1766, 3044
Lawson, David M., 583, 584
Lawton, Shailer U., 196
Layman, William A., 3137
Lazar, Gerald M., 2992
Lazarus, Arnold A., 1315, 1476
Leach, Michael, 3978
Leader, Elaine, 2044
Leaf, Earl, 4150
Leahy, Jack, 2509
LeBeuf, Jacques, 1022
Lebovitz, Phil S., 1767
Lee, Margie, 2470
Lee, Richard Borshay, 2642
Lee, Ronald R., 2216
LeFebvre, Paul, 1022
Lefkowitz, David, 308
Leggitt, Hunter, 2285
Legman, Gershon, 4090
LeGrand, Camille E., 3672
Legros, J.J., 1980, 1981
Lehman, Robert E., 3912
Lehrman, N.S., 1636
Lehtinen, Marlene Warring, 329
Leiblum, Sandra, 1558
Leibowitz, Lila, 2643
Leigh, L.H., 982
Leitch, David, 3525
LeLieuvre, Robert B., 1768
Lemere, Frederick, 567
Lemert, Edwin M., 3332
Lennox, Thomas, 503
Lentz, William D., 2074
Lenzer, Gertrud, 1055
Leon, Sidney, 693
Leonard, Wilbert M., 2315
Leroy, Bernard, 1067
Leroy, David H., 1577, 1672
Leroy, John P., 873
Leshner, Martin, 747
Lesniak, Roman, 647
Lesoualc'h, Theo, 4018
Lester, David, 1418, 2811, 3138, 3614, 3621
Lettieri, Dan J., 503
Leventhal, D.B., 1825
Lever, Janet, 276
Levin, Bernard H., 2823
Levin, Robert J., 1477, 2224
Levin, Saul M., 117
Levine, Jacob, 568
Levine, Jerome, 593
Levine, Lena, 1563
Levine, Lenore S., 1884
Lipton, Morris, 1197, 1975, 4001
Liptzin, Myron B., 1378
Liss, Edward, 1001
Liss-Levinson, Nechama, 2995
Lister, Milton, 1002
Liston, Edward H., 2523
Litman, Robert E., 1077
Little, Douglas M., 3885
Littner, Ner, 3717
Liu, William T., 3009
Livingood, John M., 904

Livsey, Clara G., 1318
Lloyd, Frederick A., 443
Lloyd, Robin, 3515
Lobell, John, 2284
Lobell, Mimi, 2284
Lobitz, W. Charles, 1524, 1525
Lock, Frank, 1384
Lockhart, William B., 4002
Lo Duca, Giuseppe, 4019, 4120
Loewe, S., 527
Loewenstein, Rudolph M., 1058
Logan, Constance, 4214
Logan, Nell, 225
Logie, P., 611
Loh, Wei P., 613
Lohrenz, John G., 481
Longford, Frank Pakenham, 3856
Longmore, Laura, 2646
Loovis, David, 948, 958
Lopez, Thomas W., 3736
LoPiccolo, Joseph, 1462, 1522, 1523, 1525, 1559, 1560, 1600, 2116, 2760
LoPiccolo, Leslie, 1462, 1600
Loraine, J.A., 883
Lord, Jere W., 675
LoSciuto, Leonard A., 3872
Losen, Stuart M., 2461
Loth, David, 3980
Love, Barbara, 938
Love, Robert E., 3871
Lowman, Annelle Zerbe, 2761
Lowry, Thea Snyder, 1479, 1640, 1674
Lowry, Thomas P., 229, 230, 1479, 1640, 1674, 3454
Luccu, Albina, 143
Luce, Ralph A., 2955
Lucie-Smith, Edward, 4047
Luckey, Eleanor B., 277
Ludovici, Anthony M., 984, 3615
Ludwig, Arnold M., 593
Ludwig, Edward G., 3045
Lukianowicz, Narcyz, 1078, 1110, 1137, 3172
Lumby, Malcolm E., 4243
Luna, Manuel, 1962
Lunde, Donald T., 1983, 1950, 2396
Lunghi, M., 1818
Luparello, Thomas J., 668
Luschen, Mary E., 1928
Lustig, Noel, 1381, 2216
Lutier, J., 3173
Luttge, William G., 1984
Lynch, W. Ware, 3652
Lyness, Judith L., 2178
Lynn, David B., 1704, 1772, 2135
Lyon, Phyllis, 887, 949
Lyons, Albert S., 656

McBee, George W., 3742
McCaffrey, Joseph A., 884
McCaghy, Charles H., 570, 3242, 3265, 3266
McCarthy, Barry W., 1526, 1593
McCartney, James L., 1645
McCary, James Leslie, 23, 52, 407,

1594, 2398, 2399, 2412, 2413, 2499, 3140
McCausland, Maureen, 3072
McClean, Donald, 2243
McClure, Robert C., 4002
Maccoby, Eleanor E., 1773, 1774
McCombie, Sharon L., 3699, 3700
McConaghy, Nathaniel, 3914
McConnell, Lawrence G., 1319, 1433–1435
McCoy, Nancy Nichols, 1480
McCoy, Ralph E., 3981
McCreary, Charles P., 3267
McCreary-Juhasz, Anne, 2179, 2485, 2504, 2553
McCrocklin, Michael T., 1481
McCubbin, Jack H., 3701
MacCulloch, M.J., 923, 4235, 4237
McCullough, Rita Colene, 1199
McDermott, John F., 2536, 4020
MacDonald, A.P., Jr., 920, 4234, 4244
MacDonald, Allen D.G., 2009
MacDonald, George J., 3800
MacDonald, John M., 3098, 3616, 3653, 3751, 3837
McDonald, Nancy P., 90
McDonald, Thomas D., 2718
MacDougal, Duncan, 4151
McDougall, Joyce, 1003
McDowell, Fletcher H., 721
McDowell, Kenneth V., 2680
Mace, David R., 1320, 1388, 1404, 1639, 2505, 2904
McEntee, Roseann, 549
McGeorge, John, 3268
McGhee, Paul E., 1727
McGrady, Patrick M., Jr., 1482
McGrath, P.G., 3801
McGuire, Linda S., 1321, 3617
Machen, Robert B., 2434
Machlowitz, Marilyn M., 1421
Machotka, Pavel, 3141
McHugh, Gelolo, 4199
McIlvenna, Ted, 1603, 1604
Macindoe, Ian, 3713
McIntire, John R., 184
MacKay, Dougal, 3802
McKee, Embry A., 2063
MacKellar, Jean S., 3577
McKenney, Mary, 1283
McKinlay, John B., 1938
McKinlay, Sonja M., 1938
Macklin, Eleanor D., 278, 330, 2180–2182
McLachlan, D.G., 1144, 1145
Maclay, W.S., 3803
MacLean, Charles J., 3174
MacLean, Paul D., 1182, 1775
McLeish, John, 985
McMahon, Judith Wantland, 2812
MacMillan, Jackie, 3333
MacNamara, Donal E.J., 62, 3516, 3549, 3836, 3838, 3839
McNamara, Patrick, 3418
McNeill, John J., 932, 2883
Maddock, James W., 1527, 2506
Madison, Jan, 3046

Madlafousek, Jaroslav, 3911
Madorsky, Martin, 408
Magal, V., 3175
Magar, Edward Magar, 2256
Maglin, Arthur, 528
Mahrer, Alvin R., 356
Maisch, Herbert, 3176
Malcarney, Courtney N., 3106
Malchanov, Elaine, 2782
Malfetti, James L., 53, 2510, 2511, 2554
Malin, Joseph M., 774
Malinowski, Bronislaw, 2647, 2648
Mandel, Adeline U., 3213
Mandel, Nathan G., 2471
Mandetta, Anne F., 2537
Mankoff, Allan H., 3480
Mann, Carola H., 409
Mann, Geoffrey Thomas, 3689
Mann, Jay, 3851, 3939, 3940
Mann, Thaddeus, 594
Manniche, Erik, 279
Mannion, Kristiann, 862
Man Thiel, David H., 570
Marcadé, Jean, 4049, 4050
Marchand, Henry L., 4091
Marcom, Betty R., 2533
Marcotte, David B., 2527, 2762, 4214
Marcus, Eric H., 3772
Marcus, Steven, 4092
Margolis, Herbert, 2289
Marin, A., 623
Marks, Isaac M., 1038, 3810
Marks, Philip A., 2719
Marmor, Judd, 825, 885, 886, 1232, 1641
Marshall, Donald S., 54, 2649
Martin, A. Joyce, 597
Martin, Clyde E., 16, 21, 22, 86, 87, 462, 857, 916, 1251, 1266, 2113, 2114, 2265, 2756, 2847, 3453, 4170, 4239
Martin, Cy, 3375
Martin, Del 887, 949, 3047
Martin, J. David, 2144
Martin, James O., 3177
Martin, Peter A., 2145
Martines, Lauro, 3055
Martino, Mario, 2086
Martinson, Floyd M., 88, 119, 198, 199
Marwell, Gerald, 1776
Marzilli, Robert, 1537
Masham, Baroness Masham of Ilton, 735
Masica, Daniel N., 1777
Mason, Karen Oppenheim, 3048
Massey, Carmen, 2183
Massey, Joe B., 3702
Mast, Marian, 1927
Masters, R.E.L., 595, 3142, 3317, 3492
Masters, William H., 24, 410, 411, 463, 476, 1183, 1200, 1208, 1322, 1483, 1484, 1528, 1529, 1642–1643, 2224, 4259
Mathiasen, Sally Ellis, 3654, 3673

Mathis, James L., 529, 766, 1323, 1778
Matthews, Joan, 836
Mattsson, Ake, 1645
May, James, 3902
Mayadas, Nazneen S., 1284
Mayer, Karl Herbert, 2650
Maykovich, Minako K., 2263, 2320
Mayle, Peter, 2372
Mazer, Donald, 356
Mazur, Ronald M., 1412, 1413, 2351, 2386, 2486, 2905, 2996
Mazur, Tom, 1988, 2065
Mead, Beverley T., 1324, 1325, 2225, 2956
Mead, Margaret, 826, 2651-2653
Meade, Marion, 3049
Meadow, Rosalyn, 3046
Mechler, Ulrich, 1018
Medea, Andra, 3618
Meeks, Linda Brower, 2328
Meeks, Wilson M., 3773
Meerdink, Robert C., 2472
Mees, Hayden, 1023, 1034, 3767, 3790
Meggitt, M.J., 2654
Mehan, Hugh, 4172
Meigs, Anna S., 2655
Melchiode, Gerald A., 57
Meldrum, S.J., 1192
Melges, Frederick T., 1929, 1985
Melikian, Levon H., 280
Mellan, Jiri, 205, 619
Mellen, Joan, 4121, 4122
Mello, Nancy, 571
Mellor, V., 4236
Melville, Robert, 4051
Mendelsohn, B., 3655
Mendelsohn, Jack A., 571
Mendelsohn, Robert A., 1779
Mendelson, Jack H., 610
Mendes, Peter, 4141
Menen, Aubrey, 3578
Menninger, W. Walter, 707
Mensch, Ivan N., 1634
Merdzhanov, Ch., 1264
Merenski, J. Paul, 2790
Meri, La, 4144
Merritt, C. Gary, 3872
Messenger, John C., 2656
Messer, Alfred A., 3143
Messinger, David, 1285
Metzger, Deena, 3656
Meuser, Wolfgang, 1986
Meyberg, Ulrich, 3922
Meyenburg, Bernd, 1336, 1500, 1587
Meyer, Jon K., 1326, 1485, 1570, 2017, 2030, 2031, 2958
Meyer, Timothy P., 3941
Meyer, V., 1540
Meyer-Bahlburg, Heino F., 1907, 1917, 1951, 1987
Meyers, David W., 2075
Meyerwitz, Joseph H., 715
Michael, Richard P., 1866, 1886, 1921, 2657
Michaux, Leon, 1039

Micheletti, V., 558
Michelson, Peter, 4093
Michielutte, Robert, 2184
Mickley, Richard R., 933
Middendorp, C.P., 2813
Middleton, Russell, 3144
Middour, Robert C., 2552
Mikesell, Richard H., 1698, 1780
Mikulas, William L., 1530
Miles, Greg J., 2432
Miller, Benjamin F., 2387
Miller, Brent C., 2820
Miller, H.R., 1432, 2350, 2355
Miller, Howard, 281
Miller, Jean Baker, 1781, 2997
Miller, Judi, 3639
Miller, Mary Susan, 2334
Miller, Merle, 888
Miller, Michael B., 412
Miller, Patricia Y., 200, 3099
Miller, Robert D., 4257
Miller, Shirley Matile, 1782
Miller, Vinnie H., 1522, 1523, 1559, 1560
Miller, Warren B., 231, 1042, 2763
Miller, William R., 2764
Millet, Kate, 3334
Milligan, Herman J., 1720
Mills, Lewis, C., 662
Milman, Doris H., 530
Milne, Hugo, 1571
Milner, Richard B., 2658, 3462
Mims, Fern, 2538, 2538
Minnigerode, Fred A., 413
Mintz, Jim, 531
Mirande, Alfred M., 2765
Mitani, Yasushi, 1930
Mitchell, Cynthia, 4262
Mitchell, Howard E., 2147
Mitchell, Leslie Howard, 1783
Mitchell, Marianne, 1436
Mitton, Jeffrey B., 2706
Mizokawa, Donald Tsuneo, 2555
Mohr, Johann W., 2054, 3100, 3243, 3269, 3298, 3299, 3752, 3794, 3803, 3804, 3822, 3825
Molnar, G., 3178
Money, John, 7, 55, 69, 201, 532, 669, 827, 1102, 1111, 1112, 1138, 1267, 1585, 1719, 1735, 1777, 1784-1792, 1858, 1904-1906, 1911, 1988, 2010, 2015, 2032, 2058, 2064, 2065, 2659, 3848
Monroe, Ruth, 1793
Monsour, Karem J., 282
Montagu, M.F., Ashley, 120, 2660, 2661
Montague, Susan P., 2662
Montgomery, Jason, 2185
Mooney, Thomas O., 736
Moor, L., 1039
Moore, Burness Evans, 1233
Moore, James E., 2444
Moore, Julie L., 367
Moore, William T., 606, 607
Moos, Rudolf H., 1931, 3849
Moran, Barbara K., 3035

Moravia, Alberto, 4094
Mordell, Albert, 4095
Morgenstern, F.S., 1157
Morgenthaler, Fritz, 1646
Morgenthau, Joan E., 138
Morin, Stephen F., 863
Morley, J.E., 611
Morokoff, Patricia, 3900
Morosco, B. Anthony, 3840
Morris, Jan, 2087
Morris, Naomi M., 2146, 2154-2156, 4178
Morrison, Eleanor S., 56, 2335, 2400, 2852
Morrison, James L., 2186
Morrow, William R., 3774, 3826
Morthland, John, 3957
Mosher, Clelia Duel, 3029
Mosher, Donald L., 331, 357, 2710, 3915, 3916, 4227
Mosovich, Abraham, 1268
Moss, Gene R., 1158
Mourad, Mahmoud, 745
Mowrer, Harriet R., 2117
Mozley, Paul D., 414
Mudd, Emily (Hartshorne), 1549, 2147
Mudd, John W., 283, 1647
Muffly, Robert B., 667
Mulas, Antonia, 4038
Mulcock, Donald, 3270
Mueller, D., 3805
Mullan, J., 517
Mullen, Stephen, 1217, 1265
Muller, Charlotte, 3050
Müller, D., 3287, 3301
Mundy, Jean, 3657
Munroe, Allan R., 3714
Munroe, Robert L., 1139, 1793
Murdock, George P., 2663
Murphy, Christine V., 1530
Murstein, Bernard I., 284
Musaph, Herman, 201, 1858
Mussen, Paul Henry, 1794, 1795
Myers, Lonny, 2257, 2285
Myers, Wayne A., 121
Myerson, Abraham, 837
Myrick, Robert D., 1796
Myron, Nancy, 3051

Nacht, Sacha, 1059
Nadelson, Carol C., 1360, 3658, 3703
Nadler, Ronald D., 1269
Naffziger, Claudeen Cline, 2957
Naffziger, Ken, 2957
Nag, Moni, 2148, 2664
Nagel, Stuart, 4003
Naiman, James, 1648
Nash, E.M., 2512
Nash, James L., 2940
Nash, Kermit B., 1437
Nass, Gilbert, 277
Natterson, Joseph, 2531
Nau, Elizabeth, 3226
Nawy, Harold, 3950
Neary, Richard S., 553
Nederlander, Caren E. Berman, 1531

Nedoma, Karel, 3271
Neef, Marian, 4003
Neeley, Roy E., Jr., 2766
Neiger, Stephen, 1327, 1532
Neimark, Paul G., 751
Nejelski, Paul, 4260
Nell, Renée, 696
Nelsen, R. Owen, 3737
Němeček, Ottokar, 2665
Neubardt, Selig B., 3052
Neubauer, Peter B., 1798
Neubeck, Gerhard, 2226, 2227, 2258
Neustadt, Rudolph, 837
Newman, Benjamin W., 426
Newman, Graeme, 2666
Newman, Gustave, 464, 465
Newman, Herbert F., 1209
Newman, Lawrence E., 832, 2038, 2051, 2052
Newman, Ronald B., 3457, 3467
Newton, Niles, 4207
Ng, Allan Y., 3619
Nichols, Claude R., 464, 465
Nichols, F.R., 2322, 2821
Nichols, Jack, 941, 2958
Nielson, Patrick A., 2187
Niemoeller, Adolf Frederick, 3335
Nieschlag, Eberhard, 1986
Nietzke, Ann, 3053
Nimmo, H. Arlo, 2667
Nims, Jerry P., 1533
Nochlin, Linda, 4040
Noe, Joel M., 2059
Noguera, Gary, 950
Nolte, Claude, 1595
Nolte, Dorothy, 1595
Norcross, Keith, 756, 1675
Norris, A.S., 1799
Norton, Rictor, 959, 962
Norwick, Kenneth P., 3982, 4004
Notman, Malkah T., 3658, 3703
Novick, Jack, 1004
Novick, Kerry K., 1004
Nuehring, Elane M., 1438
Nussel, Edward J., 483
Nutt, Roberta L., 285
Nyberg, Kenneth L., 921, 2814
Nyswander, Marie, 533, 994

Oaks, Wilbur W., 57, 534
Oberholtzer, W. Dwight, 934
Obler, Martin, 1554, 1555
Oboler, Eli M., 3983
O'Brien, Eleanor, 684
Ochsner, Alton, 618
O'Connell, Barbara E., 3054
O'Connor, John F., 1572
Oettinger, Moshe, 1937
Oetzel, Roberta M., 1683
O'Faolain, Julia, 3055
Offer, Daniel, 123, 150, 202, 203, 4188
Offer, Judith L., 203
Offir, Carole, 2945
Offit, Avodah, 1460
Ogden, Wendell, 3707
Ogren, David John, 2768

Olasov, Joseph Tigler, 4189
Oldham, James, 3706
Oliven, John F., 25, 1328, 3101, 3704
Olsen, Gunnar Aagaard, 204
Olson, David H., 3487
O'Neill, George, 2287
O'Neill, Nena, 2286, 2287
O'Neill, William, 2769, 2941
Opler, Marvin K., 2668, 2669
Oppenheim, Garrett, 1113
Oraison, Marc, 935
Orfirer, Alexander P., 666
Orö, Lars, 1873
O'Rourke, Diane M., 2435
O'Rourke, Thomas W., 2435, 2728
Orr, Douglass W., 2670
Orthner, H., 3301, 3805
Ortner, Sherry B., 2671
Osborn, Candice A., 3917
Osborne, Harold, 2170
Osofsky, Howard J., 139, 2942
Osofsky, Joy D., 2942
Ostow, Mortimer, 535
Ostwald, Hans Otto August, 3463
Oswalt, Robert M., 286
Otte, Frank, 2420
Otto, Herbert A., 58, 986
Ouelette, William, 4052
Ovenden, Graham, 4141
Oziel, Jerome L., 2747

Pacht, Asher, 3722, 3738, 3806, 3808
Packard, Vance, 26, 332, 3455
Paitich, Daniel, 2028, 3753, 4215
Palazzetti, Piero, 1385
Palm, Rose, 3620
Palmer, Eddie C., 3396, 3471
Palmieri, Vincenzo Mario, 3517
Paluszny, Maria, 1800
Panajian, Avedis, 3518
Pannor, Reuben, 1286
Paonessa, John J., 2445
Paonessa, Mary W., 2445
Papertain, Gérard, 3240
Paredes, Alfonso, 572
Parelman, Allison, 1681
Pariente, Barbara J., 3548
Park, Georgia K., 287
Park, R.L., 1068
Parker, Frederick B., 573, 574
Parker, Seymour, 1801, 3145
Parker, William, 808, 864, 4065
Parkin, Alan, 1060
Parks, R.D., 3579
Parrish, Vestal W., 2428
Parsons, Talcott, 3146
Pasamanick, Benjamin, 2774
Pasini, Willy, 1487, 1534
Patil, B.R., 3377
Paul, J.C.N., 3850, 3992
Paul, Leslie, 2853
Pauly, Ira B., 2029, 2033, 2228, 2321, 2513–2515
Pawlowski, A.W., 3309
Paykel, Eugene S., 697
Payne, Barbara, 416
Payne, David, 2433

Payne, Tyana, 2540
Peake, Richard Henry, 3378, 4134
Pearce, J.F., 1157
Pearl, Raymond, 2149
Pearlin, Leonard I., 795
Pearlman, Carl K., 466, 2150
Pearson, Manuel M., 415
Pearson, Pat (Hendricks), 3580
Peck, Alice L., 3093, 3168
Peckham, Morse, 4021
Peek, Charles W., 2947
Pekkanen, John, 3581
Peller, Robert, 2961
Peltz, Dorthyann, 2260
Perdue, William C., 3621
Perkins, Barbara B., 136
Perkins, Charles W., 694
Perkins, John C., 333, 4216
Perkins, Michael, 4096
Perkins, Worcester, 1405
Perlman, Daniel, 246, 288, 358, 4156
Perry, David G., 1802
Perry, Judith Adams, 1649
Perry, Louise C., 1802
Perry, Troy D., 936
Persky, Harold, 1932
Peruzza, Marino, 386
Peterman, Dan J., 289, 2188
Peters, Joseph J., 3102, 3272, 3300, 3305, 3659, 3807, 3809
Peterson, Donald B., 3774, 3826
Peterson, Gail Beaton, 3056
Peterson, James A., 416, 1329, 1488, 2229
Petit, Germain, 1079
Petras, John W., 1803, 2959
Pfeiffer, Eric, 378, 417–419, 467–470, 477, 478
Philbert, M., 2045
Phillip, Erhard, 3227
Phillips, Derek L., 698
Phillips, Gene D., 4123
Phillips, James K., 307
Piemme, Thomas E., 536
Pierce, David M., 1928
Pierce, Diane, 1558
Pietrofesa, John J., 124, 1439–1442
Pietropinto, Anthony, 2266, 2770, 4203
Pigg, Roger, 3934
Pilpel, Harriet F., 4005
Pinard, Leo William, 2672
Pinch, Lewis, 1907
Pinderhughes, Charles A., 699
Pinschof, J.M., 4236
Pion, Ronald J., 224
Piper, Otto A., 2907
Pirke, Karl M., 1210, 1989, 1990, 3918
Pirnay-Dufrasne, Régine, 3228
Pitt, Bruce, 471
Pittenger, Norman, 937
Pittenger, W. Norman, 2908
Pittman, David J., 3519, 4261
Pittman, Frank S., 3141, 3219
Pivar, David J., 3379
Pleck, Joseph H., 1804, 2960
Pleissner, K., 1867

Plonsky, Carolyn Giffen, 2556
Ploscowe, Morris, 3674, 3841
Ploss, Herman Heinrich, 3380
Pocs, Ollie, 290, 2771
Podell, Lawrence, 333, 4216
Podolsky, Edward, 1114, 1262
Poffenberger, Thomas, 2854
Pokrovskiĭ, N. Iû, 1489
Pollack, Robert H., 3917
Pollitt, Ernesto, 1138
Pomeroy, Wardell B., 16, 21, 22, 86,
    87, 125, 757, 857, 916, 1159, 1251,
    1263, 1266, 1395, 1490, 2053,
    2113, 2114, 2265, 2378, 2379,
    2414, 2756, 2847, 3229, 3413,
    3453, 3481, 4170, 4239
Pondelicková, J., 205
Poorkaj, Houshang, 3869
Pope, H., 4171
Pope, Michael, 3984
Potrykus, Dagmar, 3103
Poulsen, Susan B., 3012
Powell, Aaron Macy, 3381
Powell, Leslie Charles, 1535
Powell, Marion G., 2352
Powers, Ann, 1536
Powis, David, 3464
Poznanski, Elva, 3179
Praz, Mario, 4097
Presser, Carole Smith, 2076
Presser, Harriet B., 2998
Preston, Caroline E., 421
Price, Dorothy, 1805
Price, James H., 2403
Price, Mila U., 2335, 2852
Price, Quentin L., 2488
Priester, Helen Moore, 206
Prill, Hans-Joachim, 420
Primov, George, 3414
Prince, Charles (Virginia), 1129– 1131
Prince, Joyce, 3086
Prince, Virginia, 1115, 1125
Prince, Virginia (Charles), 1140
Prockaska, James O., 1537
Proctor, E.B., 1222
Prosen, Harry, 700
Prothro, Terry, 280
Pugh, Meredith D., 1845
Pullan, B.R., 3306
Puppe, George, 3582
Purdy, Strother, 4098
Putnam, Samuel, 3336

Quinn, J.T., 1491
Quinsey, Vernon L., 3273, 3310, 3311
Quirk, Barbara, 2541

Rabenalt, Arthur Maria, 4135
Rabin, Albert I., 2674
Rabin, Barry J., 637, 737
Rabkin, Judith G., 1287
Raboch, Jan, 43, 472, 473, 619, 1252,
    1991, 3415
Rabosky, John J., 3934
Rachman, Stanley, 1038
Rada, Richard T., 575, 1158, 1992,
    3583, 3622

Rado, Sandor, 828, 1806
Radzinowicz, Leon, 3104, 3739, 3827
Ragan, James Arthur, 3640
Rahav, Giora, 3421
Rainwater, Lee, 781, 805, 4261
Ram, Bali, 2675
Ramey, Estelle R., 1807
Ramey, James W., 2288
Ramsey, Glenn V., 126, 127,
    207–209, 2446
Randell, John B., 987, 1141
Ranker, Jess Elwood, 2772
Ranney, Brooks, 2437
Rapaud, G., 1039
Raphling, David L., 3203
Rappaport, Ernest A., 1005
Raschke, Vernon J., 359
Rascovsky, Arnaldo, 3204
Rascovsky, Matilde, 3204
Rashevsky, Nicholas, 1808
Raskind, Murray A., 421
Rasmussen, Paul K., 3482
Ratliff, Dale H., 1406
Rausher, Shirley R., 2557
Raven, Simon, 3520
Rawson, M., 649
Rawson, Philip, 4053–4055
Ray, Rose E., 360, 3919, 3920
Raybin, James B., 3147
Raynor, Darrell G., 1116
Ready, Jerry Lee, 2558
Rechy, John, 889
Reckless, Walter C., 3337
Redfering, David L., 2489
Reed, Charles E., 2559
Reed, David M., 422, 1492, 2151,
    4198
Reed, John P., 3873, 4006
Reed, Max R., 1809
Reed, Robin S., 3873, 4006
Rees, Bill, 2490
Rees, Jim, 3775
Rees, W. Linford, 1157
Reese, Tamara, 2088
Reevy, William R., 89, 128, 210, 291,
    334, 2118, 2773
Reich, Wilhelm, 1223, 2855
Reiche, Reimut, 899
Reichelt, Paul A., 2473, 2474
Reichlin, Seymour, 1993
Reid, John, 917
Reifen, David, 3105
Reifler, Clifford B., 1377, 1378, 3942
Reik, Theodor, 1061
Reinisch, June M., 1810, 1909, 1910
Reisner, Robert George, 4066
Reiss, Albert J., Jr., 3521, 3842
Reiss, Ira L., 27, 151, 232, 782, 796,
    1811, 2305, 2815–2820, 4191,
    4200, 4217
Reitman, Ben L., 3456, 3465
Rekers, George A., 1160, 1812
Remy, M., 3803
Rennert, Helmut, 211, 3180
Renshaw, Domeena C., 129, 130,
    423, 1493
Resko, John A., 1963

Resnick, H.L.P., 59, 1080, 3305, 3740
Resnik, Phillip J., 2521
Rettig, Salomon, 2774
Revitch, Eugene, 1024, 3274
Reyna, L.J., 699
Rhinehart, John W., 3181
Ribal, Joseph E., 81
Rice, David G., 2999
Rice, Joy K., 2999
Richards, David A.J., 4007
Richardson, Frank, 829
Richardson, Herbert W., 2856
Richart, Ralph M., 1726, 1945
Richmond, Len, 950
Richter, Lin, 1508
Rickles, Nathan King, 3754
Riddell, William Renwick, 1025
Ridley, Carl A., 289, 2188
Riegel, Robert E., 3338
Riemer, Svend, 3169, 3182
Rife, Dwight W., 3705
Rinder, Irwin D., 3186
Risher, Mary Jo, 875
Rist, Ray C., 2857, 3985
Roback, Howard Byron, 2034, 2035
Robbin, Fae, 1113
Robbins, Jhan, 1538
Robbins, June, 1538
Robbins, Mina-May Brown, 2141
Robbins, Paul R., 612
Robertiello, Richard C., 1040, 1234,
    1651, 2943
Roberts, Karlene, 1725
Roberts, Leigh M., 3808
Roberts, Ralph M., 2489
Roberts, Robert E., 3741, 3742
Robertson, Leon S., 1944
Robins, Eli, 906
Robinson, G. Erlick, 3706
Robinson, Henry A., 3106
Robinson, Ira E., 292, 335, 2754
Robinson, John P., 4173
Robinson, Paul, 28
Roby, Pamela A., 3384, 3547
Roche, Philip Q., 1041
Rockwell, Kenneth, 336, 500, 537
Rodgers, Harrell R., 3986
Rodman, Hyman, 2189, 2322, 2821
Roebuck, Julian, 3416–3418
Roeder, Fritz Douglas, 3287, 3301,
    3805
Roesler, T., 853
Roether, Hermann A., 3809
Rogawski, Alexander S., 2119
Rogers, Kenneth P., 3584
Rogers, Rex S., 2438, 2447
Róheim, Géza, 2676, 2677
Rokeach, Milton, 4174
Rolett, Karin, 716
Rolph, C.H., 3393
Romano, Mary D., 746, 1330
Romieu, Antoine, 1543
Root, Allen W., 1922
Root, Irving, 3707
Rooth, F. Graham, 3810
Ropert, Martine, 557
Rose, Al, 3385

Rose, Robert M., 1952
Rosen, Aaron, 1331
Rosen, Alexander C., 1813
Rosen, David H., 905
Rosen, Lawrence, 2261, 3874
Rosen, Marvin, 717
Rosen, Raymond C., 1211, 1218, 1558
Rosenberg, Bernard, 783, 1814
Rosenberg, Charles E., 797, 3062
Rosenberg, Edward B., 2387
Rosenberg, Gary, 2563
Rosenberg, Lois M., 2356, 2357
Rosenberg, Morris, 4190
Rosenberg, Pearl, 2356, 2357, 2528
Rosenblatt, Paul C., 2678–2680
Rosenblatt, Sidney, 576
Rosenbleet, Charles, 3548
Rosenblum, Jay A., 648, 722
Rosenblum, Karen E., 3419
Rosenblum, Leonard A., 1269
Rosene, James Melvin, 3943
Rosenfeld, David L., 3708
Rosenthal, Ted L., 3312
Rosner, Aria C., 2358
Rosner, Fred, 2875
Ross, H. Laurence, 3522
Ross, Michael W., 1815
Ross, Robert T., 293
Rossi, Lee D., 3057
Rossman, G. Parker, 3288, 3289
Roth, Edwin I., 3107
Rothman, G., 988
Rowe, George P., 96
Rowse, Alfred Leslie, 890
Roy, Della, 2858
Roy, Julie, 1623
Roy, Rustum, 2858
Rubenstein, Ben, 1652
Rubenstein, Maggie, 1601
Rubenstein, Paul, 2289
Rubin, Arline M., 2554, 2560
Rubin, Herman H., 426 ·
Rubin, Isadore, 427, 428, 474, 670, 758, 1755, 2415, 2475
Rubin, Lillian Breslow, 806
Rubin, Zick, 4185, 4262
Rubinstein, Eli A., 60
Rudy, Arthur J., 2961
Rueger, Russ, 2962
Ruether, Rosemary R., 2920
Ruff, Carol F., 3623
Ruitenbeek, Hendrik M., 29, 891
Rupp, Joseph C., 1081
Ruppel, Howard J., Jr., 798, 2822, 4165
Russell, Bertrand R., 2859
Russell, Diana E.H., 3660
Russell, Donald H., 3523
Rustad, L.C., 730
Rutherford, Eldred Eugene, 1816
Rutter, Michael, 131, 1817
Ryan, James J., 2060
Ryan, John Julian, 2884
Ryan, Mary, 1593
Ryan, Mary Perkins, 2884
Ryle, A., 1818

Rymph, David B., 1142, 2681

Saba Sardi, Francesco, 4099
Sabadini, G., 1143
Sabalis, Robert F., 2036
Sachs, Donald H., 3944
Sack, Robert L., 1042
Sackett, G.P., 1836
Sacks, Michael Paul, 3058
Sacks, Sylvia R., 1361
Sadd, Susan, 1257, 4204
Sade, Donald Stone, 3183
Sadger, J., 1006
Sadock, Benjamin J., 61, 1546, 1562, 2401
Sadock, Virginia A., 1184, 1546, 2516
Sadoff, Robert L., 3300, 3718, 3719, 3807, 3843
Sadoughi, Wanda, 747, 3549
Sagarin, Edward, 62, 1108, 1117, 1819, 3184, 3440, 3641, 3763, 3839, 4175, 4263, 4264
Sager, Clifford J., 397, 1573
Saghir, Marcel T., 906
St. James, Margo, 3550
Sales, Barbara, 598
Saltus, Carol, 3437
Salvini, Alessandro, 3185
Salzman, Leon, 2152, 2244
Sambrooks, Jean E., 4237
Sandford, Donald A., 3921
Sandford, Jeremy, 3339
Sandler, Merton, 539, 1994
Sanger, William W., 3386
Sangowicz, Jadwiga, 3211
Sannito, Thomas, 1820
Santiago, Luciano P.R., 3148
Sanville, Jean, 1658
Saperstein, Avalie, 3108
Sapp, Stephen, 2909
Sarason, Seymour, 2615
Sarembe, B., 1332, 1494
Sarrel, Lorna J., 1366–1368, 1547
Sarrel, Philip, 1185, 1366–1368, 1547, 2353
Saul, Leon J., 2232
Saunders, M., 649
Savramis, Demosthenes, 2860
Sawyer, Ethel, 844
Sawyer, Jack, 1804, 2960
Scacco, Anthony M., 3642
Scanzoni, John, 2944
Scanzoni, Letha, 2416, 2944
Scarlet, Iain, 3441
Scarlett, Sharon, 638
Scarpitti, Ellen, 3661
Scarpitti, Frank R., 3661
Schachter, M., 3230, 3524
Schaefer, Leah Cahan, 1253
Schäfer, Siegrid, 845, 846, 3923
Schaffer, Ralph S., 429
Schain, Wendy S., 680
Schalmo, Gail B., 2823
Schapera, Isaac, 2682
Schauer, Frederick F., 4008
Schechner, Richard, 3205
Schechter, Marshall D., 1082

Scheflin, Albert E., 1653
Scheidlinger, Saul, 1287
Scheimann, Eugene, 751
Scheingold, Lee Dreisinger, 430, 676
Schellen, A.M.C.M., 743
Schepp, Steven, 2365
Scherl, Donald J., 3663, 3691
Scheurell, Robert P., 3186
Schiavi, R.C., 1212, 1888, 1995
Schiebel, Douglas, 3755
Schiff, Arthur F., 3585, 3624–3626
Schill, Thomas R., 3442
Schiller, Patricia, 1443, 1444, 2334, 2336, 4192
Schindler, Gordon, 3958
Schindler, Walter, 1007, 1043
Schipper, Kristofer, 4027
Schlaegel, Jürgen, 152, 163, 212
Schlesinger, Benjamin, 2352
Schletzer, Vera M., 2258
Schmideberg, Melitta, 3811
Schmidt, Gunter, 30, 156, 157, 213, 217, 294, 846, 1449, 1996, 3922, 3923
Schmidt, Michael J., 3871
Schneck, Jerome M., 3206
Schneider, Jane, 2683
Schoenberg, B., 295
Schoenberg, Mark, 1333
Schofield, Michael, 214, 907, 2861
Schonfeld, William A., 1821, 1923
Schonfelder, Thea, 82
Schonfield, Jacob, 620
Schoof, W., 1495
Schoof-Tams, Karin, 152, 163, 212
Schoultz, Jane, 4160
Schreiber, Flora Rheta, 1031
Schroeder, Leila O., 2077
Schuckit, Marc A., 577
Schukit, Mark, 117
Schultz, LeRoy G., 44, 1495, 1497, 1578, 1586, 3109–3111, 3627, 3709–3711
Schulz, Werner, 2059
Schumacher, Sallie, 1548, 1556
Schupp, Cherie Evelyn, 2290
Schürch, Johannes, 475
Schurr, Cathleen, 3571
Schwab, John J., 3000, 3001
Schwartz, Alan U., 3970
Schwartz, Allan J., 1293, 2491
Schwartz, Barry, 3675
Schwartz, Gary E., 1211
Schwartz, Louis B., 3551
Schwartz, Martin S., 153, 807, 2476
Schwartz, Michael N., 3218
Schwartz, Neil M., 3552
Schwartz, Pepper, 276, 838, 841–843, 847, 1766, 3044
Schwartz, Ronald Alan, 752
Schwartz, Ronald M., 1396
Schwartz, Werner, 215
Schwartzman, John, 3149
Schwerner, Stephen A., 1369
Scommegna, Antonio, 1962
Scott, Daniel E., 3701

Scott, W. Clifford M., 3207
Scott, Wayne, 3707
Scott, William Henry, 2684
Scrignar, C.B., 3112
Scully, Diana, 2775
Searl, M.N., 1822
Sears, Hal D., 31
Sebba, Leslie, 3662
Sedlacek, William E., 285, 1277, 2727
See, Carolyn, 3959
Seemanová, Eva, 3231
Segel, Harold J., 1574
Seghorn, Theoharis, 3275, 3603, 3628
Segner, Leslie Louise, 3187
Seiden, Rita, 2776
Seidenberg, Robert, 431, 3208
Seidman, Jerome M., 1823
Selby, James W., 3599
Selenkow, Herbert A., 1998, 1999
Seligman, Brenda Z., 2685
Semerari, Aldo, 967
Semmens, J.P., 1334
Semper Idem, 3483
Seneca, Harry, 1889
Sepúlveda Nino, Saturnino, 3420
Serber, Michael, 1161, 1539, 3290, 3799
Servais, Jean-Fraçois, 296, 540, 1973
Seufert, Reinhard, 4142
Seward, Georgene H., 784
Shader, Richard I., 541–543
Shaffer, Helen B., 3586
Shainess, Natalie, 1235, 1236, 1335, 1824
Shamoian, Charles A., 2046
Shanahan, Louise, 3553
Shankel, L. Willard, 1083
Shapiro, David, 1211
Sharkey, Harold, 412
Sharpe, Lawrence, 1474
Sharpe, Robert, 1540
Shatin, Leo, 2439
Shaver, Philip R., 2713, 3448, 3860, 4173
Shaver, Robert, 4201
Shaw, Marvin E., 4176
Shear, Marie, 3059
Shearer, Marshall, 1549
Sheehy, Gail, 3340, 3341, 3466
Sheffield, John, 3890
Sheffield, Margaret, 2373
Shemberg, K.M., 1825
Shepard, Martin, 1655, 1656
Shepher, Joseph, 3188
Sheppard, Samona, 2492
Sher, Monroe A., 1826
Sherfey, Mary Jane, 1237, 1238, 3060
Sherman, Richard W., 1131
Sherwin, Robert Veit, 3844, 3845
Sherrod, Dale B., 3106
Sherwin, Robert Veit, 1170, 3554, 3676
Shiloh, Ailon, 63
Shipman, Gordon, 155

Shochet, Bernard R., 1657
Shoham, Shlomo, 3421
Shonick, Helen, 1387
Shoor, Mervyn, 3244, 3295
Shope, David F., 1254, 2121, 2402
Shopper, Moisy, 3677
Shor, Joel, 1658, 3002
Shore, Miles F., 1065
Shorkey, Clayton T., 3812
Shorter, Edward, 3061
Shroff, Nipank, 1203
Shugrue, Richard E., 4009
Shulman, Alix, 1239
Shulman, Bernard H., 701
Shuttleworth, Frank Kayley, 1827
Siassi, Iradj, 1659
Sibisi, H., 2455
Sidler, Nikolaus, 3150
Sidley, Nathan T., 3776
Siebenand, Paul Alcuin, 3951
Siegel, Richard, 283, 1647
Sieverts, Rudolf, 3730
Signoret, J.P., 1998
Signori, Livio, 132
Sigusch, Volkmar, 30, 82, 156, 157, 213, 216, 217, 1336, 1498, 1499, 1500, 1587, 3922, 3923
Silberman, M., 3436
Silvan, Lillian, 2269
Silverman, Ira Jay, 337, 2190
Simenauer, Jacqueline, 2266, 2770, 4203
Simmons, William L., 3949
Simon, Pierre, 32
Simon, Rita James, 3003
Simon, William, 15, 42, 123, 200, 297, 3085
Simons, G.L., 3387, 3484
Simpson, Colin, 3525
Simpson, Mary, 3442
Simpson, Ruth, 951
Sinclair, Abby, 2089
Singer, Irving, 1240, 1255, 1934
Singer, Josephine, 1240, 1255, 1934
Singer, June, 1828
Singer, Laura, 2364
Singh, B. Krishna, 2259
Sípová, Iva, 3415
Sisk, John P., 4100
Skynner, A.C.R., 1337
Slade, Joseph W., 3960
Slater, Mariam K., 2686, 2687
Sloan, Don, 1660
Sloan, Lloyd R., 3871
Sloane, Paul, 3232
Slotkin, J.S., 3151
Slovenko, Ralph, 33, 1338, 1580, 3678
Small, Iver F., 702
Small, Joyce, G., 702
Smigel, Erwin O., 2777
Smith, Alfred G., 2688
Smith, Alma Dell, 2776
Smith, Bradley, 4056
Smith, Bernard H., 723
Smith, Brenda, 1469
Smith, Carolyn, 1601

Smith, Charles E., 3777
Smith, Cyril J., 3679
Smith, Don D., 3875
Smith, Douglas K., 2078
Smith, Edward, 2745
Smith, F. Joseph, 2862
Smith, Harmon L., 185, 1353
Smith, James R., 2291, 2292
Smith, James W., 567, 578
Smith, Janet, 1801
Smith, Lynn G., 2291, 2292
Smith, Patrick B., 2191
Smith, Quentin Ted, 3113
Smith, R. Spencer, 3764
Smith, Roger A., 2742
Smith, Sidney A., 2469
Smith-Rosenberg, Carroll, 834, 3062
Smithwick, Reginald H., 725
Smukler, Arthur J., 3755
Snegroff, Stanley, 2359
Sniderman, Marlaina, 3706
Snyder, Eldon E., 2824
Soares, Anthony T., 158, 2477
Soares, Louise M., 158, 2477
Sobel, Douglas, 269
Socarides, Charles W., 835, 926, 1032, 3296
Sokoloff, Natalie J., 138
Sokolov, Jacque J., 1890
Solnick, Robert L., 476
Somerville, Don Smith, 3987
Sonenschein, David, 2689, 2690, 3952
Sontag, Susan, 432, 4101
Sorensen, Andrew A., 338
Sorensen, Robert C., 218, 4193, 4265
Sorg, David A., 433, 1256
Sorg, Margaret B., 433, 1256
Soulairac, André, 2000
Soulairac, Marie-Louise, 2000
Southard, Helen, 2388
Southworth, J.A., 2439
Spanier, Graham B., 339, 340, 2272, 2273, 2493
Spark, Geraldine M., 1397
Speed, Mary Helen, 3244, 3295
Spengler, Andreas, 1019
Spensley, James, 1126
Sperekas, Nicole B., 3690
Speigel, Jeanne, 1684
Spiers, Duane E., 830
Spillman, Emil V., 3152
Spitz, Cathy J., 2001, 2153
Spitz, Henry I., 1562
Spitz, Herman H., 3756
Spitz, Rene A., 83
Spitz, Richard, 1544
Spitzer, Stephan P., 2826
Splane, R.B., 3114
Splete, Howard, 124, 1442
Sponaugle, G.C., 2323
Sporakowski, Michael J., 320
Sporken, Paul, 2863
Sprafke, Ulrike, 219
Spreitzer, Elmer, 2824
Sprey, Jetse, 2233, 3004
Springer, Alfred, 544

Standridge, Linda Williams, 4266
Stanley, Elizabeth, 1201
Stanton, Elaine, 2192
Staples, Robert, 361, 641, 785, 786, 1829
Stárka, L., 1991
Starowicz, Zbigniew Lew, 159
Stauffer, John, 3876
Stauss, Fred F., 1592
Stayton, William R., 2337, 2507
Stearn, Jess, 3342
Stearns, A. Warren, 1084
Steckler, Allan, 184
Steele, Daniel G., 3924, 3925
Steen, Edwin Benzel, 2403
Steffensmeier, Darrell, 2825
Steffensmeier, Renee, 2825
Steg, Joseph, 1026
Steger, Jeffrey C., 2116
Stein, Conrad, 1008
Stein, Joan, 1362
Stein, Martha L., 3343, 3443
Stein, Marvin, 2147
Stein, Robert, 3209
Steiner, Betty, 2028, 2054
Steinman, Cary M., 3310
Steinmann, Anne, 1830, 2461, 2963
Steinmetz, Suzanne K., 2964, 3005
Steinmetz, Urban G., 2885
Stekel, Wilhelm, 989
Stemple, Diane, 3006
Stepan, Jan, 2431
Stephan, Walter G., 3926
Stephens, William N., 2691, 2692
Sterling, Theodore D., 621
Stern, Bernhard, 4102
Stern, Herold S., 2306
Stern, Lenore O., 1572
Stern, Michael, 3617
Stern, R.S., 509, 586
Stevens, Barbara, 2965
Stevens, Doris, 2193
Stevens, Joanne, 1445
Stevens, Kenneth R., 4010
Stevens, Maureen R., 728
Stewart, Barbara, 282
Stewart, Clarence Milton, 2440, 2561
Stewart, Cyrus S., 233, 234, 4194
Stewart, George Lee, 3444, 3485
Stewart, Karen Robb, 137
Stewart, Sidney, 1009
Stine, Diane, 703
Stinnett, Nick, 2314, 2732
Stinson, Byron, 2037
Stockowski, Benjamin L., 2387
Stocktay, G.G., 4143
Stokes, R.E., 3115
Stokes, Walter R., 434, 1388, 3007
Stolarz, Francis J., 3776
Stoll, Clarice Stasz, 3008
Stoller, Robert J., 831, 832, 1118–1120, 1127, 1162, 1831, 2011, 2038, 2052
Stolling, Frank, 301
Stone, Abraham, 1563
Stone, Alan A., 1661
Storaska, Frederic, 3587

Story, Norman L., 545
Strahan, Robert F., 4231
Strait, Joyce, 2061
Stranan, Robert F., 1832
Stratton, John R., 2324, 2826
Straus, Murray A., 4177
Straus, Robert, 579
Strauss, S.A., 2079
Strean, Herbert S., 2234
Stricker, George, 3276, 3277
Strodtbeck, Fred L., 1833
Strong, Ethelyn R., 799
Stroup, Herbert W., 1407
Struening, Elmer L., 1287
Strupp, Hans H., 1662
Stuart, Martha, 3009
Stuckey, Johanna, 3422
Sturgis, Somers H., 1939
Sturke, Robert, 350
Stürup, Georg K., 1103, 2006, 3629
Stuve, Gilbert Edmund, 2441
Stycos, J.M., 4155
Subak-Sharpe, Genell J., 622
Subrini, Louis, 1213
Suchman, Edward A., 546
Suggs, Robert, 54, 2649, 2693
Sulcov, Mark B., 2012
Sullivan, Kathleen A., 1834
Sullivan, Peter, 3778
Sulzbacher, Stephen I., 3499
Summers, Darryl L., 1835
Sunder, J.H., 2494
Sunderland, Lane V., 4011
Sunseri, A.J., 2494
Suomi, S.J., 1836
Surieu, Robert, 4022
Sutherland, Edwin H., 3779
Sutherland, Sandra, 3663
Sutker, Patricia B., 362, 787, 2778
Sutton-Smith, Brian, 1814
Suyin, Han, 3010
Sviland, Mary Ann P., 435
Swanson, Alan, 3780
Swanson, David W., 3245, 3278
Swartz, Marc C., 2694
Swearingen, Charles, 1077
Swedenborg, Emanuel, 2864
Swensen, Clifford H., 298
Swigert, Victoria Lynn, 3781
Swiller, Hillel Isaiah, 2050
Sykes, A.J.M., 2695
Symonds, Alexandra, 3063
Symonds, Carolyn, 1677, 2293
Szabo, Denis, 3189
Szasz, George, 1446
Szewczyk, Hans, 260, 436
Szkodzinsky, Wasyl, 955
Szymusik, A., 647

Taft, Kendall B., 4020
Tagliamonte, A., 1969
Talarico, June, 2339
Tallaferro, Alberto, 1268
Tamura, J., 3637
Tanck, Roland H., 612
Tappan, Paul W., 3423, 3846, 3847
Taquiri, Consuelo, 3093, 3168

Tavris, Carol, 437, 1257, 2713, 2945, 2966, 3448, 4204
Taylor, A.J.W., 1144, 1145
Taylor, Barbie J., 1663
Taylor, Brian, 3291
Taylor, David C., 650
Taylor, Donald Lavor, 64
Taylor, Michael J., 2886
Taylor, Peter, 2546
Taylor, R.W., 1339
Teal, Don, 952
Tebor, Irving B., 299, 2041
Teevan, James T., Jr., 341
Teja, Jagdish S., 1924
Tekavčič, Bogdan, 221
Templer, Donald I., 3623
Tennent, Gavin, 3814
Tennent, T.G., 3745, 3855
Tessler, Arthur N., 2057
Thaller, Barbara D., 718
Thaller, Karl E., 718
Thielicke, Helmut, 2910
Thiery, J.C., 1999
Thomas, D.R., 363
Thomas, Jerril K., 1447
Thomas, Lena B., 342
Thomas, Mivart, 1659
Thomas, Paula Jean, 1837
Thomason, Bruce, 2122, 2123
Thompson, Andrew, 1288
Thompson, C.J.S., 1121
Thompson, Ian M., 1706
Thompson, Joseph J., 3927
Thompson, Kathleen, 3618
Thompson, Linda A., 1671
Thompson, William D., 3919
Thorman, George, 2194, 2195
Thornburg, Hershel D., 2448, 2478, 2495, 2779
Thorne, Frederick C., 2780, 4218, 4224, 4225
Thorne, Melvin G., Jr., 598
Thornton, Nathaniel, 3526
Thornton, Robert Y., 3344, 3486
Thorstad, David, 947
Thurry, Cynthia, 638
Thuwe, Inga, 2080
Tickamyer, Ann R., 2994
Timms, Robert J., 628
Tinklenberg, Jared R., 3743
Tisza, Veronica B., 3070
Titus, Herbert W., 3556
Tobach, Ethel, 1838, 2696
Tobias, Jerry J., 547
Tobin, Kay, 953
Tolone, William L., 3030
Tolor, Alexander, 1839
Tomko, Michael A., 628
Toolan, James M., 222
Toon, Mark, 2887
Tordjman, Gilbert, 1214
Tormes, Yvonne M., 3116, 3233
Tourney, Garfield, 704, 1891
Toussieng, Povl W., 133
Trager, George L., 2697
Traver, Harold Henry, 3190
Travis, Patricia Y., 1341

Travis, Robert P., 1341
Trenc, Pavle, 160
Trethowan, W.H., 585
Tribe, David, 3988
Trieschmann, Robert B., 742
Tripp, Clarence A., 892
Troiden, Richard R., 1840, 3573
Trost, Jan, 2196–2199
Troyer, Beverly Jayne, 2781
Truxaw, Patsy, 1671
Tsuang, Ming T., 705
Tuchfeld, Barry, 1944
Tucker, Patricia, 1112, 1792, 2010
Turci, P.E., 1143
Turner, Edward R., 3298
Turner, Edward T., 706
Turner, Nathan W., 1342, 2337, 2507
Turner, R.E., 3269, 3299, 3752, 3794, 3815
Turner, Stanley H., 2261, 3874
Tushup, Richard, 2500
Tuteur, Werner, 2698, 3191
Twombly, Gray Huntington, 767
Tyler, Edward A., 2529
Tyler, Jane E., 3006
Tyler, Mary, 1438
Tyler, Parker, 4124, 4125

Uddenberg, Nils, 1841
Udry, J. Richard, 2154–2156, 4178
Ullian, Dorothy Z., 1760
Undeutsch, Udo, 223
Unsworth, Richard P., 2912
Updegraff, Katherine, 667
Urberg, Kathryn A., 1842
Usher, A., 1085

Vacalis, T. Demetri, 2782
Vadies, Gene, 1421
Vaitkus, Aldona, 2522
Valente, Michael F., 2888
Valentich, Mary, 2567
Valentini, Norberto, 2889
Vallery-Masson, J., 446, 614
Vanasek, Frank J., 3258, 3279, 3297
Van Bemmelen, Jacob M., 3730
Vance, Ellen Belle, 1224
Vanden Bergh, Richard L., 1010
Vanderpearl, Robert H., 3732
Vandervoort, Herb, 1603
Van Deusen, Edmund L., 2201
Vande Wiele, R.L., 1945, 1726
Van Dis, Huib, 1270
Vandiver, Richard Dale, 343, 364, 2783
Van Gelder, Lindsy, 3487
Van Ophuijsen, J.H.W., 1033
Van Waters, Miriam, 3424
Van Wert, Johanna Rucker, 300
Van Woert, Melvin H., 625, 626
Varga, Andrew C., 1400
Varni, Charles A., 2294
Vas, C.J., 724
Vasil'chenko, G.S., 1501
Vastbinder, Earl, 3079
Vayda, Andrew P., 3192
Veitch, Russell, 3902

Velarde, Albert J., 3488, 3489
Veldekens, P., 1966
Vener, Arthur M., 233, 234, 4194
Venham, Lois, 344
Vennewitz, Peter Jan, 2496
Verkuyl, A., 743
Verwoerdt, Adriaan, 468–470, 477, 478
Vestergaard, Emma, 3153
Viamontes, Jorge A., 580
Viano, Emilio C., 3680
Viernstein, Theodor, 3166
Vietze, G., 2039
Villeneuve, Roland, 4057–4059
Vincent, Clark E., 1289, 1343, 1344, 2124, 2237, 2264, 2946
Vincent, Murray L., 301
Vinson, Sarah B., 3113
Viqueira Hinojosa, Antonio, 3527
Virkkunen, Matti, 581, 3117, 3280
Voght, Martha, 3020
Vogliotti, Gabriel R., 3490
Vogt, Hermann J., 548
Vorberg, Gaston, 4060
Vorenberg, Elizabeth, 3425
Vorenberg, James, 3425
Voss, Harwin L., 2168
Voth, Harold M., 1664
Voydanoff, Patricia, 2322, 2821
Voznesenskiï, O.S., 1502
Vroegh, Karen, 1843, 1844
Vuocolo, Alfred Bernard, 3744

Waas, Emil, 4061
Wabrek, Alan J., 1241, 1345, 1370
Wabrek, Carolyn J., 1241, 1345
Wade, Carlson, 1114
Waetjen, Walter B., 2933
Waggoner, Raymond W., 1346, 1549
Wagner, Edwin E., 3757
Wagner, Nathaniel N., 65, 224, 264, 430, 676, 677, 1222, 1224, 1461, 1663
Wagner, Roland Richard, 3388
Wahle, H., 734
Wahrman, Ralph, 1845
Walczak, Leonhard, 152, 163, 212
Waldemar, Charles, 4104
Waldrop, Bernard Keith, 4103
Wales, Jeffrey B., 368
Wålinder, Jan, 1128, 2013, 2040, 2080
Walker, Alexander, 4126
Walker, C. Eugene, 351, 3896, 3920, 3925
Walker, Edith G., 2542
Walker, Marcia J., 3565, 3630
Walker, Paul A., 1163, 1911
Wall, Victor D., 2533
Wallace, Douglas H., 3877, 3878, 3928
Wallace, Jerry McLain, 161
Wallace, Robert Clayton, 162, 2479
Wallin, Paul, 479, 1244, 1252, 2097, 2099, 2124, 2125, 2130, 2157, 2158, 4158
Wallnöfer, Heinrich, 1575

Walsh, Robert H., 345, 2784, 2827, 3030
Walshok, Mary, 1259
Walshok, Mary Lindenstein, 1846, 2295
Walster, Elaine, 3926, 4186
Walter, Emil J., 3118, 3246
Walters, David R., 3119, 3281
Walton, Bonnie L., 2259
Walzer, Stanley, 1847
Wan, Livia S., 2517
Wang, Hsioh-Shan, 468, 469, 477, 478
Waniek, Marilyn Nelson, 4105
Ward, E.J., 657
Ward, Ingeborg L., 1912
Ward, Nicholas G., 1164
Ward, Richard S., 2382
Ward, Thomas J., 365, 2202
Ware, Edward E., 3932
Waring, E.M.., 3961
Warlick, Mark, 3489
Warner, Marie Pichel, 302
Warner, Ralph, 2183
Warren, Carol A.B., 908, 2390
Warring, Louise, 3599
Wasow, Mona, 438
Wasserstrom, Richard, 2307
Watson, B.W., 1192
Watson, Jan, 960
Watson, Lawrence C., 2699
Watts, Alan Wilson, 2865
Watts, G.T., 760
Watts, Parris René, 2497
Waynberg, Jacques, 1679
Wead, George, 4127
Weaver, Herbert B., 2785
Weaver, Robert G., 1892
Webb, Peter, 4023
Webb, Warren W., 1883
Weber, Ellen, 3154
Weber, Melva, 1347
Webster, Paula, 2700
Wedeck, Harry E., 4106
Weeks, Ruth B., 3120
Wehmer, Gerald, 3878
Wei, Yu, 3426
Weich, Martin J., 3210
Weightman, John, 4128, 4136
Weil, Peter M., 2701
Weimann, W., 1086
Weinberg, George, 909
Weinberg, Jack, 439
Weinberg, Martin S., 66, 480, 809, 854, 865, 896, 910, 912, 2744, 2786, 4180, 4181, 4240
Weinberg, Paul C., 768
Weinberg, Samuel Kirson, 3193, 3194
Weiner, Irving B., 3195
Weinstein, Edwin A., 651
Weis, Kurt, 3664
Weisberg, Miriam, 2246, 2248
Weisman, Avery D., 1011, 1087
Weiss, Carl, 3643
Weiss, Howard D., 1215
Weiss, Jerome, 2702, 3528

Weiss, Joseph, 3121
Weiss, Michael, 1414
Weiss, Rosalee G., 3274
Weiss, Theodore, 2535
Weissman, Myrna M., 697
Weisstein, Naomi, 1665
Weitzman, Elliott L., 2046
Welbourne, Ann, 1415, 1416
Wellisch, David K., 549
Wells, Hal, 820
Wells, James Gipson, 2828
Weltge, Ralph W., 893
Wenger, Morton G., 2795
Wepman, Dennis, 3457, 3467
Werley, Harriet H., 2473, 2474
Wessler, Martin F., 2914
West, D.J., 833, 911
West, Norman D., 440
Westermarck, Edward A., 2703
Westling, Achilles, 582
Westoff, Charles F., 2159
Westman, Jack C., 1848
Wetherbee, R. Michael, 2081
Wettstone, Richard P., 1432, 2350
Wexler, Harry, 497
Whalen, Richard E., 1186
Whales, Hugh G., 4162
Whirley, Marilyn Peddicord, 3012
Whiskin, Frederick E., 441, 3247, 3720
Whisnant, Billie, 2339
Whitam, Frederick L., 1849
White, Alice M., 2787
White, Daniel, 1995
White, Henry E., 346
White, Leslie A., 2704
Whitehead, J.A., 3446
Whitehurst, Robert N., 49, 50, 2203, 2204, 2223, 2238
Whitelaw, George P., 725
Whiting, Beatrice B., 2705
Whiting, John W.M., 1139, 2705
Whitman, Roy M., 1225
Whittaker, Peter, 3346, 3491, 3529
Wicker, Randy, 953
Wiechmann, Gerald H., 303, 2498, 2788
Wigfield, Arthur S., 3347
Wiggers, Thorne T., 1359
Wiig, Elizabeth H., 652
Wikler, Revy, 442
Wile, Ira S., 304
Wille, Warren S., 3631
Williams, Cindy Cook, 3712
Williams, Colin J., 854, 910, 912, 4181, 4240
Williams, George C., 2706
Williams, J. Sherwood, 2259
Williams, John E., 1850
Williams, Juanita H., 1851
Williams, Reg Arthur, 3712
Williams, Robert L., 459
Williams, T.M., 2913
Willis, A., 2762

Willis, Kathleen, 2971
Wills, Gary, 3945
Wilson, Cassandra, 3569
Wilson, G.T., 554, 583, 584, 3307
Wilson, John, 2866
Wilson, Margo, 1921
Wilson, Paul, 3559
Wilson, Robert Anton, 2867
Wilson, Robert R., 309, 1348, 1408, 1409, 2346, 2793
Wilson, Samuel T., 2404
Wilson, Simon, 4051
Wilson, W. Cody, 1556, 2160, 2789, 3879, 3880
Wilson, Warner, 281
Wincze, John P., 1195, 1196, 1202, 1465, 1512, 3909, 3929, 4157, 4206
Wineman, E.W., 1935
Winick, Charles, 3348–3350, 3447, 3468, 3554, 4152, 4153
Winn, Denise, 3446
Winnik, H.Z., 3175
Winokur, George, 67
Winslow, Robert W., 3351, 3589
Winslow, Virginia, 3351, 3589
Wintrob, Ronald M., 2707
Wise, Donald, 1768
Wise, Gordon L., 2790
Wiseman, Jacqueline P., 68, 1852, 2405, 2868
Wish, Peter A., 1542
Wishner, Julius, 3850, 3992
Witkin, Mildred Hope, 681
Witkowski, Gustave Joseph, 4062
Witter, Hermann, 3828
Witters, Weldon L., 550
Witton, Kurt, 551
Wöbcke, Manfred, 3103
Wojdowski, Pat, 2041
Wolf, Alexander, 2239
Wolf, Arthur P., 2708
Wolf, Katherine M., 83
Wolfe, Linda, 1503, 2246
Wolfe, Robert C., 552
Wolfe, Stephen D., 707
Wolfers, Helen, 775
Wolff, Charlotte, 840, 913
Wolff, George, 2064
Wolfgang, Marvin E., 59, 3740
Wolfish, Martin G., 243
Wollman, Leo, 1122, 1165, 1666, 2055
Wong, Amos, 3426
Wood, Clive, 1893
Wood, Frederic C., 2869
Wood, Houston, 4172
Wood, Norma Schweitzer, 1407
Woodrow, Kenneth M., 3743
Woods, Richard, 2890
Woods, Sherwyn M., 2530, 2531
Woodside, M., 1260
Woodward, Roger, 4238
Woody, Jane Divita, 2360
Woody, Robert H., 1166

Woolston, Howard Brown, 3389
Worrall, Norman, 3897
Wortis, Joseph, 2709
Wortley, Richard, 4129, 4154
Wright, Derek, 1853
Wright, J.M., 4176
Wright, Mary Ruth, 1290, 2499
Wu, Wang, 4082
Wurtman, Richard J., 645
Wyman, Rachel, 164
Wynn, John Charles, 2915
Wysor, Bettie, 894
Wyss, Rudolf, 3292

Yachnes, Eleanor, 1854
Yaffe, Maurice, 3745, 3854, 3855
Yalom, Irvin D., 1913, 3789
Yankowitz, Robert, 532
Yeaworth, Rosalee, 2539
Yoels, William C., 3781
Yorburg, Betty, 484, 1855, 2161, 3013
Yorukoglu, Atalay, 3234
Young, Allen, 944, 945
Young, Barbara Ann, 1291
Young, Frank W., 3155
Young, George H., 1856
Young, Ian, 963
Young, Marjorie A.C., 2442
Young, Rhodes C., 2568
Young, Wayland, 4107
Young, William C., 1868

Zacharias, Leona, 645
Zajac, Andrew, 2054
Zarcone, Vincent, 1216
Zechnick, Robert, 3758
Zellinger, David A., 3953
Zelnik, Melvin, 227, 235–237, 788, 2829
Zetterberg, Hans L., 34
Zieg, Patricia, 4009
Zilbergeld, Bernie, 1564
Zillmann, Dolf, 2482, 3891, 3946
Zimmerman, Robert, 1288
Zimmerman, Steve, 2490
Zimpfer, David G., 1359
Zinsser, Hans H., 658
Ziskin, Jay, 2296, 2297
Ziskin, Mae, 2296, 2297
Zuanazzi, Gianfrancesco, 3530
Zubin, Joseph, 69, 111, 513
Zuckerman, Marvin, 305, 553, 1187, 2500, 3852, 3881, 4219
Zuger, Bernard, 1857
Zupan, Irene, 638
Zumpe, Doris, 1866, 1886
Zurcher, Louis A., 3989
Zuspan, Frederick P., 3590
Zussman, Leon, 1550
Zussman, Shirley, 1550
Zwang, Gérard, 1543
Zwarensteyn, Sara B., 3080

Subject Index

The numbers refer to individual citations.

Abortion, 3559. *See also* Attitudes on; Judaic attitudes on; Legal aspects of; Medical attitudes on; Psychological effects of

Abortion laws, 3531

Absent father effects, 791, 1699, 1709, 1801

Acceptance of others test, 2463

Acculturation, 139

Adjective check list test, 2745, 4229

Adolescent behavior, 173, 1361, 2653, 4110. *See also* Problems of adolescents

Adolescent behavior bibliographies, 135, 137

Adolescent behavior problems, 176, 242, 2455, 2854, 3093, 3749, 3842

Adolescent behavior psychoanalysis, 1645

Adolescent behavior research, 212, 2601

Adrenogenital syndrome, 1717–1719, 1742

Adult behavior, 2947, 2955

Advertising, *see* Sex in

Afroamericans, 783, 791, 1280, 1835, 1837, 2658, 3041, 3043, 3457, 3467, 3725, 3734, 4105

Afroamericans and contraception, 237, 320, 788

Afroamericans and homosexuality, 3634

Afroamericans marriage and family, 641, 780, 800, 2112, 2322, 2998

Afroamericans sex attitudes, 779, 785, 787, 800, 803, 2808, 2817, 2818

Afroamericans sex behavior, 235–237, 320, 361, 362, 776, 781, 785, 788, 2998, 3591

Afroamericans sex education, 2457

Afroamericans sex knowledge, 237, 788

Age cohort studies, 3030

Aged behavior, 374, 385, 431

Aggression, 571, 1944, 1950–1952, 2661, 3012, 3595, 3884, 3895, 3934, 3936, 3937, 3941, 3946

Aggressive sex behavior, 268, 271, 502, 563, 976, 1024, 2694, 3065, 3611, 3696

Aggressiveness and sex differences, 1734, 1946, 1960, 3122, 3595

Aging, 395, 412, 416, 432, 480, 1939. *See also* Climacteric

Aging and sex behavior, 366–480, 2758

Alcohol, 530, 579, 1944

Alcohol and sex behavior, 483, 505, 520, 538, 554–584, 3592

Alcoholics, 504, 557, 559, 568, 572, 573, 576, 577, 581

Alcoholism, 516, 558

Alternative life styles perceptions scale, 2314

American Civil Liberties Union, 3539

American College Health Association, family life/sex education study, 2484

American Indians, 1100, 2598, 2633, 2635, 3321

Amphetamines, 509, 585–587

Amputees and sex behavior, 745

Amusements, 4020, 4147

Anal coitus, 2096

Anal stimulation, 975

Anatomical anomalies, 594

Anatomy and physiology, 1173, 1827. *See also* Comparative anatomy

Androgens, 704, 1810, 1880, 1884, 1891, 1947, 1950, 1961, 1972, 1995

Animal homosexual behavior, 849

Animal orgasm, 527

Animal sex behavior, 627, 1954, 2569, 3157, 3187. *See also* Hormones and animal sex behavior; Mammal sex behavior; Primate sex behavior

Animal sex differences, 1711, 1789, 1946, 1947

Animal social structure, 1711, 1952

Anorectal gonorrhea, 975

Anorexia nervosa, 1942

Anthropology, 54, 977, 2569–2709, 2855, 3185, 3192. *See also* Customs in primitive societies

Anthropology methodology, 2690

Anxiety, 195, 267, 563, 1196, 3890

Anxiety and sex differences, 1946, 3905

Aphrodisiacs, 491, 495, 505, 510, 514, 595

Art, 4012, 4018, 4024–4062. *See also* Child art; Sadomasochism in; Sex in; Sex in religious art; Sex variations in

Art exhibitions, 4042

Art history, 4036, 4042, 4043, 4051

Art of mentally ill, 3584

Art therapy, 1531

Arthritis and sex behavior, 665

Atrocities, 3578, 4245

Attitude measurement, 343, 1497, 1586, 2650, 2712, 2714, 2740, 2975, 3866, 4174, 4237, 4262

Attitude study, 919, 2319, 2731, 2767

Attitudes on abortion, 3062

Attitudes on abortion research, 282, 2532, 2536, 2765

Attitudes on censorship, 3973, 3983

Attitudes on contraception, 186, 244, 282, 301, 2482, 2556, 2564, 2568, 2808, 3050, 3062, 4162

Attitudes on erotica, 2857, 2913, 2990, 3972, 3974, 3978, 3990, 4093, 4116

Attitudes on erotica research, 792, 3607, 3864–3866, 3869, 3872, 3876, 3877, 3879, 3958, 5989

Attitudes on homosexuality, 825, 875, 882, 895, 909, 928, 930, 931, 934, 944, 1284, 3534

Attitudes on homosexuality research, 918–921, 2309, 2319, 2463, 2719, 2720, 2738, 2739, 2744, 2750, 2814, 2824, 2825, 3399, 4241–4244

Attitudes on marriage, 1371, 2203, 2222, 3000

Attitudes on marriage research, 163, 2178, 2196, 2198, 2322, 2488, 4262

Attitudes on masturbation, 372

Attitudes on masturbation research, 163, 2710, 2764

Attitudes on nonmarital sex behavior, 163, 190, 1388, 1779, 2199, 2257, 2298–2307, 3654

Attitudes on nonmarital sex behavior research, 191, 231, 278, 285, 288, 300, 306, 307, 313–315, 318, 319, 322, 326, 328, 329, 336, 343, 346, 358, 365, 796, 1311, 2170, 2180, 2182, 2191, 2259, 2263, 2308–2324, 2481, 2726, 2752, 2791–2829

Attitudes on prostitution, 3322, 3338, 3370, 3378, 3383, 3399, 3425, 3475, 3488, 3544, 3553

Attitudes on sex education, 149, 1675, 2330, 2347, 2419, 2424, 2427, 2428, 2432, 2441, 2447, 2458, 2460, 2490, 2502, 2549–2551, 2556, 2558, 2559

Attitudes on transexualism, 2065
Attitudes on venereal diseases, 3021
Audiovisual sex aids, 1327, 1539
Autoeroticism, 83
Aversion therapy, 923, 1023, 1038, 1161, 1166, 3791, 3851. *See also* Homosexuality aversion therapy; Pedophilia aversion therapy; Transvestism aversion therapy

Bantus, 2641
Bars, 3417, 3418
Behavior therapy, 693, 705, 717, 1297, 1491, 1504-1556, 1635, 1662, 1796, 2761, 3802, 4157. *See also* Aversion therapy; Desensitization; Exhibitionism behavior therapy; Fetishism behavior therapy; Homosexuality behavior therapy; Incest behavior therapy; Pedophilia behavior therapy; Sex offenders behavior therapy; Transvestism behavior therapy
Behavior therapy bibliographies, 3812
Behavioral effect of cinema, 3931
Behavioral effect of erotica, 132, 3745, 3762, 3853, 3858, 3861, 3902, 3938, 4113
Behavioral effect of erotica research, 3607, 3722, 3849-3853, 3879, 3893, 3916, 3917, 3922, 3930-3946, 3992, 4001
Bellydance, 4144
Bem sex-role inventory, 1695, 1696, 1832
Bibliophiles, 4064
Bigamy laws, 3531
Biographies of pimps, 3475
Biographies of sex criminals, 3584
Biographies of transexuals, 2082-2089
Biographies of women, 1031
Biological anthropology, 1171, 1711, 1838, 2571, 2584, 2612, 2614, 2643, 2706, 3126, 3135
Birth order, 354
Birth statistics, 2156, 2264
Bisexuality, 808-837, 855-857
Bisexuality research, 838-854, 3753
Blacks, 2189. *See also* Afroamericans; Ethnic groups
Blacky pictures technique, 3276
Blind, 3080
Blind and sex behavior, 643-645
Blind and sex education, 643
Body attitude scale, 4187
Body build research, 296, 613, 1701. *See also* Somatology
Body image, 179, 413, 432, 556, 681, 1136, 1821, 1917, 2029, 4186, 4187, 4189
Body image-1 scale, 2029
Body language, *see* Kinesics
Body type partner preference, 849
Bondage, 1066-1068, 1077
Book reviews, 3008
Bookplates, 4044
Brain diseases and sex behavior, 646-652
Brothels, 3329, 3344, 3345, 3357, 3396, 3402, 3418, 3425, 3444, 3469-3491, 3519

CPI femininity scale, 4232
California mentally disordered sex offender program, 3768
California psychological inventory, 2946
Cancer, 753
Cancer and sex behavior, 680. *See also* Urogenital cancer and sex behavior
Cardiovascular system, 674

Caricatures, 4034
Castration, 1875, 2075
Castration and sex behavior, 449, 1958
Castration complex, 100, 104, 835, 993, 1003, 1060
Castration experimentation, 1958
Castration of criminals and defectives, 3588, 3629, 3775, 3797, 3824
Catholic attitudes on contraception, 2878
Catholic attitudes on homosexuality, 932, 2890
Catholic confession, 2889
Catholic doctrine, 3356
Catholic sex attitudes, 310, 1401, 2879-2882, 3356
Catholic sex education, 2534
Catholic sex ethics, 2876-2890, 3971
Celibacy, 2880
Censored books, 3979
Censorship, 1302, 2913, 3376, 3962-3989, 4080, 4084, 4126. *See also* Attitudes on; Cinema censorship; Legal aspects of erotica; Mass media censorship
Censorship bibliographies, 3981
Censorship cases, 3994, 3996
Censorship organizations, 2757, 3971, 3989
Censorship research, 3862, 3873, 3962-3989
Ceramics, 4060
Cerebral palsy and sex behavior, 719
Changing role of homosexuals, 868
Changing role of men, 45, 1414, 1564, 1705, 1803, 1804, 2916-2967, 2994, 4234
Changing role of women, 45, 746, 1545, 1705, 2093, 2249, 2298, 2577, 2878, 2916-2946, 2968-3013, 4234
Child art, 1839
Child behavior, 93, 119, 1703, 1849
Child behavior problems, 73, 85, 90, 1152, 3073
Child behavior psychoanalysis, 71, 107, 2715
Child behavior research, 98, 3068
Child parent relationships, 85, 91, 118, 134, 149, 164, 228, 261, 290, 712, 834, 956, 1032, 1136, 1689, 1699, 1708, 1753, 1759, 1782, 1783, 1795, 1816, 1833, 1841, 2036, 2046, 2119, 2216, 2357, 2359, 2760, 2771, 3070, 3130, 3143, 3145, 3205, 3214, 3753. *See also* Parental attitudes; Single parents
Child rearing advice, 93, 103, 121. *See also* Nonsexist child rearing
Child victims, 74, 977, 1027, 3064-3121, 3154, 3230, 3233, 3268
Childbirth, 755, 4207
Children in primitive societies, 977, 2651, 2659, 3112
Christianity history, 2844
Cinema, 4113. *See also* Behavioral effect of; Homosexuality in; Sadomasochism in; Sex in; Stag films
Cinema censorship, 3964, 3971, 3993
Cinema history, 4114, 4118, 4119, 4125, 4126
Circumcision, 3124
Citizens for Decent Literature, Inc., 3959
Civil liberties, 2081, 3539, 3778, 3982, 4007, 4250
Clergy, 2779
Clients of prostitutes, 3329, 3430-3456
Climacteric, 377, 384, 394, 400, 414, 415, 425, 1936-1939, 1983
Clinical psychology, 1626
Clitoris, 1189, 1313
Clothing, 2640
Cognition, 1202, 2001
Cognition and sex differences, 1734, 1739
Coital frequency, 466, 2001, 2103, 2127-2160
Coital techniques, 381, 382, 1590
Coitally unexperienced, 226, 291, 299

Coitus, 24, 229, 230, 264, 1171-1270, 2746
Coitus physiology, 1174-1177, 1192, 1967
College student behavior, 203, 259, 267, 530, 1369, 2172, 2186, 2191, 2194, 2195
College youth study, 256, 297
Colon surgery and sex behavior, 653-658
Comarital sex behavior, 2267-2297, 2314
Comics, 220
Commission on Obscenity and Pornography, 3849, 3879, 3991, 4011
Commission on Population Growth and the American Future, 237, 788
Communes, 1801, 2169, 2922, 3188
Communication, 1291, 2482
Comparative anatomy, 1238
Conforte, Joe, 3490
Consanguinity, 2620, 3131
Continence, 664
Contraception, 690, 2343. See also Afroamericans and; Attitudes on; Catholic attitudes on; Judaic attitudes on; Legal aspects of; Mentally retarded and
Contraception acceptors, 236, 237, 244, 248, 344, 770, 775, 788, 1332, 1582, 1926, 2184
Contraception and sex behavior, 286, 2305, 3010
Contraception and sex behavior research, 189, 320, 498, 2001, 2135, 2159
Contraception bibliographies, 639
Contraception development research, 1887
Contraception for minors, 182, 216, 220, 243
Contraception history, 3034
Contraception laws, 3531
Contraception methods, 231
Contraception nonacceptors, 237, 248, 788, 2469
Contraception organizations, 1366, 1421
Coprolalia, 4100
Corporal punishment, 1027
Cosmetic surgery, 2060
Counseling, 238-243, 812, 956. See also Marriage counseling; Pastoral counseling; Peer counseling; Premarital counseling; Rape victim counseling; Sex counseling; Telephone counseling
Counselors sex education, 124, 238, 716, 1319, 1359, 1422-1447, 1485, 2503
Counselors sex education materials, 1435, 1436, 1438, 1446, 1596
Countercultures, 487, 496, 507
Courtship, 1383, 2171, 2800, 4145, 4262
Courtship customs, 2570, 2587, 2672
Couvade, 1793
COYOTE, 3314
Crime, 3470
Criminals, 3467. See also Psychology of criminals
Cryptorchidism, 993, 1907
Cryptorchidism and sex behavior, 1907
Customs in primitive societies, 78, 589, 592, 2587, 2599, 2606, 2622, 2628, 2635, 2650, 2656, 2692
Cytogenetic syndromes, 594, 859, 1899

Dancing, see Social dancing
Darwin, Charles, 1711
Dating, 177, 199, 202, 340, 3611, 4262
Dating questionnaires, 317, 4182, 4184
Defense mechanisms, 3949
Delayed puberty, 1356, 1915, 1917, 1920, 1922
Demography, 1332, 1495, 1506
Demonology, 4057
Depression, 129, 415, 423, 524, 686, 697, 1164, 1983

Desensitization, 489, 1156, 1514, 1531, 1551-1556, 2355
Determinants of sex differentiation, 811, 1171, 1184, 1704, 1707, 1711, 1717-1719, 1721, 1722, 1728, 1729, 1734, 1736, 1751-1755, 1763, 1778, 1786, 1789, 1790, 1805, 1806, 1808, 1810, 1819, 1822, 1827, 1853, 1857, 1894-1913
Deviant behavior, 232, 2666, 2718, 3351, 3416, 3417, 3421, 4181. See also Sex variations
Deviant groups, 1133, 2987, 3186
Diabetes and sex behavior, 659-662
Differential personality inventory, 1130
Differential rearing of children, 116, 1731, 1746, 1749, 1770, 1776
Digestive system, 570
Directories of physicians, 4
Directories of prostitutes, 3474
Directories of social scientists, 3, 4
Diseases and sex behavior, 534, 570, 629, 663-670, 1957. See also Brain diseases and sex behavior; Cancer and sex behavior; Cerebral palsy and sex behavior; Epilepsy and sex behavior; Heart disease and sex behavior; Metabolic diseases and sex behavior; Nervous system impairment and sex behavior; Respiratory diseases and sex behavior; Urogenital diseases and sex behavior
Divorce, 1283, 2703
Divorce statistics, 2200
Doctors sex education research, 1336, 2508-2517
Domestic relations laws, 2165, 2177, 2183
Draw-a-person test, 1724, 1761, 2745
Dreams, 3250
Dreams psychoanalysis, 492, 1057
Drug addiction, 487, 493, 522, 526, 528, 531, 549
Drug addicts, 497, 498, 504, 517, 522, 525, 529, 544
Drug therapy, 495, 499, 535, 539, 551, 595, 1164, 1994
Drugs, 265, 487, 515, 516, 533, 550, 551, 591, 3743. See also Amphetamines; Hallucinogenic drugs; Marijuana; Nicotine; Tranquilizers
Drugs and sex behavior, 336, 481-627, 648, 1994
Drugs questionnaires, 530, 611, 3782

Ejaculatory incompetence, 511, 512, 541, 1267
Ellis, Havelock, 28
Embryology, 1179
Emotions, 1931, 1983, 3736, 3915
Emotions and sex differences, 192, 1734, 1780, 1818, 2947
Endocrinology, 1721, 1859-1868, 1908, 1920, 1922, 1940, 1959, 1965, 1966, 2000
Enemas, 589
Engagement, 2680
Entrapment, 866, 3549, 3552
Epilepsy and sex behavior, 648-650, 1268
Erotica, 1118, 2628, 3124, 3848-4012, 4019, 4021, 4064, 4091, 4101, 4104. See also Attitudes on; Behavioral effect of; Homosexual erotica dealers; Obscenity; Sadomasochistic erotica; Sex offenders and
Erotica consumers, 3410, 3858, 3947-3953
Erotica dealers, 3410, 3956
Erotica distribution, 3858
Erotica industry, 986, 3858, 3861, 3954-3961, 3986
Erotica producers, 3954, 3956, 3959, 4091, 4096
Erotica production, 3858, 3961
Erotica questionnaires, 3924, 3984
Erotica research, 340, 986, 3263, 3745, 3848, 3856, 3857, 3859-3881, 3891, 3925, 3950, 3953, 3960, 4003, 4091
Eskimos, 778

Estrogens, 1878, 1890, 1910
Ethics, see Sex ethics; Social ethics
Ethnic groups, 630, 776-788, 1329. See also Afroamericans; Blacks
Ethnography, 1142, 2570, 2573, 2587, 2598, 2611, 2658, 2671, 2683, 2684, 2702
Ethnology, 78, 777, 1687, 1711, 2215, 2576, 2581, 2582, 2586, 2597, 2609, 2613, 2615, 2628, 2630-2632, 2639, 2641, 2645, 2648, 2660, 2666, 2674, 2682, 2685, 2691, 2693, 2695, 2705, 2709, 2855, 3380
Eugenics research, 3126
Eulenspiegel society, 968
Euthanasia, 2075
Evans-pritchard, E.E., 2685
Exhibitionism, 3269, 3746-3758
Exhibitionism aversion therapy, 3810
Exhibitionism behavior therapy, 3791, 3810
Exhibitionism laws, 3531
Exhibitionism psychoanalysis, 3750
Exhibitionism psychotherapy, 3748, 3758, 3815
Exhibitionism research, 2698, 3747, 3750, 3751, 3753, 3755, 5757
Exhibitionism therapy, 3751
Experimental psychology, 4174
Experimenter vs subject sex, 353, 1809, 1812, 1850, 4168
Experiments using animals, 527, 1062, 1999
Experiments using mammals, 502, 562, 1270, 1908, 1912, 1940, 1998
Experiments using primates, 604, 1836, 1866, 1963, 1988
Extramarital sex behavior, 11, 1664, 2100, 2205-2324, 3435. See also Comarital sex behavior
Extramarital sex behavior research, 2131, 2249-2266
Eysenck personality inventory, 3897

Faith in people test, 2463
Family, 2356, 3146
Family comparative research, 780, 1711, 2611, 3126, 3135
Family disorganization, 2974, 3156, 3158, 3178, 3211, 3213, 3214
Family in primitive societies, 1756, 2596, 2600, 2611, 2642, 2648, 2682-2685, 3122, 3149
Family life education, 2097, 2450, 2944
Family life education bibliographies, 636
Family life education research, 2442, 2471, 2487, 2488, 2558
Family research, 412, 641, 1833, 2922, 3199, 4177
Family therapy, 643, 1163, 3108, 3120, 3213, 3219
Fantasies, 109, 444, 445, 492, 1002, 1004, 1118
Fantasies and sex differences, 990
Female impersonation, 1089
Fertility control, 2526, 3010, 3124, 3319
Fertility control behavioral research, 498, 801, 2327
Fertility control bibliographies, 136
Fertility control conferences, 3023
Fertility control education, 165, 801, 1294, 1296, 1385, 1411, 1429, 2343, 2456, 2462, 2517, 2534
Fertility control research, 244, 282, 1869, 1887, 2466, 3042, 3061
Fertility research, 619, 621, 688, 801, 2148, 2184, 2596, 2664, 2675, 2701, 2998, 3061
Fetal hormonal functioning, 1717, 1718, 1805, 1894-1913
Fetishism, 972, 1166, 4058
Fetishism aversion therapy, 1038
Fetishism behavior therapy, 3791
Fetishism in art, 4058

Fetishism psychoanalysis, 998, 1009
Florence Crittenton Association of America, Inc., 1429
Folklore, 2455, 2574, 2583, 2623, 3467
Folksongs, 4146
Franck drawing completion test, 1793
Free love, 31, 2834
Freud, Sigmund, 92, 831, 3202
Futuristic predictions, 2838

Galvanic skin response, 1553, 2021, 3897, 3904, 3906, 3908, 3919, 3927
Gang bangs, 3430, 3648, 3684
Gender identity scale, 4211
Gender role identification, 112, 777, 827, 831, 1120, 1220, 1259, 1680-1857, 2044, 2586, 2916-3013, 3015, 3580, 3901
Gender role identification bibliographies, 1680-1684
Gender role identification problems, 832, 849, 1093, 1094, 1096, 1101, 1126, 1132, 1135, 1146, 1154, 1160, 1285, 1431, 1690, 1691, 1735, 1738, 1767, 1796, 1812, 1865, 1913, 2008, 2026, 2046, 2052, 2928
Gender role identification research, 91, 98, 116, 131, 325, 691, 784, 791, 1136, 1138, 1680-1857, 2062, 2461, 2668, 2966, 2976, 3004, 4234
Genetics, 2612, 2706, 3171
Gilyak, 2587
Glands, 1956
Gonadotrophins, 1863, 1872, 1914
Grotesque in art, 4024, 4057
Group marriage, 2274
Group sex, 2192, 2212, 2221, 2249, 2269, 2277, 2279, 2293, 2295
Group sex research, 2268, 2272, 2273, 2275, 2276, 2281, 2282, 2290, 2291, 2294
Group therapy, 295, 1330, 1365, 1371, 1522, 1523, 1555, 1557-1564, 1582, 1606, 3302, 3303, 3305, 3783, 3785, 3787, 3789, 3793, 3800, 3809, 3815
Growth, 1986
Guide books, 3480
Guyon, Rene, The Ethics of Sexual Acts, 2851
Gynecomastia, 513

Hallucinogenic drugs, 588-595
Hartogs, Renatus, 1623
Head comics, 4030
Health education, 2442
Heart disease and sex behavior, 375, 430, 519, 671-677
Heart rate response, 677, 3886, 3904, 3906, 3908, 3919
Hefner, Hugh M., 3954
Hermaphrodites in literature, 1746
Hitler, Adolf, 993
Holtzman inkblot test, 1131
Homicide, 3781
Homophobia, 195
Homosexual bars, 2573, 4180
Homosexual community, 844, 873, 884, 895, 901, 908, 938-955, 1438, 2573, 3507
Homosexual erotica dealers, 3951
Homosexual fellatio, 3521
Homosexual incest, 3141, 3147, 3212, 3218
Homosexual life styles, 429, 480, 843, 844, 889, 894, 944, 1438, 2573, 3496, 3530
Homosexual marriages, 844, 1122, 2072, 2074, 2193
Homosexual organizations, 939, 943, 951, 952, 1117, 4180
Homosexual organizations directories, 867, 2067

Homosexual pedophilia, 850, 852, 3243, 3259, 3268, 3271, 3274, 3282-3292, 3296, 3515
Homosexual prostitution, 777, 901, 2586, 2702, 3286, 3317, 3322, 3492-3530
Homosexual rape, 3568, 3632-3643
Homosexual religious organizations, 929, 993
Homosexual sadomasochism, 1012-1016
Homosexual slang, 3951
Homosexual slang dictionaries, 873, 901
Homosexual writers, 890
Homosexuality, 239, 544, 819, 837, 1358, 3463, 3559. See also Afroamericans and; Attitudes on; Catholic attitudes on; Legal aspects of; Protestant attitudes on; Religious attitudes on; Situational
Homosexuality and mental health, 392, 480, 905, 956, 1840
Homosexuality and mental illness, 877, 4251
Homosexuality and neuroses, 3505
Homosexuality and psychoses, 1012
Homosexuality aversion therapy, 1151
Homosexuality behavior therapy, 858, 1510, 3290, 4251
Homosexuality bibliographies, 858-865, 4065
Homosexuality commitment, 843-845, 853, 889, 956, 2744
Homosexuality conferences, 954
Homosexuality drug therapy, 596, 597
Homosexuality etiology, 814, 825, 858, 877, 892, 1359, 1729, 2668
Homosexuality etiology psychoanalysis, 835
Homosexuality genetic research, 594
Homosexuality history, 823, 878, 880, 882, 890, 947, 3517
Homosexuality hormonal research, 704, 1865, 1987
Homosexuality hormone therapy, 1987
Homosexuality in cinema, 3951, 4121, 4123, 4125
Homosexuality in literature, 894, 4075
Homosexuality in primitive societies, 1100, 2593, 2603, 2613, 2634, 2668, 2702
Homosexuality in theater, 4133
Homosexuality interview schedules, 846
Homosexuality laws, 8, 867, 876, 2067, 3286, 3517
Homosexuality learning theory, 852, 858
Homosexuality of prostitutes, 872
Homosexuality psychoanalysis, 814, 822, 1624, 3147
Homosexuality psychoanalytic therapy, 1607, 1621, 1646, 1648
Homosexuality psychological research, 860, 892, 900, 1840, 1865, 3753
Homosexuality psychotherapy, 1012, 1606
Homosexuality questionnaires, 401, 846, 899, 2738, 2739, 2814, 4240
Homosexuality research, 15, 401, 413, 777, 833, 846, 848, 849, 853, 854, 862, 874, 883, 892, 895-917, 926, 1730, 2096, 2586, 2613, 2690, 2738, 2747, 4180
Homosexuality surgical therapy, 3287, 3301
Homosexuality therapy, 849, 909, 922-927, 1359, 3290, 4236
Homosexuals, see Changing role of; Sex education on; Status of
Homosexuals advice, 948
Homosexuals and creativity, 890
Homosexuals as parents, 875, 1284
Homosexuals civil liberties, 867, 912, 943, 2067, 2074, 3051
Homosexuals in the military, 912
Homosexuals interest testing, 1849
Homosexuals MF scales, 1815

Homosexuals personality inventories, 2745, 3283
Homosexuals physiological testing, 1948, 2021
Homosexuals projective testing, 2745
Homosexuals psychological testing, 556, 900, 905, 3518, 4235-4239
Homosexuals sex behavior, 892, 3530
Homosexuals sex behavior research, 777, 2586
Hormonal experiments using animals, 1810, 1889, 1894, 1955
Hormonal response, 571, 608, 1174, 1175, 1206, 1885, 1948, 3886
Hormone therapy, 425, 449, 539, 1873, 1875, 1910, 1917, 1922, 1937-1939, 1941, 1943, 1957, 1960, 1994
Hormones, 827, 1791, 1858-2001, 2045
Hormones and animal sex behavior, 39, 839, 1186, 1717, 1866, 1874, 1878, 1904, 1940, 1958, 1961, 1969, 1974, 1984, 1998, 2000
Hormones and behavior, 704, 1719, 1807, 1868, 1870, 1883, 1891, 1900, 1903, 1910, 1913, 1925, 1935, 1940-1952, 1959, 1960, 1969, 1983
Hormones and sex behavior, 377, 394, 849, 1063, 1197, 1206, 1240, 1858, 1873, 1896, 1899, 1901, 1927, 1929, 1932, 1941, 1943, 1949, 1953-2001
Hypersexuality, 517, 623, 705, 3140
Hypersexuality hormone therapy, 548, 1872
Hypnotherapy, 1148, 1149, 1165, 1521, 1566, 1574, 1630, 3206
Hypogonadism, 1993
Hyposexuality, 1324, 2953
Hysterectomy and sex behavior, 763, 764

Impotence, 403, 434, 660, 724, 1323, 1863, 1956, 4221
Impotence hormone therapy, 548, 624, 1863, 1876
Impotence psychoanalysis, 1673, 3293
Impotence therapy, 391, 488, 1507, 1603, 1604, 1673, 1989
Imprinting, 3185
Inanimate fetishism, 972, 998
Incest, 2215, 2569, 2623, 2637, 2677, 2685, 2687, 2688, 2704, 3116, 3122-3240, 3300. See also Homosexual incest; Legal aspects of; Oedipus complex
Incest behavior therapy, 3211, 3212, 3215
Incest in literature, 3148, 3187, 3201, 3240
Incest laws, 2620, 3180, 3191, 3236, 3531
Incest psychoanalysis, 3130, 3139, 3156, 3158, 3161, 3172, 3175, 3181, 3196-3211, 3216, 3227
Incest psychoanalytic therapy, 3196, 3209
Incest psychotherapy, 3218
Incest research, 1633, 2574, 2583, 2602, 2708, 3069, 3093, 3130, 3145, 3156-3195, 3199, 3203, 3211, 3215, 3217, 3218, 3220-3222, 3228, 3230-3232, 3234, 3237, 3239
Incest therapy, 3198, 3211-3219
Incest victimology, 581, 3158, 3172, 3193, 3220-3234
Indeterminant sentence, 3778, 3806
Infant behavior, 79, 113
Initiation rites, 2660, 2701
Institute for Sex Research, Inc., 66, 1249, 4064
Intelligence testing, 1910, 3623
Interest testing, 2722, 3255, 3256
Interethnic marriage, 3323
International Planned Parenthood Federation, 2327
Interpersonal relations, 276, 299, 326, 549, 834, 1342, 1426, 1715, 1845, 2654, 2937, 2983, 3481
Intersex, 594, 827, 849, 1120, 1706, 1707, 1722, 1740, 1743, 1752, 1753, 1769, 1786, 1791, 1799, 1819, 1899, 1901, 1905, 1911, 2070, 2599

Interview schedules, 556, 2750, 4188
Interviewing, 757, 874, 1395, 2714, 3083, 3710, 4163, 4168, 4181
Intimacy permissiveness scale, 4165
Intracranial stimulation, 1270, 1999
Intrauterine devices, 1278
Involuntary childlessness, 2679
Ismelin, 532
It scale for children, 1716, 1809, 1816, 1826, 1835

Jealousy, 1309
Jewelry, 4029
Johnson, Virginia E., 28, 476, 1185, 1214, 1335, 1461, 1477, 1507, 1517
Joking relationships, 777, 2586, 2695
Judaic attitudes on abortion, 2872
Judaic attitudes on contraception, 2872
Judaic attitudes on sex education, 169
Judaic family life education, 2873
Judaic laws, 2871
Judaic marriage, 2871, 2872
Judaic sex attitudes, 169, 310
Judaic sex ethics, 2870-2875
Judicial definitions of obscenity, 3995, 3997, 3999, 4001, 4002, 4008
Justice administration, 3640, 3829, 3840
Juvenile delinquency, 2454, 3423, 3515, 3684, 3742, 3842, 3853
Juvenile delinquency research, 3163, 3823

Kinesics, 3039, 4815. See also Nonverbal sexual communication
Kinsey, Alfred C., 28, 1214, 3899, 4010
    Sexual Behavior in the Human Female, 1827, 2104, 2117, 2627
    Sexual Behavior in the Human Male, 1827, 2627
Kinsey scale, 4239
Kissing, 2669
Klinefelters syndrome, 1138, 1941
Kohlenberg, Robert J., 3307

L-Dopa, 623-627
LSD, 482, 596-598
Labia stretching, 2595
Latency period, 1036
Law, 3531
Law history, 4003
Learning theory, 1699
Legal aspects, see Sex laws
Legal aspects of abortion, 3042, 3551, 3677
Legal aspects of contraception, 2431, 3042
Legal aspects of cross dressing, 867, 1093, 1167-1170, 2067, 2081
Legal aspects of homosexuality, 866, 867, 875, 1284, 2067, 3136, 3501, 3511, 3517, 3525, 3539, 3549, 3635
Legal aspects of illegitimacy, 1289
Legal aspects of incest, 2620, 3125, 3178, 3180, 3190, 3235-3240
Legal aspects of marriage, 1385, 1387, 2072, 2187, 2196-2199
Legal aspects of nonmarital sex behavior, 2165, 2177, 2183, 2589
Legal aspects of obscenity, 3551, 3861, 3870, 3945, 3970, 3972, 3976, 3977, 3979, 3980, 3982, 3986, 3987, 3990-4011
Legal aspects of pedophilia, 3072, 3086, 3105, 3243, 3298

Legal aspects of prostitution, 3314, 3315, 3353, 3364, 3372, 3381, 3384, 3424, 3464, 3531-3560
Legal aspects of rape, 3083, 3089, 3097, 3532, 3567, 3570, 3586, 3596, 3609, 3610, 3624, 3625, 3637, 3647, 3649, 3651, 3654, 3661, 3662, 3665-3681, 3685, 3688, 3689, 3693, 3695, 3707
Legal aspects of sex behavior, 982, 1623, 1661, 2589, 3104, 3539, 3633, 3765, 3776-3778, 3801, 3839, 3840, 3843
Legal aspects of sex counseling, 1338, 1497, 1576-1580, 1586, 1669, 1671
Legal aspects of sex education, 1483, 1642, 2431
Legal aspects of sex reassignment, 1102, 1740, 2004, 2047, 2063, 2067-2081
Legal aspects of statutory rape, 3674, 3676, 3677, 3678
Legal aspects of voyeurism, 3764
Legal status of minors, 3075, 3077, 3110, 3114, 3677, 3842
Legal status of women, 1283, 2988, 3672
Legalized prostitution, 3543, 3553, 3554, 3558
Levi-Strauss, Claude, The Elementary Structures of Kinship, 3205
Libraries, 3984, 4064
Linguistics, 1693, 3210, 4081
Literature, 1021, 4012, 4027, 4081, 4084, 4096, 4101. See also Homosexuality in; Incest in; Men in; Motifs; Mythology; Sadomasochism in; Sex in; Women in; Writers
Literature psychoanalysis, 4087
Love, 1770, 2923, 2934, 2983, 3045, 4068, 4185
Lovelace, Linda, 3959
Lower class, 806, 2322
Lower class and sex behavior, 783, 800-807, 1260

MF scales, 91, 325, 691, 1695, 1697, 1701, 1745, 1764, 1768, 1820, 1826, 1832, 1844, 2946, 4208, 4228-4234, 4237
MMPI, 266, 296, 1144, 1813, 2034, 2035, 2167, 3267, 3755, 4220-4223
Madams, 3348, 3402
Magic, 2678
Maimonides, Moses, 2875
Male impotence test, 4220
Malinowski, Bronislaw, 977
Mammal sex behavior, 839, 1879, 1972, 2571
Marijuana, 514, 530, 602, 607, 608, 611
Marijuana and sex behavior, 599-612
Marital adjustment research, 479, 1244, 2090, 2095, 2098, 2109, 2112, 2117, 2118, 2121-2124, 2131, 2158, 2164, 2272, 2751, 2772, 2773
Marital roles, 1307, 2921, 2963, 2993, 3001, 3048
Marital sex behavior, 382, 805, 2092, 2093, 2115, 2119, 2151, 2644, 2699
Marital sex behavior research, 555, 772, 1244, 1258, 2090-2160, 2292
Marital sex problems, 775, 1293, 1301, 1304, 1305, 1307, 1314, 1320, 1325, 1339, 1343, 1522, 1523, 1527, 1546, 1666, 1762, 2115, 2124, 2147, 2205, 2935, 3438
Marks, Burton, 3959
Marriage, 11, 2226, 2836, 2859, 2864, 2898. See also Attitudes on; Homosexual marriages; Legal aspects of; Student marriages; Trial marriage
Marriage and family, 148, 2239, 2699, 2993
Marriage and family questionnaires, 2193, 2963
Marriage and family research, 608, 2199, 2686, 2944
Marriage and religion, 2910, 3000
Marriage comparative research, 2184, 2705, 2708

Marriage contracts, 2296
Marriage counseling, 758, 1304, 1318, 1332, 1337, 1341, 1344, 1372, 1373, 1377, 1384, 1445, 1470–1472, 1546, 1563, 1666, 2115, 2128, 2141, 2214, 2225, 2241, 2248, 2274, 2296, 2512, 2988, 3438
Marriage customs, 1374, 2197, 2280, 2570, 2591, 2680, 2703, 2708, 3129, 3151, 3155
Marriage effects of children, 2119
Marriage forms, 50, 2162, 2174, 2222, 2223, 2288, 2301, 2314, 2315, 2703
Marriage history, 2703, 3144
Marriage in primitive societies, 2596, 2612, 2633, 2654, 2682, 3129, 3135, 3192
Marriage laws, 2074
Marriage manuals, 2284
Marriage problems, 557, 795, 1017, 1122, 1163, 2128, 2225, 2229, 2232, 2235, 2238, 2239, 2241, 2248, 3001, 3047
Marriage reforms, 50, 2192, 2195, 2283, 2285, 2307
Marriage research, 26, 50, 795, 2173, 2174, 2189, 2222, 2223, 2254, 2282, 2287, 2292, 2922, 3188, 3737
Marriage statistics, 377, 576, 2197, 2200
Masochism, 964–1019, 1035–1065, 1077
Masochism psychoanalysis, 1036, 1044–1061
Masochism research, 1042, 1044, 1062–1065
Mass media, 3088, 3580, 3591, 4020
Mass media censorship, 3965
Mastectomy, 679
Mastectomy and sex behavior, 678–681
Masters, William H., 28, 476, 1185, 1214, 1335, 1461, 1477, 1507, 1517
    Human Sexual Response, 1172, 1233
Masters and Johnson program, 1530
Masturbation, 76, 347, 356, 526, 930, 1066, 1070, 1078, 1418, 1503, 1557, 1597, 1599, 1601, 3396. See also Autoeroticism; Attitudes on; Sex hangings
Masturbation early works, 481
Masturbation psychoanalysis, 1047
Masturbation research, 82, 263, 1072, 1730, 2096, 2764
Maternal behavior in animals, 1718, 1949
Medical attitudes on abortion, 2535, 2536
Medical care of minors, 2466
Medical ethics, 690, 1611, 1633, 1634, 1659, 3712, 4245
Medical examination, 3074, 3688, 3692
Medical jurisprudence, 3582, 3596, 3707, 3772, 3830, 3832, 3833, 3837
Medical manuals, 3038
Medical profession, 3617, 3700
Medical profession sex education, 695, 699, 758, 1339, 1344, 1492, 2228, 2505, 2512
Medical students sex education, 1339, 1345, 2518–2531, 2538, 2539, 2764
Medical students sex education curricula, 2516, 2522, 2525, 2537
Medical students sex education materials, 1305, 1326, 2521
Medical students sex education research, 283, 1336, 2508, 2518–2531, 4214
Medicine, 1583, 2875
Medicine history, 3015, 3020
Mellaril, 532
Men, 2652. See also Changing role of; Unwed fathers
Men in art, 4138
Men in literature, 4105
Men psychoanalysis, 1699, 2247, 2965, 3961
Menarche, 645, 1918, 1930
Men's magazines, 986, 2991, 3057

Menstruation, 1199, 1240, 1924–1935, 1983, 2655, 2691, 3020. See also Periodicity
Mental health, 606
Mental health and sex differences, 1798, 2927
Mental health profession, 1287
Mentally ill, 690, 691, 698, 704, 1381, 1891, 2439, 3171
Mentally ill and sex behavior, 631, 682–707, 1164, 1260, 2043, 2707
Mentally ill and sex education, 693, 703
Mentally retarded and contraception, 711, 712
Mentally retarded and sex behavior, 632, 706, 708–718
Mentally retarded and sex education, 639, 684, 692, 709, 710, 712, 714, 716, 718, 1917
Mentally retarded marriage and family, 712, 713
Mentally retarded sex education materials, 692
Mesterolone, 1876
Metabolic diseases and sex behavior, 1997. See also Arthritis and sex behavior; Diabetes and sex behavior
Metropolitan community churches, 933
Microphallus, 1784
Middle aged behavior, 396
Middle class and sex behavior, 2207
Miller, Henry, Tropic of Cancer, 3975
Miller, Marvin, 3959
Minor arts, 4029
Minors, see Legal status of
Miscegenation, 3591
Mooney problem checklist, 694
Moral development and sex differences, 145
Moral opposition to theater, 3373
Mormon Church, 1801
Mormons, 2856
Morris, Desmond, 1711, 2643
Mosher, Clelia Duel, 3029
Mosher forced choice sex guilt scale, 2782, 3871, 4226
Mosher incomplete sentences test, 3915, 4227
Mother-son interaction test, 3252
Motifs, 4115
Muria, 2601
Music, see Sex in
Musicians, 1986
Mythology, 1000

Napoleon I, 829
National Legion of Decency, 3971
Natural law, 2865
Necrophilia, 967, 1022
Nervous system, 502, 1182, 1186, 1218, 1268, 1775, 1968, 1999, 2032
Nervous system impairment and sex behavior, 532, 623, 628, 648, 719–725, 729, 730, 740, 1128
Neuroses, 517, 525, 562, 689, 2216, 3118
Nicotine, 446, 520, 613–622
Nocturnal erection, 455–458, 1180, 1888, 3612
Nonmarital sex behavior, 232, 654, 1362, 2151, 2174, 2277, 2861. See also Attitudes on; Comarital sex behavior; Extramarital sex behavior; Legal aspects of; Postmarital sex behavior; Premarital sex behavior; Singles life style
Nonmarital sex behavior research, 306, 307, 447, 682, 1361
Nonsexist child rearing, 2557, 2921
Nonverbal sexual communication, 1305, 1653, 3039. See also Kinesics
Nuclear sex, 613, 827, 1111, 1722, 1791
Nudes in art, 4036
Nudes in photographs, 3470, 3479, 4139–4142

Nudism, 3350
Nudism organizations, 2293
Nudism research, 2786
Nudity, 134, 1566
Nurses sex education, 2532-2542, 3698
Nurses sex education research, 2536
Nursing ethics, 2541, 3712
Nursing students sex education, 2532-2542

Obscene phone calls, *see* Coprolalia
Obscenity, 2639, 4006, 4081. *See also* Judaic definitions of; Legal aspects of
Obscenity laws, 3531, 3958, 3966, 3970, 3998, 4008
Obscenity trials, 3956, 4010
Obstetrics and gynecology, 1281, 2775, 3015
Oedipus complex, 1004, 2691, 3200, 3202, 3240
Oneida community, 2856
Oral contraceptives, 216
Oral contraceptives and sex behavior, 184, 1199, 2137
Oral contraceptives effects, 1870, 1925, 1926
Oral genital sex behavior, 2096
Orgasm, 1171-1270, 2595. *See also* Animal orgasm
Orgasm research, 433, 1174, 1177, 1217-1270, 1967, 2121
Orgasmic dysfunction, 433, 1267, 3007
Orgasmic dysfunction psychoanalysis, 1235
Orgasmic dysfunction therapy, 488, 489, 1230, 1241, 1461, 1503, 1507, 1557, 1597, 1600, 1679, 3912
Ovulation, 1240, 1928

P-Chlorophenylalanine, 624
Paraplegics and sex behavior, 638, 720, 726-738, 1267
Paraplegics and sex education, 720, 726, 727, 733, 735, 736
Parental attitudes, 110, 252, 339, 563, 706, 2199, 2433, 2458, 2760, 2794, 2947
Parenthood research, 1756, 3018. *See also* Absent father effects; Child parent relationships; Single parents; Unwed fathers; Unwed mothers; Unwed parents
Parents sex education, 80, 110, 220, 639, 1302, 1354, 1357, 1443, 2326, 2354-2360, 2445
Parole, 3788
Partner preference, 431, 2932. *See also* Body type partner preference
Partner preference research, 147, 284, 2804, 2828, 3898
Pastoral counseling, 1376, 1399-1407
Pedophilia, 1025, 3080, 3085, 3241-3312, 3608, 3724. *See also* Child victims; Homosexual pedophilia; Incest; Legal aspects of
Pedophilia aversion therapy, 3308-3312
Pedophilia behavior therapy, 3306, 3307
Pedophilia psychoanalysis, 3118, 3244, 3245, 3274, 3278, 3293-3296, 3304
Pedophilia psychotherapy, 3302-3305
Pedophilia research, 569, 850, 2698, 3069, 3070, 3071, 3076, 3099, 3100, 3102, 3103, 3115, 3117, 3119, 3121, 3249-3283, 3289, 3294, 3296, 3297, 3304, 3311
Pedophilia therapy, 3287, 3297-3301, 3303
Peer counseling, 1408-1415, 2351
Penile plethysmography, 459, 554, 560, 850, 1180, 1194, 1195, 1211, 2021, 3273, 3306, 3898, 3911, 3914
Penis, 476, 1209, 1213, 1264, 1775, 2640
Penis implants, 742
Penis size, 266, 296, 4186
Periodicity, 1865, 1925-1935, 1984, 2127, 2154
Periodicity and sex behavior, 351, 1188, 1199, 1240, 1866, 2139

Personal orientation inventory, 2782
Personal sex ads, 1014
Personality, 13, 106, 612, 619, 1794, 2923, 3275, 3871, 4195, 4249
Personality and sex behavior, 226, 261, 331, 347-365, 522, 553, 617, 686, 2167, 2434, 2463, 2735, 2753, 2804, 2820, 3012, 3877, 3915. *See also* Self concept and sex behavior
Personality inventories, 448, 918, 1480, 1697, 1702, 1813, 1910, 2034, 2167, 2441, 2737, 3721, 4220, 4227
Petting, 199, 291, 333, 334, 2118
Phallus cults, 2640, 2650, 2660
Photography, 1088. *See also* Sex in photographs
Photography early works, 4139, 4141
Physical fitness, 4187
Physically handicapped and sex behavior, 633, 640, 669, 727, 731, 739-747
Physically handicapped and sex education, 637, 677, 743
Physiological impotence, 513, 567, 578, 659, 720, 1989
Physiological psychology, 1171, 1196, 1870
Physiological response to auditory stimuli, 1194, 1195, 3908
Physiological response to olfactory stimuli, 1877, 1890, 1988
Physiological response to sensory stimuli, 584, 1178, 1200, 1313, 1879, 1954, 3310, 3859
Physiological response to tactile stimuli, 448, 1179, 1209, 1267
Physiological response to visual stimuli, 360, 560, 1187, 1196, 1202, 1210, 1216, 1885, 1927, 1948, 1990, 2021, 3257, 3273, 3613, 3850-3852, 3882-3929, 3939, 3942
Physiological sex differences, 837, 1184, 1734, 1870, 1895, 1955, 2643
Pimps, 2658, 3341, 3349, 3394, 3441, 3456, 3457-3468, 3552. *See also* Biographies of
Pin ups, 2991
Playboy, 3954
Poetry, *see* Sex in
Police, 3390, 3838. *See also* Entrapment
Police techniques, 3098, 3654, 3665, 3669, 3689, 3705, 3836
Polygamy, 3531
Polygyny, 398, 1756, 2596
Popular culture studies, 2991
Popular press, 3056
Popular psychology, 1482
Population, 2645
Pornography, *see* Erotica; Obscenity
Postcards, 4052, 4139, 4141
Postcoital contraceptives, 3682
Postmarital sex behavior, 422, 2249
Postmarital sex behavior research, 1249, 2264
Poverty areas and sex education, 801, 804, 2420, 2456
Precocious puberty, 80, 1871, 1915, 1917
Pregnancy, 135, 191, 618, 664, 670, 1900, 1983, 2146, 2149, 2264, 2541, 4207
Pregnancy complications, 622, 720
Premarital conception, 137, 141, 231, 788, 1378, 2578
Premarital counseling, 1371-1388, 1405, 2512
Premarital sex behavior, 138, 224, 297, 363, 483, 794, 796, 1386, 2228, 2644, 2754, 2794, 2854, 3026, 3192
Premarital sex behavior research, 9, 16, 27, 149, 151, 161, 174, 177, 213, 225-237, 249, 300, 308-346, 355, 357, 363, 782, 788, 2090. 2109, 2118, 2121, 2166, 2179, 2493, 2580, 2629, 2726, 2772, 2773, 2802, 2805, 2820
Premarital sex education, 1382, 3449

Premarital sexual permissiveness scale, 2560, 4165
Premature ejaculation, 1604
Prenatal determination of sex, 1722
Priapism, 720
Primate anatomy and physiology, 1775
Primate behavior, 1711, 1775, 1900, 1947, 1952, 2657, 3126, 3135
Primate sex behavior, 1269, 1877, 1921, 1963, 2632, 3183
Primitive art, 2650, 4055
Prison, 3632
Prison sex behavior, 3632-3637, 3639, 3641-3643
Prisoners, 3532, 3632
Probation, 3298, 3794, 3807
Problems of adolescents, 175, 188, 1361, 1447, 2653
Professional groups sex behavior, 110, 564, 1545, 2762, 2777
Professional groups sex education, 707, 714, 1349, 1354, 1443, 1548, 1578, 2337, 2440, 2501-2507, 2517, 2528
Projective testing, 91, 1705, 1714, 1716, 1723, 1724, 1761, 1768, 1793, 1795, 1809, 1812, 1826, 1843, 2674, 2782, 3524, 3620, 3757, 3871, 3884, 3915, 3944, 4162, 4189
Prostaglandins, 1869, 1873
Prostatectomy and sex behavior, 408, 450
Prostitute slang, 3407
Prostitutes, 187, 2987, 3318, 3331, 3339, 3341, 3345, 3355, 3390, 3392-3395, 3400, 3402, 3408, 3411, 3413, 3415, 3418, 3419, 3422, 3426, 3437, 3441, 3479, 3482, 3488, 3494, 3497-3499, 3516, 3519, 3520, 3522, 3523, 3557. See also Clients of; Directories of
Prostitutes psychoanalysis, 3409, 3496
Prostitutes rehabilitation, 3337, 3405, 3424, 3504, 3545
Prostitutes sex behavior, 3446, 3477, 3482, 3494
Prostitutes sex behavior research, 3392, 3398
Prostitution, 3124, 3313-3560. See also Attitudes on; Brothels; Homosexual prostitution; Legal aspects of; Proxenetism; Religious prostitution
Prostitution and venereal diseases, 3345, 3362, 3555, 3557
Prostitution bibliographies, 3314, 3483, 3538
Prostitution history, 3315, 3352-3389, 3392, 3397, 3553
Prostitution laws, 3353, 3365, 3366, 3459, 3531, 3555
Prostitution organizations, 3314, 3538, 3541
Prostitution research, 2702, 3321, 3322, 3329, 3331, 3390-3426, 3443, 3447, 3482, 3503, 3505, 3506, 3516, 3524, 3541
Protestant attitudes on homosexuality, 2897
Protestant attitudes on sex education, 2914
Protestant sex attitudes, 310, 352, 1407
Protestant sex ethics, 1407, 2891-2915
Proxenetism, 3331, 3367, 3371, 3388, 3527
Pseudocyesis, 2655
Psychiatry, 1661, 3769
Psychic masochism, 1035, 1050, 1060
Psychoanalysis, 176, 815, 1205, 1534, 1652, 1685, 1828, 2855, 3250. See also Adolescent sex behavior psychoanalysis; Child behavior psychoanalysis; Dreams psychoanalysis; Exhibitionism psychoanalysis; Fetishism psychoanalysis; Homosexuality etiology psychoanalysis; Impotence psychoanalysis; Incest psychoanalysis; Literature psychoanalysis; Masochism psychoanalysis; Masturbation psychoanalysis; Men psychoanalysis; Orgasmic dysfunction psychoanalysis; Pedophilia psychoanalysis; Psychosexual development psychoanalysis; Sadomasochism psychoanalysis; Sex offenders psychoanalysis; Sex variations psychoanalysis; Sexual symbolism psychoanalysis; Voyeurism psychoanalysis; Women psychoanalysis

Psychoanalytic therapy, 1570, 1572, 1624, 1658, 2232, 3761
Psychological effects of abortion, 2533
Psychological response to auditory stimuli, 350
Psychological response to sensory stimuli, 207, 584, 1201, 1293, 3756, 3859
Psychological response to tactile stimuli, 1224
Psychological response to visual stimuli, 275, 351, 353, 1739, 3263, 3613, 3722, 3850, 3851, 3860, 3864, 3870, 3871, 3873, 3876, 3878, 3882-3929, 3930, 3933, 3936, 3938, 3939, 3946, 4006
Psychological testing, 13, 246, 353, 612, 1035, 1710, 2489, 4174, 4176, 4195, 4220-4225, 4226
Psychology, 3185
Psychology of criminals, 1041, 3631, 3721, 3723, 3732, 3811, 3837
Psychopathology, 687, 967, 1130, 1700, 1813, 2034, 2245
Psychoses, 688, 701, 1761, 2216, 3304
Psychosexual development, 14, 15, 70, 71, 82, 90-134, 152, 163, 168, 172, 175, 212, 1233, 1281, 1352, 1689, 1694, 1703, 1736, 1743, 1747, 1759, 1760, 1766, 1771, 1788, 1811, 1814, 1908, 1911, 1929, 2438, 2846, 2933, 2955, 3066, 3068, 3069, 3071, 3092, 3128, 3631, 4087, 4110
Psychosexual development psychoanalysis, 109, 122, 123, 131, 179, 188, 192, 194, 822, 1006, 1009, 1036, 1046, 1082, 1624, 1657, 1699, 1754, 1798, 1805, 1817, 1822, 2234, 2239, 2240, 2674, 3146, 3321
Psychosomatics, 1793, 1954
Psychosurgery, 754, 3287, 3797
Psychosurgery research, 757, 3301, 3805
Psychotherapy, 1166, 1299, 1379, 1402, 1511, 1565, 1568, 1571, 1574, 1616, 1629, 1632, 1641, 1645, 1653, 1738, 2211, 3110, 3140, 3801. See also Homosexuality psychotherapy; Incest psychotherapy; Pedophilia psychotherapy; Sex offenders psychotherapy; Women psychotherapy
Pubertal hormonal dysfunction, 1821, 1859, 1884, 1914, 1915, 1917, 1922, 1924
Puberty, 127, 131, 1352, 1447, 1722, 1817, 1881, 1914-1924, 1986. See also Delayed puberty
Puberty in primitive societies, 2651, 2654
Public opinion surveying, 4162
Pupillary response, 3249, 3886, 3903

Questionnaires, 3099, 4197

Racism, 3591
Rape, 2644, 2700, 3089, 3098, 3333, 3351, 3430, 3561-3712. See also Gang bangs; Homosexual rape; Legal aspects of; Statutory rape
Rape bibliographies, 3561-3565
Rape laws, 3576, 3629, 3665, 3679, 3680
Rape research, 575, 1992, 3087, 3252, 3275, 3566, 3577, 3591-3631, 3644, 3647, 3662, 3666, 3674, 3679, 3692, 3693
Rape trials, 1630, 3097, 3652, 3665
Rape victim counseling, 3596, 3630, 3645, 3658, 3686, 3690, 3691, 3693, 3697, 3699, 3700, 3703, 3706, 3709, 3712
Rape victimology, 3089, 3090, 3106, 3107, 3111, 3113, 3566, 3572, 3574, 3585, 3590, 3593, 3596, 3597, 3598, 3609, 3626, 3627, 3630, 3638, 3639, 3644-3680, 3681-3712

Rational emotive therapy, 1379

Recidivism, 3128, 3297, 3724, 3768, 3774, 3816–3828

Rejuvenation, 1953

Religion, 2865, 4089. *See also* Christianity history; Sex in

Religion in primitive societies, 592, 2613, 2645, 2671

Religiosity and sex behavior, 146, 183, 297, 307, 312, 316, 319, 337, 339, 342, 359, 479, 1249, 2094, 2731, 2766, 2796, 2806, 2807, 2822

Religious attitudes on homosexuality, 928–937, 2893

Religious prostitution, 2676, 3377

Religious sex attitudes, 803, 1329, 1400, 1404, 1828, 2222, 2308, 2317, 2860, 2893, 2895, 3152

Religious sex ethics, 2837, 2863, 2870–2915. *See also* Afroamericans sex attitudes; Attitudes on; Catholic sex attitudes; Judaic sex attitudes; Protestant sex attitudes; Religious sex attitudes

Reproduction, 12, 1808, 1838, 1862, 2608, 2706

Reproduction research, 40, 1190, 1192, 2706

Reproductive myths and fallacies, 99, 763, 1752, 2444, 2469, 2660, 2662, 3020, 3062

Respiratory diseases and sex behavior, 667, 668

Rhythm method, 1933

Rorschach test, 1705, 3230, 3277, 3524

Ruskin, John, 3293

Sade, Donatien Alphonse Francois, Comte, called Marquis de, 970, 1021, 4086

Sadher-Masoch, Leopold, Ritter Von, 970, 1055

Sadism, 964–1034

Sadism research, 1029

Sadomasochism, 964–1087

Sadomasochism in art, 1000, 4057

Sadomasochism in cinema, 4109

Sadomasochism in literature, 973, 986, 1000, 1055, 4097

Sadomasochism in photographs, 974

Sadomasochism psychoanalysis, 984, 990–1011

Sadomasochism research, 973, 974, 999, 1007, 1014–1019

Sadomasochism therapy, 994

Sadomasochistic erotica, 1055

Sadomasochistic erotica producers, 1068

Sampling, 2716, 4169

Schmidt, Gunter, 3899

Scrotum and testes, 1881, 1889, 1892

Sculpture, 4025, 4032, 4045, 4060

Secondary impotence, 1603

Secret societies, 2701

Self concept, 344, 680, 1712, 1834, 2745, 2916, 2966, 4190, 4227

Self concept and sex behavior, 192, 194, 274, 1245, 1657, 2324, 3258

Self concept and sex differences, 325, 528, 1011, 1698, 2461, 2823

Sex aids, 48, 1227, 1530, 1567. *See also* Audiovisual sex aids; Aphrodisiacs

Sex and death, 405, 965, 1011, 1072, 1077, 1081, 3833

Sex and politics, 3384, 3437

Sex and society, 29, 112, 213, 253, 779, 783, 797, 1171, 1481, 1498, 1687, 1763, 1996, 2199, 2203, 2229, 2322, 2631, 2670, 2697, 2749, 2769, 2776, 2830, 2833, 2848, 2917, 2936, 2953, 2983, 3022, 3030, 3032, 3122, 3123, 3151, 3319, 3320, 3333, 3347, 3363, 3364, 3990, 4107

Sex assignment, 1706, 1740, 2070

Sex attitudes, 9, 26, 31, 101, 102, 115, 138, 151, 153, 154, 290, 384, 417, 599, 782, 803, 824, 1367, 1426, 1498, 2228, 2423, 2470, 2522, 2530, 2656, 2735, 2741, 2984,

3002, 3021, 3022, 3026, 3029, 3038, 3054, 3532, 4148, 4249. *See also* Afroamericans sex attitudes; Attitudes on; Catholic sex attitudes; Judaic sex attitudes; Protestant sex attitudes; Religious sex attitudes

Sex attitudes and behavior survey, 2527, 2762

Sex attitudes interview schedules, 2419, 2441, 3989, 4192

Sex attitudes questionnaires, 143, 152, 158, 164, 193, 250, 252, 328, 352, 359, 364, 1311, 1506, 2193, 2496, 2556, 2720, 2761, 2763, 2768, 2779, 2781, 2784, 2785, 2788, 2810, 2812, 2814, 2828, 3617, 3877, 3883, 4165, 4192, 4193, 4199, 4237, 4241–4244

Sex attitudes research, 13, 19, 20, 135–163, 193, 250, 253, 256, 258, 262, 269, 272, 273, 275, 277, 280, 287, 292, 304, 335, 345, 350, 352, 354, 359, 361, 364, 787, 919, 920, 1250, 1257, 1277, 1453, 1465, 1649, 1702, 2160, 2166, 2168, 2266, 2314, 2315, 2317, 2319, 2452, 2476, 2489, 2491, 2493, 2496, 2497, 2500, 2502, 2509, 2557, 2560, 2710–2829, 2840, 2889, 3045, 3532, 3599, 3647, 3920, 3924, 3938, 4195, 4199, 4234

Sex behavior, 21, 22, 40, 43, 45, 70–83, 111, 130, 136, 205, 270, 389, 409, 599, 621, 797, 823, 1220, 1247, 1253, 1321, 1357, 1743, 2172, 2523, 2570, 2632, 2724, 2919, 2930, 3029, 3112, 3151, 3319, 3439, 3448–3456, 3741. *See also* Animal sex behavior: Diseases and; Homosexuals sex behavior; Legal aspects of; Marital sex behavior; Nonmarital sex behavior; Oral genital sex behavior; Periodicity and; Personality and; Prison sex behavior; Professional groups sex behavior; Religiosity and; Sex offenders sex behavior; Social classes and; Surgery and; Tubal ligation and; Urogenital anomalies and; Urogenital impairment and; Vasectomy and

Sex behavior and health, 564, 1349

Sex behavior and obesity, 634, 748–752

Sex behavior and occupation, 2207, 2540

Sex behavior and sex differences, 157, 168, 179, 272, 274, 281, 288, 294, 313, 317, 368, 397, 468, 838, 1786, 1853, 2145, 2170, 2500, 2722, 2730, 2746, 2749, 2776, 2800, 2814, 3896

Sex behavior bibliographies, 137, 367, 638, 640

Sex behavior history, 10, 29, 869, 2305

Sex behavior in institutions, 695, 696, 707, 1502

Sex behavior in primitive socieites, 53, 563, 2271, 2569–2709

Sex behavior in the military, 3323

Sex behavior interview schedules, 1392, 3607

Sex behavior questionnaires, 19, 249, 250, 260, 300, 305, 1199, 1250, 1257, 1609, 1613, 2120, 2193, 2288, 2290, 3012, 3907, 4189, 4193, 4202, 4208, 4212

Sex behavior research, 1–69, 75, 83–89, 127, 135–139, 165–224, 234, 244–363, 366–368, 377, 412, 443–448, 465, 515, 520, 587, 710, 839, 1091, 1172, 1245, 1250, 1257, 1259, 1685, 1741, 1796, 1803, 1852, 1862, 1991, 2107, 2117, 2133, 2135, 2148, 2160, 2180, 2181, 2266, 2565, 2606, 2610, 2649, 2672, 2675, 2711–2713, 2723, 2743, 2770, 2780, 2812, 2820, 2832, 2838, 3162, 3404, 3437, 3945, 3955, 4188, 4189, 4195, 4202, 4208. *See also* Contraception and; Extramarital sex behavior research; Homosexuals sex behavior research; Marital sex behavior research; Nonmarital sex behavior research; Premarital sex behavior research; Sex offenders sex behavior research; Venereal diseases and

Sex conferences, 1452

Sex counseling, 185, 241, 421, 423, 435, 471, 523, 681,

728, 744, 793, 1159, 1229, 1271-1603, 1608, 1642, 1667, 1670, 1679, 2056, 2224, 2264, 2935, 3812, 4259. *See also* Legal aspects of; Marriage counseling; Peer counseling; Sexual history taking; Surrogate sex partners; Telephone counseling; Therapist client relationships

Sex counseling for homosexuals, 238

Sex customs, 10, 26, 34, 78, 869, 2576, 2582, 2591, 2593, 2594, 2601, 2609, 2616, 2641, 2644, 2646, 2649, 2665, 2682, 3015, 3038, 3124, 3615, 4018, 4031, 4053, 4068, 4082, 4092

Sex customs in the Bible, 2306, 2907, 2909

Sex differences, 98, 113, 152, 221, 277, 616, 920, 1171, 1222, 1682, 1686, 1714, 1725, 1726, 1728, 1729, 1736, 1764, 1770, 1773, 1774, 1801, 1807, 1810, 1853, 1902, 1954, 2652, 2945, 3003, 3014, 3030, 3599, 3901, 3923, 3944, 4234. *See also* Aggressiveness and; Animal sex differences; Anxiety and; Cognition and; Determinants of sex differentiation; Emotions and; Fantasies and; Mental health and; Moral development and; Physiological sex differences; Self concept and; Sex behavior and

Sex differences bibliographies, 1774, 1902, 1904

Sex dreams, 1212, 1215

Sex dysfunctions, 386, 410, 423, 424, 472, 473, 494, 524, 542, 577, 655, 661, 721, 793, 1212, 1236, 1308, 1312, 1315, 1320, 1334, 1345, 1448, 1459, 1508, 1509, 1518, 1538, 1544, 1547, 1564, 1582, 1591, 1867, 3056, 3137, 3709. *See also* Ejaculatory incompetence; Hypersexuality; Hyposexuality; Impotence; Orgasmic dysfunction; Premature ejaculation; Sex counseling; Marital sex problems

Sex education, 78, 228, 267, 1408, 1417, 2325-2417, 2464, 2478. *See also* Afroamericans sex education; Attitude on; Blind and; Catholic sex education; Counselors sex education; Family life education; Fertility control education; Health education; Judaic attitudes on; Judaic family life education; Legal aspects of; Medical profession sex education; Medical students sex education; Mentally ill and; Mentally retarded and; Nurses sex education; Nursing students sex education; Paraplegics and sex education; Parents sex education; Physically handicapped and; Poverty areas and; Premaritial sex education; Professional groups sex education; Protestant attitudes on; Social workers sex education; Special groups and; Teachers sex education; Venereal diseases education

Sex education advice, 379, 948, 1470, 1472, 1589-1603, 2278, 2284

Sex education bibliographies, 2345

Sex education conferences, 716, 2546

Sex education curricula, 302, 1350, 1409, 1412, 1432, 1437, 1443, 1830, 2325-2353, 2357, 2427, 2440, 2443, 2467, 2492, 2511, 3046

Sex education discussions, 94, 105, 1276, 1355, 1441, 1466, 2329, 2359, 2360, 2426, 2449, 2460, 2782

Sex education films bibliographies, 636, 2364

Sex education history, 797, 2548

Sex education laws, 2431

Sex education materials, 23, 37, 48, 52, 61, 64, 426, 550, 955-958, 1561, 1596, 1851, 2331, 2339, 2361-2417, 2437, 2511. *See also* Audio visual sex aids; Counselors sex education materials; Medical students sex education materials; Mentally retarded sex education materials; Teachers sex education materials

Sex education on homosexuals, 955-958

Sex education organizations, 37, 1415, 2545

Sex education questionnaires, 142, 716, 2332, 2456, 2458, 2490, 2501, 2547, 2558

Sex education research, 125, 142, 153, 162, 205, 207, 303, 1364, 1412, 1531, 2327, 2330, 2351, 2418-2568. *See also* Doctors sex education research; Family life education research; Medical students sex education research; Nurses sex education research; Sex knowledge research

Sex encyclopedias and manuals, 25, 1328, 1858, 2741

Sex ethics, 38, 220, 317, 1329, 1475, 1484, 1496, 1545, 1652, 1675, 2162, 2256, 2288, 2298, 2299, 2301, 2307, 2815, 2830-2915, 2917, 3124, 3157, 3197, 3347, 3533, 3559, 4259. *See also* Free love; Religious sex ethics; Social ethics; Virginity

Sex exercise, 948, 1198, 1334, 1575, 1599

Sex fantasies, 109, 1011, 1030, 1047, 1080, 1542, 1612, 3206, 4130

Sex hanging, 1011, 1066, 1069-1087

Sex hormones, 394, 837, 1792, 1864, 1866, 1867, 1869-1893, 1901, 1912, 1932, 1943, 1963, 1967, 1977, 1982-1984, 1988, 1998, 2000

Sex in advertising, 2790, 3006, 3017

Sex in art, 4013, 4015, 4018-4062, 4069, 4073, 4135

Sex in cinema, 3638, 3957, 3960, 3978, 4019, 4023, 4108-4129, 4135

Sex in literature, 2389, 3288, 3875, 3974, 3979, 3980, 3996, 4015, 4016, 4019-4023, 4063-4107

Sex in music, 3049, 4020, 4023, 4144-4154

Sex in photographs, 4015, 4137-4143

Sex in poetry, 3291, 3457, 4069, 4072, 4080

Sex in religion, 2844, 2860, 2872, 2909, 3124

Sex in religious art, 4062

Sex in theater, 3378, 4130-4136

Sex Information and Education Council of the United States, 1317, 1755

Sex knowledge, 99, 101-103, 224, 1376, 1416, 1762, 2454, 2485, 2508, 2667. *See also* Afroamericans sex knowledge; Sex questions

Sex knowledge and attitudes test, 2522, 2524, 2527, 2540, 2762, 2764, 3924, 3925, 4198

Sex knowledge inventory, 1319, 1376, 2439, 2546

Sex knowledge questionnaires, 807, 2419, 2472, 2556, 4198

Sex knowledge research, 114, 126, 142, 171, 186, 189, 231, 237, 267, 320, 340, 348, 783, 788, 807, 2184, 2419, 2434, 2439, 2459, 2470, 2472, 2474, 2476, 2485, 2488, 2491, 2493-2497, 2504, 2527, 2532, 2539, 2543, 2544, 2546, 2551, 2714, 2716, 2751, 2762, 2766, 3924

Sex laws, 8, 33, 3731, 3806, 3835, 3841, 3845. *See also* Exhibitionism laws; Homosexuality laws; Incest laws; Legal aspects of sex behavior; Rape laws; Sex psychopaths laws; Voyeurism laws

Sex offenders, 59, 441, 452, 1024, 2709, 3065, 3077, 3078, 3088, 3098, 3244, 3247, 3270, 3572, 3586, 3603, 3605, 3715-3847. *See also* Biographies of sex criminals

Sex offenders and erotica, 3263, 3613, 3745, 3938

Sex offenders behavior therapy, 3799, 3802

Sex offenders demographic research, 436, 3259, 3606, 3725, 3732, 3734, 3738, 3742, 3798, 3800, 3825

Sex offenders drug therapy, 548, 3782, 3814

Sex offenders hormone therapy, 3792, 3797

Sex offenders personality inventories, 1992, 3267, 3721, 3736, 3783

Sex offenders projective testing, 3608, 3621, 3684

Sex offenders psychoanalysis, 3102, 3262, 3275, 3285, 3583, 3738, 3777, 3781

Sex offenders psychoanalytic therapy, 3788
Sex offenders psychological testing, 3285, 3623, 3732, 3736, 3737, 3770, 3787, 3830
Sex offenders psychotherapy, 3102, 3629, 3783, 3785, 3787, 3789, 3793, 3797, 3800, 3803, 3804, 3806, 3807, 3811
Sex offenders sex behavior, 441, 3262, 3725
Sex offenders sex behavior research, 3734, 3737, 3819
Sex offenders therapy, 59, 3266, 3713, 3740, 3768, 3782-3815, 3819
Sex offenses, 33, 2630, 2641, 3104, 3162, 3463, 3605, 3668, 3713-3847, 3938
Sex offenses bibliographies, 3130, 3713, 3714
Sex organizations, 37, 48, 1416
Sex problems, see Biographies of sex criminals
Sex psychology, 15, 29, 105, 115, 210, 1201, 1227, 1228, 1241, 1253, 1321, 1339, 1448, 1533, 1755, 1796, 1828, 2226, 2670, 2682, 2963, 3615, 4226
Sex psychopaths, 3765-3781, 3817
Sex psychopaths laws, 3766, 3767, 3769, 3771, 3776, 3779, 3780, 3800
Sex questionnaires, 1504, 1506, 1531, 2266, 2491, 2770, 4201, 4215, 4218, 4242
Sex questions, 141, 1300
Sex ratio, 777, 2040, 2586
Sex reassignment, 1740, 1742, 1784, 1799, 1848, 2030, 2041, 2054. See also Gender role identification problems; Legal aspects of sex reassignment; Transexual surgery
Sex research, 7, 58, 59, 65, 68, 1484, 1687, 1765, 1790, 1852, 1858, 2275, 2627, 2689, 2690, 4155-4244, 4245-4267
Sex research bibliographies, 628
Sex research early works, 981, 2842, 3029
Sex research history, 28, 66, 1454, 4010
Sex researchers, 66, 1214, 1482, 1679, 4010
Sex revolution, 49, 138, 150, 163, 222, 311, 315, 1404, 1829, 2179, 2204, 2305, 2729, 2733, 2734, 2754, 2861, 2904, 2996, 3036, 3040
Sex role orientation, 1702, 4233
Sex role survey, 4234
Sex stereotype measure, 1850
Sex therapy, see Sex counseling
Sex variations, 10, 793, 869, 964, 981, 987, 989, 1333, 1352, 1406, 1498, 2049, 3351, 3446, 3832
Sex variations bibliographies, 3714
Sex variations etiology, 436, 838, 1024, 1063, 1119, 2698, 3093, 3157, 3165, 3193, 3222, 3303, 3607, 3754, 3764
Sex variations in art, 4024, 4034, 4059
Sex variations psychoanalysis, 1005, 2595, 3761
Sex variations research, 475
Sex variations therapy, 59, 1498, 1504, 1514, 1562, 3740, 3791, 3812
Sex variations unspecified, 1010
Sexual arousability inventory, 1465
Sexual communication, 1342, 2142
Sexual history taking, 1301, 1316, 1389-1398
Sexual humor, 107, 393, 3053, 3325
Sexual humor research, 393, 2304, 3325, 4104
Sexual interaction inventory, 1480
Sexual myths and fallacies, 404, 563, 776, 1173, 2775, 2979, 3024, 3716, 3847
Sexual nomenclature, 1119, 1787, 3240
Sexual orientation method, 4235-4238
Sexual performance evaluation, 2120
Sexual response physiology, 377, 476, 1171-1216, 1219, 1227, 1228, 1232, 1233, 1238, 1711, 2104, 3852, 4189

Sexual symbolism psychoanalysis, 616, 2715
Shakers, 2856
Sibling relationships, 3134, 3188
Single parents, 1708
Singles life styles, 819
Sittengeschichte, 4018, 4068
Situational homosexuality, 3634, 3636, 3641
Skoptsy, 988
Sleep, 455, 456, 459, 815, 1216, 1888, 3612
Social classes, 116, 780, 784, 791, 795, 1837, 3041, 3576
Social classes and sex behavior, 140, 483, 789-799, 1329, 2184, 2305, 3414. See also Lower class and sex behavior; Middle class and sex behavior
Social conditions, 31, 590, 2455, 2757, 2925, 3361, 3375, 3379, 3385, 3470, 4031, 4092
Social customs, 432, 778, 834, 1763, 2669, 4150
Social dancing, 4150, 4153
Social ethics, 106, 144, 1435, 1622, 2310, 2671, 2742, 2774, 2899, 3947, 3991, 4249
Social ethics history, 2856
Social sciences, 4070, 4172
Social sciences ethics, 1479, 1483, 1497, 1581, 1586, 1642, 4245-4267
Social sciences methodology, 232, 328, 1178, 1288, 1480, 1768, 1832, 2117, 2253, 2627, 2689, 2717, 2723, 2736, 2788, 2810, 3005, 3859, 3865, 4155-4180, 4236-4238, 4246, 4250, 4252, 4255, 4264, 4267
Social work, 1496, 1497, 1586, 3072, 3109
Social workers sex education, 728, 1294, 1296, 1422, 1475, 2349, 2352, 2562-2568
Socialization, 106, 179, 739, 1686, 1699, 1720, 1733, 1748, 1749, 1776, 1788, 1842, 2627, 3146
Sociology, 2723, 2833, 2979, 3008, 4247-4249, 4261
Somatology, 2643. See also Body build research
Special groups and sex education, 714, 741, 744, 2451
Special groups and sex education bibliographies, 628, 639, 642
Sperm, 1881, 1887
Stag films, 3960
Statistics methodology, 2138
Status of homosexuals, 868, 947, 954, 3051
Status of women, 432, 819, 946, 1598, 1665, 1682, 1766, 1839, 1851, 2577, 2777, 2803, 2815, 2920, 2921, 2925, 2927, 2936, 2968, 2970, 2975, 2977, 2982, 2988, 2993-2995, 3003, 3005, 3009, 3014-3063, 3051, 3319, 3333, 3422, 3532, 3638, 3656, 3657, 3661, 3667
Status of women bibliographies, 1283
Status of women history, 31, 2670, 2938, 2989, 3034, 3055, 3061, 3062, 3379
Status of women research, 2950, 3025, 3045, 3048
Statutory rape, see Legal aspects of
Sterility, 622
Sterilization, 766
Sterilization laws, 2075
Sterilization of criminals and defectives, 712
Sternberg, Leo, 572
Striptease, 3757, 4135, 4147, 4154
Student marriages, 279, 1377, 1378
Suicide, 405, 1011, 1082, 1084, 2811. See also Sex hanging
Surgery and sex behavior, 635, 753-759, 3287. See also Colon surgery and sex behavior; Mastectomy and sex behavior; Nervous system impairment and sex behavior; Transexual surgery and sex behavior; Urogenital surgery and sex behavior
Surrogate sex partners, 1479, 1667-1679
Swearing, 1618, 2607

Symbolism, 2671

Teachers sex education, 1276, 1443, 2326, 2348, 2543–2561
Teachers sex education materials, 709, 2328
Telephone counseling, 1416–1421, 3686
Television and radio, 3053
Testicular feminization syndrome, 1718, 1777, 1859
Testosterone, 608, 1210, 1880, 1892, 1919, 1941, 1944, 1951–1953, 1958, 1960, 1979, 1990–1992
Theater history, 3373. *See also* Sex in theater
Thematic apperception test, 583, 1144, 1801, 3944
Therapist client relationships, 283, 1479, 1483, 1605–1666
Thorne sex inventory, 2780, 4224, 4225, 4226
Tranquilizers, 490
Transexual surgery, 1150, 1154, 2030, 2033, 2047, 2056–2061, 2076, 2077. *See also* Sex reassignment
Transexual surgery and adjustment, 2062–2066
Transexual surgery and sex behavior, 658, 2064, 2066
Transexual treatment, 1101, 1154, 1162, 1735, 2033, 2044, 2047–2055, 2058, 2061, 2069
Transexualism, 832, 1093, 1098, 1110, 1111, 1117, 1120, 1121, 1141, 1154, 1159, 1960, 2002–2089. *See also* Attitudes on transexualism; Biographies of transexuals; Legal aspects of cross dressing; Gender role identification problems; Sex reassignment
Transexualism etiology, 1123, 1125, 1154, 2027, 2033, 2039, 2042–2046, 2051, 2052, 2057, 2058, 2062
Transexualism research, 1101, 1102, 1134, 1150, 1735, 2008, 2016, 2021–2042, 2063, 2069, 2081, 2598
Transexuals mf scales, 2028
Transexuals personality inventories, 1750, 2022, 2026, 2035, 2037
Transexuals psychological testing, 2021, 2029, 2032, 2047
Transvestism, 1079, 1088–1170, 2023, 2057
Transvestism aversion therapy, 1147, 1151, 1153, 1157, 1158, 1161
Transvestism behavior therapy, 1148, 1154, 1156, 1158
Transvestism bibliographies, 1110, 1143
Transvestism etiology, 1110, 1123–1128, 1139, 2044
Transvestism history, 1097
Transvestism psychoanalysis, 1078, 1083, 1093, 1137, 1146, 1155
Transvestism research, 1083, 1105, 1110, 1119, 1129–1145, 1152, 1169, 2039
Transvestism therapy, 598, 1146–1166
Transvestite organizations, 1106
Transvestites personality inventories, 1129, 1138
Transvestites projective testing, 1131, 1144
Transvestites psychological testing, 1144, 1157
Trial marriage, 278, 289, 330, 337, 365, 2161–2204
Tubal ligation and sex behavior, 762
Turners syndrome, 1905

United Ostomy Association, 654
Unplanned conception effects, 3677
Unwed fathers, 215, 1286
Unwed mothers, 173, 2237, 2766, 4171
Unwed parents, 2322
Urethra, 1193
Urinary acid phosphatase, 3885
Urogenital anomalies, 1914
Urogenital anomalies and sex behavior, 1719
Urogenital cancer, 768
Urogenital cancer and sex behavior, 761
Urogenital diseases and sex behavior, 443, 663. *See also* Venereal diseases and sex behavior
Urogenital examination, 1308, 1582, 3052, 3685, 3687, 3689, 3707
Urogenital impairment, 425, 1261
Urogenital impairment and sex behavior, 669, 1190, 1991
Urogenital mutilation, 1039, 1848
Urogenital surgery, 2060
Urogenital surgery and sex behavior, 654, 658, 761–775, 1334
Urogenital system, 79, 1184, 1214, 1239
Urolagnia, 2595

Vagina, 1190–1192, 1194, 1195, 1198, 1988
Vaginal plethysmography, 583, 1176, 1196, 1202
Vasectomy, 1290, 1893, 2940
Vasectomy and sex behavior, 770–773, 775
Venereal diseases, *see* Attitudes on
Venereal diseases and sex behavior research, 18, 219
Venereal diseases behavioral aspects research, 178, 214, 2430
Venereal diseases diagnosis and treatment, 18
Venereal diseases education, 2342
Verbal sexual communication, 2464
Victimless crimes, 3535, 3551, 3556
Victimology, 3047, 3646, 3655, 3696, 3747, 3798
Violence, 2238, 3047, 3743, 3931, 3943, 3978, 4128
Virginity, 1632, 2665, 2795. *See also* Coitally unexperienced
Voyeurism, 3749, 3759–3764, 3815. *See also* Legal aspects of
Voyeurism laws, 3531
Voyeurism psychoanalysis, 1032, 3759
Voyeurism research, 3760, 3762, 3764

War, 3578
Warhol, Andy, 4136
Werewolves, 969
Witchcraft, 4057, 4150
Wolfenden report, 876, 3534
Women, 2646, 2652, 3016. *See also* Biographies of; Changing role of; Status of
Women advice, 528, 1598, 2995
Women and crime, 2987, 3003
Women and education, 259, 2420, 2985, 3062
Women and employment, 1682, 3004, 3058
Women bibliographies, 1938
Women history, 834, 2860, 2969, 3019, 3055
Women in art, 4032, 4040, 4138
Women in cinema, 3957, 4114, 4122
Women in folklore, 3656
Women in literature, 3055, 3057, 4080
Women medical advice, 1598
Women psychoanalysis, 1002, 1052, 1188, 1664, 1781, 2240, 2242, 3027
Women psychology, 679, 766, 1040, 1253, 1281, 1282, 1665, 1851, 1924, 1928, 1929, 2763, 2968, 2973, 2978, 2985, 2987, 2992, 2999, 3002, 3009, 3014, 3024, 3027, 3032, 3033, 3043, 3053, 4207
Women psychotherapy, 1035, 2242
Working women, 1782, 3012
Writers, 1021

Zoophilia, 3206
Zoophilia in art, 4059
Zoophilia research, 558, 1005
Zuckerman heterosexual scales, 4212